BUD COLLINS'

MODERN ENCYCLOPEDIA OF TENNIS

BUD COLLINS'
MODERN ENCYCLOPEDIA OF TENNIS

Edited by Bud Collins and Zander Hollander

An Associated Features Book

DOUBLEDAY & COMPANY, INC, GARDEN CITY, NEW YORK
1980

(The chapter on equipment (8) was reprinted from *Tennis Equipment* by Steve Fiott, with permission from Chilton Book Company, Radnor, Pennsylvania. Copyright © 1978 by Tennis Research Group.)

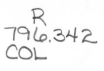
Library of Congress Cataloging in Publication Data

Collins, Bud.
  Bud Collins' Modern encyclopedia of tennis.

  "An Associated Features book."
  Includes index.
  1. Tennis—History. 2. Tennis players—Biography.
I. Hollander, Zander, joint author. II. Title.
III. Title: Modern encyclopedia of tennis.
GV993.C6 1980   796.342
Doubleday & Company, Inc.
ISBN: 0-385-13093-7
Library of Congress Catalog Card Number 79-8919

For my daughter, Suzanna

ACKNOWLEDGMENTS

The research, writing, and editing of *Bud Collins' Modern Encyclopedia of Tennis* needed more than a doubles team. It could never have been achieved without the contributions of a number of respected journalists whose names are familiar to followers of the game.

For their respective chapters and enthusiasm for the project, the editors wish to acknowledge Allison Danzig, newspaperman and author, who wrote tennis, and other sports, for forty-five years on the New York *Times*; Lance Tingay, tennis correspondent of the London *Telegraph* since 1932 and observer of every match played at Wimbledon since 1955; Stan Isaacs, tennis savant who is television sports columnist and former sports editor of Long Island's *Newsday*; Barry Lorge, tennis and feature sports-writer on the Washington *Post*, contributing editor of *World Tennis* magazine, and president of the U. S. Tennis Writers' Association; and Martin Lader, whose tennis assignments at UPI have taken him from Flushing Meadow to Wimbledon.

There were many others, touched in one way or another by the sport, who helped make the encyclopedia a reality. They include Steve Flink, associate editor of *World Tennis*, who played a major role in the compilation of records; Al Laney, tennis analyst and essayist on the late New York *Herald Tribune*; Harold Zimman, publisher of the Official U.S. Tennis Association Yearbook; Ron Bookman, editor of *World Tennis*; Aaron Elson of the New York *Daily News*; Steve Fiott, author of *Tennis Equipment*; Ed Fabricius, director of public relations, USTA; Stephanie Bostic, USTA, Phyllis Hollander, senior editor, Associated Features; and Reid Grosky of the Los Angeles *Times*.

The excitement and the legend of tennis cannot be properly portrayed without photos, and for these we thank Szilvia Szmuk, curator of the William M. Fischer Memorial Tennis Collection at St. John's University; Charles Young, curator of the New York *Herald Tribune* photo collection at the Queensboro Public Library; Pete Sansone and Marty Stern of UPI, and the various credited photographers.

B.C. and Z.H.

CONTENTS

INTRODUCTION

Either the ball goes over the net or it doesn't.

That's the essence of tennis, the simple and obvious requirement: Take a racket—an instrument that looks like an oversized magnifying glass, but with a network of strings in place of the lens—and hit a rubber ball over a rampart of netting three feet in height. Hit the ball over the net within a rectangular court one more time than your opponent, and you win a point. Win enough points and you defeat that opponent.

Should such a rudimentary exercise hold any fascination at all, or at least for very long? Spencer W. Gore remarked in 1890 that any gamesplayer worth his sweat wouldn't find tennis a satisfactory pastime for any length of time. No sour grapes for Gore, for he, an athletic Englishman, had in 1877 won the first recognized tennis tournament, one that continues highest in general esteem more than a century later: Wimbledon (properly entitled, then and now, The Lawn Tennis Championships). If Gore were a Wimbledon champion at large today, his agent would censure him for deprecatory talk about their livelihood. "Don't knock the game that feeds us, Spencer," the agent would scold. "How do you expect me to get you any more endorsement contracts if you keep saying tennis is a bore?"

The first champion's doubting statements clearly had as much impact as the *Titanic* on its icy opponent. Gore sank from view quickly, but the game flourished in the cradle, Britain, and spread throughout the planet so that today it enthralls millions upon millions of hackers (recreational players) and heroes/heroines (the professional elite) as well as millions more tennis addicts who attend tournaments and take the free fix from television.

Jimmy Connors, the irrepressible American pro who in the first seven years of his career had won more than two million dollars in prize money—this even before his 27th birthday in 1979—would not have agreed with Spencer W. Gore at all (if Jimmy could even identify that late, grumbling Gore). "I think people like to play tennis and watch tennis because it's exciting. I know that's how I feel," Connors has said.

Jimmy Connors: Colossus in the modern era.
Pete Mecca

Like other professional sports that have succeeded with the public during the years since World War II, tennis has come to be regarded as an entertainment as much as a game. At times it is raised to an art form—a competitive ballet—by the splendor in movement of such acrobatic zephyrs as Evonne Goolagong and Ilie Nastase.

Often it is sublime drama. Never more so than a chill, grim October afternoon in Bucharest in 1972 when nationalism and personal pride, strength of character, and moral outlook were all wrapped up in a game of tennis between an American, Stan Smith, and a Romanian, Ion Tiriac. Smith was the best player in the world that year, but he was out of his element. Slipping on the slow, salmon-hued European clay, he was assaulted by a canny, dark-maned lion while a feverish crowd and unfailingly patriotic officials gave him a thumbs-down treatment. Never mind the tennis match, Smith sometimes wondered whether he'd get out of town alive.

At stake was the Davis Cup. A huge sterling trophy from which world conquerors have swilled victorious champagne since 1900, it is the most difficult prize to win in tennis, a reward for the team title, pursued each year by more than 50 countries. In 1972 the United States and Romania were the finalists. The Cup would be decided by the Smith-Tiriac match, and this fact made a cauldron of the arena, an intimate 7,000-seat bowl hastily hammered together for what amounted to a state occasion in Romania. Though Tiriac, a deceptively plodding and unstylish player, wasn't in Smith's league, he lifted himself as high as his native Carpathians with one thought: His tiny homeland, producer of few world-class players besides himself and teammate Ilie Nastase, could score a fantastic victory over the mighty U.S. if he beat Smith. "I know only one way to play—to win. If I lose," Tiriac said, "then it is nothing. We don't win the Cup."

Ion orchestrated the chanting crowd and deferential line judges into a united front for himself and against Smith. He stalled, he emoted—and he played like a madman, forcing the excruciating match all the way into a fifth set. It seemed a morality play in short pants, the exemplary sportsman Smith, tall and fair-haired, against the scheming Tiriac, hulking and glaring. Somehow Smith held together amid chaos to play to his utmost, too, and win the last set in a run of six games. Considering the adverse conditions and the magnitude of the prize, Smith's triumph was possibly the most exceptional in the history of the game. "I concentrated so hard I got a headache," he said.

While Tiriac was chastized outside of Romania for a pragmatic approach to tennis, avoiding the accepted code of conduct, he was merely doing the best he could to seize a rare day for his homeland. It was only a game of tennis, but it had assumed a far greater significance for a few hours that afternoon.

The significance was global, and the internationality is a source of much of the appeal of tennis. By this, of course, I mean the established worldwide tournament game to which this encyclopedia is primarily devoted. The advance of the game since tennis was patented (as "Sphairistike") in London in 1874 by Major Walter C. Wingfield has been so complete that all continents are routinely represented in any tournament of consequence. Australians, Asians, Europeans, Africans, and North and South Americans populate a family of tournament players who work their way around the globe on an unending trek among the continents. They flit between Melbourne and Munich, Bombay and Buenos Aires, Johannesburg and Jacksonville as casually as commuters, aware that jets have made it possible to compete on one continent today and another one tomorrow.

Tennis players have been ocean-hoppers almost since the beginning, but the year 1900 seems special: A British team showed up in Boston to launch the Davis Cup by challenging the U.S. Five years later a robust Californian, May Sutton, became the first foreigner to win Wimbledon. Two years after that Norman Brookes journeyed all the way from Melbourne to London to win the singles, showing the way to the Big W for Australians, who would one day be more awesome there than any other aliens. The next year, 1908, an American, Fred Alexander, was the first outsider to win the Australian title.

The game may have been restricted to a 78-by-27-foot plot, but the players were operating on a global playground. Don Budge presented striking evidence in 1938 when he circumnavigated the initial Grand Slam by winning the Australian, French, Wimbledon, and U.S. titles all within that year. Budge traveled more leisurely, by ocean liner, but players would become winged rugbeaters in a few years, and no tournament was too far off the beaten path.

Major Wingfield's attempt to fire a tennis boom and cash in on it by patenting a set of equipment and instructions in 1874 is a convenient event in marking the start of the game we know as tennis—lawn tennis to sticklers, (mostly English,) who wish to distinguish this game from its parent, real (or court) tennis. Real tennis, a complex and beguiling game, is played with lopsided rackets in an erratically walled cement court where the balls—hard as baseballs—rattle around on sloping roofs and disappear into arcane apertures. It is still to be found in a few private clubs (six in the U.S.) where members presumably have to pass a blood test: blue-positive required.

Real tennis dates back to the Middle Ages and numbers among its stalwarts old London Fats (a.k.a. King Henry VIII), whose reputation was made in mixed doubles. Offcourt. Henry had his own tennis court at Hampton Court Palace, in use even now, and maintained the kind of edge players of today would envy by employing his own scorekeeper, one Anthony Angeley. Angeley must have been worth a couple of points a game, and what opponent would question a call made by the royal umpire?

Since kings and millionaires aren't numerous enough to carry a popular sport, real tennis never came very far out of its curiously constructed concrete closet. Actually Major Wingfield wasn't the originator of the outdoor version. He was among several who tried their hands at fresh-air tennis prior to 1874, but it was Wingfield who envisioned commercial possibilities. When he set out to market

equipment and rules for his game of Sphairistike (Greek for ball game), Wingfield realized that a profitable volume of sales would rest on attracting a broader public than that involved in real tennis and very expensive indoor courts. Not the masses, certainly, but the affluent with property large enough for one of the courts detailed in his rules.

It was natural enough in England to raise a net and outline a court on a croquet lawn—thus lawn tennis. Regardless of how far tennis would stray from a grass surface—to such exotic footing as cow dung in India, antbed in Australia, and plastic carpets for indoor play everywhere—the game was once and forever lawn tennis to the English, who would rather break their necks than tradition.

Although grass courts hold firm at Wimbledon and the Australian Open as well as at a few other tournaments in Britain and Australia, they are practically nonexistent in the U.S. and elsewhere. Steadfastly resisting the trend away from the sacred sod is Newport Casino at Newport, Rhode Island, birthplace of the American tournament game. The Casino is a hardy survivor, a gingerbread architectural gem, scene of the first U.S. tournament on grass, the men's National championships of 1881, and the last, an annual pro tour stopover called the Hall of Fame classic. Like Wimbledon, four years its senior, Newport has no intention of forsaking God's own greenery.

Lawn tennis or just-plain-tennis—whatever it is called, however the ball bounces on whichever surface—has caught on in the U.S. more widely than anywhere else. Shortly after Wingfield started peddling tennis it reached the U.S. In 1876, Dr. James Dwight, a Bostonian, won a baptismal tourney of sorts, a sociable get-together in the yard of the Appleton estate at Nahant, Massachusetts.

Feminists may have been dismayed in 1978 when an English historian, Tom Todd, asserted that it was Dwight—not Mary Outerbridge of Staten Island—who introduced tennis to America in 1874. Founding father or mother? Both Outerbridge, who usually gets credit, and Dwight have their adherents in this matter, although Dr. Richard Dwight, the son

Dr. James Dwight: Father of U.S. tennis. *USLTA*

champion, a fellow Bostonian, Dick Sears, and accompanying Sears to the national doubles championship five times between 1882 and 1887.

Although tennis drifted across the country from Staten Island and Nahant, the power remained in the Northeast. Three decades after Sears began his American championship dynasty in 1881, the American men's championship was still the property of an Ivy League crowd. Among the women, Californians May Sutton in 1904 (a year prior to her Wimbledon victory) and Hazel Hotchkiss, 1909–11, were the only early players in a similar Northeast monopoly on that title. At last, in 1912, the men's National Championships began to go truly national on the tail of the California Comet, hyperaggressive Maurice "Red" McLoughlin, and the general sporting public would soon become aware of tennis.

It was too good a game to be cloistered at Newport as a diversion of the swells, and in 1915 the National Championships for men moved to the metropolis, New York and the West Side Tennis Club at Forest Hills. There would be a country-club tinge right up to the present day of heavy money and professionalization, but at Forest Hills tennis gained exposure to larger, more diverse crowds, and a national press.

Once peacetime arrived, following World War I, the press had a tennis hero to hype— and a heroine. Big Bill Tilden, the gangling Philadelphian with a blowtorch serve, and Suzanne Lenglen, a flying Frenchwoman, worked their respective sides of the Atlantic with irresistible flair and shotmaking. Not only were Tilden and Lenglen virtually invincible champions, but also they were regal figures and somewhat mysterious. Theirs was a magnetism that pulled crowds and sold tickets, and tennis became a commercial venture. With Tilden as anchor, the U.S. went on a record rampage of seven straight Davis Cups, and it was necessary to construct a 13,000-seat stadium at Forest Hills to hold the throngs following Davis Cup matches and the National Championships.

Because of Suzanne, never beaten in singles at Wimbledon, the place seemed to shrink. It became too small for all the cus-

of the father, puts it in perspective: "Does it matter who was first as long as tennis did come to the U.S.? The fact is that both my father and Miss Outerbridge imported English sets at about the same time, and nobody can be quite sure who was first."

Papa Dwight, however, has a much more solid position in tennis annals than Mama Outerbridge. A graduate of Harvard Medical School, he was not one to let his profession stand in the way of something as important as tennis. Dwight didn't work as a physician, excusing himself on the grounds of "poor health." Instead he devoted himself to tennis, teaching the game to the first U.S. singles

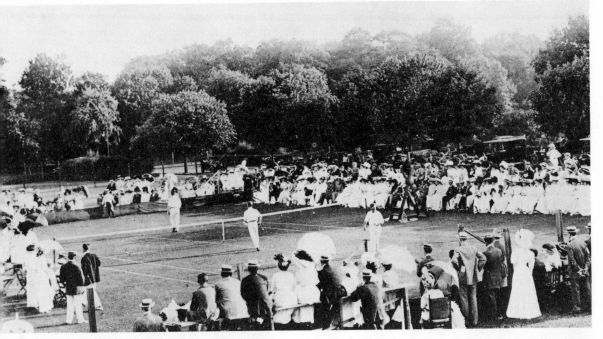

Early action at the Seabright (N.J.) Tennis Club. *Fischer Collection*

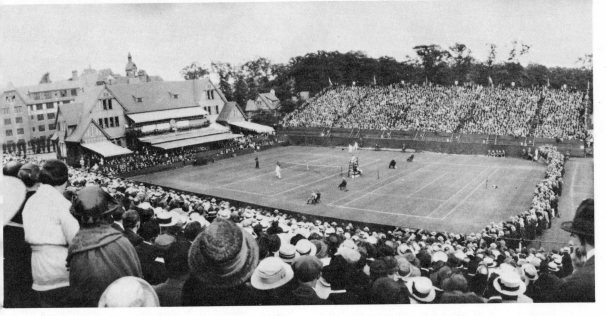

The U.S. National Championships at Forest Hills, New York, in 1920. *Fischer Collection*

tomers who wanted in. Thus the All England Lawn Tennis & Croquet Club, needing more space and seats, moved in 1922 to the present Wimbledon grounds with a Centre Court accommodating 14,000.

Tennis joined other sports as a business game, but, unfortunately, not as a profession. By 1926 it was apparent that the athletes who sold the tickets deserved to be paid. It was not apparent, however, to those volunteer officials who controlled the game and, for generations past its time, they would keep alive the fiction of "amateurism" at the upper level of tennis. Instead of prize money, the subsidy for careerists was "expenses," paid beneath the table in proportion to a player's

The legendary Bill Tilden early in his career. *Fischer Collection*

value as a gate attraction. During the 1920s Tilden made more out of tennis as an amateur than some of the better pros today. He earned it. But Tilden, a supreme individualist, showered neither gratitude nor obeisance to the amateur authorities and was eventually driven to the wilderness of outright professionalism in 1930, to take his place brilliantly on the treadmill of one-nighters.

Until 1926 the only professionals were instructors, ineligible for customary tourna-

ments. Occasionally they played small tournaments among themselves for pin money. Even though open tennis—the integration of amateurs and pros with prize money on the line—was discussed wistfully by progressives among players, officials, and *aficionados*, such a sensible arrangement was well in the future—1968. From time to time a motion to approve open tennis was even introduced within the International Lawn Tennis Federation, but the governing body was much

Suzanne Lenglen was the wonder woman of the Golden twenties. *UPI*

too narrow and steeped in the so-called gentlemanly tradition of "amateurism." The motion always failed, and "shamateurism" was maintained until 1968. Amateurs who traveled the world swinging at tennis balls, living and eating well, were nicknamed "tennis bums."

However, those who decided to accept their money above the table were considered outlaws traveling under that dirty label, "professionals." At least that was the view of amateur officials who barred pros from tradi-tional tournaments. Forced to scrape for their living outside of the usual framework of private clubs, the pros appeared mainly in public arenas, moving constantly as nomads, folding their canvas court and jaunting to the next night's location.

This way of life began in October of 1926 when La Belle Lenglen defected from amateurism to roam North America with a troupe that included her nightly foe, Mary K. Browne, the U.S. champion of 1912–14, and

Australia's Lew Hoad (right, far court) has just slammed the ball en route to a clinching doubles victory (with Rex Hartwig) over Tony Trabert (left) and Vic Seixas in the 1955 Davis Cup Challenge Round at Forest Hills. *UPI*

Vinnie Richards, the American second to Tilden. Their stopovers were regarded as exhibitions, but the pay was all right. Lenglen reportedly collected $100,000 for her year on the road. A few months after the debut of the original wandering pros, the first U.S. Pro Championship for men was thrown together at a small club in Manhattan in the summer of 1927 and won by Richards, whose reward was $1,000 from a purse of $2,000. His 1978 successor, Manolo Orantes, won $27,000, and the tournament was worth $200,000, another startling piece of inflationary evidence in men's pro tennis. Tournament prize money in 1964 was about $150,000 worldwide. In 1979 it would be $12 million. The U.S. Pro

Championships went along year after year, precariously and unprosperously, the longest-lasting of a few tourneys, but life as a pro meant barnstorming, and there wasn't enough money to support more than a handful of outlaws. The tournaments that mattered were restricted to amateurs, whose game had structure, continuity, and the attention of the press and tennis public. Interest in amateur sport was high during the 1920s and 1930s, as a reader of newspapers preserved from that time quickly ascertains.

But after World War II that interest declined. The emphasis shifted to professional sport, particularly in the U.S., and tennis, stocked with phony amateurs, didn't keep pace. While other sports gleamed in television's red eye, tennis languished away from the cameras. Three events maintained an eminence: Wimbledon, Forest Hills, and the Davis Cup finale, which became the postwar preserve of the U.S. and Australia.

As the 1950s dawned, a tidal wave swept from the antipodes of the bottom of the world: It was the Aussies, the most dynastic force ever in tennis. Their muscle lasted for more than two decades, between the Davis Cup seizure spearheaded by Frank Sedgman in 1950 and John Newcombe's U.S. Open triumph of 1973. In between were 16 Davis Cups and 14 Wimbledons for the men, two Grand Slams by Rod Laver, and a male record of 26 Big Four titles by Roy Emerson, as well as the rise and fall of Lew Hoad, and the rise and rise of ageless Kenny Rosewall. Directed by a martinet named Harry Hopman, the Aussies were hungry and superbly conditioned, and gave the impression that the primary occupations at home were tennis and beer drinking. They were world champs at both. Their women were not as pervasive successes as American females, but one of them, Margaret Smith Court, outdid everyone else: Mighty Maggie rolled up 66 Big Four titles in singles, doubles, and mixed, bracketing the singles championships of Australia, France, Wimbledon, and the U.S. in 1970 for her Grand Slam. Nobody, male or female, has come close to Court's accomplishments.

Midway through the 1960s, a period of rising acclaim for sport in general, tennis was sagging at both the amateur and professional levels. The best players were pros, but the best tournaments were amateur. Agitation for open play increased, especially in England, where Wimbledon officials, tiring of exorbitant "expense" payments to amateurs, sought to present the finest possible tennis. This was impossible as long as the professional elite—Rod Laver, Ken Rosewall, Pancho Gonzales, Lew Hoad, Butch Buchholz, and Andres Gimeno—were off in limbo as outlaws.

Impetus for the decisive move toward opens was provided startlingly in 1967 by a man unknown within tennis: Dave Dixon of New Orleans. Buoyed by Texas money supplied by petrocrat Lamar Hunt, his partner in a wildcat tennis venture, Dixon signed up amateurs John Newcombe, Tony Roche, Roger Taylor, Cliff Drysdale, and Nikola Pilic plus pros Butch Buchholz, Pierre Barthes, and Dennis Ralston as his World Championship Tennis troupe. Since another promoter, George MacCall, had enlisted amateur Roy Emerson to blend with pros Laver, Gonzales, Rosewall, Gimeno, and Fred Stolle in his National Tennis League, the amateur game was abruptly depleted of its top resources, the six best players. Even with those players entered, the 1967 Wimbledon had been dull. Now the outlook for the ultimate championship was downright barren. Herman David, the Wimbledon boss, knew what had to be done. With the backing of English tennis officials, Wimbledon announced that in 1968 it would be open to all players regardless of their status, amateur or pro. The best were welcome. When that shot was fired, the rest of the world—the membership of the International Lawn Tennis Federation—fell into line.

Bournemouth, England, was the scene of the first open, the British Hard Court Championships in April of 1968. Kenny Rosewall won the men's title, Virginia Wade the women's, and curly-headed Englishman Mark Cox wrote his footnote in sporting history as the first amateur to beat a pro at tennis. Cox, a left-hander, knocked off Pancho Gonzales and Roy Emerson on successive afternoons to upstage all else on Britain's front pages.

The Tennis Epidemic to come in the 1970s had been set in motion. In 1971 financial pioneer Rod Laver crossed the million-dollar mark in prize money after nine years as a pro. But by 1979, 15 other men and three women had followed, making theirs in shorter spans. And in 1977 Guillermo Vilas had a year that would seem a splendid career for most athletes: $800,642.

At first the boom in prize money, rising to about $20 million for tournament play in 1979, benefited principally the men. As in so many areas of life, the women were left behind. However, the tennis-playing women refused to stand at the back of the game. Guided by brainy Gladys Heldman, publisher of *World Tennis* magazine, and inspired by

Australia's Rod Laver serves against Arthur Ashe in the semifinals of the U.S. Nationals in 1969. Laver went on to stop Tony Roche for the title. *UPI*

the liberation-minded firebrand, Billie Jean King, the women divorced themselves from the conventional tournament arrangement, which had been shared unequally by the sexes. Top billing (and top dollars) had always gone to the men. Carrying the banner of Virginia Slims cigarettes, the women crusaded on a separate tour and made good artistically and economically. The Slims tour began haltingly in 1970 and picked up steam in 1971, when Billie Jean won $117,000, the first woman to earn over 100 grand in prize money. The tour was solid by 1972, when ingenue Chrissie Evert won the first eight-woman playoff at the climax. In 1973 the women demanded and got equal prize money at Forest Hills, one of the few remaining tournaments staging both male and female events.

Television didn't rush to hug tennis when the open era began, although network interest picked up. Two telecasts in particular aided in lifting the game to wide public notice: Rosewall's sensational victory over Laver for the World Championship Tennis title of 1972, and Billie Jean King's put-down of 55-year-old Bobby Riggs in the bizarre "Battle of the Sexes" in 1973. Creating one of the greatest matches, Laver and Rosewall flailed away at each other brilliantly for three and a half hours. It came down to a fifth-set tie-breaker where the 37-year-old Rosewall, seemingly beaten as Laver served at 5 points to 4, took the last three points and the championship in the closest finish of a major event. Rosewall also won $50,000, the richest prize in tennis at the time.

Bobby Riggs, well past his prime—"one foot in the grave" was one of the lines amid his con and corn—had challenged and beaten a nervous Margaret Court in what he termed the "Mother's Day Massacre" earlier in 1973. Glowing with hubris and newfound celebrity, Riggs then challenged 29-year-old Billie Jean. "Nobody knew me when I was the best player in the world in 1939, when I won Wimbledon," he said. "Now I'm over the hill but I'm a star. Everybody recognizes me—the old guy who can beat the best women."

Publicity was tremendous; super *schlock* enveloped the Astrodome in Houston where a

Bobby Riggs and Billie Jean King play the promotional bit in New York for their $100,000 "Battle of the Sexes" at the Houston Astrodome in 1973. *ABC-TV*

record tennis crowd, 30,472, assembled for the bizarre encounter. Though a meaningless match in one sense, it seemed to mean everything to millions everywhere: mankind against womankind. Billie Jean was the defender of her sex against His Piggishness, Riggs. She won easily. Tennis was the beneficiary. Laver and Rosewall had showed a TV audience how majestically the game could be played. King and Riggs lured a much larger audience because their gimmick caught the fancy of many unaware of the existence of tennis.

Tennis began to appear regularly on TV, prize money accelerated for the stars, equipment sales and participation accelerated for the hackers. Construction of public courts as well as private clubs increased, particularly in the United States, where the proliferation of indoor courts was a sporting phenomenon.

Tennis was big business, and the professional performers involved, following the example of brethren in other sports, unionized to gain a stronger position in the management of their business. The male ATP (Association of Tennis Pros) and female WTA (Women's Tennis Association) were formed as player guilds, and two new governing bodies were also formed, the International Professional Tennis Councils for men (MIPTC) and women (WIPTC), containing representatives of the unions, the ITF, and the tournament promoters. Each IPTC set down codes of professional conduct.

World Championship Tennis, which had led the way to professionalism, was still in operation in 1979, but in a lesser role as a tournament promoter. Most men's tournaments, including the WCT circuit, were under the blanket of the Grand Prix, by 1979. Conceived by Jack Kramer and set into action in 1970, the Grand Prix linked the major tournaments, offered points for each match victory, a bonus pool for the leading point scorers, and a season-ending playoff called the Masters for the top eight. The women entered into a similar arrangement called the International Series in 1977, although their winter circuit underwritten by Virginia Slims continued as a separate competition, whose sponsorship was taken over in 1979 by Avon Products.

In 1974 an ill-starred venture called World Team Tennis began in the U.S., a league of city franchises comprising teams of men and women. Most of the leading women took part, and once more the crusader, Billie Jean King, was a driving force. She was the player-coach of Philadelphia in 1974, another first: a woman in charge of a team containing male professionals. As a player she led New York to the 1976–77 titles. General lack of television and spectator interest, coupled with unrealistically high payrolls, caused the league to fold after the 1978 season.

The U.S. led in all facets of the game's development, but tennis was truly universal and well received in most tournament locations in more than 30 countries. As 1980 approached, the chief drawback, overscheduling in the men's Grand Prix, caused talk of recession. Nevertheless, growth continued generally, and Forest Hills was finally outgrown after 63 years. In 1978 the U.S. Open was relocated a few miles away, in Flushing Meadow, where the National Tennis Center is the largest of all tennis playgrounds. The main court, Louis Armstrong Stadium, surrounded by 20,000 seats, enabled the Open to set an American tournament attendance record of 275,300 in 1978. Construction of the center, shepherded by the U.S. Tennis Association's resourceful president, W. E. "Slew" Hester, produced a third style in the evolution of the game: hard courts of asphalt base.

The championship, begun in the grass period in 1881, switched to clay in 1975 as tennis lawns vanished in the U.S. For a while clay was predominant on the American outdoor circuit. Now the move is to hard paving to conform with Flushing Meadow. But more than 50 percent of professional tournaments are currently contested indoors on thin green or blue toupees—artificial rugs—covering bare floors.

It has been fascinating to watch the growth of tennis over the last quarter century, to be part of the spectacular surge transforming it from a game of a relative few to a point where pollster Lou Harris reported tennis in 1977 to be fourth among sports in American newspaper readership popularity. My old sports editor would never have believed it. He was actually apologetic in sending me forth on my first tennis assignment for the Boston *Herald* in 1955, taking pains to let me know he wasn't being punitive. The boss assiduously devoted as little space as possible to "these clubby types running around in their underwear chasing a little white ball."

Certainly then the chances that I would rove the world writing and telecasting tennis were as likely as the little white ball becoming the little yellow ball or players making 100 grand for a few hours of swatting those balls. The odds against were about as long as those facing the Newport Bolshevik, Jimmy Van Alen, who sought to chip the barnacles of ages off the game by introducing tie-breakers, which eliminated endless deuce sets and made tennis more compatible with TV. Yet all these things happened.

The Boston *Globe*, where I moved in 1963, and editor Tom Winship encouraged me to take a worldwide view of the game for its readers. Station WGBH-TV in Boston, inspired by producer-director Gret Harney, launched the Public Broadcasting Service's thorough and thoughtful pioneering of tennis

Army Lieutenant Arthur Ashe wins the crown over Holland's Tom Okker at the 1968 U.S. Nationals. *UPI*

telecasting in the U.S., well ahead of the commercial networks. That was in 1963, when I soloed as commentator at the U.S. Doubles Championships at Longwood Cricket Club in Boston, and our "network" was three stations in New England. It was rewarding to do the first PBS national telecast in 1968, the U.S. Amateur Championships, also at Longwood, as a skinny young man named Arthur Ashe made a breakthrough—the first black male to win a significant championship. Two Sundays later Arthur was in the winner's circle again at Forest Hills, and Jack Kramer and I were describing his victory in the first U.S. Open for the Columbia Broadcasting

System. Ashe was making history all over the place. That was a gripping three-week stretch of writing and talking for me, particularly since Ashe, not only an exciting player, was on his way to becoming a most distinguished representative of his race on and off the court.

Regardless of change, modernization, professionalization, commercialization, greater participation, and more intensified competition at all levels, the game is still tennis, which the original champion, Spencer W. Gore, warned us against. We didn't listen. Too bad he missed the fun of it, the countless invigorating possibilities for player and watcher within 2,106 square feet of the tennis rectangle. Apparently the old champ was oblivious to the intriguing physical and mental battle between distinct personalities, the stress and elation, the anxiety and joy. There was no danger of Gore getting hooked, becoming a tennis degenerate. For some degenerates, tennis is a way of life, even a religion.

Yet it can be stripped down to this: Either the ball goes over the net or it doesn't. . . .

BUD COLLINS

BUD COLLINS'

MODERN ENCYCLOPEDIA OF TENNIS

1 } ROOTS 1874–1918

Precisely when tennis made its debut in America is a matter of some debate, but it is safe to say that by the summer of 1876 there were two lawn tennis courts on this side of the Atlantic.

Responsible for one was Mary Outerbridge of Staten Island, New York, who had fallen in love with the new game in Bermuda, where it was the rage of the British garrison. In fact, when the S.S. *Canima* docked in New York on February 2, 1874, customs agents are said to have held up part of her luggage—rackets, balls, and a net—because they had never seen anything like it. Although they allowed her to claim it after several days, it was not until the summer that Miss Outerbridge, with the help of her brother, shipping industrialist A. Emilius Outerbridge, set up the court on a lawn of the Staten Island Baseball and Cricket Club.

Sometime between then and 1876, a court surfaced at Nahant, Massachusetts, where Dr. James Dwight, the instigator, was the winner of an informal competition on the estate of William Appleton.

The new game, taken from its stone court to the green lawns of England and then to America, was originally called Sphairistike, a name that hardly rolled off the tongue even in England, where classical education abounded. Even the more popular rendition of this Greek word for ball game—"Sticky"—soon was abandoned, and luckily so. Imagine striving to become the No. 1 "sticky" player in the world!

Sphairistike was the creation of Major Walter Clopton Wingfield, a retired regular Army man who was a member of the Corps of Gentlemen at Arms at the court of Queen Victoria. He wrote a book on the game in 1873, and on February 23, 1874, he took out papers for "A New and Improved Portable Court for Playing the Ancient Game of Tennis" at the Office of the Commissioners of Patents in London, England.

Major Wingfield was not the first in the field. As early as 1859, Major Harry Gem, a solicitor of Birmingham, England, and Mr. J. B. Perera, a merchant, marked out a lawn in Edgbaston, a Birmingham suburb, and played their version of lawn tennis.

They went farther after moving their equipment a few miles away, to Leamington in 1870. There, in 1872, they formed, with Major Gem as president, the Leamington Lawn Tennis Club, the first of its kind in the world.

Major Walter Clopton Wingfield pioneered the game. *Fischer Collection*

A.D. 1874, 23rd February. N° 685.

A Portable Court for Playing Tennis.

LETTERS PATENT to Walter Clopton Wingfield, of Belgrave Road, Pimlico, in the County of Middlesex, for the Invention of "A NEW AND IMPROVED PORTABLE COURT FOR PLAYING THE ANCIENT GAME OF TENNIS."

Sealed the 24th July 1874, and dated the 23rd February 1874.

PROVISIONAL SPECIFICATION left by the said Walter Clopton Wingfield at the Office of the Commissioners of Patents, with his Petition, on the 23rd February 1874.

I, WALTER CLOPTON WINGFIELD, of Belgrave Road, Pimlico, in the County of Middlesex, do hereby declare the nature of the said Invention for "A NEW AND IMPROVED PORTABLE COURT FOR PLAYING THE ANCIENT GAME OF TENNIS," to be as follows :—

The object and intention of this Invention consists in constructing a portable court by means of which the ancient game of tennis is much simplified, can be played in the open air, and dispenses with the necessity of having special courts erected for that purpose.

The manner by which I propose to accomplish the above object is as follows :—I insert two standards in the ground at about twenty-one feet from each other; between these two standards a large oblong net is stretched. To each of the said standards I attach a triangular shaped net in such a manner that the standard shall divide the said triangular net into two straight angle triangles, each of which is kept respectively at right angles to each side of the oblong net aforesaid by means of loops and strings, and is fixed to pegs driven in the ground.

The large oblong net forms the dividing wall of the court, and the triangular net the wings or side walls thereof, whilst the floor is marked out by paint, coloured cord, or tape into "in" and "out" courts, serving as crease, right and left courts, and boundaries. By this simple apparatus a portable court is obtained by means of which the old game of tennis, which has always been an indoor amusement, and which few can enjoy on account of the great expense of building a brick court, may be made an outdoor one, and placed within the reach of all, as the above described portable court can be erected in a few minutes on a lawn, on ice, or in any suitable sized space either in or out of doors.

The hourglass court, as
illustrated in Major
Wingfield's book.
Fischer Collection

It is now defunct, but a plaque on the wall of a hotel marks its site.

The enthusiasm at Leamington remained local. Wingfield promoted his invention industriously and the new game was written about in the press. By the midsummer of 1874, croquet, the national pastime of England on vicarage lawns, had a serious rival. Like croquet, it was played as much by women as by men.

The court was shaped like an hourglass, wider at the baseline than at the net, 30 feet narrowing to 21 feet. Its length was 60 feet.

The height of the net was four feet, eight inches at both center and sidelines. Service was from a lozenge-shaped area in midcourt on one side to a rectangular service court drawn on the baseline at the other end. Rackets scoring was used, a game comprising 15 points to be won only when serving.

Other manufacturers were soon marketing sets of lawn tennis, all with different rules. The popularity of the new game caused the Marylebone Cricket Club in November 1874 to call a meeting of interested parties with a view to laying down a common code of play.

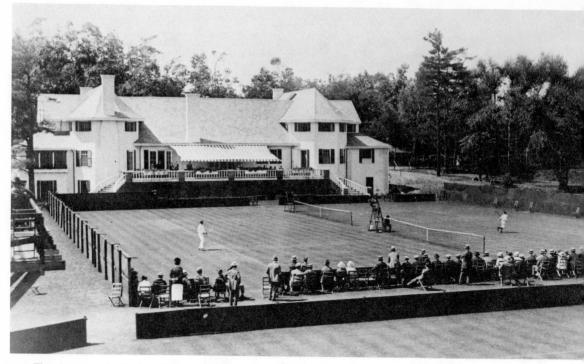

The Longwood Cricket Club had lawn tennis as early as 1878 at its original site in Boston. *Fischer Collection*

The MCC was the logical body to take such step. At that time it administered not only cricket, the major British summer sport, but also court tennis and rackets, from which the novelty was derived.

A public meeting took place in March 1875 and a committee subsequently set down the rules. The court was to be 30 feet wide at the base, the standard. The length was settled at its present 78 feet. The service court was drawn from the net, not from the baseline, to a distance of 26 feet. Service delivery had to be made with one foot outside the baseline in accordance with the rules of J. H. Hales, who was as zealous a promoter of "Germains Lawn Tennis" as was Wingfield of his "Sphairistike." Rackets scoring was retained.

In the meantime, an important event took place at the All England Croquet Club, its 12 lawns beside the London and South Western Railway in Worple Road, Wimbledon, a fast-growing London suburb. Founded in 1868, the AECC had not flourished, and to increase its membership it was agreed to set aside lawns for lawn tennis and badminton.

As in England, the game spread rapidly in America, no doubt for the same reasons. It filled a social need. It is on record that the players using the Appleton court in Nahant in 1876 organized a handicap tournament that had 15 entries. Dr. Dwight beat Fred Sears in the final.

In the same year, the first purely lawn tennis club in the U.S. was formed. This was the New Orleans Lawn Tennis Club, the most venerable of its kind in America.

The Longwood Cricket Club, then situated near Fenway Park in Boston at the corner of Brookline and Longwood Avenues, adopted lawn tennis in 1878. An older institution, the Merion Cricket Club, Philadelphia, which was founded in 1865, took up the new game in 1879. In that year a concrete court, making the name "lawn tennis" more technical than descriptive, was built in Santa Monica, California. The Orange Lawn Tennis Club in New Jersey had its beginnings in 1880.

An outstanding year in the history of the game was 1877. By then lawn tennis was so well established at the All England Croquet Club that its name was changed to the All England Croquet and Lawn Tennis Club (later to be known simply as the All England Club). Legend has it that the pony roller was in need of repair. To ease this pressing financial burden the committee, meeting in June 1877, approved a motion to stage a lawn tennis meeting open to all amateurs. One of the prime objects of its founding was the staging of a croquet championship. So why not a lawn championship?

Dr. Henry Jones, considered one of the founding fathers of the game, was appointed secretary. Jones—he was a medical practitioner—was well known for his authoritative writing on most sports and games under the pen name of "Cavendish" in the sporting weekly *The Field*. Julian Marshall and C. G. Heathcote were fellow committee members appointed to run the event.

Marshall, an old Harrovian, was a tennis and rackets player and the historian of the venerable sport of tennis, from which lawn tennis was derived. Heathcote was a court lawyer who later became stipendiary magistrate at Brighton, England, and, a few years later, a historian of lawn tennis, the sport he did much to create.

The committee members were faced with more than the normal problems of staging a tournament. They had to determine, at very short notice, under what rules lawn tennis should be played. What kind of balls? What size and shape of court? What scoring? The MCC code specifically permitted variation. There were almost as many codes of lawn tennis as there were players.

Jones was appointed referee of The Lawn Tennis Championships, and *The Field*, which had already announced the new event, added the further information that "A Silver Challenge Cup, value 25 guineas, would be given by the proprietors of *The Field*, to be competed for annually on conditions to be laid down by the committee of the AEC and LT Club."

The conditions were momentous in that they settled the future course of lawn tennis. Jones and his committee decreed a rectangular court 78 feet in length, 27 feet in width. They declared that tennis, rather than rackets, scoring should be used. On this foundation the game was built.

In the light of experience, changes were made for the Wimbledon Championships in subsequent years. Originally the height of the net was five feet at the sides, three feet, three inches at the center. It became standardized at

its present dimensions of three feet, six inches—three feet in 1882. In 1877 the distance of the service line from the net was 26 feet. By 1880 it had reduced to its present 21 feet.

Only one event was staged, the men's singles. An entry of 22 was received, and on Monday, July 9, 1877, on a fine, sunny day, The Lawn Tennis Championships began. One entrant, C. F. Buller, was absent, so there were only 10 instead of the expected 11 matches.

The 11 survivors were reduced to six on Tuesday, then to three on Wednesday. The notion of restricting byes to the first round was still some years short of coming into use. On Thursday William Marshall had a free passage into the final while Spencer W. Gore beat Heathcote, 6–2, 6–5, 6–2. Advantage sets had been adjoined, but only for the final.

The title match was held over until the following Monday. Such delay had been indicated in the prospectus to allow for the Eton and Harrow cricket match at Lords. This was the ultimate sporting event so far as the fashionable London world was concerned, and lawn tennis, itself a fashionable sport, did not dream for many years of coming into conflict with that important fixture.

Monday turned out wet, and the final was postponed until Thursday, July 19. That day was also damp, but rather than disappoint 200 spectators, each of whom had paid one shilling (then about 25 cents) to see Wimbledon's inaugural final, Gore and Marshall sportingly agreed to play. Gore, who came up to the net and volleyed—whether this was entirely sporting was a matter of some debate, as was his striking the ball before it had crossed the net—He won, 6–1, 6–2, 6–4.

Gore, an old Harrovian of 27, had played rackets at school and was a keen cricketer. He did not think much of the new game. He defended his title the next year, losing in the Challenge Round to Frank Hadow, another old Harrovian on leave from coffee planting in Ceylon, who circumvented the volleyer by lobbing. Gore later wrote:

> That anyone who has really played well at cricket, tennis, or even rackets, will ever seriously give his attention to lawn tennis, beyond showing himself to be a promising player, is

extremely doubtful; for in all probability the monotony of the game as compared with the others would choke him off before he had time to excel at it.

Those were the views of the world's first champion. Gore died in 1906, still a keen cricketer.

Competing in 1878 was a former Cambridge court tennis player, A. T. Myers. He was an innovator. He served overhead. Yet it is clear that at the time there was more of the vicarage lawn than athleticism about the infant game. In 1879 the Wimbledon champion was in fact a vicar. He was the Reverend John Hartley, yet another old Harrovian. He kept his title in 1880, and his ability to go on returning the ball was notorious.

In 1881 the game took on a new dimension. Two wealthy young twins from Cheltenham, in the west of England, initiated a dominance that endured for nearly a decade. They were William and Ernest Renshaw. In that year William won the first of his seven singles titles at Wimbledon. In the final he beat Hartley, 6–0, 6–1, 6–1, in a uniquely brief and devastating 37 minutes.

Its brevity is partly explained by the fact that at that time players changed ends only after each set. It is also explained by the difference in style. Hartley was a gentle retriever. Renshaw served hard, volleyed hard, smashed hard, and went for fast winners all round. He and Ernest created modern lawn tennis. Crowds flocked to see them play.

The Scottish Championships in Edinburgh were inaugurated in 1878. The Irish Championships in Dublin began in 1879 and were notable for initiating a women's singles as well as a mixed doubles event. The women's events, however, were restricted in some degree. While the main part of the tournament was played on courts prepared in Fitzwilliam Square and open to the public, the women were confined to the relative privacy of the Fitzwilliam Club itself. Only members and their guests were permitted the sight of well-turned ankles on display. The first woman champion of the world was May Langrishe.

The men's singles champion in the first Irish Championships was V. St. Leger Gould. In the same year he became finalist in the All Comers' singles at Wimbledon, losing to the gentle Hartley. Many years later Gould wrote a unique chapter for himself in the history of the game by being convicted of murder by a French court and getting sent to Devil's Island, where he died.

A "Championship of America" was staged in 1880. It began on September 1 on the courts at the Staten Island Cricket and Baseball Club. The prize was a silver cup valued at $100. Rackets scoring was used, with the results turning on the aggregate number of aces.

An Englishman, O. E. Woodhouse, wrote from Chicago asking if he could enter. He was a member of the West Middlesex Club, Ealing, England. He had played that year in the Wimbledon Championships and reached the All Comers' final before losing to Herbert Lawford. Woodhouse had an overhead service, a novelty to American players. With this advantage he reached the final, where he beat a Canadian, J. F. Helmuth, 15–11, 14–15, 15–9, 10–15, a score of 54 points to 50.

In October 1880 there was a tournament played in Beacon Park, Boston. The winner was Richard Sears. Tennis scoring was used. The nonstandardization of the game, both in its equipment and scoring, brought increasing difficulties as it grew. There was controversy about the correct way to play lawn tennis.

With the need for standardization in mind, a meeting was arranged at the Fifth Avenue Hotel in New York on May 21, 1881, in the name of three prominent clubs: the Beacon Park Athletic Association of Boston, the Staten Island Cricket and Baseball Club of New York, and the All Philadelphia Lawn Tennis Committee.

There were 33 clubs represented, and the U.S. National Lawn Tennis Association, as it was then named, came into being. A constitution was drawn up. The rules of the All England Club and the MCC were adopted. R. S. Oliver of the Albany Lawn Tennis Club was elected president, and Clarence Clark was elected secretary and treasurer. A vicepresident and an executive committee of three were also chosen.

This was the first national association in the world. It is the doyen of such bodies. Apart from its standardization of the game, where the British example was followed, its other major decision was to inaugurate the National Championships of the United States, men's singles, and men's doubles. As a venue it settled on the Newport Casino, Newport, Rhode Island, probably without equal at that time as the resort of wealth and fashion.

It began on August 31, 1881, with a singles entry of 25. Except for the final, the best of three sets, not of five, was played. Richard Sears won without losing a set. He was 19 years, 10 months, and the first U.S. champion would have a remarkable career. He won seven times in all, playing through in both 1882 and 1883 without losing a set. In 1884 the Challenge Round was instituted, and in the title match Sears yielded a set for the first time, to Howard Taylor. After three further victories he did not defend in 1888. Sears' unique singles record: matches played, 18; matches won, 18. From 1882 through 1887 he also won the doubles six times—five with James Dwight and once with Joseph Clark.

Sears learned to volley in 1881, the same time that the Renshaw twins were introducing their arts of aggression in England. They did so independently of each other.

The fame of the Renshaws was spread around and Americans were keen to test it. In 1883 the Clark brothers from Philadelphia, Joseph and Clarence, got the consent of the American doubles champions, Dwight and Sears, to act as American representatives, and following the championship meeting played two challenge matches against the Renshaws at the All England Croquet Club. On July 18 William and Ernest beat the Clarks, 6–4, 8–6, 3–6, 6–1. Five days later they won again, 6–3, 6–2, 6–3. The Clarks played one up, one back. The Renshaws advanced to the net side by side.

In 1884 the Wimbledon meeting was enlarged to include a women's singles and a men's doubles. The doubles cups were passed on from the tournament, which had been staged, albeit with failing interest, at Oxford since 1879 and where originally the distance was over the best of seven sets.

Among the challengers for the new doubles event at Wimbledon were Dwight and Sears. Dwight was a member of the first executive committee of the USNLTA and president of the association, 1882–84. He worked to harmonize the American and British rules of the game.

Only Dwight was a serious contender in the singles at Wimbledon and he was beaten in the second round, 7–5 in the fifth set, by Herbert Chipp. In the doubles, played as a separate event after the singles was finished, Dwight and Sears met the Renshaws in the semi-final and were roundly beaten, 6–0, 6–1, 6–2.

The other new Wimbledon event, the women's singles, was staged at the same time. The first winner, 1884, from a field of 13 ambitious and progressive-minded young ladies, was Maud Watson. She was 19 years old, and in the final she faced her elder sister, Lilian. They were the daughters of the vicar of Berkswell, a village in the heart of England. Maud won a tough match, 6–8, 6–3, 6–3.

The losing semifinalist to Watson, Blanche Bingley (later Mrs. Hillyard), became one of the most indefatigable champions of all time. She won the singles six times between 1886 and 1900 and played for the last time in 1913 when she was 49 years old.

Before winning at Wimbledon in 1884, Watson beat the first woman champion in the world, May Langrishe, the Irish wnner of 1879, in Dublin. There was coincidence in the deaths of the two women players, who have enduring fame as pioneer champions. Langrishe died at a ⁊house called "Hammersmead" in Charmouth, a small seaside resort in Devonshire, England, in 1939. Seven years later Watson died in the same house.

The women, recognized first by the Irish in 1879, made their early efforts in England and Ireland in concert with the men. In the U.S. the women came forward independently, at least in the beginning.

Four of the best Philadelphia players—Ellen Hansell, Bertha Townsend, Louise Allerdice and Margaret Ballard—were responsible for organizing the first women's singles championship of the United States at the Philadelphia Cricket Club in 1887. It was won by Hansell. The next year Townsend was the victor.

On February 9, 1889, the USNLTA carried a motion that "its protection be extended to the Lady Lawn Tennis players of the country." The tournament held later that year, when Bertha Townsend was again the winner, was the official National Championship of the U.S., and the two earlier meetings were granted retrospective recognition.

A doubles event was added to the tournament in 1890. The Roosevelt family from New York dominated both competitions, Ellen winning the singles by beating her sister Grace in the final and together taking the doubles.

Ireland's Mabel Cahill won in 1891 and again one year later. It may be noted that she beat Elizabeth Moore in 1891, 5–7, 6–3, 6–4, 4–6, 6–2. For the next eight years the women played the best of five sets.

It was not unknown in Britain, though the women at Wimbledon at no time competed over such a distance.

The growth of lawn tennis round the world was fast. Clubs were founded in Scotland, Brazil, and India in 1875. It was played in Germany in 1876. In 1877 the Fitzwilliam Club was started in Dublin, Ireland, and the Decimal Club was the first in France, in Paris. Australia, Sweden, Italy, Hungary, and Peru had lawn tennis courts in 1878, and the first tournament in Australia was the Victorian Championship meeting in 1879. Denmark and Switzerland date their beginnings from 1880, Argentina from 1881. The first club in the Netherlands was in 1882; in Jamaica in 1883; and in 1885 in both Greece and Turkey. Lawn tennis came to Lebanon in 1889, to Egypt in 1890, and to Finland in the same year. South Africa's first championship was staged in 1891.

The United States Association was a well-established body seven years before the British were similarly organized. From the first Wimbledon Championship meeting in 1877 the authority on the rules of the game was jointly the All England Croquet Club and the MCC, with the latter body taking a decreasing interest year by year. After earlier attempts

had failed, the British Lawn Tennis Association was inaugurated at a meeting in London, England, in 1888. The All England Croquet Club at once yielded its authority to the new body. William Renshaw was elected president, and Herbert Chipp was elected the honorary secretary.

The election of William Renshaw was appropriate in that his warm personality and high playing skill had, with the like qualities of his twin, Ernest, changed lawn tennis from a pastime into a popular spectator sport with crowds flocking to enjoy the magnetism of the Renshaws.

When the Renshaws held sway, the crowds at Wimbledon swelled and the London and South Western Railway built a station by the side of the All England Croquet Club to accommodate them. William won the singles seven times, 1881–89, and in doubles he and Ernest were virtually invincible. Their retirement brought a tennis slump. The nadir, so far as Wimbledon was concerned, was 1895, when the championship meeting brought a financial loss—33 pounds—for the first and only time.

In the course of time a certain measure of chauvinism was shown in the relationship of the ruling bodies of American and British tennis. At the end of the last century it was no more than a healthy rivalry between enthusiasts.

Apart from the successful intervention by O. E. Woodhouse in the unofficial American championship of 1880, there do not seem to have been any further challenges taken across the Atlantic from east to west until 1888. England's C. G. Eames competed in some U.S. tournaments that year without marked success.

In 1889 E. G. Meers, who was one of the top British players, was the first overseas challenger in the Nationals at Newport. He lost in five sets to Oliver Campbell, then 18 years old. The following year Campbell became champion for the first time and, at the age of 19½, was the youngest to do so.

(It was evidently a time that favored youth. One year later, in 1891, Wilfred Baddeley won the men's singles championship at Wimbledon at 19½. That record, like that of Campbell, has remained.)

Manlove Goodbody, one of the many Irishmen who were prominent in the game in the British Isles, gained notable success at Newport in 1893. He beat Clarence Hobart and William Larned, both players of championship ilk, and failed only in the Challenge Round, to Robert Wrenn.

In 1895 what almost amounted to a representative contest between the Americans and the British took the form of a round-robin in tournament at the Neighborhood Club, West Newton, Massachusetts. The British were from Ireland, Joshua Pim, the Wimbledon champion of 1893 and 1894, and Harold Mahony, destined to become the champion in 1896. The Americans were Larned, who later became a seven-time U.S. singles champion, Hobart, and Malcolm Chace. Pim lost only to Hobart, while Mahony, unbeaten by Americans, lost only to Pim. The first prize went to Pim, the second to Mahony.

The British challenge at Newport in 1897 was formidable, comprising Mahony, Nisbet, and Wilberforce Eaves, the last Australian-born but living in England. The British spectators, if there were any among the wealthy and fashionable who came to the Newport Casino, must have held their heads high. Eaves and Nisbet made an all-British final in the All Comers' singles. Eaves was the winner and challenged Wrenn. American pride was restored. Wrenn won in five sets as he took the title for the fourth time. It was the second occasion he had had to thwart a cross-Atlantic challenge.

Anglo-American rivalry was channeled into a team instead of an individual exercise in 1900. Dwight Davis put up his famous Davis Cup for competition in that year. He had been inspired twelve months earlier by a tennis playing tour he undertook with Holcombe Ward, Malcolm Whitman, and Beals Wright, all keen players in their early twenties. Accompanied by George Wright, the father of Beals, they traveled some 8,000 miles, from the Atlantic Coast to the Pacific and up to British Columbia.

The USNLTA accepted his offer and the International Tennis Challenge Trophy was offered to the world. They had the British primarily in mind and the British, despite the

Dwight Davis (right), donor of the Davis Cup in 1900, won the U.S. Doubles Championship with Holcombe Ward (left) in 1899, 1900, and 1901. *Fischer Collection*

Boer War then taking place in South Africa, took up the challenge.

Dwight Davis was named as the U.S. captain for the inaugural tie. He was then 21 and had reached the All Comers' singles final at Newport in 1899. Whitman, 23, the champion of 1898, and Ward, 22, doubles partner of Davis, were the other members. The venue chosen was the Longwood Cricket Club, still at its original Boston site, and the matches were arranged for early August, well before the Newport meeting at the end of the month.

The British team comprised Arthur Gore, Ernest Black, and H. Roper Barrett. The 32-year-old Gore still had a lot of tennis life in him and had not then won any of his three Wimbledon singles titles. The Scottish Black did not achieve the distinction of reaching the last eight at Wimbledon. Barrett was noted as a player of subtle abilities. It was not the best British team, since it was selected not only on playing ability but, also on a capacity to spare both the time and the money for the trip.

When the British arrived in Boston there was no one to meet them. Undaunted, they took the opportunity to pay a visit to Niagara Falls and eventually turned up at the Longwood Club in the best of spirits, though without having had much practice.

They found the courts too soft and the balls not hard enough either. They also found they had underestimated American playing skill. The American twist service, particularly that of Holcomb Ward, confounded them utterly.

The first two singles were played side by side on adjoining courts. Whitman beat Gore in three easy sets. Davis beat Black after losing the opening set. Black and Barrett could not take a set in the doubles against Ward and Davis. On the last day Davis was one set up and nine games each in the second against Gore when it rained and further play was abandoned. The U.S. had won by a mile.

Later, by the sea at Newport, Gore and Black made an effort to retrieve British honor. They clashed in the quarterfinals and Gore survived, only to lose to George Wrenn in the next round. Whitman revealed the temper of his steel. He thrust back the challenge of Larned to keep his title.

Anglo-American rivalry continued to be the international aspect of tennis for some years. There was no challenge for the Davis Cup in 1901, but in 1902 the British renewed their effort, sending Reggie and Laurie Doherty, the finest British players of all time, with Joshua Pim. They played against Whitman, Davis, and Larned at the Crescent Athletic Club in Brooklyn, New York. As in 1900 the two singles were played at the same time on adjacent courts. Fearful of Laurie's fitness, the British played Pim with Reggie Doherty in the singles. The doubles was scheduled to take place on the third day. By that time the tie was over, for Pim lost both his singles and Reggie was beaten by Whitman. The British plan to reserve Laurie's strength for the doubles had lost its point.

The classic powers of the Dohertys, which had captivated the crowds at Wimbledon and elsewhere in Britain, were again displayed to American audiences later in the month at Newport. The brothers reached the semifinals and should have played one another. Laurie gave a walkover to his elder brother and Reggie went on to beat Whitman in the final. But Reggie, though he had beaten Larned in the singles in the Davis Cup, could not repeat his success when the U.S. title was at stake.

The year 1903 was a turning point and the British challenge in the United States was as effective as it was formidable. In the Davis Cup, where the British Isles were again the only challengers, the venue was again the Longwood Club in Boston. Reggie and Laurie Doherty were put forward as a two-man side and made a daring start. Because Reggie was unfit—he was not strong—the British conceded his opening singles.

Apart from the default, the Americans, with Larned and Robert Wrenn for the singles, Robert and George Wrenn for the doubles, did not win a match. The British won, 4–1, and took the Davis Cup back with them to England.

The Doherty brothers achieved something more. In the Nationals at Newport they were again cast against one another in the quarterfinals. This time Laurie was given the walkover. He went on to reach the Challenge Round, where he dispossessed Larned of his title, 6–0, 6–3, 10–8, rather more easily achieved than his win in the Davis Cup, where his measure had been 7–5 in the fifth set.

Laurie Doherty, the first man to take the U.S. national Championship in singles overseas, was then 27 and perhaps at his peak. Reggie, three years older, won the Wimbledon singles 1897–1900. The more robust Laurie followed with a five-year sequence 1901–6. Their classic skill became a British legend and their impeccable sportsmanship became a byword. In doubles there was only one year between 1897 and 1905 when they were not Wimbledon champions. The American title fell to them in 1902 and 1903.

If 1903 was a momentous year for the U.S. Championships, that of 1905 was equally so for Wimbledon. There was an American woman challenger for the first time in 1900 when Marion Jones, then currently the U.S. champion, got as far as the quarterfinals. Five years later a chubby, robust 18-year-old from California with an intimidating forehand made a memorable appearance. She was May Sutton and she, too, was the American title-holder. She was, as it happened, English-born, having seen the light of day at Plymouth, Devonshire, as the daughter of a British naval captain who later went with his family to the U.S.

The staunch Sutton penetrated a citadel where the names of some women players were already being spoken of in bated breath. Most venerated at that time was Lottie Dod. She won the first of her five championships when only 15 years old. There was Blanche Hillyard, six times the champion. Dorothea Douglass (later Mrs. Lambert Chambers) had, when the uninhibited Sutton appeared, already won twice and was on the way to making herself a legend.

Sutton carved through all opposition and had the temerity to stop Douglass from winning for the third time. Sutton was the first overseas player to take a Wimbledon champi-

onship. This was in a year that saw the biggest overseas invasion to date, for in 1905 there were among the men five Americans, two New Zealanders, three Australians, three Belgians, two Danes, and a South African.

Tennis was in fact assuming an international role. The Davis Cup in 1905 enlarged to six nations. With the British Isles as holders, Belgium and France had challenged in 1904. So did Austria, only to withdraw before taking the court. The United States, in the position of having to be a challenger for the first time, did not then do so, for the difficulties of finding a team to cross the Atlantic proved overwhelming.

But in 1905 teams from the U.S., France, Austria, and Australasia converged on London. Belgium should have done so but in the event conceded a walkover to the U.S. At Queen's Club in July, after the Wimbledon meeting was finished, the four nations played a knock-out competition to decide the best fitted to challenge the British Isles for the trophy. The U.S. beat France, 5–0. Australasia beat Austria, 5–0. The U.S. then beat Australasia, 5–0. In the Challenge Round the British beat the U.S., 5–0. It all took place in 12 days, July 13–24.

The Australasian side (until 1923 New Zealand and Australia functioned as a single entity for tennis) included Norman Brookes and Tony Wilding. Each was to impress himself deeply in the history of the game. New Zealand's Wilding combined athletic skill, good looks, and a personality that made him a teen-age idol long before such a phenomenon was known to exist.

In 1907 the men's singles at Wimbledon was won by Brookes. He was one of the world's all-time great volleyers, a left-hander of consummate skill. Brookes and Wilding took the men's doubles. May Sutton, who had lost her women's singles in 1906 to Dorothea Douglass, won it back again. All three championship titles at Wimbledon—at that time the women's and mixed doubles did not have the same high status—went overseas. A contemporary wrote that a new epoch had been initiated in the history of lawn tennis.

In the U.S., the championship meeting at Newport settled back after the Doherty sortie

The British-born May Sutton, the first American to win at Wimbledon, in 1905 and again in 1907, won the U.S. Singles title in 1904. *Fischer Collection*

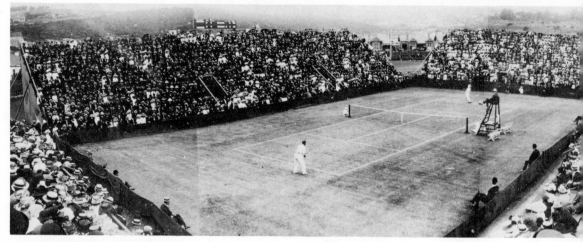

New Zealand's Tony Wilding (foreground), representing Australasia, vanquishes England's M. H. Long in 1909 Davis Cup play at Sydney, Australia. *Fischer Collection*

of 1903 to control its own destinies. The outstanding player of the first decade of the century was Larned. This graduate of Cornell won the Inter-Collegiate Championship, a title established as early as 1883, in 1892. A New York stockbroker, he won the U.S. singles for the first time in 1901 when he was 28. He equaled the record of Richard Sears by taking it seven times, the last in 1911.

Larned competed first at Newport in 1891. He played 72 singles in all and won 61. Only William T. Tilden, the other seven-time winner along with Sears, did better, playing the same number of singles, 72, and winning 67. Larned had an unbroken sequence of 11 victories from 1907, when he played through and won, to his success in his last Challenge Round of 1911.

The popularity of the Newport singles reached unprecedented heights during his career. The entry passed 128 for the first time in 1908. It peaked at 202 in 1911, and this was the last year of the Challenge Round.

The winner in 1912 was a Californian, Maurice McLoughlin. His dynamic serving brought a new dimension to the game and so, perhaps, did his background. He was the first public parks player to take a title that had been dominated by men from wealthy families. With McLoughlin's game, service and volley came first. "The California Comet," as he was known, electrified tennis prior to the First World War.

He was a precociously skilled player. He took the Pacific Coast Championship, an event dating from 1889, in 1907, when he was 17. His triumph at Newport in 1912 came after losing the All Comers' final to Bill Clothier in 1909, after yielding in the quarterfinal to Beals Wright in 1910 and after taking the All Comers' event and losing to Larned in the Challenge Round of 1911.

In 1913 McLoughlin made his only appearance in Europe. Wimbledon spectators

Maurice McLoughlin won his second U.S. Singles title in 1912 when, two sets down, he took the next three against Wallace Johnson in the final. *Fischer Collection*

were awestruck by his serving, and the word "cannonball" was used for the first time. His reputation preceded him and he did not disappoint. Before record crowds he came through the All Comers' singles and challenged Wilding, the title-holder since 1910, for the crown. "The history of the match," it was written at the time, "may be succinctly stated by saying that McLoughlin ought to have won the first set and was very near to winning the third. He lost both of them, and the second into the bargain, and so Wilding retained the honors." The score: 8–6, 6–3, 10–8.

Wilding's invincibility at Wimbledon was brought to an end in 1914 by his Davis Cup colleague, Norman Brookes. The great Australian was 36 years old when he won his second Wimbledon singles championship. Later that year he and Wilding were in America challenging the U.S. for the Davis Cup. They played at the West Side Tennis Club, Forest Hills, a few days after the start of World War I. (Wilding was killed, aged 31, on May 9, 1915, at Neuve Chapelle on the Western Front.)

McLoughlin won both his singles against Australasia. In the first, he beat Brookes, 17–15, 6–3, 6–3, and the strength of his service and volley had never been so devastatingly displayed. Nonetheless, Australasia won, 3–2. The International Team trophy had been in contention 13 times, with three successes for the U.S., five for the British, and five for Australasia.

The West Side Tennis Club staged its first Davis Cup in 1911 when America beat the British Isles, 4–1. The famous club was founded in 1892, when 13 founder members rented three clay courts on Central Park West between 88th and 89th Streets, Manhattan. By the end of that season there were 43 members, five courts, and the initiation fee was $10, with a yearly subscription of the same amount.

A move was made to a site near Columbia University at 117th Street between Morningside Drive and Amsterdam Avenue in 1902. Six years later a further move took the club to 238th Street and Broadway, where there was room for 12 grass and 15 clay courts. The shift to Forest Hills in Queens was made in 1913. Until the building of the concrete stadium in 1923 the main courts were in front of the clubhouse, flanked by temporary stands.

The West Side Tennis Club became the host of the National Men's Singles Championship in 1915. In 1914, the last year at Newport, Norris Williams reversed the outcome of the final of the preceding year and beat McLoughlin to take the title. In the first meeting at Forest Hills, McLoughlin was again the losing finalist, this time to Bill Johnston.

The Newport Casino, after 34 years as the home of America's most prestigious event, had outlived its purpose. The age it represented, of wealth and fashion and leisure, was passing. The victory by McLoughlin, the public parks player, had been significant.

In due course—1920—the West Side Tennis Club became the home of the U.S. Women's Championships as well. Until that time the Philadelphia Cricket Club was the site. The champion of 1908, Maud Barger Wallach, took a special place in the roll of winners. She was 37 when she won the title, having taken up the game as late as 30. When she was 44 she still ranked No. 5 in the U.S.

The successor to Mrs. Wallach was Hazel Hotchkiss, who became Mrs. George W. Wightman in 1912 and in the course of her career the winner of innumerable national titles. Her name would have survived as a valiant and stalwart champion even without the Wightman Cup she later founded.

Hazel Wightman was succeeded as national singles champion in 1915 by the Norwegian-born Molla Bjurstedt. As Molla Mallory she took the fame of the American women's game into the postwar years. Her record, though, was not exclusively as an American. When the Olympic Games were staged in Stockholm in 1912 she represented Norway and won the bronze medal for the women's singles on indoor courts.

Tennis was featured as part of the Olympic Games from the first in Athens in 1896 to the Paris event of 1924. At the prewar games British players predominated except for those at St. Louis in 1904. Only men took part and the gold medalists were exclusively American, Beals Wright taking one for the singles and, with E. W. Leonard, the doubles.

In international administration 1913 was an

important year. It marked the founding of the International Lawn Tennis Federation. Prior to this time the world governing body, so far as there had been one, had been the British Lawn Tennis Association. Its membership included clubs and associations from all round the world.

In 1913 the BLTA members included the associations of Australasia, Belgium, Bohemia, Ceylon, Chile, Finland, Hungary, Ireland, Jamaica, Mauritius, Netherlands, Norway, the Riviera, Russia, South Africa, Spain, and Switzerland, as well as 26 individual clubs from 15 countries.

The ILTF had its inaugural meeting in Paris on March 1, 1913. Its founder members were Australasia, Austria, Belgium, the British

Mary Browne (left) was U.S. Singles champion in 1912, 1913, and 1914, and with Louise Williams (right) won the doubles in 1913, 1914, and 1921. *Fischer Collection*

Isles, Denmark, France, Germany, Netherlands, Russia, South Africa, Sweden, and Switzerland. The U.S. was voteless and was only informally represented—by one of the British delegates, H. Anthony Sabelli, secretary of the British LTA.

The absence of the U.S. resulted in the Davis Cup organization developing along different lines from the ILTF, parallel but separate. (The merger between the two international bodies did not take place until 1978, and even then the difference of voting procedure was left to mark the original reluctance of America to yield any of its independence to the world's governing body.)

The reluctance of the U.S. to join the ILTF was occasioned by the allocation of various "World Championship" titles. The Wimbledon meeting was granted ("in perpetuity") the description of "The World Championships on Grass." There was a "World Championship on Hard Court," which was staged mainly in Paris, and also a peripatetic "World Championship on Covered Courts." When these grandiose titles were abolished soon after World War I, the U.S. found its way clear to become a member of the ILTF.

An early winner of the women's singles in the World's Hard Court Championships in Paris was a promising girl who was only 15 years old. She won the women's doubles with an American, Elizabeth Ryan. She was from Picardy and her name was Suzanne Lenglen, the greatest player in the history of the women's game.

Ryan's name was also to echo reverberatingly in the annals of tennis. Even before 1914 this Californian had laid the foundation of her career as an assiduous, effective competitor.

The doubles events at Wimbledon, the women's and mixed, became full championship competitions in 1913 when officially the World title on grass belonged to it. In 1914, the indefatigable Ryan partnered A. M. Morton to win the women's doubles, the first of 19 titles she was to gain at Wimbledon.

The Riviera season was by then a well-established feature of the game, reflecting the world of fashion, wealth, and leisure, of which tennis had become as much a part in

Europe as it had in the U.S., where Newport had been for so long a center.

Immediately prior to the First World War, however, it was perhaps Imperial Russia that represented the high point of tennis in its smart social context. A party of British men who played in what was then St. Petersburgh in the Russian Championships of 1913 recorded that the ball boys were footmen in ornate uniforms who passed the balls on silver salvers. Ryan was the last women's champion of Imperial Russia, a title she was never able to defend.

Ryan was overshadowed at this time, like all other women, by Dorothea Lambert Chambers, as Dorothea Douglass had become. She made 13 attempts to win the Wimbledon singles between 1902 and 1920, and she was beaten only six times. At the age of 24 she won for the first time, in 1903. Her seventh success was in 1914. She was the precursor of great, near-invincible players.

Yet at this period it was still possible to be near invincible and excel at other sports. Mrs. Lambert Chambers was one such, for she was a champion at badminton and a top-class field hockey player.

The Davis Cup strongly helped boost tennis as an international sport. Prior to 1914, when the war brought the competition to a temporary halt, nine nations participated: the U.S., the British Isles, Belgium, France, Australasia, Austria, Germany, Canada, and South Africa.

The Australian Championships were staged first in 1905. Four years earlier the former British colonies of Victoria, New South Wales, and others united in a federal government.

A notable woman champion of New Zea-

Norris Williams and Gustav Touchard are playing in the U.S. Nationals at the Newport Casino. Williams won the championship in 1914 and 1916. *Fischer Collection*

land was K. M. Nunneley. She took the title first in 1895 and for the 13th successive year in 1907. Rose Payten was prominent in Australian tournaments in the early 1900s and an Australian, Stanley Doust, who was familiar with playing standards in Australia, Europe, and America, averred that she was as good as any of the top players elsewhere, Mrs. Lambert Chambers, Molla Mallory, and the like. But the women's game in the Southern Hemisphere was a long way short of reaching outside its own orbit.

The French, prior to the war, made an impact on the world with men of high caliber, Andre Gobert and Max Decugis most notably. They won the men's doubles at Wimbledon in 1911. A German pair, Heinrich Kleinschroth and Frederik Rahe, were runners-up for the title in 1913. In 1912 Kleinschroth competed in the U.S. Nationals at Newport but did not survive the opening round.

The German Championships was an event favored by British players and among the fashionable happenings of season. They were staged in Hamburg from 1892.

Canada's first championships were held two years earlier, in 1890. The first tournament staged was on the turf of the Montreal Cricket Club in 1878. Like those in the U.S., the first official championships followed the founding of the Canadian Lawn Tennis Association in Toronto in 1890. The first women's championship was held in Toronto in 1892.

In Europe the outbreak of the war in 1914 brought a halt to competitive tennis. Australia, more remote, staged its championships for the 1914–15 season, and a Britisher, Gordon Lowe, was the winner.

In the United States the game was affected to a lesser degree. Inevitably the international field dried up. In 1917, when America became directly involved in the war, there was a break. The National Championships were not staged as such that year, though the continuity of the events was not broken. The events were known as "Patriotic Tournaments," with the winners not taking full championship status.

In 1918 a tall, slightly ungainly man from Philadelphia, William Tatem Tilden II, did well in the National Singles at the West Side Tennis Club. He reached the final, where he was beaten by R. Lindley Murray, left-hander with a big service. Murray had revealed his aggressive qualities by taking the patriotic event the year before.

Tilden was not all that young to make his mark. He was, in fact, 25 years old. He was a late developer. His record was to surpass, by far, that of Larned and Sears.

Tennis players all (left to right): Lieutenant Colonel Dwight Davis, Major R. D. Wrenn, Major Bill Larned, Captain Watson Washburn, Captain Norris Williams, Captain O. S. Walters, Lieutenant Dean Mathey, Colonel Wallace Johnson. *USLTA*

2 } WAS IT REALLY GOLDEN? 1919 –1945

They called it "The Golden Age of Sport." Though we tend to look back today with some skepticism on the hyperbole of the purple prose of the past, there is a large measure of truth in that phrase. The titans of the twenties—Babe Ruth, Jack Dempsey, Bobby Jones, Red Grange, and, in tennis, Bill Tilden, Suzanne Lenglen, and Helen Wills Moody—were golden because people wanted to believe they were that. It was the era after World War I when a measure of prosperity gave people more leisure, when the opening of society created a demand for heroes, and first loves are the ones who loom largest down through the years.

1919

This was the year of the arrival of Suzanne Lenglen on the world tennis stage she would dominate until she turned pro in 1926. A product of constant drilling by her father, a well-to-do Frenchman, she had style as well as ability and would come to be ranked with Helen Wills Moody as one of the two greatest women players of all time.

Lenglen appeared in her first tournament at 12 and won the singles and doubles in the World Hard Court Championships at 15, so she was not an unknown quantity when she came to Wimbledon upon the resumption of play after a four-year lapse because of World War I. Playing on grass for the first time, Lenglen won the title in a match that is still regarded as one of the greatest Wimbledon women's finals of all time.

Lenglen was no beauty. She had a long, Gallic nose, a large mouth, and a prominent chin. She was stocky and swarthy, with thick shoulders. She also possessed a short-temper fuse and a fiery disposition. She was 20 and advanced to the challenge round to play the seven-time champion, Britain's Mrs. Dorothea

"Little Bill" Johnston was the first post-World War I U.S. champion. He defeated "Big Bill" Tilden in the 1919 final. *UPI*

Lambert Chambers, who had won her first Wimbledon title in 1903.

Lenglen's dress created a sensation. The British had been accustomed to seeing their women in tight-fitting corsets, blouses, and layers of petticoats. When Suzanne stepped onto the center court in a revealing one-piece dress, with sleeves *daringly* just above the elbow, her hemline *only* just below the knee, reaction ranged from shock on the part of most women spectators—some reportedly walked out during her matches, muttering "shocking"—to delight, among most of the men.

Attending the matches were King George V and Queen Mary. Everybody was impressed by the young French women's grace and disciplined shotmaking. She won the match, 10–8, 4–6, 9–7; it wasn't until Margaret Court beat Billie Jean King, 14–12, 11–9 in 1970, that a Wimbledon women's final saw more games. After losing the second set, Lenglen sipped brandy during the interval. She took a 4–1 lead in the final set, then Lambert Chambers fought back to lead, 6–5, with two match points at 40–15. A lucky wood shot and slashing backhand winner pulled Lenglen back to deuce and she went on to win the set, the last game to love.

In the Wimbledon men's championship, Australian Gerald Patterson advanced to the Challenge Round by beating Britain's Algernon Kingscote and then met countryman Norman Brookes, who won the title in 1914, the last Wimbledon before the war. As champion, Brookes did not have to play until the Challenge Round. Patterson beat him, 6–3, 7–5, 6–2.

In the resumption of Davis Cup play after a four-year hiatus, Australasia, a combination of Australia and New Zealand, retained the Cup it had won in 1914, beating the British Isles, 4–1. Patterson was the dominant player, winning both singles and combining with Brookes to win the doubles. The Australian title went to Kingscote.

The U.S. Nationals final at Forest Hills between the 1915 champion, 5-foot, 7-inch William "Little Bill" Johnston, and 6-foot, 1½-inch William "Big Bill" Tilden, was billed in the New York *Times* as the battle for

the title, "William the Conqueror." It was the first of six meetings between the two Bills in the national finals, the only one Johnston would win. Tilden had first played in the National in 1916 and lost in straight sets in the first round to Harold Throckmorton. In 1918 he lost in the finals to R. Lindley Murray. By 1919 he was already being called the greatest player of all time. Johnston, however, spotted a weakness in Tilden, a backhand that was totally defensive, hit invariably with underspin. Johnston pounded away at the weakness nad won relatively easily, 6–4, 6–3, 6–3. Tilden would go up to a friend's indoor court in Providence Rhode Island, later in the year, work for months to correct the flaw, and come away with an improved backhand that would enable him to become the dominant tennis figure over the next decade.

For the women's championship the Challenge Round was abolished and Mrs. Hazel Hotchkiss Wightman won the title, interrupting a seven-year reign by Molla Bjurstedt of the United States, who had won in 1915, 1916, 1917, and 1918 and who would, as Mrs. Molla Mallory, win in 1920, 1921, and 1922 and then again in 1926. Miss Marion Zinderstein eliminated the defending champion in the semifinals and was beaten in the finals by Wightman, 6–1, 6–2.

1920

William Tatem Tilden II, born in 1893, the son of a Philadelphia wool merchant and prominent civic figure, came of age at 27 when he won at Wimbledon and Forest Hills and helped the United States win the Davis Cup for the first time since 1913.

In the All-Comers final at Wimbledon against the Japanese Zenzo Shimizu, Tilden fell behind in all three sets, 1–4, 2–4, 2–5, but rallied in each and won the match, 6–4, 6–4, 13–11. It became the mark of Tilden to put on a show and entertain the crowd as well as win at tennis. In his remarkable biography of Tilden, *Big Bill Tilden*, Frank Deford wrote, "Nobody realized it at the time, but it was one of Tilden's amusements, a favor to the crowd, to give lesser opponents a head start." Tilden had whipped Shimizu, 6–1,

Bill Johnston (left) and Bill Tilden sail for Auckland, New Zealand, where they swept Australasia for the Davis Cup in 1920. *Fischer Collection*

6–1, in a preliminary tournament to Wimbledon. In the final, Tilden defeated the defending champion, Australian Gerald Patterson, 2–6, 6–3, 6–2, 6–4. The Associated Press reported that "Tilden in the first set opened with experiments all around the court and then settled down mercilessly to feeding his opponent's backhand, and, as the game progressed, Patterson got worse and worse. . . . Tilden exploited his famous cut-stroke to his opponent's backhand again and again."

The British marveled at Tilden, acclaimed him the greatest player of all time, and one observer rhapsodized, "His silhouette as he prepares to serve suggests an Egyptian pyramid king about to administer punishment."

In the American championships, Tilden beat Bill Johnston in a dramatic five-set final, 6–1, 1–6, 7–5, 5–7, 6–3, that was regarded as the greatest championship final up to that time. During the match a Navy plane crashed while making passes over Forest Hills and two men were killed.

It was the first of seven straight national titles for Tilden. A flamboyant, controversial figure who dominated any match, win or lose, he came to be regarded along with Babe Ruth, Jack Dempsey, Bobby Jones, and Red Grange as one of the great names of the 1920s, America's Golden Age of Sport.

Tilden, who would not lose an important match until 1926, teamed with Johnston in a 5–0 Davis Cup sweep of Australasia. He and Johnston each took a pair of singles matches and a doubles over Norman Brookes and Gerald Patterson.

In the women's championship at Wimbledon, Mrs. Dorothea Lambert-Chambers defeated Elizabeth Ryan and Molla Mallory of the United States on the way to a return match with Suzanne Lenglen in the Challenge Round. Lenglen beat her, 6–4, 6–0. Mallory won the American title, defeating Marion Zinderstein, 6–3, 6–1.

1921

Suzanne Lenglen, who hadn't lost a match to anyone since the end of the war, came to the United States for the first time, and lost a match on a default. It was one of the most stunning developments tennis had seen up to that time, and was long talked about and cited whenever Lenglen was discussed.

The position occupied by Lenglen at the time of the great default was described by Al Laney, the eminent tennis writer. "She probably did more for women's tennis than any girl who ever played it. She broke down barriers and created a vogue, reforming tennis dress, substituting acrobatics and something of the art of the ballet where decorum had been the rule. In England and on the Continent, this slim, not very pretty but fascinating French maiden was the most popular performer in sport or out of it on the postwar scene. She became the rage, almost a cult . . . Even royalty gave her its favor and she partnered King Gustav of Sweden in the mixed doubles more than once."

Lenglen was beaten by the defending champion, Molla Mallory, in the second round of the first women's championships played at Forest Hills. Lenglen lost the first set, 6–2, seeming weak and nervous, coughing from time to time, causing some concern by those who had seen her play before. She played better in the first point of the second set, but lost the point and the game at love. Then, when she lost the first point of the second game and double faulted on her serve to trail,

Molla Mallory (left) won her sixth U.S. Singles title in 1921. Along the way she ousted Marion Jessup (right). *USLTA*

2–6, 0–1, and 0–30, she started weeping. She went to the umpire's chair and, speaking French, said she was too ill to go on. As she and the disappointed Mallory walked off the court, there was a faint hissing sound in the stands from the crowd of 8,000, the largest ever to witness a women's match in the United States.

The newspapers reported she told the umpire that she was unable to breathe and that she coughed the night before. Others recalled her saying she did not feel like playing and had been listless in a practice session. If she were suffering from menstrual cramps, that was not mentioned beacused it was a taboo subject in the public prints at the time. It was also pointed out that she had arrived in the United States only four days before her first scheduled match. Her opponent defaulted, so she did not have a warmup before her match

with Mallory, which was in the second round because there was no seeding in those days.

Lenglen incurred criticism because she appeared at Forest Hills the next day in good spirits, continuing to attend parties. Despite her signs of physical distress in the match, it was not considered acceptable to default, and there arose speculation about whether Lenglen could accept defeat. For some time the phrase "to cough and quit" was current in New York; in France there were accusations of mistreatment by the Americans and the charge that her first-round opponent had purposely defaulted to help set up Lenglen for defeat.

Mallory went on to win the U.S. Championship, her sixth, with a 4–6, 6–4, 6–2 victory in the final over Mary Browne. Lenglen had breezed to her third Wimbledon title with a 6–2, 6–0 victory over Elizabeth Ryan of the United States.

Bill Tilden retained his Wimbledon Championship, coming out of a sickbed to defend against South African Babe Norton in the Challenge Round. Tilden won, 4–6, 2–6, 6–1, 6–0, 7–5. After losing the first two sets, Tilden gave up his normal hard-hitting game, took to chops and slices, and turned the match around. This displeased the crowd, which booed Tilden despite the remonstrations of the referee that he was playing quite fairly and within the rules. Norton recovered in the last set, led 5–4 with two match points, but Tilden rallied and prevailed. F. P. Adams wrote, "He is an artist, more of an artist than nine tenths of the artists I know. It is the beauty of the game that Tilden loves; it is the chase always, rather than the quarry."

Tilden won the Nationals at Forest Hills over Wallace Johnson in straight sets and teamed with Bill Johnston to dominate a 5–0 Davis Cup victory over Japan. Tilden lost the first two sets and was within two points of defeat before beating Japan's Zenzo Shimizu in five sets in the first singles match. R. Norris Williams and Watson Washburn took the doubles. R. H. Gemmell won the Australian Championship.

Australia's Gerald Patterson won Wimbledon for the second time in 1922. *Fischer Collection*

1922

After playing at the Worple Road site in the London suburb of Wimbledon since 1877, the All England Croquet and Lawn Tennis Club moved to its present site in a picturesque hollow at the foot of Church Street near Wimbledon Common. King George V and Queen Mary attended the opening on June 22 at the new Centre Court holding 14,750 seats (the previous arena had 8,500) and saw the first match, played by Leslie Godfree and Algernon Kingscote of Great Britain.

For the first time the Challenge Round was abolished and players were seeded. Bill Tilden did not choose to make the transatlantic crossing to defend his title, and it was won by Australian Gerald Patterson, whom Tilden had dethroned in 1920. Patterson defeated Great Britain's Randolph Lycett in the final, 6–3, 6–4, 6–2.

Suzanne Lenglen avenged her controversial default to Molla Mallory at Forest Hills the year before when she trounced Mallory in the Wimbledon final, 6–2, 6–0. Lenglen's appeal was such that before her first-round match with Kathleen McKane there was a line from the underground station to the entrance to the All England Croquet Club waiting to get in. Wimbledon official Duncan Macaulay wrote, "People used to call it the 'Leng-len trail a-winding' after the famous war song of those days."

Lenglen won three Wimbledon titles for the second time. She teamed with Pat O'Hara Wood to win the mixed doubles and won the women's doubles with Elizabeth Ryan, an American who would never win a singles title at Wimbledon or Forest Hills, but who would set a record of 19 titles in women's doubles and mixed doubles at Wimbledon that Billie Jean King would surpass by one in 1979.

After her loss to Lenglen at Wimbledon,

Mallory returned to Forest Hills to win her sixth U.S. Nationals, defeating 16-year-old Helen Wills in the final, 6–3, 6–1.

The meeting between perennial rivals Bill Tilden and Bill Johnston in the U.S. Nationals at the Germantown Cricket Club was called "a match for the Greek gods." They played for a coveted championship bowl, which each had won twice and which would be retired permanently by any three-time winner. Tilden advanced to the final, beating Wimbledon champion Gerald Patterson, while Johnston defeated promising newcomer Vincent Richards. Tilden lost the first two sets, then came back to win the match, 4–6, 3–6, 6–2, 6–3, 6–4. Afterward, Johnston said, "I can't beat him, I just can't beat him." The trophy gained by Tilden had on it the names of previous winners William Larned and R. Lindley Murray (once) and Maurice McLaughlin, R. Norris Williams, and Johnston (twice each).

In the Davis Cup, Australasia advanced past Spain to the Challenge Round, where it was beaten by the United States, 4–1. In those days when there was more interest in Davis Cup play, something of a stir was created by the loss of the doubles by the U.S. team of Tilden and Richards to Gerald Patterson and Pat O'Hara Woods. Tilden and Johnston swept Patterson and James Anderson in the singles.

1923

A new stadium was constructed at the West Side Tennis Club grounds in Forest Hills. Built at a cost of $250,000, the concrete bowl that would eventually seat 14,000 opened on August 10 with the inauguration of the Wightman Cup matches.

The competition was the brainchild of Hazel Hotchkiss Wightman, who was a ladies champion in pre-World War I days and who would compete until she was past 70, winning the last of her 45 national titles at the age of 68. She had conceived the idea of a women's competition the equivalent of the Davis Cup in 1920 and donated a trophy similar to the Davis Cup, but the idea lay fallow until it was seized upon by Julian Myrick, U.S.

Lawn Tennis official, as a way of launching the new Forest Hills stadium.

The competition between Great Britain and the United States consisted of five singles matches and two doubles, and though Wightman hoped to make it an international tournament by bringing in France, that never came to pass. With Wightman as a captain, the American team of Molla Mallory, Helen Wills, and Eleanor Goss scored a 7–0 sweep, starting with an inaugural match before 5,000 in which Wills beat Kathleen McKane, 6–2, 7–5.

Wills won the first of her seven U.S. national titles, defeating Mallory, 6–2, 6–1. Suzanne Lenglen breezed through the Wimbledon field, losing only 11 games in the 12 sets she played, defeating McKane in the final, 6–2, 6–2.

With Bill Tilden, universally regarded as the kingpin of tennis, absent again from Wimbledon, Bill Johnston won for the second time. In straight sets he swept past countryman Vincent Richards, South Africa's Babe Norton, and then Frank Hunter of the United States in a final that was completed in 45 minutes. Johnston's success at Wimbledon could not carry over to the U.S. Nationals, where he was crushed by Tilden in the final, 6–4, 6–1, 6–4. Pat O'Hara Wood won the Australian title.

In a Davis Cup field increased to 17 countries from 11, Australia beat France to challenge the U.S. The U.S. won, 4–1, with Tilden winning both singles and Johnston losing one of his singles to James Anderson. In the doubles, Tilden and R. Norris Williams won the first set, 17–15 (still the most ever for a Davis Cup final), lost the second, 11–13, and the third, 2–6, before winning the final two sets from Anderson and John Hawkes.

These Davis Cup results read almost as footnotes in tennis history, because it is hard today to realize how significant the Davis Cup used to be when there was no open tennis or team tennis and when there were not so many tournaments that players could choose to skip competitions with $100,000 prizes. After World War I an atmosphere of international good fellowship took hold for a time and the Davis Cup acquired tremendous significance,

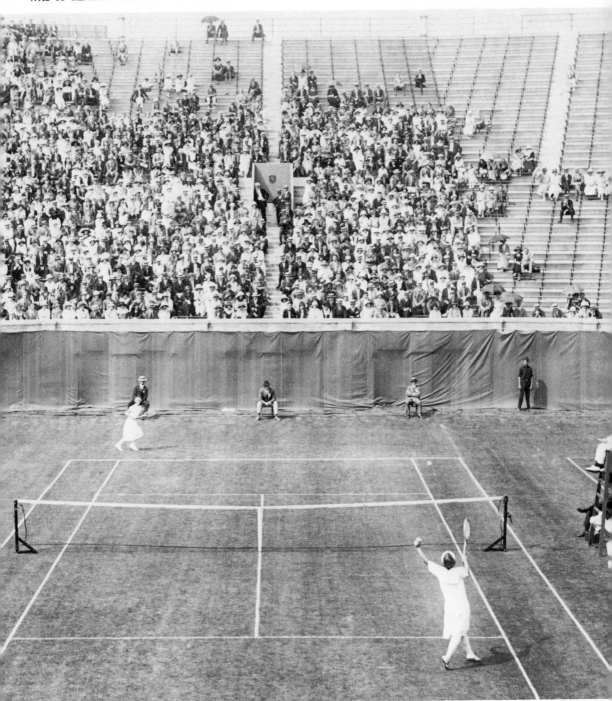

Helen Wills readies a smash against Kitty McKane in the inaugural match at the new stadium in Forest Hills in 1923. *UPI*

Flanking the Wightman Cup won by the U.S. in 1923 are (left to right): Helen Wills, Molla Mallory, Hazel Hotchkiss Wightman (the donor), Geraldine Beamish, and Mrs. R. Clayton. *UPI*

Bill Tilden won the U.S. crown for the fourth year in a row and led the Americans' Davis Cup triumph in 1923. *UPI*

partly because of the U.S. dominance of the competition. It was front-page news then and controversies such as Tilden's threats to quit were almost looked upon as national calamities.

1924

In the latter part of the 1920s, when the French would dominate men's tennis, each of the three great Frenchmen would win two Wimbledon championships, and it started this year with an all-French final in which 25-year-old Jean Borotra defeated 19-year-old René Lacoste, 6–1, 3–6, 6–1, 3–6, 6–4.

Borotra, the colorful Bounding Basque who wore a beret while playing, and Lacoste, the Crocodile, were two of the Four Musketeers along with 22-year-old Henri Cochet and 29-

The Crocodile, René Lacoste, one of the Four Musketeers, lost to fellow Frenchman Jean Borotra in an all-French Wimbledon final in 1924. *Fischer Collection*

year-old Jacques "Toto" Brugnon, who was essentially a doubles specialist. Wimbledon Secretary Duncan Macaulay wrote in *Behind the Scenes at Wimbledon*: "They were all very different in style and temperament, and they sometimes clashed bitterly with one another on the courts. But whenever they felt they were playing for France . . . they always put France first. Thus it was the combined pressure of Lacoste and Cochet which began to rock the great Bill Tilden on his pedestal, and which finally toppled him off it."

Tilden, becoming increasingly at odds with the tennis establishment, sent a letter of resignation to the United States Lawn Tennis Association, bowing out of the Davis Cup because of a proposed ban on his writing about tennis as a conflict with amateur rules. The threat of not having Tilden's gate appeal in the Davis Cup competition forced the tennis body to cave in. Tilden and Bill Johnston

President Calvin Coolidge makes the 1924 Davis Cup draw at the White House. *Fischer Collection*

swept the Australian team of Gerald Patterson and Pat O'Hara Wood, 5–0.

Underdog rooters hopeful that Little Bill Johnston would break the spell held over him by Tilden had reason to believe that Johnston would crash through in the U.S. Championships, the first played in the new West Side Tennis Club Stadium at Forest Hills. Tilden's feud with the USLTA and the increased time he was devoting to a theatrical career led to charges that he was out of shape. He came to the final with a desultory five-set victory over Vincent Richards, while Johnston routed Australia's Gerald Patterson. In the final, however, Tilden crushed Johnston, 6–1, 9–7, 6–2, in a stunning display that tennis savant Al Laney later called "Tilden at his absolute peak, and I have not since seen the like of it." Patterson said, "Tilden is the only player in the world . . . [the rest of us are] second-graders."

Suzanne Lenglen, a five-time winner at Wimbledon, weakened by an attack of jaundice earlier in the year, was forced to drop out after winning a quarterfinal match over Elizabeth Ryan of the United States in which Lenglen was extended, 6–2, 6–8, 6–4. That was the first singles set she lost—except the one to Molla Mallory in her great default at Forest Hills in 1921—since 1919. Britain's Kathleen McKane got a walkover in the semifinals and then defeated Helen Wills in the final, 4–6, 6–4, 6–4.

They had met only a few days earlier in Wightman Cup play at Wimbledon, McKane winning, 6–2, 6–2. The British evened the series at one-all, winning the competition, 6–1. The United States' only point came on a doubles triumph by Wills and Hazel Wightman over McKane and Evelyn Colyer. The 19-year-old Wills won her second successive U.S. title, defeating Molla Mallory, 6–1, 6–2.

In Australia, the men's championship was won by James Anderson, the women's by Sylvia Lance. Norman Brookes, the 47-year-old Australian immortal who had first played at Wimbledon 20 years before, highlighted early-round Wimbledon play with an upset victory over Frank Hunter, who had been a finalist in 1923.

1925

The French dominated Wimbledon as it never had been dominated before. They scored almost a clean sweep of the championships, winning the men's singles and doubles, the mixed doubles and women's singles—and half of the women's doubles.

Suzanne Lenglen, reaching the zenith of her career, lost only five games in sweeping through five opponents. She scored a 6–0, 6–0 triumph over Kathleen McKane, who had won the title after Lenglen was incapacitated the previous year, and defeated Joan Fry in the final, 6–2, 6–0. Lenglen combined with American Elizabeth Ryan to win the women's doubles for the sixth time, and Lenglen won the mixed doubles with Jean Borotra for Lenglen's third Wimbledon triple crown.

Helen Wills made it three in a row in U.S. singles in 1925. *Fischer Collection*

The men's final was a rematch of the previous year. This time, René Lacoste scored a 6–3, 6–3, 4–6, 8–6 victory over Borotra, who was troubled by foot-fault calls. In the quarterfinal round Henri Cochet began to gain a Tilden-like reputation for comebacks, losing the first two sets to John Hennessy, then sweeping the last three. In the first year that the French Championships were opened to players from all countries, René Lacoste triumphed. James Anderson won his second straight Australian title and Daphne Akhurst the first of her five Australian championships.

Bill Tilden achieved the distinction of winning 57 straight games during the summer. The stage was set for another Big Bill-Little Bill confrontation in the U.S. Nationals at Forest Hills after semifinals in which Tilden beat Vincent Richards and Bill Johnston advanced past R. Norris Williams. Despite an injured shoulder, which prevented him from holding hardly more than half his service games in a long, five-set match, Tilden defeated Johnston, 4–6, 11–9, 6–3, 4–6, 6–3.

Johnston said immediately afterward, "I can't beat him, I can't beat the sonofabitch, I can't beat him." It was the last of Tilden's six straight U.S. titles and the last time he and Johnston would contest the title. Tilden, like most tennis people, admired Johnston greatly, and, after Johnston's premature death from tuberculosis, dedicated his memoirs to him.

The French made their first breakthrough into the Davis Cup Challenge Round. Though the Four Musketeers—Lacoste and Borotra in singles, and Cochet and Jacques Brugnon in doubles—were swept by Tilden and Johnston in singles and R. Norris Williams and Vincent Richards in doubles, both Frenchmen extended Tilden to five sets. Tilden rallied for a 3–6, 10–12, 8–6, 7–5, 6–2 victory over Lacoste. Borotra extended him 4–6, 6–0, 2–6, 9–7, 6–4.

Helen Wills won her third straight U.S. Championship, defeating Kathleen McKane of Great Britain, 3–6, 6–0, 6–2, in the final. Wills won both her matches in Wightman Cup play at Forest Hills, but Great Britain won the competition for the second straight year, 4–3. Mrs. Dorothea Lambert Chambers, 47, who lost an epic singles confrontation

with Suzanne Lenglen in 1919, won a singles match and participated in one of Britain's two doubles victories.

1926

Suzanne Lenglen and Helen Wills met in what would be the only confrontation between the two women generally recognized as the two greatest players of all time. One writer called this match "the most important sporting event of modern times exclusively in the hands of the fair sex"—this five decades before one of the fair sex met Bobby Riggs.

Spectators unable to purchase tickets for the Lenglen-Wills match in Cannes found another way in March 1926. *UPI*

Wills took off early in the year for a trip to southern France to participate in invitation tournaments on the Riviera and what some observers regarded as a chance for a showdown with Lenglen. "This gal must be mad," Lenglen told a close friend. "Does she think she can come and beat me on my home court?"

In a dramatic match played at the Carleton Club in Cannes, Lenglen, the favorite of the European crowd, won, 6–3, 8–6. Wills, who had appeared nervous in the first set, began chasing her opponent around the court and was leading, 5–4, at set point when she hit what appeared to be a winner. It wasn't called in her favor, however. Lenglen recovered, went on to win, and broke down in tears

Football immortal Red Grange (left) and promoter C. C. (Cash and Carry) Pyle welcome Suzanne Lenglen as she turns pro in September 1926. *UPI*

afterward. Wills said, "She is terrific. I think it was one of my greatest matches."

Lenglen's brilliant amateur career came to a sad end amid controversy and incriminations at Wimbledon when she failed to show up on time for a women's doubles match at which the King and Queen were present. Due to a mixup after a scheduling change, Lenglen arrived at Centre Court after the King and Queen had left. This drew a reprimand and she became hysterical. She never quite recovered, though the officials agreed to pospone her match. Meeting hostility from the crowds and in the press, Lenglen lost her doubles match. She won a first-round singles match and an opening mixed doubles, but then scratched from the tournament. She never played amateur tennis again, signing on as a pro with American promoter C. C. (Cash and Carry) Pyle. She went on a tour in which she was opposed by Mary Browne and with a troop of five Americans, including Vincent

Richards. After debuting at Madison Square Garden where they grossed $40,000, the tour was such a success that Lenglen was paid a $25,000 bonus over her $50,000 guarantee. Pyle pocketed $80,000.

With Lenglen out of Wimbledon, the title was won by Kathleen McKane Godfree of Great Britain over Lili d'Alvarez of Spain, 6–2, 4–6, 6–3. The U.S. National title, which had been the property of Helen Wills, was opened to others when Wills was sidelined after an appendicitis operation. Molla Mallory came back to win the championship for a record eighth time. The sentimental favorite of the crowd, she beat Elizabeth Ryan, 4–6, 6–4, 9–7, after trailing, 4–0, in the third set.

The six-year reign of Bill Tilden came to an end in the United States Championships when he was eliminated in the quarterfinals by Henri Cochet, 6–8, 6–1, 6–3, 1–6, 8–6. In many ways Tilden came to be more popu-

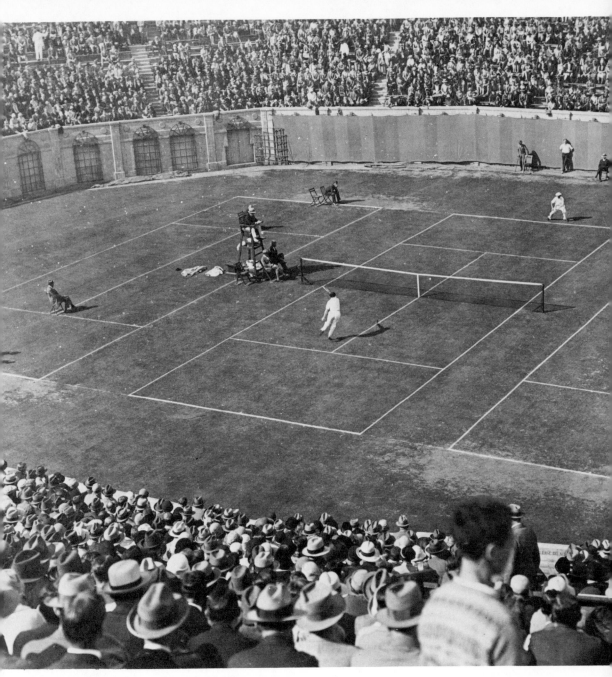

In an all-French final at Forest Hills, René Lacoste (far court) won the U.S. crown in 1926 in straight sets over Jean Borotra. *Fischer Collection*

lar in defeat than he had been as the kingpin of the sport. Allison Danzig wrote of the Tilden-Cochet match, "The climax of the match, the point at which the gallery broke into the wildest demonstrations, was during the final set when Tilden, trailing at 1–4, rallied to volley Cochet dizzy with one of the most sensational exhibitions he ever gave at the net and pull up to 4-all. Every winning shot of the American was greeted with roars

of applause. Tilden, 33, then led, 40–15, on Cochet's serve, but then fell back."

Bill Johnston also lost in the same round, to Jean Borotra in five sets. Borotra advanced to make it an all-French final by eliminating Vincent Richards. René Lacoste eliminated Henri Cochet in the semifinals and then beat Borotra for the title, 6–4, 6–0, 6–4.

It was the first time since 1917 that Tilden did not make the U.S. finals, the first time since 1920 he didn't win; it was the first of three years in which Forest Hills and Wimbledon would be swept by the French.

With Lacoste ill and unable to defend his title at Wimbledon, Borotra met American Howard Kinsey in the final, and Borotra's dynamic volleying and smashing subdued Kinsey's strong defense and clever lobbing. Borotra won, 8–6, 6–1, 6–3. Kinsey, who in 1924 achieved a No. 4 U.S. ranking, reached the finals of the singles, doubles, and mixed doubles and lost in all. The men's doubles was notable for the entry of the Duke of York, later King George VI, teamed with Louis Grieg. They lost in the first round. Leslie and Kathleen Godfree won the mixed doubles crown, the only time a married couple won that competition at Wimbledon.

In Davis Cup play at the Germantown Cricket Club, the U.S. extended its winning streak to seven, a record that still stands. The U.S. won, 4–1. Tilden suffered the only loss, to Lacoste, 4–6, 6–4, 8–6, 8–6, his first defeat in an important match since 1919. Johnston won both his singles, over Lacoste and Borotra, and R. Norris Williams and Vincent Richards beat Cochet and Jacques Brugnon in the doubles. The French championships went to Cochet; John Hawkes won the Australian title.

Though playing without Helen Wills, the U.S. tied the Wightman Cup competition at 2-all, defeating Great Britain at Wimbledon, 4–3, with a pair of doubles and singles triumphs. Elizabeth Ryan split in singles and won her doubles match teamed with Mary K. Browne. She and Browne also won the Wimbledon women's doubles, and Ryan teamed with Eleanor Goss to win the U.S. crown. Ryan would go on to win 19 championships at Wimbledon, but she never won a singles title at either Wimbledon or Forest Hills.

1927

One of the most astounding turnarounds in the history of tennis occurred in the semifinals at Wimbledon. Bill Tilden at 34 was no longer the supreme tennis player in the world, but he was a legendary figure, imposing and formidable still, seeded second only to René

Henri Cochet overcame two-set deficits against Frank Hunter, Bill Tilden, and Jean Borotra to capture Wimbledon in 1927. *UPI*

Lacoste in his first appearance at Wimbledon since he won there in 1921. Playing fourth-seeded Henri Cochet, Tilden won the first two sets, reached 5–1, 15-all in the third set, and then lost, probably as great a collapse as any outstanding tennis figure would ever experience. On Cochet's service Tilden hit out on three drives and lost the game. Cochet then won 17 consecutive points and went on to win, 2–6, 4–6, 7–5, 6–4, 6–3.

Tilden later wrote: "I have heard many interesting, curious, quite inaccurate accounts of what happened. One ingenious explanation was that King Alfonso of Spain arrived at 5–1 in the third set and I decided to let him see some of the match . . . Ridiculous! I didn't even know he was there. Another was that a group of Hindus hypnotized me. If they did, I didn't know it, but they certainly did a swell job. Personally, I have no satisfactory explanation. All I know is my co-ordination cracked wide open and I couldn't put a ball in court."

Before surprising Tilden, Cochet had come from behind a two-set deficit to beat Frank Hunter. Cochet then added a third sensational comeback by losing the first two sets in the final to Jean Borotra and then rallying from 5–2 in the fifth set, surviving *six* match

points, to win his first Wimbledon title. The
score: 4–6, 4–6, 6–3, 6–4, 7–5.

Wimbledon Secretary Duncan Macaulay
wrote, "Cochet was incredibly cool in a
crisis—so much that I sometimes wondered
whether he really knew what the score was."
Footnote: In the doubles final, Cochet and
Jacques Brugnon led Tilden and Frank
Hunter, two sets to love, 5–3, 40–15, on
Cochet's serve for the match, only to be upended, 1–6, 4–6, 8–6, 6–3, 6–4.

René Lacoste (the Crocodile) won three
great matches over Tilden this year to establish his own supremacy in the sport. He won
the French and United States Championships
in extraordinary finals and also beat Tilden in
a crucial Davis Cup match. The French finale
was a 61-game, five-set duel with Lacoste
winning the last set, 11–9. In the Forest Hills
final, Lacoste may have played the best tennis
of his life, defeating Tilden, 11–9, 6–3, 11–9.

"It was a match," Allison Danzig wrote,
"the like of which will not be seen again
soon. . . . On the one side of the net stood
[Tilden], the perfect tactician and most ruthless stroker the game probably has ever seen,
master of every shot and skilled in the necro-
mancy of spin. On the other side was the
player who has reduced the defense to a
mathamatical science; who has done more
than that, who has developed his defense to
the state when it becomes an offense, sub-
conscious in its workings but none the less
effective in the pressure it brings to bear as
the ball is sent back deeper and deeper and
into more and more remote territory."

Lacoste, whose career was cut short by
illness and who became famous for his sports-
shirt line with the crocodile emblem on the
chest, never played at Forest Hills again.

America's record seven-year reign came to
an end in the Davis Cup. France broke
through in its third challenge with a 3–2 victory over the U.S. team that included the two
men who had brought America the Cup in
1920, Tilden and Johnston. Lacoste beat
Johnston, then Tilden beat Cochet, then the
Americans took a 2–1 lead on a doubles victory by Tilden and Frank Hunter over Jean
Borotra and Jacques Brugnon. Tilden could
not come through with another victory,

however. He fell to Lacoste, 6–3, 4–6, 6–3,
6–2, and the Cup moved to France when
Johnston was beaten by Cochet, 6–4, 4–6,
6–2, 6–4 in a dramatic match in which the
overflow crowd of 15,000 at the Germantown
Cricket Club was so carried away cheering for
an American victory that, a report said, "it
broke all bounds of tennis etiquette and
cheered madly both Johnston's winning shots
and Cochet's mistakes."

With Suzanne Lenglen off in the professional ranks, Helen Wills (called Little Miss
Poker Face because of her lack of expression
on the court) assumed complete dominance of
the women's ranks at 22. She began a string
of four Wimbledon titles with a 6–2, 6–3
victory over Lili d'Alvarez. Wills won her
fourth straight American Championship, defeating 19-year-old Helen Jacobs in the semifinal and Betty Nuthall of England in the final,
6–1, 6–4.

The United States went ahead in Wightman
Cup play, 3–2, beating the British, 5–2, at
Forest Hills. Wills and Molla Mallory both
won a pair of singles matches, and Wills
teamed with Hazel Wightman for a doubles
triumph. Gerald Patterson won an 18–16
fourth set in a five-set over defender John
Hawkes for the Australian title. The women's
championship went to Esna Boyd.

1928

Controversy raged much of the year between Bill Tilden and the United States Lawn
Tennis Association over Tilden's writing
newspaper articles about tennis as a violation
of amateur rules. Tilden was suspended, missing the interzone matches with Italy. As the
matches with France approached, other members of the American team threatened to
strike; René Lacoste announced he would not
defend his title at Forest Hills. He said, "We
would rather lose the Davis Cup than retain it
where there may be some excuse in the absence of Tilden."

The French had built a new stadium at
Roland Garros, which needed Tilden's presence to fill; France's protests and American
public opinion supporting Tilden forced the
USLTA to back down and permit Tilden to

Helen Wills (left), with Lili d'Alvarez, her victim in the Wimbledon final, also won the U.S. and French titles in 1928. *UPI*

play, though it would later keep him out of the U.S. Championships.

Tilden then went out and played what teammate George Lott called his greatest match of all time as he defeated Lacoste on clay, 1–6, 6–4, 6–4, 2–6, 6–3. Afterward, Lacoste said, "Two years ago I knew at last how to beat him. Now, he beats me. I never knew how the ball would come off the court, he concealed it so well. I had to wait to see how much it was spinning—and sometimes it didn't spin at all. Is he not the greatest player of all time?"

That victory was not enough. Tilden lost to Henri Cochet; both Lacoste and Cochet beat John Hennessey, and the Cochet-Jean Borotra team beat Tilden and Frank Hunter for a 4–1 French triumph. The ranks of the Davis Cup,

which was contested for by six countries in 1920, had now swelled to 33 participants.

French supremacy carried to the major championships where, for the first time, one country's representative swept all four major championships. Cochet won the American and French crowns, Lacoste won his second Wimbledon title and Borotra won the Australian Championship.

With Tilden and Lacoste missing from Forest Hills, Cochet won by beating Frank Shields in the semifinal and Frank Hunter in the final, 4–6, 6–4, 3–6, 7–5, 6–3. It was the third straight victory by a Frenchman at Forest Hills, and it would turn out to be the last; there would be no outstanding Frenchman to play in the United States, let alone win, after the retirements of Lacoste, Cochet, and Borotra. At Wimbledon, a Lacoste-Cochet final was set up when Lacoste scored a five-set victory over Tilden, and Cochet beat Christian Boussus. Lacoste won, 6–1, 4–6, 6–4, 6–2.

In the Wightman Cup matches Great Britain evened the series again, 3-all, with a 4–3 victory gained on two doubles triumphs. The Americans' victories came as Helen Wills won both her singles and Helen Jacobs won in Wightman Cup play for the first time. Both lost in separate doubles matches, and 36-year-old Molla Mallory lost twice in the singles.

Wills won both at Wimbledon and Forest Hills for the second straight year and also won the French title. She beat Lili d'Alvarez in the Wimbledon final and, in the beginning of a classic rivalry, trounced Jacobs at Forest Hills, 6–2, 6–1. Wills so dominated the sport that as much attention was given to her reserved manner as to her skills. W. O. McGeehan wrote in the New York *Herald Tribune*, "She is powerful, repressed and imperturbable. She plays her game with a silent, deadly earnestness, concentrated on her work. That, of course, is the way to win games, but it does not please galleries. Of course, there is no reason why an amateur athlete should try to please galleries." Wills did not play in the Australian Championships won by Daphne Akhurst.

Vinnie Richards succeeded C. C. Pyle as a promoter of professional matches and im-

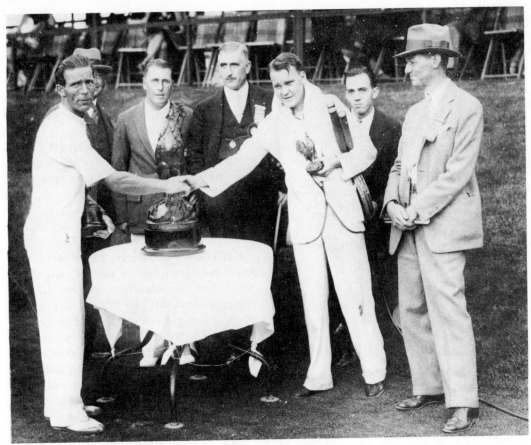

Czechoslovakia's Karel Kozeluh (left) is congratulated by Vinnie Richards after Kozeluh won the pro championship at Forest Hills in 1929. *UPI*

ported Karel Kozeluh, a Czech who was being acclaimed as a great player even though he had not played long on the amateur circuit. In a head-to-head duel with Richards, Kozeluh proved superior on clay and hardwood, winning a majority of the matches, but he lost on grass to Richards in the match billed as the Professional Championship of the World.

1929

In the years the French were dominating Wimbledon and Forest Hills, Tilden was still the most dynamic figure in the sport. René Lacoste wrote, "He seems to exercise a strange fascination over his opponents as well as his spectators. Tilden, even when beaten, always leaves the impression on the public mind that he was superior to the victor."

The French had broken Tilden's six-year dominance at Forest Hills, and now Tilden ended the three-year French reign. He won the United States title for the seventh time, coming back from 2-1 deficits against John Doeg in the semifinals and against Frank Hunter in a 3–6, 6–3, 4–6, 6–2, 6–4 finals triumph. At 36, he was the oldest man to win the U.S. crown, a distinction that still holds.

After Lacoste succumbed to illness after winning the French championship, Henri Cochet became the No. 1 Frenchman. He won the last all-French final at Wimbledon, beating Jean Borotra, 6–4, 6–3, 6–4, after defeating Tilden in the semifinals. Great Britain's future great, Fred Perry, made his Wimbledon debut, losing in the third round to John Olliff.

France was extended in winning a third successive Davis Cup competition over the United States. Cochet beat Tilden, 6–3, 6–1,

Time marches on: An electronic scoreboard was installed at Wimbledon in 1929. *UPI*

6–2, then Borotra beat American newcomer George Lott, 6–1, 3–6, 6–4, 7–5. The U.S. doubles team of John Van Ryn and Wilmer Allison beat Cochet and Borotra, 6–1, 8–6, 6–4, and then Tilden beat Borotra, 4–6, 6–1, 6–4, 7–5, tying the competition at 2-all. In the deciding match, Cochet defeated the 22-year-old Lott, 6–1, 3–6, 6–0, 6–3.

Helen Wills was never more supreme. She swept Wimbledon and Forest Hills for the third straight year and the French Championships for the second. In the first of four Wimbledon finals she would win over Helen Jacobs, she romped, 6–1, 6–2. At the U.S. Championships, Jacobs was eliminated in the semifinals by Britain's Phoebe Watson, and Wills shut out Molla Mallory, 6–0, 6–0. Wills then beat Watson, 6–4, 6–2. Billie Tapscott caused an echoing wave of criticism by being the first player to be seen at Wimbledon without stockings.

Wills led the American team to a 4–3 Wightman Cup victory on the strength of singles superiority. Wills beat Watson and Betty Nuthall, Jacobs beat Nuthall, and Edith Cross beat Mrs. Peggy Michell. The English won

two doubles matches, and Watson beat Jacobs in the other singles. The U.S. led in the series, 4–3, no team having taken a more than one-match lead since the first Wightman Cup inaugural in 1923.

Colin Gregory of Great Britain and Australian Daphne Akhurst won the respective Australian singles titles.

In what still was a minor aspect of the sport, the pro championship was contested for again by Vinnie Richards and the Czech Karel Kozeluh. This time Kozeluh won.

1930

Bill Tilden's magnificent career as an amateur came to an end on the last day of the year when he officially announced he was turning professional. He bowed out after one of the most glorious victories of his career. He won his third Wimbledon, becoming, at 37 years, five months, the oldest man ever to win the Wimbledon singles title, a distinction that still stands, though Ken Rosewall would reach the 1974 final in his 40th year.

Tilden beat Texan Wilmer Allison 10 years and six days after he had defeated Gerald Patterson to win his first Wimbledon. Before defeating Allison, 6–3, 9–7, 6–4, Tilden had to survive a tough five-set match with France's Jean Borotra in which Tilden trailed, 3–1, in the final set. The London *Daily Mail* reporter called this the greatest match he had seen at Wimbledon, one of many matches in Tilden's career that struck some observers as the "greatest."

Tilden had his most successful European tour, winning the Austrian, Italian, and Dutch Championships, losing to Henri Cochet in the French final. Ranked first in the United States for the 10th time—nobody ever has come close to dominating the rankings for such an extended period—Tilden wanted badly to break a tie with William Larned and Richard Sears by winning the U.S. title for an eighth time. He came a cropper against 21-year-old California John Doeg, a big left-hander with a powerful serve, a formidable opponent when he had control of his ground game. Doeg made 20 aces, 12 in the final set, losing his service only once in 29 games, and beat

Bill Tilden's valedictory as an amateur saw him win his third Wimbledon in 1930, over Wilmer Allison (right). *UPI*

Tilden, 10–8, 6–3, 3–6, 12–10. Doeg hit his serve so hard, it was reported that he turned the ball into an ellipse; it was called his "egg ball." The loss marked the first time Tilden had been beaten by a countryman in a U.S. Championship since Bill Johnston beat him 11 years earlier. Doeg then beat Frank Shields in the final, 10–8, 1–6, 6–4, 16–14.

Tilden's record in U.S. Championships showed 80 matches, at least one every year since 1916, except for 1928, when he was suspended. He won 73, lost seven. He won 203 sets and lost 59.

Tilden, who had long had a love-hate relationship with crowds that admired his gallant efforts in the face of defeat and his sportsmanship, but didn't like some of his showboating histrionics, now had no great goals to achieve as an amateur. Frank Deford wrote in his remarkable biography of Tilden:

"Frustrated by the reductions of age, ap-pearing more effeminate in his gestures (Tilden would die a lonely, broken figure at 60 after two convictions on morals charges), he became testier, even petty, on the court. Once, on the Riviera, in a match of no consequence, the umpire, an Englishman, finally just got up and departed when Tilden kept fussing. Once, at Orange, New Jersey, he rudely informed the tournament chairman that Big Bill Tilden was not accustomed to competing on grass that had the texture of cow pasture, and had to be coaxed back onto the court."

Earlier in the year, Tilden played in his 11th consecutive and last Davis Cup final round. Despite an injured ankle, he came back from a slow start to beat Jean Borotra in four sets. He then lost to Henri Cochet in four sets, his final Davis Cup appearance. George Lott, who would come to make his mark as a doubles player, was beaten in both singles by Cochet and Borotra, and the French doubles team of Cochet and Jacques Brugnon beat Wilmer Allison and John Van Ryn for a 4–1 victory, France's fourth in a row.

The year marked the first appearances in the American Top Ten rankings of Sidney Wood, fourth; Ellsworth Vines, eighth; and Bitsy Grant, 10th.

Queen Helen, now Mrs. Helen Wills Moody, won Wimbledon for the fourth straight year without working up too much of a sweat in a 6–2, 6–2 finals triumph over Elizabeth Ryan. She and Ryan teamed to win the doubles over Edith Cross and Sarah Palfrey, making her Wimbledon debut at 17. Wills did not play at Forest Hills, and Britain's 19-year-old Betty Nuthall became the first foreigner ever to win a U.S. Championship in singles. Daphne Akhurst won the Australian women's title for the third straight year, and E. F. Moon defeated Harry Hopman for the Australian men's crown.

For the fifth time in the eight-year rivalry, Wightman Cup competition ended in a 4–3 score, Great Britain evening the series at 4-all. Moody won her two singles matches, Helen Jacobs split her two matches, and the pair suffered one of the two doubles defeats when they played together in a loss to Phoebe Watson and Kathleen Godfree. Watson and

Phyllis Mudford won singles matches over Jacobs and Palfrey, respectively.

Women's dress continued to be less cumberson. Lili d'Alvarez was wearing a pagodalike trouser dress. Eileen Bennett and Betty Nuthall showed up at Wimbledon with open-backed tennis dresses, and necklines continued to drop.

1931

Sidney Wood first appeared at Wimbledon as a 15-year-old wearing white knickers on the Centre Court and losing to René Lacoste. Wood returned for the first time at 19, became the youngest player in this century to win and the only one ever to win a Wimbledon final in a walkover.

Wood, who was seeded seventh, advanced to the final with a four-set victory over 22-year-old Fred Perry, a winner in an early round over a promising young German, Gottfried von Cramm. The other semifinal went to American Frank Shields over Jean Borotra, who had won the French Championship for the first time. Shields strained a leg muscle against Borotra, however, and had to scratch out of his final with Wood.

Ellsworth Vines, who had been ranked eighth in 1930 and hadn't been picked for the Davis Cup team early in the year, came into his own at 19 when he won the United States Championship in September. Vines, from Pasadena, California, was a lanky 6-foot-1, weighing only 145 pounds, who had a great cannonball serve. Analyst Julius Heldman wrote, "He had the flattest set of ground strokes ever seen and they were hit so hard, particularly on the forehand, that they could not clear the net by more than a few inches without going out."

He had a scare in the semifinal, losing the first two sets to Fred Perry before rallying. In the final Vines met George Lott, who advanced by eliminating defending champion John Doeg. Vines won, 7–9, 6–3, 9–7, 7–5. Jack Crawford took the Australian title.

Playing without Bill Tilden, the United States didn't appear in the Challenge Round of the Davis Cup for the first time since 1919, the year before Tilden joined the team. It

Nineteen-year-old Sidney Wood made history when he won the 1931 Wimbledon. *UPI*

appeared the U.S. would have a crack at the French in the Challenge Round when, in the Inter-Zone final, after a loss by Sidney Wood to Great Britain's Bunny Austin, the U.S. took a 2–1 lead as Shields beat Perry, and the American doubles team of Lott and John Van Ryn beat George Hughes and Perry. Britain prevailed, however, as Perry beat Wood, and Austin defeated Shields. In the Challenge Round, France won, 3–2, for the fifth straight time, on a doubles victory and two singles triumphs by Henri Cochet, the second over Perry in the climactic match.

With Helen Wills Moody choosing not to play at Wimbledon, it appeared that Helen Jacobs would have an excellent opportunity to win, particularly after she beat Betty Nuthall, the 1931 Forest Hills winner, in a quarterfinal. Jacobs lost, however, in the semifinal to Hilde Krahwinkel, and the first all-German Wimbledon saw Cilly Aussem defeat Krahwinkel, 6–2, 7–5. Aussem had beaten Nuthall in the French finals; Mrs. Coral Buttsworth won the Australian Championship.

Wills Moody, who went into the Forest Hills Nationals without a major title because she had not played there in 1930 and had skipped Wimbledon and the French Championships earlier in 1931, rectified that by winning the U.S. crown with a 6–4, 6–1 victory over Britain's Eileen Whittingstall. By the end of the year Moody had gone four years without losing a set of singles.

As the U.S. and Great Britain prepared for the Wightman Cup matches, they were tied at 4-all. The U.S. won the matches, 5–2, with both Moody and Jacobs winning a pair of singles. This was the start of a 21-year string of U.S. Wightman Cup victories that would not be broken until 1958.

Bill Tilden made his long-awaited debut as a professional in the midst of the Depression. A part promoter of his tour with entrepreneur William O'Brien, Tilden opened against Czech Karel Kozeluh at Madison Square Garden on February 18 before a crowd of 13,000 paying $36,000. Tilden won his debut, 6–4, 6–2, 6–4, then ran off 16 straight victories and went on to beat Kozeluh before big galleries at almost every stop of a cross-country tour that grossed $238,000.

Frank Hunter, Robert Siller, and Emmett Pare played subordinate roles on the tour. Other professionals at the time were Roman Najuch of Germany; Albert Thomas and Edward Burke of France; and Major Rendell of England. At Forest Hills during the summer, the U.S. Pro championships drew a field of 44, Tilden trouncing Richards, 7–5, 6–2, 6–1 in the final.

Forest Hills and Wimbledon were 21-year-old Ellsworth Vines' conquests in 1932. *UPI*

1932

Ellsworth Vines became the first man since Bill Tilden in 1921 to win both the Wimbledon and Forest Hills Championships. Competing in his first Wimbledon at 21, Vines was so impressive that some English reporters were calling him the greatest player of all time.

He defeated Australia's Harry Hopman in an early round and sailed through Australia's Jack Crawford and Britain's Bunny Austin in the last two rounds in straight sets. Vines scored 30 service aces against Austin, who broke his serve only once. Vines' match point was a service ace, and Austin said, "I saw him swing his racket and I heard the ball hit the back canvas. The umpire called game, set, and match, so I knew it was all over, but

I never saw the ball." Vines' serve was measured at 121 miles per hour (Pancho Gonzales' serve was measured at 118 miles per hour later).

Crawford, the winner of the Australian Championship, had beaten Fred Perry in the quarterfinals. An oddity of the tournament was Henri Cochet losing in the second round, then entering the All England Plate competition for also-rans eliminated in the first two rounds, and winning. He became the first ex-champion to win the Plate.

Americans were so impressed with Vines at Wimbledon that hopes were high the U.S would win back the Davis Cup after the U.S. had advanced past Great Britain in the Inter-Zone final. Vines showed himself to be less than invincible, however, losing to Jean Borotra in the first singles, 6–4, 6–2, 3–6, 6–4. When Cochet beat Wilmer Allison in the second singles, it looked as if France would win easily. A doubles triumph by Allison and John Van Ryn over Cochet and Jacques Brugnon, however, tightened things and set up one of the controversial episodes in Davis Cup history.

First, the groundskeepers heavily watered the clay at Roland Garros Stadium in the hopes of slowing the court down to hamper Vines in his final match. The slow court served instead to bother Borotra in the third singles against Allison. Borotra lost the first two sets, then rallied to take the next two. Allison went to hold a commanding 5–3 lead in the final set, but blew three match points, once when a Borotra shot hit the tape and fell over safely. The final blow came on a match point against Borotra's serve. Borotra hit his first ball into the net and his second seemed long, so long Allison didn't hit it, and most observers thought the ball was out and the match completed. But the linesman said it was good, Borotra was saved again, and he came on to give France her third victory of the competition. Fans were left to debate whether Cochet, who won the first two sets and then lost the final match to Vines, would have been able to pull through if France needed that point. This was the sixth straight Davis Cup triumph for France, and her last.

Vines, who often wore a white cap, had a curious windmill stroke in which the racket made an almost 360-degree sweep. Starting on high as though he were going to serve, he brought the racket head back almost to the ground and swept up to the ball. He put no spin on it, however, thereby hitting a flat shot with tremendous force that made him unbeatable when he was on.

Opponents came to realize that the way to beat Vines was to keep the ball in play, hitting him soft stuff until he started making errors. A harbinger of all that came in one of the memorable semifinals at Forest Hills, when Cliff Sutter of New Orleans won the first two sets before losing in an exhausting two-and-a-half-hour match that had a packed stadium roaring. As Vines made error after error, Sutter kept the ball in play, avoiding deep shots as much as possible because he knew Vines was unbeatable at the base line. Because of the length of that match, the other semifinal, in which Cochet beat Allison, was postponed because of darkness.

When they resumed the next day, Cochet completed a five-set victory, then complained bitterly that he had to compete on the same day in the final against Vines, who disposed of him in straight sets, 6–4, 6–4, 6–4. Cochet was tired. Twice he was unable to move out of the way in time to avoid being hit by Vines' blinding serve. The last two aces of the match by Vines were so hard that they bounced into the stands. Cochet never returned to Forest Hills.

Helen Wills Moody returned to Wimbledon after a one-year absence and won her fifth title. She lost only 13 games in the 12 sets she had to play. For the second time in the final she met Helen Jacobs, and won, 6–3, 6–1. Moody also won her fourth French Championship. Jacobs raised eyebrows playing in what now are regarded as Bermuda shorts.

With Wills Moody absent from Forest Hills, Jacobs won the U.S. Championship for the first time, defeating third-seeded Carolin Babcock in the final, 6–2, 6–2. Alice Marble made her first appearance in the U.S. rankings at No. 7, and was a finalist in the women's doubles at Forest Hills. Mrs. Coral Buttsworth won her second successive Australian title.

The U.S. took a 6–4 lead in Wightman Cup play on a 4–3 victory. Wills Moody won two singles matches, Jacobs and Mrs. Anna Harper one each. Bill Tilden continued to dominate the thin professional ranks with a mixture of tennis skill and theatrical showmanship. He and Vinnie Richards grossed $86,000 on their tour.

1933

Helen Wills Moody and Suzanne Lenglen are regarded by many long-time observers as the two greatest women players of all time. It is an irony that both are best remembered for matches they lost—in which they defaulted and walked off the court. Lenglen defaulted to Molla Mallory at Forest Hills in 1921, and Moody quit in the middle of her final with Helen Jacobs in 1933.

The two Helens—Moody, almost 28, tall, dark-haired, and coldly methodical, and Jacobs, 25, stocky, blond, and outgoing—were natural rivals. They both came from the San Francisco Bay area. Both had the same teacher, Pop Fuller. When they met for the

Helen Wills Moody's default to Helen Jacobs (left) marked Moody's last appearance in a Forest Hills final, in 1933. *New York Herald Tribune*

second time in this U.S. final, Moody had long been the dominant figure. She had won her sixth Wimbledon title earlier in the year, she had won seven U.S. titles, and she had never lost to Jacobs after trouncing her, 6–0, 6–0, the first time they played. She beat her in two Wimbledon finals and the 1928 Forest Hills finale. Jacobs had won Forest Hills in 1932 when Moody did not compete.

Though Jacobs insisted there was no feud, she wanted badly to beat Moody. She went to none other than Lenglen, who drilled her in hitting cross court so that she would avoid giving Moody the back-court dominance she liked best. Jacobs, being faster, was determined to play the net as often as possible.

In the semifinal Moody ahd lost her first set in seven years at Forest Hills to Betty Nuthall. Jacobs proceeded to take her first set ever from Moody, 8–6. Moody won the second, 6–3, using drop shots to tire her opponent. Given a respite in the intermission, Jacobs broke Moody's service in the opening game and then again for a 3–0 advantage. In his history of tennis, Will Grimsley wrote: "At this point Moody strode to the umpire's chair and put on her sweater. 'I am sorry, my back pains me. I cannot go on,' she said tersely. That was all she said. Wearing a long coat, her familiar eyeshade pulled low, she strode to the dressing room. She declined an interview."

It was reported that Jacobs pleaded with her to continue. Jacobs denied this, saying she merely inquired if she would like to rest. Moody said no and walked away without shaking hands. The fans were stunned. The press lambasted her for not trying to finish the match. She was accused of being a poor sport, a quitter, ungracious. Later she said, "I feel that I have spoiled the finish of the national championships and wish that I had followed the advice of my doctor and returned to California. I still feel I did right in withdrawing because I was on the verge of collapse on the court."

The loss was her first since she had been beaten by Lenglen in 1926. Earlier, Moody had won the Wimbledon final over Dorothy Round, 6–4, 6–8, 6–3, for her sixth title. Joan Hartigan won the Australian championship, Britain's Margaret Scriven the French crown.

Playing without Moody, who injured her back, and Alice Marble, the U.S. defeated Great Britain in Wightman Cup play, 4–3, as Jacobs won singles matches over Round and Scriven, Sarah Palfrey scored a key victory over Scriven, and the doubles team of Jacobs and Palfrey beat Round and Mary Heeley.

Before Don Budge was to come along and popularize the notion of the Grand Slam—victories in the Australian, French, British, and American championships—Australia's Jack Crawford came within a set of achieving that sweep, missing out only at Forest Hills in a five-set loss to Fred Perry.

Wimbledon Secretary Duncan Macaulay wrote in *Behind the Scene at Wimbledon:* "Jack Crawford was one of the most popular champions who ever appeared at Wimbledon. Although he was only 25 when he won the title, he always seemed much older. Perhaps it was the effect of his hair, parted in the middle, the sleeves of his cricket shirt buttoned at the wrists (though he was known to roll them up in moments of crisis) and , most of all, the old-fashioned square-headed racquet with which he always played. In a long match he liked to have a pot of tea, complete with milk and sugar, and reserves of hot water, by the umpire's chair, instead of the iced beverages and other revivers favored by the moderns."

English authority Max Robertson wrote in 1974 that if a poll were taken about the best men's singles final at Wimbledon, "the Crawford-Ellsworth Vines match in 1933 would probably head it; certainly it would have to be included in the top six." Vines' service earned him 13 aces and he ran out 11 service games at love. Crawford played a defensive game against Vines' power, concentrating on Vines' relatively weak backhand. They split the first two sets, then the next. Then Crawford changed tactics, rushing the net. He broke Vines at the end, winning the last game at love on Vines' serve. The score: 4–6, 11–9, 6–2, 2–6, 6–4.

The crowd exulted over the first victory by a player from the British Empire since another Australian, Gerald Patterson, won 10 years

His leap says it all for Fred Perry, winner over Jack Crawford in the 1933 U.S. final.
New York Herald Tribune

earlier. Macaulay wrote, "The cheering of the spectators went on and on, and their enthusiasm was so great there appeared to be a distinct danger that the sacred turf of the Centre Court would be invaded by the multitude."

There were two innovations at Wimbledon. Vivian McGrath, an Australian, showed his two-handed backhand. Britisher Bunny Austin wore shorts for the first time on the Centre Court. Henri Cochet put on a pair, but only for the mixed doubles, and his opponent, Norman Farquharson, rolled up his trousers.

A big disappointment at Wimbledon was fourth-seeded Fred Perry, who lost in the second round to Farquharson, a South African. Perry finally achieved his first major title, at Forest Hills, when he outlasted Crawford in a grueling match, 6–3, 11–13, 4–6, 6–0, 6–1. Defending champion Vines lost in the fourth round in straight sets to Bitsy Grant in what was called a Mutt & Jeff match.

Perry spearheaded Britain's first Davis Cup triumph since 1912. The British ended France's six-year reign by a 3–2 margin.

Perry won in five sets over Henri Cochet and then defeated 19-year-old André Merlin in the climactic singles. Austin beat Merlin and lost to Cochet; Jean Borotra and Jacques Brugnon won the doubles over Harry Lee and Pat Hughes.

Bill Tilden's opponent on the professional tour was Hans Nusslein of Germany. Tilden dominated, though gross receipts dropped from $86,000 the year before to $62,000. Henri Cochet also turned pro and was beaten by Tilden in his debut in Paris.

1934

Fred Perry brought England its first Wimbledon championship since 1909, the year he was born. He won the Australian and United States Championships and teamed with Bunny Austin to spearhead a successful defense of the Davis Cup.

In his history of Forest Hills, Robert Minton wrote, "Perry combined speed with a wristy forehand developed from first playing table tennis, of which he became the world champion. He was an enormous crowd pleaser, handsome enough to be a movie star, and a cocky showman in a white blazer and an unlit pipe, as though he were a Lord, and not the son of a Labor Party member of Parliament. He never ruffled anyone with a display of temper, for he was phlegmatic and won his matches by outlasting his opponents. His physical condition was second to none."

Perry's opponent in the Wimbledon final was Jack Crawford, who had lost to Perry in the finals of the Australian Championships and to Gottfried von Cramm in the French final. Reporter Ferdinand Kuhn said of Perry's 6–3, 6–0, 7–5 triumph: "Perry was always the complete master. He didn't make a half-dozen bad shots in the whole match. He was lithe as a panther, always holding the opponent in check and beating Crawford at his own cool, cautious game. Once he performed the amazing feat of capturing 12 games in a row." Perry said, "If I live to be 100, I'll never play so well again."

At the end, with Crawford serving at match point, he hit what looked like an ace, but he was called for a foot fault. He was so shaken

Australia's Jack Crawford, No. 1 in the world rankings in 1933 after missing a Grand Slam, lost to Fred Perry in the 1934 Wimbledon final. *UPI*

by the call, he then served into the net, the first time anybody could remember a Wimbledon final ending on a double fault.

Britain's joy was complete when Dorothy Round won the women's title, and afterward, to a tumultuous ovation, she and Perry were summoned to the Royal Box to be presented to the King and Queen.

The women's final had come down to a meeting between Round, who had been beaten in the 1933 final by Helen Wills Moody, and Helen Jacobs, who had lost to Moody in the 1929 and 1932 finals. Playing before the King and Queen in a scene much like Virginia's Wade's Wimbledon Centennial victory in 1977, Round won the first set, 6–2, lost, 7–5; then triumphed in the finale, 6–3.

By now shorts and bare legs were much in evidence at Wimbledon. The Prince of Wales said, "I see no reason on earth why any woman should not wear shorts for lawn tennis. They are very comfortable and quite the most practical costume for the game; and I don't think the wearers lose anything in looks."

Elizabeth Ryan teamed with Simone Mathieu to win the women's doubles crown, her 19th at Wimbledon, a record that Billie Jean King later would tie and surpass. Ryan won 12 doubles and 7 mixed-doubles titles. Wimbledon official Duncan Macaulay discussed why Ryan, so strong in doubles, never won a major singles championships. "Firstly, her era coincided with that of two superlative singles champions, Miss Lenglen and Mrs. Moody; and secondly, Miss Ryan's only stroke on the forehand was a sizzling chop, very effective in doubles—particularly against women—but not so effective in singles as a good flat or topspin drive such as Lenglen or Moody played to perfection."

At Forest Hills, Perry won in the semifinals over Vernon Kirby, who earlier had eliminated 19-year-old Don Budge, making his first appearance in the Nationals. Wilmer Allison beat Sidney Wood in the other semi, then put Perry to the test before losing, 6–4, 6–3, 3–6, 1–6, 8–6.

George Lott won his fifth U.S. doubles title, teaming with Lester Stoefen. That pair gave the U.S. its only point in a 4–1 Davis Cup loss to the British. In singles Perry and Austin swept Wood and Frank Shields.

The United States increased its Wightman Cup lead to 8–4 with a 5–2 triumph powered by Helen Jacobs and Sarah Palfrey. Each won singles over Dorothy Round and Peggy Scriven, and they combined to win a doubles match.

The pro tour needed some new blood and got it with the arrival of Ellsworth Vines. With much fanfare before a Madison Square Garden crowd of 14,637, the largest ever to see a tennis match in the United States, Vines, 23, made his debut against Bill Tilden, 41. The match grossed $30,125 and Tilden won, 8–6, 6–3, 6–2. They went on a tour of 72 cities, grossing $243,000, the most ever for the pros, and Vines beat Tilden, 47 matches to 26. Vines won a match in Los Angeles, 6–0, 21–23, 7–5, 3–6, 6–2. Another memorable match between old adversaries Tilden and Henri Cochet took place at the Garden before a crowd of 12,663 paying

$20,000, and Tilden outlasted the 32-year-old Cochet, 7–9, 6–1. 4–6, 6–3, 6–3.

1935

Probably no player ever suffered as much frustration against an archrival as Helen Jacobs did against Helen Wills Moody. The only time Jacobs beat Moody, the victory was less than fully satisfying because it came as a result of a default when back trouble forced Moody to quit the 1933 final at Forest Hills while losing. All other times Jacobs lost to her, and among the toughest setbacks was the 1935 Wimbledon final.

Moody had played little the year before and was seeded only fourth in pursuit of her seventh Wimbledon title. Early in the season she had lost a set to Mary Hardwick, had lost a match to Kay Stammers, and in an early Wimbledon round against unknown Czech Slenca Cepkova she lost the first set and was within a point of trailing 4–1 in the second set before rallying.

In the final Jacobs, seeded third, fell be-

Wilmer Allison won his only U.S. singles title in 1935. *USLTA*

hind, 4–0, almost tied at 4–4, then faltered and lost the first set 6–3. Of the second set British authority Max Robertson wrote in his Encyclopedia of Tennis, "Jacobs' length improved; her favorite forehand chop became as dangerous as a scimitar. Mrs. Moody tried to come to the net but she was never able to run up and down the court as well as she could cover it from side to side." Jacobs won the second set.

Jacobs took a 4–2 lead, knocking the racket from Moody's hand on one powerful serve. She then broke Moody to lead, 5–2, but Moody broke to 3–5 where she faced a match point at 30–40, and flicked a desperation lob with Jacobs at the net. It looked like a simple smash, but a gusty wind caused the ball to sink swiftly, so that Jacobs had to drop to her knees to hit it—into the net. That turned the match around. Jacobs went down fighting, serving two aces when trailing, 5–6, but lost the set and match, 6–3, 3–6, 7–5. It was her fourth loss to Moody at Wimbledon, the third time in a final. She also lost to her in the 1928 Forest Hills final.

With Moody again absent from Forest Hills, Jacobs went on to win the title for the fourth successive year, beating Sarah Palfrey, 6–1, 6–4. Jacobs had a hand in a 4–3 Wightman Cup victory by the United States over Great Britain, winning in singles over Dorothy Round and teaming in the doubles with Sarah Palfrey. Palfrey and Mrs. Ethel Arnold also won in singles, as did Stammers (over Jacobs) and Round (over Arnold) for the British.

The second of Fred Perry's three-year reign in the men's division saw him win the French and Wimbledon Championships, lose the Australian final to Jack Crawford and lose at Forest Hills in the semifinals when hampered by a kidney injury. He led Britain to a 5–0 sweep over the U.S. in the Davis Cup.

At Wimbledon, Perry beat Crawford in four sets, then trounced Gottfried von Cramm, the first German to make the final, 6–2, 6–4, 6–4. Von Cramm had eliminated Don Budge in a semi, and it was Budge, unseeded, who created the sensation of the tournament by beating Bunny Austin in a quarterfinal. It was

in that match that there was an interruption for the Queen to take her seat in the Royal Box. It was written by one British reporter the next day that Budge had waved to the Queen. The story grew that Budge even said, "Hi, Queenie," and Budge took pains in his autobiography to point out that he did not wave, that he did wipe his brow, a reflex gesture with him. Two years later, though, when Budge was again at Wimbledon and met the Queen, she told him, he said, "You know, Mr. Budge, I did not see you a few years ago when you waved to me, but had I, I want you to know that I would have waved back."

The Wimbledon mixed finals was marked by the appearance of Mr. and Mrs. Harry Hopman of Australia; they were beaten by Perry and Dorothy Round.

At Forest Hills, Perry fell on his side heavily at 3–3 against Wilmer Allison in the semifinals. A doctor was brought to the sidelines to keep an eye on Perry, who kept putting his hand to his back (it turned out to be a displaced kidney). He lost to Allison, who he had beaten the previous year, and in the Davis Cup, in straight sets. Allison then beat Sidney Wood, 6–2, 6–2, 6–3, and thereafter confined himself to doubles.

The United States was shut out for the first time in the Davis Cup since 1911, losing to Great Britain as Perry and Austin swept Allison and Budge in singles, and Pat Hughes and Raymond Tuckey defeated Allison and John Van Ryn.

George Lott and Lester Stoefen joined the professional ranks. Tilden beat Lott, 6–4, 7–5, before a crowd of 16,000 in Madison Square Garden, and Tilden and Ellsworth Vines defeated the newcomers in their specialty, doubles. The pros' cross-country tour grossed $188,000.

1936

Fred Perry turned pro late in the year after dominating tennis in the four previous years as few men have over such a span. He won three successive Wimbledon titles, three American titles, a French and an Australian

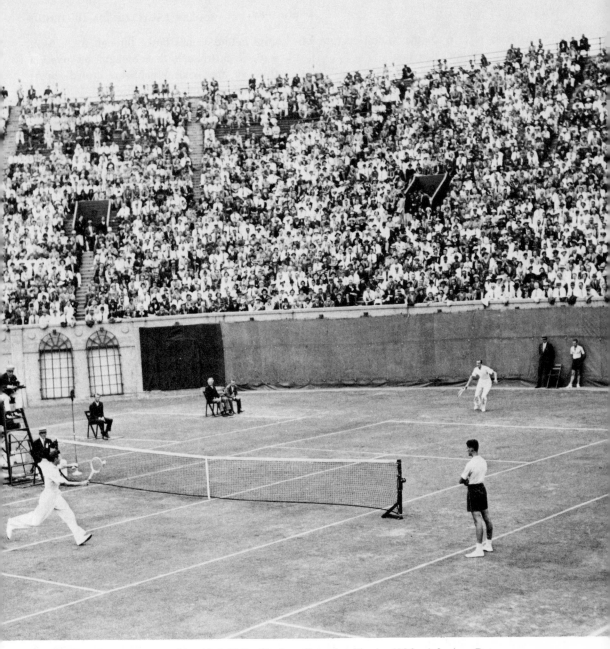

Fred Perry (far court) won his third U.S. Singles Championship in 1936, defeating Don Budge. *UPI*

title, and nine out of 10 Davis Cup Challenge Round victories.

Perry had laid off for seven months after his injury at Forest Hills in 1935, and when he was beaten in the French final by Gottfried von Cramm, there was some question that he could retain his old form. At Wimbledon, however, he quickly established that he would be formidable by sailing through early-round

opponents. He beat Bitsy Grant in straight sets, then had what would turn out to be his only difficult moments of the tournament, losing the first set to fifth-seeded Don Budge in the semifinals. Perry rallied to win in four sets, 5–7, 6–4, 6–3, 6–4. He then had an easy time in the final when von Cramm hurt his leg in the second game of the first set. Von Cramm continued on a bad leg and Perry won, 6–1, 6–1, 6–0, the widest margin of victory in a Wimbledon final.

It was the first time since the pre-World War I days that somebody had won three straight Wimbledons, and Perry was on hand in 1978 as a radio commentator when Bjorn Borg did the same.

Perry and Budge met again in a Forest Hills final that represented Budge's last chance to beat Perry in a major international tournament before Perry turned pro. They played a classic five-set match twice interrupted by rain. Budge won the first set, 6–2, Perry the second by the same score. Budge won, 8–6, then Perry, 6–1.

Of the fifth set, Budge later wrote, "We held serve to 3–2, my favor, and then I got the break for 4–2. Promptly, I permitted Fred to break me back. My serve was a dishrag. However, tired as I was, I was able to break him back again, so I stood at 5–3, serving for the National Championship of my country against the No. 1 player in the world. All I had to do was hold my serve one more time. I could not. I was so exhausted in reaching up to hit my serve that I felt as if I were leaning on the ball. There was no life in my shots. The stretching and reaching for the serve particularly wore on me. He broke me again—our fourth loss of service in a row—held his own serve at last, and tied the set at 5-all."

Budge came to within two points of victory at 8–7, but couldn't break through, and Perry finally won, 10–8, for his third Forest Hills title. Nobody has won it three times since. Budge later beat Perry on cement in Los Angeles. Only Perry beat him on grass.

A loss to Australia in the Inter-Zone final knocked the United States out of the Davis Cup final for the first time since 1933. Great Britain defended successfully, though pressed. After Bunny Austin beat Jack Crawford and Perry beat Adrian Quist, the Aussies rallied to take the doubles, Crawford and Quist over Pat Hughes and Raymond Tuckey, and Quist beat Austin. Perry prevailed, however, whipping Crawford in straight sets.

Helen Jacobs' quest for a Wimbledon Championship finally was successful after 10 years. She and Mrs. Hilde Sperling split the first two sets and were tied at 5-all in the third before Jacobs broke through for a 6–2, 4–6, 7–5 triumph that brought an ovation from an approving Wimbledon crowd. Sperling had won the French title.

Jacobs did not win a fifth straight United States championship because she ran into 22-year-old Californian Alice Marble, who would become the new queen of tennis. Marble was making her return to the championship after a two-year absence because of illness. Playing a man's game with a strong serve and constant rushing of the net, she started slowly and then prevailed, 4–6, 6–3, 6–2. Marble, an attractive blonde, wore the shortest shorts yet seen on a woman. Joan Hartigan won the Australian crown.

The Wightman Cup competition came down to its closest finish ever. The U.S. was hard-pressed because Jacobs was beaten by both Kay Stammers and Dorothy Round. Victories by Sarah Palfrey Fabyan and Carolin Babcock in singles, and a doubles win by Babcock and Mrs. Margorie Van Ryn evened the match at 3-all. Jacobs and Fabyan then teamed to beat Stammers and Freda James in a match that went 5-all into the final set before the Americans won.

The pros continued to struggle in their quest for gate attractions. Promoter Bill O'Brien brought women players back for the first time since 1926, and Ethel Burkhardt Arnold defeated Jane Sharp at Madison Square Garden. Bruce Barnes was added to the troup led by Tilden, but the tour lost $22,000.

1937

The line of dominant players, which started with Bill Tilden in the 1920s and continued through the French trio of René Lacoste, Henri Cochet, and Jean Borotra, then Ellsworth Vines and Fred Perry, added the imposing red-headed figure of Don Budge. Budge, 22, swept Wimbledon and Forest Hills and sailed through all Davis Cup competition, winning what many rate as the greatest Davis Cup match ever played.

With Perry moving to the professional ranks, it was obvious that Great Britain would yield the Davis Cup to the strong challenger that emerged from the Inter-Zone final. Budge

Princess Helena Victoria presents the Davis Cup to nonplaying captain Walter Pate in 1937 as (left to right) Don Budge, Gene Mako, Frank Parker, and Bitsy Grant look on.
Fischer Collection

spearheaded United States victories over Japan and Australia, beating Aussies Jack Crawford and John Bromwich, to set up a showdown against Germany.

Before Davis Cup play, there was the Wimbledon championships in which Budge was seeded first and Gottfried von Cramm second. On his way to the final Budge lost only one set, to Frank Parker in the semifinals, while von Cramm was extended to five sets by Crawford. Budge then defeated von Cramm, 6–3, 6–4, 6–2. Budge also became the first man ever to score a Wimbledon triple, adding the men's doubles title with Gene Mako and the mixed doubles with Alice Marble.

On to the Davis Cup and a match that had implications beyond the tennis court. "War talk was everywhere," Budge recalled. "Hitler was doing everything he could to stir up Germany. The atmosphere was filled with tension although von Cramm was a known anti-Nazi and remained one of the finest gen-

tlemen and most popular players on the circuit."

On the first day von Cramm beat Bitsy Grant, and Budge beat Henner Henkel, the Australian champion, in straight sets. Budge and Mako then defeated von Cramm and Henkel in four sets. Henkel, however, defeated Grant easily, setting up the concluding match on the Wimbledon Centre Court, July 30, with Queen Mary in attendance. Just before Budge and von Cramm went out to the court, von Cramm was called to the telephone. It was a long-distance call from Adolph Hitler exhorting von Cramm to win for the Fatherland. Budge recalls that "Gottfried came out pale and serious and played as if his life depended on every point." (Von Cramm would later be sent to a concentration camp.)

Von Cramm won the first two sets. Budge rallied, took the next two, then fell behind, 4–1, in the fifth. At this point he decided to take desperate measures. Attacking von Cramm's service and going to the net behind it, he got the matching break in the seventh game, making the score, 3–4, and held service to tie, 4-all. The score went to 5–5, then 6–6. In the 13th game Budge achieved another break. He then reached match point five times on his own service only to see von Cramm fight back to attain the sanctuary of deuce. "The crowd was so quiet I am sure they could hear us breathing," Budge recalled.

"On the sixth point, there was a prolonged rally," Will Grimsley recorded in his book *Tennis: Its History, People, and Events.* "Von Cramm sent up a lob. Budge raced back and returned it. Von Cramm then hit a forehand crosscourt. Budge tore after the ball, got his racket on it and took a desperate swing, sprawling to the court. it was a placement—game, set, match and the Davis Cup series. The final score was 6–8, 5–7, 6–4, 6–2, 8–6. The match ended at 8:45 P.M. in semi-darkness. The two players went to their dressing rooms, relaxed, dressed and returned more than an hour later to find most of the crowd still on hand, buzzing over the spectacular final."

Because von Cramm was the underdog and the British thought they might have a better chance in a Davis Cup final against the Germans, the crowd slightly favored von Cramm. An oddity of the competition was that the Germans were coached by Bill Tilden. It was not unusual for a pro in one country to coach another country's Davis Cup team, but it was uncommon for a coach to hold the post when it meant working against his own nation. At one point Tilden was animated in his rooting to the point of infuriating American show-business celebrities Jack Benny, Paul Lukas, and columinist Ed Sullivan, who challenged Tilden to a fight. Tilden later told Budge this was the greatest tennis match ever played.

The U.S. went on to defeat the British and win the Davis Cup trophy for the first time since 1926. In a 4–1 triumph, Budge scored singles triumphs over Charlie Hare and Bunny Austin; Budge teamed with Mako in the doubles for another point, with Frank Parker splitting his singles assignments.

The Americans returned with the trophy to a ticker-tape parade in New York, and Budge later was greeted with a parade in his hometown of Oakland, receiving a signet ring that featured the city seal flanked by diamonds. At Forest Hills von Cramm had a third crack at Budge, but only after he survived an 0–6, 8–6, 6–8, 6–3, 6–2 semifinal over Bobby Riggs, who had gained a place in the Top Ten rankings at No. 6 the previous year. Von Cramm extended Budge to five sets, yet Budge said he felt none of the trauma he found at Wimbledon, which he had won in straight sets. The score this time: 6–1, 7–9, 6–1, 3–6, 6–1. The packed crowd of 14,000 (5,000 were turned away) roared all the way for Budge. He was voted athlete of the year and became the first tennis player to win the Sullivan Award, annually presented to the country's outstanding amateur athlete. Budge lost for the first time that year in a small tournament in Chicago to Henkel. Vivian McGrath won the Australian title; Henkel, the French.

Despite the victory by Alice Marble over Helen Jacobs at Forest Hills the year before, Jacobs was seeded first at Wimbledon and Marble fifth. Neither player reached the final. Marble lost in the semifinals to Jadwiga Jedrzejowska of Poland; Jacobs went out in the quarterfinals against Britain's Dorothy Round, who went on to beat Jedrzejowska in the final, 6–2, 2–6, 7–5.

At Forest Hills, Jedrzejowska beat Jacobs in the semifinal, then lost, 6–4, 6–2, to Anita Lizana of Chile, making her first appearance in the championships. The French title having been won by Mrs. Hilde Sperling of Denmark and the Australian title by Nancye Wynne of Australia, this marked the first time since the end of World War I that no American woman won one of the four major championships.

International success came in Wightman Cup play with a 6–1 victory over Great Britain, the United States' seventh straight for an 11–4 edge in the series. Marble and Jacobs won twice in singles from Kay Stammers and Mary Hardwick; Sarah Palfrey Fabyan defeat Margot Lumb; and Marble and Fabyan won a doubles point. Interest in professional tennis revived with the debut of Fred Perry playing a cross-country tour against Ellsworth Vines, promoted by Frank Hunter, Bill Tilden's old doubles partner, and S. Howard Voshell. Perry opened at Madison Square Garden in fine fashion, defeating Vines, 7–5, 3–6, 6–3, 6–4, before a crowd of 17,630 paying $58,120, a record for the tour. Perry won the first six matches, but Vines finished strong, winning the series, 32–29. The tour grossed $412,181. Perry, under his guarantee, receiving the bigger slice, $91,335, while Vines got $34,195.

Though Vines was regarded as the "official" pro champion at this time, Tilden scheduled himself against Perry in the Garden later in the year. Tilden was 44, Perry 28, and though the crowd of 15,132 cheered mightily for the old guy, he was outclassed. He lost in the Garden for the first time, 6–1, 6–3, 4–6, 6–0. Al Laney wrote in that period, "All they can do is beat him, they cannot ever be his equal." It was estimated that Tilden had netted $500,000 (in Depression dollars) since turning pro six years before.

The Grand Slam at 23 for Don Budge in 1938. *UPI*

1938

Don Budge at 23 had the single most successful year of any player in tennis history. He won the four major championships—of Australia, France, Great Britain and the United States—a feat that came to be known as tennis' Grand Slam after Budge accomplished it. He also won the triple crown at Wimbledon for the second straight year and he helped the U.S. retain the Davis Cup.

Budge had been offered his first substantial offer to turn professional in 1937. He turned it down because he felt he owed a debt to amateur tennis to the extent of helping defend the Davis Cup trophy the U.S. had won in 1937 for the first time since 1926. "The Grand Slam then occurred to me as something of an afterthought," Budge said. He laid his plans carefully, telling only his friend Gene Mako, resolving not to extend himself at any time, so that he shouldn't tire along the way, as Jack Crawford had in 1933 when he won the first three titles, but lost in the final at Forest Hills.

Budge started in Australia, after losing frequently in leisurely tune-ups, he swept through the championships, beating John

Bromwich, 6–4, 6–1, 6–1. Shortly after the players' return to their home countries, Gottfried von Cramm of Germany, Budge's friend, was arrested and thrown in jail for refusing to become a Nazi. Budge led a committee of athletes appealing without success for von Cramm's release.

In the French Championships, though Budge suffered from diarrhea, he had a fairly easy time. Extended to five sets by a Yugoslavian lefty, Franjo Kukulevitch, Budge was never behind and said later he never felt threatened. Where von Cramm might have been his opponent in the final, he faced 6-foot-4 Czech Roderich Menzel, an outstanding clay court player. Budge romped, 6–3, 6–2, 6–4, in less than an hour. He recalled best about that feat the party afterward at which cellist Pablo Casals gave a concert in Budge's honor in Casals' apartment within view of the Eiffel Tower.

At Wimbledon, Budge won without losing a set, yet there was a time in the tournament when he said he was near panic because he had been having trouble with his backhand, his most celebrated weapon, considered by many to have been the greatest backhand of them all. He had been undercutting the stroke, and only while watching an older woman member of the all England Club on a sidecourt hitting with topspin on her backhand did he realize his error. He won his second successive Wimbledon by sailing through Britain's Bunny Austin in the final, 6–1, 6–0, 6–3, then completed another triple with Mako in the men's doubles and Alice Marble in the mixed.

Before Forest Hills, Budge faced the Australian Davis Cup challenge at the Germantown Cricket Club outside Philadelphia. The U.S. won, 3–2, as Bobby Riggs beat Adrian Quist in a key four-set opening victory, and Budge beat Bromwich in four sets and Quist in straight sets. The Budge-Mako team lost to Bromwich-Quist, and Bromwich beat Riggs.

Budge had been suffering from the flu and a loss of voice off and on during the year. Before Forest Hills, he had a tooth removed, eliminating his hurts. He proceeded to romp through the U.S. championships, defeating Welby Van Horn, Bob Kamrath, Charlie Hare, Harry Hopman, and Sidney Wood to reach the final against his pal Mako, who had become the first unseeded player ever to reach the finals at Forest Hills.

To some it looked like a setup for Budge, but he responded, "Gene was as likely to roll over and play dead for me as peace was to come in our time." Mako actually won the second set, only the second one Budge lost in the four tournaments. Budge then had to explain that he did not intentionally throw a set to his friend, certainly not at Forest Hills with so much at stake. "And I had too much respect and affection for Gene to treat him as if he were an inferior player who could be given a set for his troubles, rather like a condescending pat on the head."

Aside from Budge's heroics, Wimbledon was marked by what may have been the strongest women's field of all time, featuring the return after a two-year's absence of 32-year-old Helen Wills Moody, seeking a record eighth title. Though she had been extended by Kay Stammers in Wightman Cup play and had lost in a minor tournament to Hilde Sperling, she was seeded No. 1. Behind her came Alice Marble, Jadwiga Jedrzejowska of Poland, and Sperling. Sarah Palfrey Fabyan was seeded seventh; not seeded at all was Helen Jacobs.

The semifinals came down to these match-ups: Moody vs. Sperling, and Marble vs. Jacobs. Had Moody and Marble won, it would have brought a meeting of the longtime queen of tennis, Moody, and the bright new face who had succeeded her and Jacobs. Despite a struggle, Moody prevailed, 12–10, 6–4, but Marble lost to Jacobs, 6–4, 6–4, giving Jacobs what would be her fourth and last chance in a Wimbledon final against the woman who had been her lifelong nemesis.

The day before the final Jacobs worked out with Bill Tilden, who had been cultivating a flat forehand drive in her game, and she came up with a slight strain of her Achilles tendon. She came on the court with her ankle bandaged, she had trouble with it during the match, stopping to change the bandage at one point, and after holding even at 4-4 in the first set, she eventually deteriorated and lost, 6–4, 6–0. It was Moody's fiftieth successive match win, a record, and fifty-sixth in 57 matches at Wimbledon, concluding her career in major events. In the middle of the tournament, word came that Suzanne Lenglen had died from pernicious anemia. She was 38.

The Australian Championship went to Dorothy Bundy of the United States, the French title to Simone Mathieu of France. With Moody absent from the U.S. Championships, Marble won for the second time. She beat Sarah Palfrey Fabyan in the semifinals after losing the first set, then won the final over Australian Nancye Wynne.

An eighth straight Wightman Cup success for the United States over Britain, this time 5–2, consisted of two singles triumphs by Moody in her first appearance since 1932, a split in singles by Marble, a singles triumph by Fabyan, and a doubles victory by Marble and Fabyan. Moody lost with Bundy in doubles, Moody's seventh defeat in 10 Wightman Cup doubles matches. Moody's overall singles record: 18–2.

A pro tennis pattern had been set. The tour would flourish with the arrival of a new amateur champion, then taper off until a new face appeared. Fred Perry, in his second year, became co-promoter with Ellsworth Vines, the

Holcomb Ward, president of the USLTA, presents the U.S. singles trophy to Bobby Riggs, victor over Welby Van Horn in 1939. *UPI*

champion. Vines won 48 matches, Perry 35 on a tour that brought in $175,000, considerably less than the previous year, and the pair split $34,000.

1939

With the departure of Don Budge to the professional ranks, amateur tennis turned up another great player in Bobby Riggs, though his cocky attitude served to delay for a long time the fact that he was a quality player deserving of a ranking not far behind Bill Tilden, Don Budge, Jack Kramer, and Pancho Gonzales in the all-time lists.

Riggs was a key figure in the Davis Cup challenge by Australia, and at Wimbledon and Forest Hills. In the Davis Cup competition at the Merion Cricket Club in Philadelphia, the United States won the first two singles, then lost the doubles and the final two singles, enabling Australia, captained by Harry Hopman, to reclaim the Davis Cup for the first time since 1919.

Riggs, instrumental in winning the Cup for the U.S. the previous year by beating Adrian Quist, failed this time by losing to Quist, a heavy underdog. Riggs beat Australian champion John Bromwich in straight sets and then Frank Parker came through with a big victory with a five-set success over Quist. Joe Hunt

and Jack Kramer, who had yet to gain a Top Ten ranking, lost the doubles to Quist-Bromwich, so a Riggs victory over Quist was needed because Parker was not expected to beat Bromwich.

Riggs lost the first two sets, Quist running off 10 straight games at one point. Riggs then won the next two. The final set had the crowd reeling as Riggs won the first game, lost the next five, and then battled back up to 4–5, saving a match point in the ninth game. Quist wouldn't break, however, and he then held serve to win the match. Bromwich defeated Parker, 6–0, 6–3, 6–1.

Riggs was a wily player, compact, versatile, a great all-court retriever and completely self-confident. He preferred to play from the baseline, but he had a better serve than many people thought, and it kept getting better. He also could play the net, particularly when his opponent least expected it. He was a compulsive gambler. At Wimbledon, he reportedly won more than $100,000 from English bookies in 1939 when he bet he would win the singles, doubles, and mixed doubles. In the singles, he trailed two sets to one before rallying to beat his doubles partner, Elwood Cooke. After he and Cooke won the men's doubles, Riggs paired with Alice Marble to win the mixed doubles, becoming the only man other than Budge to win a Wimbledon triple. Marble became the only woman to win a triple other than Suzanne Lenglen.

Marble won Wimbledon for the first time, and in such convincing fashion that the British experts were ready to accord her a place with the all-time greats. She beat Mrs. Hilde Sperling, 6–0, 6–0, then romped in the final, 6–2, 6–0, over Kay Stammers, who had eliminated Helen Jacobs and Sarah Palfrey Fabyan. Marble and Fabyan won their second Wimbledon doubles crown.

Don McNeill, who won the French title, beating Bobby Riggs, was eliminated in an opening round at Wimbledon, entered the All-England Plate for also-rans, and won that.

At Forest Hills, Riggs ran into a bright young hope in 19-year-old Welby Van Horn, an unseeded player who beat Bromwich, Wayne Sabin, and Cooke on his way into the finals. Riggs eliminated Joe Hunt in the semis. Van Horn opened with two aces, and the supportive crowd roared with approval. Riggs then took charge. As Robert Minton wrote in *A History of Forest Hills*, "Serving a high twist ball to Van Horn's backhand, keeping the ball down the middle to his forehand, to increase the youngster's tendency to crowd his powerful drive, interspersing drop shots, throwing up lobs and constantly mixing his speed and length, Riggs won the match not so much on his ability to finish off the rallies as on his success in prodding Van Horn into mistakes." The score: 6–4, 6–2, 6–4.

In the women's championships, Marble, completing one of the most powerful successes ever enjoyed by a woman in one season, was threatened by Helen Jacobs, the 32-year-old four-time champion who reached the final by overcoming Stammers, her conqueror at Wimbledon. After losing the first set, 6–0, Jacobs won the second, 10–8, and took a 3–1 lead in the third set before Marble recovered to win.

Allison Danzig wrote in *The New York Times:* "Here was one of the most dramatic battles that women's tennis had produced in years, fought out for an hour and a half in gusty cross-currents of wind that raised havoc with the strokes, while the gallery roared and screamed its encouragement at Miss Jacobs. The crescendo of the enthusiasm was reached in the final game, a furiously disputed 20-point session in which Miss Jacobs five times came within a stroke of 5-all and twice stood off match point, only to yield finally to Miss Marble's more powerful attacking weapons."

Thus, Marble completed her second straight U.S. triple, having won in Boston the women's doubles with Sarah Palfrey Fabyan for the third straight year, and then the mixed doubles, not with Riggs, but with the 33-year-old Australian, Harry Hopman.

When Don Budge made his pro debut in Madison Square Garden in January, he was a slight underdog to Ellsworth Vines, the champion. A crowd of 16,725 paid $47,120, and many of them were U.S. Lawn Tennis Association officials who showed their devotion to Budge for his loyalty in putting off his departure from the amateur ranks a year in order to defend the Davis Cup. Budge trounced Vines,

6–3, 6–4, 6–2, and it may have been because Vines had played only eight matches with Fred Perry in South America that summer.

Later, Budge made a second Garden appearance against Perry, who had been his master as an amateur. Budge won easily, 6–1, 6–3, 6–0. On the tour played mostly in big cities, Budge asserted his superiority, beating Vines, 21–18, and Perry, 18–11. Budge collected more than $100,000, including a $75,000 guarantee from the $204,503 gross. Vines got $23,000, then deserted tennis for a successful pro golf career.

1940

Bombs fell on Wimbledon. The start of World War II a year earlier forced the cancellation of Wimbledon and the French Championships between 1940 and 1945, though the French held a tournament that was closed to non-nationals. The Australian Championships were halted in 1941. Bombs first hit Wimbledon on October 11, causing damage to the competitors' stand, and the club was hit three more times this year and in succeeding years.

International play ceased. This took something away from the quality of play, and it enabled the United States, which ran its National Championships without interruption

Don McNeill took the U.S. title in 1940.
Fischer Collection

through the war, to dominate through the postwar years.

Defending champion Bobby Riggs suffered a costly loss in the U.S. Championships in 1940 because his defeat by Don McNeill in the final took some of the luster off his record and he had to wait a year before turning pro. McNeill, a 22-year-old Oklahoman, fought one of the great come-from-behind battles against Riggs in a match marked by some outstanding sportsmanship. McNeill won, 4–6, 6–8, 6–3, 6–3, 7–5.

With the score tied at 4-all and deuce in the final set, McNeill hit a shot to Riggs' sideline that the linesman first called out. As Riggs turned his back and prepared to serve, the official reversed his call, declaring it safe. Riggs did not know of the change until he heard the call, "Advantage McNeill." Allison Danzig wrote, "The defending champion, who rarely questions a decision, turned at the call and then walked back toward the linesman, asking him why he had changed his ruling. The official maintained that the ball was good and Riggs, without further quibbling, accepted the costly decision and lost the next point and the game."

Then, in the opening rally of the final game, Riggs had to hit a ball that was falling just over the net and he gingerly endeavored to keep from touching the tape as he made his volley. The umpire instantly announced his foot had touched the net and he lost the point. "At that critical stage," Danzig wrote, "it was a bitter pill to swallow, but Riggs took it without arguing. McNeill, however, apparently did not like to win the point that way, even though the ruling was correct, and when he knocked Riggs' next service far out of court, the stadium rang with applause."

After losing the first set, McNeill rallied from 1–5 and 15–40 in the second set to tie, saved four set points, went on to take a 6–5 lead, but then dropped the set anyway. Down by two sets, he still came back, and with the crowd almost completely behind the valiant underdog, he pulled out the final set and the match.

Alice Marble won the singles, doubles, and mixed doubles for the third straight year, equalling the feat of Hazel Hotchkiss in

Sarah Palfrey Cooke displays the form that won her the U.S. crown over Pauline Betz in 1941. *UPI*

1909–11. In the singles final she won a return match with Helen Jacobs, 6–2, 6–3; she and Sarah Palfrey Fabyan won a third straight doubles, and she and Riggs won the mixed. She turned pro at the end of the year. In Australia, Adrian Quist won the men's title, Nancye Wynne Bolton the women's.

There was little pro tennis action of any note in 1940, although Don Budge won his first U.S. Pro title, over Fred Perry in Chicago.

1941–45

The United States Championships at Forest Hills was the only major tournament outpost during the World War II years. Old champions went off to war, new ones emerged, and though there were no sellout crowds, there were outstanding matches among fine players.

The Top Ten rankings for 1941 give some indication of the names that would dominate the sport during the war years: The men: 1. Bobby Riggs, 2. Frank Kovacs, 3. Frank Parker, 4. Don McNeill, 5. Ted Schroeder, 6. Wayne Sabin, 7. Gardnar Mulloy, 8. Bitsy Grant, 9. Jack Kramer, 10. Bill Talbert. The women: 1. Sarah Palfrey Cooke, 2. Pauline Betz, 3. Dorothy Bundy, 4. Margaret Osborne, 5. Helen Jacobs, 6. Helen Bernhard, 7. Hope Knowles, 8. Mary Arnold, 9. Virginia Kovacs, 10. Louise Brough.

1941—Riggs regained the title he had won in 1939 and then relinquished in 1940 to Don McNeill. In the semifinals Riggs beat Ted Schroeder in five sets, while McNeill was eliminated by the colorful Kovacs. Riggs then took apart Kovacs' game after the first set, winning 5–7, 6–1, 6–3, 6–3.

Sarah Palfrey Fabyan, now divorced and remarried as Sarah Palfrey Cooke, won the women's title, the first Easterner to achieve that distinction since Mrs. Maud Barger-Wallach in 1908. Cooke was 28, a year older than Bill Tilden when he won his first U.S. crown. She had been a contender for the championship since she was 14; she had been a runner-up to Helen Jacobs in 1934 and 1935. Victory came by a 7–5, 6–2 score over Pauline Betz. She also won the women's doubles with Margaret Osborne, her ninth title with her fourth partner in this competition. She won with Betty Nuthall in 1930 and 1933, Jacobs in 1934 and 1935, and with Alice Marble from 1937 through 1940.

Jack Kramer and Ted Schroeder won their second straight doubles championship.

Marble joined the pros and beat Britain's Mary Hardwick, 8–6, 8–6, in their debut at Madison Square Garden. Bill Tilden, 48, came out of semiretirement to face Don Budge and lost, 6–3, 6–4. The tour was a relative bust, Budge winning 51 of 56 matches. Budge wrote: "Tilden was still capable of some sustained great play that could occasionally even carry him all the way through a match. Most of the time he could, at his best, hang on for at least a set or two. Despite his age, he was no pushover. The people came out primarily for the show—to see me at my peak, and to see Tilden because they might never have the chance again. . . . Bill could invariably manage to keep things

close for a while. It was seldom, however, that he could extend me to the end."

1942—Californians Ted Schroeder and Pauline Betz won the singles championships. Schroeder with a fine net game and great determination, beat less gifted but diligent Frank Parker in the final, 8–6, 7–5, 3–6, 4–6, 6–2. Early favorite Jack Kramer, who had not lost a match all year, missed the tournament with appendicitis. A few weeks later, Kramer was inducted into the U. S. Coast Guard.

Betz defeated 19-year-old Louise Brough, 4–6, 6–1, 6–4; Brough and Margaret Osborne won the doubles for the first time. Mulloy and Bill Talbert won the men's dou-

Sergeant Frank Parker won the Nationals in 1944 and 1945. *New York Herald Tribune*

bles (shifted from Longwood to Forest Hills), Schroeder and Brough the mixed.

Bobby Riggs and Frank Kovacs turned pro in late 1941, but the entrance of the U.S. into the war cut down the scope of the tour. Budge won, finishing ahead of Riggs, Perry, and Kovacs in that order. They played 71 cities, drew only 101,915 customers, and that was the end of the pro tour for the remainder of the war, although Budge won his second U.S. Pro title over Riggs at Forest Hills.

1943—Kramer, on leave, was topseeded at Forest Hills, but he ate a plateful of bad clams the night before the semifinals and came down with food poisoning. He managed to beat Pancho Segura in the semis but was so sick he could hardly get out of bed for the final, in which Navy Lieutenant Joe Hunt beat him, 6–3, 6–8, 10–8, 6–0. It was Hunt's last major tournament. He was killed in an airplane training accident in February 1945.

Pauline Betz won her second straight women's title, again downing Brough in the final, 6–3, 5–7, 6–3. Kramer and Frank Parker won the doubles, Bill Talbert and Margaret Osborne the mixed.

1944—Sergeant Frank Parker at 28 won the men's singles championship on his thirteeneth try. Pauline Betz won her third successive women's title. Bill Talbert ousted No. 1-seeded Ecuadorian Pancho Segura in a five-set semifinal; Parker advanced past Don McNeill. Parker then defeated Talbert, 6–4, 3–6, 6–3, 6–3. It was the only tournament in which he competed. Betz won her final over Margaret Osborne, 6–3, 8–6. Osborne and Brough won the women's doubles, McNeill and Bob Falkenburg the men's doubles, and Talbert and Osborne their second mixed doubles.

Though there was no pro activity, pro champion Don Budge and Cadet Jack Kramer

Lieutenant (j.g.) Don McNeill (left) and Private Frank Kovacs appeared at Forest Hills as part of a tennis program benefiting the Red Cross Victory Fund. *New York Herald Tribune*

played a war charity exhibition at Madison Square Garden. Kramer won, 6–3, 6–2.

1945—In a repeat of the previous men's final, Sergeant Frank Parker defeated Bill Talbert, and Sarah Palfrey Cooke ended Pauline Betz' three-year reign. Parker beat Mrs. Cooke's husband, Elwood, in the semifinals and then defeated Talbert, 14–12, 6–1, 6–2. Talbert had eliminated Pancho Segura. Talbert and Gardnar Mulloy won the men's doubles, Brough and Osborne the women's doubles, and Talbert and Osborne the mixed.

3 } THE 25 GREATEST PLAYERS 1914–45

They changed a game played at moderate pace into one of thunder and lightning, fire and guts. They revolted against playing in long dresses or in long-sleeved shirts. One player used a flat-top racket, another played wearing a white cap, still another wore a white eyeshade. They had nicknames such as the Wizard, Big Bill, Little Miss Poker Face, the Baron. They all had one thing in common: They were champions, the best tennis players in the years 1914 to 1945.

To select the 25 top players from this period is a challenging task, for there was an unusually large number of performers of first class in the world. Tennis had its full share of all-time greats during the Golden Twenties and in the 30s, too.

There are no such things as Grand Prix points and professional earnings by which to rank these players. The professional game carried small weight and small money except for the top two or three touring pros. More important to prestige was amateur competition in the major national tournaments and in Davis and Wightman Cup play. When a woman wins Wimbledon eight times, when a man becomes the first to complete the Grand Slam, there can be little doubt of his or her greatness. A champion who played the big game of serve and volley 25 years before it became the standard method of play certainly deserves recognition among the best.

It is much harder for me to draw the line and leave out so many of the following who deserve mention but who did not make the top 25, players like Mary K. Browne and Hazel Hotchkiss Wightman, both trailblazers in women's tennis, both national champions before World War I, and both prominent afterward . . . Elizabeth Ryan, one of the best volleyers in the 1920s . . . Lili d'Alvarez of Spain, whose carefree style of playing in the late 1920s was so captivating . . . Cilly Aussem, the only German to capture the Wimbledon crown, winning in 1931 . . . Simone Mathieu of France, six times a Wimbledon semifinalist . . . Anita Lizana of Chile, who won the 1937 U.S. title . . . Jadwiga Jedrzejowska, the hard-hitting Pole of the 30s and 40s.

Among the men left out were Wilmer Allison, the 1935 U.S. champion and a formidable doubles player with John Van Ryn . . . John Bromwich and Adrian Quist, the tough Australian duo of the late 30s and the 40s . . . Vivian McGrath, the 1937 Australian champion and the first of the two-handed hitters to win renown . . . Bunny Austin, a Davis Cup mainstay for Great Britain in the 1930s . . . Frank Parker, a U.S. Davis Cupper in the late 1930s who blossomed into the U.S. singles champion in 1944 and 1945 . . . Sidney Wood and Frank Shields, native New Yorkers who both advanced to the 1931 Wimbledon final round . . . Vincent Richards, a great volleyer of the 1920s and one of the first pros . . . George Lott, a dynamic doubles player in the 1930s . . . Frank Hunter, a late bloomer born in 1894 who didn't make his big tennis moves until the late 1920s and the 1930s . . . and John Doeg, the smooth lefty who was 1930 U.S. champion.

Allison Danzig

JEAN BOROTRA (1898–   )

In many ways, Jean Borotra fit the image of the cosmopolitan Frenchman: a spectacular, debonair personality, a gallant kissing ladies' fingertips, a host of elegant parties aboard the *Ile de France* or at his fashionable residence in Paris.

Borotra was spectacular, too, on the tennis court in the 1920s and early 30s. He won Wimbledon in 1924 and 1926 and was runner-up in 1925 and 1927. He won the championship of France in 1924 and 1931 and the Australian title in 1928. And he was a demon in international play, a member of the Four Musketeers who in 1927 broke the U.S. grip on the Davis Cup and brought it to France for the first time.

Born on August 13, 1898, at Arbonne, Basque Pyrenees country near Biarritz, France, he first attracted wide attention when he played in the 1921 covered court championship in Paris. Standing out with a dramatic, aggressive style of play—and with the blue beret he always wore—Borotra became known as the "Bounding Basque from Biarritz."

His energy on the court was limitless, marked by headlong assaults and dashes for the net, both on his service and return of service, then a stampede back to retrieve lobs. No player could start faster or dash so madly. His service was not a rifled cannonball, but it was not to be trifled with. His backhand return of service and backhand volley were vividly individual, thrusts for the kill.

Borotra was named to France's Davis Cup team in 1922, and in 1923 he assembled with René Lacoste, Henri Cochet, and Jacques Brugnon, a great doubles player, to form the Four Musketeers. Not only did the French win their first Cup in 1927, but they also held it for five years thereafter.

In the 1932 Challenge Round, Borotra reached heights of inspiration against the U.S. He defeated Ellsworth Vines, the winner of Wimbledon and the U.S. championship that year. On the final day, Borotra lost the first two sets to Wilmer Allison, and with the Texan at match point in the fifth set, Borotra's second serve appeared to be out. Alli-

Jean Borotra: Bounding Basque in a blue beret. *Fischer Collection*

son ran forward for the handshake, thinking he had won, but the linesman insisted the serve was good and play resumed. Borotra pulled out the victory and France retained the Cup.

With his dazzling performances, Borotra was popular everywhere. This included the Seventh Regiment Armory in New York, where he was in his element on the fast board courts and four times won the national indoor championships. He was not rated quite the player that Cochet and Lacoste were, but Borotra's celebrity endured and the legs that ran like fury kept him active in tennis into his 70s as a competitor in the veterans' division at Wimbledon. He was among the champions honored at the 1977 Wimbledon Centennial, a year after he was enshrined with the three other Musketeers in the International Tennis Hall of Fame at Newport.

NORMAN BROOKES (1877–1968)

They called him the Wizard. A figure of heroic stature, Norman Everard Brookes was renowned both as a player—for many years Australia's best—and as an administrator. He was of sallow complexion and pale blue eyes, austere in bearing, rather taciturn, a man of

Norman Brookes: An unorthodox southpaw. *UPI*

strength and character to command respect and win honors.

And win honors he did. Born on November 14, 1877, at Melbourne, Australia, he became in 1907 the first male from overseas to win the championship at Wimbledon. He won Wimbledon again in 1914 and was runner-up in 1919 after returning from World War I. Long ranked as the ablest of left-handed players, he was a member of the Australasian and Australian Davis Cup teams between 1905 and 1920 and played in eight challenge rounds.

He was an exponent of the serve and volley game, the "big game" that was supposed to have originated after World War II. Brookes played that type of game in 1914, but he had more than a serve and volley. He had ground strokes adequate to hold his own from the back of the court. Because his serve was so big an asset and he volleyed so much, his methods were characterized as unorthodox when he was in his prime.

Germany's Otto Froitzheim, a player of skill and quickness, put Brookes to a severe test in an 8–6 fifth set in the 1914 Wimbledon championships, the Australian's first appearance there since his 1907 victory. Brookes demonstrated the all-around strength of his game preparatory to wresting the championship from Tony Wilding of New Zealand in straight sets with a display of faultless ground strokes. Brookes' durability was demonstrated again in 1926 at Wimbledon when, at the age of 49, he ousted Frank Hunter, a good player 18 years his junior.

The honors didn't stop for the man who seemed to command them. In 1926, he was named president of the Lawn Tennis Association of Australia, a post he held until 1955. He was decorated with the French Legion of Honor for his services in the war as a captain in the British Army and, in 1939, he was knighted.

He died in 1968, a patriarch of tennis.

DONALD BUDGE (1916–   )

In sheer achievement, James Donald Budge accomplished what nobody before 1938 had been able to do—he won the Grand Slam of tennis, capturing the championships of Australia, France, England, and the United States in the same year. People were suddenly speaking of Budge in the same breath with the already immortal Bill Tilden.

Born on June 13, 1916, in Oakland, California, Budge had been less interested in tennis than in baseball, basketball, and football while growing up in the California city, where his Scottish-born father, a former soccer player, had settled.

Don Budge: The grandest slam of all. *UPI*

When he turned to tennis, his strapping size enabled him to play a game of maximum power. His service was battering, his backhand considered perhaps the finest the game has known, his net play emphatic, his overhead drastic. Quick and rhythmic for his size, he was truly the all-around player and, what is more, was temperamentally suited for the game. Affable and easygoing, his concentration could not be shaken from the objective of winning without any fuss or waste of time, with the utmost application of hitting power.

The red-haired young giant was a favorite wherever he played, and he moved quickly up the tennis ladder. At the age of 19, he was far enough advanced to be named to the Davis Cup team. The next year, 1936, he lost at Wimbledon and Forest Hills to Fred Perry, the world's No. 1-ranked amateur, but beat Perry in the Pacific Southwest tournament.

In 1937 Perry turned pro and Budge earned the world's No. 1 ranking. He won at Wimbledon and Forest Hills and led the U.S. to the Davis Cup Challenge Round with a comeback victory over Gottfried von Cramm in one of Budge's many classic matches with the German ace. In a culmination to a fantastic year, Budge received the Sullivan Award as America's top amateur athlete, the first tennis player to be so honored.

The high regard in which Budge was held by fellow players, spectators, and officials was evidenced following the loyalty he demonstrated in 1937. He was a big attraction for pro tennis but decided against leaving the amateur ranks for another year. The United States had the Davis Cup and he decided that, in return for all tennis had done for him, he must help in the defense of the Cup for at least another year.

So he turned down the professional offers, aware that poor fortunes in 1938 could hurt, if not end, his earning power as a pro. As it turned out, 1938 would be his most glorious year. He defeated John Bromwich in the Australian final, losing only one set in the entire tournament. In the French championship he beat Roderic Menzel of Czechoslovakia in the final and yielded three sets in the tournament. At Wimbledon he did not lose a single set, beating Bunny Austin of Britain for the title,

and at Forest Hills he gave up but one set—to Gene Mako in the final—in winning the U.S. crown.

Budge had won the Grand Slam and was the toast of the tennis world. After helping the U.S. retain the Davis Cup, he left the amateur ranks, with the blessing and good wishes of the United States Lawn Tennis Association. The association president, Holcombe Ward, and the Davis Cup captain, Walter L. Pate, extolled Budge's character and achievements and wished him well in his pro career.

He made his professional debut at Madison Square Garden in New York early in 1939 and, before a crowd of 16,725, defeated Ellsworth Vines, 6–3, 6–4, 6–2. On tour, Budge defeated Vines, 21 matches to 18, and also defeated Perry, 18–11. On tour with the 47-year-old Tilden, Budge beat him, 51–7.

Budge conquered Bobby Riggs, 6–2, 6–2, 6–2, for the U.S. Pro title at Forest Hills in 1942, the same year Budge enlisted in the Air Force. After the war, his playing career slumped off as he concentrated more on teaching, but he reached the pro final three more times and left little doubt as to his greatness. "I consider him," said Bill Tilden, "the finest player 365 days a year who ever lived."

DOROTHEA DOUGLASS LAMBERT CHAMBERS (1878–1960)

Considered to be the outstanding woman tennis player prior to World War I, Dorothea Douglass Lambert Chambers came within a stroke of defeating one of the greatest postwar players in a match that marked the evolution of the women's game.

The date was 1919, in the Wimbledon Challenge Round, with Lambert Chambers, a seven-time champion, defending the title against the 20-year-old sensation from France, Suzanne Lenglen. With King George, Queen Mary, and the Princess Royal in the committee box, one of the finest matches to be played at Wimbledon, by men or women, was enacted.

Against the all-court game of Lenglen, Lambert Chambers delighted the gallery with

Dorothea Lambert Chambers: Ageless champion.
UPI

superb resistance. She drove with such power and length from both forehand and backhand, passed so accurately, put up lobs so irretrievable, and had so much tough on her drop shot that her youthful opponent was showing signs of physical distress and found herself in danger of losing.

After two sets, the match was even and Lenglen was sipping brandy to ease her peril. In the third set, trailing, 4–1, the 40-year-old Lambert Chambers put on a remarkable comeback for a player of her age and seemed to have the victory in hand at 6–5, 40–15 on her service at double match point. But, just as remarkably, Lenglen rallied and pulled out the match by the scores of 10–8, 4–6, 9–7. Both players were so exhausted that when asked to come to the royal box, they said they were physically unable to do so. It had been an epic struggle between the past and the future in tennis.

Born on September 13, 1878, at Ealing, England, Lambert Chambers won Wimbledon for the first time as Dorothea Douglass in 1903 and repeated in 1904. After losing to May Sutton of California in the 1905 final,

she defeated Sutton in 1906, then lost to her again in the 1907 title round as Mrs. Lambert Chambers. Her other victories came in 1910, 1911, 1913, and 1914, before the Wimbledon Championships were suspended because of World War I.

Again, in 1920, a year after her unforgettable match, she faced Lenglen for the title. To get to the final, she defeated Molla Mallory and Elizabeth Ryan, and the strain of playing through the tournament took its toll. She won only three games in losing the match to the French queen of the courts.

In 1900, she had been a quarterfinalist at Wimbledon. In 1925, she was a quarterfinalist in the U.S. Championship and played on the British Wightman Cup team. She was on the team again in 1926, at the age of 47.

She died in 1960, in her 82nd year, one of the remarkable figures of tennis.

HENRI COCHET (1901–   )

It could be said that Henri Cochet had as pronounced a gift for playing tennis as anyone who attained world supremacy. A racket in his hand became a wand of magic, doing the impossible, most often in a position on the court considered untenable, and doing it with nonchalant ease and fluency. He took the ball early, volleys and half volleys rippling off the strings. His overheads invariably scored, though his service seemingly was innocuous.

He developed his skills early in Lyons, France, where he was born on December 14, 1901, and where his father was secretary of the tennis club. Henri worked at the club as a ballboy and practiced with his friends and sister when nobody was using the courts. In 1921 he went to Paris where he and Jean Borotra, both unknowns, reached the final of the covered court championship. Cochet was the winner.

The next year, he and Borotra played on the Davis Cup team, and in 1923 they joined with René Lacoste and Jacques Brugnon in the origin of the Four Musketeers. Cochet won 10 successive Davis Cup Challenge Round matches from the time the Musketeers wrested the Cup from the U.S. in 1927.

A sensitivity of touch and timing, resulting

Henri Cochet: The Little Musketeer.
Fischer Collection

in moderately hit strokes of genius, accounted for the success the little Frenchman had in turning back the forceful hitters of the 1920s and early 30s. Following a stunning victory over Bill Tilden in the quarterfinals of the 1926 U.S. championships, ending Tilden's six-year sway, and a triumph over William Johnston in the 1927 challenge round, Cochet established himself in 1928 as the world's foremost player. Winner of the U.S. and French Championships that year, and runner-up at Wimbledon, he became more of a national hero than ever as he scored three victories in the Davis Cup Challenge Round.

With Lacoste's retirement from international play in 1929, Cochet was France's indispensable man. He led his country to victory over the United States in the Challenge Round in 1929, and 1932, and over the British in 1931.

He was champion of France five times and won the Wimbledon and U.S. titles once. His triumph over Bill Tilden in the 1927 Wimbledon semifinals, after losing the first two sets and trailing by 1–5 in the third, was one of the most remarkable comebacks in tennis. "In these inspired moments of his," said Tilden, "Cochet is the greatest of all the Frenchmen and in my opinion is possibly the greatest player who has ever lived."

After France lost the Davis Cup to Great Britain in 1933, Cochet turned professional. He did not have much of a career as a pro, however, and after the war, in 1945, one of the most naturally gifted tennis players in history received reinstatement as an amateur, a role in which he had once ruled the tennis world.

SARAH PALFREY FABYAN COOKE (1912–   )

If any player may be said to have been the sweetheart of tennis, as Mary Pickford was of the movies, her name was Sarah Palfrey.

Twice national champion, twice a runner-up for the title to Helen Jacobs, nine times national doubles champion, and twice doubles champion at Wimbledon, she was an international attraction on both sides of the Atlantic and west to the Pacific.

Born on September 18, 1912, at Sharon, Massachusetts, she was a carefully reared girl of upper-register Boston and a protégé of Hazel Hotchkiss Wightman. The galleries loved her radiant smile and her unfailing graciousness in triumph and defeat alike, and they marveled at the cleverness and dispatch she used in the volleying position and at the execution of her sweeping backhand. She was one of the most accomplished performers around the net, thanks in part to the instruction of Wightman, a pioneer in introducing the volley as a major component of the women's game. A slip of a girl, Sarah was remarkable in the way she stood up to the more powerful hitters.

Sarah was so prized as a doubles partner in the 1930s and 1940s that she had the pick of the best. Seven times in Wightman Cup play she teamed with Jacobs, three times with Alice Marble, and once with Helen Wills

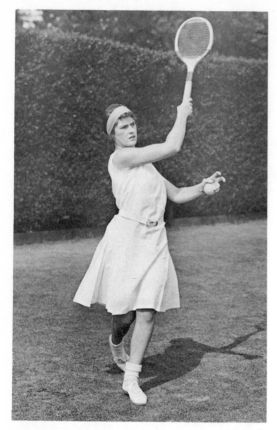

Sarah Palfrey: The sweetheart of tennis. *USLTA*

sportsman, as well as a handsome figure on the court in his long, white flannels and button-down, long-sleeved shirt. And he moved easily, gracefully, over the turf with his flat-topped racket, a model of early vintage.

Crawford, born on March 22, 1908, at Albury, Australia, was a masterful player from the back of the court, driving the ball with length and pinpoint control with seemingly little strain. He played the classical game of solid, fluent strokes, and he played it so well that he came within one set of completing a Grand Slam five years before Don Budge accomplished the feat of winning the four major championships.

Crawford's bid came in 1933, starting with a victory over Keith Gledhill in the Australian final. Next Crawford won the French Championship, beating Henri Cochet for the title. At Wimbledon came a legendary final against Ellsworth Vines that Crawford won, 4–6, 11–9, 6–2, 2–6, 6–4.

So Crawford moved on to Forest Hills and the United States Championship with an opportunity to complete the ultimate sweep. After defeating Frank Shields in the semifinals, Crawford faced Fred Perry as the last obstacle in his path. Crawford lost the first set, but then won the next two, 11–9, 6–4, and was one set away from a slam. But his strength

Moody. But prestige comes from superiority in singles play, and in this she ranked no less than 13 times in the Top Ten of the United States. She was No. 1, No. 2, or No. 3 numerous times.

After her playing career she was a successful business executive and (as Mrs. Jerry Danzig) was available for committee work in the tennis associations, the International Tennis Hall of Fame, and for organizations devoted to public service and charity. Her writings appear in books and magazines. In 1963 she was voted into the International Tennis Hall of Fame.

JACK CRAWFORD (1908–   )

Few players so completely won the gallery to them as did John Herbert Crawford, called by one commentator the "most popular Wimbledon winner in history."

Indeed, Jack Crawford was an exemplary

Jack Crawford: Picture player. *UPI*

faded, owing in part to the asthma and insomnia he had at the time. Perry went on to victory in the next two sets, dashing Crawford's hopes.

Still, the gallery loved this man from Down Under. He won the championship of his country four times, he almost won the Grand Slam, and he did it all his way, seemingly never hurried, his every move appearing effortless, his serve belonging in a picture book. Jack Crawford was one of the greats of his time while playing tennis in the style of a gentleman of the old school.

KITTY McKANE GODFREE (1898–   )

The only player to defeat Helen Wills Moody at Wimbledon, where the Californian won a record eight titles, was Kathleen McKane Godfree, the foremost woman player in Britain in the 1920s.

The year of Kitty's triumph over Wills was 1924, when Helen played at Wimbledon for the first time. McKane won, 4–6, 6–4, 6–4. A player of courage and fighting qualities, McKane defeated Wills in the Wightman Cup

Kitty McKane Godfree: Dynamic Britisher. *UPI*

matches that year and triumphed over Molla Mallory, too.

The following year, McKane lost to Wills in the final of the U.S. Championships, 3–6, 6–0, 6–2, after eliminating Mallory and Elizabeth Ryan. McKane also got to the final of the French Championships before bowing to Suzanne Lenglen.

Born on May 7, 1898, in London, she would win Wimbledon a second time. That was in 1926 when, as Mrs. Godfree, she defeated Lili d'Alvarez of Spain in the final, 6–2, 4–6, 6–3, after the Spanish beauty had come within a stroke of a 4–1 lead in the third set.

Kathleen was in a third Wimbledon final. In 1923 she got there by beating Elizabeth Ryan, 1–6, 6–2, 6–4, and then lost to Lenglen. In the U.S. Championships that year, Kathleen offered a dangerous challenge to Wills, coming from 2–5 to 5-all in the third set before losing.

She was a member of the British team that played the United States for the Wightman Cup in the inaugural matches in 1923 in the Forest Hills stadium. She lost to Wills and Mallory, both members of the host team.

The following year, in the first of these international team competitions held in Britain, Kitty beat both Wills and Mallory. The home team won by a surprising margin of 6–1, and then in 1925 the British won again in a close series, with Kathleen defeating Mallory and losing to Wills. In 1926 Kathleen beat both Mary K. Browne and Ryan, but the British lost the series at Wimbledon despite Kathleen's heroics.

She was among the champions of the past who received Centennial medallions on Wimbledon's Centre Court in 1977 and was inducted into the International Tennis Hall of Fame in 1978.

HELEN JACOBS (1908–   )

Helen Hull Jacobs had the misfortune to be a contemporary of Helen Wills Moody. Four times in the battle of Helens in the final round at Wimbledon, Jacobs lost. She also lost to her archrival at Forest Hills in the 1928 U.S. Championships.

On top of all those defeats to Helen the

Helen Hull Jacobs: Artist at the net. *New York Herald Tribune*

First, Jacobs was beaten in a Wimbledon final by Dorothy Round of Britain, and three times she was turned back in a U.S. final by Alice Marble.

Particularly bitter for her to take was a defeat in the 1935 Wimbledon final. Moody that season was struggling, and in the final round Jacobs led at match point, 5–3. Victory seemed at hand when Wills threw up a lob that barely got to the net, and Jacobs waited to smash it for the final point. But a wind current caught the ball and Jacobs, off balance, hit it into the net. Moody rallied and went on to her seventh Wimbledon title. At the time, Jacobs had none.

In spite of so much adversity, Jacobs, born on August 6, 1908, at Globe, Arizona, was as stout of heart as any champion. She won at Forest Hills four years in a row, 1932–35, a rare achievement, and she was finally

crowned at Wimbledon in 1936, beating Hilde Sperling.

Jacobs' unflagging courage, her iron will to win, was her biggest asset. She had little of the power that Moody applied, and Jacobs' forehand stroke was so unsatisfactory that she forsook it for a sliced cut at the ball, not too effective either to stand off a full-blooded drive or to repel a volleyer. Her backhand, while not severe, was steadfast, reliable against any amount of pressure, and she won heavily with it.

It was at the net where she was most effective. She was not as conclusive with her volley or her smash as Marble, but she was a determined, skilled foe at close quarters, and her fighting traits counted most, whatever her position on the court. Even when afflicted with injuries, she refused to be discouraged. Her admirable qualities, including her sportsmanship and great self-reliance, had a strong appeal for tennis galleries.

A feud was built up in publications between the two Helens that Jacobs said never existed. Moody was pictured as resenting Jacobs following in her footsteps—both played at the Berkeley (Calif.) Tennis Club, each won the national junior championship two years in a row, and both attended the University of California. The Jacobs family lived in the Wills' former home. The two Helens did not see each other except in connection with tennis.

Jacobs finally got the victory she was after in the 1933 U.S. Championships, although even then it was not a complete one. She won the first set against Moody, 8–6, and lost the second, 6–3. When the score went to 3–0 in Jacobs' favor in the third set, Moody walked to the umpire's stand, informed the official that because of pain in her back she was unable to continue, and conceded the match. Jacobs had dealt Moody her first big defeat since 1926.

BILL JOHNSTON (1894–1946)

William M. Johnston's name is inevitably associated with Bill Tilden's. Tilden was "Big Bill" and Johnston "Little Bill," and they were the twin terrors who turned back the

Bill Johnston: Tops with topspin forehand.
Fischer Collection

Australasians, French, and Japanese in the Davis Cup Challenge Round from 1920 through 1926, a seven-year span of invincibility unequaled in international team matches.

Big Bill and Little Bill were teammates and they were also rivals. It was Johnston's bad luck that his career was contemporaneous with the player commonly regarded as the greatest ever. Otherwise Johnston might have won the national tennis championship most of the years it fell to Tilden, from 1920 to 1925. As it was, Little Bill won it twice, in 1915 and in 1919, defeating Maurice McLoughlin the first time and Tilden in the 1919 final. Johnston was runner-up six times, and in five of those years it was Tilden who beat him in the final.

Until the French began to catch up to Big Bill and Little Bill in 1926, Johnston had been winning his Davis Cup matches with the loss of very few sets. In seven challenge rounds, he won 11 of 14 matches in singles. He lost only once until 1927, when his age and his health began to tell.

The top-spin forehand drive he hammered

with the western grip was one of the famous and most effective shots in tennis history. No other player executed it as effectively as he did, taking the ball shoulder high and leaping off the ground on his follow-through. He was also one of the best volleyers the game has known, despite meeting the ball near the service line, where he stationed himself because of his short height of 5-8.

Johnston was born on November 2, 1894, in San Francisco and developed many of his skills on public parks courts. His whole game was aggressive and he played to win on the merit of his strokes rather than on the opponent's errors. Though he did not have a big serve, overhead he was secure and angled his smash effectively. He had as much fight as anyone who was ever champion, and many times when he came off the court, dripping with perspiration after a prolonged struggle, he was five to eight pounds below his usual weight of 125.

Such was the case in his U.S. National final with Tilden in 1922 at the Germantown Cricket Club in Philadelphia in which Johnston won the first two sets and led by 3–0 in the fourth. It seemed that every spectator in the stands was cheering for Johnston, the favorite of galleries virtually every time he went on the court. Both he and Tilden had two legs on the challenge trophy, and Little Bill had his heart set on retiring it for his permanent keeping in this match. It was a crushing disappointment when he lost in five sets.

Following the 1927 season, Johnston retired from competition. His health had not been robust from the time he served in the Navy in World War I. He died in 1946 at the age of 51 and seven years later was enshrined in the International Tennis Hall of Fame. Little Bill had made a big name in tennis.

RENÉ LACOSTE (1905–   )

He was not particularly athletic in build or in his movements, and as a reserved and rather shy youth he seemed to be more fitted for the world of education, law, or medicine than for athletic achievement. But Jean René Lacoste, known as the Crocodile, would win

René Lacoste: As relentless as a crocodile. *Fischer Collection*

Wimbledon twice and the French and U.S.
titles twice and would become a member of
the Four Musketeers, the scourges of the tennis world in the 1920s.

Lacoste would be a self-made champion, a
player who won world renown through sheer
hard work and devoted application rather than
through the benefit of natural talent. Born in
Paris on July 2, 1905, he did not go on a
court until he was 15 years old, while on a
trip with his father to England, and his development after that was slow.

His father, a wealthy manufacturer of
motor cars, agreed to his son's devoting himself to tennis, but with the understanding that
he must set himself the task of becoming a
world champion and must achieve his goal
within five years or drop it.

In his determination to excel, Lacoste
trained faithfully and read and observed
everything, even keeping a notebook on the
strengths and weaknesses of his contemporaries. He became a master of the backcourt
game, choosing to maintain a length of inex-
orable pressure to exact the error or the open-

ing for the finishing shot, and repelling the
volleyer with passing shots and lobs.

His successes began to build. He joined the
French Davis Cup team, forming the Four
Musketeers with Jean Borotra, Henri Cochet,
and Jacques Brugnon. He lost to Borotra in
the 1924 Wimbledon final, then avenged the
defeat the next year to win Wimbledon. The
French title fell to Lacoste in 1925 and also in
1927 and 1929. He won Wimbledon for the
second time in 1928.

But perhaps his most stirring victory came
in the 1927 U.S. championships, where the
efficiency of his backcourt game thwarted the
great Bill Tilden in the final. The 34-year-old
Tilden attacked for close to two hours and
volleyed far more than was his custom, but
despite efforts that brought him to the point of
exhaustion, he could not win a set. The
sphinxlike Lacoste, 22 years old, kept the ball
going back the full length of the court with
the inevitability of fate and hardly an inex-
cusable error. The scores of the fabulous
match were 11–9, 6–3, 11–9, enabling Lacoste to retain the U.S. title he had won the
previous year against Borotra.

Lacoste also defeated Tilden two other
times in 1927—in the French Championships
and in Davis Cup play in which France beat
the U.S. In 1928, Lacoste lost the opener in
Davis Cup play to Tilden, and it marked the
Frenchman's last appearance in international
team matches, owing to his health. After winning the French title in 1929 he withdrew
from competition, having more than fulfilled
the goal he once never seemed suited for—
that of a tennis champion.

SUZANNE LENGLEN (1899–1938)

In the days of ground-length tennis dresses,
Suzanne Lenglen played at Wimbledon with
her dress cut just above the calf. She wept
openly during matches, pouted, sipped brandy
between sets. Some called her shocking and
indecent, but she was merely ahead of her
time, and she brought France the greatest
global sports renown it had ever known.

Lenglen won Wimbledon every year but
one from 1919 through 1925, the exception
being 1924, when illness led to her with-

Suzanne Lenglen: The magnificent swinger.
Fischer Collection

drawal after the fourth round. Her 1919 title match, at the age of 20, with the 40-year-old Dorothea Lambert Chambers is one of the hallmarks of tennis history.

Lambert Chambers, the seven-time champion, was swathed in stays, petticoats, high-necked shirtwaist, and a long skirt that swept the court. The young Lenglen was in her revealing dress that shocked the British at the sight of ankles and forearms. After the second set, Lenglen took some comfort from her brandy and won, 10–8, 4–6, 9–7, in a dramatic confrontation.

After her victory, Lenglen became easily the greatest drawing card tennis had known, and she was one of those who made it a major box-office attraction. Along with a magnetic personality, grace, and style, she was the best woman player the world had seen.

Lenglen, born on May 24, 1899, in Paris, played an all-court game such as few had excelled at. She moved with rare grace, unencumbered by the tight layers of garments others wore. She had extraordinary accuracy with her classical, rhythmic ground strokes. For hours daily her father had her direct the ball at a handkerchief he moved from spot to spot. Her control was so unfailing that she thought it shameful to hit the ball into the net or beyond the line. In addition, she had so keen a sense of anticipation that she invariably was in the right position to meet her opponent's shot.

Her 1926 match against Helen Wills in a tournament at Cannes, France, caused a sensation. Tickets brought unheard-of wealth to scalpers, and the roofs and windows of apartments and hotels overlooking the court were crowded with fans. Lenglen, on the verge of collapse during the tense match, but saved by smelling salts and brandy, defeated the 20-year-old Wills, 6–3, 8–6.

Lenglen's career was not free of setbacks, however. In the 1921 U.S. Championships, having lost the first set badly to Molla Mallory, Lenglen walked weeping and coughing to the umpire and said she could not continue, defaulting the match. She made up for it the next year at Wimbledon by defeating Mallory in the final and did not lose another match for the remainder of her amateur career.

In the 1926 Wimbledon, Lenglen had a terrifying ordeal. She kept Queen Mary waiting in the royal box for her appearance when, owing to a misunderstanding or a failure of communications, Lenglen did not have the correct information about the time she was to be on court. The ghastly error was too much. She fainted and Wimbledon saw her no more as a competitor. She withdrew from the tournament, and that year went on a tour for money in the United States under the management of C. C. Pyle. It marked the start of professional tennis as a playing career.

At the age of 39, Lenglen died of pernicious anemia. It was speculated that her health had been undermined by her long hours of practice as a young girl. But as a young woman she had brought the glamor of the stage and the ballet to the court, and queues formed at tennis clubs where before there had been indifference. She had emancipated the female player from layers of starched clothing and set the short-hair style as well. She had brought the game of tennis into a new era.

MOLLA BJURSTEDT MALLORY (1892–1959)

Molla Bjurstedt Mallory had less in the way of stroke equipment than most players who have become tennis champions. But the sturdy, Norwegian-born woman, the daughter of an army officer, had the heart and pride of a gladiator, could run with limitless endurance, and was a fierce competitor. She won the U.S. Championship the same number of times as did Helen Wills Moody, seven, and she administered the only defeat that Suzanne Lenglen suffered as an amateur.

It was her match with Lenglen in the second round of the U.S. Championship at Forest Hills in 1921 that won Mallory her greatest celebrity. She won the first set, 6–2, playing with a fury that took her opponent by surprise, running down the ball interminably to wear out the French girl in long rallies, and hitting her mighty topspin forehand down the line for blazing winners. Lenglen, the Wimbledon queen, out of breath from running, coughing, and weeping, walked to the umpire's stand after several points of the second

Molla Mallory: A striking force out of Norway.
UPI

set and informed the official that she was ill and could not continue. This was as sensational a reversal as ever recorded on the courts.

Mallory, whose game was developed in Norway, where she was born in 1892, came to the United States in 1915 as Molla Bjurstedt and won the U.S. tournament each year through 1918. Some credit her with winning a total of eight U.S. Championships, but the 1917 tournament was held as a "Patriotic Tournament" during the war, with no title at stake.

Mallory was a player of the old school. She held that a woman could not sustain a volleying attack in a long match and she put her reliance on her baseline game. That game amounted to a forehand attack and an omnivorous defense that wore down her opponents. She took the ball on the rise and drove it from corner to corner to keep her rival on the constant run and destroy her control. The quick return made her passing shots all the more effective.

In her first U.S. National Championship final—in 1915, against Hazel Hotchkiss Wightman, who had won the title three times—Mallory yielded only the first set, after which Wightman began to tire and could not get to the volleying position.

Eleanor Goss in the 1918 final and Marion Zinderstein in the 1920 final were strong volleyers, like Mrs. Wightman, but neither could win a set against the Norwegian native.

Mallory yielded her title to Helen Wills in 1923, after defeating her in the 1922 final, and lost to her again in 1924. In 1926 Mallory hit one of the heights of her career when she came back from 0–4 in the third set of the final against Elizabeth Ryan and won for her seventh championship. Never had a gallery at Forest Hills in the years of her triumphs cheered her on as it did in this remarkable rally.

Mallory reached the final at Wimbledon in 1922 and lost to Lenglen, 6–2, 6–0. Mallory was twice a semifinalist at Wimbledon, and she played on the Wightman Cup team in 1923, 1924, 1925, 1927, and 1928. She died in 1959, a player who had more than made her mark.

ALICE MARBLE (1913–   )

One of the most attractive players to grace the courts, Alice Marble was deceptive. Her blond loveliness, her trim athletic but feminine figure belied the fact that she played tennis in the late 1930s in a masculine manner that more closely approximated the game of Don Budge or Ellsworth Vines than it did the game of any woman.

There had been women before her who could volley and hit overheads—Suzanne Lenglen and Helen Wills Moody among them—but none played the "big game," the game of the big serve and volley, as it was to be called years later, as their standard method of attack the way Marble did regularly. No woman had a stronger service. Her first serve was as severe as any, and she delivered the taxing American twist serve as few women have been able to do. She followed it to the net for emphatic volleys or the strongest kind of overhead smash.

Pressing the attack without a letup, she could win from the back of the court as well as at the net. Her ground strokes, made with a short backswing and taking the ball on the

Alice Marble: The lady was a tiger. *UPI*

rise, were not overpowering, and her forehand was not always steadfast against the many fine backcourt players of her day, in part because of her daring in playing for winners. But in the aggressive all-court game she played, with her speed and agility and with her skill in the use of the drop shot, they served to carry her to four U.S. titles and to the Wimbledon Championship. World War II brought about tournament suspension or she might have added appreciably to her major conquests.

Her dominance is evidenced by her record of invincibility in 1939 and 1940. She did not lose a match of consequence either year. In winning her fourth U.S. title in 1940, she did not yield a set. She was voted by sportswriters the woman athlete of the year in 1939 and 1940.

Born on September 28, 1913, at Plumes County, California, she achieved a place high among the world's best after she had been stricken with an illness that threatened to end her career before the age of 21. In 1933 at a tournament at East Hampton, New York, she had to play the semifinals and finals of singles and doubles in one day with the temperature on the court more than 100 degrees. She played an almost unbelievable 108 games, and then collapsed. She was so weakened that she had to withdraw from the Wightman Cup team.

In the spring of 1934, playing in a Franco-American series near Paris, she was taken ill and removed to a hospital, where her illness was diagnosed as pleurisy. She was cautioned not to play more tennis that year when she left. It was feared her career might be at an end. But in 1935 she began to play again in California and changed to the eastern grip. In 1936 she returned to the East. Officials of the U.S. Lawn Tennis Association were fearful that she might jeopardize her health permanently if she returned to serious competition. But she was determined, and with the assistance of her coach, Eleanor Tennant, she undertook to re-establish herself and get back to the top.

At Forest Hills in 1936 she came up against Helen Jacobs in the U.S. final. Jacobs had held the title four years in a row, raising serious doubts about Marble's chances. But Marble won the match, 4–6, 6–3, 6–2, to attain the No. 1 ranking. In 1937 she lost in the quarterfinals but again was ranked No. 1, and she held the top spot in 1938, 1939, and 1940, winning the U.S. crown all three years and winning Wimbledon in 1939. In four years of Wightman Cup play she lost but one match in singles and one in doubles.

She made her bow as a professional late in 1940, touring with Mary Hardwick, Budge, and Bill Tilden. When the United States entered the war, she enlisted in the Hale American movement and played exhibitions in training stations and camps. She was elected to the International Tennis Hall of Fame in 1964 and was among the past champions present at Wimbledon in 1977 to receive Centennial medallions on the Centre Court, where she had defeated Kay Stammers in the 1939 final. No one there seemed happier or was more joyously greeted by the other champions than was the attractive woman who had once played tennis like a man.

MAURICE McLOUGHLIN
(1890–1957)

He came out of the West with a cannonball service, spectacular volleys, and overhead smashes. He created great excitement in the East and abroad at Wimbledon with the violence of his attack. And more than anything else, Maurice "Red" McLoughlin, known as the California Comet, opened the eyes of the public to tennis as a demanding game of speed, endurance, and skill.

Tennis at the turn of the century was a moderately paced game contested from the back of the court. But McLoughlin carried his attack forward, projecting the cannonball serve and rushing in behind it to meet the return near the net with a cataclysmic smash overhead or a masterful volley. The volley was not new to the game (it had been used in the first championship in 1881), but it had not nearly been the finishing stroke that Red Mac made it.

Born on January 7, 1890, in Carson City, Nevada, McLoughlin polished his game on the public parks courts of northern California,

Maurice McLoughlin: The California Comet. *USLTA*

and this in itself was a departure in the direction of democratizing the game. Most of the top-ranking players had developed their games on the turf of exclusive clubs in the East or their own private family courts.

Before he was 20, he had developed sufficiently to be named to the Davis Cup team. He won the U.S. championship in 1912 and 1913 at Newport, Rhode Island, but the Comet lost in a hard fight at Wimbledon against the champion, Tony Wilding. McLoughlin's style of play created a big stir at Wimbledon, however, and brought out large crowds. An attendance record was set at his match with Wilding, and McLoughlin's sunny disposition made him something of a favorite with the British gallery.

McLoughlin reached his peak the next year in 1914 Davis Cup play at Forest Hills. The matching of McLoughlin and Norman Brookes of Australasia brought forth tennis that was a revelation to the thousands who attended. The match was characterized as "never been equaled." McLoughlin won, including a first-set victory of 17–15. The matches attracted 14,000 people daily, and McLoughlin was given much of the credit for the large crowds.

After the Davis Cup success, the 1915 Tennis Guide said, "In McLoughlin America undoubtedly has the greatest tennis player of all time." Yet he never was to be again the player he once was. Absent from the East for several years, he returned after World War I and was hardly recognizable. He had lost his cannonball and his punch. Gone was his whirlwind speed. After he was defeated by Dick Williams decisively in a tournament, he left the tennis scene for golf, where he soon was shooting in the low 70s. His tennis career had come to a premature end. Some said he was burned out from his violent exertions on the court.

In 1957 the Comet died. But in the short time that he had lighted the tennis firmament, as no one before him, he had started the sport on its way to becoming a popular game for the masses.

HELEN WILLS MOODY (1905–   )

It scarcely seems possible that two players of the transcendent ability of Helen Wills Moody and Suzanne Lenglen could have been contemporaries. They have been ranked for close to half a century as the two best female tennis players of all time. Their records are unmatched and hardly have been approached.

While indeed comtemporaries, they were rivals in only one match, played in 1926 and won by Lenglen, 6–3, 8–6, at Cannes, France. Lenglen, not yet 27, was at the crest of her game, with six Wimbledon championships in her possession. Wills' game at 20 had not quite attained full maturity, though she had won Wimbledon once of the record eight times she was to triumph there. Their rivalry was limited to the single meeting, for later that same year Wills was stricken with appendicitis and Lenglen turned pro.

It would be difficult to imagine two players of more different personalities of types of game. Quiet, reserved, and never changing expression, Wills, known as Little Miss Poker Face, played with unruffled poise and never

Helen Wills Moody: Little Miss Poker Face. *USLTA*

exhibited the style, the flair, or the emotional outbursts that Lenglen did. From her first appearance in the East in 1921, when she was national girls' champion, Wills' typical garb on the court was a white sailor suit, white eyeshade, and white shoes and stockings.

The game she played was one of sheer power, which she had developed in practice against men on the West Coast. From both forehand and backhand she hammered the ball almost the full length of the court regularly, and the speed, pace, and depth of her drives, in conjunction with her tactical moves, sufficed to subdue her opponents. She could hit winners as spectacularly from the baseline on the backhand as on the forehand.

She went to the net occasionally, not nearly as often as Lenglen, and Wills was sound in her volleying and decisive overhead with her smash. Her slice service, breaking wide and pulling the receiver beyond the alley, was as good as any female player has commanded.

Her footwork was not so good. She did not move with the grace and quickness of Lenglen, and opponents fared best against her who could use the drop shot or changes of length to draw her forward and send her running back. Anchored to the baseline, she could run any opponent into the ground. Because of her exceptional sense of anticipation, she seemed to be in the right spot, and it was not often that she appeared to be hurried in her stroking.

She was born on October 6, 1905, in Berkeley, California and the facts of her invincibility are stark. She won the Wimbledon title a record eight times in nine tries, her only loss coming on her first appearance, in 1924. She won the U.S. championship seven times. From 1927 to 1932 she did not lose a set in singles anywhere. She won seven U.S., five Wimbledon, and four French championships without loss of a set until Dorothy Round of Britain extended her to 6–4, 6–8, 6–3 in the 1933 Wimbledon final.

In Wightman Cup play from 1923 to 1938, she won 18 singles matches and lost two, both in 1924. She won the Olympic singles and doubles in Paris in 1924. When she scored her first Wimbledon victory, in 1927, she was the first American woman to be crowned there since May Sutton in 1905.

Two of her three most remarkable matches were her meeting with Lenglen in 1926 and her default because of back pain to rival Helen Jacobs when trailing 0–3 in the third set of the 1933 U.S. Championships. The third remarkable match was in the 1935 Wimbledon final in which Jacobs led, 5–2, in the third set and stood at match point, only to see the then Mrs. Moody rally and add one more victory to her astounding record.

Betty Nuthall: Serving with distinction. *USLTA*

BETTY NUTHALL (1911–   )

Until Betty Nuthall came along from England, no one had ever taken the women's national championship out of the United States.

But the British prodigy changed all that before her 20th birthday, defeating Mrs. Lawrence A. Harper in the final of 1930.

In 1927, at the age of 16, she had reached the final of the U.S. Championships and lost to Helen Wills Moody. She played Moody again in the semifinals in 1933 and took the opening set from her. It was considered a surprise when Moody lost a set.

Nuthall represented Britain in the Wightman Cup matches eight times from 1927 to 1939. She was the youngest player, at 61, ever to get into the international team matches, and that year she scored a victory over Helen Jacobs, 6–3, 2–6, 6–1. In 1931 Nuthall won the French Championship.

The main strength of her game was her forehand. Holding the racket out with extended arm, she used it as a flail and hit the ball with great power. Speed was the essence of her game and there was no temporizing. She hit with length and with discernment, and she was resourceful and wise in the tactics of tennis.

Born on May 23, 1911, at Surbiton, Surrey, in England, she took up the game at the age of seven with her father's guidance. As a teen-ager she was too short to serve overhand effectively. Accordingly, she used an underhand service in the finals of the U.S. Championships at Forest Hills in 1927.

She accomplished little in 1928 after her success the previous year when she had ousted Molla Mallory at Wimbledon, got to the U.S. final, and won the British hardcourt championship. It was not until she had been bypassed for the Wightman Cup team in 1930, newcomers being picked instead, that she decided to take matters into her own hands and campaign on her own.

Packing her trunk and accompanied by her brother Jimmy, the junior champion, she sailed for America, and her perseverance, initiative, and faith in herself were rewarded. When she won the championship of the U.S. in 1930, this time beating Helen Wills Moody, she was serving overhand and had established herself as among the game's most distinguished performers.

As Betty Nuthall Shoemaker, she was elected in 1977 to the International Tennis Hall of Fame.

FRED PERRY (1909–　　)

It was the technique of one particular stroke that was the making of Fred Perry as a world champion—and as a tennis player considered perhaps the best Great Britain has produced.

The knack of making the stroke baffled the promising Briton for so long that he was on the verge of giving up in despair. He had been advised that to get very far he would have to learn to take the ball early on his continental forehand, the racket making impact instantly as the ball rose from the court.

For months he could not master the timing. Then suddenly, like riding a bicycle, it came to him and he was on his way—on his way to

Fred Perry: Great Britain's finest. *UPI*

the net on a running forehand, going forward with the swing of the racket to gain good volleying position if the drive did not win outright. And on his way to three Wimbledon Championships, three U.S. Championships, an Australian title, a French title, and a lucrative pro career.

Born on May 18, 1909, in Stockport, England, Frederick John Perry did not take up tennis until he was 18 years old. But he had good coaching and took to the game quickly, for he had been playing table tennis for years and winning tournaments and recognition.

Perry developed an undercut backhand that came off with surprising pace. He hit the ball smartly with good length and regularity on the service, was sharp and sound with his smash, perfect in his footwork and timing, and volleyed with dispatch. None of his strokes was overpowering, but his attack was impetuous and relentless, ever challenging, and he ran like a deer in retrieving.

He was the completely equipped and efficient adversary, jaunty, a bit cocky in his breezy self-assurance, with gallery appeal. He could be sarcastic and some thought him egotistical, but it was a pose and he had an ever-ready grin. He cut a handsome figure with his regular features, raven black hair, and a physique that was perfection for the game. Once he developed the stroke that had eluded him, he was virtually unstoppable.

In 1933 Perry led the British Isles to a 4–1 victory over the United States in the Inter-Zone final and to the glorious victory over France that brought the Davis Cup back to Britain after a wait of 21 years. Britain retained the Cup through 1936 as Perry won every singles match he played in the four challenge rounds. England had not produced a Wimbledon singles champion for a quarter century, but Perry took care of that, too. He won three straight Wimbledon finals without loss of a set, defeating John Crawford in 1934 and Gottfried von Cramm in 1935 and 1936.

Perry was also impressive elsewhere, winning the U.S. Championship in 1933, 1934, and 1936, an assault interrupted only in 1935, when he suffered a painful injury and lost in the semifinals. In 1934 he won the Australian Championship and in 1935 the French Championship.

When Perry joined the professional tour, he drew huge crowds to see him play Ellsworth Vines and Bill Tilden. Perry won the U.S. Pro championship in both 1938 and 1941.

After his playing career, he became associated with the manufacture of tennis clothes, was a tennis correspondent for a London newspaper, and took part in radio and television coverage of tennis events. He was elected to the International Tennis Hall of Fame in 1975.

BOBBY RIGGS (1918–   )

Though he had little of the power of Don Budge and Jack Kramer, and though his physique was hardly comparable to that of these six-footers, Bobby Riggs was one of the smartest, most calculating, and resourceful court strategists tennis has seen, particularly in his defensive circumventions. And he had a temperament that was unruffled in all circumstances, hung in the fight without showing a trace of discouragement other than a slight shake of the head, and won the championship at Wimbledon and twice at Forest Hills.

Budge, with his vast power, usually had to work his hardest to turn back the little Cal-

Bobby Riggs: The canny campaigner. *New York Herald Tribune*

ifornian, whose forte was to subdue the fury of the big hitters. Riggs had both the brains and the shots to quell the cannonaders, particularly the drop shot from both forehand and backhand, and a lob matched by few in the way he masked it and his control of its length. Most often Budge required four sets, if not five, to win when they were amateurs. When they met as pros, Riggs won his full share.

Born on February 25, 1918, in Los Angeles, Robert Lorimer Riggs first began to make tennis progress at the age of 12, when Dr. Esther Bartosh saw him hitting balls and took over his instruction. In 1934, at 16, he beat Frank Shields, a finalist at Wimbledon and Forest Hills. Two years later Riggs was ranked fourth in the country, and he was second to Budge in 1937 and 1938.

Riggs had the best record of any amateur in the world in 1919 in winning the Wimbledon and U.S. Championships. After yielding his U.S. title to Don McNeill in the 1940 final, he regained it in 1941, beating Frank Kovacs, a spectacular shotmaker, and his career as an amateur soon ended. Riggs was in demand on the pro circuit.

In 1942 he competed in the U.S. Pro championship and lost in the final to Budge. The next time they met was after World War II, in 1946, and this time Riggs beat Budge in the pro final at Forest Hills. They went on tour and Riggs won 23 matches to 21 for Budge. Again in 1947 they met in the final of the pro championship and Riggs won in five long sets. Late in the year Jack Kramer made his pro debut at Madison Square Garden in New York and Riggs beat him before a crowd of 15,114 who plowed through 25 inches of snow on the streets in a blizzard.

After losing to Kramer in the pro final at Forest Hills and regaining the title in 1949 against Budge, Riggs began to taper off as a player and tried his hand as a promoter when Gussy Moran and Pauline Betz made their debuts as pros in 1950. Years later, after fading into virtual obscurity as a senior player who would make a bet on the drop of a hat, Riggs was back, taking on first Margaret Court and then Billie Jean King in mixed singles matches that gave tennis much publicity. He defeated Mrs. Court, but Mrs. King made him look like Humpty Dumpty. Few things ever fazed Riggs, though, or made him unhappy. And nothing ever made him forget his good manners and sportsmanship in the years when he was playing serious tennis.

DOROTHY ROUND (1909–   )

Dorothy Round was the leading British female player at the time Helen Wills Moody ruled the courts in the 1930s. Round distinguished herself on several counts, among them that she was the only British player besides Kathleen McKane Godfree to win Wimbledon twice since World War I, and she was in 1935 the only player from overseas to win the Australian Championship.

Born on July 13, 1908, at Dudley, Worcestershire, in England, she developed a ground-stroke game of power and precision and volleying ability equaled by few. She won the Wimbledon crown in 1934 and repeated in 1937. Her play at the net was a factor in her victory over Helen Jacobs in the 1934 final, 6–2, 5–7, 6–3. In the 1937 final, she defeated the strong Polish player, Jadwiga

Dorothy Round: All-around game. *UPI*

Jedrzejowska, 6–2, 2–6, 7–5, overcoming a 1–4 deficit in the final set.

To get to the Wimbledon final of 1937, Round defeated Jacobs and Simone Mathieu, France's leading player. Round appeared to rise to her best form when confronted by Jacobs or Moody. In 1933 Round got to the final at Wimbledon and gave Moody one of the most challenging fights of her career, yielding at 6–4, 6–8, 6–3. That same year in the U.S. Championships, she lost to Jacobs, 6–4, 5–7, 6–2, in the semifinals.

Round was not as successful, however, in Wightman Cup matches as in tournaments for the championship of England, America, and Australia.

She was a member of the British team from 1931 to 1936. She lost to Jacobs four times before defeating the American in 1936, in her final appearance in the international team matches, 6–3, 6–3. Round (later Mrs. Little) probably relished that victory particularly, for it was the year Jacobs finally achieved her ambition of winning Wimbledon.

BILL TILDEN (1893–1953)

If a player's value is measured by the dominance and influence he exercises over a sport, then William Tatem "Big Bill" Tilden

Bill Tilden: The greatest of all? *UPI*

Tilden, born on February 10, 1893, in Philadelphia, had the ideal tennis build, standing over six feet tall, with thin shanks and big shoulders. He had speed and nimbleness, coordination and perfect balance. He also had marked endurance despite smoking cigarettes incessantly when not playing. In stroke equipment, he had the weapons to launch an overpowering assault and the resources to defend and confound through a variety of spins and pace when the opponent was impervious to sheer power.

Nobody had a more devastating service than Tilden's cannonball, or a more challenging second serve than his kicking American twist. No player had a stronger combination of forehand and backhand drives, supplemented by a forehand chop and backhand slice. Tilden's mixture of shots was a revelation in his first appearance at Wimbledon. Gerald Patterson of Australia, the defending champion, found his backcourt untenable and was passed over and over when he went to the net behind his powerful service. Tilden won, 2–6, 6–3, 6–2, 6–4.

The backcourt was where Tilden played tennis. He was no advocate of the "big game," the big serve and rush for the net for the instant volley coup. He relished playing tennis as a game of chess, matching wits as well as physical powers. The drop shot, at which he was particularly adroit, and the lob were among his disconcerting weapons.

His knowledge and mastery of spin has hardly ever been excelled, as evidenced not only on the court but also in his *Match Play and the Spin of the Ball,* a classic written half a century ago. Yes, Tilden was a writer, too, but he craved to be an actor above anything else. Unsuccessful in his efforts to the point of sinking most of his family wealth, his tennis earnings, and his writing royalties in the theater, he was happiest when playing on the heartstrings of a tennis gallery.

Intelligent and opinionated, he was a man of strong likes and dislikes. He had highly successful friends, both men and women, who were devoted to him, and there were others who disliked him and considered him arrogant and inconsiderate of officials and ballboys who served at his matches. He was constantly

II could be considered the greatest player in the history of tennis.

From 1920 through 1926, he dominated the game as has no player before or since. During those years he was invincible in the United States, won Wimbledon both times he competed there, and captured 13 successive singles matches in the Davis Cup Challenge Round against the best players from Australia, France, and Japan.

When he first won Wimbledon, in 1920, he was 27 years old, an advanced age for a champion. But he had a long and influential career, and at the age of 52, in 1945, he was still able to push the 27-year-old Bobby Riggs to the limit in a professional match.

wrangling with officers and committeemen of the United States Lawn Tennis Association on Davis Cup policy and enforcement of the amateur rule, and in 1928 he was on the front pages of the American press when he was removed as captain and star player of the Davis Cup team, charged with violating the amateur rule with his press accounts of the Wimbledon Championships, in which he was competing. So angry were the French over the loss of the star member of the cast for the Davis Cup Challenge Round—the first ever held on French soil—that the American ambassador, Myron T. Herrick, interceded for the sake of good relations between the countries, and Tilden was restored to the team.

When Tilden, in the opening match, beat René Lacoste, the French gallery suffered agony and cursed themselves for insisting that "Teel-den" be restored to the team. It all ended happily for them, however, as the French won the other four matches and kept the Davis Cup. On Tilden's return home, he was brought up on the charges of violating the rule at Wimbledon. He was found guilty and was suspended from playing in the U.S. Championships that year.

Eligible for the U.S. title again in 1929, after the lifting of his suspension, he won the crown for the seventh time, defeating his doubles partner, Frank Hunter. In 1930 he won Wimbledon for the third time, at the age of 37. After the U.S. Championships, in which he was beaten in the semifinals by John Doeg, he notified the tennis association of his intention to make a series of motion pictures for profit, thus disqualifying him for further play as an amateur.

In 1931 he entered upon a professional playing career, joining Vincent Richards, Hans Nusslein, and Roman Najuch of Germany and Karel Kozeluh of Czechoslovakia. Tilden's name revived pro tennis, which had languished since its inception in 1926 when Suzanne Lenglen went on tour. His joining the pros paved the way for Ellsworth Vines, Fred Perry, and Don Budge to leave the amateur ranks and play for big prize money. Tilden won his pro debut against Kozeluh, 6–4, 6–2, 6–4, before 13,000 fans in Madison Square Garden.

Joining promoter Bill O'Brien, Tilden toured the country in 1932 and 1933, but the Depression was on and new blood was needed. Vines furnished it. Tilden and O'Brien signed him on, and in 1934 Tilden defeated Vines in the younger man's pro debut, 7–9, 6–1, 4–6, 6–3, 6–3. That year Tilden and Vines went on the first of the great tennis tours.

The tours grew in the 1930s and 40s, and Tilden remained an attraction even though he was approaching the age of 50. For years he traveled across the country, driving by day and sometimes all night and then going on a court a few hours after arriving. At times, when he was managing his tour, he had to help set the stage for the matches.

Tragically, his activity and fortunes dwindled after his conviction on a morals charge in 1951. He died of a heart attack under pitiful circumstances, alone and with few resources, on June 5, 1953, in Los Angeles. His bag was packed for a trip to Cleveland to play in the U.S. Pro championship when perhaps the greatest tennis player of them all was found dead in his room.

ELLSWORTH VINES (1911–   )

One night in 1929, an 18-year-old lad sat in a rocking chair on the porch of the Peninsula Inn in Seabright, New Jersey, looking out to sea and thinking that his tennis dreams were shattered.

"I guess I'm just a flash in the pan like they say," said Ellsworth Vines.

Weeks earlier they had been calling him another California Comet. He had come out of the West, a lanky youth who had the kick of a mule in his cannonball service and who terrorized the eastern grass court circuit.

Vines, born on September 29, 1911, at Los Angeles, ambled along mournfully like slow molasses when not in hot pursuit of a tennis ball. But on the court he was devastating, wherefore came the comparisons to Maurice McLoughlin, the original California Comet.

Vines had easily disposed of Frank Shields and Frank Hunter, two of the best players in the East. But now at the Seabright tournament, he had incredibly lost to Sidney Wood,

Ellsworth Vines: Master gambler. *UPI*

Moreover, his disposition and temperament were foolproof. Where others might explode in protest against a line call, Vines would slowly turn his head and grin under his white cap at the linesman.

He was a gambler on the court. He hit his forehand flat, with all his whizzing might, and closer to the net and the lines than anyone dared. At his best he was equal to beating any player, but his margin of safety was so thin that on days when he did not have the feel and touch, his errors could be ruinous.

Wimbledon crowds marveled at the devastating fury of his attack in beating Bunny Austin in the 1932 Wimbledon final, which ended with a service ace. The ball catapulted by Austin so fast that the Briton said afterward he did not know whether it went by him to the left or to the right. Yet, the very next year, Vines lost to both Fred Perry and to Austin in Davis Cup play and to Bitsy Grant in the fourth round at Forest Hills. Disgusted, Vines could not wait to cut the gut out of his rackets and leave for home, his tennis career as an amateur soon at an end.

He signed a professional contract to go on tour with Bill Tilden and won their opening match, 8–6, 6–3, 6–2, before 14,637 fans at Madison Square Garden. Vines beat the aging Tilden, 47 matches to 26. A match in the Garden between Vines and Perry drew 17,630.

Near the end of the decade, Vines' interest in tennis waned. He turned to golf and became about the best golfer who was ever a top tennis player. For years he prospered as a teaching pro, and he was good enough to reach the semifinals of a Professional Golf Association championship.

He was enshrined in the International Tennis Hall of Fame in 1962. In 1977, he attended the Wimbledon Centennial and was one of the former champions to receive commemorative medals. He had turned out to be much, much more than a flash in the pan.

BARON GOTTFRIED VON CRAMM (1909–76)

If any player was the prince charming of tennis, he was Gottfried von Cramm, a baron

unable to cope with Wood's seemingly innocuous game of moderate strokes. Vines could never get his confidence or control against Wood's tactics, and some were saying the new Comet had burned out already.

Vines didn't settle for being a flash in the pan, however. A year later, after practicing all winter and spring back in California against slow-ball strategy, Vines came East again and won a ranking of No. 8 nationally. In 1931 he was the U.S. champion and No. 1 in America, and Wood was Wimbledon champion. In 1932, Vines won at Wimbledon and Forest Hills. He had become the world champion.

Vines played amateur tennis on the grass circuit only five years, 1929–33. But in those five years he established at Forest Hills and Wimbledon that he had one of the best serves, if not the very fastest serve ever turned loose, with almost no spin. He also had as fast and as risky a forehand as ever seen, a murderous overhead, and a skill in the volleying position to compare with the best.

Gottfried von Cramm: The Baron. *Fischer Collection*

of the German nobility, six feet tall, with blond hair, green eyes, and a magnetism that, in the words of Don Budge, "made him dominate any scene he was a part of."

The most accomplished tennis player Germany has known, von Cramm must be one of the finest players never to have won the Wimbledon Championship, for which he was runner-up three years in a row—to Fred Perry in 1935 and 1936, and to Budge in 1937.

Von Cramm, who was known as The Baron, was also runner-up to Budge for the U.S. Championship in 1937 and runner-up yet again to Budge in what has been termed the greatest Davis Cup match ever played, the fifth and deciding match in the 1937 Inter-Zone final between the United States and Germany. Budge came from 1–4 and had match point five times before he hit the final shot, racing across the court beyond the alley, and he lay sprawled on the ground as the umpire declared the United States to be the winner. The score of the match: 6–8, 5–7, 6–4, 6–2, 8–6.

Said the Baron at the end, when he stood at the net waiting for Budge to pick himself up from the ground: "Don, this was absolutely the finest match I have ever played in my life.

I'm very happy I could have played it against you, whom I like so much. Congratulations." The next moment, their arms were around each other.

Von Cramm, born on July 7, 1909, at Nettlingen, Hannover, in Germany, was noted on the court for his endurance and tenacity. In recalling their thrilling Cup match, Budge related how he put four successive first serves in play, his very best, and all four came back for winners for von Cramm.

When von Cramm won the French Championship in 1936, he was carried to five sets in round after round, and in the final he beat Perry in the fifth set, 6–0. Von Cramm had also won the French title in 1934; he was champion of Germany from 1932 to 1935, and in 1948 and 1949, at the age of 40. He was a member of Germany's Davis Cup team between 1932 and 1953.

Von Cramm, at the height of his career when Hitler was preparing for Germany to launch World War II, declined to speak for Nazism in his tennis travels and was imprisoned by the Gestapo in 1938. After the war, he had a successful business career and was an administrator in tennis, serving as president of Lawn Tennis Terner Club Rot-Weiss in Berlin. The Baron died in an automobile crash near Cairo, Egypt, in 1976, and a year later was enshrined in the International Tennis Hall of Fame.

TONY WILDING (1883–1915)

The British idolized Tony Wilding. He was a superb figure of a man, his sportsmanship was exemplary, and, besides, he learned his tennis at Cambridge University.

Anthony Wilding, born on October 31, 1883, at Christchurch, New Zealand, stood with Norman Brookes as two of the foremost players in tennis for nearly a decade. Four straight times, 1910–13, he won the Wimbledon Championship. In the 1913 Wimbledon against Maurice McLoughlin, the formidable California Comet, Wilding was particularly impressive. "He was in prime physical condition," wrote distinguished British tennis authority A. Wallis Myers. "All his best fighting instincts were aroused, his tactics

Tony Wilding: Wimbledon hero. *UPI*

were as sound as his strokes and he won a great victory, the greatest of his career, in three sets."

Wilding lost his title to Brookes in 1914 and joined with the Australian "wizard" to win the Davis Cup back from the United States that very year. Wilding's triumph over Dick Williams of the U.S. on the first day of the Cup was a shock. Williams was one of the most daring and brilliant shotmakers in history, but Wilding, playing almost errorlessly, won quickly.

Wilding played the classic game in vogue at the time. His drives were the strength of his attack and his defense was outstanding. He could hit with immense pace and overspin, but when prudence and judgment dictated security of stroke rather than speed, as against a player of Williams' daring, Wilding could temper his drives and play almost faultlessly from the baseline.

Wilding made his debut on the Australasian Davis Cup team at the age of 21 in 1905. In 1906 he won the Australian Championship and a year later he and Brookes won the Davis Cup for Australasia for the first time, defeating the British Isles. Wilding-Brookes

retained the Cup in 1908 against the United States, and repeated in 1909, a year in which Wilding won the Australian Championship a second time.

Wilding's 1914 appearance in the Davis Cup was his last. Following their victory at Forest Hills, he and Brookes went to war. Wilding never came back. At the age of 31, on May 9, 1915, he was killed in action in France.

R. NORRIS WILLIAMS (1891–1968)

Richard Norris Williams II survived the sinking of the *Titanic,* and after that harrowing experience, tennis must have seemed easy, for he became one of the outstanding players of his time.

Born of American parents in Geneva, Switzerland, on January 29, 1891, he left for the United States in 1912 aboard the S.S. *Titanic,* which struck an iceberg and sank. His father went down with the ship, but young Williams was rescued from the icy North Atlantic.

He lived a long life, until 77, and for that the tennis world was always grateful.

Williams had learned to play in Switzer-

Norris Williams: Unsinkable. *UPI*

land, using the Continental grip and hitting his ground strokes with underspin. He developed his game further as a Harvard University undergraduate, winning the intercollegiate championship in 1913 and 1915, and he was accepted for the U.S. Championships at Newport, in 1912, getting to the quarterfinals.

The next year, he was runner-up at Newport, but in 1914 he won, defeating Maurice McLoughlin, 6–3, 8–6, 10–8, in a stirring final before a record crowd on the new championship court at the Casino. Throughout the three sets Williams maintained a terrific pace and marvelous control, averting the loss of the final set several times with bursts of speed and master strokes that thwarted even so aggressive and courageous a foe as the Comet.

In 1916 he won the U.S. title again, this time over Little Bill Johnston, and attained the No. 1 ranking. Following World War I, Williams was in the Top Ten from 1919 to 1925. He played on Davis Cup teams from 1913 to 1926, and was captain of the team in 1921–26 and in 1934. With Bill Tilden and Johnston as contemporaries, Williams played doubles on many of the Cup squads, teaming with his two famous mates and with Watson Washburn.

Williams had a daring style of play, taking every possible ball (when not in volleying position) on the rise with hair-trigger timing. Always he hit boldly, sharply for the winner, and that included serving for the winner on both the first and second ball. He did not know what it was to temporize.

On occasion, his errors caused by his gutsy tactics might bring defeat by opponents of inferior ability. But it was the commonly held opinion that Williams, on his best days, when he had the feel and touch and his breathtaking strokes were flashing on the lines, was unbeatable against any and all.

4 } UNDER THE TABLE 1946–1967

International tennis resumed after the disruptions of World War II in much the same format as in the immediate prewar years. The game was essentially divided into two parts: the "amateur" fixtures, and a struggling band of gypsy professionals who wandered rather anonymously from city to city and continent to continent, playing one-night stands. They may have been the best players in the world, but their gigs received almost no attention outside the town they happened to be playing on a given night.

The major international events—the "Big Four" tournaments (Australian, French, Wimbledon, Forest Hills) and the Davis Cup and Wightman Cup competitions—were ostensibly amateur. Only a handful of top stars made a living playing tennis; the rest were "tennis bums" on a lark for several years before settling down and getting jobs. All were paid, according to previously established reputation, "under the table" by an Establishment of amateur officials. Major-league tennis was not big-time at all; it was very much a game of country club and old school tie.

1946

The year 1946 was one of reconstruction for international tennis. The French and Wimbledon championships and the Davis Cup had last been played in 1939, the Australian Championships in 1940. The U.S. Championships had continued uninterrupted.

Jack Kramer, who had entered the service as a seaman and was discharged as a lieutenant after seeing action in the Pacific, returned at the age of 24 to claim the No. 1 U.S. ranking that had been predicted for him since 1942. Ted Schroeder was No. 1 in 1942, Joe Hunt in 1943, and Frank Parker in 1944–45.

It was comparatively easy restarting championships in countries that had not been ravaged by the war. In Australia, John Bromwich—a highly unorthodox player who hit a two-fisted forehand—re-established a thread with the prewar era. He had been the 1939 singles champion, and regained the Australian title with a five-set victory over his countryman Dinny Pails, 5–7, 6–3, 7–5, 3–6, 6–2. In doubles, it was as if the war had never occurred: Adrian Quist, the last prewar

singles champion, who had won his national doubles title with Don Turnbull in 1936–37 and with Bromwich in 1938–40, successfully teamed with Bromwich once again, re-establishing a monopoly that lasted through 1950.

In Paris, French tennis fans crowned the first native champion since Henri Cochet in 1932: left-hander Marcel Bernard. He upset Czech Jaroslav Drobny, 3–6, 2–6, 6–1, 6–4, 6–3, and teamed with countryman Yvon Petra to win the doubles.

More startling was Petra's triumph in the singles at Wimbledon, the first Frenchman to win there since Cochet beat Jean Borotra in the all-French final of 1929. (Borotra was refused entry to Wimbledon in 1946 because he had been Minister of Sport in the Vichy government of France, though he was later a Nazi prisoner.)

Kramer, though seeded second, was the favorite, but he was done in by a nasty blister on his right hand that had caused him to default at the Queen's Club tune-up tournament the week before. Drobny beat him in the

Ashore at last, Jack Kramer wins the U.S. Singles crown, defeating Tom Brown in 1946. *UPI*

round of 16, 2–6, 17–15, 6–3, 3–6, 6–3, after Kramer had lost only five games in the three previous rounds despite his handicap.

Pails, 25, was the top seed, but he got lost on the London Underground on his way to Wimbledon for his quarterfinal match and arrived late. Unsettled, he lost to Petra in four sets. Petra—a tall, lanky player with less than polished strokes—then reached the final by beating San Franciscan Tom Brown after losing the first two sets. Petra did not figure to have a chance in the final against Australian Geoff Brown, a player of medium build with a devastating serve and great pace on the rest of his shots, but Brown made the curious tactical miscalculation of trying to slow-ball during the first two sets. He did win the third and fourth, but by that time was psychologically exhausted, and when he dropped his serve in the opening game of the fifth set, Petra ran out the match, 6–2, 6–4, 7–9, 5–7, 6–4.

Kramer, playing with his damaged racket hand encased in bandages and a glove, dominated the doubles final, teaming with Tom Brown for a straight-sets victory over Geoff Brown and Pails.

There had been some reluctance on the part of the All England Lawn Tennis & Croquet Club to stage "The Championships" at all in 1946. The club had been heavily damaged by German bombs, and a gaping hole in the Centre Court competitors' stand and adjacent seats had to be cordoned off. The organizing committee did not want to have a tournament if Wimbledon's pre-war standards of pre-eminence could not be maintained. Colonel Duncan Macaulay, who returned as the club's full-time secretary after the war, summarized the obstacles in his book *Behind the Scenes at Wimbledon:*

"The groundsmen were not back from the war, the mowers wouldn't work, the rollers wouldn't roll, nothing would function. We were surrounded by bomb-shelters, improvised buildings and huts of every sort. The back part of the Club was covered with broken glass as a result of flying bombs. Britain was under a tight wartime economy and nothing could be obtained without a license or a coupon. There was the difficulty of supplies of balls and rackets and the printing of tickets. Paper was very short . . . Soap, too, was strictly rationed—and we needed a lot of it. Clothes were rationed and tennis flannels and costumes were almost non-existent. And of course food was rationed too—and there would be hungry thousands to be fed each day. The Club's ration of whisky was one bottle a month!"

Nevertheless, with customary efficiency and industry, the championships were staged and again established as a showcase of the tennis world. There was considerable drama on court, both because of the early upsets of the favorites and the uncertainty of form that resulted from the wartime hiatus.

One fact that was amply demonstrated was the superiority of American women players, who put a stranglehold on the distaff game in the immediate postwar years and maintained it through the 1950s, until Australia, Latin America, and Europe again began producing champions in the early 1960s.

Macaulay explained the phenomenon quite logically. "Least upset by the war of all the lawn tennis-playing nations was the United States. America's young tennis-playing men were, of course, called up for service in the armed forces. But whereas lawn tennis in Britain and on the Continent closed down completely during the war and only started up again with many creaks and groans, with ruined courts and grave shortages of equipment, the American lawn tennis courts and clubs remained in being and the American Championships continued all through the war . . . It was in the sphere of women's tennis that the United States gained such a tremendous advantage during these years.''

Few non-Australian women ventured Down Under in those days, so the Australian Championship remained a native affair, but American women won just about every title of consequence, setting the pattern for ensuing years.

Margaret Osborne defeated Pauline Betz, 1–6, 8–6, 7–5, in the French final, and the two of them teamed with Louise Brough and Doris Hart to rout Great Britain in the resumption of the Wightman Cup at Wimbledon. The Americans did not lose a set in romping, 7–0. None of the four had ever been to England before, but this was the strongest Wightman Cup team assembled to date, and they would all leave their mark.

Betz, an accomplished groundstroker, lost only 20 games in six matches in winning her first Wimbledon title, and overcame netrusher Brough in the final, 6–2, 6–4. Betz had won the U.S. Championship in 1942–44, beating Brough the first two years and Osborne the third, but had been runner-up to Sarah Palfrey Cooke in 1945. In '46, Betz won Forest Hills again, for the fourth and last time, beating Patricia Canning, 11–9, 6–3.

Brough and Osborne teamed to win the first of their three French and five Wimbledon doubles titles. They also maintained an incredible streak in the U.S. Doubles they had started in 1942; they won the title nine straight years, until Shirley Fry and Doris Hart took over in 1951–54, and then won three more in a row for a total of a dozen titles together.

Osborne and Billy Talbert won their fourth consecutive U.S. Mixed Doubles title (Osborne had teamed successfully with Tom Brown at Wimbledon), and the tactically as-

Gardnar Mulloy (left) and Billy Talbert took their third U.S. Doubles title at Longwood in 1946. *UPI*

tute Talbert and Gardnar Mulloy defended the U.S. Men's Doubles crown they had won in 1942 and 1945, and would again in 1948.

Don Budge and Bobby Riggs, the best players in the world immediately before the war, were now teamed up again on the pro circuit. Riggs, who had succeeded Budge as Wimbledon and Forest Hills champ in 1939 and won the U.S. crown again in 1941, was signed by promoter Jack Harris when he got out of the service. In an abbreviated tour against Budge, Bobby won, 18 matches to 16, lobbing incessantly to take full advantage of Budge's ailing shoulder. He trounced Budge, 6–3, 6–1, 6–1, in the final of the U.S. Professional Championship, which went virtually unnoticed at the West Side Tennis Club.

The tournament that did draw attention at Forest Hills, naturally, was the "amateur" Nationals—as America's premier tennis event was called before it became the U.S. Open in 1968. It was here that Jack Kramer finally assumed the crown and top ranking that had been more or less reserved for him, as Hannibal Coons intimated in an article in *Collier's* in August 1946:

"Six feet one, powerfully built and a natural athlete, Jack Kramer has been the logical heir to the American tennis throne since he was fourteen. Successively National Boys' Champion, National Interscholastic Champion, a Davis Cup veteran at 18, and three times National Doubles Champion, twice with Schroeder and once with Parker, Kramer has for four years been shoved away from the singles title only by the whim of circumstance."

Kramer had re-established himself as a force in the game after his three-year military service by winning the singles, doubles (with Schroeder), and mixed doubles (with Helen Wills Moody Roark) without losing a set at the Southern California Championships at Los Angeles in May. His Wimbledon blisters had extended his reputation as "the hard-luck kid," but at Forest Hills there was no stopping him. Kramer had developed his aggressive, hard-hitting game on the cement courts of the Los Angeles Tennis Club under the watchful eye of the longtime iron-handed developer of Southern California junior talent, Perry T. Jones, and his coach and onetime idol Ellsworth Vines. Kramer always had a thunderous serve and forehand, and with the formidable backhand he developed on a South American exhibition tour in 1941 also in harness, he ravaged Tom Brown—who had beaten defending champ Frankie Parker and Gar Mulloy—in the Forest Hills final, 9–7, 6–3, 6–0.

There was one task left for Kramer in 1946: recovery of the Davis Cup. He had been an 18-year-old rookie for the U.S. in 1939, playing only doubles, teaming with Joe Hunt in a four-set lost to Adrian Quist and John Bromwich as Australia won, 3–2. Now Kramer and his friend Schroeder, 12 days his senior, went to Kooyong Stadium (the name, in the aboriginal tongue, means "haunt of the wild water fowl") in December and socked it to the Aussies, 5–0, inaugurating a four-year U.S. reign. Kramer beat Dinny Pails and Bromwich, and teamed with Schroeder for revenge against Bromwich and Quist in the deciding match, all in straight sets.

Kramer and Schroeder were the first Davis Cuppers to fly to Australia—then a four-day trip in a propeller-driven aircraft, complete with sleeping berths. Prior to 1946, tennis players had gone to Australia by boat, making the journey in a leisurely month, stopping off and playing exhibitions at ports en route to stay sharp. Kramer and Schroeder were the

first airborne tennis stars, but they could hardly have imagined that they were the forerunners—or forefliers—of an age in which players would become true jet-setters, frequently playing matches on one continent one day and across the ocean the next.

1947

The tennis world returned to normalcy in 1947. Of the nine countries (Germany, Italy, Japan, Bulgaria, Finland, Hungary, Romania, Thailand, and Libya) that had been expelled from the International Lawn Tennis Federation at the ILTF's first postwar meeting in 1946, four (Italy, Hungary, Finland, and Romania) were readmitted, reflecting a cooling of hatreds that had been kindled by the war. This trend would continue.

If 1946 had marked Jack Kramer's emergence, 1947 verified his greatness. He dominated the amateur game, paving the way for the most significant pro-contract signing of the era. Kramer did not play the Australian or French Championships, but he won the singles and doubles titles of Wimbledon and the United States, and won both his singles (over Dinny Pails and John Bromwich) in straight sets as the U.S. defended the Davis Cup with a 4–1 victory over Australia at the West Side Tennis Club.

Jack Kramer holds the Challenge Cup presented to him by King George VI and Queen Elizabeth after he won at Wimbledon in 1947. *UPI*

Pails and Bromwich were again the finalists in the Australian Championships, but this time Pails reversed the decision of the previous year in another five-setter, 4–6, 6–4, 3–6, 7–5, 8–6, for his only Grand Slam singles title. Nancye Bolton beat Nell Hopman, wife of the Australian Davis Cup captain, 6–3, 6–2, for the fourth of her six Australian singles titles (1937, 1940, 1946–48, 1951). She also teamed with Thelma Long for the sixth of their 11 doubles titles together, regrasping the championship they had captured in 1936–39 under their maiden names of Nancye Wynne and Thelma Coyne.

Readmission of Hungary to the ILTF permitted Jozsef Asboth, an artistic clay court specialist, back into the international fixtures, and he won the French Championship over South African Eric Sturgess, a slim but accomplished player with superbly accurate ground strokes. Pat Canning Todd, a statuesque and graceful Californian who was largely overshadowed by her American contemporaries, beat Doris Hart for the French women's title, 6–3, 3–6, 6–4.

Hart, a remarkable player who had been stricken with a serious knee infection at age 11 and took up tennis to strengthen her right leg, beat Louise Brough, 2–6, 8–6, 6–4, in the semifinals at Wimbledon, but had little left for Margaret Osborne in the final and was relegated to being runner-up as at Paris, 6–2, 6–4. Brough and Osborne had successfully defended their French doubles title, but were dethroned in the Wimbledon final by Hart and Todd.

The U.S. Wightman Cup team—again a powerhouse with Brough, Osborne, Hart, and Todd replacing Betz (who had been suspended by the U.S. Lawn Tennis Association for *talking about* turning pro)—overwhelmed Great Britain, 7–0, at Forest Hills, but this time conceded a couple of sets in the process.

Kramer's domination of Wimbledon was so great that John Olliff, longtime tennis correspondent of London's *Daily Telegraph*, referred to him as "a presence of unutterable awe." In his book *The Romance of Wimbledon*, Olliff recalls: "It became almost boring to watch him mowing down his victims when it was so obvious that nothing short of a physical injury could possibly prevent him from winning. . . . He was an automaton of crushing consistency."

Kramer lost only 37 games in seven matches. In the quarterfinals he beat Geoff Brown, the 1946 runner-up, 6–0, 6–1, 6–3; in the semis, Dinny Pails, 6–1, 3–6, 6–1, 6–0, and in the final, Tom Brown, 6–1, 6–3, 6–2, in just 48 minutes. King George VI and Queen Elizabeth were in the Royal Box, and His Majesty presented the champion's trophy to Kramer, the first titlist to have worn shorts instead of long white flannels. It was the King's first visit to Wimbledon since, as the Duke of York, he had played in the men's doubles in 1926.

Ted Schroeder did not play Wimbledon, but Kramer teamed with Bob Falkenburg—another tall American with a big serve—to win the doubles without losing a set. In the Davis Cup Challenge Round, Kramer and Schroeder won all four singles but lost the doubles to Bromwich and Colin Long. Jack and Ted then teamed to win the National Doubles for the third time at Longwood.

And so on to Forest Hills. Kramer was again top-seeded and considered a cinch winner; in fact, he had already signed on September 3, 1947, with promoter Jack Harris to play a tour against Bobby Riggs in 1948. Riggs had beaten Don Budge on a short tour for the second consecutive year, 23 matches to 21 this time, and had edged Budge for the U.S. Pro title, 3–6, 6–3, 10–8, 4–6, 6–3. Kramer was to be the new challenger for pro king Riggs, but the deal had to be hushed up until after the U.S. Nationals, which ended September 14.

Everything went according to plan until, as Kramer recalled in a *Sports Illustrated* article, "I almost blew the whole thing sky high. Here I was, signed and sealed for delivery to Riggs, and I lost the first two sets in the final to Frankie Parker. He was playing his best, but I did my best to help him. I can still remember looking up into the first row of the stadium seats and seeing the top of Jack Harris' bald head. The reason I could look up and see the top of his bald head was because he had it bowed forward in despair." But Kramer pulled himself together, starting the third set with two aces and the first of many winning drop shots. He purged the errors from his game and brought Harris back to life by winning the last three sets easily.

Allison Danzig, the venerable tennis writer of *The New York Times*, reported on the final: "Not since Sidney Wood tamed the lethal strokes of Ellsworth Vines at Seabright in 1930 with his soft-ball strategy and reduced the Californian to a state of helplessness, has so cleverly designed and executed a plan of battle been in evidence on American turf as Parker employed in this match.

"In the end, the plan failed, as the challenger's strength ebbed and the champion, extricating himself from a morass of errors, loosened the full fury of his attack to win at 4–6, 2–6, 6–1, 6–0, 6–3. But the gallery will long remember the thrill and the chill of those first two sets and also the tense final chapter as the 31-year-old Parker gave his heavily favored and younger opponent the scare of his life."

1948

Perhaps the most unforgettable event of the tennis year 1948 actually took place on December 26, 1947: Jack Kramer's professional debut against Bobby Riggs at Madison Square Garden as a raging blizzard buffeted New York.

" . . . The city lay paralyzed by the heaviest snowfall in its history," esteemed columnist Red Smith recalled the night in the New York *Times* 30 years later. "Yet with taxis, buses, commuter trains and private cars stalled and the subways limping, 15,114 customers found their way into the big barn at Eighth Avenue and 50th Street."

Kramer, the top amateur of 1947, had been signed to face 1946–47 pro champ Riggs on a long tour. Francisco "Pancho" Segura of Ecuador and Australian Dinny Pails came along as the preliminary attraction—"the donkey act," in the vernacular of the tour. As was customary, the long and winding road of one-

Jack Kramer (far right) joins Pancho Segura, Bobby Riggs, and Dinny Pails on the pro circuit. *UPI*

night stands began in the Garden, then the American Mecca of pro tennis.

Riggs won the opener, 6–2, 10–8, 4–6, 6–4, but Kramer gradually got accustomed to the grind of the tour and the style that playing night after night on a lightning-fast canvas court required. He learned to hit a high-kicking second serve to keep the quick and clever Riggs from scooting in behind his return, and to attack constantly, rushing the net on virtually every point and hammering away at Riggs' backhand.

"I began to really get comfortable with this new style around the time our tour reached San Francisco, when we were tied at 13 matches apiece," Kramer reminisced in *Sports Illustrated*. "I won there, and then we flew to Denver, and Bobby got something started with the stewardess, and that gave me Denver, and then we went into Salt Lake City, where we played on a tremendously slick wood surface. Bobby couldn't handle my serve there, and all of a sudden it was 16–13. And that was it. Now he had to gamble on my serve. He had to take chances or I could get to the net, and he was dead. He was thoroughly demoralized."

By the time the tour worked its way through the hinterlands, Riggs was "tanking" matches. Kramer won 56 of the last 63, finishing with a 69–20 record, the last amateur to overthrow the pro king. Kramer, whose cut of the opening-night receipts at the Garden had been $8,800, earned $89,000. Riggs made $50,000.

Kramer also won the U.S. Pro Championship at the West Side Tennis Club. He had a tough match against Welby Van Horn in the quarterfinals, then beat aging but still formidable Don Budge in the semifinals, 6–4, 8–10, 3–6, 6–4, 6–0. Al Laney, who covered tennis for 50 years, many of them for the New York *Herald Tribune*, made no secret of his low regard for the pros "because for so many years they have preferred exhibitions to real tournaments," but he begrudgingly put this one on his list of all-time memorable matches. The next day Kramer put away Riggs, 14–12, 6–2, 3–6, 6–3, becoming the undisputed ruler of the pros as he had been of the amateurs.

With Kramer out of the amateur ranks, three other Americans took major titles. Frankie Parker won the French over Jaroslav Drobny in four sets; Bob Falkenburg startled Wimbledon by taking the men's singles over John Bromwich, 7–5, 0–6, 6–2, 3–6, 7–5, saving three match points; and Richard "Pancho" Gonzales stormed to the first of his back-to-back Forest Hills titles, over Eric Sturgess, 6–2, 6–3, 14–12.

Adrian Quist, the last prewar champ, had regained the Australian singles title over doubles partner Bromwich, but was able to win only one set in the Davis Cup Challenge Round as Australia fell to the United States, 5–0, at Forest Hills. Parker—who had been denied a singles berth in 1946–47—and Ted Schroeder beat Quist and Bill Sidwell to sweep the four singles matches. Bill Talbert-Gardnar Mulloy won the clinching doubles point over Sidwell and Colin Long.

Falkenburg, 23, was a tall and skinny Californian who dawdled between points, sometimes apparently stalling to upset opponents; and threw games or whole sets to grab a breather and pace himself. He later moved to

Twenty-year-old Pancho Gonzales (right) was the victor, Eric Sturgess the vanquished, in the 1948 U.S. Singles Championships. *UPI*

Rio and played in the Davis Cup for Brazil. Seeded seventh, he beat Frank Sedgman in the fourth round, Lennart Bergelin (conqueror of Parker in five sets) in the quarters, and Mulloy in an acrimonious semifinal. Then he met Bromwich, 29, in the final. Lance Tingay, in his book *100 Years of Wimbledon*, described the match-up:

"Bromwich was a much-loved player. Not only did he have a gentle personality but a persuasively gentle game. Craft and skill and guile were his all, never muscle and pace. His racket was light-weight, the grip small and could have been a girl's. He was double-fisted on the forehand. His ability to tease pace-making opponents into defeat by the accuracy of his slow returns was entrancing to watch.

"Falkenburg, having won the first set 7–5, palpably threw the second at 6–0. The tactics were legitimate but they hardly endeared him to the crowd. He took the third set 6–2. Bromwich won the fourth 6–3. By then the effectiveness of Falkenburg's big serve had declined. And he was missing much with his forehand volley. . . . Bromwich controlled the fifth set decisively, so much so that he led 5–2, 40–15, on his own service. On the two match points Falkenburg played shots that were pure gambles, screaming backhand returns of service. Bromwich had his third match point at advantage and Falkenburg repeated his performance. The Australian 'died' as an effective player from that stage. Falkenburg devoured the remaining games. If Bromwich was heart-broken he shared the sentiment with nearly every spectator round the court."

Bromwich never did win the Wimbledon singles, but he salvaged some consolation by taking the doubles title with the 20-year-old Sedgman, and successfully defended the mixed doubles title with Louise Brough.

After all the Wimbledon surprises, Forest Hills in 1948 was considered a wide-open affair. Ted Schroeder, generally regarded as Kramer's heir apparent, did not play. Frank Parker was the top-seeded American, ahead of Falkenburg. Virtually ignored was Gonzales, 20, one of seven children of a poor Mexican-American family from Los Angeles. His father wished he would give up tennis and get

an education, but Pancho preferred to be a truant, going to movies or developing the blazing serve that was his hallmark.

Gonzales—a lean 6-foot-3, 185-pounder whose theatricality, smoldering Latin temper, sex appeal, and combination of power and touch gave him a kind of animalistic magnetism—upset Parker in the quarterfinals, Drobny in the semis, 8–10, 11–9, 6–0, 6–3, and the South African Sturgess in the final. A friend had once described Gonzales as "even-tempered—he's always mad." The fact that his worthiness as champion was questioned because Schroeder had not played made him an even angrier young man.

American women continued to rule international tennis, although Nancye Bolton recovered the Australian title and Frenchwoman Nelly Adamson Landry won in Paris, beating Shirley Fry by the bizarre score of 6–2, 0–6, 6–0, the only non-American to win between 1946 and 1958. The U.S. clobbered Great Britain again in the Wightman Cup, 6–1, at Wimbledon. Louise Brough won her first major singles title overseas, starting a three-year Wimbledon reign by beating Doris Hart, 6–3, 8–6. Then Margaret Osborne, who had become Mrs. duPont, beat Brough in a scintillating Forest Hills final, 4–6, 6–4, 15–13, the first of her three consecutive triumphs there.

Louise Brough dominated women's play in 1948. *New York Herald Tribune*

Hart and Pat Todd dethroned Brough-du-Pont at the French Championships, as they had at Wimbledon the year before, but Brough-duPont turned the tables at Wimbledon. When Brough left the Centre Court at 8:15 P.M. on the final Saturday of Wimbledon, after defending her title with Bromwich over Sedgman and Hart, she was the reigning singles, doubles, and mixed champion of both the United States and Great Britain, a feat previously achieved only by Alice Marble before the war.

1949

Ted Schroeder won the Wimbledon singles on his first and only attempt, and Pancho Gonzales proved that he was not the "cheese champion" some had called him, but 1949 will always be remembered as the year of "Gorgeous Gussy" Moran and the lace-trimmed panties that shocked Wimbledon.

Couturier Teddy Tinling, a tennis insider since he umpired matches for Suzanne Lenglen on the Riviera decades earlier, had waged a one-man battle against the unflattering white jersey and skirt that pretty much constituted women's tennis attire. He had ex-

Gussy Moran's lace-trimmed panties stirred staid Wimbledon in 1949. *UPI*

perimented with touches of color on the dresses he made for Englishwoman Joy Gannon in 1947, without objection, but ran into problems in 1948 when Mrs. Hazel Wightman, captain of the U.S. team playing for the cup she had donated, objected to bits of color on the Tinling frock of British No. 1 Betty Hilton. This resulted in Wimbledon officials issuing an "all-white" rule.

In 1949, unable to use color as requested by the attractive and sexy Gertrude Moran of Santa Monica, California, Tinling put a half inch of lace trim around her knickers, trying to satisfy Gussy's wish for some distinctive adornment. This was done innocently, but when the flamboyant Gussy posed for photographers at the pre-Wimbledon garden party at the Hurlingham Club, she caused a sensation. The first time she twirled on Centre Court a tremor went through the staid old arena. "Tennis was then suddenly treated to the spectacle of photographers lying flat on the ground trying to shoot Gussy's panties," Tinling remembered in a 1953 interview. The "coquettish" undergarment became the subject of Parliamentary debate and photo-stories on front pages around the world.

"No one in their wildest dreams could have foreseen the furor, the outcry, the sensation . . ." Tinling wrote in the 25th anniversary issue of *World Tennis*. "Wimbledon interpreted the lace as an intentional device, a sinister plot by Gussy and myself for the sole purpose of guiding men's eyes to her bottom. At Wimbledon I was told that I had put 'vulgarity and sin' into tennis, and I resigned the 'Master of Ceremonies' job I had held there for 23 years." Fortunately, he continued designing, dressing most postwar women champions.

The year had begun with Frank Sedgman, age 21, winning his first Grand Slam title, beating John Bromwich, 6–3, 6–3, 6–2, in the final of the Australian Championships. Bromwich was thus runner-up for the third straight year after winning in 1946, but again captured the doubles with Adrian Quist—which seemed almost a formality by now. So it was as well for Nancye Bolton and Thelma Long in the women's doubles, but Doris Hart ended Bolton's quest for a fifth consecutive singles title. Her 6–3, 6–4 triumph in the final made Hart the first overseas champion since Californian, Dodo Bundy in 1938.

Frank Parker defended his French singles title over the elegant Budge Patty, 6–3, 1–6, 6–1, 6–4, and teamed with Gonzales to win the doubles. Margaret duPont recovered the singles title she had won in Paris in 1946, dethroning Nelly Landry, 7–5, 6–2, and teamed with Louise Brough to regain the doubles title they had won in 1946–47.

At Wimbledon, spectators were anxious to see the man Americans called "Lucky" Schroeder. Though almost 28, he had never played the world's premier championship, but was well-known worldwide for his Davis Cup exploits. "Rather stocky, he had a rolling gait which made him look as though he had just got off a horse," remembers Lance Tingay. "Except when he was actually playing he always seemed to have a pipe in his mouth, a corn cob as often as not." Britons found him an intriguing character.

Seeded No. 1, Schroeder lost the first two sets of his first-round match to the dangerous Gardnar Mulloy, whom he had beaten in the final at Queens Club just two days earlier. In the quarters, he was again down two sets to Frank Sedgman, trailed 0–3 in the fifth, and had a match point against him at 4–5. He was called for a foot fault, but coolly followed his second serve to the net and hit a winning volley off the wood. He saved another match point at 5–6, this time with a bold backhand passing shot, and finally pulled out the match at 9–7, never having led until the final minutes.

Schroeder continued to live precariously, coming back from two sets to one down against Eric Sturgess in the semifinals. In the final, he had his fourth five-setter in seven matches, edging the popular Jaroslav Drobny, 3–6, 6–0, 6–3, 4–6, 6–4, after being within a point of a 0–2 deficit in the final set. "Lucky" Schroeder, indeed, he was always living on the edge of the ledge.

The women's final came down to a memorable duel between the No. 1 seed, Louise Brough, and the No. 2, Margaret duPont. Brough won the first set, 10–8, duPont the second, 6–1, and at 8-all in the third the difference between them was no more than the breadth of a blade of Wimbledon's celebrated grass. Brough served out of a 0–40 predicament like a champion, and then broke for the match and successful defense of her title.

Parker and Gonzales added the Wimbledon doubles title to the French they had won earlier, while Brough and duPont joined forces to defend their title over Pat Todd and Gussy Moran. The scores were 8–6, 7–5—close enough to prevent anyone from quipping that the champs had beaten the lace panties off Gorgeous Gussy.

The American women continued their relentless domination of the Wightman Cup, drubbing Great Britain, 7–0, at Philadelphia. Schroeder and Gonzales gave the U.S. all four singles points as the U.S. men made it for four straight victories over Australia in the Davis Cup Challenge Round at Forest Hills. Schroeder was up to his usual five-set highjinks in the opening match, beating Bill Sidwell, 6–1, 5–7, 4–6, 6–2, 6–3, but he put away Sedgman in straight sets to clinch. The Americans lost only the doubles; Sidwell and Bromwich, who also won the 1949 U.S. National Doubles at Longwood, beat Bill Talbert and Gar Mulloy in a long five-setter.

There was keen interest in a Schroeder-Gonzales showdown at Forest Hills. Because Gonzales, seeded second at Wimbledon, had gone out to Geoff Brown in the round of 16, there was speculation that his 1948 U.S. victory had been a fluke. One writer flatly called him a "cheese champ"—which is how Gonzales got his nickname of "Gorgo." It was short for "Gorgonzola."

Gonzales was taken to five sets by Art Larsen and by Parker, who let him off the hook in the semis. Schroeder was pushed to the limit by Sedgman in the quarters and Billy Talbert in the semis. But finally the men people wanted to see arrived safely in the final.

The old 15,000-seat horseshoe stadium at the West Side Tennis Club was packed and tense as Schroeder and Gonzales fought to 16-all in the first set. Gonzales fell behind 0–40, but three big serves got him back to deuce. A net-cord winner gave Schroeder another break point, and Gonzales lost his serve on a volley

Ted Schroeder had his day at Wimbledon in 1949, but Forest Hills was spoiled for him by Pancho Gonzales. *UPI*

that he thought was good. A linesman called it wide. Schroeder served out the set, then donned spikes on the slippery turf and quickly ran out the second set, 6–2. Gonzales seethed.

But "Gorgo" always had a knack of channeling his temper, and he turned the rage surging within him to his advantage. Serving and attacking furiously, he achieved one of the great Forest Hills comebacks, 16–18, 2–6, 6–1, 6–2, 6–4.

Margaret duPont, meanwhile, won her second "Big Four" title of the year with an easy 6–4, 6–1 victory over Doris Hart in the women's final.

Jack Harris had quit the promotional game after the successful Kramer-Riggs tour. The new promoter was Riggs, who had won the U.S. Pro title at Forest Hills over Don Budge, 9–7, 3–6, 6–3, 7–5, while Kramer sat out, awaiting a new amateur king.

That was supposed to be Schroeder, who actually had signed after winning Wimbledon but then changed his mind, deciding that his intense constitution was not suited for the nightly grind of the tour. It he had won Forest Hills, Schroeder undoubtedly would have signed so as not to leave his old friend Kramer in the lurch; Kramer thinks that in the back of his mind, Schroeder wanted to lose to Gonzales for that reason.

But in any event, Gonzales—as two-time Forest Hills champ—became the only viable alternative, and Riggs signed him for the longest head-to-head tour yet. Frank Parker came along to play Segura in the prelims. The tour stretched from October 1949 to May 1950, and Kramer clobbered the talented but surly and immature Gonzales, 96 matches to 27. Both players made $72,000, but the future seemed a dead end for Gonzales, who was only 21 years old.

1950

The year 1950 was in many ways not only the start of a new decade, but also of a new era in tennis. With Kramer, Gonzales, and Parker now pros, the American stranglehold on the international game was loosened. A new crop of Yanks was coming along—led by touch artists Art Larsen and Herbie Flam, the expatriate Californian Budge Patty, and the

Southpaw Art "Tappy" Larsen outplayed fellow Californian Herbie Flam for the U.S. Singles title in 1950. *UPI*

forthright Tony Trabert and Vic Seixas. But Frank Sedgman, Ken McGregor, and Mervyn Rose signaled a powerful new line of Australian resistance.

Germany and Japan were readmitted to the International Lawn Tennis Federation, indicating that wartime wounds had healed. The Italian Championships were played for the first time since 1935, revived by the energetic promotion of Carlo della Vida, who was intent on building them into one of the international showcases. Despite rains that threatened to flood the sunken *campo centrale* (center court) at Rome's Il Foro Italico, the tournament was a success, won by the clay court artistry of Jaroslav Drobny.

The self-exiled Czech, who traveled on an Egyptian passport until becoming a British citizen in 1959, also won the German championship, which had started to rebuild slowly as a Germans-only affair in 1948–49. The elegant and sporting prewar star, Baron von Cramm, had won both years. The Hamburg and Rome tournaments were destined to rise simultaneously to a stature just below the French championships as the most important clay court events of Europe.

Sedgman, an athletic serve-and-volleyer with a crunching forehand, defeated McGregor for his second straight Australian singles title, while Adrian Quist and John Bromwich won their eighth doubles title.

J. Edward (Budge) Patty, an urbane California native who lived in Paris, won the French championship over Drobny in a duel of enchanting shotmaking, 6–1, 6–2, 3–6, 5–7, 7–5. Patty then became the first player since Don Budge in 1938 to win the Paris-Wimbledon "double," beating Frank Sedgman on grass, 6–1, 8–10, 6–2, 6–3, as gracefully as he had overcome Drobny on clay.

Patty was a great stylist, fluent on all his strokes and mesmerizing with the effortlessness of his forehand volley. He was also a painter and patron of the arts—"I have a way to go to catch Rembrandt, but Renoir doesn't stand a chance," he commented once, upon the opening of an exhibition of his canvases in Paris. "He gave the impression," noted Tingay, "of being the most sophisticated champion of all time."

Unsophisticated, flaky, eccentric, and totally original was Art "Tappy" Larsen, so nicknamed because of his habit, one of many superstitions, of tapping objects from net posts to opponents in ritualistic "good luck" sequences. Patty was known as a suave playboy who only occasionally trained; Larsen was an eager if unpolished ladies' man who *never* trained. But he had a great gift for the game, and magnificent touch, as he amply demonstrated in winning the Forest Hills title over his pal Flam in a lovely match of wits and angles, 6–3, 4–6, 5–7, 6–4, 6–3.

In doubles, Bill Talbert partnered his athletic Cincinnati protégé, Tony Trabert, also a star basketball guard, to the French title. Quist and Bromwich won their only Wimbledon title together, outlasting Geoff Brown and Bill Sidwell, 7–5, 3–6, 6–3, 3–6, 6–2. Bromwich and Sedgman won the U.S. Doubles over four-time champs Bill Talbert and Gardnar Mulloy.

Australia ended the four-year American grip on the Davis Cup with a 4–1 victory in the Challenge Round at Forest Hills. Sedgman walloped Tom Brown, 6–0, 8–6, 9–7, and McGregor ambushed Ted Schroeder, 13–11, 6–3, 6–4, in the opening singles, and then Sedgman and Bromwich sealed the Aussie triumph by beating Schroeder and Mulloy in the doubles, 4–6, 6–4, 6–2, 4–6, 6–4.

America's women extended their monotonous superiority over Great Britain with another 7–0 Wimbledon, and hoarded all the "Big Four" titles in singles and doubles. The Australian final was an unusual all-American affair, Brough succeeding Doris Hart as champion with a 6–4, 3–6, 6–4 victory over the defender. They then teamed to win the doubles, interrupting the long reign of Nancye Bolton and Thelma Long.

Hart won her first French singles, over Pat Todd, 6–4, 4–6, 6–2. Brough won her third straight Wimbledon title, beating Margaret duPont, 6–1. 3–6, 6–1, while duPont took her third straight Forest Hills crown, dispatching Hart in the final, 6–3, 6–3.

Hart and Shirley Fry began a four-year rule in the French doubles, while duPont and Brough won their third consecutive Wimbledon and ninth consecutive U.S. doubles

In 1951, Althea Gibson became the first black to play in the U.S. Nationals and came within one game of defeating Louise Brough in the second round. *UPI*

crowns. Brough also teamed with Eric Sturgess for her fourth Wimbledon mixed doubles title in five years, with three different partners.

Jack Kramer again passed up the U.S. Pro Championships, and Pancho Segura won the title over Frank Kovacs, who retired at 4–4 in the fourth set with cramps at the Cleveland Skating Club.

There was no amateur to challenge Kramer for supremacy of the pro game, but Riggs put together a tour with Segura—the swarthy little Ecuadorian with bowed legs, a murderous two-fisted forehand, and enormous competitive heart—as the challenger at $1,000 per week against 5 per cent of the gate. Kramer got 25 per cent. Unfortunately, the cunning "Segoo" simply could not handle Kramer's big serve on fast indoor courts, and the tour was not competitive. Riggs tried to spice it up

by signing Gussy Moran to a lucrative contract—$35,000 guaranteed, against 25 per cent of profits—to play Pauline Betz. Gussy got tremendous publicity as the glamor girl of the lace pants, but she was not in the same class with Betz, who was overwhelming even after Riggs suggested she try to "carry" her fashionable but outclassed opponent.

The tour was an artistic, competitive, and financial flop. Kramer was still the king, Segura went back to being a prelim boy, Moran tried to make it in showbiz, and Betz, who married noted Washington *Post* sportswriter Bob Addie, became a respected teaching pro in Washington.

Two other events were worthy of note. In Europe, the Galea Cup was started as a kind of Davis Cup for juniors. And in the United States, the U.S Lawn Tennis Association demonstrated its iron hand in matters of discipline by suspending Top Tenner Earl Cochell from tournaments for life, though the sentence was commuted some years later.

Cochell's behavior in a match against Gardnar Mulloy was extreme, especially for the day. He argued many line calls, erupted in bursts of temper, argued with the umpire and spectators, tried to climb the umpire's chair and grab his microphone to lecture the crowd, and blatantly threw a number of games, batting balls into the stands. What really did him in was his abusive verbal attack on the referee, Dr. Ellsworth Bunker, who reprimanded him. Even so, a life sentence seemed excessive punishment.

1951

The new era continued to take shape on the world's tennis courts in 1951. American Dick Savitt surprisingly won the Australian and Wimbledon singles titles, but Frank Sedgman and Ken McGregor helped forge the founda-

Dick Savitt, Australian and Wimbledon champion in 1951, wore a bonnet to withstand the heat in a Davis Cup match against Japan's Jiro Kumamaru in Louisville. *UPI*

tion of a new Australian dynasty, holding onto the Davis Cup and fashioning the first Grand Slam of doubles. Meanwhile, American women continued their postwar supremacy, but the dominance of Louise Brough, Margaret Osborne duPont, Doris Hart, and Shirley Fry was challenged by a stirring new teen-age talent: Maureen Connolly.

Savitt, 24, a rawboned and hulking competitor from Orange, New Jersey, and Cornell University, sported a big serve, solid ground game, and an impressive, hard-hit backhand. He was the first American to win the Australian singles—in fact, the first non-Australian finalist—since Don Budge in 1938.

Like Ted Schroeder two years earlier, Savitt won Wimbledon on his first attempt. He was aided by Herb Flam's defeat of Sedgman from two sets down in the quarters, Englishman Tony Mottram's third-round upset of Jaroslav Drobny, and defending champion Budge Patty's demise in the second round, at the hands of former Tulane star and Rhodes scholar Ham Richardson.

Savitt also had a narrow escape from Flam, whom the BBC's extraordinary radio commentator Max Robertson called "the Paul Newman of tennis players, with hunched and self-deprecating look." Savitt trailed 1–6, 1–5 in the semifinals before salvaging the second set, 15–13, to turn the match around. "A couple of points the other way and my whole life might have been different," Savitt mused on the occasion of Wimbledon's Centennial "parade of champions" in 1977. As it happened, he lost only five games in the third and fourth sets against Flam and then chastened McGregor in the final, 6–4, 6–4, 6–4.

Drobny—the crafty left-hander with the sad countenance, spectacles, and wonderful repertoire of touch and spin to go with his tricky serve—defeated Eric Sturgess, 6–3, 6–3, 6–3, to win the French singles for the first time after being runner-up in 1946, 1948 and 1950.

Sedgman, the personification of robust Australian fitness with an unerring forehand volley, atoned for his Wimbledon failure by winning the first of back-to-back Forest Hills titles.

He was the first Australian player to win the U.S. Nationals, the first in the final since Jack Crawford in 1933. Sedgman got there in devastating form, ravaging defending champion Art Larsen in the semifinals, 6–1, 6–2, 6–0, in just 49 minutes, the worst beating ever inflicted on a titleholder. Wrote Allison Danzig in *The New York Times,* "The radiance of the performance turned in by the 23-year-old Sedgman has not often been equaled. With his easy, almost effortless production of stabbing strokes, he pierced the dazed champion's defenses to score at will with a regularity and dispatch that made Larsen's plight almost pitiable."

In the final against Philadelphian E. Victor Seixas, Sedgman was nearly as awesome, winning 6–4, 6–1, 6–1. Sexias had played superbly until then, beating McGregor, Flam, and then Savitt in the semifinals, 6–0, 3–6, 6–3, 6–2. Savitt was the No. 1 seed, but severely hobbled by an infected left leg, which had to be lanced the day before he faced Seixas.

Savitt had played Zone matches against Japan (readmitted to the Davis Cup, along with Germany, for the first time since the war) and Canada, but was passed over—much to his chagrin—for the Challenge Round in Sydney. Seixas handled Mervyn Rose, and Sedgman beat Ted Schroeder to make it 1–1 after the opening singles, but the match hinged on the doubles. Schroeder had one of his worst days—"I wanted to cry for him, he was so bad," recalls old friend Jack Kramer—and he and Trabert were beaten by Sedgman and McGregor, 6–2, 9–7, 6–3. Schroeder did pull himself together after a nervous, sleepless night and beat Rose with a courageous performance, but Sedgman rolled over Seixas in the fifth match, 6–4, 6–2, 6–2, for a 3–2 Australian victory.

It was appropriate that Sedgman-McGregor won the pivotal doubles, for this was their year as a tandem. They swept the Australian, French, Wimbledon, and U.S. doubles titles, the only pair ever to do so. They ended the eight-year monopoly of Adrian Quist-John Bromwich in the Australian final, beating the champions, 11–9, 2–6, 6–3, 4–6, 6–3, then went on to capture the French over Savitt and

Gardnar Mulloy, and Wimbledon over Drobny and Sturgess, 3–6, 6–2, 6–3, 3–6, 6–3. They completed the Slam by making the U.S. title over Don Candy and Merv Rose, 10–8, 4–6, 6–4, 7–5, the final having been moved to Forest Hills after heavy rains at Longwood.

U.S. women—Doris Hart, Shirley Fry, Maureen Connolly, Pat Todd, and Nancy Chaffee—cruised by Great Britain again, 6–1, in the Wightman Cup at Longwood.

In the absence of an overseas challenge, Nancye Bolton recaptured the Australian singles title over her partner Thelma Long, but Americans again won everything else. Fry, persistent as ever from the backcourt, beat Hart in the French final, 6–3, 3–6, 6–3, but got her comeuppance at Wimbledon, where Hart thrashed her, 6–1, 6–0. This was Hart's only singles title—she had been runner-up in 1947–48—and she parlayed it into a "triple," taking the women's doubles with Fry (starting a three-year rule) and the mixed doubles with Sedgman (first of her five successive triumphs, two with Sedgman and three with Vic Seixas).

In fact, Hart-Fry and Hart-Sedgman swept the women's and mixed doubles titles of France, Wimbledon, and the U.S. in 1951. Hart was the No. 1 seed at Forest Hills, and thought she was the best woman player in the world, but was given a rude jolt in the semifinals by 16-year-old Maureen Connolly of San Diego. Blasting her flawless ground strokes from both wings, Connolly overcame a 0–4 deficit to win the first set on a drizzly, miserable day, 6–4. Hart asked several times that the match be halted, and then won the second set the following afternoon. In the final, the tenacious and mentally uncompromising Connolly beat Fry, 6–3, 1–6, 6–4, for the first of three straight championships. "I later kidded Maureen that she was lucky to beat me in '51," Hart has said. "But after that she became, unquestionably, the greatest woman player who ever lived."

1952

Another patch in the nearly complete postwar reconstruction of tennis was put in place

Maureen Connolly, at 16 the youngest until 1979 to win the U.S. title, is shown in 1951 in Los Angeles (after capturing the Pacific Southwest crown) with former U.S. champions May Sutton, Helen Wills Moody, and Marian Jones. *UPI*

in 1952 when the King's Cup, a European team competition for a trophy donated by Swedish monarch and tennis patron Gustaf V in 1936, was resumed. But other than Jaroslav Drobny's second straight French title, Europe had little impact on the world tennis stage. Australian men and American women dominated the major championships.

Among the men, it was Frank Sedgman's year. The aggressive, diligent Aussie was in all of the "Big Four" finals, singles and doubles, and led Australia's successful Davis Cup defense.

He was on the losing end of the first two singles finals, however, beaten by his partner McGregor in the Australian, 7–5, 12–10, 2–6, 6–2, and by the ever-dangerous Drobny on

the salmon-colored clay of Paris, 6–2, 6–0, 3–6, 6–3.

Sedgman got his revenge on "Old Drob" in the final at Wimbledon, 4–6, 6–2, 6–3, 6–2, becoming the first Aussie champ there since Jack Crawford in 1933. Two other Aussies— Lew Hoad (who, with Ken Rosewall, was making his first overseas tour; they reached the semifinals in doubles) and McGregor— gave Drobny trouble en route. Hoad took him to four tough sets in the fourth round, and McGregor came within two points of beating him in the quarters. American Herbie Flam also pushed him to the five-set limit in the semis.

Drobny took the first set of the final, but Sedgman seized control of the match in a

Frank Sedgman prevailed at Wimbledon and here against Gardnar Mulloy (far court) in the final at Forest Hills in 1952. *UPI*

swirling wind on Centre Court when he got hold of his crushing overhead smash. Sedgman, in fact, lost only two sets at Wimbledon, underscoring his superiority, and rolled impressively to his second straight Forest Hills title. He crunched countryman Merv Rose in the semis and made the final against surprising Gardnar Mulloy look as easy as one, two, three . . . 6–1, 6–2, 6–3.

Sedgman, who also won the Italian Championship in his last year as an amateur, defended his Wimbledon doubles title with McGregor and the mixed with Doris Hart, becoming one of only three men to achieve such a "triple." (The others were Don Budge in 1937–38 and Bobby Riggs in 1939.) Sedgman-McGregor again won the Australian and French doubles but were denied a second consecutive doubles Grand Slam when the unusual Australian-American alliance of Merv Rose and Vic Seixas beat them in the final of

the U.S. National Doubles at Longwood. Sedgman-Hart did defend their U.S. mixed title, however, as they had the French and Wimbledon.

Sedgman beat both Seixas and Tony Trabert in straight sets, and partnered McGregor to a four-set triumph in doubles, as Australia won the Davis Cup Challenge Round for the third year in a row, 4–1. Seixas salvaged the only point for the United States, beating McGregor in the meaningless fifth match.

American women again avoided the long journey to Australia, allowing Thelma Long to win her first singles title and team with Nancye Bolton for their 10th doubles title together. (Long later won two more.)

But U.S. women were oppressive in the other major championships, as had become their custom. Doris Hart won her second French singles title, reversing the final-round result of a year earlier to beat Shirley Fry,

Lew Hoad and Maureen Connolly reach for the ball in mixed doubles against Rex Hartwig and Julie Sampson at Forest Hills. The championship went to Frank Sedgman and Doris Hart in 1951 and 1952. *New York Herald Tribune*

6–4, 6–4. Maureen Connolly ascended to the world No. 1 ranking at age 17 by beating three-time champ Louise Brough, 7–5, 6–3, in the Wimbledon final, and Hart 6–3, 7–5, to defend her Forest Hills crown.

Connolly's first appearance at Wimbledon, seeded No. 2 behind Hart, was a celebrated event. "The pressures under which she played were enormous," noted Lance Tingay in *100 Years of Wimbledon*. "There was the basic pressure of being expected to win. There was a blaze of publicity because Miss Connolly, for reasons of her skill, her charm and achievement, was 'news' in everything she did. And her guidance went sour at this her first Wimbledon challenge." Her coach—the strong-willed, overly protective, and domineering Eleanor "Teach" Tennant, who had also developed Alice Marble and imbued her with "killer" psychology—advised Connolly to withdraw because of a mild shoulder strain.

Maureen refused and parted company with Tennant forever, removing a stifling weight from her personality.

Connolly lost sets to Englishwoman Susan Partridge, who slow-balled her, giving neither the pace nor angle on which Maureen thrived, and to Thelma Long in the quarterfinals. Partridge, the Italian champion, proved her toughest foe, taking her to 6–3, 5–7, 7–5. Hart was beaten in a long quarterfinal by Pat Todd, leaving Connolly to mow down Fry and Brough in straight sets in the final two rounds. Connolly's scythelike strokes were as deadly as the British had heard; in fact, in three years, she never lost a singles match in Great Britain.

Hart and Fry extended their streaks in the French, Wimbledon, and U.S. doubles, and the United States again rolled over Great Britain in the Wightman Cup, losing only one set in a 7–0 triumph at Wimbledon.

Bobby Riggs had tried to sign Sedgman and McGregor to tour as pros with himself, Pancho Gonzales, and Pancho Segura in 1952, dismissing Jack Kramer by saying he had retired. Riggs struck a deal, but later Gonzales wanted to change the agreed-upon terms, and Riggs—who was about to remarry—got disgusted and left the promoting business.

There was no pro tour in 1952, but Segura startled Gonzales in the final of the U.S. Pro Championship, 3–6, 6–4, 3–6, 6–4, 6–0, at Lakewood Park in Cleveland. Kramer, who had no intention of retiring, took over as player-promoter, signing Sedgman to a contract ($75,000 guarantee) that was announced right after the Davis Cup Challenge Round. McGregor also turned pro to face Segura in the prelims on the 1953 tour.

1953

The year 1953 provided the tennis world with lovely days of "Mo" and Rosewall.

The incomparable Maureen Connolly, nicknamed "Little Mo" because she was as invincible as the World War II battleship *Missouri* ("Big Mo"), swept the Australian, French, Wimbledon, and U.S. Singles, and won 10 of 12 tournaments, compiling a 61–2 record. This was the crowning year of an abbreviated career that was to end tragically, after 3½ awesome seasons, in 1954.

Meanwhile, Kenneth Robert Rosewall, 21 days older than his fellow Australian "Whiz Kid" Lew Hoad, took the Australian and French singles titles, the first major accomplishments of a career matchless in its longevity. Rosewall would still be going strong a quarter of a century later, nine years after Connolly's death from cancer at age 34.

Connolly, at 18, was the first woman to emulate Don Budge, who took the "Big Four" singles titles in 1938 and popularized the feat by calling it the "Grand Slam." In doing it, she trampled 22 opponents, losing just one set and 82 games.

"Little Mo" started in Australia, demolishing her partner Julie Sampson, 6–3, 6–2, before they teamed up to win the doubles. In the quarterfinals at Paris, Connolly lost that lone set—to Susan Partridge, her toughest rival at Wimbledon the year before, who by this time had married French Davis Cupper Philippe Chatrier. She slow-balled again, but Connolly hit her way out of trouble, blasting her ground strokes even harder, deeper, and closer to the lines than usual, prevailing by 3–6, 6–2, 6–2. Then she drubbed Doris Hart in the final, 6–2, 6–4.

Hart was also her final-round opponent at Wimbledon and Forest Hills. "The Wimbledon final was the finest match of the Slam: 8–6, 7–5. . . . The two great players called it the best of their life," noted Bud Collins in a silver anniversary tribute to Little Mo's wondrous 1953 record. "In the homestretch at Forest Hills, Connolly won driving, as they say at the racetrack, 6–2, 6–3 over Althea Gibson in the quarters; 6–1, 6–1 over Shirley Fry; and 6–2, 6–4 over Hart."

In fact, Connolly lost only two matches during the year: to Hart in the final of the Italian Championships, and to Fry in the Pacific Southwest at Los Angeles.

Connolly and Hart teamed for the French doubles title, but Little Mo—never a great doubles player because of her distaste for net play—was not destined for a doubles Slam. Hart and Fry won their fourth consecutive Wimbledon doubles, whitewashing Connolly and Sampson, 6–0, 6–0, minutes after Maureen had gotten a telephone call from her fiancé, Olympic equestrian Norman Brinker, telling her he was being sent to Korea by the U. S. Navy. Hart and Fry also won the third of their four successive U.S. National Doubles titles.

Rosewall, 18, a 5-foot-7, 145-pounder with an angel face and neither a hair nor a footstep out of place, took the first of his four Australian singles titles, spanning 19 years, by beating left-hander Mervyn Rose, 6–0, 6–3, 6–4. Rosewall beat Vic Seixas, 6–3, 6–4, 1–6, 6–2, in the French final, the first tournament covered by a new magazine, *World Tennis*, which debuted in June 1953 and which was to become an influential force in the game. The story, under Gardnar Mulloy's byline, described Rosewall as "a young kid with stamina, hard-hitting groundstrokes, and plenty of confidence."

The Wimbledon and U.S. titles came back into American possession, property of Vic Seixas and Tony Trabert.

Seixas, according to Lance Tingay's official history of Wimbledon, was "hardly the prettiest player in the world, for his strokes smacked more of expediency than fluency and polish, but he gave the impression of being prepared to go on attacking forever. He edged Hoad in the quarters and Rose in the semis, both in five long sets. In the final, he beat Dane Kurt Nielsen—whose chopped forehand down the middle of the court had upset top seed Rosewall in the quarters—9–7, 6–3, 6–4.

The match of the tournament was the third-round classic in which Jaroslav Drobny defeated his good friend and constant touring companion, Budge Patty, 8–6, 16–18, 3–6, 8–6, 12–10. The herculean epic began at 5:00 P.M. and ended in twilight some 4½ hours later. Its 93 games, played at a consistently high standard, were the most in any Wimbledon single to that time. But Drobny had ruptured a blood vessel, and, after limping through victories over Australian Rex Hartwig and Swede Sven Davidson, lost to the surprising Nielsen in the semis.

Trabert did in Rosewall, and Seixas beat Hoad in the semifinals at Forest Hills, and then Trabert—serving and volleying consistently and returning superbly whether Seixas charged the net or stayed back—beat the Wimbledon champ in the final, 6–3, 6–2, 6–3, in just one hour. Trabert was less than three months out of the U. S. Navy, but he had trained hard to regain his speed and match fitness, and he leveled Seixas with a vicious onslaught from backcourt and net, off both wings—especially his topspin backhand.

Hoad and Rosewall captured the Australian, French, and Wimbledon doubles titles, but their countrymen Hartwig and Rose took the U.S. title over Bill Talbert and Gar Mulloy.

Australia was favored in the Davis Cup Challenge Round at Melbourne but nearly threw it away when the team selectors ordered captain Harry Hopman to nominate Hartwig and Hoad, both right-court players, as his doubles team instead of either of the experienced pairs available: Rosewall-Hoad or Hart-

Jaroslav Drobny (left) and Budge Patty wearily leave the court at Wimbledon after their 93-game marathon match in 1953. *UPI*

wig-Rose. The confused Aussie duo lost to Trabert-Seixas, 6–2, 6–4, 6–4.

Hoad had beaten Seixas, and Trabert had stomped Rosewall the first day, but Australia won from 1–2 down, Hoad beating Trabert, 13–11, 6–3, 2–6, 3–6, 7–5 in the pivotal fourth match—one of the greatest in Davis Cup history. As a huge crowd huddled under newspapers to protect themselves from rain, Trabert lost his serve at love at 5–6 in the desperate final set, double faulting to 0–40 and then netting a half volley off a return to his shoetops.

Meanwhile Frank Sedgman, the Davis Cup hero of a year earlier, lost a pro tour to Jack Kramer, 54 matches to 41, but earned $102,-000, the highest total to date. The tally was closer than it might have been because Kramer was bothered by an arthritic back and was as interested in promoting as playing. Pancho Gonzales won the U.S. Pro title over Don Budge, 4–6, 6–4, 7–5, 6–2, at Lakewood Park in Cleveland, the first of eight triumphs in nine years for Gonzales in this affair for teaching pros and present and former touring pros.

1954

The quotation that hangs above the competitors' entrance to the Centre Court at Wimbledon, and was also adopted for a similar exalted position in the marquee at the Forest Hills stadium, is from a poem by Rudyard Kipling. It says, "If you can meet triumph and disaster, and treat those two impostors just the same . . ." The words seldom seemed more appropriate than in 1954, for it was a year of continued triumph and then sudden disaster for Maureen Connolly.

"Little Mo" did not go to Australia to try for another Grand Slam—in her absence, the experienced Thelma Long won her second Aussie singles title—but Maureen successfully defended her French and Wimbledon titles, and also took the Italian crown that had eluded her in 1953. At Wimbledon she defeated Louise Brough in the final, 6–2, 7–5. Historian Lance Tingay wrote, "The whole event was accounted a trifle dull because of

Vic Seixas, 31, in his 14th try, won his first U.S. Singles in 1954. *UPI*

the inevitability of the eventual winner. Miss Connolly, without losing a set, won 73 games and lost but 19."

Little did anyone know that this would be Little Mo's last major title. Between Wimbledon and Forest Hills, she was riding her horse Colonel Merryboy—a gift from a group of San Diegans after her 1952 Wimbledon triumph—and was struck by a truck. Most people thought she would return in 1955, but in her autobiography Maureen wrote that she knew she was finished: "My right leg was slashed to the bone. All the calf muscles were severed and the fibula broken. Eventually, I got on-court again, but I was aware that I could never play tournament tennis."

Bud Collins summed up Little Mo's achievements in *World Tennis*: "It was the shortest of great careers, but few got more done in many more years. During those 3½ years when she was undisputed No. 1, Maureen won Wimbledon in 1953–55, Forest Hills in 1951–53, all seven of her Wightman Cup singles in 1951–54, the Irish singles of 1952 and 1954, and the U.S. Clay Courts in 1953–54."

Mervyn Rose won his only Australian singles title in 1954, over countryman Rex Hartwig, 6–2, 0–6, 6–4, 6–2. Rugged Tony Trabert—firing like the 16-inch guns that adorned the aircraft carrier on which he had served the year before—blasted fellow American Art Larsen in the French final, 6–4, 7–5, 6–1. But the year ultimately belonged to three players who savored sentimental triumphs that came when they were seemingly a shade past their prime: Jaroslav Drobny, Vic Seixas, and Doris Hart.

Drobny, age 34, still had a punishing serve, though not as oppressive as it had been before a shoulder injury. He was seeded only No. 11 in his 11th appearance at Wimbledon, but upset Lew Hoad in the quarterfinals and beat old rival Budge Patty in the semifinals. In the final Drobny defeated Ken Rosewall, 13–11, 4–6, 6–2, 9–7, in two hours, 35 minutes, becoming only the second left-handed champion. No one could have imagined that Rosewall, in the final for the first of four times at age 19, would never win the singles title he coveted most. The galleries loved

Drobny, the expansive Czech refugee in dark glasses. "No better final had been seen since Crawford and Vines 21 years before," judged Lance Tingay. ". . . The warmth of Drobny's reception as champion could not have been greater had he been a genial Englishman. In a sense he was, for he had married an English-woman and lived in Sussex."

The triumphs of Vic Seixas and Doris Hart at Forest Hills were just as popular with the American audience. Seixas, age 31 and com-peting in his Nationals for the 14th time, fi-nally won in his third appearance in the final. He stopped Rex Hartwig, who had upset de-fending champion Tony Trabert and Rose-wall, 3–6, 6–2, 6–4, 6–4. Hart, runner-up five times in 16 appearances but never before champion, survived three match points and outlasted Louise Brough, 6–8, 6–1, 8–6. In a courtside box, Hart's brother and Seixas's wife and parents were thrilled.

Seixas, according to Allison Danzig's re-port in the New York *Times*, "made the most of his equipment and he never lagged in car-rying the attack to his opponent. His speed and quickness, the effectiveness of his serv-ice, his strong return of service and his staunch volleying all contributed to the vic-tory. Too, he found a vulnerable point in his opponent's game and exploited it by directing his twist service to Hartwig's backhand."

Hart and Brough played a patchy match. Brough had one match point in the 10th game of the final set and two more in the 12th. Each time she netted a backhand return of serve, and Hart gave her no more opportuni-ties.

Hart and Seixas teamed for the mixed dou-bles title of the U.S. at Longwood, as they had at Wimbledon. Both also won the dou-bles, Hart with Shirley Fry for the fourth consecutive year and Seixas with Trabert, whom he had also partnered to the French title. Elsewhere, Hartwig and Rose won the Australian and Wimbledon men's doubles; Connolly and Nell Hopman took the women's doubles at the French, while at Wimbledon, Brough and Margaret duPont recaptured the title they had won in 1948–50.

Connolly, in her last Wightman Cup ap-pearance, led the United States to a 6–0 frolic over Great Britain at Wimbledon. The U.S. also recovered the Davis Cup after four straight losses, upsetting Australia, 3–2, in the Challenge Round at Sydney. Trabert and Seixas, who earned his spot because of his Forest Hills form, were the conquering he-roes. Trabert beat Hoad, and Seixas upset Rosewall, both in four tough sets, and they combined to beat Hoad-Rosewall, 6–2, 4–6, 6–2, 10–8, in the decisive doubles. The largest crowds ever to watch men play tennis, 25,578, jammed White City Stadium each day.

Jack Kramer retired as undefeated pro champion and promoted a round-robin tour involving Pancho Gonzales, Frank Sedgman, Pancho Segura, and Don Budge. Gonzales won it, narrowly defeating Sedgman, and thus gained a previously unheard-of second life in the head-to-head pro tour. He also won the U.S. Pro title over Sedgman, 6–3, 9–7, 3–6, 6–2, at the Cleveland Arena.

1955

At the midpoint of the postwar decade, 1955, American Tony Trabert established himself as the best player in the world, his Australian rivals snatched back the Davis Cup with a vengeance, and a couple of gallant American women who had left a considerable legacy—Louise Brough and Doris Hart—took their final bows as soloists in the world tennis arena.

Tony Trabert soared in 1955 winning the French, Wimbledon, and U.S. Singles. *UPI*

Ken Rosewall beat Lew Hoad, 9–7, 6–4, 6–4, for his second Australian singles title, but Trabert—the All-American boy from Cincinnati with his ginger crewcut, freckles, and uncompromisingly aggressive game—won the French, Wimbledon, and U.S. singles.

In the Italian Championships, two of the most unorthodox but combative clay court specialists of Europe—tall and gangly Fausto Gardini ("The Spider") and tiny, gentle Beppe Merlo ("The Little Bird")—met in an all-native final before a raucous Roman crowd. They had their customary epic battle—"We were always like a dog and a cat," Merlo recalls—with Gardini claiming victory as Merlo collapsed with cramps. To make sure his opponent could not recover and win, Gardini counted off one minute while Merlo writhed in pain, then rolled down the net and raised his arms triumphantly.

There were no such histrionics in Paris, where Trabert bulled his way to the French title over Swede Sven Davidson, 2–6, 6–1, 6–4, 6–2. At Wimbledon, Trabert eliminated defending champion Jaroslav Drobny in the quarters and Budge Patty (conqueror of Hoad) in the semis.

In the final Trabert expected to meet Rosewall, but instead came up against 1953 runner-up Kurt Nielsen, who beat the Australian champ in the semis. "Nielsen clearly remembered his success against the Little Master in 1953, when he hit his approach shots down the middle and came to the net, making it difficult for Rosewall to play his favorite passing shots decisively," wrote Max Robertson in his book *Wimbledon, 1878–1977.* "He pursued the same tactics and with the same result; for the *second* time he had reached the final unseeded—a record which could stand forever." Trabert denied him a more satisfying immortality, however, 6–3, 7–5, 6–1.

The only real stain on Trabert's record for the year came in late August, in the Davis Cup Challenge Round at Forest Hills. After Rosewall had beaten Vic Seixas, 6–3, 10–8, 4–6, 6–2, Trabert went down in straight sets to Hoad in the critical second match; Hoad, it must be said, played with immense power and brilliance.

The next afternoon, Hoad and Rex Hartwig—who two years earlier had been thrown together as first-time doubles partners, with disastrous results—blended beautifully to clinch the Cup with a 12–14, 6–4, 6–3, 3–6, 7–5 victory over Seixas and Trabert that had 12,000 spectators howling with delight through five scintillating sets. The Aussies had their cake and put frosting on it too, running up a 5–0 final margin the next day.

Trabert had the last laugh, though, banishing Rosewall in the final of Forest Hills, 9–7, 6–3, 6–3. That set him up as the new amateur champ. Actually, promoter Jack Kramer had signed Hoad and Rosewall as well, to tour with him and Trabert playing a Davis Cup-style format, but the deal fell through. Slazenger, the racket company that Rosewall represented, gave him a bonus, and Jenny Hoad persuaded her husband to make one more grand tour as an amateur. So Trabert's indoctrination into the pros in 1956 wound up taking the more conventional form of a head-to-head tour against the champ.

On the women's side, new singles champions were crowned in Australia, where Beryl Penrose defeated Thelma Long, 6–4, 6–3, and in France, where England's Angela Mortimer topped Dorothy Head Knode, 2–6, 7–5, 10–8.

At Wimbledon, 1948–50 champion Louise Brough, seeded second, defeated demonstrative newcomer Darlene Hard in the semis, reaching the final for the seventh time. Her opponent was ambidextrous, free-swinging, light-footed Beverly Baker Fleitz, who upset top seed Doris Hart in the semis.

"Louise was always prone to tighten up at important points but had a greater breadth of stroke and experience at her command, which just saw her through a keenly fought struggle," reported Max Robertson. "In the sixth game of the second set, for example, it was only after nine deuces and five advantages to Fleitz that she wrong-footed her near exhausted opponent with a backhand slice down the line to lead 4–2. This was the major turning point and Louise went on to win her fourth singles, 7–5, 8–6."

That was Brough's last major singles title. Doris Hart, also a majestic champion, won her last one at Forest Hills, site of her narrow and jubilant victory over Brough the year before. This time it was much easier; Doris routed Patricia Ward, the Italian titleholder, 6–4, 6–2. Hart also made her last appearance in the Wightman Cup in 1955 as the U.S. defeated Great Britain, 6–1, at Westchester Country Club in Rye, New York. She had been on the U.S. team since 1946, compiling a record of 14–0 in singles and 8–1 in doubles. She became a pro at the end of the year.

As for doubles titles in 1955, Brough and Margaret duPont, who had reigned nine successive years between 1942 and 1950, regained the U.S. title, starting a new three-year run. Seixas and Trabert won the Australian and French titles, but Hoad and Hartwig, presaging their Davis Cup heriocs, won Wimbledon. The little-known team of Kosei Kamo and Atsushi Miyagi won the U.S. doubles, primarily because they were willing to hang around Longwood Cricket Club through a hurricane as most of the favored teams fled Boston. When the waters that turned the grass courts into ponds finally receded, the Japanese pair triumphed. World War II truly was a long time past.

1956

In 1956, the 21-year-old former "Whiz Kids" of Australia, Lew Hoad and Ken Rosewall, had clearly grown up into the best amateur tennis players in the world. They smothered the United States in the Davis Cup Challenge Round, 5–0, for the second straight year, and played each other in three of the "Big Four" singles finals. Ultimately, on the last day of Forest Hills, it was Rosewall who prevented his three-weeks-younger countryman from pulling off the Grand Slam.

This was the Diamond Jubilee year of the U.S. Championships, and Rosewall captivated a crowd of 12,000 at the Forest Hills stadium with his 4–6, 6–2, 6–3, 6–3 victory in the first all-foreign final since 1933, when Britain's Fred Perry thwarted Australian Jack Crawford's bid for a Grand Slam.

"If there were any doubts about the little Australian measuring up to the caliber of a truly great player they were dispelled by his play in the championship," wrote Allison

Ken Rosewall lost to Lew Hoad in 1956 in the Wimbledon and Australian finals, but Rosewall repulsed his countryman at Forest Hills. *UPI*

Danzig in his vivid and authoritative story "A Grand Slam Trumped" in the New York *Times*. "His performance in breaking down the powerful attack and then the will to win of the favored Hoad was even more convincing, considering the conditions, than his wizardry in his unforgettable quarterfinal round match against Richard Savitt.

"Against the powerful, rangy Savitt, Rosewall's ground strokes were the chief instruments of victory in a crescendo of lethal driving exchanges seldom equaled on the Forest Hills turf. Yesterday's match between possibly the two most accomplished 21-year-old finalists in the tournament's history was a madcap, lightning-fast duel. The shots were taken out of the air with rapidity and radiance despite a strong wind that played tricks with the ball.

"The breakneck pace of the rallies, the exploits of both men in scrambling over the turf to bring off electrifying winners, their almost unbelievable control when off balance and the repetition with which they made the chalk fly on the lines with their lobs, made for the most entertaining kind of tennis. In time the gallery was so surfeited with brilliance that the extraordinary shot became commonplace, particularly by Rosewall. . . ."

So it had been much of the year . . . the blond-haired, blue-eyed, muscular, and positively engaging Hoad rousing galleries around the world with his remarkable weight of shot and free-wheeling attack . . . the immaculate, compact, and quicksilver Rosewall challenging him but constantly being rebuffed, until now.

Hoad had beaten Rosewall in the finals of the Australian, 6–4, 3–6, 6–4, 7–5, and Wimbledon, 6–2, 4–6, 7–5, 6–4. He had beaten Sven Davidson in the French final, 6–4, 8–6, 6–3. He had won the Italian and German titles on clay as well. But finally Rosewell got him, and with Hoad changing his mind again about signing a pro contract with Kramer, it was Rosewall who signed on to face Pancho Gonzales the following year.

Doris Hart, who had climaxed 17 appearances with back-to-back Forest Hills titles in 1954–55, had, like Trabert, turned pro at the end of the year. In her absence, her old doubles partner, Shirley Fry, took the Wimbledon and Forest Hills singles titles for the first and only time. At Wimbledon, she beat Englishwoman Angela Buxton, 6–3, 6–1, and at Forest Hills, her final victim was Italian and French champion Althea Gibson of Harlem, the first black champion of international tennis, 6–3, 6–4.

Fry—who attained her first singles title, as Hart had two years previous, on her 16th attempt—had beaten Gibson at Wimbledon and the U.S. Clay Court. This time Fry maintained her mastery by attacking the net constantly in the first set, then staying back and

Shirley Fry took over at Wimbledon and Forest Hills in 1956. *UPI*

thwarting Gibson's attack with deep, accurate ground strokes in the second.

The addition of Buxton, Shirley Bloomer, and Angela Mortimer (runner-up to Gibson in the French) made the British Wightman Cup team more competitive than it had been at any time since the war, but the U.S. still prevailed, 5–2, at Wimbledon.

Gibson teamed with Buxton to win the French and Wimbledon doubles titles, but Louise Brough and Margaret duPont continued their unmatched supremacy in the U.S. National Doubles.

Hoad and Rosewall won the Wimbledon and U.S. doubles titles, and single-handedly achieved the Davis Cup shutout of the United States in the Challenge Round at Adelaide. Hoad beat Herbie Flam easily, Rosewall kayoed Vic Seixas in four sets, and Hoad and Rosewall thumped Seixas and Texan Sammy Giammalva in a four-set doubles to make sure that the contest was decided before the third day.

Pro promoter Jack Kramer would have liked to sign Hoad, no doubt, but Rosewall was a fine attraction to oppose Pancho Gonzales in 1957. Kramer had started training to play 1955 amateur king Tony Trabert in 1956, but was persuaded by Gonzales' wife to let Pancho face Trabert on the head-to-head tour. Kramer, now badly afflicted with arthritis, was just as happy to do the promotion and let the strong and hungry Gonzales play.

Gonzales, very likely the best player in the world even though few realized it, crushed Trabert, 74 matches to 24. Gonzales also won the U.S. Pro Championship over Pancho Segura at Cleveland, and beat Frank Sedgman, 4–6, 11–9, 11–9, 9–7, in a match of remarkably high quality at Wembley, England.

"Wembley, a London suburb of fast-fading respectability, is a shrine of English soccer. In those days its indoor arena was also a shrine of pro tennis," wrote Rex Bellamy in *World Tennis* more than two decades later. "That night, public transport ceased long before the match did. Stranded spectators did not much mind. They were unlikely to see such a match again."

1957

The order that had prevailed in international tennis in the early part of the 1950s was changing rapidly by 1957. A year that began with Lew Hoad and Shirley Fry on top of the world ended with Althea Gibson as the dominant woman and surprising Mal Anderson challenging Ashley Cooper for the top spot among the men.

Any designs Hoad may have had on the Grand Slam he had come within one match of achieving in 1956 were shattered quickly. The "baby bull" was upset in the semifinals of the Australian singles by a promising young left-hander, Neale Fraser, son of a prominent Labor politician. Cooper—a rather mechanical but solid and determined player who, with Fraser and Anderson, represented the new products off Harry Hopman's Australian Davis Cup assembly line—then won his first Grand Slam title by beating Fraser in the final, 6–3, 9–11, 6–4, 6–2. Hoad and Fraser took the doubles.

Shortly after the pro tour between Pancho Gonzales and Ken Rosewall—which Gonzales would win, 50–26—had begun in Australia at the New Year, Hoad had a friend contact promoter Jack Kramer and tell him that he was again interested in turning pro. Kramer was baffled, since Hoad had recently turned down his entreaties, but later figured that Hoad was starting to encounter the back problems that eventually cut short his career, and decided he'd better get his payday while he still could.

Kramer signed Hoad—sending Ted Schroeder to the bank with him to make sure he cashed a $5,000 advance, which would provide proof of a contract if Hoad changed his mind again—but agreed to keep the pact secret until after Wimbledon.

Sven Davidson, the Swedish Davis Cup stalwart who was runner-up the previous two years, won the French singles over Herbie Flam, the last American man in the Paris final for 19 years, 6–3, 6–4, 6–4. Anderson and Cooper were the doubles titlists.

Hoad, whose season had been erratic, made his last amateur tournament a memorable one. At Wimbledon he lost only one set, to fellow

Althea Gibson made it to the top in 1957. *UPI*

Aussie Merv Rose in the quarters. Then he routed Davidson, the only non-Australian semifinalist, while Cooper won a tougher semifinal in the other half over Fraser. In the final, Hoad was brilliant, humbling Cooper, 6–2, 6–1, 6–2, in a mere 57 minutes. "It was a display of genius and it is to be doubted if such dynamic shotmaking was sustained with such accuracy before. If Cooper felt he had played badly, he had no chance to do anything else," wrote Lance Tingay in *100 Years of Wimbledon*. "Hoad was 'superhuman.' It never began to be a contested match."

Gardnar Mulloy, age 43, and Budge Patty, 10 years younger, won their only Wimbledon doubles title—an exciting and sentimental occasion—over Fraser and Hoad, 8–10, 6–4, 6–4, 6–4.

Hoad joined the pros, Kramer carefully trying to get him ready for a serious run at Gonzales the following year. "I used him in a couple of round robins in the States, and then I made myself into a sparring partner and, with Rosewall and [Pancho] Segura, we took off on an around-the-world tour to get Hoad in shape for Gonzales," Kramer recalled in *Sports Illustrated*. "If Hoad could beat Gonzales, that was my chance to get rid of that tiger. Gonzales knew what I was doing, too, and he was furious. We played a brutal death march, going to Europe, then across Africa, through India and Southeast Asia, all the way to Manila. I was impressed by how strong Hoad was. He was personally as gentle as a lamb, but on the trip his body could tolerate almost anything.''

With Hoad gone, the 20-year-old Cooper was the top seed and heavy favorite to win Forest Hills, But he was upset by Anderson, thought to be the first unseeded champion of the U.S. Nationals.

Anderson, a country boy from a remote Queensland cattle station, had lost to Cooper in five of six previous meetings. But in the month before Forest Hills, the thin, quick, dark-haired lad of 22 had become an entirely different player. Early in the year he had suffered from nervous exhaustion and heat prostration. At Wimbledon he broke a toe. But at Newport, Rhode Island, on the U.S. Grass Court circuit, he beat U.S. No. 1 Ham Richardson and got a confidence-boosting title under his belt.

At Forest Hills, he clobbered Dick Savitt, who had a virus cold, 6–4, 6–3, 6–1, then put on a dazzling display of piercing service returns and passing shots to crush Chilean Luis Ayala, 6–1, 6–3, 6–1. In the semifinals, he overcame Sven Davidson—conqueror of Vic Seixas at Wimbledon—from a 1–2 deficit in sets, 5–7, 6–2, 4–6, 6–3, 6–4.

In his 10–8, 7–5, 6–4 triumph over Cooper, Anderson was so good that he inspired rhapsodic prose and superlatives from Allison Danzig in the next day's New York Times: "Anderson's performance ranks with the finest displays of offensive tennis of recent years. His speed of stroke and foot, the inevitability of his volley, his hair-trigger reaction and facileness on the half-volley, the rapidity of his service and passing shots and the adroitness of his return of service, compelling Cooper to volley up, all bore the stamp of a master of the racket. It was offensive tennis all the way, sustained without a let-up. The margin of safety on most shots was almost nil. The most difficult shots were taken in stride with the acme of timing, going in or swiftly moving to the side.''

Less artistically satisfying, but just as dramatic, was Althea Gibson's 6–3, 6–2 victory in the women's final over Louise Brough. In 1950, when Gibson made history as the first black player admitted to the U.S. Nationals, she had gained widespread attention by nearly beating Brough, then the Wimbledon champion.

At the start of the year, Shirley Fry captured the Australian Championship, the only one of the Grand Slam singles titles she had not previously won, over Gibson, 6–3, 6–4. They teamed to win the doubles; these were Fry's last big titles before retiring to become a housewife and teaching pro in Connecticut.

Englishwoman Shirley Bloomer, whose victory in the Italian Championships had been overshadowed by the first men's title of the stylish Nicki Pietrangeli, took the French over Dorothy Knode, 6–1, 6–3, and teamed with Darlene Hard for the doubles crown. But thereafter Gibson reigned supreme, clobbering Californian Hard, 6–3, 6–2, in the Wimbledon final, winning two singles and a doubles as the U.S. defeated Great Britain, 6–1, in the Wightman Cup, and then winning Forest Hills. Althea also won the Wimbledon doubles with Hard, but they lost in the U.S. Doubles final to Louise Brough and Margaret duPont, who took their last title: the third straight and 12th in all.

Fifteen years earlier, Gibson had been playing paddle tennis on the streets of Harlem. She had as difficult a path to the pinnacle of tennis as anyone ever did. She had to stare down bigotry as well as formidable opponents. Some tournaments had gone out of existence rather than admit her. But finally, at age 30, she was standing on the stadium court at Forest Hills, already the Wimbledon champion, accepting the trophy that symbolized supremacy in American women's tennis from Vice President Richard Nixon. The cup had white gladiolas and red roses in it, and "Big Al" had tears in her eyes.

There was one other important piece of silverware at stake in 1957. With Hoad and Rosewall gone, Australia was vulnerable to a U.S. raiding party invading Melbourne for the Davis Cup Challenge Round. But Anderson edged big-serving Barry MacKay, 6–3, 7–5,

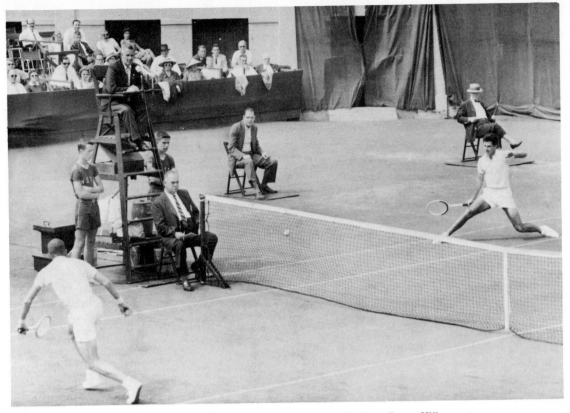

Ashley Cooper, netting the ball against Neale Fraser in the 1958 semifinals at Forest Hills, went on to win the championship in his finest year. *New York Herald Tribune*

3–6, 7–9, 6–3; Cooper bumped 34-year-old Vic Seixas in a similarly torturous match, 3–6, 7–5, 6–1, 1–6, 6–3; and Anderson and Merv Rose—chosen even though Cooper and Fraser had won the U.S. Doubles—combined to demoralize MacKay and Seixas, 6–4, 6–4, 8–6.

Seixas beat Anderson and MacKay edged Cooper, both in five sets, to make the final score respectable, 3–2 for Australia, but it all had been decided on the second day. The second-largest Davis Cup crowds—22,000 a day—witnessed the four singles marathons and the decisive, straight-sets doubles. There were no flowers in the cup, but for the third straight year Aussies drank libations of victory beer from it.

1958

In 1958, Australians Ashley Cooper, Mal Anderson, and Mervyn Rose were the top men in amateur tennis, and American Althea Gibson the outstanding woman. By the end of

the year, they had all turned professional, underscoring the rapidly growing distance in quality between the small band of pros who wandered around the world playing one- and two-night stands as official outcasts and the amateurs who basked in the limelight of the traditional "fixtures."

The previous year the issue of "open competition" between amateurs and pros was raised formally within the councils of the U.S. Lawn Tennis Association for the first time since the 1930s; a "special committee" report favored open tournaments. This document was promptly tabled, the leadership of the Association not being nearly as progressive as the committee, but the ferment that ultimately led to the open game a decade later had started, and not only in America.

With Hoad and Rosewall touring professionally with Jack Kramer's World Tennis, Inc., Cooper took over the top amateur ranking by winning the three legs of the Grand Slam played on grass courts: the Australian, Wimbledon, and Forest Hills.

He reversed the result of the 1957 Forest

Hills final and took the Australian singles by beating Mal Anderson, 7–5, 6–3, 6–4, and then teamed with Neale Fraser for his only national doubles title.

At Wimbledon, Anderson injured himself in the quarterfinals, and Cooper very nearly stumbled in the same round, probably coming within one point of defeat against Bobby Wilson, the pudgy but talented Englishman who delighted British galleries with his deft touch. Wilson had a break point for 6–5 in the fifth set, but Cooper rifled a backhand cross-court winner within an inch of the sideline, and thereafter fortune favored the bold. Cooper dominated Rose after losing the first set, and then beat Fraser—who had won a gallant semifinal over Kurt Nielsen—in the final, 3–6, 6–3, 6–4, 13–11.

Cooper and Fraser were beaten in the doubles final, however, as the title went to an unseeded pair for the second straight year, the strapping Sven Davidson and Ulf Schmidt becoming the first Swedes to have their names inscribed on a Wimbledon championship trophy.

At Forest Hills, Cooper and Anderson advanced to the final for the second consecutive year, but this time Cooper prevailed in the longest final since Gonzales-Schroeder in 1949, 6–2, 3–6, 4–6, 10–8, 8–6. Gardnar Mulloy, reporting the match for *World Tennis*, wrote that the final set had "all the drama of a First Night," and suggested that Cooper merited an Oscar for his theatrics. The even-tempered Anderson served for the match at 5–4, but lost his serve at love. At 6–6, 30–15, Cooper apparently twisted an ankle, writhed in pain, hobbled to the sideline, and finally went back out to play after several minutes, to tumultuous applause. He "ran like a deer and served as well or better than he had all afternoon," opined Mulloy, a bit skeptical about the "injury." Cooper promptly held serve and then broke Anderson for the match. "Cooper is strong, tenacious, smart, and merciless," wrote Mulloy. "And don't forget his famous one-act play, 'The Dying Swan,' a real tear-jerker which clinched the championship for him."

Ham Richardson and Alex Olmedo foreshadowed a U.S. revival in the Davis Cup by winning the National Doubles at Longwood in their first tournament together, beating Sammy Giammalva and Barry MacKay in the final after bumping Cooper and Fraser in a four-set semi.

Merv Rose, with his tormenting left-handed serve, was the leading Aussie on clay, winning both the Italian title and the French, ripping the fiery Chilean Davis Cupper Luis Ayala in the Paris final, 6–3, 6–4, 6–4. The most astounding match of the tournament was Frenchman Robert Haillet's resurrection from 0–5, 0–40 down in the fifth set to beat Budge Patty. Cooper and Fraser won the doubles, as they had in Australia, but were to advance no farther toward a Grand Slam. The only "Slam" this year was in the junior ranks, Earl "Butch" Buchholz, Jr., of St. Louis becoming the first player to win the 18-and-under titles of Australia, France, Wimbledon, and the U.S.

Australia was heavily favored to defend the Davis Cup at the end of the year, but the United States had a potent and somewhat controversial weapon—the sleek, bronze-skinned, outgoing Alejandro "Alex" Olmedo, 22, from Arequipa in the snowcapped Peruvian Andes. The nimble 6-foot, 160-pounder was a student at the University of Southern California, and since Peru did not have a Davis Cup team, he was permitted to play for the U.S. "The Chief," as he was called because of his regal Inca appearance, had lost a tough five-setter to Fraser at Forest Hills, but in the Davis Cup Olmedo was magnificent.

In the opening singles, before a capacity crowd of 18,000 at the Milton Courts in Brisbane, Olmedo stunned Anderson, 8–6, 2–6, 9–7, 8–6. Cooper beat MacKay in four sets to make it 1–1, but on the second day Olmedo teamed with Richardson to outlast Fraser and Anderson, 10–12, 3–6, 16–14, 6–3, 7–5. Olmedo, the U.S. Intercollegiate champion, then capped his herioc performance by clinching the Cup with a 6–3, 4–6, 6–4, 8–6 victory over Cooper. Anderson beat MacKay to make the final margin for the U.S. 3–2. Olmedo was rewarded with the No. 1 ranking.

No. 1 among the women, in the U.S. and the world, was clearly the 5-10½, 145-pound Gibson, who used her thunderous serve and overhead, long reach and touch on the volley, and hard, flat, deep ground strokes to defend the Wimbledon and U.S. singles titles. At Wimbledon she beat Angela Mortimer—who had won the Australian title over Lorraine Coghlan—in the final, 8–6, 6–2. At Forest Hills, Gibson's final victim was Darlene Hard, 3–6, 6–1, 6–2. Gibson teamed with Maria Bueno—an enchanting Brazilian who, making her first overseas tour at age 18, had won the Italian title—for the Wimbledon doubles title, but they were beaten in the final of the U.S. Doubles by Jeanne Arth and Hard. This was the first of Hard's five successive National women's titles; she won six in all, with four partners.

Gibson lost only four matches during the year, three in the early season (to Beverly Baker Fleitz and Janet Hopps twice), but the one that hurt was to tall Englishwoman Christine Truman in the pivotal match of the Wightman Cup. The British had a fine young team with Truman, Shirley Bloomer (runner-up to Hungarian Suzie Kormoczi in the French Championships), and left-hander Ann Haydon, even though Angela Mortimer didn't play. To the glee of the crowd at Wimbledon's Court No. 1, the British won the Cup for the first time since 1930, 4–3. Truman's 2–6, 6–3, 6–4 upset of Gibson paved the way, and the left-handed Haydon's scrambling 6–3, 5–7, 6–3 triumph over Mimi Arnold was the clincher.

After Forest Hills, Gibson announced her retirement "to pursue a musical career." She needed a source of income. The next year she accepted an offer to turn pro and play pregame exhibitions at Harlem Globetrotters' basketball games against Karol Fageros, a popular glamor girl noted for her gold lamé panties, but not a player of Gibson's standard.

Lew Hoad found pro tennis much more lucrative. Even though he lost his 1958 tour against Gonzales, 51–36, Hoad made $148,-000. Gonzales, who rallied from a 9–18 deficit after Hoad developed a stiff back in Palm Springs, California, made over $100,000.

"That was the last tour to make any real money, though," promoter Kramer later said. It had been a doozy. In Australia at the start of the year, Hoad was awesome, winning

eight of 13 matches against a stale and overweight Gonzales. In San Francisco, on a canvas court indoors, Hoad won, 6–4, 20–18, to inaugurate the U.S. segment of the tour. The next night Gonzales won in his hometown of Los Angeles, 3–6, 24–22, 6–1. Before a crowd of 15,237 at Madison Square Garden, Gonzales won the only best-of-five-setter, . . . 7–9, 6–0, 6–4, 6–4.

Then Hoad, strong as an ox and beating Gonzales in every department—serve, overhead, volley, ground strokes—surged to an 18–9 lead. But the bad back got him, and he was never again the factor he had been. Gonzales won the tour and beat Hoad in the U.S. Pro Championship at the Arena in Cleveland, 3–6, 4–6, 14–12, 6–1, 6–4. Gonzales was the best in the world, and the next year—when Cooper, Anderson, and Rose came aboard for a round-robin—he proved it decisively.

1959

The folly of the uneasy arrangement between amateur officials and pro promoter Jack Kramer during the "shamateur" days of the late 1950s and -early 1960s was apparent in

Dick Savitt congratulates Alex Olmedo after the Peruvian won the U.S. Indoors in 1959.
New York Herald Tribune

this passage from a 1958 *Sports Illustrated* story on Kramer by Dick Phelan:

" 'I look on the amateurs as my farm system,' he says flatly, and this has been true particularly in Australia. There he is denounced as a public enemy because his money tempts the best Australian players to abandon their amateur status and thus their eligibility for Davis Cup play. Then when his troupe arrives in Australia the very public that reviled him flocks to his matches and profits mount. This leads the amateur tennis officials, whose own tournaments sometimes follow Kramer's and don't draw nearly so well, to lambaste him afresh. But they let him come back. Their share of his gate receipts helps support the Australian amateurs."

After the heady peak of the Pancho Gonzales-Lew Hoad tour in 1958, the profits of Kramer's World Tennis, Inc., started to dwindle, despite his personal flair for promotion. Anderson and Cooper joined the vanquished Hoad and the victorious Gonzales in a round-robin tour, but the thrill was gone. They did not draw well, nor did similar tours with other personnel. If they had, it might have hastened the willingness of the amateur officials to consider open tennis. With Cooper, Anderson, and Mervyn Rose gone, Alex Olmedo and Neale Fraser ruled the amateur roost, sharing the world stage with the fiery Latin grace of Maria Bueno.

Olmedo, still buoyed by his herculean accomplishment in the Davis Cup Challenge Round at the end of 1958, stayed and took the 1959 Australian singles title over southpaw Fraser, 6–1, 6–2, 3–6, 6–3. Rod Laver and Bob Mark took the first of their three straight Aussie doubles titles.

Olmedo then returned to the United States and won the U.S. Indoors at New York, 12–10 in the fifth set over Dick Savitt. Olmedo did not play the Italian Championship, where Luis Ayala prevailed over Fraser, or the French, where the great Italian artist Nicola Pietrangeli beat Fraser in the semis and then South African Ian Vermaak in the final, 3–6, 6–3, 6–4, 6–1. Pietrangeli and Italian Davis Cup teammate Orlando Sirola won the doubles over the champions of Italy, Fraser and Roy Emerson.

Olmedo's 1958 Davis Cup triumph for the United States made him a national hero in his native Peru, and he made a triumphant tour there along with 1958 Junior Grand Slammer Butch Buchholz, Davis Cup captain Perry Jones, and the Cup itself. Olmedo added to his skyrocketing reputation by winning Wimbledon, beating Emerson in the semifinal, and Laver, a left-hander of enormous but as yet unconsolidated talent, in the final, 6–4, 6–3, 6–4. Emerson took the first of his eventual 16 Grand Slam men's doubles titles, alongside Fraser.

Wimbledon was the peak of Olmedo's year, however. Fraser beat him in the finals of Forest Hills, 6–3, 5–7, 6–2, 6–4, the Chief's serve lacking its customary zip because of a shoulder strain he had suffered in a mixed doubles match the night before.

Australia regained the Davis Cup at Forest Hills, 3–2, Olmedo never finding the form to which he had risen deep in the previous December. Fraser beat him again in the opening match, 8–6, 6–8, 6–4, 8–6. Barry MacKay, the hulking "Bear" of Dayton, Ohio, served mightily in beating Laver, 7–5, 6–4, 6–1, but in the doubles Emerson and Fraser outclassed Olmedo and Buchholz, 7–5, 7–5, 6–4. The Aussies had prevailed in the U.S. National Doubles by the breadth of their fingernails, 3–6, 6–3, 5–7, 6–4, 7–5, but this time the nails became claws.

Olmedo raised his game to beat Laver, 9–7, 4–6, 10–8, 12–10, to tie the series at 2-all, but Fraser clinched by beating MacKay in a match that was played over two days. They split sets before darkness forced a postponement, but after a long rain delay, Fraser won the last two sets easily for a soggy 8–6, 3–6, 6–2, 6–4 victory.

On the women's side, Mary Carter Reitano won the Australian singles over South African Renée Schuurman, who teamed with her countrywoman Sandra Reynolds for the doubles crown. Englishwoman Christine Truman won both the Italian and French titles, dethroning the clay court specialist Suzie Kormoczi in the Paris final, 6–4, 7–5. Reynolds and Schuurman won the doubles.

Thereafter the season belonged to the incomparably balletic and flamboyant Bueno.

Volleying beautifully, playing with breathtaking boldness and panache, the lithe Brazilian became the first South American woman to win the Wimbledon singles, beating Darlene Hard in the final, 6–4, 6–3. Hard did team with Jeanne Arth to add the Wimbledon doubles to the U.S. crown they captured the previous year, and won the mixed with Laver.

Bueno then inspired the galleries at Forest Hills as she had at London, beating the tall and sporting Christine Truman in the final, 6–4, 6–1. Hard and Arth repeated as doubles champions at Longwood.

The United States regained the Wightman Cup from Great Britain with a 4–3 victory at the Edgeworth Club in Sewickley, Pennsylvania. The British won the final two matches, but only after Hard's 6–3, 6–8, 6–4 victory over Angela Mortimer and Beverly Baker Fleitz's 6–4, 6–4 conquest of Truman had given the Americans an unbeatable 4–1 lead.

Gonzales remained the pro champion. He beat Hoad for the second straight year in the final of U.S. Pro Championship at Cleveland, 6–4, 6–2, 6–4, after romping in the round-robin tour against Hoad, Cooper, and Anderson.

1960

Once again, the start of a new decade was the dawn of a new era in tennis. As 1950 had been, so 1960 was an eventful year.

It began with an Australian Championships that heralded a man and woman who would be king and queen of tennis. Rod Laver beat fellow Aussie left-hander Neale Fraser in an epic final, 5–7, 3–6, 6–3, 8–6, 8–6, to take the first of his eventual 11 Big Four singles titles. Margaret Smith, who would later become Mrs. Barry Court, beat her countrywoman Jan Lehane, 7–5, 6–2, for the first of seven consecutive Australian titles and 26 Big Four singles titles in all— both records.

It would have been much more of a landmark year but for five votes at the annual general meeting of the International Lawn Tennis Federation. By that slim margin, a proposal calling for sanction of between eight and 13 "open" tournaments in which pros and amateurs would compete together failed to

Darlene Hard and Neale Fraser made off with the silverware at the 1960 U.S. Nationals. *USLTA*

muster the two-thirds majority needed for passage. The proposal had the backing of the U.S., British, French, and Australian associations, and the proponents of the "open" movement were bitterly disappointed when it failed.

Another proposal put forth by the French Association, calling for creation of a category of "registered" players who could capitalize on their skill by bargaining with tournaments for appearance fees higher than the expenses allowed amateurs, was tabled. The USLTA had voted to oppose this resolution on the basis that "registered player" was just another name for a pro.

Maria Bueno did not reach the semifinals of the Australian singles, but she teamed with Christine Truman to win the doubles over Margaret Smith and Lorraine Coghlan Robinson, 6–2, 5–7, 6–2. That was the first leg of a doubles Grand Slam by Bueno. She went on to win the French, Wimbledon, and U.S. titles with American Darlene Hard, losing only one more set along the way—to Karen Hantze and Janet Hopps in the semifinals at Wimbledon.

Hard won her first Big Four singles title at Paris, struggling through three three-set matches in the early rounds and then whipping Bueno in the semis and the quick little Mexican Yola Ramirez in the final, 6–3, 6–4. Hard also won her first U.S. National singles at Forest Hills, beating Bueno, 6–4, 10–12, 6–4, after the final was postponed nearly a week by Hurricane Donna.

At Wimbledon, where American women had been so dominant for more than a decade after the war, not one of the 10 American girls who entered reached the semifinals. This had not happened since 1925. Hard, the best U.S. hope, lost in the quarterfinals to South African Sandra Reynolds, who reached the final but lost to Bueno, 8–6, 6–0. A year earlier, Lance Tingay had pointed out that the difference between being very good or very bad was, for Bueno, a thin line based on her timing. "Mundane shots did not exist for her," he observed. "It was either caviar or starvation." For the second year in a row it was mostly caviar, and a feast for the spectators. Her Wimbledon performance was good enough to earn Bueno the No. 1 ranking by a shade over Hard.

Britain won the Wightman Cup for the second time in three years, snatching a 4–3 victory at Wimbledon by winning the final two matches. Hard had given the U.S. a 3–2 lead with a 5–7, 6–2, 6–1 triumph over Ann Haydon, but Angela Mortimer beat Janet Hopps, 6–8, 6–4, 6–1, and Christine Truman paired with Shirley Bloomer Brasher to beat Hopps and Dorothy Head Knode, 6–4, 9–7.

Nicki Pietrangeli defended his French singles title over Luis Ayala, runner-up for the second time in three years, 3–6, 6–3, 6–4, 4–6, 6–3. Ayala was also second best in Rome, where Barry MacKay served and volleyed on the slow clay, winning the final by a most peculiar score: 7–5, 7–5, 0–6, 0–6, 6–1. MacKay had won the U.S. Indoors in February in a splendid five-set final over Dick Savitt, so within four months he took titles on just about the fastest and slowest court surfaces in the world. Roy Emerson and Neale Fraser combined for the French doubles title, the first of six straight for Emerson, with five partners.

Fraser took over as the No. 1 man in the amateur ranks by winning Wimbledon and the U.S. Championship.

As with the women, no American man got to the semis at Wimbledon. MacKay was beaten in the quarterfinals by Pietrangeli, and Butch Buchholz, 19, led Fraser by 6–4, 3–6, 6–4 in the same round and had six match points in the fourth set before being seized with cramps that left him unable to continue.

Fraser, 26 and playing for the seventh time, was a sporting and popular champion. His left-handed serve had a wicked kick, and he was a daring and resourceful volleyer. He beat Laver, five years his junior, in the final, 6–4, 3–6, 9–7, 7–5.

A small measure of U.S. pride was saved when Dennis Ralston, 17, teamed with agile 21-year-old Mexican Rafael Osuna to win the men's doubles, the youngest pair ever to do so. They beat Britons Humphrey Truman and Gerald Oakley in the first round, 6–3, 6–4, 9–11, 5–7, 16–14, and second-seeded Laver and Bob Mark, the Australian champions, 4–6, 10–8, 15–13, 4–6, 11–9, in the semifinal. After that pulsating contest, the final was comparatively easy: 7–5, 6–3, 10–8 over Welshman Mike Davies and Englishman Bobby Wilson.

Laver foreshadowed greatness to come by ripping up the U.S. Eastern Grass Court circuit, winning consecutive titles at Merion, Southampton, Orange, and Newport. Laver and Mark got revenge on Ralston and Osuna in the semis of the U.S. Doubles at Longwood, but lost the final to Fraser and Emerson.

At Forest Hills, Laver got to the final by beating Buchholz, who had three set points before again suffering a debilitating attack of cramps. Fraser beat the precocious Ralston and then, after sitting around through a week of hurricane rain and wind, slogged to the title over Laver, 6–4, 6–4, 10–8.

For the first time since 1936, the United States failed to reach the Challenge Round of the Davis Cup, falling to Italy, 3–2, in the Inter-Zone semifinals at Perth, Australia, in December.

Buchholz beat the lanky Orlando Sirola in the opening match, and MacKay gave the U.S. a 2–0 lead in an all-time classic, saving eight match points in beating Pietrangeli, 8–6, 3–6, 8–10, 8–6, 13–11. But Sirola and

Pietrangeli beat Buchholz and Chuck McKinley in a long four-set doubles, Pietrangeli beat Buchholz in five sets to even the series, and then Sirola—a definite underdog on grass instead of his preferred clay—served and played like a dream to upset MacKay, 9–7, 6–3, 8–6.

Italy's first appearance in the Challenge Round a couple of weeks later was less auspicious. Australia won, 4–1, Fraser and Emerson clinching the doubles point over Pietrangeli-Sirola for an unbeatable 3–0 lead. Pietrangeli beat Fraser in four sets in the final match, but the Australian No. 1 had started things off with a decisive four-set win over Sirola.

This time the Aussies suffered no defections to the pro tour immediately after the Davis Cup, but the Americans did. MacKay and Buchholz, undoubtedly thinking that open tennis was near and wanting a piece of Jack Kramer's checkbook before it arrived, signed to make a tour in 1961 with Lew Hoad, Frank Sedgman, Tony Trabert, Ashley Cooper, Alex Olmedo, and the Spaniard Andres Gimeno.

Meanwhile, the 1960 tour won by Pancho Gonzales over Olmedo, Pancho Segura, and Ken Rosewall was not a financial success. Olmedo, the Wimbledon champ a year before, beat Trabert in the U.S. Pro final, 7–5, 6–4, at Cleveland.

1961

In 1961, the amateur tennis Establishment was stunned and smarting from a wholesale raid on its ranks by pro promoter Jack Kramer, who in 1960 signed to contracts several middling players: Spaniard Andres Gimeno, Welshman Mike Davies, Frenchman Robert Haillet, and Dane Kurt Nielsen. Kramer tried without success to lure into his fold Australian Neale Fraser, the Wimbledon and Forest Hills champion; Italian Nicki Pietrangeli, champion of France; and Chilean Luis Ayala, runner-up in the 1960 Italian and French Championships. But at the end of the year he did sign young American Davis Cuppers Barry MacKay (the Italian champ) and Butch Buchholz.

When a proposal for introducing "open tournaments" was unexpectedly stymied by

Unseeded teen-agers in 1961, Karen Hantze (left) and Billie Jean Moffitt won the women's doubles at Wimbledon. *UPI*

just five votes at the 1960 ILTF annual meeting, there was relatively little official grieving among the member national associations and their officials. However, Kramer's response of taking out his wallet and waving it in front of practically every player of moderate reputation—which the amateur powers-that-be thought both irresponsible and reprehensible—started alarm bells sounding. Suddenly the national associations saw their tournaments, and hence their revenues, in grave danger. Kramer became Public Enemy No. 1.

But if his motive was to force the ILTF into open competition by his mass signings, as most suspected, he failed. Amateur officials did not like being bullied. A new "open tournament" proposal was rejected at the 1961 ILTF annual meeting at Stockholm. Delegates approved a resolution agreeing "to the principle of an experiment of a limited number of open tournaments," but referred the matter to a committee for another year of study to see how the experiment might be conducted. A U.S.-sponsored "home rule" resolution, which would have permitted national associations to stage open tournaments at their own discretion, was defeated. The ILTF was able to stand up to Kramer because he had been able to sign only two of the previous year's top handful of players: No. 3, MacKay, and No. 5, Buchholz. The amateurs still had Fraser, Rod Laver, Pietrangeli, Roy Emerson, and Ayala. But the battle lines had been drawn. Instead of the uneasy coexistence of the past, the amateur associations and Kramer were now at war.

Emerson—a magnificently fit and affable fellow with slick black hair that shone like patent leather and a smile that sparkled with gold fillings—served and volleyed relentlessly to defeat his fellow Queenslander Laver in the Australian final, 1–6, 6–3, 7–5, 6–4. This was the first of six Australian titles in seven years for "Emmo," the first of 12 Grand Slam singles titles in all. Laver and Bob Mark annexed the doubles crown for the third straight year. On the women's side, "Mighty Margaret" Smith beat Jan Lehane again in the singles final, 6–1, 6–4, and teamed with Mary Carter Reitano for the first of Smith's eight Australian Doubles titles.

In Paris, the two greatest European virtuosi of the 60s met in the final. English writer Rex Bellamy was there and remembered it some years later in *World Tennis*:

"Nicola Pietrangeli, the favorite to win for the third consecutive year, was beaten by the young Manuel Santana, the first Spaniard to win a major title. The match lasted five sets. Santana and Pietrangeli were like artists at work in a studio exposed to a vast public in the heat of the afternoon. Each in turn played his finest tennis. The flame of Pietrangeli's inspiration eventually died, his brushstrokes overlaid by Santana's flickering finesse. But long before that, these two Latins had established a close rapport with a Latin crowd enjoying a rare blend of sport and aesthetics. At the end there was a tumult of noise. Santana, his nerves strung up to the breaking point, dropped his racket and cried. And Pietrangeli, disappointed yet instantly responsive to the Spaniard's feelings, went around the net, took Santana in his arms, and patted him on the back like a father comforting a child."

The scores were 4–6, 6–1, 3–6, 6–0, 6–2, but bald numbers could hardly convey the emotion of this long afternoon . . . especially for the toothy Santana, who got to the final by upsetting cannonball-serving Englishman Mike Sangster, Emerson, and Laver (runner-up to Pietrangeli in Rome).

A vivid contrast in style to the gliding and caressing strokes of the singles finalists was provided by Laver and Emerson, who bore in on the net for murderous volleys in winning the doubles. Ann Haydon showed the legs, heart, and brain of a clay court stalwart in beating agile volleyer Yola Ramirez, 6–2, 6–1, for the women's title. South Africans Renée Schuurman and Sandra Reynolds won the doubles.

Maria Bueno, who had beaten Australian Lesley Turner in the Italian final, lost to Suzie Kormoczi in the quarterfinals at Paris and then was bedridden with hepatitis. Lacking funds to pay for hospital care, she was confined to a tiny hotel chamber for a month, with the rest of the floor quarantined, until she was able to go home to Brazil.

Bueno was thus unable to defend her Wimbledon title. Darlene Hard, her doubles partner and the Forest Hills champ, also withdrew and stayed in Paris to care for her friend. Karen Hantze was the only American to reach the women's quarterfinals; Schuurman, who had beaten Haydon, did her in. This was the 75th-anniversary Wimbledon, and through the wreckage came Angela Mortimer and Christine Truman, opponents in the first all-British women's final since 1914.

The crowd adored Truman, a tall and smiling lass with a big forehand and attacking game who epitomized all the best British sporting traits, and they moaned when she fell awkwardly on a rain-slicked court in the third set of the final. That tumble cost her the momentum she had built up against the more defensive Mortimer, who didn't hesitate to lob and drop-shot in a 4–6, 6–4, 7–5 victory.

Hantze, age 18, and bouncing, bubbly Billie Jean Moffitt, 17, won the doubles unseeded, the youngest pair ever to seize a Wimbledon crown. Eighteen years later, Billie Jean Moffitt King's tenth doubles title would give her the all-time record for career Wimbledon titles in all events: 20.

Laver, the red-haired Queenslander called "Rocket" because of the velocity of his shots, won the men's title for the first time, over American Chuck McKinley, 6–3, 6–1, 6–4. This was the start of an unprecedented reign: Laver would win 31 singles matches without a defeat at Wimbledon in five appearances to the fourth round in 1970, winning four singles titles plus a BBC-sponsored pro tournament in 1967. Fraser, who had lost his title in the round of 16 to Englishman Bobby Wilson, captured the doubles with Emerson, but then returned home to Australia to tend to an ailing knee.

Great Britain had both Wimbledon singles finalists and the French champion on its team, but was startlingly ambushed in the Wightman Cup by a "mod squad" of eager American Juniors. Hantze beat Haydon and Truman, Moffitt beat Haydon, and 18-year-old St. Louis lefty Justina Bricka shocked Mortimer, the first British Wimbledon champ since 1937. Hantze-Moffitt clobbered Truman-Deidre Catt, and the U.S. won the final doubles when Mortimer defaulted with foot cramps. Truman's singles win over Moffitt was the only one the shellshocked English could salvage in the 6–1 massacre at Chicago's Saddle and Cycle Club.

Texan Bernard "Tut" Bartzen won his fourth U.S. Clay Court singles since 1954, beating Donald Dell, who earlier in the year had gone with doubles partner Mike Franks on a State Department tour of South Africa, the Middle East, and the Soviet Union, the first Americans to play in Russia since the 1917 Revolution.

McKinley and Dennis Ralston won the rain-delayed U.S. Doubles over Mexicans Rafe Osuna and Antonio Palafox. Hard teamed with Turner for her fourth successive women's doubles title, and was supposed to play with Ralston against Margaret Smith and Bob Mark in the mixed final, at Longwood instead of Forest Hills for the first time. But rain postponed it until after Forest Hills, and Ralston was unable to play because he was suspended for his behavior earlier, in a Davis Cup match against Mexico.

At Forest Hills, Whitney Reed—a spacey, unorthodox player who never trained, partied all night, but had such wonderful touch that he earned the No. 1 U.S. ranking—upset McKinley in the third round. He fell to Osuna, and Dell to Laver, leaving no Americans in the men's semis. Emerson just got by the catlike and clever Osuna, 6–3, 6–2, 3–6,

5–7, 9–7, in a rousing semifinal. Emerson grabbed the first two sets in just 35 minutes, but Osuna kept scrambling for every ball, even making shots from flat on his back. He saved two match points in the fourth set and leveled after trailing 0–3 in the fifth. Finally three fine passing shots brought Emerson to match point again at 8–7, and this time he wouldn't let it get away. Then the speedy and powerful Emerson overwhelmed Laver in the final, 7–5, 6–3, 6–2, to lay claim to the No. 1 ranking among amateurs.

Darlene Hard, the only American in the women's quarterfinals, battled past Ramirez, 6–3, 6–1; Smith, 6–4, 3–6, 6–3; and Haydon in the final, 6–3, 6–4, for her second straight title.

With MacKay and Buchholz professionals, U.S. Davis Cup captain David Freed named a 14-man squad that accented youth. The U.S. beat British West Indies, Ecuador, Mexico (losing Ralston via suspension), and India, but again lost to Italy in the Inter-Zone semifinals, 4–1. Jon Douglas astonishingly upset Fausto Gardini on the clay at Rome's Il Foro Italico, 4–6, 3–6, 7–5, 10–8, 6–0, but Pietrangeli beat Whitney Reed—who trained for the occasion, and later said he couldn't play because of it—2–6, 6–8, 6–4, 6–4, 6–4. Orlando Sirola and Pietrangeli beat Reed and Dell in the doubles, and Pietrangeli spanked Douglas in straight sets to clinch. Gardini came from behind to beat Reed, 3–6, 7–5, 3–6, 8–6, 6–4, as a raucous Italian crowd exulted in his adding to the margin of victory.

Gardini refused to go to Australia for the Challenge Round unless he was assured of a singles berth. However, he wasn't, and Pietrangeli and Sirola never got a set on the grass at Melbourne until Emerson and Laver in singles and Emerson and Fraser in doubles had closed out the Aussie defense of the Cup. The final score was 5–0.

Kramer's expanded traveling circus—with Pancho Gonzales, Lew Hoad, Frank Sedgman, Tony Trabert, Ashley Cooper, Alex Olmedo, Gimeno, MacKay, and Buchholz as the principals and the others "Big Jake" had signed out of spite as lesser lights—did not make enought to cover his vastly increased overhead. Gonzales beat Sedgman, 6–3, 7–5, in Cleveland for his eighth and last U.S. Pro title, but the pros were in trouble, and Kramer's grandstand play of the previous autumn had not helped the cause of open competition.

1962

The Australian grip—both hands firmly around the throat of players of any other nationality—was in vogue in 1962, the season of Rod Laver's first Grand Slam and Margaret Smith's first near-Slam.

Laver duplicated Don Budge's supreme feat of 1938, sweeping the singles titles of Australia, France, Great Britain (Wimbledon), and the United States (Forest Hills). He also won the Italian and German titles, not to mention the less prestigious Norwegian, Irish, and Swiss, and led Australia to a 5–0 blitz of upstart Mexico in the Davis Cup Challenge Round. In all, Laver won 19 of 34 tournaments and 134 of 149 matches during his long and incomparably successful year.

Smith was staggered in the first round of Wimbledon by the pudgy chatterbox who would grow up to be her archrival—Billie Jean Moffitt—but otherwise won just about everything in sight. Smith's only other loss was to another young American, Carole Caldwell, but "Mighty Maggie" won 13 of 15 tournaments, including the Australian, French, and Forest Hills, and 67 of 69 matches.

Laver, the "Rockhampton Rocket" from that Queensland town, started his Slam at White City Stadium in Sydney, beating Roy Emerson, 8–6, 0–6, 6–4, 6–4. Emerson and Neale Fraser took the doubles.

Laver lived precariously in Paris, the only leg of the Slam on slow clay. He saved a match point in beating countryman Marty Mulligan in the quarterfinals, 6–4, 3–6, 2–6, 10–8, 6–2. He also went five sets with Fraser in the semis, 3–6, 6–3, 6–2, 3–6, 7–5, and with Emerson again in the final, 3–6, 2–6, 6–3, 9–7, 6–2. Emerson and Fraser racked up another doubles title.

At Wimbledon, Laver lost only one set, to Manuel Santana in a 14–16, 9–7, 6–2, 6–2 victory. There were no Americans in the

Rod Laver: Grand Slam in 1962. *UPI*

quarterfinals for the first time since 1922. There was hardly room for anyone but Australians: six of them. There were only Aussies in the semis: Laver, Mulligan (who advanced over Emerson, who had an injured toe), Neale Fraser, and his brother John Fraser, a doctor by profession who got an uncommonly lucky draw. Laver beat Neale Fraser, 10–8, 6–1, 7–5, and trampled Mulligan in the final, 6–2, 6–2, 6–1. With Emerson sidelined, Aussies Bob Hewitt and Fred Stolle won the doubles.

At Forest Hills, Laver lost only one set again en route to the final—to gangly American Frank Froehling in a 6–3, 13–11, 4–6, 6–3 quarterfinal victory. The athletic Emerson was back, but Laver repelled him as he had in Sydney, Rome, and Paris. Laver hit four fearsome backhand returns to break serve in the first game and dominated the first two sets with his varied backhand, either bashed or chipped, a topspin forehand, and ruthless serving and net play. Emerson, always barreling forward and battling, aroused a crowd of 9,000 by winning the third set, but Laver closed out the match and the Slam, 6–2, 6–4, 5–7, 6–4, and was greeted by Budge in the marquee.

Astonishingly, there were again no Aussies in the U.S. Doubles final at Longwood, where the "Mexican Thumping Beans," collegians Rafe Osuna and Tony Palafox, out-hustled temperamental Americans Chuck McKinley and Dennis Ralston, reversing the previous year's final result, 6–4, 10–12, 1–6, 9–7, 6–3.

Osuna and Palafox had scored a victory of much greater import over Ralston-McKinley earlier in the year, in the pivotal match of Mexico's 3–2 upset of the U.S. in the Davis Cup. Palafox beat Jon Douglas in the rarefied atmosphere of Mexico City after McKinley had disposed of Osuna in three straight sets in the opener. The doubles point provided the impetus, and then Osuna was carried off on the shoulders of his jubilant countrymen when he outnerved Douglas, 9–7, 6–3, 6–8, 3–6, 6–1, for the clinching 3–1 point. This was the first time Mexico had won the American Zone, and Osuna and Palafox lugged their adoring nation past Yugoslavia, Sweden, and India to the Challenge Round. But Laver and Neale Fraser in singles and Laver-Emerson in doubles had too much serve-and-volley power on the slick grass at Brisbane, winning 5–0.

Margaret Court drubbed Jan Lehane, 6–0, 6–2, in the final of the Australian, but had a much closer final in Paris against another countrywoman, Lesley Turner. Smith had shown she could play on clay too, however— she had won the Italian title as a tune-up— and she prevailed, 6–3, 3–6, 7–5.

By that time Smith, just shy of 20, must have been entertaining thoughts of duplicating the Grand Slam accomplished by only one woman previously, Maureen Connolly in 1953. But 18-year-old Billie Jean Moffitt, who had had a premonition weeks earlier that she would draw Miss Smith in her opening match at Wimbledon, rudely wrecked the dream. It was the first time that the No. 1 seed had failed to survive one round, and established "Little Miss Moffitt" as a force to be reckoned with on the Centre Court that already was her favorite stage.

It was Karen Hantze Susman, with whom Moffitt repeated as doubles champion, who took the singles title at age 19. An outstanding volleyer, Susman captured the title with a 6–4, 6–4 victory over unseeded Vera Sukova of Czechoslovakia, who had scored successive upsets over defending champ Angela Mortimer, Darlene Hard, and Maria Bueno.

Smith was back in form at Forest Hills. With her enormous reach, athleticism, weight of shot, and solid arsenal from the backcourt and net alike, she beat Hard in a nerve-wracking match, 9–7, 6–4, to become the first Australian woman to win the U.S. singles. She saved a set point in the 10th game of the first, and benefited from 16 double faults by Hard, who was perplexed by numerous close line calls and burst into prolonged tears in the sixth game of the second set.

Hard beat Christine Truman, 6–2, 6–2, and Ann Haydon, 6–3, 6–8, 6–4, as the United States edged Britain, 4–3, in the Wightman Cup at Wimbledon. Captain Margaret Osborne duPont, age 44, teamed up with Margaret Varner to show that she could still win at doubles.

While the interest generated by Laver and Smith signaled a banner year for amateur tennis, the pros were struggling. Pancho Gonzalez had retired for the time being, leaving Butch Buchholz to win the U.S. Pro title over Pancho Segura, 6–4, 6–3, 6–4, in Cleveland.

Jack Kramer had also given up the ghost as promoter. "We had all the best players, but the public didn't want to see them," he recalled in *Sports Illustrated*. ". . . There was no acceptance for our players. The conservative and powerful amateur officials were secure. Among other things, they had succeeded in making me the issue. If you were for pro tennis, you were in favor of handing over all of tennis to Jack Kramer. That was the argument."

That is vastly oversimplified, of course. Kramer in many ways had only himself to blame for antagonism. But name-calling aside, the pro game was in sorry shape.

Ken Rosewall was the top dog, but he had little flair for promotion, and the top amateurs no longer were tempted to turn pro and face an uncertain, anonymous future. Under-the-table payments afforded a comfortable if not lavish lifestyle for the top "amateurs." For the first time in the postwar era, there was no pro tour in the United States. Rosewall and

Lew Hoad were contemplating retirement. Their only chance at reviving interest, they thought, was to induce Laver to join them, and they pooled resources and personally guaranteed him $125,000 to come aboard for 1963.

1963

With Rod Laver out of the amateur ranks, another Australian—the peerlessly fit and universally popular Roy Emerson of rural Blackbutt, Queensland—set his sights on the Grand Slam that Laver had achieved in 1962. Emerson won the first two legs, but was thwarted at Wimbledon as Australian supremacy waned. By the end of the year Latin America had scored a unique "double" at Forest Hills, and the United States had both recovered the Davis Cup and captured the inaugural Federation Cup, its women's equivalent.

Politically, it was not a progressive year. With Jack Kramer retired from promoting, amateur officials worldwide felt they had won a battle against some dark specter, and the

Chuck McKinley returned the U.S. to Wimbledon supremacy in 1963 after a long drought. *UPI*

movement for open competition lagged. In the United States, which had supported the principles of "self-determination" and experimentation with open tournaments, the Old Guard reasserted itself and repudiated USLTA president Ed Turville, a supporter of open tennis. The USLTA instructed its delegates to the ILTF to oppose "opens" and "home rule."

Emerson, 26, romped to the Australian title over countryman Ken Fletcher, 6–3, 6–3, 6–1, while Bob Hewitt and Fred Stolle took the doubles. Margaret Smith ritually slaughtered two-fisted Jan Lehane, 6–2, 6–2, for the fourth straight year in the women's final, and teamed with Fletcher to beat Lesley Turner and Stolle in the first leg of a mixed doubles Grand Slam. They took the French, Wimbledon, and U.S. titles as well.

Emerson won the French over the first native to reach the men's final since 1946: the suave and sporting Pierre Darmon, who in the 1970s would return to Roland Garros as tournament director and preside over the greatest period of prosperity in the tournament's history. The scores were 3–6, 6–1, 6–4, 6–4, and Emerson then teamed up with Spaniard Manuel Santana for the doubles title.

Smith's designs on a singles Slam were upset by the steadiness of Vera Sukova, the unseeded Wimbledon finalist of 1962, who was more at home on Parisian clay. The title did remain in Australian hands, however, Lesley Turner beating Ann Haydon Jones, 2–6, 6–3, 7–5. Jones teamed with Renée Schuurman for the doubles trophy.

Wimbledon, which had seen five all-Australian men's singles finals in seven years, got its first American male champion (discounting the Peruvian Alex Olmedo in 1959) since Tony Trabert in 1955: 22-year-old Chuck McKinley, a Missourian attending Trinity University in San Antonio, Texas. He was the first since Trabert to win the title without losing a set, but it was a peculiar year. No seeded players wound up playing each other in the men's singles. Emerson, the favorite, ran into Germany's Wilhelm Bungert on a hot day and was beaten in the quarters, 8–6, 3–6, 6–3, 4–6, 6–3. McKinley, a little but athletic man who charged the net like a toy top gone wild, was too sure in his volleying for Bungert in the semis and Fred Stolle in the final, 9–7, 6–1, 6–4. This was the first of three straight years as runner-up for the tall, angular Stolle, who never did win the singles. Mexican Davis Cuppers Rafe Osuna and Antonio Palafox won the doubles.

Margaret Smith, who had already won four Australian, two Italian, one French, and one U.S. title, became the first Australian woman to win the Wimbledon singles. In the final, she avenged her early defeat by Billie Jean Moffitt the year before, 6–3, 6–4. The title was not decided until the start of the third week because of rain, and thus Miss Smith did not get to dance the traditional champions' first foxtrot with McKinley at the Wimbledon Ball. He was perhaps relieved, since he was four inches shorter than Smith; instead, he guided his wife around the hardwood floor.

The Federation Cup was inaugurated to celebrate the 50th anniversary of the International Lawn Tennis Federation. The United States blanked the Netherlands, Italy, and Great Britain, then upset Australia, 2–1, in the women's international team competition, which drew 16 nations. It was set up to be more compact than the Davis Cup—played in best-of-three (two singles, one doubles) series instead of best-of-five, with all participating countries together at one site for one week. Smith blitzed U.S. No. 1 Darlene Hard, 6–3, 6–0, in the opening match, but then Moffitt upended Turner, 5–7, 6–0, 6–3, and teamed with Hard to take the excruciating doubles from Smith and Turner, 3–6, 13–11, 6–3, at London's Queen's Club.

The U.S. also beat Britain, 6–1, in the Wightman Cup at the Cleveland Skating Club. Ann Jones beat Hard in the opening match, 6–1, 0–6, 8–6, but Moffitt beat Christine Truman, 6–4, 19–17 (the second set a Wightman record) to turn things around for teammates Hard, Nancy Richey, and Donna Floyd Fales. Richey won the first of her six consecutive U.S. Clay Court titles.

For the first time, the U.S. did not have a woman in the semifinals at Forest Hills. Hard, a finalist the last three years and champion twice, was beaten by Jones in the quarters. Even more curious, Australia was shut out of the men's quarterfinals after having had both

finalists in six of the previous seven years.

This was a south-of-the-border year, Rafe Osuna becoming the first Mexican to take the men's singles, and Brazilian Maria Bueno recapturing the women's title she had won in 1959 with a breathtaking display of shotmaking.

Osuna, a gallery favorite because of his quickness of hand, foot, and smile, ousted Wimbledon champ McKinley in the semis and unseeded Floridian Frank Froehling III in the final, 7–5, 6–4, 6–2. Froehling had served devastatingly to upset top seed Emerson, but Osuna cleverly neutralized his power with wonderfully conceived and executed tactics, especially lobbed service returns from 10 to 12 feet behind the baseline. Occasionally Osuna would stand in and take Froehling's serve on the rise, chipping the backhand, but more often he lobbed returns to disrupt Froehling's serve-volley rhythm and break down his suspect overhead. In fact, Osuna climbed the walls of the stadium to retrieve smashes and float back perfect lobs, frustrating Froehling with his nimble speed around the court, touch, and tactical variations.

Bueno was also brilliant, especially in the second set of her 7–5, 6–4 victory over Smith. "With the score 1–4 and 0–30 against her, Miss Bueno set the gallery wild with the dazzling strokes that stemmed from her racket," wrote Allison Danzig in the next morning's New York Times. "Her service was never so strong. Her volleys and overhead smashes were the last word, and she hit blazing winners from the backhand and threw up lobs in an overwhelming assault."

At Longwood, Hard was not able to snag a sixth straight women's doubles title; she and Bueno fell in the final to Smith and Robyn Ebbern. McKinley and Dennis Ralston met Osuna and Palafox for the third straight year in the men's final, saving a match point in recapturing the title, 9–7, 4–6, 5–7, 6–3, 11–9, before a record crowd of 7,000.

That was immediately after they combined to beat Osuna and Palafox, 4–1, in a Davis Cup match at Los Angeles. Captained by Bob Kelleher and coached by Pancho Gonzales, the Americans also conquered Iran, Venezuela, Britain, and India to return to the Challenge Round for the first time in three years.

It had been a long campaign, taxing competitively and medically. Ralston nearly lost an eye in England, McKinley had dysentery in India, Froehling needed his abscessed backside lanced, and McKinley had back spasms. But the squad persevered and took the Cup back from Australia, which had held it in a Melbourne bank vault 11 of the last 13 years.

Ralston beat 19-year-old Cup rookie John Newcombe in five sets in the opening match, and McKinley and Ralston took the key doubles over Emerson and Neale Fraser, 6–3, 3–6, 11–9, 11–9. Emerson kept the Aussies alive to the final match with his second singles win, but McKinley preyed on Newcombe's backhand for the decisive point, 10–12, 6–2, 9–7, 6–2.

In the pro ranks, Laver was beaten regularly by both Ken Rosewall and Lew Hoad, who had staked him to a $125,000 bankroll to try to keep the fading pro game alive. They succeeded, but barely. Rosewall was supreme, beating Laver in the final of the U.S. Pro Championship at Forest Hills, 6–4, 6–2, 6–2, but the tournament went bust, and at presentation time Rosewall got only a handshake.

1964

As if any additional evidence were necessary to prove the depth of tennis talent in Australia, the Davis Cup went back Down Under for the 11th time in 14 years even though three members of the Aussie squad fled to other countries because of an altercation with the autocratic Lawn Tennis Association of Australia.

Roy Emerson, Fred Stolle, Marty Mulligan, Bob Hewitt, and Ken Fletcher were all suspended by the LTAA for the grievous offense of leaving for the overseas tournament circuit earlier than permitted. Emerson and Stolle were reinstated after reaching the Wimbledon final—Emerson beat Stolle in the singles finals of the Australian, Wimbledon, and U.S. Championships in 1964—and they were the core of the raiding party that took the Cup back from the United States in Cleveland, the

Roy Emerson led the Aussie raiding party in 1964. *UPI*

first time a Challenge Round in the U.S. was played out of the East and off grass.

The other three continued to have problems. Mulligan moved to Italy, where he married, became a successful businessman, and played in Davis Cup competition in 1968, nicknamed "Martino Mulligano." (He had been on the Australian squad but had never played, so he was eligible to play for Italy when he became a citizen.) Hewitt married a Johannesburg model and became a mainstay of the South African Davis Cup team, continuing to develop into one of the world's best doubles players. Fletcher took up residence in Hong Kong. It is a measure of the strength of Aussie captain Harry Hopman's production line that Australia won the Cup four years in a row, never missing this trio of talented players.

The affable Emerson—strong enough to quaff beer and sing choruses of "Waltzing Matilda" into the wee hours of the morning, then get up early to train and play magnificently athletic tennis—ruled the amateur world in 1964. He won 55 straight singles matches in one stretch, finishing the year with 17 tournament championships and a 109–6 record, including two singles victories in the Davis Cup Challenge Round.

"Emmo" thumped Stolle in the Australian final, 6–3, 6–4, 6–2; at Wimbledon, 6–4, 12–10, 4–6, 6–3; and at Forest Hills, 6–4, 6–1, 6–4. He also took the French doubles, practically an annual acquisition, with

Fletcher. Hewitt and Stolle took the Australian and Wimbledon doubles, while Chuck McKinley and Dennis Ralston captured the U.S. title at Longwood for the third time in four years, the first three-timers since Bill Talbert and Gardnar Mulloy (1942, 1945–46, 1948).

A preview of America's Davis Cup fate was offered in the most dramatic match of the U.S. Nationals, a quarterfinal in which Ralston fought back from two sets down against Stolle, saved a match point at 3–5 in the fifth, and hauled himself back to 7–7 before the gripping encounter was halted by darkness. Ralston had two break points at 15–40 as Stolle served the first game of the resumption the next morning, but the lean Aussie with the pained gait and delightful wit held and broke Ralston in the next game for the match.

It was the 25-year-old Stolle's 7–5, 6–3, 3–6, 9–11, 6–4, triumph over Ralston on a clay court at newly built and jampacked (7,000 a day, at top dollar) Harold T. Clark Stadium in Cleveland that broke America's back in the Challenge Round. On a gray day, after a long rain delay, they played a majestic match for a national television audience. Ralston saved one match point, serving at 4–5 in the fifth, but Stolle blasted a forehand cross-court passing shot by him on the next. Emerson wrapped up a 3–2 Australian victory the next afternoon, running like a greyhound and whacking piercing ground strokes and volleys to sear McKinley, 3–6, 6–2, 6–4, 6–4, sending the Davis Cup back to Melbourne.

The French, Italian, and German titles, the three biggest on continental clay, all went to Europeans. Manolo Santana beat Nicki Pietrangeli, 6–3, 6–1, 4–6, 7–5, in a rematch of their more memorable meeting in the Parisian final three years earlier. Jan Erik Lundquist of Sweden won in Rome, and Wilhelm Bungert took his national title in Hamburg.

Among the worldly women of tennis, Margaret Smith had an awesome record, losing only two matches during the year, but those were at Wimbledon and Forest Hills. Maria Bueno won those titles, and thus took back the No. 1 world ranking that illness and Smith had stripped from her.

Smith beat her countrywoman Lesley Turner, 6–3, 6–2, in the Australian singles, and Bueno, 5–7, 6–1, 6–2, at Paris. Bueno beat Smith only once in three meetings, but it was the most important: the final at Wimbledon, 6–4, 7–9, 6–3. This was a match of almost unbearable tension, a patchwork of glorious shots and awful ones, and Bueno ultimately controlled her nerves better. Smith seemed more serene beforehand, but her anxiety showed in her usually oppressive serve. She was a little tentative, and double-faulted badly on several key points. "I guess I beat myself. I felt pressure all the way," she said afterward. "It was like beating my head against a wall."

Karen Hantze Susman, the 1962 Wimbledon champion who was back for a fling after temporary retirement for childbirth, troubled Smith in the first round at Wimbledon and beat her in the fourth round at Forest Hills. That paved the way for Bueno, who raced through the championship without losing a set. In the final she met surprising Carole Caldwell Graebner, who had resolutely upset Susman and Nancy Richey despite suffering from painful second-degree sunburns of the arms, face, and hands. In the final, it was not the sun's rays but Bueno who blistered her, 6–1, 6–0, in just 25 minutes.

Bueno thus usurped Smith's throne as the No. 1 player, even though her record of 82–10 and seven titles was not quite as formidable as Smith's 67–2 and 13 championships. Smith had a 39-match winning streak at one point in the season.

Lesley Turner blended with Judy Tegart to win the Australian doubles and with Smith to win at Paris and Wimbledon, but she was denied a Grand Slam in the finals of the U.S. Championships by Susman and Billie Jean Moffitt, 3–6, 6–2, 6–4.

With Darlene Hard, the U.S. No. 1 of the past four years, retired to a teaching pro career, the United States relinquished the Federation Cup to Australia, 2–1, in the final of a 24-nation assemblage in Philadelphia. Smith beat Moffitt, 6–2, 6–3, and Turner did in top-ranked American Nancy Richey, 7–5, 6–1, rendering Moffitt-Susman's three-set victory over Smith-Turner meaningless.

Richey and Moffitt won both their singles, over Deidre Catt and Ann Haydon Jones, and Carole Graebner added a victory over Elizabeth Starkie as the U.S. swept the singles and the Wightman Cup at Wimbledon, 5–2.

Most of the men pros were scattered around the globe, playing the odd exhibition here and there, badly disorganized. Ken Rosewall, the pro king, was observed playing Pancho Segura in a shopping-center parking lot in Los Angeles.

One who thought this was wrong was Ed Hickey of the New England Merchants National Bank in Boston, who convinced his boss to put up $10,000 in sponsorship money to revive the U.S. Pro Championship. John Bottomley, president of Longwood Cricket Club, threw his support to the project. Jack Kramer was enlisted to contact the farflung gypsies and put together a short summer tournament circuit with $80,000 in prize money. A dozen pros were assembled, and Rod Laver won the climactic event at Longwood over Pancho Gonzales, 4–6, 6–3, 7–5, 6–4, in a rainstorm that turned the grass into a quagmire.

It was a humble renaissance, but the U.S. Pro was to become a fixture at Longwood, as was Laver. He won there four more times. It wasn't strawberries-and-cream, à la Wimbledon, but the pros were on the rocky road to a comeback.

1965

The gloom of a drizzly, gray September afternoon in Forest Hills was pierced by Spanish singing and dancing, and the unmistakable click of castanets filled the old cement stadium of the West Side Tennis Club. There were loud choruses of "¡Olé!" and "¡Bravo, Manolo!" The discreet charm of the bourgeoisie that so long characterized tennis audiences gave way to unabashed Latin celebration as Manuel Santana beat South African Cliff Drysdale in four absorbing sets, 6–2, 7–9, 7–5, 6–1, to become the first Spaniard to win the U.S. singles title.

The balletic and crowd-pleasing Santana, age 28, provided other occasions for rejoicing in 1965, but few places came alive as Forest

The Spanish reign: Manuel Santana defeats South Africa's Cliff Drysdale for the 1965 U.S. Singles crown. *UPI*

Hills did when a troupe of entertainers from the Spanish Pavilion at the nearby World's Fair arrived to urge him on with an up-tempo Latin beat. Santana was arguably the No. 1 amateur in the world, winning 10 of 16 tournaments, compiling a 71–7 record, and a 25-match winning streak, longest of the season. He did not enter Wimbledon, devoting his summer instead to Davis Cup preparation and duty on clay. Such diligence paid off. Santana and teammates Juan Gisbert and José Luis Arilla bumped off the United States in the Inter-Zone semifinals in Barcelona and carried Spain to the Challenge Round for the first time.

Not that Spanish music replaced "Waltzing Matilda" as the anthem of the world tennis empire. Australia won the Cup again, for the 14th time since 1950, as Roy Emerson and Fred Stolle gunned down Santana & Company, 4–1, at Sydney. Australians also captured the Federation Cup and all the other Grand Slam singles titles, men's and women's. Most of the finals were all-Aussie affairs.

Emerson outslugged Stolle, who seemed

capable of beating anybody else, from two sets down in the Australian final, 7–9, 2–6, 6–4, 7–5, 6–1. John Newcombe and Tony Roche, the latest in a long line of great Aussie pairs, took their first major doubles title.

Roche, a ruggedly muscular left-hander with an unerring backhand volley, spoiled Emerson's vision of a Grand Slam in the French semifinals. With his chief nemesis out of the way, Stolle prevailed in Paris over Roche, 3–6, 6–0, 6–2, 6–3—winning his first major title after being runner-up in one Australian, two Wimbledons, and one Forest Hills. Emerson and Stolle took the doubles, Emerson's sixth in a row in Paris with five partners.

Emerson powered his way through the Wimbledon draw again, a *tour de force* justifying his top seeding, and made Stolle the bridesmaid for the third consecutive year. This time it was easier than in 1964, 6–2, 6–4, 6–4. Newcombe and Roche won the first of their five Wimbledon doubles titles together.

At Forest Hills, where there had been all-Aussie finals seven of the last nine years, none of the men from Down Under made the semis, however. Charlie Pasarell ambushed Stolle in the second round, and Arthur Ashe, who was to gain the No. 2 U.S. ranking behind Dennis Ralston, delivered big serves and fatal backhands in enough glorious clusters to topple Emerson.

Santana, shrewdly changing speeds and spins as he danced around the turf, erased Ashe in a four-set semifinal. Drysdale, who had beaten Ralston in a five-set quarterfinal, got by Mexican Rafe Osuna in the other half. Santana vs. Drysdale was thoughtful tennis, much of it from the backcourt, between two intelligent and stylish men. Rain interrupted the match and made the footing slick, but it couldn't dampen Santana's flashing shotmaking or the castanets.

Emerson and Stolle were unbeaten in doubles on the U.S. circuit, winning six tournaments and 31 matches, a run climaxed by a 6–4, 10–12, 7–5, 6–4 triumph over Pasarell and Frank Froehling in the National Doubles final at Longwood.

Emerson won seven of 22 tournaments in singles for an 85–16 record. He was 0–2 against Santana, demolished on clay in the Swedish Championship final and edged, 2–6, 6–3, 6–3, 15–13, on grass at Sydney in the Davis Cup final. Emmo's win over Gisbert, Stolle's over Santana in the opener, and Newcombe-Roche's over Arilla-Santana in the doubles had already given Australia a 3–0 lead and continued possession of the Cup.

Spain had similarly won the first three matches against the U.S., heralding three years of nightmares for the Americanos on red clay in Latin countries. Chuck McKinley had retired to stockbrokering, leaving Ralston to head the U.S. contingent, and it was his demise to the inspired play of Gisbert after leading 6–3, 4–1 that paved the way for a 4–1 U.S. defeat. Santana jolted Froehling in three straight sets and joined with Arilla to break the hearts of Ralston and Clark Graebner, 4–6, 3–6, 6–3, 6–4, 11–9.

Australia beat the United States, 2–1, in the final of the Federation Cup at Kooyong in Melbourne. Lesley Turner beat Carole Graebner, 6–3, 2–6, 6–3, and Margaret Smith stopped Billie Jean Moffitt, 6–4, 8–6, in the singles.

Smith, 23, won three of the "Big Four" singles titles in one season for the second time in her still ascending career. She beat Maria Bueno, who retired with an injury while trailing 2–5 in the final set in the Australian final; Bueno again at Wimbledon, 6–4, 7–5; and Moffitt at Forest Hills, 8–6, 7–5. The only match that prevented her from a Grand Slam was the final of the French, which she lost to Turner, 6–3, 6–4. After that, Smith didn't lose another all year, piling up 58 consecutive victories for a season record of 103–7, including 18 titles in 25 tournaments.

Bueno, 25, won the Italian Championship and two other of the 11 tournaments she entered, finishing 40–8 in a year in which she was hampered by a knee injury that required surgery. She played Forest Hills against the advice of her doctor, losing to Moffitt in the semis.

Moffitt led Smith by 5–3 in both sets of the Forest Hills final, and had two set points in the second. Even though she lost, Moffitt

Maria Bueno (left) and Billie Jean Moffitt won the Wimbledon doubles in 1965, marking the fourth time that the Brazilian beauty had been a winner in this event. *UPI*

later said this was a turning-point match in her career, adding a great deal to her self-awareness. She knew that the forehand she had gone to Australia to rebuild from scratch the previous year was coming around, complementing her exquisite backhand and volleying, and that she had the ability to rival Smith for No. 1. Billie Jean married Larry King shortly after Forest Hills, and she knew she was coming of age as a player.

She was coranked No. 1 in the U.S. with Nancy Richey, an unprecedented decision by the USLTA ranking committee. Moffitt had shone on the grass court circuit, which Richey avoided after winning the National Indoors and Clay Courts. Both were 1–1 in singles in the 5–2 U.S. victory over Britain in the Wightman Cup.

Richey and Carole Graebner (whose husband, Clark, ranked No. 13 among U.S. men and would return to the Top Ten the next year) earned the top U.S. ranking in doubles after winning the Nationals at Longwood.

They beat defending champs Moffitt and Karen Susman in the final, 6–4, 6–4.

Turner teamed with Judy Tegart to win the Australian doubles and with Smith to take the French. Moffitt captured her third title at Wimbledon with her second partner, Maria Bueno. Smith and Ken Fletcher won the French, Wimbledon, and U.S. mixed doubles. They might well have repeated their 1963 Grand Slam, but the mixed final of the Australian was abandoned because of bad weather.

The itinerant pros of tennis were still trying to organize, Mike Davies, Butch Buchholz, and Barry MacKay among the driving forces behind the "International Professional Tennis Players' Association," organized in 1965 to try to give some structure to the amorphous, struggling pro game. The U.S. Pro Championship returned to Longwood, Ken Rosewall regaining the title he had won in 1963—and getting paid, albeit modestly, this time—by beating Rod Laver, 6–4, 6–3, 6–3.

Patrician scoring reformer James Van Alen of Newport, Rhode Island, whose "Van Alen Streamlined Scoring System" (VASSS) became the basis for "sudden death" tie-breakers in 1970, hosted a pro tournament at famed Newport Casino, where the U.S. Championships had been played from their inauguration in 1881 until 1914. Van Alen put up $10,000 in prize money, on the condition that the pros use his radical VASSS round-robin, medal-play format, in which every point counted and was worth $5. The players were happy to play any way as long as they were paid, though Pancho Segura spoke for most of his colleagues when he disparaged the Van Alen system, saying "It seems half-VASSS to me."

1966

If variety is indeed the spice of life, 1966 was a flavorful year for international tennis. There were no one-man or one-woman gangs, as the game's major titles got spread around. For the first time since 1948, no player, man or woman, captured more than one of the Grand Slam singles crowns.

Fred Stolle, thought to be past his prime at

Australia's Fred Stolle, unseeded, defeated country-men Roy Emerson in the semis and John New-combe in the final to win at Forest Hills in 1966. *UPI*

age 27, didn't win a single tournament until August, then came on like the old Australian Mafia. He won the German Championship on clay and took the U.S. title at Forest Hills unseeded. There he routed nemesis Roy Emerson in the semifinals, 6–4, 6–1, 6–1, with an astounding display of power and con-trol, and withstood 21 aces served by the similarly unseeded John Newcombe to win the final, 4–6, 12–10, 6–3, 6–4. Thereafter Stolle won tournaments in California on ce-ment and Australia on grass, and beat both Ramanathan Krishnan and Jaidip Mukerjea as Australia pummeled India, 4–1, in the Davis Cup Challenge Round. That was the climax of his amateur career as he turned pro at the end of the year.

Stolle's Davis Cup accomplice, Emerson, started the year by grabbing his national championship for the fourth consecutive time. In the final he extinguished Arthur Ashe—who had burned up the Australian circuit, winning four of seven tournaments—6–4, 6–8, 6–2, 6–3. Emmo teamed with Stolle to

win the doubles, and they went on to post the year's best doubles record, adding the Italian, South African, and U.S. Championships.

Emerson was perhaps never in better condi-tion or form than at the start of Wimbledon, where he was keen to become the first man to win three successive singles titles since Fred Perry in 1934–36. He looked as if he would until fate and his own eagerness intervened during his quarterfinal against fellow Aussie Owen Davidson. Richard Evans described what happened in *World Tennis*:

"The first set took Emerson precisely 14 minutes to win 6–1. His first service was going in, his volleys were crisp and accurate, his ground-strokes laden with power and spin. There was no danger in sight unless it lay in the greasy, rain-slicked turf and of this, surely, Emerson was aware. So it surprised many people when he raced for a Davidson drop-volley in the third game of the second set. And it horrified us all when he skidded headlong into the umpire's chair and brought the BBC microphone crashing down on top of him. He was up in a moment, flexing his left shoulder and telling Davidson that he thought he had heard something snap. In fact he had torn the shoulder ligaments—an injury that, in a fatal second, had shattered a dream, ruined weeks of arduous preparation and deprived Wimbledon of its champion."

Manuel Santana, the clay court artist who had proved himself a man for all surfaces by winning Forest Hills on grass the previous year, inherited the throne that Emerson abdi-cated, and he was a popular champion. Grin-ning and playing extraordinary shots when behind, he beat Ken Fletcher and then David-son, both in deuced fifth sets, to get to the final. There he eliminated Dennis Ralston, who had more firepower but less control, 6–4, 11–9, 6–4.

Santana had his own problems with injuries during the season, though—a bad shoulder that plagued him as Spain, the 1965 runner-up, went out to Brazil in the Davis cup elim-ination rounds, and a bad ankle that reduced his Forest Hills defense to a limp.

It was not Santana but Australian lefty Tony Roche who was the 1966 man of the year on clay. He won the Italian and French singles, beating Hungarian roadrunner Istvan Gulyas in the Paris final, 6–1, 6–4, 7–5. Thereafter ankle problems sapped his effectiveness as well.

So who was the world's No. 1 amateur? Take your pick. Stolle won four of 19 tournaments, 70 of 85 matches; Emerson won eight of 16 tournaments, including the rising South African Championships, and 67 of 78 singles; Santana was 52–16, winning only two of 17 tournaments, but one of those was the biggest: Wimbledon; Roche played the most ambitious schedule, winning 10 of 29 tournaments and 106 of 125 matches.

Ralston, generally considered No. 5 in the world, was top-ranked in the U.S. for the third year in a row, the first man so honored since Don Budge in 1936–38, but frustrated by his failure to win a Grand Slam singles title. He turned pro with Stolle at the end of the year, leaving Ashe—a lieutenant in the U. S. Army—as heir apparent.

Ralston did have one particularly satisfying doubles triumph, teaming with Clark Graebner to become the first American champions of France since 1955. Their final-round victims, little known until later, were the hulking Romanian Ion Tiriac and his wet-behind-the-ears but gifted protégé, Ilie Nastase. Ralston and Graebner were runners-up for the U.S. title at Longwood to Emerson-Stolle, 6–4, 6–4, 6–4. Newcombe, separated from regular partner Roche, won the Wimbledon doubles anyway, with Ken Fletcher.

It was a dark year for the U.S. in the Davis cup as Captain George MacCall's team was bushwhacked, 3–2, by unheralded Brazil at Porto Alegre. Cliff Richey was upset in singles by both Edison Mandarino and Tom Koch, and Mandarino took Ralston in the fifth match, 4–6, 6–4, 4–6, 6–4, 6–1.

The most successful American player was the No. 1 woman, Billie Jean King, who won her first Wimbledon singles title at age 23 and spearheaded successful team efforts in the Federation and Wightman Cups. A virus infection diminished her effectiveness later, but Billie Jean won 10 of 16 tournaments and compiled a 57–8 record, best in the world.

Nancy Richey, co-ranked No. 1 with Billie

Jean in 1965, slipped to No. 2 despite reaching the finals of the Australian, French, and U.S. singles, and winning six of 14 tournaments, with a 55–9 record. She also won her fourth straight U.S. Clay Court title (her younger brother Cliff won the men's title for an unprecedented family "double"), and won three of the "Big Four" doubles titles: the Australian with Carole Graebner, and Wimbledon and the U.S. with Maria Bueno.

Margaret Smith won her seventh consecutive Australian singles title, by default over Richey, and her third consecutive French doubles (with Judy Tegart), but was increasingly burdened by the pressure and loneliness of big-time tennis competition. Shortly after being beaten by King, 6–3, 6–3, in the semifinals of Wimbledon, she announced her retirement at age 24 to open a dress boutique in Perth—the first of several short-lived retirements, as it turned out.

Ann Haydon Jones won her second French singles over Richey, 6–3, 6–1, the American having spent herself in a semifinal victory over Smith.

King was magnificently aggressive at Wimbledon, grass staining her knees on the low volleys she played better than anyone else, as her husband of less than a year sat nervously in the competitors' guest stand. Having dispatched one old rival, Smith, in the semis, she did in another, Bueno, in the final, 6–3, 3–6, 6–1, then tossed her racket high in the air and squealed with glee.

King, Julie Heldman, and Carole Graebner carried the United States to a 3–0 victory over surprise finalist West Germany in the Federation Cup on clay at Turin, Italy. King, Richey, Mary Ann Eisel, and Jane Albert were the Americans who played in a 4–3 Wightman Cup victory over Great Britain at Wimbledon. Richey and Eisel contributed the decisive point in doubles, over Elizabeth Starkie and Rita Bentley.

Maria Bueno captured her fourth Forest Hills title—the last of her seven Grand Slam singles crowns—by beating Richey, 6–3, 6–1, with an all-court display of grace and shotmaking magic that completely thwarted Richey's backcourt game. They had teamed for the doubles title at Longwood, 6–3, 6–4, over the new but potent partnership of King and Rosemary Casals, but in the singles final Bueno treated Richey more like a stranger, winning in just 50 minutes. The best match of the tournament had been Bueno's 6–2, 10–12, 6–3 victory over the diminutive, 17-year-old Casals, a feast of dazzling footwork and shot-making that captivated a crowd of 14,000.

Also noteworthy in 1966 were the longest matches on record in major competition: Roger Taylor of Britain defeated Wieslaw Gasiorek of Poland, 27–29, 31–29, 6–4, on a slick wood surface in a King's Cup match that stretched until the early hours of a bitterly cold Warsaw morning, and American Kathy Blake outlasted Elena Subirats of Mexico, 12–10, 6–8, 14–12, on grass at the Piping Rock Country Club.

The pros had decided to cast their fate to small tournament-format events rather than head-to-head tours, as in the past, but the going was still rough. The U.S. Pro at Long-wood remained an encouraging beacon, light-ing the future, and Rod Laver signaled his takeover from Ken Rosewall as the pro king, beating "Muscles," 6–4, 4–6, 6–2, 8–10, 6–3.

1967

By sweeping the singles titles at Wimble-don and Forest Hills, Australian John New-combe and Californian Billie Jean King reigned as the king and queen of amateur tennis in 1967, the last year of the amateur era. By the end of the year two professional troupes—World Championship Tennis (WCT) and the National Tennis League (NTL)—had been formed, Newcombe and a half dozen other leading amateur men had turned pro, and a successful eight-man pro tournament had been played on the Centre Court at Wim-bledon. These were all factors in a rebellion destined to change forever the old order in tennis.

The call to revolution was sounded in De-cember 1967. Despite a threat of expulsion from the International Lawn Tennis Federa-tion, which had again voted against Open Tennis at its midyear annual meeting, the

Billie Jean King and John Newcombe display their silver in 1967 after winning the U.S. Singles Championships at Forest Hills. *UPI*

British Lawn Tennis Association voted at year's end to remove the distinction between amateur and professional players in their country. It declared that tournaments in Brit-ain in 1968, including Wimbledon, would be open to pros and amateurs alike. This hard-line stand by one of its oldest and most influ-ential member nations ultimately forced the ILTF's hand on the "open" question that had been festering for four decades. Progressives, when they got the enormous prestige of Wim-bledon behind them, finally carried the day.

Early in the year, such upheaval did not seem to be in prospect. The U.S. Lawn Ten-nis Association hired Robert Malaga, a suc-cessful promoter of Wightman Cup and Davis Cup matches in his hometown of Cleveland, as its first full-time executive secretary and signed a product-endorsement agreement with Licensing Corporation of America.

The competitive year began the same way the previous four had, with Roy Emerson winning his native Australian singles title. Arthur Ashe was his victim in the final for the second straight year, this time in straight sets: 6–4, 6–1, 6–4. The triumph was Emerson's sixth in seven years, but he was unable to defend his doubles crown. Newcombe and Tony Roche, who would go on to win the French and U.S. doubles as well, beat Owen Davidson and Bill Bowrey in a rousing final, 3–6, 6–3, 7–5, 6–8, 8–6.

Nancy Richey, runner-up as Margaret Smith won her seventh consecutive singles title the year before, took advantage of Margaret's temporary retirement to capture the women's title with a 6–1, 6–4 triumph over Lesley Turner. Turner and Judy Tegart captured the doubles.

Turner upended Maria Bueno, 6–3, 6–3, in the Italian final and won the first set of the French final before losing it to Françoise Durr, whose 4–6, 6–3, 6–4 victory was the first by a native woman at Paris since Simone Mathieu in 1939. Durr teamed with Australian Gail Sheriff, who was later to marry Frenchman Jean Baptiste Chanfreau and move to France, for the first of five consecutive doubles titles—two with Ann Jones and then two more with Mme. Chanfreau.

Emerson, fit as ever, powered his way to the French men's singles title, dethroning fellow Aussie Roche in the final, 6–1, 6–4, 2–6, 6–2. Roche had earlier lost his Italian title to Marty "Martino Mulligano" Mulligan.

Having cleared the troublesome hurdle of Parisian clay, Emerson set his sights on the elusive Grand Slam, but his vision was shattered in the fourth round at Wimbledon by tall Yugoslav Nikki Pilic. Emerson was the favorite after the startling first-round ambush of Manolo Santana by American Charlie Pasarell in the curtain-raiser on Centre Court, the first time a defending champion and No. 1 seed was ever beaten in the first round at Wimbledon.

That was the prelude to an upset-filled fortnight. By the quarterfinals, there were no seeded players left in the top half of the draw. The only meeting of seeds came in the quarterfinals, No. 3 Newcombe overpowering No. 6 Ken Fletcher. Pilic and rugged Yorkshireman Roger Taylor, both left-handers, were unseeded semifinalists, as was Germany's Wilhelm Bungert.

Bungert erased Taylor, but was spent by the final and offered only token, halfhearted resistance as Newcombe claimed the title, 6–3, 6–1, 6–1, equaling the most lopsided postwar men's finals (Lew Hoad over Ashley Cooper in 1957 and Rod Laver over Mulligan in 1962).

In doubles, Newcombe and Roche—re-united and favored to regain the title—fell in the quarters to Englishmen Graham Stilwell and Peter Curtis. The title went to the newly minted South African Davis Cup team of Bob Hewitt (who, as an Australian, had won twice with Fred Stolle) and Frew McMillan. They drubbed Emerson and Fletcher, winner the previous year with Newcombe, 6–2, 6–3, 6–4.

Cumulative attendance for the last amateur Wimbledon exceeded 300,000 for the first time, as 301,896 spectators went through the turnstiles.

Newcombe took the No. 1 world ranking at age 23 by winning eight of 24 tournaments and 83 of 99 matches. A sciatic nerve condition nearly cost him the U.S. Doubles championship, which was decided for the 50th and last time at Longwood Cricket Club, but he and Roche pulled through over Bowrey and Davidson. His lower back was still worrying "Newc" going into the U.S. singles, but he experienced no ill effects in plowing to victory at Forest Hills with the loss of but four sets.

It was Emerson who was plagued first by back problems, then by torn thigh muscles suffered in his quarterfinal loss to Clark Graebner. Graebner, one of several players using the new steel T-2000 racket recently introduced by Wilson Sporting Goods, crunched 25 aces in his 8–6, 3–6, 19–17, 6–1 victory, and three in a row from 30–40 to end his scintillating 3–6, 3–6, 7–5, 6–4, 7–5 semifinal victory over Jan Leschly, the clever and sporting left-handed Dane. Newcombe outslugged Graebner, seeking to become the first native champ since 1955, in a serve-and-volley final, 6–4, 6–4, 8–6.

Sharing attention with the winners at Forest Hills were the much-publicized steel rackets used by women's champ Billie Jean King, Rosemary Casals, Graebner, and Gene Scott, among others. Wilson's equipment innovation, adapted from a French design pioneered by clothier and ex-champion René Lacoste, was the harbinger of a wave of new racket designs and materials that flooded the market in the next decade. Scott, then a 29-year-old Wall Street lawyer and part-time player who would later become the self-styled Renaissance Man of pro tennis in the 70s, fulfilled many a Walter Mitty fantasy by working mornings in his office and taking the train to Forest Hills, where he reached the semis before Newcombe jolted him back to reality. Scott predicted that wood rackets would soon be obsolete, but his prophecy did not come to pass.

Woman-of-the-year in tennis in 1967 was Billie Jean Moffitt King, 24, who scored "triples"—victories in singles, doubles, and mixed doubles—at both Wimbledon and Forest Hills. Only Don Budge in 1938 and Alice Marble in 1939 had achieved this feat previously.

Billie Jean also won all her singles in leading the United States to victories in the Federation and Wightman Cups. She teamed with Rosie Casals to sweep past Rhodesia, South Africa, Germany, and Great Britain without losing a match in the Fed Cup on clay at Berlin, and with Nancy Richey, Carole Graebner, and Mary Ann Eisel for a 6–1 triumph over Great Britain at Cleveland. Richey won the decisive fourth point with a gritty 3–6, 8–6, 6–2 victory over Virginia Wade despite a pulled muscle in her back that pained her through the last six games.

King compiled a 68–5 record during the ranking season and won 10 tournaments. In addition to seizing the Wimbledon and Forest Hills titles without losing a set, she won the U.S. Indoors and the South African Championship, and had the season's two longest winning streaks: 23 and 25 matches. In Johannesburg she scored another "triple," teaming triumphantly with Casals (her partner in U.S. and Wimbledon doubles victories) and Aussie Owen Davidson (her partner in French, Wimbledon, and U.S. Mixed Doubles Championships). Davidson scored a Mixed Grand Slam, having first teamed with Lesley Turner to win the Australian title.

King beat Ann Jones, the tenacious British left-hander, in the Wimbledon final (6–3, 6–4) and again in the Forest Hills title match (11–9, 6–4). In the latter, Jones ignored a pulled hamstring and gallantly fought off nine match points before succumbing. Injuries had influenced the women's singles from the outset, four-time champion Maria Bueno pulling

out with tendinitis in the right arm and Nancy Richey with the back ailment sustained in the Wightman Cup.

Richey had earlier won her fifth consecutive U.S. Clay Court title, gunning down Casals after little Rosie conquered King in the semis. Arthur Ashe, whose duties as a lieutenant in the U. S. Army kept him out of Wimbledon and Forest Hills, won the men's title for the only time, beating Marty Riessen. Ashe was ranked second in the U.S. behind Pasarell, who beat him twice in three meetings: in the finals of the U.S. Indoors and in the Richmond Indoors, in Ashe's hometown.

The U.S. outdoor season saw what is believed to be the longest (147 games) tournament match of all time, in the doubles of the Newport (R.I.) Casino Invitational. Dick Leach and Dick Dell defeated Len Schloss and Tom Mozur, 3–6, 49–47, 22–20. The marathon consumed six hours and 10 minutes over two days, and undoubtedly provided impetus for the scoring reform championed by Newport's Jimmy Van Alen—whose "sudden death" tie-breaker, designed to terminate such monster matches, was finally adopted in 1970.

For the third consecutive year under hapless captain George MacCall, the U.S. Davis Cup team was upset on foreign soil—slow, red clay. The 1967 loss to Ecuador at Guayaquil was the most ignominious of all, undoubtedly the most startling upset in the long history of Davis Cup competition. Ecuador's two players, Pancho Guzman and Miguel Olvera, were barely known internationally.

Cliff Richey, the most comfortable of the Americans on clay, won the first and inconsequential fifth matches, but the middle three spelled disaster for the United States. Olvera, a 26-year-old who had been sidelined by tuberculosis, beat Ashe—who had not lost a set in his 10 previous Cup matches—4–6, 6–4, 6–4, 6–2. Ecuadorian captain Danny Carrera was so thrilled he attempted to leap the net to embrace Olvera, tripped, and broke his leg. Still, the 1–1 score did not seem too worrisome for the U.S. until the scrambling Olvera and his 21-year-old sidekick Guzman overcame a 0–6, 2–5, deficit and stunned Americans Riessen and Graebner, 0–6, 9–7, 6–4, 4–6, 8–6, setting the stage for a raucous third day. The giddy crowd of 2,200 at the Guaya-quil Tennis Club cheered wildly for their sud-den heroes and unsettled the Americans with a shower of abuse. Panic set in on MacCall as the slow-balling Guzman withstood two rushes from Ashe and won the decisive match by a score as bizarre as the whole series: 0–6, 6–4, 6–2, 0–6, 6–3.

With the U.S. out, South Africa was ex-pected to reach the Challenge Round against Australia. Bob Hewitt, Cliff Drysdale, and young Ray Moore gave the South Africans three formidable singles players, and Hewitt-McMillan was the doubles team of the year. (Their 53–1 record included victories in the Italian, Wimbledon, and South African Cham-pionships, plus seven other tournaments. Newcombe-Roche won 12 of 19 tournaments, including the Australian, French, and U.S.)

But Hewitt broke his ankle in the quarterfi-nal series against India and was unavailable for the semis, in which Spain eliminated South Africa, 3–2. In Australia for the Chal-lenge Round for the second time in three years, Spain was outclassed again. Emerson took advantage of one of Santana's rare poor matches and won the opener in a rout, 6–4, 6–1, 6–1. Newcombe swamped 18-year-old Cup rookie Manuel Orantes, 6–3, 6–3, 6–2, then teamed with Roche to scald Santana-Orantes, 6–4, 6–4, 6–4, losing only 16 points in 15 service games. The 3–0 lead assured Australia's 15th Cup victory in 18 years.

Emerson blasted Orantes, ending a peerless Davis Cup career in which he won 11 of 12 singles matches plus six doubles matches in nine Challenge Rounds, eight of them won by Australia. Newcombe's last match as an ama-teur was not as successful. He lost to San-tana, making the final score 4–1.

Immediately after the Challenge Round, Newcombe, Roche, Emerson, and Davidson turned pro. Newcombe and Roche signed with New Orleans promoter Dave Dixon, who—bankrolled by Texas oilman Lamar Hunt and his nephew, Al Hill, Jr.—had founded World Championship Tennis, Inc. Emerson signed with George MacCall, who had corralled Rod Laver, Ken Rosewall, Pancho Gonzales, An-dres Gimeno (runner-up to Laver in the U.S. Pro final), Fred Stolle, and a few others for

his National Tennis League. Davidson became the pro at the All England Club and Britain's national coach.

The formation of WCT's "Handsome Eight" barnstorming troupe had an enormous impact on the amateur tennis establishment. In one day, Dixon and his partner Bob Briner, a tennis neophyte who would later become executive director of the Association of Tennis Professionals, signed Newcombe, Roche, Nikki Pilic, and Roger Taylor, ac-counting for three of the 1967 Wimbledon semifinalists. Dennis Ralston had been their first signee, and they soon added Cliff Drys-dale, Butch Buchholz, and Pierre Barthes.

"We had in one fell swoop taken all the stars out of the game. . . . If anyone was ever going to see them again at Wimbledon and Forest Hills, the ILTF had to make an accom-modation," Briner remembers. "Open tennis came about so fast after that, it was pitiful."

The stage for the "British Revolution" that ultimately pierced the reactionary armor of the ILTF had been set for some time. The press was agitating against the hypocrisy of the "shamateur" system. For years Herman David, chairman of the All England Club, had denounced shamateurism as "a living lie" and urged open competition. He allowed Wimbledon's Centre Court to be used for an eight-man pro tournament sponsored and tele-vised by the British Broadcasting Corporation in August 1967. Laver, who had won 14 straight singles matches at Wimbledon in his last amateur appearances (1961–62), beat Rosewall in a final of much higher standard than Newcombe's romp over Bungert a month earlier. This whetted the public's appetite for open tennis.

When the ILTF, at its 1967 annual meeting in Luxembourg, turned down by a 139–83 vote a British proposal for a limited number of open tournaments in 1968, the British re-fused to accept the verdict.

"It seems that we have come to the end of the road constitutionally," said Herman David, who vowed that Wimbledon would continue to be the world's premier tourna-ment, with a field commensurate with that reputation, even if it had to "go it alone" as a pioneer of open competition. Britain's LTA took an unconstitutional, revolutionary step by voting overwhelmingly at its December meeting to make British tournaments open in '68.

The ILTF threatened to expel the British from the international organization, but its hand had been forced. A number of compromises later, open tennis became a reality in 1968, though in a much more limited and qualified way than the British had envisioned.

5 } THE OPEN ERA 1968–1979

In the 1970s, tennis became truly the "in" sport of the great middle class, first in the United States, then abroad. In a single decade, the sport threw off and trampled its starched white flannel past and became a favored diversion of not the masses, but the modern leisure class—attired in pastels and playing tie-breaker sets in public parks and clubs. They were equipped with a bewildering variety of gear, from optic yellow, heavy-duty balls to double-strung graphite rackets.

All this was inspired by the advent of Open Tennis in 1968. If competition between amateur and professionals did not trigger the tennis boom single-handedly, it unquestionably fueled it. By making tennis at the top level professional, honest, and unabashedly commercial, open competition ushered in an era of dramatic growth and development.

For an expanding group of pros, this was boomtime, a veritable bonanza of opportunities. They enjoyed and reaped the benefits of a Brave New World of televised matches and two-fisted backhands, evolution of technique and technology, full-blown tours for women and over-45s, exposure and prize money undreamed of even by Wimbledon champions in the pre-open era.

1968

The advent of "open competition" between amateurs and professionals, some 40 years after the issue was first raised, made 1968 truly a watershed year for tennis.

The British "revolt" of December 1967, reinforced by the USLTA's vote in favor of Open Tennis at its annual meeting in February 1968, led to the emergency meeting of the ILTF at Paris and approval of 12 open tournaments for 1968.

Unfortunately, the hypocrisy and confusion of the "shamateur" period was not done away with quickly and cleanly. Rather than accept the British proposal that all competitors would be referred to simply as "players," abolishing the distinction between amateur and professional, the ILTF bowed to heavy pressure from Eastern European countries and their voting allies and effected a compromise that called for four classifications:

1. Amateurs, who would not accept prize money.

2. Teaching professionals, who could compete with amateurs only in open events.

3. "Contract professionals," who made their living playing tennis but did not accept the authority of their national associations affiliated to the ILTF, signing guaranteed contracts instead with independent promoters.

4. "Registered players," who could accept prize money in open tournaments but still accepted the authority of their national associations and retained eligibility for amateur events including the Davis, Federation, and Wightman Cups.

The prime example of this strange and short-lived new breed was Dutchman Tom Okker, who won the Italian and South African Championships (not yet prize-money events) and was runner-up to Arthur Ashe in the first U.S. Open at Forest Hills. Okker pocketed $14,000 in prize money while Ashe, then a lieutenant in the U. S. Army and a member of the Davis Cup team, had to remain an amateur (the USLTA had not yet

It was a landmark year for tennis, and Lieutenant Arthur Ashe, winning the first U.S. Open in 1968, helped make it memorable. *UPI*

adopted the "registered player" concept) and received only $28 per day expenses.

Other ludicrous examples abounded. Margaret Court, for instance, won and accepted nearly $10,000 in open tournaments in Britain, then came to America and played in the U.S. Amateur for expenses only, beating old rival Maria Bueno in the final.

But despite such anomalies of the transition period, great progress had undeniably been made toward a more honest and prosperous international game.

The first open tournament, a month after the concept was approved at the conference table, was the British Hard Court Championships (in Europe, "hard court" refers to a clay surface, not concrete or similar hard surface as the term is used in the U.S.) at the coastal resort of Bournemouth. History was made on a drizzly, raw Monday, April 22. The "open era" began with an undistinguished young Briton, John Clifton, winning the first point but losing his match against Australian pro Owen Davidson—then the British national coach—on the red shale courts of the West Hants Lawn Tennis Club.

The field at Bournemouth was not as distinguished as the historic nature of the occasion warranted. The "Handsome Eight" of World Championship Tennis were off playing their own tour, leaving the professional portion of the field to come from George MacCall's National Tennis League, plus Davidson and former Chilean Davis Cupper Luis Ayala, then a coach in Puerto Rico, who paid his own way to take part. The top-line amateurs, wary of immediate confrontation with the pros, stayed away. None of the world's Top Ten amateurs entered, and Englishman Bobby Wilson was the only amateur seeded. On the women's side, the only four pros at the time—Billie Jean King, Rosemary Casals, Françoise Durr, and Ann Haydon Jones, who had just signed contracts with MacCall—were otherwise engaged.

The male pros were expected to dominate the amateur field of Englishmen and a few second-line Australians. But many of the pros were nervous; they knew their reputations were on the line, and the most discerning realized they were ill prepared, given long absence from best-of-five-set matches and exposure to new faces and playing styles.

Pancho Gonzales particularly recognized the hazards posed by sudden emergence from a small circle of familiar opponents, with its well-established pecking order. It didn't take long for his apprehension to prove justified. In the second round, Mark Cox, a Cambridge-educated, 24-year-old English left-hander ranked only No. 3 in Britain, outlasted Gonzales, 0–6, 6–2, 4–6, 6–3, 6–3, becoming the first amateur to topple a pro.

Gonzales, only a month from his 40th birthday, hadn't played a 5-set match in five years, but his defeat sent shock waves through the tennis world. Buoyed by his instant celebrity, Cox ousted first-year pro Roy Emerson the next day to reach the semifinals.

Obviously the pros were not invincible—a notion that would be reinforced convincingly throughout the year. But the best of their number, Rod Laver and Ken Rosewall, proved they still inhabited the top echelon. Laver canceled Cox's heroic run in the semis, 6–4, 6–1, 6–0, and Rosewall—a man for all seasons whose longevity at the top level of international competition is unsurpassed—beat Laver in the title match, 3–6, 6–2, 6–0, 6–3.

Rosewall beat Laver again in the final of the second open, the French Championships, also on clay. The first of the traditional "Big Four" tournaments to be open, its field still lacked most of the top American men and Okker, but was stronger than Bournemouth had been.

The French was also memorable because it was played during the general strike and student riots of 1968. Paris was a troubled, crippled city, without public transportation or essential services, but record crowds flocked to Stade Roland Garros on the western outskirts of the city—many by bicycle or on foot—because literally nothing else of a sporting nature was happening. Players, many of whom had harrowing true-life adventures getting to Paris, found accommodations within walking distance of the courts.

"Roland Garros was a port in a storm," recalled Rex Bellamy of the London *Times*. "One thought of Drake and his bowls, Nero and his fiddle. In a strife-torn city, the soaring center court blazed with color. People even perched on the scoreboards, which was as high as they could get without a ladder.

"So the fortnight's excitement was two-edged: a revolution on the courts, and a whiff of revolution in the streets. . . . The first major open was played in the sort of environment that nightmares are made of. But the tennis was often like a dream."

In the quarterfinals, Laver was taken to five sets by the lumbering Romanian Ion Tiriac, one of numerous protracted struggles that kept the packed galleries gasping appreciatively. Laver then easily handled Gonzales, who had enchanted spectators earlier, but in the final Rosewall again asserted his clay court mastery, 6–3, 6–1, 2–6, 6–2.

The women's singles was also full of surprises. Amateurs Gail Sherriff (later Gail Chanfreau Lovera) and Elena Subirats eliminated pros Françoise Durr and Rosie Casals in straight sets. Nancy Richey, a clay court specialist, beat Billie Jean King, who always preferred faster and more sure-footed surfaces, in the semifinals and won the title over the last of the four women pros, Ann Jones, who had been considered the world's leading lady on clay, 5–7, 6–4, 6–1. In the first set, Jones led, 5–1, but lost 11 of the next 13 points. In the second she led, 4–2, then lost 15 of the ensuing 16 points. "A fortnight earlier," Bellamy recalled of Richey, "she had

asked anxiously: 'How do we get out of here?' Like the rest of us, she was glad she stayed."

There was more upheaval on the courts, amid the giddy jubilation of a once-in-a-life-time occasion, at the first open Wimbeldon. This was a richly sentimental fortnight, as legendary champions who had been stripped of their All England Club membership upon turning pro were welcomed back to the shrine of the game and again permitted to wear its mauve-and-green colors. Even old-time champions no longer able to compete came back for the festivities surrounding the enactment of a long-held dream. The tournament began with five days of intermittent rain, which held down crowds, but even this couldn't dampen soaring spirits.

Wimbledon was also the first of the open tournaments that every player of consequence entered. The seeding list for the men's singles read like a Who's Who of the present and immediate past: Laver, Rosewall, Andres Gimeno, defending champion John Newcombe, Emerson, Manuel Santana, Lew Hoad, Gonzales, Dennis Ralston, Butch Buchholz, Fred Stolle, Okker, Ashe, Cliff Drysdale, Tony Roche and Nikki Pilic.

There were numerous surprises, none more unsettling to the pros than the third-round defeat of Gimeno, the elegant Spaniard who was regarded as just a shade below Laver and Rosewall, by long-haired, unheralded, 21-year-old South African Ray Moore. Hoad was beaten by Bob Hewitt, and Gonzales by Soviet Alex Metreveli in the same round, demonstrating again that the pros were unaccustomed to this Brave New World. Indeed, in the quarterfinals only two old pros—Laver and Buchholz—shared the stage with two recent pros (Ralston and Roche), three amateurs (Graebner, Ashe, and Moore), and the lone "registered player," Okker.

Rosewall, who had won everything but Wimbledon as an amateur in the 50s, was upset in the fourth round by the tricky left-handed spins of Roche, who went on to beat Buchholz and unseeded Clark Graebner (conqueror of Santana, Stolle, and Moore) to reach the final. Laver got there by beating Gene Scott, Stan Smith, Marty Riessen, Cox,

Ralston, and Ashe, then clobbered Roche, 6–3, 6–4, 6–2, to again command the stage he had made his in 1961–62, and in the 8-man BBC pro event the summer before.

Having artfully made the pros' return to the premier championship of the game triumphant, Laver received $4,800, but said decisively that money had never entered his thoughts. "Wimbledon's first open tournament enabled this fine left-hander to prove his magnificent worth. Wimbledon endorsed his quality," wrote Lance Tingay of London's *Daily Telegraph*. "Equally Laver endorsed Wimbledon's renewed status as the *de facto* world championship."

The cream also rose in the women's singles. Billie Jean King won her third consecutive singles title, equaling a feat last achieved by Maureen Connolly in 1952–54, over a surprise finalist: seventh-seeded Judy Tegart. An accomplished doubles player, this affable Australian earned her day in the sun by beating second-seeded Margaret Court in the quarters and third-seeded Nancy Richey in the semis, but King was not to be denied her throne. The scores of the final were 9–7, 7–5.

Billie Jean, weary and ill three weeks before the tournament, was pressed to three sets only in the semifinals. Ann Jones led her, 6–4, 5–4, 15–15, three points away from the match on her own serve. But BJK saved the next point with a lob and was off on a 13-point binge that carried her to 1–0 in the final set and out of trouble on a July 4 she could truly celebrate.

King also repeated her doubles triumph of 1967 with Casals, but was unable to defend the mixed doubles title with Owen Davidson for a second consecutive "triple." Australians Ken Fletcher (then playing out of Hong Kong) and Court ended their reign in the semis and went on to defeat Metreveli and Olga Morozova, the first Soviet players to reach a Wimbledon final, 6–1, 14–12. Newcombe and Roche beat Rosewall and Stolle in a doubles final made up entirely of Aussie pros.

There was one more great "first open" of 1968—the $100,000 U.S. Open at Forest Hills, richest of the year's events, which was lavishly promoted by Madison Square Garden in the first year of an ultimately uneasy five-year contract with the USLTA.

By the end of the summer, observers were no longer startled when amateurs knocked off pros, as Ray Moore did in repeating his Wimbledon victory over Andres Gimeno, this time in the first round. The biggest upsets were the fourth-round knockouts of the Wimbledon men's singles finalists—a badly off-form Laver by Cliff Drysdale, 4–6, 6–4, 3–6, 6–1, 6–1, and Roche by the clever and rejuvenated Gonzales, 8–6, 6–4, 6–2.

Gonzales, 40, the graying but still glorious "old wolf," was the darling of the crowds in the stadium where he had prevailed as a hungry young rebel with a cause in 1948–49, but the speedy "Flying Dutchman," Okker, was too fresh for him in the quarters. Gonzales melted in a broiling sun, 14–16, 6–3, 10–8, 6–3.

Joining Okker in the semis were Rosewall (over Ralston), Ashe (over Drysdale), and Graebner (over defender John Newcombe). Okker was too quick for Rosewall, and Ashe was too powerful for Graebner in four-set

The aging Pancho Gonzales, still a crowd favorite, was able to provide excitement in a new era. *UPI*

semis. Ashe simply had too much flashing firepower—26 aces, a lightning backhand, and superior volleying—for Okker in a superb final, 14–12, 5–7, 6–3, 3–6, 6–3. That was the first five-set final since Ashley Cooper over Mal Anderson a decade earlier, and produced the first native champion since Tony Trabert in 1955.

Ashe and Gimeno, an unlikely duo, survived two match points and beat Graebner and Charlie Pasarell, 6–4, 3–6, 4–6, 20–18, 15–13, in the semifinals of the doubles, the longest match in Forest Hills history to that point. But they had little left for the final; Stan Smith and Bob Lutz, ascending 21-year-old Californians who had won the U.S. Amateur Doubles two weeks earlier without losing a set, took the title, 11–9, 6–1, 7–5. They won 11 of 19 tournaments, 57 of 66 matches on the season, to claim the No. 1 U.S. doubles ranking for the first time.

Billie Jean King was unable to defend her title as she had done at Wimbledon. Like Laver, she was far from peak form and struggled three sets with Maryna Godwin in the quarters and Maria Bueno in the semis. Virginia Wade, a 23-year-old Englishwoman of regal bearing recently graduated from Sussex University with a degree in math and physics, beat BJK in the final, 6–4, 6–2. Wade had won at Bournemouth, but this was infinitely more impressive, as she beat Casals, Tegart, Jones, and King in succession. Court and Bueno dislodged the defending champs, King and Casals, in the women's doubles finals.

There was only one other open tournament in the U.S., the Pacific Southwest at Los Angeles, and form held truer on cement, Laver beating Rosewall in the final, 4–6, 6–0, 6–0. Casals beat Bueno for the women's title, 6–4, 6–1.

Despite Laver's Wimbledon triumph and No. 1 world ranking, Ashe was the man of the year in tennis, winner of 10 tournaments to earn the No. 1 U.S. ranking for the first time after three straight years at No. 2. The first black male to win one of the Grand Slam titles, he triumphed at Forest Hills while commuting to his Army duties as a data processing instructor at West Point, New York. Ashe won 30 straight matches from the start of the

Pennsylvania Grass Courts through the Inter-Service Championships (he beat Pfc. Pasarell, who plunged from No. 1 to No. 7 in the U.S. rankings, in the final), the U.S. Amateur, U.S. Open, and the Las Vegas Invitational, to the semis of the Pacific Southwest. Also included were singles victories over Juan Gisbert and Manuel Santana in the 4–1 U.S. victory over Spain in the Davis Cup.

Ashe and Graebner were the singles players for the U.S. as it recaptured the Davis Cup for the first time since 1963 at Adelaide in December, recording a 4–1 victory over an Australian team depleted by the defection of Newcome, Roche, Emerson, and Davidson to the pro ranks. Imbued with great *esprit de corps* and dedication by 29-year-old Donald Dell, a former player, the Americans, (Ashe, Graebner, Smith, Lutz, and Pasarell) trained hard and made winning back the Cup into, as Ashe called it, "a quest." They lost only three matches plowing through the West Indies, Mexico, Ecuador, Spain, India, and Australia to end the three years of U.S. Davis Cup disaster.

Graebner beat Bill Bowrey (who had won the Australian Championships in January, before open competition was approved), and Ashe topped lefty Ray Ruffels, both after losing the first set, to give the U.S. a 2–0 lead. Smith and Lutz clinched the Cup by gunning down the makeshift pair of Ruffels and 17-year-old John Alexander, 6–4, 6–4, 6–2, in just 66 minutes.

There were a couple of other notable achievements during this landmark season.

Nancy Richey made one of the fantastic comebacks in tennis history to beat Billie Jean King, 4–6, 7–5, 6–0, in the semifinals of the Madison Square Garden International. BJK had a match point at 5–1 in the second set, and apparently had the match won with an angled overhead. Richey retrieved it and lobbed again, however, and this time King bungled the smash, then inexplicably collapsed. Richey ran 12 straight games thereafter, 39 of the last 51 points.

That was King's last match as an amateur. Within days she signed with George MacCall. Richey, who beat Tegart in the Garden final, took over the No. 1 ranking and finished 2–0 for the year over King by thwarting BJK's hoped-for revenge in the French. Richey also won her sixth straight U.S. Clay Court title, something only one player had previously achieved, Bill Tilden in 1922–27.

With King and Casals unavailable for duty in the still amateur women's team competitions, the U.S. relinquished both the Federation Cup (Holland beat the U.S. in the semis at Paris, then lost the final to Australia, 3–0) and the Wightman Cup (Wade and Christine Truman Janes led the British to a 4–3 victory at Wimbledon, their first since 1960).

The longest match on record, in terms of elapsed playing time, took place at Salisbury, Maryland, when Englishmen Bobby Wilson and Mark Cox defeated Pasarell and Graebner, 26–24, 17–19, 30–28, in the U.S. Indoor Doubles. The match consumed six hours, 23 minutes, and is the longest in terms of games in a U.S. Championship event.

1969

The second year of Open Tennis was one of continued progress but lingering confusion on the political front, and indisputably towering oncourt performances by Rod Laver and Margaret Court.

There were 30 open tournaments around the world, and prize money escalated to about $1.3 million. Laver was the leading money-winner with $124,000, followed by Tony Roche ($75,045), Tom Okker ($65,451), Roy Emerson ($62,629), and John Newcombe ($52,610).

The Davis Cup and other international team competitions continued to be governed by reactionaries, however, and admitted only players under the jurisdiction of their national associations. This left the "contract pros"— who were paid guarantees and committed by contract to play where scheduled by independent promoters—on the outs, while players who accepted prize money but remained under the aegis of their national associations were allowed to play. At the end of the year a proposal to end this silly double standard and allow "contract pros" back in was defeated by the Davis Cup nations on a 21–19 vote.

The "registered player" concept, borne of

Rod Laver, returning the ball to fellow Australian Tony Roche in the 1969 U.S. Open final, took home the most money. *UPI*

compromise a year earlier, persisted until finally being abolished by a newly elected and more forward-looking ILTF Committee of Management in July. Still, the public found it difficult to understand who was and who was not a pro. In the United States, those who took prize money but remained under the authority of the USLTA were officially called "players." Under the leadership of Captain Donald Dell, the members of the U.S. Davis Cup team preferred to call themselves "independent pros," making it clear that they were competing for prize money.

The USLTA leadership would have preferred to keep the U.S. tournament circuit amateur, paying expenses only, except for five open events given ILTF sanction (Philadelphia Indoors, Madison Square Garden, U.S. Open, Pacific Southwest, Howard Hughes Invitational). This would have kept down spiraling overhead costs, a threat to the exclusive clubs, which resisted sponsorship but did not want to lose their traditional events. Dell and the Davis Cup team refused to play in tournaments that offered expenses and guarantees instead of prize money, however, and thus effectively forced a full-prize-money circuit into being in the U.S.

Dell led the way by organizing the $25,000 Washington *Star* International in his hometown. It was a prototype tournament in many ways: commercially sponsored, played in a public facility for over-the-table prize money rather than under-the-table appearance fees. Other tournaments followed suit, and a new and successful U.S. Summer Circuit began to emerge. In all, 15 U.S. tournaments offered $440,000 in prize money, with the $137,000 U.S. Open again the world's richest event. In 1968, there had been only two prize-money open tournaments in the U.S., with combined purses of $130,000.

A few peculiar hybrid events—half amateur and half pro—remained. The most obviously unnecessary was the $25,000 National Singles and Doubles at Longwood Cricket Club, which welcomed amateurs and independent pros but excluded the "contract pros." Stan Smith beat Bob Lutz, and Margaret Court prevailed over Virginia Wade for the singles titles, but the grandly named tournament was essentially meaningless and vanished from the scene the next year in a natural sorting-out process.

If the labels put on tournaments and players boggled the public mind, there was no doubt as to who the world's No. 1 players were: Australians Laver and Court were truly dominant.

Laver repeated his 1962 Grand Slam, something only he and Don Budge (1938) had achieved, by sweeping the Australian, French, Wimbledon, and U.S. titles the first year that all four were open.

Laver also won the South African Open and finished the season with a 114–17 record for 32 tournaments, 18 of which he won. He didn't lose a match from the start of Wimbledon in June until the second round of the Pacific Southwest Open in late September, when Ray Moore ended the winning streak at 31 matches.

During that stretch, Laver won seven tournaments, including his fourth Wimbledon (where he had not lost since the 1960 final), his second Forest Hills, and his fifth U.S. Pro Championship. By the time he got to Los Angeles, Rod just wanted to get 45 minutes farther south to his adopted home of Corona Del Mar, California, where his wife, Mary, had just presented him with his first child, Rick Rodney.

The most difficult match for Laver of the 26 that comprised the Slam came early, in the semifinals of the Australian. He beat Tony Roche, 7–5, 22–20, 9–11, 1–6, 6–3, in a match that lasted more than four hours in the sweltering, 105-degree heat of a Brisbane afternoon. Both players got groggy in the brutal sun, even though they employed an old Aussie trick of putting wet cabbage leaves in their hats to help stay cool. It was so close that it could easily have gone either way, and a controversial line call helped Laver grasp the final set. Having survived, Laver beat Andres Gimeno in the final, 6–3, 6–4, 7–5.

His tall countryman Dick Crealy took the first two sets from Laver in a second-rounder at the French Championships, but the red-haired "Rocket" accelerated and ultimately played one of his best clay court matches to beat Ken Rosewall in the final, 6–4, 6–3, 6–4.

An unheralded Indian named Premjit Lall similarly captured the first two sets in the second round at Wimbledon, but Laver awoke to dispose of him, 3–6, 4–6, 6–3, 6–0, 6–0. Stan Smith took Laver to five sets in the quarterfinals, and Arthur Ashe and John Newcombe to four in the semis and final, respectively. But despite Newcombe's thoughtful game plan of using lobs and changes of pace instead of the straightforward power for which he was known, Laver prevailed, 6–4, 5–7, 6–4, 6–4.

Then it was on to Forest Hills, where Philip Morris and its tennis-minded chairman of the board, Joe Cullman, had infused heavy promotional dollars into the U.S. Open and brought flamboyant South African promoter Owen Williams in from Johannesburg to run a jazzed-up show and foster corporate patronage. They drew record crowds until the weather turned surly. Rain inundated the already soft and uneven courts, played havoc with the schedule, and pushed the tournament three days past its scheduled conclusion.

Despite the trying conditions and the imminent birth of his son on the West Coast, Laver remained intent on the task at hand. He was taken to five sets only by Dennis Ralston in the fourth round. After that Laver disposed of Roy Emerson in four sets, Arthur Ashe in three straight, and—after two days of rain—donned spikes in the second set to climb over Roche, 7–9, 6–1, 6–3, 6–2 on a gloomy Tuesday, before a crowd of only 3,708 fans who sat through rain delays of 90 and 30 minutes.

The weather certainly dampened the occasion, but it was appropriate that Roche—clearly No. 2 in the world, and regarded as Laver's heir apparent until a series of arm injuries started to plague him the next year—provided the final hurdle. The ruggedly muscular Roche was the only player with a winning record (5–3) for the year over Laver, and Roche got to the final by beating his doubles partner, John Newcombe, in a splendid marathon, 3–6, 6–4, 4–6, 6–3, 8–6.

Laver shed a few tears as USLTA President Alastair Martin presented him the champion's trophy and check for $16,000, saying, "You're the greatest in the world . . . perhaps the greatest we've ever seen."

"I never really think of myself in those terms, but I feel honored that people see fit to say such things about me," said Laver shyly. "Tenniswise, this year was much tougher than '62. At that time the best players—Ken Rosewall, Lew Hoad, Pancho Gonzales—were not in the amateur ranks. I didn't find out who were the best until I turned pro and had my brains beaten out for six months at the start of 1963."

Now, in the open era, there was no question who was best.

Margaret Court, who had returned to action following a brief retirement (the first of several in her long career), was almost as monopolistic as Laver. She lost only five matches the entire season, winning 19 of 24 tournaments and 98 of 103 matches.

She won the Australian over Billie Jean King, 6–4, 6–1, after trailing Kerry Melville, 3–5, in the final set in the semis. In the French, Court beat Pat Walkden, Melville, defending champ Nancy Richey, and Ann Jones—all splendid clay court players—in the last four rounds.

Court's dream of a Grand Slam ended at Wimbledon, however, where Ann Jones beat her in the semifinals, 10–12, 6–3, 6–2. To the unbridled joy of her British countrymen,

the left-handed, 30-year-old Mrs. Jones then won her first Wimbledon title after 14 years of trying, squashing Billie Jean King's bid for a fourth consecutive crown, 3–6, 6–3, 6–2. Billie Jean was shaken by the noisy partisanship of the customarily proper British gallery and what she thought were some dubious line calls, but the British extolled the popular Jones as a conquering heroine.

Court won the U.S. Open without losing a set. In fact, she lost more than two games in a set only twice in six matches, in beating fellow Aussie Karen Krantzcke in the quarters, 6–0, 9–7, and Virginia Wade in the semis, 7–5, 6–0. Nancy Richey—eschewing her usual baseline game for net-rushing tactics quite foreign to her—helped out by eliminating King in the quarters, 6–4, 8–6, but found herself passed repeatedly in the final by some of Court's finest ground stroking. The scores were 6–2, 6–2.

But if Laver and Court clearly reigned supreme, there were other notable heroes and achievements in 1969.

Pancho Gonzales, at 41, buried Peter Curtis, John Newcombe, Ken Rosewall, Stan Smith, and Arthur Ashe in succession to win the $50,000 Howard Hughes Open at Las Vegas. Gonzales also won the Pacific Southwest Open and had a 2–0 record over Smith, who was ranked No. 1 in the U.S. for the first time. Gonzales was the top U.S. money-winner with $46,288, and might have returned to the No. 1 spot he occupied in 1948–49 if the USLTA had included "contract pros" in its rankings.

Gonzales' most dramatic performance, however, came at Wimbledon, where he beat Charlie Pasarell in the first round in the longest match in the history of the oldest and most prestigious of championships. It consumed 5 hours and 12 minutes over two days. Gonzales lost a marathon first set and virtually threw the second, complaining bitterly that it was too dark to continue play. He was whistled and hooted by the normally genteel Centre Court crowd, but won back all his detractors the next day with a heroic display. Pasarell played well, but Gonzales was magnificent. In the fifth set he staved off seven match points, twice serving out of 0–40 holes, and won, 22–24, 1–6, 16–14, 6–3, 11–9. Again the darling of the crowds, Gonzales lasted until the fourth round, when his protégé, Ashe, beat him in four sets.

Stan Smith won eight tournaments, including the National Indoors, to replace Ashe atop the U.S. rankings. Ashe, bothered by a nagging elbow injury and numerous nontennis distractions following his big year in 1968, won only two tournaments but had an 83–24 match record, and more wins than any other American. He was a semifinalist at Wimbledon and Forest Hills, losing to longtime nemesis Laver at both, and was ranked No. 2, ahead of Cliff Richey and Clark Graebner, even though they had more tournament victories—eight and seven, respectively.

The United States defeated long-shot Romania, 5–0, in the Davis Cup Challenge Round on a fast cement court at Cleveland, painted and polished to make it even slicker, to the home team's benefit. Ashe defeated Ilie Nastase in the opening singles, 6–2, 15–13, 7–5, and Smith escaped the hulking and wily Ion Tiriac, 6–8, 6–3, 5–7, 6–4, 6–4, in the pivotal second match. Smith and Lutz closed out the Romanians, 8–6, 6–1, 11–9.

President Richard M. Nixon, a bowler and golfer who secretly despised tennis, had both teams to a reception at the White House. This was a nice gesture, but the Chief Executive caused a few awkward stares when, as a memento of the occasion, he presented each player with a golf ball. Perhaps these were left over, some speculated, from the golf-happy Eisenhower administration.

Tiny Romania, with the lion-hearted Tiriac and the immensely talented Nastase its only players of international standard, was proud to have gotten past Egypt, Spain, the Soviet Union, India, and Great Britain (which, with a heroic 10–2 singles run from unranked Graham Stilwell, reached the semifinals for the first time since relinquishing the Cup in 1937) to the final. Never before had Romania won more than two rounds.

Australia failed to reach the final for the first time since 1937—beaten in its first match for the first time since 1928 by Mexico, 3–2. Rafael Osuna, Mexico's popular tennis hero,

defeated Bill Bowrey in the fifth match, 6–2, 3–6, 8–6, 6–3, and was hailed triumphantly by his countrymen. This was the engaging Osuna's last hurrah, however; he died tragically shortly thereafter, at age 30, when a private plane carrying him on a business trip crashed into the mountains outside Monterrey.

In another significant development, the Davis Cup nations voted South Africa and Rhodesia out of the competition for 1970–71 because demonstrations against their racial policies, and the refusal of some nations to play them, made their presence in the draw disruptive.

Nancy Richey was upset in the semifinals of the National Clay Courts by Gail Sheriff Chanfreau, ending her record winning streak in a U.S. Championship event at 33 straight matches over seven years. She was trying to become only the second player to win seven consecutive titles, matching the feat of Richard Sears in the first seven U.S. Men's Championships (1881–87). Clark Graebner, winner of the Clay Court doubles three times with Marty Riessen and once with Dennis Ralston, teamed with Bowrey for Graebner's fifth title, eclipsing the record set by Bill Talbert in 1946.

Richey retained the No. 1 U.S. women's ranking, winning four of 13 tournaments for a 46–10 record and splitting four matches with old rival Billie Jean King, who as a "contract pro" was not ranked. Richey teamed with Julie Heldman and Peaches Bartkowicz to regain the Federation Cup at Athens and the Wightman Cup at Cleveland.

Richey was undefeated in singles, and Heldman lost only to Margaret Court as the U.S. defeated Bulgaria, Italy, Holland, and upset Australia, 2–1, for the Federation Cup. Richey and Bartkowicz, an unlikely doubles team made up of two confirmed baseliners, upset the world's No. 1 team—Court and Judy Tegart—in the final match, 6–4, 6–4. Bartkowicz stayed in the backcourt throughout, even when Richey served, but the Americans astonishingly won the curious match witn energetic retrieving and deft lobbing.

Heldman, a clever player who nicknamed herself "Junkball Julie," set the tone of the

5–2 Wightman Cup victory by upsetting Wade in the opening match. Ranked No. 2 nationally with eight victories in 20 tournaments and a 67–13 match record, Heldman also became the first American woman to win the Italian Championship since Althea Gibson in 1956, beating three outstanding clay courters—Lesley Turner Bowrey (wife of Bill), Ann Jones, and Kerry Melville.

One of the most remarkable and crowd-pleasing victories of the year was that of Darlene Hard and Françoise Durr in the U.S. Open women's doubles. They were a "pick-up" team: Hard, now a 33-year-old teaching pro, had entered as a lark. Out of tournament condition, she was an embarrassment in losing the first eight games of the final, but seemed suddenly to remember the skills and instincts that had made her the world's premier doubles player in her time, winner of five previous U.S. women's titles. As the crowd loudly cheered their revival, Hard and Durr stunned heavily favored Court and Wade, 0–6, 6–3, 6–4.

Forest Hills had begun with a match of record duration—F. D. Robbins defeated Dick Dell, younger brother of Donald, 22–20, 9–7, 6–8, 8–10, 6–4, the longest in number of games in the history of the U.S. Championships. When the tournament ran three days over, the men's doubles finished in a disgraceful shambles, Ken Rosewall and Fred Stolle beating Denny Ralston and Charlie Pasarell, 2–6, 7–5, 13–11, 6–3, before a few hundred spectators on a soggy Wednesday. Pasarell-Ralston got defaults from Wimbledon champs Newcombe and Roche in the quarters and Australian Open winners Laver and Emerson in the semis.

Newcome-Roche were urged to leave waterlogged New York by their employers, WCT, in order to meet other commitments, a decision that rankled the ILTF in its increasingly uneasy dealings with the new pro promoters. After all, it was unseemly for the No. 1 team—they had repeated at Wimbledon, over Tom Okker-Marty Riessen, and won four other tournaments, including the Italian and French—to walk out on one of the "Big Four" showcase championships.

1970

As in 1950 and 1960, the beginning of a new decade also was, in many ways, the start of a new era for tennis. In 1970, the professional game for both men and women fitfully began to assume the structure that would characterize the decade of its most rapid growth.

This was the first year of the men's Grand Prix—a point system, under the aegis of the International Lawn Tennis Federation, that linked together tournaments, leading to year-end bonus awards for the top finishers in the standings and berths in a new tournament at the end of the year: the Grand Prix Masters.

The brainchild of Jack Kramer, the Grand Prix was announced late in 1969 and sponsored by Pepsi-Cola. Players earned points, round by round, in the Grand Prix tournaments they entered, and at season's end the top men received cash awards scaled according to their order of finish. Cliff Richey, for example, collected $25,000 for topping the standings; Arthur Ashe earned $17,000 for placing second, Ken Rosewall $15,000 for coming in third, etc. There were 19 tourna-

Margaret Smith Court, with her U.S. Open trophy, was the leading lady in 1970. *UPI*

ments in the Grand Prix in 1970. The "bonus pool" totaled $150,000, and there was another $50,000 at stake in the six-man Masters.

The underlying intent of the Grand Prix, it was clear, was to keep players from signing guaranteed contracts with the professional troupes, World Championship Tennis (WCT) and the struggling National Tennis League (NTL). WCT, which loomed as an ever more formidable rival to the ILTF and its member national associations for control of the burgeoning pro game, responded by swiftly signing more players to contracts, then increasing its "stable" to 30 players by swallowing the NTL in May.

Mike Davies, executive director of WCT, became a member of the ILTF scheduling committee, but wariness and distrust between the maneuvering giants continued. It became increasingly difficult for traditional tournaments to count on the participation of the WCT players because of the "management fees" demanded by WCT in order to cover their guarantees to the players.

In September, at the U.S. Open, WCT took the wraps off a Grand Prix-style competition of its own, announcing a "million-dollar circuit" for 1971. The first World Championship of Tennis, for 32 players to be selected by an international press panel, would consist of 20 tournaments with uniform prize money and point standings, leading to a rich, nationally televised playoff with a $50,000 first prize.

This was considered a declaration of war by WCT against the ILTF, especially since Davies had never mentioned it to the ILTF calendar committee. The battle intensified when, shortly thereafter, WCT announced that it had signed Arthur Ashe, Charlie Pasarell, and Bob Lutz to five-year contracts in a package deal.

The ILTF went ahead and announced an expanded Grand Prix, worth $1 1/2 million, in 1971, but the battle lines had already been drawn.

The beneficiaries of the infighting, of course, were the players, who found themselves the objects of a giddy bidding war between the ILTF, which offered ever-bigger prize money tournaments but no guarantees, and WCT, with its long-term, guaranteed contracts.

Rod Laver did not retain any of the "Big Four" titles he monopolized in 1969, but still became the first tennis player to crack the $200,000 barrier in winnings. He collected $201,453, compared to the $157,037 won by Lee Trevino, top earner on the professional golf circuit. This had heretofore been considered unimaginable. But prize money was escalating at a rate no one had foreseen—nearly $1 million was up for grabs in U.S. tournaments alone—and three players (Laver, U.S. Open champ Ken Rosewall, and Arthur Ashe) won more than $100,000.

Growing along with the total purses, however, was the disparity in prize money for men and women. Despite Margaret Court's fulfillment of a long-held ambition—a singles Grand Slam of the Australian, French, Wimbledon, and U.S. Open titles—1970 was for the majority of women players the autumn of their discontent. A group of pioneers, led by the strong-willed Gladys Heldman—a tough, shrewd businesswoman who had founded *World Tennis* magazine in 1953—decided that the women would have to split away from mixed tournaments and found their own tour if they were ever to corner a significant share of the sport's mushrooming riches and publicity. This was a bold step, but the women decided to take it in September, and from a little acorn—a $7,500 renegade tournament for eight women in Houston—there eventually grew a mighty oak: the women's pro tour in the U.S.

The political kettle was boiling, but 1970 was also a spectacularly eventful year on the court. It was made singularly exciting by the advent of the game's first major scoring innovation—tie-breakers—and towering performances by several players, notably Rosewall and Court.

"Mighty Margaret" had twice before won three of the "Big Four" singles titles in a season. In 1970, at age 28, she finally corralled the Grand Slam previously achieved by only one woman—Maureen Connolly in 1953. Court compiled a 94–5 record, winning 19 of 24 matches, and had the season's longest winning streak: 39 matches.

Court lost only three sets during the Slam, none in winning her ninth Australian singles title. She defeated Kerry Melville—one of only four women to beat her during the season—in the final, 6–3, 6–1, and teamed with Judy Dalton to win the doubles by the same score over Melville and Karen Krantzcke.

In the French, only Russian Olga Morozova pushed Court to three sets, in the second round. Court's next four victories were all in straight sets, German Helga Niessen falling in the final, 6–2, 6–4. Françoise Durr won her fourth consecutive doubles title, alongside Gail Sheriff Chanfreau.

At Wimbledon, the tall, languid Niessen—not considered a threat on grass courts—took the first set from Court in the quarterfinals, but did not get another game. The final between Court and Billie Jean King was a masterpiece of drama and shotmaking under duress. Both players were hurt. Court had a painfully strained and swollen ankle tightly strapped as she went on court; she had taken a pain-killing injection beforehand. King was hobbling on a deteriorated kneecap, which required surgery immediately after Wimbledon.

Nevertheless, BJK broke service in the first set three times. Each time Court broke back. Their injuries partially dictated the pattern of play, but both players produced magnificent shots under pressure. It was the longest women's final ever at Wimbledon, Court finally winning by 14–12, 11–9, in 2 1/2 hours, after the anesthetic effects of her injection had worn off. King saved three match points with gutsy shots worthy of the contest. "It was a bit like one of those 990-page novels that Trollope and Arnold Bennett used to write," suggested British journalist David Gray, who in 1977 would become general secretary of the ILTF. "It started a little slowly, but had so many fascinating twists of character and plot that in the end it became a matter of utter compulsion to see how it all ended."

King took her sixth doubles title, her third with Rosemary Casals (who teamed with Ilie Nastase to win the mixed). Billie Jean was the only player who truly challenged Court, splitting their four matches during the year, but King was still recuperating from her post-Wimbledon surgery in September and missed the U.S. Open. In her absence, Court completed the Slam, losing only 13 games in mowing down Pam Austin, Patti Hogan, Pat Faulkner, Helen Gourlay, and Nancy Richey

to reach the final. Casals, attacking furiously, won the middle set of the final, but it was a futile effort. "Her arms seemed a mile long," shrugged the diminutive "Rosebud," only 5-foot-2 to Court's 5-foot-11, after her 6–2, 2–6, 6–1 beating. Court also took the doubles, in tandem with Judy Dalton, and the mixed doubles with Marty Riessen.

Court won approximately $50,000 in prize money on the year, about one quarter of what Laver earned for a far less productive season. In most tournaments, the women's share of the prize money was one quarter or less that of the men's. In the Italian Open, for example, Billie Jean King received a mere $600 for beating Julie Heldman in the final, while Ilie Nastase earned $3,500 for whipping Jan Kodes in the men's final.

Court, never a crusader or champion of causes, wanted no part of a "women's lib" movement in tennis, but King and several others resented the growing inequity in prize-money ratio between men and women. They enlisted fiery activist Gladys Heldman as their negotiator and spokeswoman, and focused on the Pacific Southwest Open at Los Angeles—which favored men by an eight-to-one ratio—as an example of their plight.

Heldman tried to get tournament chairman Jack Kramer to raise the women's purse. He would not. At a highly publicized Forest Hills press conference, a group of eight women declared they would boycott the Los Angeles tournament and play in a $7,500 event in Houston, sponsored by Virginia Slims cigarettes. The USLTA said it would not sanction this rebel event. The women said they would play anyway—and did. After signing token one-dollar contracts with Heldman, the Houston Eight (King, Casals, Kristy Pigeon, Peaches Bartkowicz, Judy Dalton, Valerie Ziegenfuss, Kerry Melville, and Nancy Richey) competed in an event that was unexpectedly successful, paving the way for the first Virginia Slims circuit the next year.

Meanwhile, in men's tennis, the Grand Slam singles titles monopolized by Laver in 1969 went to four different players:

■ Arthur Ashe, the runner-up in 1966–67, became the fourth American to win the Australian singles, the first since Dick Savitt 19 years earlier. Laver did not defend, and Dennis Ralston eliminated Newcombe in a marathon quarterfinal. Ashe took out Dick Crealy in the final, 6–4, 9–7, 6–2, while Stan Smith and Bob Lutz captured the doubles, the first American men to do so since Vic Seixas and Tony Trabert 17 years earlier.

■ With Laver, Rosewall, and their fellow "contract pros" out of the French Championships because their bosses could not come to a financial accommodation with the French Tennis Federation for their appearance, Czech Jan Kodes, Yugoslav Zeljko Franulovic, American Cliff Richey, and Frenchman Georges Goven reached the semifinals of the richest ($100,000) tournament outside America. Kodes beat Franulovic, 6–2, 6–4, 6–0, for the $10,000 top prize. Romanians Ilie Nastase and Ion Tiriac took the doubles.

■ At Wimbledon, Laver's 31-match winning streak in the world's most important tournament, dating back to 1961, was snapped when he came up badly off-form against Englishman Roger Taylor in the fourth round and tumbled, 4–6, 6–4, 6–2, 6–1. John Newcombe withstood five break points in the fifth set of an excruciating three-hour quarterfinal against fellow Aussie Roy Emerson, won it by 6–1, 5–7, 3–6, 6–2, 11–9, then crushed Spaniard Andres Gimeno (conqueror of Ashe) and beat Rosewall, 5–7, 6–3, 6–2, 3–6, 6–1. This was the first five-set final in 21 years, and the 10th All-Aussie men's final in 15 years.

Rosewall had beaten left-handers Tony Roche and Taylor to reach the final for the third time, 14 years after losing to fellow Aussie "Whiz Kid" Lew Hoad, but again failed at the final hurdle. Newcombe and Roche teamed for their third consecutive doubles triumph, the first to achieve this since Reg and Laurie Doherty, the English brothers in 1903–5.

■ Rosewall, two months shy of his 36th birthday, reigned at Forest Hills, where 14 years earlier he had halted Hoad's Grand Slam bid. It was a wild tournament, the richest in the world with a $176,000 pot. Pastel clothing was permitted in lieu of the traditional "all white," and red flags flew every time a set reached 6–6 and went into the "sudden death" best-of-nine-points tie-breaker.

Record crowds totaling 122,996 came out to see all the revolutionary happenings, but Rosewall interjected a reactionary note. After Dennis Ralston had achieved one of his career high points, knocking off defending champ Laver in a five-set quarterfinal to lead a charge of four Americans into the last eight, Rosewall took over. He blasted Stan Smith and Newcombe in straight sets, then relegated Roche to the runner-up spot for the second consecutive year, 2–6, 6–4, 7–6, 6–3. Rosewall was the oldest champ at Forest Hills since Bill Tilden, who was 36 when he won for the seventh and last time in 1929.

The men's doubles event was notable for several reasons. Pancho Gonzales, the oldest man in the tournament at 42, entered with a then unknown protégé, Jimmy Connors, who at 18 was the youngest man in the tournament. They reached the quarters. Nikki Pilic of Yugoslavia and Pierre Barthes of France slew Emerson and Laver in the final, 6–3, 7–6, 4–6, 7–6, to become the first European team ever to win the U.S. Doubles. The victors won eight of their 15 sets in the tie-breakers, the scoring innovation that was given its first wide spread exposure in the U.S. Pro Championships and U.S. Open.

Players were skeptical—"It's like rolling dice," said Newcombe—but spectators, schedule-makers, and television producers loved them, so tie-breakers were here to stay—although the more conservative 12-point, win-by-two method gradually won favor over nine-point sudden death in professional tournaments.

■ Laver, at 32, did win five significant tournaments on four continents, but in addition to losing his Grand Slam titles, he gave up his four-year stranglehold on the U.S. Pro title. Roche beat him in the final at Longwood, 3–6, 6–4, 1–6, 6–2, 6–2. Laver also won the "Tennis Champions Classic," a series of head-to-head winner-take-all challenge matches played in seven cities. He beat Rosewall for the $35,000 top prize at Madison Square Garden.

■ Nastase underscored his emerging brilliance by winning titles on one of the world's fastest courts—the canvas of the U.S. Indoors at Salisbury, Maryland, where he escaped a two-set deficit and a match point in the fourth set to beat Cliff Richey, 6–8, 3–6, 6–4, 9–7, 6–0—as well as one of the slowest, the red clay of Foro Italico in Rome.

Richey, a scrappy Texan with more tenacity than natural talent, earned the No. 1 U.S. ranking, thereby establishing a unique family achievement. His sister, Nancy, had been the top-ranked U.S. woman in 1964–65 and 1968–69.

Richey won eight of 27 tournaments he played during the season, was runner-up in five more, and went farther than any other American man at Forest Hills: the semifinals. His match record for the year was 92–10.

Even so, he did not clinch the top ranking until the Pacific Coast Championships at Berkeley in late September, when he played Stan Smith—who had beaten him in two of three previous 1970 meetings—in the semifinals. Both men knew the No. 1 ranking hinged on this match, and what an extraordinary battle it turned out to be! After a long afternoon of furious scrambling and shotmaking, it all came down to four points apiece in the sudden-death tie-breaker: simultaneous match point for both players. Richey served to Smith's backhand and charged the net. Smith cracked a backhand return cross-court that Richey could barely get his racket on. He nudged the ball cross-court, and Smith lashed what appeared to be a winning passing shot down the line. Richey dived for the ball, throwing everything into a desperate last lunge, and astonishingly volleyed a winner to seize the match, 7–6, 6–7, 6–4, 4–6, 7–6.

Richey also was the unlikely hero of the lackluster 1970 Davis Cup Challenge Round. U.S. Captain Ed Turville agonized over the selection, but finally chose Richey over Smith to face upstart Germany on a fast asphalt court at Cleveland. Richey, who felt he had been slighted by not being chosen in 1969, responded by clobbering Christian Kuhnke, 6–3, 6–4, 6–2, and Wilhelm Bungert, 6–4, 6–4, 7–5, to spearhead a 5–0 U.S. victory. Arthur Ashe beat Bungert, 6–2, 10–8, 6–2 in the opener and erased Kuhnke, 6–8, 10–12, 9–7, 13–11, 6–4, in the meaningless fifth

match, the longest singles ever in Davis Cup. Smith and Bob Lutz beat Bungert and Kuhnke, 6–3, 7–5, 6–4, becoming the first doubles team to clinch the Cup three straight years.

It was a disappointing final, concluding a tarnished Davis Cup campaign. The exclusion of contract pros, even though all major tournaments were now "open," left the Davis Cup a second-rate event. Australia, denied the services of perhaps its 10 best players, fell pathetically to India. Other countries suffered a similar fate. Kuhnke and Bungert, moonlighting from their full-time occupations as lawyer and sporting-goods merchant, respectively, were hailed as "the last of the great amateurs" as they surged through six matches, then played like halfhearted amateurs in the finale. Future political turmoil within the Cup was also foreshadowed as South Africa was expelled for two years because the apartheid racial policy of its government was considered disruptive to the competition, and Rhodesia withdrew to avoid political problems.

Largely because contract pros were excluded from the Davis Cup, a new competition—grandly misnamed the World Cup—was organized as a charity event in Boston. It put a two-man team of Australian pros—Newcomb and Fred Stolle—against U.S. Davis Cuppers Richey, Smith, Ashe, and Clark Graebner for $20,000 in prize money. The Aussies won, 5–2, at Harvard University's indoor courts and, even though the ILTF opposed the event, a new Australian-U.S. pro team rivalry had begun.

Australia won the Federation Cup at Freiburg, West Germany, even though Margaret Court opted not to play. Judy Dalton and Karen Krantzcke swept through the competition without losing a match, whitewashing West Germany—2–1 victors over Americans Peaches Bartkowicz, Julie Heldman, and Mary Ann Eisel Curtis—in the final.

With Billie Jean King winning two singles and collaborating with Bartkowicz for the first time to win the decisive doubles, the U.S. scored a 4–3 Wightman Cup victory over Great Britain at Wimbledon. King beat Virginia Wade in the opening singles, but had to

stop Ann Jones and then team with Bartkowicz for a 7–5, 3–6, 6–2 triumph over Wade
and Winnie Shaw to salvage victory after
Wade's singles win over Nancy Richey gave
the British a 3–2 lead.

The season ended with the first Grand Prix
Masters tournament, a six-man round-robin in
Tokyo. Cliff Richey, who topped the Grand
Prix point standings, was ill and could not
participate. Stan Smith and Rod Laver both
had 4–1 records in the round-robin, but Smith
took the $15,000 first prize because of his
head-to-head win over Laver.

The next year, because of the growing
strain of the tug-of-war between WCT and the
ILTF, Smith and Laver would not be playing
in the same season-ending playoff tournament. There were negotiations throughout the
fall of 1970, trying to develop an accord, and
in December WCT and the ILTF issued a
joint communiqué pledging that they would
"work together toward the development and
spectator appeal of the game throughout the
world." An agreement in principle for the
appearance of WCT contract pros in the 1971
French, Wimbledon, and U.S. Open Championships also was announced, but the cautious
harmony turned out to be short-lived.

1971

In 1971, both men's and women's professional
tennis were split into rival camps. It was an
uneasy, acrimonious year politically, but the
game prospered.

On court, there were many highlights: John
Newcombe's second consecutive Wimbledon
triumph, after he trailed Stan Smith by two
sets to one in the final; Smith's impressive
triumph at Forest Hills; the first "World
Championship of Tennis," in which Ken
Rosewall upset Rod Laver in the final; a new
women's pro tour, dominated by the indefatigable Billie Jean King; and the emergence
of Evonne Goolagong, who won the French
Open and Wimbledon at age 19, and Chris
Evert, who reached the semifinals of the U.S.
Open at 16.

Rosewall, who in 1970 had captured his
second U.S. Championship 14 years after the
first, continued to perform geriatric marvels.

Evonne Goolagong, 19, was No. 1 in 1971. *UPI*

He dethroned Arthur Ashe in the Australian
Open final, 6–1, 7–5, 6–3, regaining a title
he first held in 1953. Newcombe and Tony
Roche won the third of their four Australian
doubles titles.

Unfortunately, for much of the season the
34 men under contract to World Championship Tennis and the "independent pros" who
remained under the authority of their national
associations played separate tournaments.

WCT's new "World Championship of Tennis"—a million-dollar series of 20 tournaments in nine countries on four continents—
got off to a promising start with the Philadelphia Indoors, where Newcombe beat Laver
for only the second time in a dozen career
meetings.

Meanwhile, the independent pros were
playing on an expanding indoor circuit promoted by Bill Riordan under the aegis of the
U.S. Lawn Tennis Association. The highlight
was the U.S. Indoor at Riordan's hometown
of Salisbury, Maryland, where Clark Graebner came from two sets down to upend Romanian Ilie Nastase in the semifinals, then saved
two match points in beating Cliff Richey for
the title, 2–6, 7–6, 1–6, 7–6, 6–0.

The Italian Open at Rome was one of several strange hybrid events—copromoted by

WCT as part of its 20-tournament series, but also open to noncontract pros. This made for a week of exceptional matches and excitement on the red clay of Il Foro Italico. Record crowds and profits were recorded before Laver defeated Czech Jan Kodes in the final, 7–5, 6–3, 6–3.

Only a few of the WCT players entered the French Open. After five months of a grueling travel and playing schedule, Ashe—never a factor on European clay—was the only one of WCT's top "names" who opted to go to Paris for two weeks of physically demanding best-of-five-set matches. The mass nonappearance of the "contract pros" infuriated the ILTF, and was a major factor in polarizing opposition to WCT. Meanwhile, the dour but energetically industrious Kodes won his second straight French title, beating the more gifted but less persistent Nastase, 8–6, 6–2, 2–6, 7–5, in an absorbing final. Ashe and Marty Riessen, the top two WCT players entered, won the doubles. (Both had been beaten in singles by surprising Frank Froehling, who survived a match point against Ashe in the quarterfinals.)

At Wimbledon, No. 1 seed Laver was ambushed by the inspired serving and volleying of American Tom Gorman in the quarterfinals. The best match was an enchanting four-hour quarterfinal in which Rosewall finally outstroked Richey, 6–8, 5–7, 6–4, 9–7, 7–5. The final between Newcombe and Smith had fewer breathtaking rallies, and was dominated by slam-bang points accentuating each's serve-volley power, but it also became gripping in the end. Smith seemed in control after a seven-game run that took him to 1–0 in the fourth set, but this was his first major final and he got "a little tired mentally." Newcombe was tougher and seized control, ending his 6–3, 5–7, 2–6, 6–4, 6–4 triumph with an ace. Roy Emerson, twice a winner with Neale Fraser (1959–61), partnered Laver to the latter's first Wimbledon doubles title over Ashe and Dennis Ralston, 4–6, 9–7, 6–8, 6–4, 6–4.

The U.S. Open—minus Laver, defending champ Rosewall, and Emerson, who opted to rest—was less than three hours old when Wimbledon champ Newcombe was rudely dismissed by Kodes—who was unhappy about being unseeded, even though he said tennis on grass courts was "a joke" that he found totally unfunny. This was the first time in 41 years that a top seed failed to survive his opening match—No. 1 foreign seed Jean Borotra lost in the 1930 opening round to Berkeley Bell—but Kodes proved it was no fluke. He came back from two sets down against Pierre Barthes, and from two sets to one and a service break down in the fourth to beat Arthur Ashe in the semifinals. Kodes also wön the first set of the final against Smith, but the 6-foot-4 Californian had learned from his near miss at Wimbledon; unflinching on the crucial points, he erased the "bouncing Czech," 3–6, 6–3, 6–2, 7–6.

Smith and Erik van Dillen were even at two sets apiece against Newcombe and Englishman Roger Taylor in the doubles final when darkness forced a halt. Rather than resume the next day, it was agreed that a nine-point sudden-death tie-breaker would decide the championship. Newcombe-Taylor won it, 5–3.

It was indeed a curious year for men's tennis, climaxed by separate playoffs for the leading "contract" and independent pros:

Laver, Tom Okker, Rosewall, Cliff Drysdale, Ashe, Newcombe, Riessen, and Bob Lutz were the top eight men in the WCT standings. They had their playoffs in Houston and Dallas, Rosewall playing two magnificent tie-breakers to seize the $50,000 top prize at Dallas Memorial Auditorium over Laver, 6–4, 1–6, 7–6, 7–6.

Smith, Nastase, Zeljko Franulovic, Kodes, Richey, Barthes, and Gorman were the seven men who made the round-robin Grand Prix Masters at Paris. Smith collected the $25,000 top bonus prize from the season-long point standings, but Nastase went 6–0 in the Masters, whipping Smith, 5–7, 7–6, 6–3, and collected the tournament's $15,000 top prize. It was the first of Nastase's four victories in the Masters.

At year's end Newcombe and Smith shared "Player of the Year" honors, but there was no clear-cut No. 1.

The Italian was Laver's biggest title, but he won seven of 26 tournaments, 82 of 100 matches, and was far and away the leading money winner with $292,717, which made him tennis's first career millionaire. His nine-year pro winnings: $1,006,974. His most astounding string came in the second and last "Tennis Champions Classic," a series of head-to-head, winner-take-all matches in various cities, leading to a four-man playoff in Madison Square Garden. Laver incredibly swept all 13 of his matches, against top opponents, to win $160,000 in this one event.

Rosewall won seven of 23 tournaments, including the Australian and South African Opens and his third U.S. Pro Championship, and 70 of 86 matches. He earned $138,371 and would have been unchallenged as "Old Man of the Year" had not Pancho Gonzales—43, and already a grandfather—beaten Roscoe Tanner, Richey, and Jimmy Connors (conqueror of Smith in the semis) in succession to win the $10,000 top prize in the Pacific Southwest Open at Los Angeles.

Newcombe captured five of 19 tournaments, 53 of 67 matches, and amassed $101,514. Smith, who missed the early season because he was in basic training with the U. S. Army, won six tournaments and compiled a 79–15 record that included beating Nastase in the opening match and Ion Tiriac in the decisive singles of the 3–2 U.S. Davis Cup Challenge Round victory over Romania. Smith earned

Stan Smith, in the Army now, took the U.S. Open and more than $100,000 in 1971. *UPI*

$100,086. Nastase, who finished the season spectacularly, was the top "independent" earner with $114,000 in winnings.

Relations between the ILTF and WCT, strained at the start of the year and aggravated by the French Open, broke down completely at Wimbeldon. In a bitter, turbulent press conference, fueled by misunderstanding over several WCT "points of negotiation" that were falsely interpreted by the ILTF as "demands," both sides admitted that talks aimed at establishing a unified circuit for 1972 had failed miserably.

Two weeks later, at its annual meeting in the northern Italian resort town of Stresa, the ILTF voted to ban WCT's "contract pros" from all tournaments and facilities controlled by the ILTF and its 93 member national associations, effective at the start of 1972. After 3 1/2 years of "open" tournaments, the contract pros were to be made outcasts again.

In November, new ILTF president Allan Heyman announced that Commercial Union Assurance, a London-based worldwide insurance group, was taking over sponsorship of the Grand Prix from Pepsi, and expanding the financial commitment to more than $250,000. WCT, meanwhile, said that it would focus its attention on strengthening its own tournament series, which it shifted to a May windup in 1972 for maximum TV exposure in the U.S. In the first week of 1972, Ken Rosewall won his second consecutive Australian Open; ironically, the man who had won the first Open tournament in 1968 also won the last of the now interrupted Open era.

Meanwhile, women's tennis—which a year earlier seemed to be overshadowed by the men's game and suffering from a dearth of refreshing young talent—took a dramatically vibrant upturn. From the renegade Virginia Slims of Houston tournament the previous September sprang a new women's tour with $309,000 in prize money. Billie Jean King, who energetically promoted the Virginia Slims Circuit—one observer suggested that she "single-handedly talked it into prominence"—won the lioness's share of the rewards: $117,000. She became the first woman athlete to break the $100,000-in-a-year milestone.

Publisher Gladys Heldman was the behind-the-scenes driving force, arranging 14 tournaments with combined prize money of $189,-100 for the first four months in 1971, while King was the oncourt dynamo and chief drumbeater. Trumpeting that she had her "wheels back" after knee surgery in July 1970, Billie Jean won the first five tournaments on the new tour, at San Francisco, her native Long Beach, Milwaukee, Oklahoma City, and Chattanooga. She beat Rosemary Casals in the first four finals, then Ann Jones, and teamed with Casals to win the doubles at the first seven Slims tournaments.

At Philadelphia—where word came that the U.S. Lawn Tennis Association had lifted its suspension of the "rebel" women—Françoise Durr snapped King's singles streak in the semifinals, and Casals won the tournament. King, who had been ineligible as a "contract pro" for two years, then recovered the U.S. Indoor title she had held in 1966–68, beating Casals again in the final. Rosie, so long the whipping girl, got revenge in the tour's disappointing New York stop at the dingy old 34th Street Armory. In all, King won eight of the inaugural 14 tournaments. Ann Jones won the biggest prize ($9,000) at Las Vegas, and amateur Chris Evert was the most surprising winner, striking down Durr, Judy Alvarez, an ailing King, and Julie Heldman to capture the first pro tournament she entered, at St. Petersburg.

The winter/spring tour—which captured a great deal of media attention, thanks to the clever and energetic promotion of Heldman and King and the emerging fascination with "women's liberation"—was so successful that the women's tour added five summer tournaments, starting with a $40,000 Virginia Slims International at Houston. King captured the $10,000 first prize there, beating Australian Kerry Melville in the final, and went on to take the $10,000 top bonus in the first women's Grand Prix. King's total of $117,000 in prize money was the highest sum for any American, male or female.

While King and Company were pioneering under the banner of "Women's Lob," Margaret Court and Evonne Goolagong dominated the traditional early season. Court beat Ann Jones in three tough sets, Goolagong walloped Virginia Wade, and Court teamed with hometown girl Lesley Hunt to beat Wade and Winnie Shaw as Australia won the 1971 Federation Cup at Perth, actually played the last week in 1970, with a 3–0 victory over Great Britain in the final. With most of the top U.S. players suspended as part of the new women's pro group, the USLTA sent a young team of Patti Hogan and Sharon Walsh, who lost to Britain in the semis.

The Australian Open was played in March, three months later than usual, and Court beat Goolagong, 2–6, 7–6, 7–5, to take her sixth consecutive Grand Slam singles title (1969 Forest Hills, 1970 Australian, French, Wimbledon, and U.S., '71 Australian). Margaret beat Evonne again in the final of the South African Open (Goolagong, of one-eighth aboriginal descent, was the first "nonwhite" woman to compete in Johannesburg); and they teamed to win the doubles.

Virginia Wade won the Italian Open and Billie Jean King the German, both over Helga Niessen Masthoff in the finals, and then Court's Grand Slam winning streak was surprisingly terminated in the third round of the French by Gail Chanfreau, who played the match of her life to win, 6–3, 6–4. She lost in the next round to Helen Gourlay, who went on to beat 1968 titlist Nancy Richey in the semis. Goolagong came through the other half easily and beat Gourlay in the final, 6–3, 7–5, the first player since Althea Gibson in 1956 to win the tournament the first time she played. Durr, alongside Chanfreau, won her fifth consecutive doubles title.

Having won the most prestigious clay court title, Goolagong cemented the No. 1 women's ranking for the year by winning Wimbledon in her second appearance on the grass of the All England Club. The most ethereal of tennis players, graceful, smiling, and free-spirited, she captivated the galleries in dismissing Nancy Richey Gunter in the quarters, 6–3, 6–2; Billie Jean King in the semis, 6–4, 6–4; and Court in the final, 6–4, 6–1. Couturier Teddy Tinling made Goolagong a special dress for the final, white with a scalloped hem and lilac lining and adornments; his staff worked through the night to get it ready, and sent it to Wimbledon with a "good luck" message sewn in, and a silver horseshoe. Such was the spirit of the occasion as Evonne became the youngest champion since Karen Susman in 1962. King and Casals collaborated on their fourth Wimbledon doubles title, and King-Owen Davidson took the mixed over Court-Marty Riessen, 3–6, 6–2, 15–13, the final set being the longest in any Wimbledon final to date.

Despite her triumphs in Paris and London, Goolagong's coach, Vic Edwards, adhered to his long-range plan of not having Evonne play the U.S. circuit until 1972. Therefore, she did not enter the U.S. Open. Neither did Margaret Court nor Ann Jones, both of whom were pregnant. But just when it appeared that Billie Jean King would have the stage to herself, another appealing young rival emerged: Chris Evert.

A 16-year-old high-school student from Fort Lauderdale, Florida, she had beaten Court on clay in Charlotte, North Carolina, the previous fall and won the Virginia Slims tournament at St. Pete on the same surface. But she gained national attention for the first time as the heroine of the 4–3 U.S. Wightman Cup victory over Great Britain on an ultraslow rubberized court in Cleveland in August. Three months younger than Maureen Connolly had been in her debut 20 years earlier, Chris crunched Winnie Shaw, 6–0, 6–4, in the opener and a nervous and off-form Virginia Wade, 6–1, 6–1, in the decisive sixth match, which clinched victory for the injury-riddled U.S. team.

Evert then moved on to the Eastern Grass Court Championships at South Orange, New Jersey, and won there, even though her only previous tournament on grass had been the National Girls singles. At Forest Hills, she immediately became the darling of the crowds, the star of the show since three prominent men were missing. Playing every match in the old concrete stadium, she beat Edda Buding, 6–1, 6–0; Mary Ann Eisel, 4–6, 7–6, 6–1, after Eisel had six match points; Françoise Durr, 2–6, 6–2, 6–3; and Lesley Hunt, 4–6, 6–2, 6–3, to supplant Little Mo Connolly of 1951 as the youngest semifinalist ever. Eisel, Durr, and Hunt all

departed in tears, intimidated by Chrissie's nerveless backcourt stroking and the wildly partisan crowds cheering for "Cinderella in Sneakers."

King had too much of a fast-court arsenal for Evert and ended her fairy tale in the semis, 6–3, 6–2. BJK wrapped up her second Forest Hills title by beating Casals, 6–4, 7–6, sealing the No. 1 U.S. ranking for the fifth time. Her record for the season was 111–10, including victories in 19 out of 30 tournaments.

King's persistent drive to the $100,000 landmark was slowed when she and Casals walked off the court because of a line call dispute at 6–6 in the first set of the final of the Pacific Southwest Open, which they had boycotted the year before. It was one of the strangest episodes in U.S. tournament history, and both players were later fined for their "double default." BJK finally went over the 100-grand mark at Phoenix, where she again beat Casals in the final. King celebrated with champagne in the dressing room, and at a news conference in New York the following week received a congratulatory phone call from President Richard Nixon.

1972

In 1972, a peace agreement was reached between the International Lawn Tennis Federation and World Championship Tennis, reintegrating a men's game that had briefly and regrettably regressed into segregated "contract pro" and "independent pro" circuits, but not in time for the 32 WCT contractees to participate in the French Open or Wimbledon. Stan Smith's triumphs over Ilie Nastase in the Wimbledon final and the Davis Cup gave him the edge over the mercurial Romanian, who won the U.S. Open, for the No. 1 men's ranking. Meanwhile, Billie Jean King swept the French, Wimbledon, and U.S. Open titles and again dominated the ascending Virginia Slims circuit, emphatically ruling women's tennis and giving the U.S. dual supremacy in men's and women's tennis for the first time since 1955.

Despite the unsatisfactory separate circuits for men most of the year, prize money kept

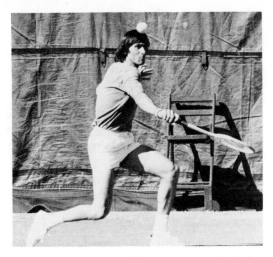

Romania's Ilie Nastase led the run to the bank in 1972, winning at Forest Hills, the first European to do so since Spain's Manuel Santana in 1965. *UPI*

spiraling, to more than $5 million worldwide. Nastase was the top earner at $176,000, with Smith second at $142,300, even though he was in the U. S. Army. Four other men (WCT employees Ken Rosewall, Arthur Ashe, John Newcombe, and Rod Laver) and one woman (King) collected more than $100,-000.

It also was a year of outstanding matches, none finer than the three-hour 34-minute classic between Rosewall and Laver in the final of the WCT Championships at Dallas in May. Laver was favored to grab the $50,000 plum that had eluded him the previous November, but Rosewall—an enduring marvel at age 38—again stole it. Laver revived himself from 1–4 in the final set, saved a match point with an ace, and had the match on his racket at 5–4 in the best-of-12-point tiebreaker, with two serves to come. He pounded both deep to Rosewall's backhand corner, but tennis's most splendid antique reached down for vintage return winners. Laver failed to return the exhausted Rosewall's last serve and it was over, 4–6, 6–0, 6–3, 6–7, 7–6. This had been a duel of torrid, exquisite shotmaking on a 90-degree Mother's Day afternoon, and the sellout crowd at Moody Coliseum and a national television audience of 21 million were enthralled. Many old hands said it might have been the greatest match of all time, and it was

certainly the one that put tennis over as a TV sport in America.

In order to restructure its season for a spring windup, the most advantageous time for U.S. television, WCT counted the last 10 tournaments of 1971 and 10 between January and April 1972 in its point standings. Laver won the Philadelphia opener, rechristened the U.S. Pro Indoor, and four more tournaments to top the point standings heading into the Dallas playoffs. Behind him were Rosewall, Tom Okker, Cliff Drysdale, Marty Riessen, Arthur Ashe, Bob Lutz, and John Newcombe.

Meanwhile, the "independent pros" were playing the USLTA Indoor Circuit organized by Bill Riordan. Smith played only five of 13 events, but won four in a row, starting with the U.S. Indoor over Nastase, 5–7, 6–2, 6–3, 6–4. Also prominent were rookie pro Jimmy Connors—he dropped out of UCLA after becoming the first freshman to win the National Intercollegiate singles in 1971—and "Old Wolf" Pancho Gonzales, who beat Frenchman Georges Goven from two sets down to win the Des Moines Indoors.

Rosewall had begun the New Year by beating 37-year-old fellow Aussie Mal Anderson in the final of the Australian Open, the last ILTF tournament open to WCT pros before the ban voted the previous July went into effect. Rosewall's last Australian championship came 19 years after his first, an unprecedented span between major championships.

Another veteran Aussie, 35-year-old Roy Emerson, saved a match point and beat Lutz, 4–6, 7–6, 6–3, to give Australia the pivotal point in a 6–1 victory over the U.S. in a World Cup marked by Laver's first appearance.

A contemporary of Laver and Emerson, the elegant Spaniard Andres Gimeno, who had left WCT to return to "independent pro" status, won his only Grand Slam singles title, taking the French Open at age 35 over surprising Frenchman Patrick Proisy, 4–6, 6–3, 6–1, 6–1. Proisy had ended Jan Kodes' 17-match French winning streak and bid for a third successive title in the quarters, and had eliminated Italian and German champ Manuel Orantes in the semis. Bob Hewitt and Frew McMillan captured their first French doubles title, and within a month would add the Wimbledon crown.

Smith, runner-up to the now disenfranchised Newcombe (who went to court to try to break the ILTF ban and get a crack at a third straight title) the previous July, was an overwhelming favorite at Wimbledon. The men's singles was dull until the final—the first ever played on Sunday, after a rain delay—when Smith and Nastase went after each other for five absorbing sets. It was Smith's serve-volley power and forthright resolve against Nastase's incomparable speed, agility, and eccentric artistry. The fifth set was electrifying. Smith escaped two break points in the fifth game, which went to seven agonizing deuces, the first with a lunging volley off the frame of his wood racket. Nastase brushed aside two match points on his serve at 4–5, saved another after having 40–0 at 5–6, then netted an easy, high backhand on match point No. 4. The scores of Smith's scintillating triumph: 3–6, 6–3, 6–3, 4–6, 7–5.

Back in America, Lutz won the U.S. Pro Championship at Longwood, ending a nine-year Australian rule to become the first American champ since Butch Buchholz in 1962. But it was the U.S. Open that commanded the most attention.

Lamar Hunt, the Texas millionaire who bankrolled WCT, and Allan Heyman, the Danish-born English lawyer who was president of the ILTF, had been meeting secretly throughout the winter and spring, prompted by Americans Donald Dell and Jack Kramer to find a solution to reunify the men's game. In April, they reached an accord to divide the season into two segments, starting in 1973. WCT would have free reign the first four months of the year, expanding to two groups of 32 players each that would play 11-tournament series to qualify four men from each group for the May WCT finals in Dallas. During that period, no other tournaments with more than $20,000 would be sanctioned. The last eight months of the year would belong to the ILTF for its Grand Prix and Masters.

With this agreement—later modified considerably, under pressure of an antitrust suit by Bill Riordan, who felt he had been sold down the river—the ban of WCT players

from the traditional circuit was removed in July, making Forest Hills the year's only biggie open to everybody.

It turned out to be a wild tournament. No. 2 seed Rosewall was beaten by Mark Cox in the second round; No. 3 Laver by Cliff Richey in the fourth; No. 1 Smith by Ashe in the quarters; No. 5 Newcombe by Fred Stolle; No. 7 Tom Okker by Roscoe Tanner; and No. 8 Kodes by Sandy Mayer, all in the third round. Three Americans (Ashe, Richey, and Tom Gorman) made the semis for the first time in 21 years, but the lone foreigner, Nastase, won the tournament.

"Nasty" incurred the enmity of 14,690 spectators with temper tantrums early in the final but gradually won them over with his shot-making genius. He trailed by two sets to one, 1–3 in the fourth set, and had a break point against him for 1–4. Ashe failed to get a backhand return in play, and faded thereafter, Nastase running five straight games for the set and recovering quickly after losing his serve in the first game of the fifth. Nasty became the first European since Manuel Santana in 1965, and the first ever from Eastern Europe to triumph on the soft grass at Forest Hills, 3–6, 6–3, 6–7, 6–4, 6–3. Roger Taylor, champ with Newcombe the year before, teamed up with Cliff Drysdale to whip Newcombe and Owen Davidson in the doubles final.

Smith sealed his No. 1 ranking in the fall, winning the Pacific Southwest Open, Stockholm and Paris Indoors, and giving a towering performance in the Davis Cup final at Bucharest.

The Davis Cup nations had voted in 1971 to do away with the "Challenge Round"—in which the defending nation sat out and waited for a challenger to plow through the Zone competitions. Thus the U.S. had to follow an unprecedented road for a defending champion: five matches, all in the opponents' backyards. The U.S. didn't lose a match in sprinting past Commonwealth Caribbean, Mexico, and Chile to the semifinals against Spain, but only a gritty five-set victory by Cup rookie Harold Solomon over Juan Gisbert in Barcelona salvaged a 3–2 U.S. victory and a trip to Bucharest for the final.

Romania, with the brilliant Nastase and the menacing Ion Tiriac at home on the red clay of the Progresul Sports Club, was a heavy favorite. Nastase boasted, "We cannot lose at home"—and his record of 19 straight Cup singles victories and 13 consecutive Romanian triumphs in Bucharest seemed to support his braggadocio. Slow clay, an adoring and vocal home crowd, and notoriously patriotic linesmen all favored Nastase and Tiriac.

This was the first Davis Cup final in Europe in 39 years, and perhaps the greatest international sporting occasion ever in Bucharest, where likenesses of Nastase and Tiriac were everywhere. But the pressure of great expectations worked in reverse. Smith played undoubtedly his finest match on clay, while Nastase was high-strung and erratic as the American took the critical opener, 11–9, 6–2, 6–3. Tiriac, the brooding former ice hockey international who claims kinship with Dracula, used every ploy of gamesmanship, orchestrating the crowd and the linesmen, to come from two sets down and beat Tom Gorman in the second match, but the doubles was a Romanian disaster.

Once one of the world's premier teams, Nastase and Tiriac had fallen out as friends, and their incompatibility showed as Smith and Erik van Dillen, playing with skill and élan, humiliated the home team, 6–2, 6–0, 6–3. Tiriac summoned all his wiles and battled heroically in the fourth match, but Smith was too good for him and clinched the Cup, 4–6, 6–2, 6–4, 2–6, 6–0. Nastase beat Gorman in the meaningless fifth match.

It had been a wild weekend in Bucharest—made unforgettable by the fervor of the fans, the thievery of the linesmen, the machinations of Tiriac, and extraordinarily heavy security in the aftermath of the Olympic massacre at Munich (there had been rumors of threats against two Jewish members of the U.S. team, Solomon and Brian Gottfried)—but in the end, captain Dennis Ralston's brigade could savor the finest victory ever by a U.S. team away from home.

Once again there were separate playoffs for "contract pros" and "independents" at the end of the year. WCT scheduled a makeshift "winter championship" in Rome for the top eight men in a summer-fall circuit that filled the gap before the new two-group format started in 1973. Ashe won the $25,000 first prize, beating Nikki Pilic, Okker, and Lutz.

The Commercial Union Masters was played in Barcelona with a new format—two four-man round-robin groups, with the two players with the best records in each advancing to "knockout" semis and final. Gorman had Smith beaten in one semi, but hurt his back and defaulted so as not to wreck the final. Nastase repeated as champion, beating Smith in a rousing final, 6–3, 6–2, 3–6, 2–6, 6–3, but it was his only victory in five meetings on the year with the tall Californian.

One of the most significant developments of 1972 was the formation, at the U.S. Open, of a new players' guild—the Association of Tennis Professionals. Some 50 players paid $400 initial dues, and Washington attorney Donald Dell—former U.S. Davis Cup captain, now personal manager for a number of top players—enlisted Jack Kramer as executive director. The urbane Cliff Drysdale was elected president, and Dell became the Association's legal counsel. Other players' associations had come and gone in the past, but the ATP was carefully constituted and loomed as a major new force in the pro game's politics and administration.

The politics of women's tennis in 1972 began with conciliation and ended with a major new rift.

Early in the year Gladys Heldman, organizer of the rebel women's pro tour the year before, was appointed by the USLTA as coordinator of women's tennis and director of the women's tour in a peace effort. Thus empowered, she expanded the winter tour to $302,000 in prize money. But by September the honeymoon was over, Mrs. Heldman resigned her USLTA post amid mutual mistrust, and formed the Women's International Tennis Federation. She took the USLTA to court for alleged antitrust violations. Meanwhile, the USLTA appointed U.S. Wightman Cup captain Edy McGoldrick to form a women's tour in opposition to Mrs. Heldman's in the winter-spring of 1973.

On the tennis court, there was no question who was boss in '72. King did not play the

Australian Open, but swept the rest of the Grand Slam singles titles with the loss of only one set, to Virginia Wade in the quarterfinals at Wimbledon. Billie Jean won 10 of 24 tournaments, compiled an 87–13 record, ran away with the women's Grand Prix top prize, and exceeded her prize money landmark of 1971, earning $119,000. Against her greatest career rivals, she was 3–2 over Margaret Court (back on the circuit after the birth of her first child, Daniel) and 4–3 over Nancy Richey Gunter for the year.

Wade won her first Australian Open title, over Goolagong, 6–4, 6–4. King won her first French Open title—joining Doris Hart, Maureen Connolly, Shirley Fry, and Court as the only women to have won all four Grand Slam singles titles—with a 6–3, 6–3 triumph over Goolagong. BJK also dethroned Goolagong at Wimbledon by the same scores, after Evonne had thrillingly won her first meeting with Chris Evert in the semis.

At the U.S. Open, King beat Wade in the quarters, 6–2, 7–5; Court in the semis, 6–4, 6–4; and Kerry Melville—who ripped Evert in the semis by skidding clever slices short, low, and wide to Chrissie's two-fisted backhand—for the $10,000 first prize, 6–3, 7–5.

Dutchwoman Betty Stove was the lady of the year in doubles, teaming with King to win the French and Wimbledon and with Françoise Durr to take the U.S. Open. She was the first woman to win all three in a season since Darlene Hard and Maria Bueno did so in 1960.

Evert, still an amateur at age 17, was the only player with a winning record over King for the year: 3–1, including a 6–1, 6–0 victory in the final of the Virginia Slims tournament in her hometown of Fort Lauderdale. She also won the richest women's tournament, the $100,000 Virginia Slims Championship at Boca Raton, Florida—beating King and Melville in the final two rounds after her 15-year-old sister, Jeanne, erased Court in the third round—but could not accept the $25,000 first prize.

Evert ranked third in the U.S. behind King and Gunter (who beat her all three times they played), compiling a 47–7 record, winning four tournaments. She spearheaded the 5–2

U.S. Wightman Cup victory over Great Britain at Wimbledon, beating Wade and Joyce Williams in singles, and then beat Court and Goolagong for the only two U.S. victories in a 5–2 loss to Australia in the inaugural Bonne Bell Cup at Cleveland. Evert also won her first adult national title—the first of four consecutive U.S. Clay Court singles at Indianapolis—by beating Court in the semis and Goolagong in the final.

The Maureen Connolly Brinker Indoor at Dallas was the first tournament in which both Goolagong and Evert competed, but King delayed their first meeting. She fought off a 1–3, 15–40 deficit and later cramps in the final set to beat Evert in the quarters, and came from behind again to beat Goolagong in the semis. Exhausted, she fell easily to Gunter in the final.

The magical first encounter between the two radiant new princesses of women's tennis came, appropriately, in the semis at Wimbledon. It was a majestic match worthy of the occasion, Goolagong winning, 4–6, 6–3, 6–4, after trailing 0–3 in the second and 2–3 (down a break) in the third. Evert promptly won the next two meetings, however, setting the tone for their career rivalry.

The Virginia Slims circuit continued to grow, offering $525,775 in prize purses for 21 tournaments, but the appeal of Evert and Goolagong—who could not be enticed by Heldman to side with her in a war against the ILTF establishment—made them the cornerstones of the rival USLTA circuit in 1973.

1973

Tennis celebrated a Centennial in 1973—commemorating the accepted, if historically debatable, origin of the modern sport at a shooting party in Wales in 1873, where Major Walter Clopton Wingfield introduced the game he later patented as Sphairistike—with undoubtedly the most peculiar season in its history.

The landmark match of the year did not come in any of the traditional major tournaments. There was nothing traditional at all about the celebrated "Battle of the Sexes" between 29-year-old Billie Jean King and 55-

In the "Battle of the Sexes" in 1973, Bobby Riggs cleared the net, and Billie Jean King cleared $100,000. *UPI*

year-old Bobby Riggs, the self-proclaimed "king of male chauvinist pigs," at Houston's Astrodome the night of September 20. But this spectacle—roughly equal parts tennis, carnival, and sociological phenomenon—captured the fancy of America as no pure tennis match ever had. The crowd of 30,472, paying as much as $100 a seat, was the largest ever to witness a tennis match. Some 50 million more watched on prime-time television. The whole gaudy promotion was worth perhaps $3 million, and King collected a $100,000 winner-take-all purse, plus ancillary revenues, for squashing Riggs, 6-4, 6-3, 6-3.

Riggs, the outspoken hustler who had won Wimbledon and the U.S. Championship in 1939, created the bonanza by a challenge proclaiming that women's lib was a farce and that the best of the female tennis pros couldn't even beat him, "an old man with one foot in the grave." He challenged Margaret Court to a winner-take-all challenge match on Mother's Day at a California resort he was plugging;

she was the ideal victim for his well-perfected "psych job" and assortment of junk shots. Margaret choked and Riggs won, 6-2, 6-1. That set the stage for the challenge against Billie Jean, the leading voice of women's lib in sports.

The whole ballyhooed extravaganza was just right for the times, and it became a national media event, front-page news in papers and magazines across the country. King exulted in her victory, not as a great competitive triumph but as "a culmination" of her years of striving to demonstrate that tennis could be a big-league entertainment for the masses, and that women could play.

Tennis was clearly the "in" sport of the mid-70s. Sales of tennis equipment, clothing, and vacations were burgeoning, and though the pro game remained plagued with disputes—notably an antitrust suit in women's tennis and a boycott of Wimbledon by the men's Association of Tennis Professionals—it continued to grow quickly. Prize money in 1973 rose to nearly $6 million.

World Championship Tennis introduced the new format agreed to in its 1972 accord with the International Lawn Tennis Federation: a January-through-May series with a field of 64 players split into two groups of 32, playing parallel tours of 11 $50,000 tournaments. The top four men of each group (Stan Smith, Rod Laver, Roy Emerson, and John Alexander of "A"; Ken Rosewall, Arthur Ashe, Marty Riessen, and Roger Taylor of "B") went to Dallas for the $100,000 finals.

Smith, who had won a record four consecutive tournaments and six of 11 to top Laver (three victories) in his group, took the $50,000 top prize by beating Ashe, 6-3, 6-3, 4-6, 6-4. Ashe had ended Rosewall's bid for a third straight Dallas title in a five-set semi, and Smith waylaid Laver.

For the first time WCT also conducted a doubles competition, using the same format as singles. Smith and Lutz won the $40,000 first prize in the playoffs at Montreal, beating Riessen and Tom Okker, 6-2, 7-6, 6-0.

Running concurrently with the WCT tour for three months was the USLTA Indoor Circuit of Bill Riordan, who refused to be dealt out by the WCT-ILTF deal dividing the season, and threatened restraint-of-trade proceedings if forced to limit the prize money in his tournaments. His headliners were Jimmy Connors and Ilie Nastase, both of whom he managed at the time. Connors won six of the eight events he played, including the U.S. Indoor over Germany's Karl Meiler.

John Newcombe started the year by winning his first Australian Open title over New Zealander Onny Parun, 6–3, 6–7, 7–5, 6–1, and sharing the doubles with countryman Mal Anderson. Newcombe also won the French doubles with Okker, but slumped badly until rededicating himself late in the year, winning the U.S. Open and teaming with Laver to return the Davis Cup to Australia in the first year it was open to "contract pros."

On balance, the No. 1 ranking had to go to Nastase, the volatile Romanian (he accumulated fines totaling $11,000) who won 15 of 31 tournaments, 118 of 135 matches, and led the money earning list with $228,750, including a $55,000 bonus for topping the Grand Prix standings. He clobbered Manuel Orantes in the Italian Open final, 6–1, 6–1, 6–1, swept through the French Open without losing a set (Nikki Pilic was his final victim, 6–3, 6–3, 6–0), topped the Grand Prix standings, and won the Masters for the third straight year, beating Newcombe in the round-robin and personal nemesis Okker in the final, 6–3, 7–5, 4–6, 6–3, at Boston.

"Contract pro" John Newcombe made the winner's circle at the 1973 U.S. Open and helped bring the Davis Cup back to Australia. *UPI*

Nastase played indifferently at Wimbledon, where he was considered a shoo-in because of the boycott, but was beaten in the fourth round by Sandy Mayer, and at Forest Hills, where Andrew Pattison ambushed him in the second round. But his overall record was the best.

The No. 1 U.S. men's ranking was shared for the first time in history. The ranking committee could not choose between Smith, who won eight of 19 tournaments and 81 of 103 matches but lost his world-beating form after peaking in May, and Connors, who won 10 of 21 tournaments and 81 of 97 matches, capturing the U.S. Pro and South African Open titles.

Connors, just 20, was the brightest of several ascending youngsters, including Bjorn Borg and Brian Gottfried (winner of the $30,000 first prize at the ATP's Alan King Classic in Las Vegas, over Ashe). Connors was the youngest man atop the American rankings since one of his mentors, Pancho Gonzales, ruled at 20 in 1948, and Smith was the first to be No. 1 four times since Bill Tilden gained the top spot for the 10th time in 1929.

Connors, brimming with confidence after his fine showing on the less-strenuous-than-WCT U.S. Indoor circuit, knocked off top-seeded Smith in the first round of the U.S. Pro Championship and went on to whip Ray Moore, Dick Stockton, Cliff Richey, and Arthur Ashe for the title. He saved a match point in beating Smith again at the Pacific Southwest, and escaped another match point in beating out Smith for a semifinal berth in the Grand Prix Masters, giving him a 3–0 record against Stan for the calendar year. (Smith was the only player to reach both the WCT and Masters playoffs.)

The already turbulent political waters in tennis were muddied further by formation of a league called World Team Tennis, which planned to start intercity team competition using a unique, Americanized format in 1974. Dennis Murphy, who had helped found the American Basketball Association and the World Hockey Association, envisioned 16 teams with six players apiece under contract competing in a May-through-August season.

Jack Kramer and the ATP board came out stanchly opposed to WTT, saying it would harm the long-range players' interest in a healthy worldwide tournament circuit, but even as discussions between the ILTF and ATP about team tennis were scheduled, a more immediate problem arose.

When ATP member Nikki Pilic was suspended by the Yugoslav Tennis Federation for allegedly failing to participate in a Davis Cup series to which he had committed himself, ATP members objected, claiming that this was precisely the sort of arbitrary disciplinary power by a national association that the players' association had been formed to counteract. An ATP threat to withdraw all its 70 members from the French Open if Pilic was barred from the tournament was averted by a delaying tactic: an appeal hearing before the ILTF Emergency Committee, which reduced Pilic's suspension from three months to one month.

This did not satisfy the ATP board, which contended that only their own association should have disciplinary authority over players. Many also felt that the one-month suspension, which included Wimbledon, was devised by the ILTF to demonstrate its muscle because it believed the players would never support a boycott of the world's premier tournament. Thus "the Pilic Affair" became a test of the will and organization of the new association. Many ATP leaders felt that if they gave in on this first showdown, they would never be strong, whereas if they held firm and proved to the ILTF that even Wimbledon was not sacred, the Association's unity and power would never be doubted in the future.

After days of tortuous meetings and attempts to find compromises, including the ATP's seeking an injunction in Britain's High Court forcing Wimbledon to accept Pilic's entry, ATP members voted to withdraw en masse if Pilic were barred from Wimbledon. Seventy-nine men did withdraw their entries, including 13 of the original 16 seeds; Ilie Nastase, Englishman Roger Taylor, and Australian Ray Keldie were the only members who did not withdraw. (They were later fined by the ATP.)

Amid ferocious press criticism and bitter-ness, the tournament was played with a second-rate men's field. The British public, taking up the press crusade that "Wimbledon is bigger than a few spoiled players," turned out in near-record numbers. They made heroes of Nastase, Taylor, and such bright newcomers as Connors and Swedish teen-ager Borg, who became the immediate heartthrob of squealing British schoolgirls.

Nastase, an overwhelming favorite, was beaten at the end of the first week by collegian amateur Mayer, who went on to reach the semifinals. Jan Kodes won the championship, the first Czech to do so since expatriate Jaroslav Drobny in 1954, beating Soviet No. 1 Alex Metreveli, 6–1, 9–8, 6–3, in a predicatably uninspiring final. Nastase and Connors clowned their way to a five-set victory over Australians John Cooper and Neale Fraser in the doubles final.

In one sense, the success of the boycotted Wimbledon was a triumph for the tournament, proving again what an unshakable institution it is, an important part of British summer life. But in the long run, the boycott made the ATP. The players' message to the ILTF was clear: They were finally united in an organization to influence their own destiny; if they could stand up to Wimbledon, they could stand up to any authority. The Association was established as a political force to be reckoned with in the future.

Meanwhile, with Wimbledon sacrificed for one year, the U.S. Open became the men's most important competitive test of 1973. Nastase, coseeded No. 1 with Smith, squandered a two-set lead and lost to journeyman Pattison. Kodes, who resented being downgraded as a "cheese champion" at Wimbledon, returned serve spectacularly in going all the way to the final, saving a match point at nightfall to outstroke Smith, 7–5, 6–7, 1–6, 6–1, 7–5, in the semifinals. Kodes almost repeated his 1971 upset over Newcombe, this time in the final instead of the first round, but the rugged Australian ultimately had too much firepower and won a spectacular finale, 6–4, 1–6, 4–6, 6–2, 6–3. Newcombe and Davidson beat countrymen Laver and Rosewall in the doubles final.

Newcombe and Laver also performed heroically in the Davis Cup. Laver, representing his country for the first time since 1962, won all his singles in a 4–1 semifinal victory over Czechoslovakia in Melbourne and a 5–0 whitewash of the United States in the final, ending the Americans' five-year reign. In the Cup's first indoor final, before a disappointing crowd at Cleveland's Public Auditorium, Newcombe set the tone by beating Smith in the opener, 6–1, 3–6, 6–3, 3–6, 6–4. Artistically, this might well have been the match of the year, Newcombe—an enforced absentee from Davis Cup competition since 1967—coming back from 1–3 and a break point in the fifth set with some sublime play. Laver beat Tom Gorman, 8–10, 8–6, 6–8, 6–3, 6–1, in the second match, then surprisingly teamed with Newcombe to pummel Smith and Erik van Dillen in the decisive doubles, 6–1, 6–2, 6–4. (Earlier in the year, in the American Zone final, Smith and van Dillen had beaten Chileans Jaime Fillol and Patricio Cornejo, 7–9, 37–39, 8–6, 6–1, 6–3, in the longest Davis Cup match on record.)

Captain Neale Fraser's "Australian Antique Show" was so strong that evergreen Ken Rosewall—whose brilliant singles victories over Marty Riessen and Smith and inspired doubles alongside John Alexander had spurred Australia to a 5–2 World Cup triumph over the U.S. at Hartford in March—couldn't crack the lineup. Newcombe and Laver handled the stunned Gorman and Smith in the final singles for the 5–0 sweep.

At year's end, the ATP board remained opposed to World Team Tennis and to guaranteed contracts for players—a stance it was forced to reverse the next year, under growing pressure from members who wanted to accept guarantees. WTT named former U.S. Davis Cup captain George MacCall as its commissioner, announced that it would begin operations in May 1974, and signed such prominent players as Newcombe, Rosewall, Billie Jean King, and Evonne Goolagong to lucrative contracts.

In women's pro tennis, two separate tours were played in the winter and spring of 1973. The Virginia Slims Circuit consisted of 14 events, starring Billie Jean King and Margaret Court, conducted under the auspices of the

"Women's International Tennis Federation" (WITF), incorporated as an autonomous body by Gladys Heldman. The USLTA—claiming that it had been hoodwinked and double-crossed by Mrs. Heldman—hastily arranged a circuit of eight tournaments featuring Chris Evert, Evonne Goolagong, and Virginia Wade.

In Mrs. Heldman's suit against the USLTA in Federal District Court in New York, Judge Milton Pollack ruled against her, rendering the WITF short-lived. The players who signed with WITF were declared ineligible for the 1973 Commercial Union Grand Prix (won by Chris Evert), but by June an agreement was reached between the USLTA and Philip Morris, Inc., parent company of Virginia Slims, for a single women's tour under USLTA/ILTF auspices starting in September 1973. Part of the compromise was that Mrs. Heldman would not be involved.

Out of wreckage of the WITF, a new women players' guild—the Women's Tennis Association—was formed at Wimbledon. With Billie Jean King as its first president, the WTA worked closely with the USLTA's Edy McGoldrick in organizing a strong women's circuit for 1974 and beyond.

It is ironic that, because of Bobby Riggs, 1973 will be remembered as the year of Court's humiliation and King's triumph. In fact, Court was the dominant women's player of the season—winner of the Australian, French, and U.S. Opens, 14 of 18 tournaments on the Virginia Slims Circuit, and $204,000 in prize money. Dating from her loss to Jeanne Evert in Boca Raton the previous fall, Court won 59 consecutive matches. For the calender year her record was 102–6, and she beat King in three of four meetings.

Court started the year by beating Evonne Goolagong in the final of the Australian Open for the third consecutive year, 6–4, 7–5. She then teamed with Virginia Wade to win the doubles for the eighth time in 13 years, with her sixth different partner.

Court was down 3–5 in the final of the French, but recovered to beat Evert, 6–7, 7–6, 6–4, and became the only woman other than Suzanne Lenglen to win five singles titles in Paris. This was a battle of torrid ground-stroking, the most memorable women's match of the year. Court also won her fourth French doubles title, with Wade.

Only Wimbledon prevented Court from recording a second Grand Slam. All eight seeds advanced to the quarterfinals, and the only reversal of form was Evert's 6–1, 1–6, 6–1 defeat of No. 1 seed Court in the semis—as unexpected a result on the grass that Margaret likes so much as was her comeback in the French final on Chrissie's beloved clay. King, superbly conditioned physically and mentally and operating at a high emotional pitch, beat Goolagong in the semifinals, 6–3, 5–7, 6–3, and blasted Evert in the final, 6–0, 7–5. BJK became the first five-time singles winner since Helen Wills Moody four decades earlier, and also teamed with Rosemary Casals to win the doubles and with Owen Davidson to capture the mixed, her third Wimbledon "triple." The women's doubles triumph was King's ninth, with four partners, and fifth with Casals.

At the U.S. Open, 1971–72 champion King walked off court while trailing Julie Heldman, 1–4, in the final set of a fourth-round match played in exhausting heat and humidity. Heldman complained, as was her right under the rules, that King was taking far more than the one minute allowed at changeovers. "If you want the match that badly, you can have it," seethed King, who later said she was suffering from a virus that had sapped her strength. King's defeat—3–6, 6–4, 4–1, ret.—recalled two other celebrated surrenders by champions: Suzanne Lenglen to Molla Bjurstedt Mallory in 1921, and Helen Wills Moody to Helen Jacobs in 1933.

Court beat Wade in two tie-breakers in the quarterfinals, avenged her Wimbledon defeat by Evert, 7–5, 2–6, 6–2, in the semis, and made Goolagong a bridesmaid again in the final, 7–6, 5–7, 6–2. For her victory Margaret received $25,000, the same as Newcombe, as the women achieved prize money parity with men in a major championship for the first time. The singles triumph was her 26th, and last, in a Big Four event. Court teamed with Wade for Court's 21st and last Big Four doubles title.

King, despite being hampered by injuries in the early season, won seven of 17 tournaments and 56 of 65 matches. Including her $100,000 triumph over Riggs, she earned $197,000 for the year. In earning the No. 1 U.S. ranking for the seventh time, she equaled a feat previously achieved only by Mallory (between 1915 and 1926) and Moody (between 1923 and 1931).

Evert—who turned pro on her 18th birthday, December 21, 1972—earned $151,352 in her rookie season. She virtually monopolized the USLTA winter tour, winning six of seven tournaments, beating Goolagong in the final of the last three. Evert went on to win 12 of 20 tournaments, 88 of 97 matches, including the Virginia Slims Championship at Boca Raton over her personal nemesis, Nancy Richey Gunter. Evert was disappointed to lose three major finals in a row at midseason—the Italian Open to Goolagong, the French to Court, and Wimbledon to King—but she took her first significant international title in the autumn, the South African Open over Goolagong. During this tournament she also announced her engagement to Jimmy Connors, later called off.

Evert also led the U.S. to a 5–2 victory over a young and, except for Virginia Wade, inexperienced British team in the Wightman Cup. This was the 50th anniversary of the competition, and was therefore played at Longwood Cricket Club, only yards from the home of Cup donor Hazel Hotchkiss Wightman, who was present and active in the celebrations at age 86.

Australia, led by Evonne Goolagong, defeated South Africa, 3–0, in the final of the Federation Cup at Bad Homburg, Germany, and Goolagong's 6–2, 6–3 victory over Evert and Kerry Melville's triumph over Julie Heldman spearheaded an Australian comeback and 6–3 victory over the U.S. in the second Bonne Bell Cup, at Sydney.

Other notable happenings during the year: Rosie Casals took the biggest check, $30,000, for beating King in the semis and Gunter in the final of the Family Circle Cup at Hilton Head, South Carolina. Goolagong beat Evert in the final of the Western Championships at Cincinnati, Chris's last defeat on clay for nearly six years. Evert won her second U.S. Clay Court title the next week, beginning an astounding streak on her favorite surface that had stretched to 25 tournaments and 125 matches (including the only three U.S. Opens played on clay) until her defeat by Tracy Austin in the Italian Open semifinals in May 1979.

Kathy Kuykendall turned pro at age 16, and then Californian Robin Tenney did her one better, becoming the youngest pro to date at age 15—though three years later, having been unsuccessful on the tour, she applied for and was granted a return to amateur status in order to play college tennis.

Although Arthur Ashe was beaten by Connors in the South African Open final, he was the first nonwhite to reach the men's final there, and the first to win a men's title, the doubles with Tom Okker. Ashe's first appearance in South Africa was an emotional pilgrimage for him to a country he had long studied, but had heretofore been denied a visa to visit.

The king and queen of Wimbledon: Jimmy Connors and Christ Evert in 1974. *UPI*

1974

Two young Americans—21-year-old Jimmy Connors and 19-year-old Chris Evert, who had announced their engagement late in 1973 but called it off before getting to the altar the next fall—reigned as the king and queen of tennis in 1974. And as the American game celebrated its Centennial, two startling surveys revealed just how popular the game had become in the United States.

The respected A. C. Nielsen Company made its first survey of tennis in 1970, estimating that 10.3 million Americans played occasionally and projecting that the number would increase to 15 million by 1980. A second survey in 1973 indicated that the growth rate was much faster, and fixed the number of players at 20.2 million. A third study, released in September 1974, indicated a staggering 68 per cent increase to 33.9 million Americans who said they played tennis "from time to time," and a more significant estimate that 23.4 million played at least three times a month.

Almost as surprising as the rate of the participation boom was a Louis Harris survey that indicated a substantial rise in tennis's popularity as a spectator sport. "The number

[of sports fans] who say they 'follow' tennis has risen from 17 to 26 per cent just in the last year, by far the most dramatic change in American sports preferences," the Harris organization said.

This growth was reflected in the tennis industry, as new companies rushed in to offer a dizzying variety of equipment to the burgeoning market, and in the professional game, where prize money continued to skyrocket. Four men and one woman exceeded the $200,000 prize money barrier, which had seemed unattainable just a few years earlier. Connors ($281,309) and Evert ($261,460) led the parade of six-figure earners.

Connors rampaged to the most successful season of any American player since Don Budge in his Grand Slam year of 1938, and also became the center of a new political storm in men's tennis.

Connors won 99 of 103 matches during the year, 14 of 20 tournaments, including the Australian Open, Wimbledon, U.S. Open, U.S. Indoor, U.S. Clay Courts, and South African Open. He was denied a chance at the Grand Slam when the French Tennis Federation, led by the strong-willed Philippe Chatrier, barred any player who had signed a contract to compete in the new World Team

Tennis league in the U.S., which Europeans viewed as a threat to their major summer tournaments.

Thus Connors, who had signed to play some matches with the WTT Baltimore Banners, and Evonne Goolagong, contracted to the Pittsburgh Triangles, were kept out of the world's premier clay court championship after having won the Australian at the start of the year. Bill Riordan, the maverick Connors' maverick manager, knew there was no way he could sue the French Federation directly, but filed a $40 million antitrust suit against Association of Tennis Professionals officers Jack Kramer and Donald Dell (who had been anti-WTT activists) and Commercial Union Assurance, sponsor of the ILTF Grand Prix, alleging a conspiracy to monopolize professional tennis and keep Connors (and other WTT players) out of the French.

Few envisioned what a world-beating year it would be for the brash left-hander Connors when he beat Australian Phil Dent, 7–6, 6–4, 4–6, 6–3, for the Australian title. Aussies Geoff Masters and Ross Case took the doubles at Kooyong in Melbourne, their first Grand Slam title.

Connors dominated Riodan's USLTA Indoor Circuit—which was played at the same time as an expanded, three-group World Championship Tennis circuit—winning seven of the nine tournaments he played, including the U.S. Indoor over Frew McMillan.

At Wimbledon, Connors came within two points of defeat at the hands of Dent in the second round, but pulled away to win from 5–5, 0–30 in the fifth set. He beat Jan Kodes in five rugged sets in the quarterfinals, Dick Stockton (conqueror of Ilie Nastase) in a four set semi, and then ravaged 39-year-old Ken Rosewall, 6–1, 6–1, 6–4, in the final.

Rosewall had masterfully beaten 1970–71 champ and top seed John Newcombe in the quarters and come from two sets and a match point in the third-set tie-breaker down to beat 1972 champ Stan Smith, 6–8, 4–6, 9–8, 6–1, 6–3, in one of Wimbledon's most memorable comebacks.

But Connors' ferocious returns of Rosewall's unintimidating serves kept the old man constantly on the defensive, the young lion always on the attack. Consequently, Connors became the youngest champion since Lew Hoad beat Rosewall at age 22 in the 1956 final, and Rosewall—the sentimental choice who had been runner-up in 1954, '56, and '70—remained, along with Pancho Gonzales, "the greatest players who never won Wimbledon."

Meanwhile, Newcombe captured his sixth doubles title, the fifth with fellow Aussie Tony Roche.

Connors had a virus infection that left him doubtful for the last U.S. Open played on grass courts. He lost a great deal of weight, but turned out to be lean and mean as he barreled through the tournament without serious danger, beating Alex Metreveli in the quarters, Roscoe Tanner (who had stopped Nastase and Smith) in the semis, and Rosewall again in the final.

Rosewall, two months shy of his 40th birthday, trimmed Newcombe (who had beaten Arthur Ashe in a marvelous five-set quarterfinal) in the semis, but was humiliated by Connors, 6–1, 6–0, 6–1, the worst final-round flogging in the history of the U.S.

Roscoe Tanner ousted Ilie Nastase and Stan Smith before losing to Jimmy Connors in the 1974 U.S. Open semifinals. *Jack Mecca*

Championships. Connors became the youngest Forest Hills Champion since, ironically, Rosewall in 1956. The doubles title also stayed in America, Smith and Bob Lutz regaining the prize they first won in 1968.

Connors was the main man, but there were other outstanding performers during the year. Bjorn Borg, the ascending "Teen Angel" from Sweden, became the youngest player to win the Italian and French Opens and the U.S. Pro Championship. He celebrated his 18th birthday during the French, where he lost the first two sets of the final and then stomped Manuel Orantes, 2–6, 6–7, 6–0, 6–1, 6–1. He had been 17 when he won the Italian, dethroning Nastase in the final, 6–3, 6–4, 6–2. At the U.S. Pro, Borg beat Tom Okker, 7–6, 6–1, 6–1, after resurrecting himself from 1–5 in the fifth set to beat Jan Kodes in an astonishing semifinal, 7–6, 6–0, 1–6, 2–6, 7–6.

Borg won six tournaments and was runner-up in four more, including the WCT finals at Dallas. There he coolly beat Ashe and Kodes before running up against Newcombe, 30, who won this one for the older generation, 4–6, 6–3, 6–3, 6–2.

Borg was also runner-up to Connors in the U.S. Clay Court, their only meeting of the year. Borg had won their first meeting in the quarterfinals of the 1973 Stockholm Open, but now Connors was off on a seven-match run in what would develop into the rivalry of the '70s in men's tennis.

Newcombe was the dominant player of the WCT season, winning five of the 11 tournaments in his group (Nastase and Laver won four each in theirs), but the new format of tricolor groups (Red, Blue, Green) each playing 11 tournaments to qualify their two point leaders plus two "wild cards" for the eight-man Dallas finals was not very successful. The product was too diluted, difficult to follow, and the zigzagging global travel schedule taxed the players. WCT, which two years before had the inside track in the men's pro game, had overexpanded and suffered in prestige in the process.

Bob Hewitt and Frew McMillan won the WCT doubles final at Montreal, sharing $40,000 for beating Newcombe and Owen

Davidson in the final, 6–2, 6–7, 6–1, 6–2. A makeshift young doubles team of Brian Gottfried and Mexican Raul Ramirez was formed in the spring and immediately proved to be a successful partnership, winning the first of four consecutive Italian doubles titles and several other tournaments.

After Wimbledon, another 22-year-old left-hander arose and edged out Connors for the $100,000 top prize in the Commercial Union Grand Prix. Guillermo Vilas of Argentina, who had shown promise of things to come by knocking out defending champ Andres Gimeno at the French Open in 1973, ruled the U.S. Summer Circuit and won six of his last 15 tournaments.

The attractive and sensitive young South American, a former law student and part-time poet, also won the Grand Prix Masters at Melbourne, which Connors boycotted. (He claimed a dental problem, but most blamed his suit against sponsor Commercial Union for his absence.) Even though Vilas did not like grass courts, which were not well suited to his heavy topspin game, he beat Newcombe, Borg, and Onny Parun to win his round-robin group, then Ramirez in the semis and Nastase in a brilliant final, 7–6, 6–2, 3–6, 3–6, 6–4, to claim his biggest title to date.

At season's end, Vilas was not far behind Connors on the money list, having earned $271,327. Newcombe was third with the $273,299, Borg fourth with $215,229. Laver won six tournaments, including the U.S. Pro Indoor over Ashe (his fifteenth consecutive victory over Arthur in 15 years) and the rich Alan King Classic, and temporarily remained the all-time money winner with a career total of $1,379,454. Connors would catch him soon enough.

Meanwhile, World Team Tennis made its raucous debut in May, offering players a lucrative alternative to tournaments during the summer. Sixteen teams embarked on a schedule of 44 contests each, the format being five one-set matches (men's and women's singles and doubles, plus mixed doubles), with the cumulative games won in all five deciding the outcome.

The Philadelphia Freedoms, with Billie Jean King as player-coach, defeated Ken

Rosewall's Pittsburgh Triangles in the ballyhooed opener at Philadelphia's Spectrum, 31–25. Philadelphia had the best season record, 39–5, but lost the playoffs in two straight to the Denver Racquets, who promptly moved to Phoenix. No team made money, and the average loss per franchise was estimated to be $300,000. The league was cut down to 12 teams in 1975, and only one came back for the second season with the original owners.

A more traditional team competition, the Davis Cup, continued to be tarnished by political problems and cumbersome scheduling that often left countries playing matches without their best players, who had conflicting commitments elsewhere. Such was the case with both the United States, which was ambushed by Colombia, 4–1, at Bogota in January, and Australia, which traveled to India undermanned and was beaten by the same score.

For the first time in the 74-year history of the competition, the Cup was decided by default. South Africa became the fifth nation to hold the sterling silver punchbowl when the Indian Government refused to let its team play the final, in protest of South Africa's apartheid racial policies.

Connors declined to play for the U.S. in either the Davis Cup or the World Cup—won by Australia at Hartford, 5–2, with Newcombe spearheading the attack, beating both Ashe and Smith in singles and teaming with Roche to beat them in doubles.

Evert became the youngest woman to gain the No. 1 U.S. ranking since Maureen Connolly reigned supreme in 1951–53. Chrissie won 13 tournaments—including Wimbledon, the French, Italian, and U.S. Clay Courts—and was never beaten before the semifinals in compiling a 71–7 record in 20 tournaments. Her $261,460 in prize money far outdistanced Margaret Court's record of the previous year.

Evert did not have things entirely her own way, even though she did compile a 56-match winning streak in midseason. Evonne Goolagong beat her in four of six meetings, including the finals of the Australian Open and the Virginia Slims Championship at Los Angeles, and the semifinals of the U.S. Open.

Billie Jean King won the Open and took two of three from Evert, including the final of the U.S. Indoor, which BJK captured for the fifth time.

Goolagong played inspired tennis in celebrating the New Year with a 7–6, 4–6, 6–0 triumph over Evert at Melbourne, winning her native title for the first time after being runner-up the previous three years. Evonne also paired with American Peggy Michel, her Pittsburgh Triangles teammate and partner in WTT, to win the Australian and Wimbledon doubles.

With Goolagong, King, Kerry Melville (who would marry her Boston Lobsters teammate Raz Reid), and most of the other leading women playing WTT during the summer, Evert had the European clay court season pretty much to herself. She beat Martina Navratilova, the promising young Czech lefthander who had played the USLTA women's circuit at age 16 in 1973, in the Italian Open final, 6–3, 6–3, and Soviet No. 1 Olga Morozova in the French Open final, 6–1, 6–2. Evert and Morozova won both doubles titles.

Evert barely survived her opening match at Wimbledon—she squeezed by Lesley Hunt, 8–6, 5–7, 11–9, in a thrilling match that was delayed for several hours by rain, breathtakingly played despite a slippery court, and suspended overnight by darkness at 9–9 in the third set—but went on to complete her European hat trick by crunching Morozova in the final, 6–0, 6–4.

Evert did not have to play her two greatest rivals, King and Goolagong, because they both came up flat and were stunned in the quarterfinals—King by Morozova, 7–5, 6–2, and Goolagong by Melville, 9–7, 1–6, 6–2. Evert beat Melville, and Morozova erased Virginia Wade in the semis, and Evert got to dance the champions' traditional first foxtrot at the Wimbledon Ball with her fiancé, Connors. The "lovebird double," a Connors-Evert parlay, paid bettors 33–1 in England's legalized gambling shops.

Evert won 10 consecutive tournaments after losing the U.S. Indoor to King, but her streak ended at 56 matches in the semifinals at Forest Hills. Goolagong raced to a 6–0, 4–3 lead before rain suspended their match. The next day, Evert pulled level after Goolagong served for the match at 5–4 in the second set, four times reaching deuce, and came within two points of victory twice more when she served at 6–5. Evert broke again, won the tie-breaker by 5 points to 3, but could not contend with Goolagong's outstanding volleying in relinquishing the excruciating final set, 6–3.

King avenged her bitter loss of the year before by beating Julie Heldman, 2–6, 6–3, 6–1, in the other semifinal, and toppled Goolagong, 3–6, 6–3, 7–5, in a final of thrilling shotmaking that delighted a Monday sellout crowd of 15,303. Vastly more entertaining than the massacre of a men's final, this one was alive until the very end; Goolagong broke at love when King served for the match at 5–4, but BJK won eight of the last nine points to seal her fourth singles title. She also collaborated with Rosemary Casals for their second U.S. doubles crown. Bulldozers moved into the stadium at the West Side Tennis Club the next day to dig up the grass courts, which were to be replaced with synthetic clay.

Goolagong beat Evert in the final of the Virginia Slims tournament at Denver and again in the Slims playoff, where she took the richest women's prize to date—$32,000—with a 6–3, 6–4 victory over the 1972–73 champ. That evened their career rivalry at 8–8 over three years.

Melville, who had been runner-up to Evert for the $30,000 top prize in the Family Circle Cup in the spring, won the South African Open, her biggest international title, over Australian teen-ager Dianne Fromholtz, 6–3, 7–5. Fromholtz had eliminated Margaret Court, making a comeback after the birth of her second child.

America's top two players, Evert and King, sat out the Federation, Wightman, and Bonne Bell Cups. Player-captain Heldman beat both Goolagong and Hunt in leading the U.S. to a shock 5–4 victory over Australia in the third Bell Cup, at Cleveland, after which the competition was unfortunately abandoned.

Great Britain, psyched by player-captain Virginia Wade's 5–7, 9–7, 6–4 victory over Heldman, sprinted to a 6–1 victory in the Wightman Cup, only their eighth in 46 meetings with the U.S., at Deeside, Wales. Cup donor Hazel Wightman died at age 87 in December, shortly after the series.

Heldman and Jeanne Evert—Chrissie's younger sister, who ranked No. 9, making the first time since Ethel and Florence Sutton in 1913 that sisters were among the U.S. Top Ten simultaneously—got to the final of the Federation Cup at Naples, Italy, before falling to Australia, 2–1. Goolagong beat Heldman for her 13th straight Fed Cup singles without a loss and teamed with Janet Young for the clincher after Evert guttily beat Fromholtz.

Chris Evert was elected to succeed the more activist King as president of the Women's Tennis Association at Wimbledon, where the women threatened to boycott in 1975 unless they received "equal parity" with the men in prize money, as Evert put it. That was about the only political story in the women's game, however, and it turned out to be no more than a mild tempest in a teapot, solved by teatime.

1975

Jimmy Connors joined world leaders as a cover subject for *Time* magazine in 1975, as he beat first Rod Laver and then John Newcombe (avenging a loss in the Australian Open final) in ballyhooed "Heavyweight Championship of Tennis" challenge matches in Las Vegas.

These extravaganzas—the focal point of a TV sports scandal two years later because of erroneous reporting of the purse structure—gained high ratings and massive exposure. Connors and his clever, prizefight-style manager Bill Riordan—who were to split bitterly before the end of the year as Connors dropped the controversial antitrust suit he filed in 1974—were the kings of hype. But the ruler of men's tennis was King Arthur Ashe.

At age 32, after nearly 15 years in the big time, Ashe finally fulfilled the promise that had been acclaimed for him in 1968 and gradually abandoned. Seemingly a perennial bridesmaid, loser of 14 of his last 19 final-round matches coming into the year, Ashe became the best man by dedicating himself to training and positive thinking as never before.

Spain's Manuel Orantes overcame every obstacle in 1975, including Jimmy Connors, at Forest Hills. *Peter Mecca*

In 29 tournaments he got to 14 finals, winning nine of them, including the two he really set out to win: the WCT finals at Dallas (over Bjorn Borg, 3–6, 6–4, 6–4, 6–0) and Wimbledon (over Connors in a stunner, 6–1, 6–1, 5–7, 6–4). Ashe's $338,337 earnings for the year boosted his total in seven years as a pro to $1,052,202, making him the sport's third million-dollar winner.

Meanwhile, despite Billie Jean King's dramatic sixth Wimbledon singles title, a postwar record, Chris Evert was the indisputable sovereign of women's tennis.

Before celebrating her 21st birthday on December 20, Chrissie defended her Italian and French Open titles, won the first U.S. Open on clay by outgritting archrival Evonne Goolagong, dethroned Goolagong to recapture the Virginia Slims throne, won 16 of 22 tournaments for the year and set an all-time single-season-winnings record of $350,977. She didn't lose a match the last sixth months of the season after succumbing to King in the Wimbledon semis, and was never beaten before the quarterfinals of a tournament.

Ashe was the man of the year, but the season began with another self-reclamation project. John Newcombe, who was slowed by injuries after winning the WCT title in May 1974, and who was to miss Wimbledon and the U.S. Open with new ailments, flogged himself into shape for the Australian Open by doing miles of roadwork and charging countless times up the hill behind his attractive split-level home in the Sydney suburb of Pymble. He struggled to the final, but was ready for Connors, serving ferociously to win, 7–5, 3–6, 6–4, 7–5.

Already set before the loss to Newcombe was the first of Connors' challenge matches at Caesar's Palace, the Las Vegas hotel-casino. The opponent was Laver, the Grand Slammer of 1962 and 1969—a "natural" pairing since they had never played each other. Connors won, 6–4, 6–2, 3–6, 7–5, seizing what was said to be a $100,000 "winner take all" purse, but it was widely reported that both players took home big checks from "ancillary" revenues.

The success of the venture on CBS-TV made a second "Heavyweight Championship" inevitable, Newcombe being the logical challenger after his popular victory at Melbourne on New Year's Day. Connors won again, 6–3, 4–6, 6–2, 6–2. Connors was said to receive a $250,000 "winner take all" purse, but it was later revealed that the match had been structured like a championship prize fight, each player receiving a pre-agreed percentage, win or lose. Connors made $480,-000, Newcombe, $280,000.

Although he won these indoor bouts amid the heavyweight hoopla on which he thrives, Connors lost in the finals of the three major championships he had swept the previous year. Newcombe set the tone in Australia. Ashe, considered a prohibitive underdog, came up with a tactical masterpiece at Wimbledon. He changed speed and spin smartly, fed junk to Connors' forehand, exposing the vulnerability of that wing to paceless shots, and sliced his serves wide to Connors' backhand, exploiting the slightly limited reach of his two-handed shot.

This was an extraordinary final, the first ever between litigants in a lawsuit since President Ashe, along with other officers of the Association of Tennis Professionals, were named in the $40 million antitrust suit Connors and Riordan had filed against attorney Donald Dell, Jack Kramer, and Grand Prix sponsor Commercial Union. There were several other suits and counterclaims associated with this one, but all were quietly settled, out of court and without payment of damages, not long after Ashe's emotion-charged and enormously popular victory.

Ashe was not considered a serious threat at the U.S. Open after the grass courts at the West Side Tennis Club in Forest Hills were dug up immediately after the 1974 tournament, replaced with a synthetic clay called Har-Tru, which became the predominent surface of the U.S. Summer Circuit. Sure enough, clay specialist Eddie Dibbs—one of a group of scrappy young Americans coming up to succeed Ashe's generation—beat Arthur in the fourth round.

Forest Hills, previously dominated by grass-loving Americans and Australians, suddenly became a happy hunting ground for clay-reared Europeans and South Americans. The most successful was Manuel Orantes, the elegant left-hander from Barcelona. In the semifinals, he revived himself from two sets and 0–2 down, and from 0–5 in the fourth set, saving five match points to beat Argentinian left-hander Guillermo Vilas, 4–6, 1–6, 6–2, 7–5, 6–4. That three-hour, 44-minute marathon did not end until 10:40 P.M. on Saturday—the installation of all-weather courts permitted floodlighting and night play for the first time—and Orantes did not get to bed until 3:00 A.M. because of a plumbing failure in his hotel room. He was assumed to be a lamb going to slaughter in the final against Connors, who had hammered Borg in the other semifinal, 7–5, 7–5, 7–5, early the previous afternoon.

But taking his cue from Ashe's strategy at Wimbledon, Orantes slowballed Connors and cleverly mixed up his game. He drop-shotted and lobbed, chipped and passed, traded ground strokes and sometimes dashed in to take away the forecourt, snaring Connors in his butterfly net.

It was 10 years to the day since Manuel Santana had become the first Spaniard to win at Forest Hills, and again the old concrete stadium was filled with Latin chants and shouts of "*¡Bravo!*" as 15,669 spectators roared Orantes to an astonishing 6–4, 6–3, 6–3 victory. At the end, he fell to his knees, jubilantly, his toothy Latin face the definitive portrait of ecstasy. Why not? His last 24 hours had constituted the most remarkable feat of any player in a major championship since Wimbledon in 1927, when Frenchman Henri Cochet elevated himself from two sets and 1–5 down to beat Bill Tilden in the semifinals, then from two sets down to overhaul Jean Borotra in the final.

Connors lost his stranglehold on men's tennis, but did not have a bad year by anyone's standards except his own. He entered 18 tournaments and won nine—five of them on Riordan's USLTA Indoor circuit, including the U.S. Indoor over Vitas Gerulaitis, 5–7, 7–5, 6–1, 3–6, 6–0. Connors was runner-up in six others, including the Australian, Wimbledon, and U.S. Opens. Connors compiled an 84–10 record and, made well over a half-million dollars with all his "special" matches, but Ashe was the prize-money leader with $306,712.

Connors also split with Riordan in the fall. He had prospered, financially and competitively, under Riordan's tutelage, but also had become the isolated man of the locker room, despised and openly cold-shouldered by his colleagues. With the divorce from his manager, Connors gradually came in from the cold, re-establishing cordial if never close relations with his fellow players. "I think Jimmy just decided that it wasn't worth going through life hated," said his contemporary, Roscoe Tanner.

Ashe, who had been one of the first to recognize that a deep freeze by his peers would be the most effective way of ending the divisive lawsuits Connors fronted for Riordan, won four of eight tournaments in his group during the WCT season, while Connors was playing the smaller Riordan-organized tour. Laver set a WCT record by winning four consecutive tournaments and 23 straight matches, but Ashe earned a solid gold tennis ball, valued at $33,333, as the top point-winner on the tour, which was divided into three groups (Red, Blue, and Green) playing a total of 25 tournaments. He won the

$50,000 top prize in the WCT finals at Dallas by beating Mark Cox, John Alexander, and Bjorn Borg.

Ashe also played a substantial number of events in the $4 million dollars Commercial Union Grand Prix, which embraced 42 tournaments in 19 countries during its May-through-December calendar, boosting the total prize money available in men's tennis to more than $8 million dollars. Ashe compiled a 16-match winning streak in the fall, winning tournaments at Los Angeles and San Francisco, and qualified for the eight-man Grand Prix Masters playoff at Stockholm. He had visions of a unique WCT-Masters "double," but was upended in the semis of the Masters by Borg and concluded, "I don't think anybody is strong enough, mentally and physically, to win WCT and the Masters in the same year."

Borg was runner-up in both—to Ashe in Dallas and to Ilie Nastase (who came back from a disqualification against Ashe in his opening round-robin match of the Masters) in Stockholm. "Teen Angel" was in the waning days of his 18th year when he beat Laver in a magnificent four-hour semifinal at Dallas, perhaps the year's finest match, 7–6, 3–6, 5–7, 7–6, 6–2. He had turned 19 by the time he clobbered Guillermo Vilas, 6–2, 6–3, 6–4, for his second consecutive French Open title. Later he steamrolled Vilas again, 6–3, 6–4, 6–2, to defend his U.S. Pro crown. Borg won five of 23 tournaments on the year, amassed a 78–19 record, and carried Sweden to its first possession of the Davis Cup, winning all 12 of his singles matches against Poland, West Germany, the Soviet Union, Spain, Chile, and Czechoslovakia. His record of 16 consecutive Davis Cup singles victories over three years eclipsed the all-time Cup record of 12 set by Bill Tilden between 1920 and 1926.

Vilas didn't win any of the big international titles, but won six of 23 tournaments—including Washington and Louisville during a 16-match winning streak early in the U.S. Summer Circuit—and reached at least the quarter-finals of 21 to seize the $100,000 top prize in the Commerical Union Grand Prix for the second straight year. Orantes, who counted the German, Swedish, Canadian, British,

U.S. Clay Court, and U.S. Open titles among the seven tournaments he won, finished second in the Grand Prix standings.

Nastase won the Masters for the fourth time in five years, coming back from his opening disqualification. (Ashe, disgruntled by Nastase's behavior and stalling, uncharacteristically stormed off the court, but was declared the winner the following day.) "Nasty" beat Orantes and Adriano Panatta in his remaining round-robin matches, Vilas in the semifinals, and a badly off-form Borg in the final, 6–2, 6–2, 6–1. This was by far the biggest of Nastase's seven tournament victories for the year, but he set a dubious achievement record by being defaulted three times, quitting his semifinal match in the Italian Open to ultimate champion Raul Ramirez, and "tanking" the Canadian Open final to Orantes after getting upset by a line call in the first-set tie-breaker. For this unprofessional conduct, Nastase was fined $8,000 by the newly formed Men's International Professional Tennis Council, a tripartite body made up of three representatives each of the male players, the ILTF, and worldwide tournament directors. Nastase's lawyers appealed, and the fine was reduced, but the "Pro Council" had established itself as an important new administrative and judicial force in the men's game. It was designed to be legislative as well, and became the autonomous governing body of the Grand Prix circuit.

It was a peculiar year in men's doubles. Australians John Alexander and Phil Dent won their national title for the first time, but Brian Gottfried and Raul Ramirez were the Team of the Year. They began their reign in the U.S. Pro Indoor at Philadelphia, and won the WCT doubles title at Mexico City over Mark Cox and Cliff Drysdale. Gottfried-Ramirez also won a special "Challenge Match" during the WCT singles finals at Dallas, necessitated because South African Davis Cuppers Bob Hewitt and Frew McMillan had been rudely kicked out of Mexico shortly after their arrival for the doubles playoff—a clumsy power play by the Mexican Government to protest the apartheid racial policies of South Africa.

Gottfried-Ramirez also won the French title, over Alexander-Dent, and the U.S. Pro, but they came up flat at the end of the year, failing to win a match in the Masters as a four-man doubles playoff was inaugurated alongside the singles. The doubles was a round-robin affair, which proved to be an unsatisfactory format when three teams tied with identical 2–1 records. Spanish Davis Cuppers Orantes and Juan Gisbert were declared champions on the basis of having the best percentage of games won for their three matches, even though they were beaten head-to-head by the spirited new American tandem of Sherwood Stewart and Freddie McNair. (The Masters doubles was changed to a knock-out format in succeeding years.)

The Wimbledon doubles turned into a wildly unpredictable scramble as only one seeded team reached the quarterfinals. Alex Mayer and Vitas Gerulaitis, who had not blended well earlier in the year, became the first American champions in 18 years with a 7–5, 8–6, 6–4 victory in the final over similarly unseeded Allan Stone of Australia and Colin Dowdeswell of Rhodesia, who had never even met each other until introduced in the tea room the first day of the tournament. Their regular partners were injured, so they formed a makeshift alliance and filled a late vacancy in the draw.

Connors got his only "Big Four" title of the year by teaming with Nastase to win the U.S. Open doubles over Marty Riessen and Tom Okker. Connors seldom played doubles thereafter, a trend soon followed by Borg and Vilas as top players began to concentrate singularly on singles.

Connors also ended—only temporarily, as it turned out—his one-man boycott of the U.S. Davis Cup team. Former French, Wimbledon, and U.S. champion Tony Trabert replaced Dennis Ralston as the American captain after Raul Ramirez led a 3–2 Mexican ambush of the U.S. at Palm Springs in February 1975, ironically the same weekend that Connors was beating Laver in the first Las Vegas Challenge Match.

Trabert coaxed Connors, who had long feuded with Ralston (this was really a proxy fight between Riordan and Ralston's agent, former Cup captain Donald Dell), onto the American squad for a first-round conquest of undermanned Venezuela at Tucson. But the notion that Connors' presence alone assured victory in the American Zone was dispelled as Ramirez, an inspired Davis Cup player, teamed with Marcelo Lara and led his nation to another 3–2 upset in the second round of the 1976 competition, which was actually played December 19–21, 1975. It all came down to the No. 1 players of the two countries in the decisive fifth match, and Ramirez was as high as the six-thousand-foot altitude of Mexico City as he beat Connors, 2–6, 6–3, 6–3, 6–4, in a match suspended overnight by darkness.

The 1975 final was played the same weekend at Stockholm's Kungliga Tennishallen. Borg whipped both Jiri Hrebec and Jan Kodes in singles and teamed with towering Ove Bengtson to dispatch Kodes and shaky Vladimir Zednik in doubles as Sweden defeated Czechoslovakia, 3–2, to become the sixth nation to hold the Davis Cup. Both teams were first-time finalists.

The Davis Cup continued to be plagued by political turmoil. Mexico, after eliminating the U.S., refused to play South Africa. Colombia similarly defaulted, putting South Africa—winner of the Cup by default the previous year—into the American Zone final without playing a match. But the South Africans were eliminated by Chile at Santiago. Chilean No. 1 Jaime Fillol received a death threat from opponents of the military junta in his homeland, and it was only with massive security precautions that Chile was able to play the semifinal in Sweden. The stadium at Baastad was kept almost empty except for thousands of police and troops; boats patrolled the harbor, aircraft hovered overhead, and huge nets around the stadium protected the players from projectiles hurled by anti-Chile demonstrators, who chanted and set off firecrackers a block away. In this unnerving atmosphere, Borg and Birger Andersson—who helped win four of Sweden's matches along the way, but sat down in favor of Bengtson in the final—whipped the Chileans and set up the final in Stockholm just before Christmas.

The ATP, in a rather clumsy effort to force a consolidation of the Davis Cup into a one-

or two-week showdown at one site, staged a new competition with just such a Federation Cup-style format, calling it the Nations Cup. The American team of Ashe and Tanner defeated Great Britain's Roger Taylor and Buster Mottram, 2–1, in Jamaica, but the competition was not a success. Meanwhile, Laver and 40-year-old Ken Rosewall helped Australia to a 4–3 victory over the U.S. in the World Cup at Hartford, showing that the Aussie dynasty was not entirely dead—though a group of younger Aussies was beaten by Czechoslovakia in the semifinals of the Davis Cup at Prague.

World Team Tennis, despite the huge financial losses of its inaugural season and a ludicrous player draft (numerous showbiz personalities were named by teams in a publicity stunt that made a mockery of the league), surprised many by coming out for a second season. There were 12 teams, four fewer than in 1974, and only one returned with the original ownership, but the league staggered along. Pittsburgh, led by Vitas Gerulaitis and Evonne Goolagong, beat the San Francisco Bay Area's Golden Gaters in the championship series.

Goolagong started the season by repeating as Australian Open champion, beating Martina Navratilova, 6–3, 6–2, in an emotional final (Evonne's father had been killed in an auto accident, and Evonne cried on the shoulder of her coach and guardian, Vic Edwards, at the presentation ceremonies). Goolagong also successfully defended her doubles title with WTT teammate Peggy Michel.

Evert won the biggest checks for women in "special events"—$50,000 for winning the four-woman L'Eggs World Series over King at Lakeway, Texas, 4–6, 6–3, 7–6, and $40,000 for adding her third triumph in the Virginia Slims Championship at Los Angeles, over Navratilova, 6–4, 6–2. Navratilova won the U.S. Indoor at Boston, beating Virginia Wade, Margaret Court, and Goolagong, but she lost again to Evert in the final of the rich Family Circle Cup at Amelia Island, Florida.

With most of the top women committed to World Team Tennis, Evert and Navratilova were the class of the women's field in the Italian and French Opens. They reached the singles finals of both, Evert winning in Rome by 6–1, 6–0 and in Paris by 2–6, 6–2, 6–1. Chris and Martina then teamed up to win both the doubles titles.

King always considered the Centre Court at Wimbledon her favorite stage, and she never performed more majestically there than she did in coming from 0–3 down in the third set to beat Evert in the semifinals, and burying Goolagong, 6–0, 6–1, in the most lopsided women's final since 1911. BJK's sixth singles title was her 19th in all at Wimbledon, tying the career record of Elizabeth Ryan, who never won the singles but captured 12 doubles and seven mixed crowns between 1914 and 1934. King said this was her last appearance in singles because of a deteriorating knee—"I want to quit on top," she said, "and I can't get much higher than this"—but she eventually returned, in 1977.

The women's doubles champions turned out to be as unlikely as the men's, Kazuko Sawamatsu of Japan and Ann Kiyomura, an American of Japanese ancestry, teaming to upset Françoise Durr and Betty Stove in the final. Margaret Court teamed with Marty Riessen for the mixed doubles title over Stove and Allan Stone.

Evert won the U.S. Open, dropping only one set. That was in the final, where her 5–7, 6–4, 6–2 victory over Goolagong relegated Evonne to the record books as the first woman to lose three consecutive U.S. singles finals. Chris was just too formidable on the clay she loves so well, as she demonstrated by grinding out the last four games of the match in a baseline duel. Court and Wade took the doubles title over King and Casals; this was the last of Court's record 66 Big Four titles in singles and doubles.

More important than tennis was Navratilova's decision, announced at Forest Hills, to defect from her native Czechoslovakia and seek U.S. citizenship. She made the decision after the Czech tennis federation, chiding her for becoming "too Americanized," initially refused her a visa to compete in the U.S. Open. Navratilova felt she had to follow the lead of the great Czech player Jaroslav Drobny, who defected in 1949, if she were to develop as a tennis

Martina Navratilova made a big decision in 1975—
she defected from Czechoslovakia. *UPI*

player and as a person, but the decision was painful. She knew that her action meant that it would be years before she would see her parents and younger sister, Jana, again.

Navratilova and Renata Tomanova had led Czechoslovakia past Ireland, The Netherlands, West Germany, France, and Australia to win the 30-nation Federation Cup at Aix-en-Provence in southern France. Australia beat the United States in the semifinals, Goolagong and Helen Gourlay stopping U.S. captain Julie Heldman and Janet Newberry, 11–9, 6–1, in the doubles that swung a 2–1 decision. That put the Aussies in the final for the 10th time, but Navratilova ended Goolagong's 16-match unbeaten streak in Fed Cup singles, 6–3, 6–4, and Tomanova ambushed Gourlay, 6–4, 6–2. The Czechs then teamed to beat Gourlay and Dianne Fromholtz for a 3–0 verdict, clinching the Cup for the first time.

Great Britain also humbled the U.S. in the Wightman Cup for the second straight year, its first back-to-back wins since 1924–25. Evert won both her singles, over Wade and Glynis Coles, in straight sets, but with Held-

man sidelined with a sore shoulder, the U.S. did not have the depth it needed to contend with Wade, Coles, and Ann Jones, who returned to the battle at age 37. Coles' 6–3, 7–6 victory over Mona Schallau was the clincher in a 5–2 British victory at Cleveland's Public Auditorium.

The most spectacular comeback of the year belonged to Evert, who trailed Nancy Richey Gunter, 6–7, 0–5, 15–40—double match point—in the semifinals of the U.S. Clay Courts at Indianapolis. After that, Chrissie didn't make a mistake in roaring back to win, 6–7, 7–5, 4–2, ret., Gunter finally having to quit with cramps. Evert went on to thrash Fromholtz in the final for her fourth consecutive U.S. Clay Court crown.

A couple of administrative happenings during 1975 are worthy of note. Over the protests of tournament chairman and director Bill Talbert, the U.S. Open adopted a 12-point tiebreaker (win by two) instead of the nine-point "sudden death" that had been in use since 1970. This was a victory for the ATP, whose members preferred the less nerve-wracking "lingering death." The change of the surface at Forest Hills permitted night play there for the first time, and a resultant dramatic increase in total attendance, to 216,683. Finally, the U.S Lawn Tennis Association voted to drop the "Lawn" from its name, becoming simply the USTA. This was the beginning of a fashion that would, in 1977, see the International Lawn Tennis Federation become the ITF.

1976

Jimmy Connors returned to the pinnacle of men's tennis in 1976, and Chris Evert consolidated her stranglehold on the women's game. But the most bizarre and compelling story of the year was the emergence of professional sport's first transsexual.

Richard Raskind, a 41-year-old ophthalmologist, was a good enough player to captain the Yale University varsity in 1954, play at Wimbledon and Forest Hills, and reach the semifinals of the National 35-and-over championships in 1972. In August 1975, he had sex reassignment surgery and moved west to

Dr. Richard Raskind, an ophthalmologist, switched to a career in tennis as Renée Richards. *Peter Mecca*

Newport Beach, California, to start a new life and practice as Dr. Renée Richards.

In July 1976, Dr. Richards—a 6-foot, 2-inch left-hander—entered and won a local women's tournament in La Jolla, California. A former acquaintance noticed her resemblance in playing style to Richard Raskind, verified her identity, and tipped off a San Diego television sportscaster, who broke the story.

Dr. Richards, who had sought a clean start in California, far from her former wife and 4-year-old son in New York, decided to "go public" and put aside her brilliant career as an eye surgeon in order to play professional tennis.

"I started getting letters, poignant letters from other transsexuals who were considering suicide, whose friends and families won't see them," she explained to *Newsday* reporter Jane Gross, explaining her decision. "I realized that this was more than just a tennis thing, my hobby; I could easily give that up. But, if I can do anything for those people, I will. I am in a position to try and make people see that such individuals should be allowed to hold up their heads. I realize this is important from a social standpoint."

The Richards case caused an extraordinary, highly publicized stir in women's tennis. The Women's Tennis Association (WTA) opposed her eligibility for tournaments, and sided with the U.S. Tennis Association in its hasty ruling that women would have to pass an Olympic-style chromosome test before being accepted for women's national championships, including the U.S. Open. Dr. Richards refused to take the test, claiming that it was an unsatisfactory means of determining gender, given the advances of modern medicine.

Many women felt that Dr. Richards would have an unfair competitive advantage because of her size, strength, and past experience in competition against men. Others feared that her acceptance would set a bad precedent, paving the way for a younger, stronger transsexual to dominate women's tennis in the future. Many WTA members liked Richards personally, admired her courage, but still opposed her acceptance in tournaments.

Dr. Richards was denied admission to the U.S. Open—she took her case to court, and was admitted in 1977 by court order—but did play in a pre-Forest Hills tournament at South Orange, New Jersey. Most WTA members withdrew in protest, but the tournament attracted national television coverage and massive publicity. Richards was beaten in the semifinals by 17-year-old Lea Antonoplis, early evidence that fears Dr. Richards would upset the competitive balance of the women's game were unfounded. Richards played several other tournaments, winning one at Kauai, Hawaii, at the end of the year over Kathy Kuykendall, ranked No. 10 in the U.S.

Along more conventional lines, Jimmy Connors recaptured the No. 1 world ranking even though he won only one major championship, the U.S. Open, in which he edged his major rival, Bjorn Borg, in a superlative final, 6–4, 3–6, 7–6, 6–4.

Connors compiled a 100–12 record, winning 13 of 23 tournaments he played. He won the only two World Championship Tennis events he entered, the two big-prize-money events put on by the Association of Tennis

Professionals (American Airlines Games at Palm Springs, Alan King Classic at Las Vegas), and six of the 10 Commercial Union Grand Prix events he played. He collected $303,335 in tournament prize money, plus more than double that amount in exhibitions—including $500,000 for beating up on Spaniard Manuel Orantes in another "Heavyweight Championship of Tennis" Challenge Match at Las Vegas. (Orantes, guaranteed more than $250,000 just for showing up, did little more than that, winning three games in three pathetic sets.)

More important in deciding the global game of king-of-the-hill, Connors was 3–0 in head-to-head clashes with Borg. Connors vanquished the young Swede in the U.S. Pro Indoor final at Philadelphia, the American Airlines Games, and the Forest Hills final.

Otherwise, Borg had an outstanding season, winning seven of 19 tournaments and 63 of 77 matches. He continued his domination of his good friend and sometimes doubles partner, Guillermo Vilas, to win the WCT Finals at Dallas in May, 27 days before his 20th birthday. He failed in his bid for a third consecutive French Open title, but prepared diligently on grass courts and became the third youngest champion in the history of Wimbledon, the first man to sweep through the most prestigious of championships without losing a set since Chuck McKinley in 1963. Borg pulled a muscle in his lower stomach in a doubles match the first week, but deadened the pain in his last four singles matches by taking prematch cortisone injections and spraying his abdomen at changeovers with an aerosol freeze spray. Despite the injury, he never served or smashed more authoritatively than in routing Brian Gottfried, Vilas, Roscoe Tanner (quarterfinal conqueror of Connors), and Ilie Nastase in the final, 6–4, 6–2, 9–7.

After a seven-week layoff to recuperate—a period during which Sweden relinquished the Davis Cup—Borg extended his winning streak to 19 matches, winning a third consecutive U.S. Pro title (another lopsided thrashing of Vilas) and reaching the final of the U.S. Open. That match hinged on a tingling third set tiebreaker in which Connors escaped four

set points and finally prevailed, 11–9, tilting a majestic epic his way.

The year began with perhaps the most startling result ever in one of the Grand Slam championships, 21-year-old Australian Mark Edmondson—an anonymous serve-and-volleyer recently removed from employment as a janitor and odd-jobs man—winning the Australian Open. He beat two former champions, 42-year-old Ken Rosewall in the semifinals and defender John Newcombe, 6–7, 6–3, 7–6, 6–1, in a final played in fierce winds and the eerie weather of a gathering storm.

Edmondson was hardly a Grand Slam threat. He quickly found his level again, losing in the first round of the French Open to Paraguayan Victor Pecci. Adriano Panatta, the handsome and dashing Italian No. 1, won the French during a dazzling 16-match winning streak that established him as the king of European clay for the year.

Panatta withstood 11 match points against Aussie Kim Warwick in the first round of the Italian Open, then went on to win the title before his adoring hometown fans in Rome, beating Vilas in the final, 2–6, 7–6, 6–2, 7–6. Panatta was nearly a goner in the first round in Paris, too, saving a match point against an unorthodox and virtually unknown Czech, Pavel Hutka, with a desperate, lunging volley winner. After that narrow escape, however, Panatta was superb, dispatching Borg in the quarterfinals, Eddie Dibbs in the semis, and gritty Harold Solomon, 6–1, 6–4, 4–6, 7–6, in the final. (Solomon, who roared from behind in five of his seven matches, was the first American finalist at Paris since Herb Flam in 1957.)

Arthur Ashe, No. 1 in the world in 1975, got off to the best start of his career, winning five of his first six tournaments and 29 of 30 matches. He again topped the WCT point standings, earning a $50,000 bonus, but lost his crown in the first round of the WCT playoffs at Dallas, beaten by Solomon, and did little thereafter. His fade was in part attributed to inflammation of a chronic heel injury that required surgery in February 1977.

A pinched nerve in his elbow slowed another of 1975's heroes, Orantes, much of the

Harold Solomon ousted Arthur Ashe in the 1976 WCT playoffs and reached the finals of the French Championships against Adriano Panatta. *Richard Pilling*

season, but therapy and a switch to a lighter aluminum racket revived him in the autumn. The elegant left-hander won five of his last eight tournaments (including the year's longest winning streak: 23 matches), reached two other finals, and resurrected himself from 1–4 down to win a stirring Grand Prix Masters final at Houston over Poland's Wojtek Fibak, the most improved pro of the year, 5–7, 6–2, 0–6, 7–6, 6–1.

The Houston Masters culminated five years of Grand Prix sponsorship by the Commercial Union Assurance group, which withdrew because of flagging profits in the insurance business and was replaced by Colgate-Palmolive, which already had undertaken sponsorship of a women's Grand Prix, known as the Colgate International Series. Commercial Union's swan song was soured when Connors decided to pass up the Masters for a third consecutive year (thereby forfeiting the $60,000 he already had earned from the Grand Prix bonus pool for finishing third in the season-long

standings), and Borg and Nastase chose to play exhibitions in the fall instead of Grand Prix tournaments that could have qualified them for the eight-man Masters.

Mexican Raul Ramirez won only four of 32 tournaments, but he was a tireless and consistent campaigner. His diligence paid off as he earned both the $150,000 prize for topping the Grand Prix singles standings and the $40,000 award for heading the doubles standings, a unique accomplishment. In all, the Grand Prix encompassed 48 tournaments (and produced 23 different winners) in 22 countries, with more than $5 million in prize purses. With the WCT (24 16-man tournaments) and U.S. Indoor circuits added in, more than $9 million was available in men's tournaments worldwide.

The riches available were demonstrated graphically when Ilie Nastase collected $180,000 in a single tournament: the WCT-run Avis Challenge Cup, a series of winner-take-all round-robin matches played throughout the winter and spring in Hawaii. Nastase beat Ashe in a five-set final on asphalt; on the year Nastase won five of 23 tournaments, compiled a 76–17 record, reached the final at Wimbledon and the semifinals at Forest Hills, and was the only player with a winning record over Connors (4–1).

In doubles, John Newcombe and Tony Roche won their fourth Australian championship, but team-of-the-year honors were shared by Ramirez-Brian Gottfried and Sherwood Stewart-Freddie McNair, who underscored the old axiom that two ordinary singles players can blend extraordinarily in doubles.

Stewart-McNair won the French Open, dethroning Gottfried-Ramirez, 7–6, 6–3, 6–1, and came back from 1–4 in the fourth set to stun the same team in the Masters doubles final, 6–3, 5–7, 5–7, 6–4, 6–4. Those triumphs earned Stewart-McNair the No. 1 U.S. ranking in doubles. (Connors was No. 1 in singles, regaining the spot he occupied in 1973–74.)

Fibak and Karl Meiler won the WCT doubles at Kansas City, after beating Gottfried-Ramirez in a five-set semifinal. Gottfried-Ramirez won their third straight Italian title, over Newcombe-Geoff Masters, even though completion of the final was delayed by darkness and continued four months later at The Woodlands, outside Houston. They also won Wimbledon, knocking off curiously unseeded Newcombe-Roche (five-time champions) in the first round and Masters-Ross Case in a rousing final, 3–6, 6–3, 8–6, 2–6, 7–5, and the $100,000 ATP Doubles at The Woodlands. Tom Okker and Marty Riessen took the U.S. Open, over surprising Aussies Paul Kronk and Cliff Letcher, 6–4, 6–4.

It was a quiet year politically, in men's tennis, aside from the Davis Cup and storms arising from Nastase's tempestuous behavior. The rambunctious Romanian was at his worst in an ugly second-round victory over Germany's Hans Pohmann at Forest Hills. Nastase's gamesmanship and outbursts of obscene language, gestures, and spitting, along with delays when Pohmann suffered cramps that should have disqualified him, caused this match to get out of control. Nastase was eventually fined $1,000, which increased his aggregate disciplinary fines for a 12-month period to more than $3,000 and triggered an automatic 21-day suspension, under provisions of a new Code of Conduct enacted by the Men's International Professional Tennis Council. The suspension was a joke, however, since it applied only to Grand Prix tournaments; Nastase played exhibition tournaments and earned more than $50,000 during the time he was supposed to be disciplined.

In the Davis Cup, Mexico—after upsetting the United States in the American Zone—refused to play South Africa for the second consecutive year, and defaulted. When the Davis Cup nations refused to take action against Mexico at its annual meeting, the United States led a walkout of the major Cup nations, including France and Great Britain, for 1977. A compromise was worked out within two weeks, however, and these nations returned. The Soviet Union defaulted its semifinal series to Chile in protest of the military junta that had overthrown the Marxist regime of Salvador Allende in Santiago in 1973. This was precisely the sort of political disruption that the U.S. was opposing, and a reconstituted Davis Cup Committee of Management

threw the U.S.S.R. out of the 1977 competition.

Italy, runner-up in 1960–61, won the Davis Cup for the first time, beating Chile, 4–1, in a final distinguished more by the enthusiasm and sportsmanship of the sellout crowds at Santiago than by the quality of play. Corrado Barazzutti upset Chilean No. 1 Jaime Fillol, and Panatta beat game but overmatched Patricio Cornejo, then teamed with Paolo Bertolucci to down Cornejo-Fillol for an unbeatable 3–0 lead as captain Nicola Pietrangeli, the star of the 1960–61 Italian teams, exulted at courtside. The political situation had been tense, Italian leftists opposing the matches, but the Italians' joy at winning was unrestrained.

Earlier in the year Connors had made his first appearance for the U.S. in the World Cup. Both he and Ashe thrashed Newcombe and Roche in singles, leading Captain Dennis Ralston's American squad to a 6–1 victory over declining Australia before sellout crowds in Hartford, Connecticut.

World Team Tennis was more stable in its third season, but even with Chris Evert as a shining new attraction and the respected Butch Buchholz aboard as commissioner, all of the 10 franchises continued to operate in the red. The New York Sets—led by league most valuable player Sandy Mayer, Billie

Captain Tony Trabert talks strategy with doubles players Bob Lutz (center) and Stan Smith, winners over Mexico in 1976 Davis Cup competition. Italy won the Cup for the first time. *UPI*

Jean King, Virginia Wade, and Phil Dent—captured the league title with a 3–0 sweep of the Golden Gaters (San Francisco Bay Area) in the playoff final series. Evert, of the Phoenix Racquets, was the female MVP, her singles winning percentage (.700) the best of any player in WTT.

Evert was unquestionably the queen of tournament tennis as well. She won 75 of 80 matches, 12 of 17 tournaments, including three of the year's four most important: Wimbledon, the U.S. Open, and the rich Colgate Inaugural at Palm Springs in October, which launched the new Colgate International Series, and was to serve thereafter as its climactic playoff. Its $45,000 top prize was the biggest of the year in women's tennis. It boosted Evert's season winnings to $289,165 and her career winnings to $1,026,604, making her the first woman to earn more than $1 million in prize money.

Only four players—Evonne Goolagong Cawley (twice), Wade, Martina Navratilova, and Dianne Fromholtz—were able to beat Evert during the year.

Goolagong started the year by winning her third straight Australian Open title, a 6–2, 6–2 rout of Czechoslovakia's Renata Tomanova, and teaming with Helen Gourlay to defend the doubles title she had won the previous two years with Californian Peggy Michel.

The lithe Australian was at her best during the January through April Virginia Slims circuit, winning 38 of 40 matches, dropping only 10 sets, and at one point running off 16 consecutive victories without loss of a set. She climaxed her record $133,675 Slims season (en route to a $195,452 year) by beating Evert, 6–3, 5–7, 6–3, in a magnificent match at the Los Angeles Sports Arena, the final of the Virginia Slims championship. That was the high point of Goolagong's year.

On the season, Evonne won eight of 13 tournaments, 58 of 64 matches. She reached the final of every tournament she played, was 7–0 vs. Virginia Wade, 6–0 vs. Rosemary Casals, 4–0 over Navratilova, and 4–0 over Sue Barker. Evonne had the second best winning percentage in singles among WTT players, and aside from one-set WTT matches lost

to only two players: Evert five times, and Billie Jean King in the Federation Cup at Philadelphia. This was Evonne's most consistent season but still, as she announced at season's end that she was taking maternity leave, she was overshadowed by Evert.

After losing the Virginia Slims final, Chrissie won her next six tournaments in a dazzling 36-match winning streak, and lost only one more match the rest of the year.

Her streak began with her third consecutive triumph in the Family Circle Cup, over Australian Kerry Melville Reid, 6–2, 6–2, at Amelia Island, Florida.

At Wimbledon, where all eight seeds reached the quarterfinals, Evert beat Olga Morozova in the quarterfinals, Martina Navratilova in the semis, and Goolagong, 6–3, 4–6, 8–6, in a thrilling final that ended Evonne's 25-match streak. This was Evert's first triumph ever over Goolagong on grass. Then Evert and Navratilova took the doubles title over Betty Stove and Billie Jean King—who did not play singles, and was thwarted in her attempt to seize a record 20th career Wimbledon title—6–1, 3–6, 7–5. (King and her New York Sets teammate Sandy Mayer were upset in the second round of the mixed doubles by South Africans Bob Hewitt and Greer Stevens, leaving BJK tied with Elizabeth Ryan, who never won the singles but captured 19 Wimbledon doubles and mixed titles between 1914 and 1934.)

Evert was at her dominating best on the artificial clay at Forest Hills, winning her second consecutive U.S. Open title with the loss of only 12 games in six matches. (The only more devastating run through the field was accomplished by Helen Wills, who gave up only eight games in six matches in 1929.) Evert stomped Goolagong, 6–3, 6–0, in the most lopsided final since 1964, running the last 10 games. This extended Evert's astounding clay court winning streak to 21 tournaments and 101 matches, dating to August 1973.

Delina "Linky" Boshoff and Ilana Kloss startlingly won the doubles title over Wade and Morozova, 6–1, 6–4, becoming the first South African women to win a U.S. title. King and another WTT teammate, Phil Dent, won the mixed doubles over Stove and Frew McMillan.

King came out of her self-imposed singles retirement in the Federation Cup at Philadelphia in August. Colgate assumed sponsorship of this women's team competition, and infused it with prize money for the first time: $130,000 for teams representing 32 nations, $40,000 to the winners. Unfortunately, a political hassle developed when the Soviet Union reneged on a previous promise and led a four-nation walkout (1975 champion Czechoslovakia, Hungary, and the Philippines joined the U.S.S.R. in refusing to play) to protest the inclusion of South African and Rhodesia in the draw. The defaulting nations were subsequently fined by the International Lawn Tennis Federation, but they had succeeded in making the draw a shambles.

King filled in unexpectedly in singles for Evert, who withdrew with a sore wrist. King, playing for the U.S. for the first time since 1967, teamed with old doubles partner Rosie Casals in a two-woman *tour de force*. They sprinted through four 3–0 victories to a meeting with favored Australia in the final. Kerry Reid beat Casals, but King found a wellspring of her old inspiration to beat Goolagong, 7–6, 6–4, in a match of exceptionally high standard. King-Casals then toppled Reid-Goolagong, 7–5, 6–3, for the championship.

After rare back-to-back losses in 1974–75, the U.S. regained the Wightman Cup with a 5–2 victory over Great Britain, indoors at London's Crystal Palace. Evert led the way, beating Wade and then Sue Barker in the decisive match, 2–6, 6–2, 6–2. (In the absence of the leading women, who were contracted to WTT, Barker had won the German and French Opens, sharing with Italian Open champ Mima Jausovec pre-eminence on European clay for the year.)

Evert was ranked No. 1 in the U.S., of course, but Nancy Richey achieved a milestone in earning the No. 3 ranking. It was the 16th time she figured in the U.S. Top Ten, a record for consistency at the top previously held only by Louise Brough.

A major innovation in equipment was introduced in 1976. New rackets in a dizzying variety of designs and materials—wood, metal, Fiberglas, alloys, composites—had been marketed over the previous decade, but the biggest stir since the introduction of Wilson's steel T-2000 in 1967 was created by the Prince racket, with its oversized head. Howard Head, founder of Head Ski and architect of that company's headlong plunge into tennis equipment, joined forces with the manufacturer of Prince ball machines to produce the revolutionary and subsequently imitated new racket, which had much the same balance as conventional rackets but twice the hitting area.

1977

By any standard, 1977 was a landmark year for tennis. Wimbledon, the oldest of tournaments, celebrated its Centennial. The U.S. Open was played at Forest Hills for the last time. And a technological innovation, the "double strung" or "spaghetti" racket, caused such a stir that it was banned from tournament play several months after gaining notoriety, and led to the definition of a racket for the first time in the official rules of the game.

Three men—Bjorn Borg, Guillermo Vilas, and Jimmy Connors—waged their own version of the year's hit movie, the science-fiction classic *Star Wars*. They were in a stratospheric super class, a galaxy above anyone else in tennis.

Borg won Wimbledon and had the most solid record, including winning margins against both his rivals. Vilas won the French and U.S. Opens and fashioned the longest winning streak of the 10-year-old Open era. Connors won the World Championship of Tennis in Dallas and the Grand Prix Masters, and was runner-up at Wimbledon and Forest Hills. The debate as to who was No. 1 continued right through the Masters which, because of U.S. television considerations, was moved back by new Grand Prix sponsor Colgate-Palmolive to the first week of January 1978.

There was no similar disagreement as to who was the ruler of women's tennis. Chris Evert remained the indisputable No. 1, despite Virginia Wade's coronation—after 15 years as the lady in waiting—as the queen of Wimbledon.

Bjorn Borg won Wimbledon in its Centennial year. *Jack Mecca*

The celebrations of Wimbledon's Centenary fortnight began with the All England Lawn Tennis and Croquet Club honoring 41 of the 52 living singles champions at a luncheon. Afterward, a crowd of 14,000 in the packed Centre Court rose, and their applause swelled. As the Band of the Welsh Gaurds, resplendent in scarlet uniforms and polished brass, played "The March of the Kings" from the opera *Aida*, a wonderfully nostalgic "Parade of Champions" began, the former winners striding out onto the most famous lawn in the tennis world to receive commemorative medals from the Duke of Kent in a brief, dignified ceremony.

In a touching final gesture, medals were presented to Elizabeth "Bunny" Ryan, 85, and Jacques "Toto" Brugnon, 82, "representing all the doubles champions." Ryan—winner of 12 women's doubles and seven mixed titles between 1914 and 1934—moved slowly, on walking sticks, but cast them aside to wave to the crowd. Brugnon—who won Wimbledon doubles titles twice each with fel-

low French "Musketeers" Henri Cochet and Jean Borotra—used a cane and later held the arm of the fourth "Musketeer," René Lacoste. Toto died the next winter, but for this moment he was ebullient. When the presentations were over, the band started to play again, softly. The champions posed for photos, then joined arms and sang "Auld Lang Syne."

The tournament was also richly memorable. Left-hander John McEnroe, 18, of Douglaston, New York, became the youngest semi-finalist in Wimbledon's 100 years, the first player ever to come through the qualifying rounds and get that far. He won eight matches in all before Connors brought him back to reality, 6–3, 6–3, 4–6, 6–4. In the other semifinal, Borg defeated the swift and flashy Vitas Gerulaitis, 6–4, 3–6, 6–3, 3–6, 8–6, in a breathtaking match. The sustained quality of the shotmaking and drama made this, in the opinion of longtime observers, one of the all-time Centre Court classics.

The final also lived up to a majestic standard, Borg and Connors—destined to be remembered as the archrivals of the 70s in tennis—battling each other from the baseline in torrid rallies seldom seen on grass courts. Connors seemed out of it at 0–4 in the fifth set, but roused himself for one last challenge and came back to 4–4 before a crucial double fault in the ninth game cost him his momentum, his serve, and the match, 3–6, 6–2, 6–1, 5–7, 6–4.

In the women's singles, 14-year-old Californian Tracy Austin became the youngest player ever to compete at Wimbledon. She defeated Ellie Vessies-Appel, then showed tremendous poise and groundstrokes in losing a Centre Court match to defending champion Evert, 6–1, 6–1. That match, and her first victory ever over Billie Jean King on grass—6–1, 6–2 in the quarterfinals—took an enormous emotional toll on Evert, and left her curiously flat for her semifinal against Wade.

"Our Ginny," as the British affectionately call Wade, had never prepared better for a tournament, nor felt more self-confident. She had never gone beyond the semifinals in 15 previous Wimbledons, but she kept the pressure on with bold approach shots and magnifi-

Only 14, Tracy Austin became a crowd favorite from Wimbledon to Forest Hills. *Peter Mecca*

cent net play to beat Evert, 6–2, 4–6, 6–1. Wade was much more passive in the final against 6-foot, 160-pound Betty Stove—the first Dutch finalist at Wimbledon—but settled down and let her erratic opponent make the mistakes. Wade won nine of the last 10 games and the match, 4–6, 6–3, 6–1.

The tennis was commonplace, but the occasion unforgettable. Wade, the first Englishwoman to win her national title since Ann Jones in 1969, accepted the gold championship plate from Queen Elizabeth II, who was making her first appearance at Wimbledon since 1962 in honor of the Centenary and her own Silver Jubilee celebration. British reserve gave way to an unbridled outpouring of patriotic sentiment. The Duchess of Kent waved excitedly to Wade from the Royal Box, and thousands of delighted Britons broke into a spontaneous, moving chorus of "For She's a Jolly Good Fellow."

Stove wound up a three-time loser, runner-up with Martina Navratilova in the women's doubles to unseeded JoAnne Russell and

Helen Gourlay Cawley, 6–3, 6–3, and with Frew McMillan in the mixed doubles to Bob Hewit and Greer Stevens, 3–6, 7–5, 6–4. In the men's doubles, defending champions Brian Gottfried and Raul Ramirez fell in the first round, paving the way for an all-Australian final. Ross Case and Geoff Masters, runners-up in five sets the previous year, beat John Alexander and Phil Dent in another thriller, 6–3, 6–4, 3–6, 8–9, 6–4.

Wimbledon was the highlight of the year, but the most impressive achievement was the winning streak Vilas compiled the last six months of the year, after losing listlessly to Billy Martin in the third round at Wimbledon.

Vilas started the year as runner-up to Roscoe Tanner, the hard-serving left-hander, in the Australian Open, 6–3, 6–3, 6–3. By winning the French Open in the absence of Borg and Connors—Vilas lost only one set in seven matches, and his 6–0, 6–3, 6–0 victory over Brian Gottfried in the final was the most decisive since the tournament went international in 1925—Vilas shed his image as "The Eternal Second" and removed an enormous psychological burden.

Driven by his coach-manager, the hirsute and menacing Romanian Ion Tiriac, Vilas became the fittest and most iron-willed player on the professional circuit. His last six months of 1977 were a *tour de force*. He won 12 of 13 tournaments, 76 of 77 matches, including the U.S. Open. His 50-match, July-through-September winning streak was by far the longest since the advent of Open tennis, eclipsing Rod Laver's 31 straight matches of 1969, previously the male record.

It ended the first week in October in the final of a tournament at Aix-en-Provence, France, Vilas defaulting after losing the first two sets to Ilie Nastase, who was using the "spaghetti" racket that had been barred, effective the following week.

The crowning glory of Vilas's streak was winning the U.S. Open, which was played at the West Side Tennis Club in the Forest Hills section of New York's borough of Queens for the last time, after 54 consecutive years there. Clumsy last-ditch efforts by the club's officials to retain the Open could not compensate for their years of foot-dragging on making

Argentina's Guillermo Vilas made money, and Jimmy Connors furious, in 1977. *Peter Mecca*

physical improvements. W. E. "Slew" Hester of Jackson, Mississippi, president of the U.S. Tennis Association, decided that the West Side Tennis Club was too congested, its management too stubbornly old-fashioned, to accommodate America's premier tournament, which was given 28 hours of television coverage by CBS-TV under a new five-year, $10 million rights contract. Hester set in motion ambitious plans for building a new USTA National Tennis Center in nearby Flushing Meadow Park, site of the 1939-40 and 1964-65 New York World's Fairs.

Vilas helped make "the last Forest Hills" memorable. He lost only 16 games in five matches up to the semifinals, in which he beat Harold Solomon in straight sets. In the final, Vilas displayed great physical and mental stamina and a new technical weapon—a fine sliced backhand approach shot—to beat Connors in a match of brutish grace, 2-6, 6-3, 7-6, 6-0. The sellout crowd of more than 16,000 cheered for the popular Argentinian

left-hander against "the ugly American." After the last point, many Latins in the crowd hoisted Vilas to their shoulders and carried him around the old horseshoe stadium like a conquering hero. Connors, furious at both the outcome and the reception given the victor, left in a huff, not bothering to wait for the trophy presentation ceremonies.

Vilas dominated the Grand Prix point standings, winning the $300,000 prize earmarked as the top share of the $1.5 million bonus pool put up by Colgate, which took over from Commercial Union Assurance as the Grand Prix sponsor. On the year, Vilas won 17 tournaments and $800,642 in prize money—more than he had earned in five previous pro seasons. He played the most ambitious tournament schedule of any of the top men and finished with a 140-14 record, including Davis Cup matches. (With Vilas and Ricardo Cano playing singles, Argentina upset the United States in the American Zone final to reach the Cup semifinals for the first time.) During his 50-match streak, Vilas won an astonishing 109 of 125 sets. Starting with the French Open, he won 57 consecutive matches on clay.

But even though *World Tennis* magazine declared him No. 1 for the year, most other authorities disagreed and bestowed that mythical honor on Borg, who defaulted in the fourth round of the U.S. Open with a shoulder injury. The 21-year-old Swede had the best winning percentage for the season—.920, on a record of 81-7. He won 13 of the 20 tournaments he played. Including the Masters—played in 1978, but considered the climax of the 1977 season—Borg was 3-0 over Vilas (two victories in the spring, the third in the semis of the Masters) and 2-1 over Connors, who beat him in the Masters final, 6-4, 1-6, 6-4, before a crowd of 17,150 at Madison Square Garden.

Connors may have had the season-ending last laugh, but he finished No. 3 after having been the best player in the world in 1974 and 1976 and No. 2 to Arthur Ashe in 1975. Connors won eight of 21 tournaments, 70 of 81 matches, and was in four big finals (winning the WCT playoffs over Dick Stockton, 6-7, 6-1, 6-3, 6-3, and the Masters, losing to Borg at Wimbledon and to Vilas at Forest Hills). But Connors was 1–2 head-to-head against Borg and 0–2 against Vilas, including a gripping match in the round-robin portion of the Masters, won by Vilas, 6–4, 3–6, 7–5. This spellbinder kept a record tournament crowd of 18,590 riveted to their seats in the Garden until 12:42 A.M. on a Friday morning.

While Borg, Vilas, and Connors comprised the ruling triumvirate of men's tennis, there were other noteworthy performers. Spaniard Manuel Orantes underwent surgery to repair a pinched nerve in his left elbow in the spring, but came back splendidly to bedazzle Connors, 6–1, 6–3, in the U.S. Clay Court final at Indianapolis and to topple Eddie Dibbs in the 50th U.S. Pro Championships. Vitas Gerulaitis became the first American since 1960 to win the Italian Open, on slow clay, and later demonstrated his versatility by winning the second Australian Open of the calendar year—the tournament was moved up to mid-December so that it could be included in the Grand Prix—on grass at Melbourne. Floridian Brian Gottfried won four tournaments in a six-week span early in the year and reached 15 finals during the season, winning five of them and compiling a 108–23 record.

In doubles, South Africans Bob Hewitt, 37, and Frew McMillan, 35, won 13 tournaments, even though separated for four months during the summer because McMillan played World Team Tennis. Their biggest victory came at Forest Hills, where they captured their first U.S. Open doubles title over Gottfried and Raul Ramirez, 6–4, 6–0. Hewittt and McMillan also won the Masters over Stan Smith and Bob Lutz, 7–5, 7–6, 6–3.

Gottfried and Ramirez won the Italian Open doubles for a record fourth consecutive year, and recaptured the French Open title. Arthur Ashe and Tony Roche won the Australian Open title in January, and Aussies Allan Stone and Ray Ruffels took it over in December. Vijay Amritraj and Dick Stockton made their only doubles victory together count, collecting $40,000 apiece for beating the makeshift pair of Adriano Panatta and Gerulaitis in the WCT Doubles finals at Kansas City, 7–6, 7–6, 4–6, 6–3.

The Colgate Grand Prix embraced 76 tournaments, with total prize money of approximately $9 million. Worldwide, men's tournaments offered about $12 million, excluding World Team Tennis and exhibition matches. Fifteen players made more than $200,000 in prize money, including Hewitt ($234,184), whose earnings came mostly in doubles. Five players (Vilas, Borg, Ramirez, Smith, and Orantes) crossed the once-unimaginable $1 million career earnings mark, increasing the number of tennis millionaires to 13 since Laver first broke the milestone in 1971.

In team competitions, Australia recovered the Davis Cup for the first time since 1973 and tied the U.S. for the most possessions (24). John Alexander and Phil Dent spurred the Aussies past Argentina, 3–2, in the semifinals at Buenos Aires. For the finale at Sydney, Captain Neale Fraser surprisingly called on veteran left-hander Tony Roche, who responded by toppling Adriano Panatta in the opening match, 6–3, 6–4, 6–4. Alexander beat Corrado Barazzutti in the second match and clinched a 3–1 triumph with an epic 6–4, 4–6, 2–6, 8–6, 11–9 triumph over Panatta.

The U.S., undermanned, was ambushed on the road again—this time by Argentina, 3–2, at Buenos Aires. Ricardo Cano beat Dick Stockton in the prophetic first match. This was the third consecutive year that U.S. failed to survive the American Zone, eclipsing 1965–67 as the dimmest period in U.S. Davis Cup history.

World Team Tennis completed its fourth season, with the Boston Lobsters topping the East Division, and the Phoenix Racquets the West Division. Ten teams played 44 matches each, and again all operated in the red. The New York Apples, led by Billie Jean King and Sandy Mayer, won the league championship, defeating Phoenix in the final round of the playoffs.

Chris Evert won three of the four biggest tournaments in women's tennis: her fouth Virginia Slims Championship, played at Madison Square Garden, over Englishwoman Sue Barker, 2–6, 6–1, 6–1; her third consecutive U.S. Open, matching a feat last accomplished by Maureen Connolly in 1951–53, over Australian Wendy Turnbull, 7–6, 6–2; and the

Colgate Series Championship—eight-woman finale of the Colgate International Series, the women's equivalent of the men's Grand Prix—over Billie Jean King, 6–2, 6–2, at Rancho Mirage, California.

Evert represented the United States for the first time in the Federation Cup, which attracted 42 nations to the grass courts of Devonshire Park in Eastbourne, England, the week before Wimbledon. Chrissie did not lose a set in singles as the United States romped past Austria, Switzerland, France, South Africa, and Australia. Evert defeated Kerry Reid, 7–5, 6–3, and King disposed of Dianne Fromholtz, 6–1, 2–6, 6–2, to clinch the championship before the Americans lost the meaningless final doubles.

Evert also led America's 39th victory in the 54-year-old Wightman Cup rivalry against Great Britain, played on the West Coast for the first time, at Oakland Coliseum. Chrissie opened with a 7–5, 7–6 victory over Wade, King blistered Barker, 6–1, 6–4, and a 7–0 rout was on. Even though the outcome was already decided, a record Wightman Cup crowd of 11,317 turned up on the final evening of the three-day event to see King beat Wade in a glorious match, 6–4, 3–6, 8–6.

In all, Evert at age 22 won 11 tournaments, 70 of 74 matches, and $453,134 in prize money. She was ranked No. 1 in the U.S. for the fourth consecutive year, and No. 1 in doubles for the first time, with Rosemary Casals. Evert won the U.S. Open without losing a set for the second straight year, and stretched her remarkable clay court winning streak to 23 tournaments and 113 matches, dating back to August 1973. Even though Fromholtz surprised her in the round-robin portion of the Colgate Series Championships, Evert reached the final with a bitterly fought 1–6, 6–4, 6–4 victory over Wade, and went on to claim the richest prize in women's tennis: $75,000.

Although Evert was the dominant force, and Wade the sentimental success story, there were other notable achievements in women's tennis in 1977.

■ Tracy Austin, 5 feet tall and weighing 90 pounds, reached the quarterfinals of the U.S. Open, beating No. 4 seed Barker en route. The 14-year-old took enough time off from her eighth and ninth-grade classes in Rolling Hills, California, to play 10 professional tournaments and wound up ranked 12th in the world on the computer of the Women's Tennis Association, and No. 4 in the United States—the youngest ever to crack the Top Ten.

■ Martina Navratilova, starting the season slimmed down and determined to make up for a disappointing 1976, won four of 11 tournaments on the Virginia Slims circuit, beating Evert in the final of the season opener at Washington, D.C.

■ Sue Barker, with an improved backhand to go with her already devastating forehand, won two Slims tournaments and lost three finals to Navratilova. Barker finished third on the circuit, but beat Navratilova to get to the final of the Slims Championships.

■ Wendy Turnbull, so swift afoot she was nicknamed "Rabbit," emerged as a player to be reckoned with by upsetting Casals, Wade, and Navratilova to reach the U.S. Open final.

■ Transsexual Renée Richards won her year-long legal struggle for acceptance in women's tournaments when a New York judge ruled that she could not be barred from the U.S. Open because she could not pass the Olympic chromosome test. The court ruled that medical evidence proved that Richards was "female," and the U.S. Tennis Association and Women's Tennis Association dropped efforts to bar her. She lost in the first round of the Open singles to Wade, but reached the doubles final with Californian Bettyann Stuart before losing to Navratilova and Stove, 6–1, 7–6. (Stove also won the mixed doubles, with Frew McMillan, over King and Gerulaitis, 6–2, 3–6, 6–3.) Thereafter, Richards became a regular competitor on the women's circuit, though several players defaulted against her to protest her inclusion in their tournaments.

■ King, recovered from knee surgery the previous November, worked her way back into shape and won three consecutive tournaments and 18 straight matches in the autumn to reach the playoff finale of the $2 million Colgate Series, which carried a $600,000 bonus pool. She was 0–4 on the year against Evert, but 2–0 against WTT teammate Wade, 3–0 against Navratilova, 1–0 against Barker, and 4–0 against Stove. King finished the year with a 53–6 record, ranked No. 2 in the U.S. and again a major factor in the women's game.

■ Kerry Reid, at 29, won the Australian Open for the first time, over fellow Aussie Dianne Fromholtz, 7–5, 6–2. Fromholtz and Helen Gourlay Cawley captured the doubles.

■ Evonne Goolagong Cawley, kept out of the January version of the Australian Open because she was pregnant, gave birth to her first child—daughter Kelly— in May, and launched a comeback in the fall. She won the December version of the Australian Open over Gourlay (formally, it was Cawley vs. Cawley), 6–3, 6–0. This was Evonne's fourth Australian title, and she extended her unbeaten streak in the tournament to 20 matches.

The hottest political controversy of the year concerned the rise and fall of the "double strung" or "spaghetti" racket, which was actually a radical stringing technique that could be applied to any standard racket frame. There were several versions, but they all used two sets of vertical strings, supported by five or six cross strings threaded through them, and braced with fish line, adhesive tape, rope, or other protuberances, including a plastic tubing called "spaghetti." While rackets thus strung generally had a very low tension—between 35 and 55 pounds—they were able to generate tremendous power because of a "trampoline effect," the ball sinking deep in the double layer of strings and being propelled out. Because the dual layer of strings also moved, they were able to "brush" the ball, artificially imitating a heavy topspin stroke. Thus, some players were able to hit the ball extremely hard from the backcourt and still keep it in play. The "spaghetti" racket was all the more maddening to play against because the ball came off it with a dull thud that made it difficult to judge.

The "double strung" racket was invented in West Germany by a former horticulturist named Werner Fisher, and it created a major

The controversial spaghetti racket, now banned, was used by France's Christopher Roger Vasselin in the 1977 Poree Cup finals in which he lost to Guillermo Vilas. *UPI*

scandal in club and national tournaments there as second- and third-line players became champions with it. An adaptation of the racket was first used in a major tournament by Australian Barry Phillips-Moore, in the French Open. A number of professional players used it in Europe during the summer, and it gained further notoriety at the U.S. Open when an obscure American player named Mike Fishbach used his homemade version to trounce Billy Martin and seeded Stan Smith in the first two rounds.

A couple of weeks later. Ilie Nastase was beaten by a player using a "spaghetti" racket in Paris, and swore he would never play against it again. The following week he turned up with one and used it to win a tournament at Aix-en-Provence, ending Guillermo Vilas's long winning streak in the final. Vilas quit after two sets, claiming that playing against the exaggerated spin injured his elbow.

The International Tennis Federation—which dropped "Lawn" from its name earlier in the year—had already acted by that time, however, putting a "temporary freeze" on use of the double-strung rackets in tournaments, effective October 2. The ITF based its decision on a report by the University of Brunswick in West Germany, which indicated that every hit with the racket was in fact a "double hit," in violation of the rules.

The ITF made its "ban" permanent the following June by adopting a definition of a racket for the first time: "A racket shall consist of a frame, which may be of any material, weight, size or shape and stringing. The stringing must be uniform and smooth and may be of any material. The strings must be alternately interlaced or bonded where they cross. The distance between the main and/or cross strings shall not be less than one quarter of an inch nor more than one-half inch. If there are attachments they must be used only to prevent wear and tear and must not alter the flight of the ball. They must be uniform with a maximum protrusion of .04 of an inch."

"The best player in the world the last four months of 1978," Arthur Ashe said of young John McEnroe. *Peter Mecca*

1978

In 1978, as Wimbledon began its second century, Stade Roland Garros in Paris—home of the French Championships—celebrated its 50th anniversary, and the U.S. Open moved to the new USTA National Tennis Center in Flushing Meadow, Queens, New York, the most important new arena for international tennis in half a century.

Bjorn Borg and Jimmy Connors continued their spirited battle of king-of-the-hill in men's tennis, Martina Navratilova and Chris Evert waged a similarly lovely little war for the No. 1 ranking among the women, and several precocious young talents blossomed— 19-year-old John McEnroe starting to challenge the top men, and high-school girls Tracy Austin and Pam Shriver asserting themselves in women's tournaments.

Perhaps nothing better symbolized what happened to the once-elitist, white-flanneled sport of tennis in the 1970s than the fact that the U.S. Open, America's premier tournament, moved to a public park. The National Tennis Center was built, remarkably, in one

year on 16 acres of city-owned land in Flushing Meadow Park, site of the 1939–40 and 1964–65 New York World's Fairs, and adjacent to Shea Stadium.

After 98 years in patrician clubs—first the Newport Casino amid the coastal mansions of Rhode Island, and then the West Side Tennis Club in Forest Hills, Queens, for the previous 54 years—the Open was moved to its new home by W. E. "Slew" Hester. The drawling, cigar-chomping, 66-year-old wildcat oilman from Jackson, Mississippi, sounded like a southern conservative, but proved in a memorable two-year term to be perhaps the most progressive president in the history of the U.S. Tennis Association.

Many people second-guessed Hester in September 1977 when, fed up with the reactionary board of governors of the West Side Tennis Club, he announced that the Open would not be played again at Forest Hills. Few thought the new complex Hester envisioned a couple of miles away could be completed in 12 months, and many considered the project "Hester's Folly." But Hester's per-

The new home of the U.S. Open—The National Tennis Center in Flushing, New York.
Jack Mecca

severance and leadership, despite arthritis so severe it was difficult for him to walk, enabled the USTA to cut through bureaucratic red tape, union disputes, and cost overruns and get the splendid facility built in time for the 1978 Open.

The National Tennis Center was dedicated on August 30, 1978. Its main arena—Louis Armstrong Stadium, site of the Singer Bowl for the 1964–65 World's Fair and named for the late jazz great who lived nearby—accommodated nearly 20,000 spectators, with barely a bad seat in the house. In addition to the steeply banked, red, white and blue stadium, the complex included a 6,000-seat grandstand, 25 additional lighted outdoor courts, and nine indoor courts, all with the same acrylic asphalt surface that approximates the hard courts most Americans play on. Under a 15-year lease agreement between the USTA and the city of New York, the facility is open to the public year-round and is available to the USTA for tournaments and special events 60 days a year, at a modest fee. The USTA, in turn, spent $10 million to renovate and enlarge a stadium that was intended for concerts but that had fallen into terrible disrepair.

The result was the most significant new venue for world tennis since the modern All England Club was opened in the London suburb of Wimbledon in 1922 and Stade Roland Garros was dedicated as a civic monument in Paris for the 1928 Davis Cup Challenge Round.

Roland Garros celebrated its golden anniversary during the 1978 French Open Championships. On balance, this was a dull tournament, but on a day when 32 past champions were honored in gala center court ceremonies, Bjorn Borg asserted himself as one of the greatest by winning the most important clay court test of Europe for the third time, five days past his 20th birthday.

Two weeks after winning the Italian Open in five sets over Roman matinee idol Adriano Panatta, Borg repeated the arduous clay court "double" he had first achieved in 1974. He swept through seven matches in Paris in 21 straight sets, dropping only 32 games. In the final, he trounced defending champion Guillermo Vilas, 6–1, 6–1, 6–3.

Bjorn Borg wins in 1978 for the third straight year at Wimbledon as Jimmy Connors, his victim, stonily departs the scene. *UPI*

Borg went on to become the first man since Rod Laver in 1962 to sweep the Italian, French, and Wimbledon singles titles in one season. In dominating the grass of Wimbledon as he had the clay in Rome and Paris, Borg also equaled a more important milestone. He became the first man since Englishman Fred Perry in 1934–36 to win the Wimbledon singles three successive years.

Borg's dream of duplicating Perry's feat nearly ended in the first round. Victor Amaya, a 6-foot-7, 220-pound left-hander with a thunderous serve, led him by two sets to one, 3–1, in the fourth, 30–40 on Borg's serve. Borg escaped a second service break only by the margin of a bold second serve, then broke Amaya and came back to win.

Thereafter, Borg grew increasingly sharper and stronger. He routed a rejuvenated Tom Okker in the semifinals and thrashed archrival Connors, 6–2, 6–2, 6–3, in the final. Never before had Borg served, volleyed, and smashed with such authority, and he also displayed a new weapon—a sliced backhand approach shot to Connors' vulnerable forehand, which stayed low on the fast grass. "The way Borg played today," marveled Perry, who hustled down from behind his microphone in the BBC radio commentary booth to congratulate the young Swede on Centre Court, "if he had fallen out of a 45th-story window of a skyscraper, he would have gone straight up."

At the midpoint of the season, it seemed that Borg, with his beefed-up serve, had begun to dominate his grand rivalry with Connors. Despite a loss in the 1977 Grand Prix Masters the first week of the new year, Borg had won five of their last six meetings, giving up only 11 games in the last six sets, through Wimbledon.

But Connors immediately began to train for another showdown, vowing to "follow that sonofabitch to the ends of the earth" for revenge. He worked on adding oomph to his serve—which had deserted him in the Wimbledon final—and shoring up his forehand. Having won 18 straight matches going into the Wimbledon final, he didn't lose another the rest of the summer, winning Grand Prix tournaments at Washington, Indianapolis (the U.S. Clay Court), and Stowe, Vermont, as he groomed his game to peak at the U.S. Open.

Connors' moment of truth at the Open came in a fourth-round victory over Panatta, the dashing and talented Italian. Panatta served for the match at 5–3 in the fifth set of this 3-hour, 36-minute epic, came within two points of victory at 30–30, and later fended off four match points. Connors got to the fifth with an astounding shot: a backhand down the line on the dead run from 10 feet out of court, which he somehow reached and drilled one-handed around the net post for a winner.

Moments later, Connors had the match, 4–6, 6–4, 6–1, 1–6, 7–5, and that, he said later, gave him the impetus to steamroll through the final three rounds without losing a set to Brian Gottfried, John McEnroe, and Borg. Never before were Connors' skill, will, and churning internal aggression better showcased than in the final. He annihilated Borg, who had a blister on the thumb of his racket hand, almost as badly as he had been ravaged at Wimbledon, 6–4, 6–2, 6–2.

Connors, the first man since Bill Tilden in the 1920s to reach the singles final five consecutive years, thus became the first man since Perry in 1933–34 and 1936 to win three U.S. Singles titles, and the first American to do so since Tilden. By quirk of history, Connors also gained the singular distinction of having won on grass (1974), clay (1976), and hard courts (1978).

The U.S. Open final was the last meeting of the year between Borg and Connors. The last four months of the season belonged to McEnroe, the brash left-hander from Douglaston, New York, who was the first man since Ken Rosewall in the 1950s to have reached the semifinals at both Wimbledon and the U.S. Championships while still a teenager.

After losing to Connors in the Open, McEnroe won four Grand Prix tournaments (Hartford, San Francisco, Stockholm, London) in singles, seven in doubles, led the U.S. to its first possession of the Davis Cup since 1972 with a spectacular singles debut, and won both the singles and doubles titles at the Colgate Grand Prix Masters at Madison Square Garden the second week in January 1979. His singles record over that stretch was 49–7. In the six months since turning pro in June, after winning the National Intercollegiate Singles title as a Stanford University freshman, McEnroe collected $463,866.

At Stockholm, on a fast tile court, he won his first meeting with Borg, 6–3, 6–4. His left-handed serve, sliced low and wide so that it skidded away from Borg's two-fisted backhand, was so effective that McEnroe lost only seven points in 10 service games. It was the first time that Borg, 22, had lost to a player younger than he.

McEnroe made his Davis Cup debut in doubles in September, partnering Brian Gottfried to the decisive point in America's 3–2 victory over Chile in the American Zone final at Santiago. McEnroe made his singles debut in the finals at Rancho Mirage, California, and lost his serve only once in demoralizing John Lloyd, 6–1, 6–2, 6–2, in the opening match, and Buster Mottram, 6–2, 6–2, 6–1, in the clincher of the 4–1 U.S. victory over Great Britain. This ended a five-year drought

Slew Hester, whose dream of a USTA National Tennis Center became a reality in 1978, beams as Jimmy Connors displays the U.S. Open trophy he won at the facility's inaugural. *Jack Mecca*

for the U.S. and gave it possession of the trophy symbolizing international team supremacy in tennis for a record 25th time. As for McEnroe's dominance, it should be noted that never before in 67 Davis Cup finals had a player lost as few as 10 games in two singles matches.

McEnroe went into the season-ending Masters playoff eager for a showdown with Connors, who had beaten him in all four of their career meetings. The Masters, designed to bring together the top eight finishers in the previous year's Grand Prix standings for a $400,000 shootout, had lost much of its luster because Borg and Guillermo Vilas declined invitations. They had not played the minimum 20 Grand Prix tournaments required to qualify for shares of the $2 million Grand Prix bonus pool, and so turned their backs on the showcase finale. Connors did not qualify for his bonus either, but was coaxed at the eleventh hour into defending his title.

The Connors-McEnroe duel was seen as the savior of a disappointing tournament, but it also fizzled because Connors aggravated a blood blister on his foot in the first set of their meeting in the round-robin portion of the tournament, and defaulted while trailing, 5–7, 0–3. McEnroe went on to beat Eddie Dibbs in the semifinals and comebacking Arthur Ashe, 6–7, 6–3, 7–5, in a scintillating final, McEnroe reviving himself from 1–4 down and two match points in the final set.

But even if McEnroe was, as Ashe called him, "the best player in the world the last four months of 1978," he was not in the running for Player of the Year honors based on his full-season record of 75–20. The run for the No. 1 ranking was strictly a match race between Borg and Connors.

Tennis magazine's ranking panel voted for Connors, but *World Tennis* and the International Federation—which instituted a "world champion" award—went for Borg.

The "world champion" title was a new honor to be awarded annually by the ITF for men and women, intended to establish an official No. 1 player for each calendar year, eliminating the confusion caused by diverse and often contradictory sets of unofficial rankings.

Borg was the unanimous choice of the selection committee of three former champions: Fred Perry, Australian Lew Hoad, and Californian Don Budge. Their decision was based primarily on his superior record in traditional major events, although Borg also held a 3–2 edge over Connors in head-to-head meetings, including three four-man "special events."

Borg's record for the entire season was 85–8, including a 10–0 singles record in spurring Sweden to the semifinals of the Davis Cup. Excluding four-man events, he was 72–7. From March through the U.S. Open final, he had a 55-match winning streak, although twice during that period he defaulted matches before going oncourt because of infected blisters.

Connors was 82–7 overall, 76–5 excluding four-man events. He monopolized the U.S. Indoors, Clay Court, and Open titles. Following the Wimbledon final, he compiled a 32-match winning streak.

Other notable achievements in men's tennis in 1978:

■ "Broadway Vitas" Gerulaitis, the flamboyant 23-year-old New Yorker, got a default over Borg in the semifinals and captured the $100,000 top prize in the eight-man World Championship of Tennis finals at Dallas with an impressive 6–3, 6–2, 6–1 victory over Eddie Dibbs. Gerulaitis also collected the $100,000 top prize in WCT's 12-man, $300,000 invitational tournament at Forest Hills in July, beating Ilie Nastase in the final, 6–2, 6–0.

■ Dibbs won four Grand Prix tournaments (Tulsa, Cincinnati, North Conway, Toronto), 77 of 100 matches in 27 tournaments, and finished third in the Grand Prix standings. Because Connors and Borg did not qualify, Dibbs received the top prize of $300,000 from the bonus pool and headed the Association of Tennis Professionals' "official money" list (tournament winnings and bonuses only) with $575,273. Borg ($469,441), Raul Ramirez ($463,866) and McEnroe were also over the $400,000 mark. Connors ($392,153) led a parade of six more players who won in

Vitas Gerulaitis won the Italian Open and the second Australian Open of the year in 1978. *Jack Mecca*

excess of $300,000. Fourteen players were over $200,000, and a total of 34 collected over $100,000. In all, more than $12 million was at stake in 93 Grand Prix tournaments around the world.

■ Guillermo Vilas won seven tournaments, including the German Open and the Australian Open, which ended January 3, 1979. His 6–4, 6–4, 3–6, 6–3 triumph over unseeded John Marks, and a semifinal victory over Arthur Ashe in five sets gave him his third Big Four singles title, to go along with his French and U.S. Open crowns of 1977.

■ Ashe, the Wimbledon champion and World No. 1 of 1975, started the year ranked only No. 257 on the computer printout of the Association of Tennis Professionals because he had missed almost the entire 1977 season after surgery on a chronic heel ailment. He won three Grand Prix tournaments (San Jose, Columbus, Los Angeles), reached the Masters final, and finished the season ranked No. 11.

Bob Hewitt and Frew McMillan won seven doubles titles, including their third at Wimbledon. Tom Okker and Wojtek Fibak also won seven tournaments, including the WCT finals at Kansas City, for which they split an $80,000 prize. Stan Smith and Bob Lutz captured their third U.S. Open doubles, and won crucial Davis Cup matches in America's 3–2 victory over Sweden in the semifinals at Gothenburg and the 4–1 victory over Great Britain. John McEnroe and Peter Fleming were the hottest team the second half of the season, winning six tournaments together between August and December, plus the 1978 Masters early in January. Brian Gottfried and Raul Ramirez, a standout team the previous four years, won only the U.S. Indoor at Memphis together in 1978 and split up their partnership after the French Open.

In women's tennis, the first half of the year belonged to Martina Navratilova, the second half to Chris Evert.

With Evert taking the first three months of the year as a vacation, Navratilova, at age 21, began to fulfill her rich promise. She dominated the Virginia Slims winter circuit—the last under the cigarette company's sponsorship—winning the first seven tournaments and the $150,000 final playoff at Oakland, California, over Evonne Goolagong, 7–6, 6–4. That was Navratilova's most important victory to date, an important psychological breakthrough for the expatriate Czech left-hander.

Evert returned to competition in the spring, but Navratilova, supremely fit and confident, beat her in the final of a pre-Wimbledon grass court tournament at Eastbourne, England, coming back from 1–4 in the final set and saving a match point.

They met again in the Wimbledon final, and this time Navratilova came back from 2–4 in the final set, serving magnificently and outsteadying as well as overpowering Evert to win, 2–6, 6–4, 7–5. Navratilova, whose emotions had regularly overwhelmed her abundant talent, won 12 of the last 13 points. She held at love the last two times she served, missing only one first serve, while Evert made three uncharacteristic unforced errors to lose her serve to 5–6 in the most crucial game of an absorbing match.

When it was over, Navratilova looked ecstatically toward her friend and manager, Hall of Fame golfer Sandra Haynie, an important stabilizing influence in her life who sat beaming in the competitors' guest box. Then Martina shed a flood of tears into a towel, and was puffy-eyed when she received the championship trophy from the Duchess of Kent.

"I don't know if I should cry or scream or laugh. I feel very happy that I won, but at the same time I'm very sad that I can't share this with my family," said Navratilova, who had not seen her parents or her 15-year-old sister since defecting to the United States during the 1975 U.S. Open Championships. Her victory, predictably, was all but neglected in the government-controlled media of Czechoslovakia, but her parents watched it on German television by driving to a town near the German border.

Navratilova and Billie Jean King—again foiled in her attempt to win a record-setting 20th career Wimbledon title—were upset in the quarterfinals of the Wimbledon women's doubles by Mona Guerrant and Sue Barker, but they did win the U.S. Open title, over Wimbledon champs Kerry Reid and Wendy Turnbull, 7–6, 6–4. Australians Reid and Turnbull took the Wimbledon crown with a 4–6, 9–8, 6–3 thriller over French Open champs Mima Jausovec and Virginia Ruzici. Betty Stove and Frew McMillan won the mixed doubles at both Wimbledon and Flushing Meadow.

Navratilova won her first 37 matches of the year, but the winning streak finally came to an end in the quarterfinals of the Virginia Slims in Dallas. She was beaten by 15-year-old Californian Tracy Austin, 6–3, 2–6, 7–6. The tingling match before 10,000 enthralled spectators went down to the final point of a best-of-nine-point tie-breaker, simultaneous match point for both players.

The Dallas tournament produced several startling upsets and three teen-aged semifinalists—Austin, 15-year-old Pam Shriver of Lutherville, Maryland, and 18-year-old Anne Smith of Dallas. Goolagong, 26, eventually beat Austin in the final, 4–6, 6–0, 6–2. "Someday, that tournament may be looked upon as a landmark, the beginning of a new order," predicted women's tennis pioneer Billie Jean King.

Those words appeared prophetic as Austin, Shriver, and Smith all landed in the U.S. Top Ten rankings for 1978—Austin at No. 3, Shriver at No. 5, and Smith at No. 8. They appeared to be the vanguard of a wave of promising young women players, a notion fortified by the victory of 13-year-old Andrea Jaeger in the 18-and-under division of the prestigious Orange Bowl junior tournament at the end of the year.

Austin rose to No. 6 in the world before turning 16 on December 12, 1978. She beat Shriver in the finals of the U.S. Girls' 16 and 18 Championships, increasing her record total of U.S. junior titles to 27. She turned pro in October, won her first tournament as a professional at Stuttgart, Germany, and collected $70,000 in prize money within three months.

Shriver, while 0–9 against Austin in their junior careers, one-upped her at the U.S. Open, becoming the youngest finalist in the tournament's history. Shriver upset Kerry Reid, an injured Lesley Hunt, and Navratilova, 7–6, 7–6, in a rain-interrupted semifinal. That was arguably the greatest upset in women's major tournament history. Playing nervelessly and aggressively with her Prince (oversized head) racket, Shriver used her serve-and-volley game to extend Evert to 7–5, 6–4 before losing an exciting final.

Both Austin and Shriver, who remained an amateur, were named to the U.S. Wightman Cup team, which was upset by Great Britain, 4–3, at London's Royal Albert Hall. Evert routed Sue Barker, 6–2, 6–1, and Virginia Wade, 6–0, 6–1, but the British preyed on the inexperience of the American teen-agers. Michele Tyler upset Shriver, Wade and Barker each beat Austin, and Wade and Barker teamed up to beat Shriver and Evert, 6–0, 5–7, 6–4, in the decisive doubles match.

Austin also joined Evert and Captain Billie Jean King as the U.S. won the Federation Cup for the third straight year, at Melbourne, Australia. The U.S. nipped Australia, 2–1, in the final, Evert and King teaming for the decisive point over Reid and Turnbull, 4–6, 6–1, 6–4.

Evert did not lose a tournament match after

A future queen, 16-year-old Pam Shriver had to settle for roses after a noble try against Chris Evert in the 1978 U.S. Open final. *UPI*

the Wimbledon final, winning her last 34 of the year, including three over Navratilova. Evert finished with a 56–3 record, six victories in 10 tournaments, and $443,540 in prize money. She became only the third woman to win the U.S. singles four consecutive years, the first since Helen Jacobs in 1932–35. Evert won the U.S. Open without losing a set for the third consecutive year, an astonishing feat, especially since the surface was changed from clay (on which she had not lost since August 1973) to the medium-fast hard courts that are not ideally suited to her backcourt game.

Evert finished the year with a 3–2 record against Navratilova and was voted the ITF "world champion" by unanimous vote of a panel of three former women champions: Ann Jones, Margaret Court, and Margaret Osborne duPont.

Evert also was voted the most valuable player in World Team Tennis, leading her Los Angeles Strings to their first championship of the intercity league. The Strings beat the Boston Lobsters in the playoff finale.

But after five years of financial losses, WTT was on shaky ground as the year ended. Half of the league's 10 teams announced that they were ceasing operations in the fall, and despite some optimistic noises from the commissioner's office in St. Louis, the chances of finding replacements appeared slim. Plans for a seven-week, $1 million women's tournament circuit in Europe in the spring gave Evert, Navratilova, and the other women stars of WTT a lucrative alternative. The failure of the league to sign top players for 1979 caused several influential owners to give up the ghost, and the league seemed to unravel quickly after the Boston Lobsters and the New York Apples folded.

Virginia Slims, which had pioneered the promotion of women's tennis since 1971, startlingly departed from the sponsorship scene in April when the Women's Tennis Association board of directors voted not to renew its contract for the winter circuit. The WTA cited "differences in philosophy on the structure of the circuit" for the divorce from the company, which had poured more than $8 million into women's pro tennis over eight years.

Some women players thought the termination of the contract was a grave mistake and that no comparable patroness of the women's game could be found. But in June it was announced that Avon—the huge cosmetic and costume jewelry firm that had for two years sponsored the "Futures" satellite circuit—had signed a two-year contract, with additional renewal options, to take over sponsorship of the major circuit as well as the "Futures." Avon's $2.2 million annual commitment was to fund 11 "Championship" tournaments with purses between $125,000 and $200,000, leading to a $325,000 singles and doubles championship playoff, and an expanded circuit of $25,000 "Futures" tournaments.

Despite growing pains, sometimes acute, it was obvious that professional tennis was still on the rise as the 1980s approached.

1979

The United Nations designated 1979 as the "International Year of the Child," and in tennis, youth was well served. This was most evident at the U.S. Open, where 16-year-old Tracy Austin became the youngest women's singles champion in the history of America's premier championships, and 20-year-old John McEnroe reigned as the youngest men's champion since Pancho Gonzales in 1948.

But while firmly establishing themselves as

Tracy Austin is a study in concentration during her straight-set victory over Chris Evert Lloyd in the U.S. Open final. *UPI*

contenders for the No. 1 world rankings, the "kids" were not ready to ascend the throne quite yet. The positions of honor in the last year of tennis' remarkable "growth decade" belonged to "old-timers" Martina Navratilova, 22, who won the Avon Championships climaxing the women's indoor circuit and her second consecutive Wimbledon title, and the irrepressible Bjorn Borg, 23, who captured his fourth French Open title and his fourth in a row at Wimbledon, a feat no man had accomplished since before World War I.

Still, it was an exceptional season for those youthful overachievers, Austin and McEnroe. In addition to her triumph in the Open, Tracy was runner-up to Navratilova in the Avon Championships and snapped Chris Evert Lloyd's six-year, 125-match clay court winning streak en route to victory in the Italian Open, her first major international title.

McEnroe, who had started the year by winning the 1978 Grand Prix Masters, added the World Championship of Tennis (WCT) title, beating Jimmy Connors and Borg back-to-back, and teamed with Peter Fleming to win the Wimbledon and U.S. Open doubles. Prodigious in their successes, they were clearly the best doubles pair in the world.

The rapid ascendance of Austin and McEnroe did symbolize a significant change in the old order that had ruled much of the latter part of the decade.

Chris Evert and Jimmy Connors—who had reached the pinnacle of the game in 1974 as "the lovebird double," young champions engaged to wed—finally did get married . . . but not to each other. Evert became the bride of British Davis Cup player John Lloyd. A few weeks earlier, Connors revealed that he had secretly married former *Playboy* magazine Playmate-of-the-Year Patti McGuire in Japan the previous autumn. The couple's first child, Brett David, was born in August.

Meanwhile, though still formidable players, neither Evert Lloyd nor Connors were quite the force they had been. Their marriage and apparent off-court happiness seemed to coincide with a slight but noticeable decline in their competitive fires.

Evert Lloyd said she was no longer obsessed with the ambition to be the No. 1 player in the world. She did recapture the French Open title in the absence of Navratilova and Austin, but never really resembled her dominant and awesomely consistent form of the prior five years. She failed to reach the semifinals of the Avon Championships, was runner-up to Navratilova at Wimbledon for the second straight year, and succumbed to Austin one hurdle short of an unprecedented fifth consecutive U.S. Open title.

Connors, after being in the finals at Wimbledon four of the five previous years and at the U.S. Open five straight times, fell in the semis of each, and at the same stage in the WCT playoffs and French Open as well. Moreover, Borg established indisputable superiority in their long-running and splendid rivalry—crushing Connors in straight sets in four meetings on four different surfaces (clay at Boca Raton, Florida, cement at Las Vegas, grass at Wimbledon, indoors in Tokyo), never losing more than three games in a set.

Connors did defend his titles in both the U.S. Pro Indoors at Philadelphia and the U.S. Indoor Championships at Memphis, beating Arthur Ashe—who had made an impressive comeback from heel surgery, but shockingly suffered a mild heart attack at age 36 in August—in both finals. Connors romped in Philly, 6–3, 6–4, 6–1. Memphis was closer, Ashe fighting valiantly for the only U.S. National singles title he had never won before losing, 2–6, 6–4, 6–4.

It was at Moody Coliseum in Dallas, at the end of the winter-spring men's indoor season, that McEnroe gave a convincing glimpse of great things ahead. Playing in the WCT Finals for the first time, he beat Australian John Alexander, 6–4, 6–0, 6–2; Connors, 6–1, 6–4, 6–4; and Borg, 7–5, 4–6, 6–2, 7–6, to win the $100,000 first prize with the kind of lefthanded serve-and-volley attack—rich in variations of speed and spin, touch and improvisation—not seen since the salad days of Rod Laver.

Navratilova was the prevailing figure on the 12-week, $2.2 million Avon Championship Series, winning four of seven tournaments she played plus the showcase $275,000 finale at Madison Square Garden. In the climactic match, Martina clinched the $100,000 top prize by overcoming her own shaky backhand and Austin's persistent backcourt game, 6–3, 3–6, 6–2. Veterans Betty Stove and Francoise Durr won the doubles over Sue Barker and Ann Kiyomura, 7–6, 7–6.

The most startling development of the Avon Championships, which climaxed a successful first year for the cosmetics firm as heir to Virginia Slims in sponsoring the women's indoor circuit, was the failure of Evert to get through the round-robin portion of the playoffs to the semifinals. Until 1979, Chrissie had never lost two matches in a row in her professional career. That astounding landmark of consistency was broken when she was beaten by Navratilova in the final of an Avon tournament at Oakland and then by Greer Stevens in the first round at Hollywood, Florida. In the playoffs at New York, Evert—whose mind was obviously more on her upcoming wedding than on her tennis—lost listlessly on successive nights to Austin and Australian Dianne Fromholtz.

Evert did regroup to win her last tournament before her April 17 nuptials, coming from behind to beat Fromholtz (conqueror of Navratilova), 3–6, 6–3, 6–1, for the $100,000 first prize in the four-woman Clairol Crown special event at Carlsbad, California.

After a two-week honeymoon, Evert Lloyd teamed with Austin, Billie Jean King, and Rosemary Casals to give the United States its fourth consecutive triumph in the Federation Cup, on clay at Madrid. In the final, the American juggernaut overwhelmed Australia (Fromholtz, Wendy Turnbull, Kerry Reid), 3–0. Later in the year, an expanded U.S. squad also whitewashed Great Britain, 7–0, in the Wightman Cup at Palm Beach, Florida.

This was the year the Women's Tennis Association (WTA) embarked on a bold experiment of breaking away from joint events with the men in the major championships of Europe and playing their own separate tournaments, except in Paris. After years of secondary billing and proportionally low prize money, the women concluded they were ready to go it on their own in the European clay court tournaments, even though interest in women's tennis was traditionally lacking in Latin countries.

Attendance at the new women's-only events was generally disappointing. This was especially true in Rome, where the paid attendance was only about 5,000 for the week, despite the glorious semifinal in which Austin defeated Evert Lloyd, 6–4, 2–6, 7–6, 7 points to 4 in the final set tiebreaker. This was on May 12, and it marked the first time Evert Lloyd had lost a match on a clay court since August 12, 1973, when Evonne Goolagong beat her in the final of the Western Championships at Cincinnati. Evert Lloyd's incredible streak had covered 25 tournaments and 125 matches over nearly six years, only eight of which went to three sets. Evert Lloyd said she was more relieved than stunned when the streak finally ended. Austin was thrilled, and celebrated the next day by beating West German lefthander Sylvia

Hanika—voted the most improved player of the year by the WTA—in the final.

It was a shame that the streak ended before such a sparse and seemingly disinterested audience, however. There were only about 1,500 spectators at Il Foro Italico, compared with a howling sell-out throng of more than 9,000 for the final of the men's Italian Open two weeks later. That was a glorious match too. Vitas Gerulaitis, the flamboyant New Yorker, defeated Guillermo Vilas, 6–7, 7–6, 6–7, 6–4, 6–2, in an enthralling battle of wit and grit that began in the midafternoon sunshine and ended 5 hours and 10 minutes later in the cool of evening. This was thought to be the longest final ever in major tournament history, in terms of playing time: 4 hours and 53 minutes, not counting the 17-minute intermission between the third and fourth sets.

Interest in the women's matches was also clearly secondary in the French Open at Stade Roland Garros, where the center court was enlarged to 17,000 seats as part of a major renovation targeted at producing a second "show" arena in 1980. Twelve of the tournament's 14 days were sold out, the French Open having become almost as much of an "in thing" in Paris as Wimbledon is in London, but only 10,000 spectators turned out on the final Saturday to view the women's singles final. This was a terribly tedious match in which Evert Lloyd monotonously ground down erring Wendy Turnbull, 6–2, 6–0. Evert Lloyd, the champion of 1974–75, lost only one set in regaining the title she had abdicated in order to play in World Team Tennis, the American intercity league, which was gasping for breath at the end of 1978 and was pronounced officially dead early in 1979.

The men's singles in Paris was expected to produce another duel between Borg and Connors, who entered the premier clay court championship of the world for the first time since 1973. Instead, it was exciting primarily because of Victor Pecci, a 6-foot-3-inch Paraguayan with a diamond in his right ear who entered the tournament ranked No. 30 in the world and unseeded. He knocked off four seeds in succession—1978 semifinalist Corrado Barazzutti, 1976 runner-up Harold Solomon, and 1977 champion Guillermo Vilas in straight sets, and Connors in four. In the final, Pecci stirred a capacity crowd on a drizzly day by coming back from two sets and 2–5 down to push Borg before bowing, 6–3, 6–1, 6–7, 6–4. American brothers Gene and Sandy Mayer won the men's doubles over Australians Ross Case and Phil Dent, while Betty Stove and Wendy Turnbull won the women's doubles over Virginia Wade and Francoise Durr, 2–6, 7–5, 6–4.

McEnroe, who had missed Rome and Paris because of a pulled groin muscle, returned to action and won a Wimbledon tune-up tournament on grass at London's Queen's Club over Pecci—and was simultaneously grilled in the British press for his surly deportment. Dubbed "Superbrat," he dominated pre-Wimbledon publicity and was seeded No. 2 to Borg, largely because Connors did not reveal until after the draw was made whether he would play or remain a home with his expectant wife.

McEnroe, still bothered by the groin pull, was upset in the fourth round by Tim Gullikson, culminating a first week that was tumultuous for the men (10 of the 16 seeds were beaten in the first five days) and formful for the women. Most observers thought the semifinal between Borg and Connors, who had met in the previous two finals, would be the *de facto* title match, but Borg was in his most devastating form and annihilated his longtime arch rival, 6–2, 6–3, 6–2.

Lefthander Roscoe Tanner, a semifinalist twice before, came through the wreckage in the other half of the draw to reach the final for the first time. Attacking at every opportunity, playing thoughtfully and well, he pushed Borg to the limit in an absorbing final that kept 15,000 spectators and a live television audience in 28 countries spellbound for 2 hours, 29 minutes. Half an hour after his 6–7, 6–1, 3–6, 6–3, 6–4 triumph, which made him the first man since New Zealander Tony Wilding in 1910–13 to win the Wimbledon singles four years running, Borg said: "I feel much, much older than when I went on the court. Especially at the end of the match, I have never been so nervous in my whole life. . . . I almost couldn't hold my racket." That was a revealing admission from the as-

tonishing Swede who, after a narrow second-round escape against Vijay Amritraj, the only man in four years to have a match game against Borg at Wimbledon, had said he gets more relaxed when matches are at their tightest.

Coupled with Navratilova's 6–4, 6–4 victory over Evert Lloyd in the women's final the previous day, Borg's victory marked the first time that both the men's and women's singles champions had successfully defended their titles since Bill Tilden and Suzanne Lenglen won in 1920–21.

Navratilova was entitled to a first-round bye, but chose instead to play a match in order to enjoy the champion's traditional honor of playing the opening contest on center court. She had good reason for making this decision: watching her from the competitiors' guest box was her mother, whom she had not seen in nearly four years, since defecting from Czechoslovakia during the 1975 U.S. Open. Mrs. Jana Navratilova was granted a two-week tourist visa to visit her daughter in London with the personal approval of Czechoslovakian Prime Minister Dr. Lubomir Strougal. "Winning here last year was the greatest moment of my career," a tearful Navratilova said after an unexpectedly tense 4–6, 6–2, 6–1 victory over qualifier Tanya Harford, "but yesterday [her airport reunion with her mother] was one of the greatest moments of my life."

Fighting a cold, Navratilova struggled into the semifinals, losing sets to Greer Stevens and Dianne Fromholtz. But she did not lose a set in the last two rounds, beating Austin and Evert Lloyd. Her father and 16-year-old sister, who were not granted visas, watched the match live on West German television in the border town of Pilsen, as they had the year before. But this time, instead of ignoring the expatriate's victory, the government-controlled Czech media gave it prominent attention in newspapers and on television.

Navratilova had another thrill in partnering Billie Jean King to the women's doubles title, 5–7, 6–3, 6–2, over Turnbull and Stove. This was King's twentieth Wimbledon title in singles (6), doubles (10) and mixed doubles (4), giving her a long-sought record for career titles in the world's most prestigious tournament. But the occasion was saddened by the death the previous day of 87-year-old Elizabeth Ryan, with whom King had shared the record since 1975.

Miss Ryan, a native Californian who lived in London, was stricken with a heart attack while watching the women's singles final, collapsed in a ladies room at the All England Club, and died on the way to a hospital. Winner of 12 women's doubles and seven mixed doubles titles between 1914 and 1934, but never the singles, Miss Ryan had told friends of a premonition that this would be the year King broke her cherished record. She dreaded the moment, but never saw it. She died less than 24 hours before being erased from the record book.

Back in the United States, Connors won the National Clay Court singles for the fourth time, beating Vilas in the final, 6–1, 2–6, 6–4. Evert Lloyd—returning after a 3-year absence—won her fifth title, extending her personal winning streak in the tournament to 26 straight matches. Both joined 16 other former champs in ceremonies dedicating a superb new 10,000-seat stadium at the Indianapolis Sports Center.

The U.S. Open was played for the second time at the National Tennis Center in Flushing Meadow, New York, and amid the cacophony of planes roaring overhead and spectators moving about during play, the youngsters came to the fore.

McEnroe's toughest battle came in the second round against Ilie Nastase, no longer the exquisite shotmaker he once was, but still a tempestuous personality. McEnroe won, 6–4, 4–6, 6–3, 6–2, in a stormy match that could be completed only after the crowd of 10,000 spectators at a night session—many of them heavily into their cups—had booed veteran umpire Frank Hammond from the chair amid a shower of beer cans, paper cups, and other unidentified flying objects. After more than 2½ hours of tennis charged with a constant undercurrent of psychological warfare, Hammond lost his temper and control of the match in docking Nastase a "penalty game" for alleged stalling. The predominantly pro-Nastase crowd rebelled, objected vociferously when

The U.S. Open trophy and a smile say it all for John McEnroe after his straight-set conquest of Vitas Gerulaitis. *UPI*

Hammond tried to default Nastase, and did not calm down until the tournament director had overruled the default and replaced Hammond as the umpire.

McEnroe—at home on the asphalt-based courts less than 15 minutes from his front door in Douglastown, Long Island, but never a favorite with the home crowds because of his incessant pouting and grousing—won two matches by default, including his quarterfinal over Eddie Dibbs. But he stayed sharp playing doubles, and in the semifinals routed Connors, who was inhibited by back spasms, 6–3, 6–3, 7–5. He won the final with similar ease over his Long Island neighbor Gerulaitis, 7–5, 6–3, 6–3.

Gerulaitis had made a magnificent comeback from two sets and a service break down in the semifinals to beat Tanner, who had served magnificently in upsetting No. 1 seed Borg in the quarterfinals, 6–2, 4–6, 6–2, 7–6. Borg—who hates playing at night, especially against a big server like Tanner—was

Martina Navratilova won Wimbledon for the second year in a row. *UPI*

thus foiled for the second straight year in his attempt to nail down the third leg of a possible French-Wimbledon-U.S.-Australian Grand Slam, and failed to win his first U.S. Open.

In the women's singles, Pam Shriver—who a year earlier had become the youngest finalist in the tournament's history at 16 years, 2 months of age—lost in the first round to qualifier Julie Harrington. Shriver had played only 24 matches in the year between Opens because of first school commitments and then a persistent shoulder ailment that robbed her of her oppressive serve. Seven of the top eight seeds reached the quarterfinals, but Austin upset Navratilova in the semis, 7–5, 7–5, and Evert Lloyd in the final, 6–4, 6–3. At 16 years, 9 months of age, the cool Californian became the youngest champion ever, three days younger than May Sutton in 1904 and several months younger than Maureen Connolly in 1951.

"I thought the title might intimidate her," said Evert Lloyd, who until a three-set victory over Sherry Acker in the fourth round had not lost a set in the U.S. Open since the 1975 final. "But she was out there like it was just another tennis match."

McEnroe and Fleming won the men's doubles over fellow Americans Stan Smith and Bob Lutz, 6–2, 6–4. The sentimental story of the doubles, however, was the reunion of Australians Roy Emerson, 42, and Fred Stolle, 40, who had last played together in the U.S. Doubles when it was played in Boston. They were the champions of 1965–66, and added four more victories to reach 15 in a row before Smith and Lutz toppled them in the semifinals, 7–5, 3–6, 7–5. Stove-Turnbull reversed the result of the Wimbledon final, beating King-Navratilova for the women's doubles title, while Greer Stevens and Bob Hewitt repeated their Wimbedon victory over Stove and Frew McMillan in the mixed doubles final.

In Davis Cup ploy, McEnroe and Gerulaitis in singles and Smith-Lutz in doubles cinched the Cup with a 5–0 shutout of Italy. The U.S. team did not allow Italy a single set in 15 sets. It may have been the last of Cup competition for veterans Smith and Lutz.

Not long after the U.S. Open, Volvo, the Swedish auto manufacturer, announced that it would assume and expand sponsorship of the men's Grand Prix of tennis, following Colgate-Palmolive's decision to drop out of the men's game after three years of Grand Prix sponsorship. The advent of the fourth Grand Prix sponsor in 11 years (Pepsi-Cola, Commercial Union, Cogate, Volvo) promised continued growth of the $12 million men's major tournament circuit in the 1980s, despite the persistence of troubling political problems and battles for control of the men's game.

6 } THE 25 GREATEST PLAYERS 1946–79

Athletes in all sports are better every year, measurably in some, apparently in others. Certainly more exceptional tennis players abound today than ever before. With only a few exceptions, I believe, the best tennis players have appeared since World War II, and even better ones are on the way. Thus a selection of the foremost 25 (15 men and 10 women) is inevitably unfair to some of them.

The game, with its broadened schedule, increased competition, and staggering prize money, is more demanding than ever. My faith in the current crop is such that I have chosen six players yet active among the 25, three of them—Evert, Borg, and Connors—theoretically with their best tennis still ahead.

While narrowing the all-timers since World War II to 25, I recognize that numerous others made records that merit mention and possibly inclusion. It wouldn't be right not to point to such as: Arthur Ashe, the first black male champion who won Forest Hills in 1968, Wimbledon in 1975, and played on three U.S. teams that won the Davis Cup . . . Stan Smith, winner of Forest Hills in 1971, Wimbledon in 1972, and mainstay of six winning U.S. Davis Cup teams as well as holder of 23 various American titles . . . Bill Talbert, who ranked in the U.S. Top Ten 13 times between 1941 and 1954, who won 21 American titles (including the U.S. doubles four times with Gardnar Mulloy), and who played on two winning Davis Cup teams . . . Nicola Pietrangeli of Italy, who won the French (1959–60) and Italian (1957–61) singles twice each and played and won more Davis Cup singles (78–32) and doubles (42–12) than anyone else . . . Tony Roche, who won the Italian and French singles in 1966, the U.S. Pro singles in 1970 as well as five Wimbledon doubles with John Newcombe, and who helped Australia win five Davis Cups . . . Darlene Hard, who won Forest Hills twice (1960–61), the U.S doubles five straight years with three different partners, and who helped the U.S. win four Wightman Cups and one Federation Cup . . . Shirley Fry, one of the few to win all Big Four singles (between 1951 and 1957), and a member of six winning U.S. Wightman Cup teams . . . Evonne Goolagong, the Australian zephyr who won Wimbledon (1971) and Aussie singles (1974–77) titles and helped her country take three Federation Cups . . . Virginia Wade, who won the Wimbledon (1977), Australian (1972), U.S. (1968), and Italian (1971) singles and helped Britain seize four Wightman Cups . . . Nancy Richey Gunter, who ranked in the U.S. Top Ten 16 times between 1960 and 1976, won the U.S. Clay Court title a record six straight times as well as the Australian (1967) and French (1968) singles and played on eight winning Wightman Cup teams . . . Rosie Casals, who won 13 various U.S. titles between 1965 and 1975, and 25 of other countries, mostly in doubles, and helped win four Wightman and four Federation Cups for the U.S.

BUD COLLINS

PAULINE BETZ (1919–   )

Many believe Pauline May Betz was the finest of the post-World War II players of the U.S., even though her career was cut short in her prime by a controversial ruling by the U.S. Lawn Tennis Association. In 1947 she was declared a professional for merely exploring the possibilities of making a pro tour.

There was no pro tennis as such for women at the time, but she did make two tours of one-night stands against Sarah Palfrey Cooke in 1947, and Gussy Moran in 1951, dominating both opponents. Then she became a teaching professional and married Bob Addie.

Born August 6, 1919, at Dayton, Ohio, she grew up in Los Angeles, and became noted for her extreme speed and mobility. She was quick to the net, a pleasure to watch as she attacked with sureness and a firm finishing touch.

World War II deprived her of the chance for much international play, but she won Wimbledon the only time she entered, in 1946, without losing a set. Her closest match was the 6–2, 6–4 final with Louise Brough. In Betz's only Wightman Cup match against Britain, in 1946, she helped the U.S. win by

taking both her singles matches and her doubles.

Betz was first ranked in the American Top Ten, at No. 8 in 1939, and stayed in that select group for seven more years, standing at No. 1 in 1942–44 and 1946, the years she won the U.S. Championship in singles at Forest Hills.

Two other years, 1941 and 1945, she was runner-up, thus setting a Forest Hills record of six straight years in the final. In playing Forest Hills eight times, she won 33 of 37 matches.

She captured 19 U.S. titles on various surfaces, including the Clay Court singles in 1941 and 1943 and the Indoor singles in 1939, 1941, 1943, and 1947. Twice she scored triples at the Indoor Championships, winning the singles, doubles, and mixed doubles in 1941 and 1943, a feat equaled only by Billie Jean King in 1966 and 1968.

Tennis historian Jerome Scheuer called her "the fastest woman on foot ever to play the game."

She was selected for the International Tennis Hall of Fame in 1965.

BJORN BORG (1956–   )

Before he was 21, Bjorn Rune Borg had registered feats that would set him apart as one of the greats when his playing career ended.

Tennis is filled with instances of precocious achievements and championships, but none are quite as impressive as those of Borg, the seemingly emotionless Swede. Just before his 18th birthday he was the youngest winner of the Italian Championship, and just after, two weeks later, he was the youngest winner of the French Championship. Eighteen months later, at 19, he climaxed a Davis Cup record winning streak of 19 singles by lifting Sweden to the Cup for the first time in a 3–2 final-round victory over Czechoslovakia.

Although Lew Hoad and Ken Rosewall were a few months younger in 1953 when they won the Davis Cup for Australia, both were beaten during the final round. But Borg won both his singles and teamed with Ove Bengtson for the doubles win. Borg's Davis

Pauline Betz: Speediest afoot.
New York Herald Tribune

Bjorn Borg: Cool and confident. *Jack Mecca*

Cup debut at 16 in 1972 as one of the youngest ever in that competition was phenomenal: a five-set win over seasoned pro Onny Parun of New Zealand. Borg was also the youngest winner of the oldest professional championship, the U.S. Pro, whose singles he took in 1974 at 18 (and, subsequently, 1975 and 1976).

A player of great strength and endurance he has a distinctive and unorthodox style and appearance. He is bowlegged, yet very fast. His muscular shoulders and well-developed torso give him the strength to lash at the ball with heavy topspin on both forehand and backhand. He uses a two-handed backhand, adapted from the slap shot in hockey, a game he favored as a child. By the time he was 13 he was beating the best of Sweden's under-19 players, and Davis Cup captain Lennart Bergelin cautioned against anyone trying to change Borg's rough-looking, jerky strokes. They were effective. Through 1977 he had never lost to a player younger than himself.

Born June 6, 1956, at Sodertalje, Sweden, where he grew up, Bjorn was fascinated by a tennis racket his father had won as a prize in a Ping-Pong tournament. His father gave him the racket and that was the start.

Borg prefers to battle from the baseline, trading groundstrokes tirelessly in long rallies, retrieving and waiting patiently to outlast the opponent. Volleying, with his Western grip forehand and two-fisted backhand, was troublesome, and his serve was not impressive at first. He didn't do much on grass until 1976, when he was determined to win Wimbledon, and did after devoting himself to two weeks of solid practice on serve-and-volley tactics. He won the most important tournament without loss of a set, beating favored Ilie Nastase in the final, 6–4, 6–2, 9–7. Borg was the youngest champion of the modern era at 20 years, 1 month, although Wilfred Baddeley had won in 1891 at 19.

Borg repeated in 1977, although the tournament was more demanding. His thrilling five-set victories over Americans Vitas Gerulaitis in the semifinals and Jimmy Connors in the final were considered two of the best ever played at Wimbledon. By that time Borg had more confidence and proficiency in his volleying. Borg repeated over Connors in 1978, becoming the first to win three successive years since Fred Perry (1934–36). He made it four in a row with a five-set triumph over American Roscoe Tanner in the 1979 Wimbledon final, thus becoming the first player since Tony Wilding (1910–13) to win four straight years. Borg's four-set defeat by Connors in the 1976 U.S. Open final at Forest Hills was one of the most thrilling championship matches there. His duels with Connors have been marked by incredibly hard hitting by both.

At the close of 1979, after seven seasons as a pro, Borg had amassed more than $2 million in prize money. His first significant check was for $20,000, as the surprising runner-up to John Newcombe for the 1974 World Championship Tennis title. Borg was also runner-up in 1975 for the WCT title to Arthur Ashe, but won it the following year over Guillermo Vilas.

Through 1979 Borg had eight of the Big Four titles: the French singles in 1974–75 and 1978–79 as well as Wimbledon, 1976–79. In 1977 he played World Team Tennis for Cleveland.

LOUISE BROUGH (1923–   )

One of the great volleyers in history was Althea Louise Brough, whose handiwork at

Louise Brough: The volley her forte.
New York Herald Tribune

the net earned her 13 titles at Wimbledon alone, in singles, doubles, and mixed doubles, including a rare triple—championships in each event—in 1950.

Of America's foremost females, none lasted longer. She ranked in the Top Ten 16 times between 1941 and 1957, and held the No. 1 position in 1947. She was selected for the Wightman Cup team 10 times and compiled the best U.S. record against Britain: 12 singles and 10 doubles wins against no defeats.

Louise Brough was born March 11, 1923, at Oklahoma City, Oklahoma, but grew up in Southern California, where she came to prominence as a junior, winning the national 18-and-under title in 1940 and 1941.

Wimbledon was not held during World War II, but when the tournament reopened in 1946 Brough was ready to play a dominant role for a decade in the leading tournament, and is recalled by the British as one of the most overwhelming players to compete there. In that first postwar visit she appeared in every final and just missed out on a triple, losing the singles final to Pauline Betz. But Brough won the doubles with Margaret duPont and the mixed doubles with Tom Brown. During the Brough decade a Wimbledon final without her was unusual. Between 1946 and 1955, she

won her way into 21 of the 30 finals, taking the singles in 1948–50 and 1955, the doubles also in 1948–50 and 1954 with duPont, and the mixed doubles also in 1947–48 with John Bromwich and in 1950 with Eric Sturgess.

Although she won the U.S. Singles Championship at Forest Hills only in 1947, she was a finalist on five other occasions. Doubles was the stage for her utmost success in the U.S., allied with duPont in possibly the finest female team ever, certainly the most victorious in major events. They won 20 Big Four titles together (12 U. S., five Wimbledon, three French), a mark unapproached by any other team. Included in their record dozen U.S titles was the longest championship run in any of the Big Four events: nine straight doubles between 1942 and 1950. (Max Decugis and Maurice Germot won the French doubles 10 straight times between 1906 and 1920, but competition then was restricted to French citizens.) Brough and duPont did not enter the U.S. doubles in 1951 and 1952, but they returned to increase their record match winning streak to 41 before narrowly losing the 1953 final to Doris Hart and Shirley Fry, 6–2, 7–9, 9–7. As a team in the U.S doubles they won 12 of 14 times entered and 58 of 60 matches, losing but five sets.

Altogether Brough won 35 of the Big Four titles in singles, doubles, and mixed doubles to rank fourth on the all-time list behind Margaret Court (66), duPont (37), and Billie Jean King (36). Brough won the Australian singles in 1950. Her various U.S. titles amounted to 18, and she was inducted into the International Tennis Hall of Fame in 1967.

A willowy blonde, she was quiet and diffident, but she was the killer in the left court when at play alongside duPont. Despite their close friendship and partnership, they were keen rivals in singles, and Brough's most difficult Wimbledon triumphs were the three-set wins over duPont in 1949–50, the most stirring the 10–8, 1–6, 10–8 decision in 1949.

After retiring from the amateur circuit she married Dr. A. T. Clapp, and later occasionally played in senior (over-40) tournaments, winning the U.S. Hard Court Doubles in that category in 1971 and 1975 with Barbara Green Weigandt.

MARIA BUENO (1939–   )

Maria Esther Andion Bueno came swirling out of Brazil as a teen-ager to quickly establish herself as one of the world's most graceful and proficient athletes, a delight to watch and dangerous to deal with since she had a wide repertoire of shots and the skill and grace to deliver them constantly.

As the São Paulo Swallow, she was slim and quick, swooping to the net to conquer with piercing volleys. She was a blend of power and touch, a woman of superb movement and rhythms. Stylishly gowned by the tennis couturier, Ted Tinling, she was the frilly treasure of Wimbledon's Centre Court, where she was at her best and won eight titles: three in singles (1959, 1960, and 1964), and five in doubles.

Grass was her favorite surface, suiting her attacking nature. Born October 11, 1939, at São Paulo, she was clearly the best female player to come from Latin America, and was rated No. 1 in the world in 1959, 1960, 1964, and 1966. She was agreeable, but reserved

Maria Bueno: Fluidity and artistry. *Peter Mecca*

and distant, a private person who underwent a number of physical agonies, harming her career, without complaint. Her best days were as an amateur. By the time open tennis and prize money dawned in 1968 she was hobbled by a variety of arm and leg injuries. After a long retirement, she felt sufficiently well to try the pro tour in 1975, and returned to Wimbledon for a spiritual triumph in 1976 after a hiatus of seven years. There were glimpses of the wondrous Maria as she won three rounds, and most spectators were gratified to see her again. "In her day she was so marvelous to watch," said Billie Jean King, an old rival and doubles accomplice, after defeating Maria at Wimbledon in 1977. "But it was painful to play her today. I wanted to remember her as she was."

Bueno seemed undismayed to be a loser. "I have always loved tennis, and still enjoy playing. I've had my glory," she said.

At 18, in the company of Althea Gibson, Maria won her first Wimbledon prize, the doubles of 1958. In all she won 20 Big Four titles in singles, doubles, and mixed, including the U.S. Singles at Forest Hills in 1959, 1963–64, and 1966. She and American Darlene Hard were one of the best teams, taking the Wimbledon title twice and the U.S. twice. Maria's skill at doubles was such that she won her 12 Big Four titles with six partners.

She represented Brazil in the Federation Cup, the worldwide team competition, in 1964, winning her only singles, but there was no other Brazilian capable of supporting her, and the team lost in the first round. Perhaps it was a fluke that she alone of Brazilian women rose as a world class player.

In her regal choreography, unapproached by others, Bueno was one of a triumvirate of women—including Frenchwoman Suzanne Lenglen and Australian Evonne Goolagong—whose fluidity and artistry set them apart.

MAUREEN CONNOLLY (1934–69)

A brief flash on the tennis scene was that of Maureen Catherine Connolly, but it was of

Maureen Connolly: The power of a battleship. *UPI*

such incandescence that she may have been the finest of all female players.

Nicknamed "Little Mo" for her big-gunning, unerring ground strokes (it was an allusion to "Big Mo," the battleship *Missouri*), she was devastating from the baseline, and seldom needed to go to the net. Small and compact (5-5, 127 pounds), she won her major singles championships as a teen-ager: three successive Wimbledons, 1952–54, and U.S. Championships at Forest Hills, 1951–53. At 16 years, 11 months, she was the youngest U.S. champ ever until Tracy Austin won in 1979 at 16 years, 9 months. In addition, Connolly won three other American titles, and held the No. 1 U.S. rankings of 1951–53. She was undisputed world leader in 1951–54.

Connolly was born September 17, 1934, at San Diego, California, and grew up there. She was a pupil of Eleanor "Teach" Tennant, an instructor who had guided a previous world champ, Alice Marble. Connolly first came East in 1949 to win the U.S. junior title, and would soon dominate the world while still technically a junior, not yet 19.

A cheerful and sporting competitor, she

crushed the opposition, never losing an important match, only occasionally losing a set. She helped the U.S. beat Britain in the Wightman Cup matches of 1951–54, winning all seven of her singles.

Fifteen years after Don Budge scored the first Grand Slam, Connolly traveled the same route in 1953, winning the Big Four singles championships (Australian, French, Wimbledon, U.S.) within a calendar year to achieve the first female Slam. She lost only one set in doing so.

By 1954 her playing career was over, aborted by an unusual traffic accident: The horse she was riding was struck by a truck, and she received a severe leg injury. By then she was Mrs. Norman Brinker. She recovered sufficiently to give tennis instruction, and helped a number of players with their games, but she died at 34 in 1969 of cancer.

She was inducted into the International Tennis Hall of Fame in 1968, and is memorialized by the Maureen Connolly Brinker Cup, an international team competiton between the U.S. and Britain for girls under 21.

"Whenever a great player comes along, you have to ask, 'Could she have beaten Maureen?'" is the standard of Lance Tingay, the tennis authority of the London *Telegraph*. "In every case the answer is, 'I think no.'"

JIMMY CONNORS (1952–   )

One of the most controversial players of his day, James Scott Connors is also one of the most dynamic shotmakers in the history of the game. A left-hander with a crushing baseline game, he can pound high-speed shots incessantly throughout a long match, and is particularly dangerous with his two-fisted backhand.

He was raised to be a tennis player by his mother, a teaching pro named Gloria Thompson Connors. Connors grew up in Belleville, Illinois, across the Mississippi from St. Louis. Although he was always smaller than his contemporaries on his way up the ladder, he made up for that through determination and grit. He played in his first National Championship, the U.S. boys' 11-and-under of 1961,

Jimmy Connors: Two-fisted backhander.
Russ Adams

when he was only eight. He was born September 2, 1952, at East St. Louis, Illinois, and claimed to have begun playing when he was two. "My mother rolled balls to me, and I swung at them. I held the racket with both hands because that was the only way I could lift it."

Connors became known as a maverick when he refused to join the Association of Tennis Pros, the union embracing most male professionals, and avoided the mainstream of pro tennis to play in and dominate a series of smaller tournaments organized by his manager, a clever promoter named Bill Riordan. In 1974 he and Riordan began bringing lawsuits, eventually amounting to $10 million, against the ATP and its president, Arthur Ashe, for allegedly restricting his freedom in the game. It stemmed from Connors' banning by the French Open in 1974 after he had signed a contract to play World Team Tennis for Baltimore. Connors had sought to enter the French, the only Big Four championship he did not win that year, but because the ATP, and French administration, opposed World Team Tennis—conflicting with their

tournament—the entries of WTT players were refused. The 1975 Wimbledon final, then, was unique, a duel between opponents in a lawsuit. Ashe won, and shortly thereafter Connors dropped the suits, and parted with Riordan.

Despite his absence from the French, Connors enjoyed in 1974 one of the finest seasons ever, the best by an American since Tony Trabert's 1955. Connors lost only four matches in 20 tournaments, while winning 99. Among the 15 tournaments he won were the Australian, Wimbledon, the South African, the U.S. at Forest Hills, the U.S. Clay Court, and the U.S. Indoor. He was clearly the No. 1 player in the world, a status he also held in 1976 after beating Bjorn Borg, the Wimbledon champion, in an exciting four-set final at Forest Hills, during which Connors saved four set points in the third-set tie-breaker. He was regarded by many as No. 1 for 1978, too, after crushing Borg in the U.S. Open final at the new site, Flushing Meadow. This was Connors' third U.S. Open title and made him unique, the only person to win it on grass (1974), clay (1976), and the newly laid hard court (1978). By winning the U.S. Indoor singles three straight years (1973–75) he tied a record set by Gus Touchard (1913–15). Connors also won that title in 1978–79, tying Wylie Grant, who won five Indoors between 1903 and 1912, and the U.S. Clay Court in 1974, 1976, 1978–79, his four titles the most since Frank Parker's five between 1933 and 1947.

Connors seemed to delight in keeping the public off-balance. He annoyed numerous tennis fans in the U.S. with his sometimes vulgar oncourt behavior, and his refusal to play Davis Cup (except briefly in the 1976 season), and he was booed at Wimbledon—a rare show of disapproval there—for snubbing the Parade of Champions on the first day of the Centenary in 1977.

But his tennis was unquestionable. Over a seven-year span, beginning in 1973, he won 73 of 141 tournaments he entered and took seven of the Big Four titles in singles and doubles. He won the World Championship Tennis title in 1977, and helped the U.S. win the World Cup, the annual team competition against Australia, in 1976–78, winning all six of his singles.

Jimmy went to college one year at the University of California at Los Angeles, where he won the National Intercollegiate Singles in 1971 and attained All-American status.

It was in 1973 that he made his first big splash by winning the U.S. Pro Singles, his first significant title, at 20, toppling Ashe, the favorite, in a five-set final. Ashe said, "I've played them all, and I never saw anybody hit the ball so hard for so long as Jimmy did." That year Connors was ranked co-No. 1 in the U.S. with Stan Smith, but was No. 1 alone in 1976–78, and most of that time was listed as No. 1 on the ATP computer ranking all the pros.

After irritating sponsors and tennis officials by shunning the climactic Masters for three years, Connors entered and won the 1977 event over Bjorn Borg, having qualified by finishing among the top eight in the worldwide Grand Prix series of first-flight tournaments.

His two crushing final-round victories over Ken Rosewall in 1974 (6–1, 6–1, 6–4 at Wimbledon, and 6–1, 6–0, 6–1, at Forest Hills) made Connors seem invincible. His manager, Bill Riordan, proclaimed Jimmy "heavyweight champion of tennis," and arranged a series of challenges over three years at Las Vegas and Puerto Rico in which Connors retained his "title" by defeating Rod Laver, John Newcombe, Manolo Orantes, and Ilie Nastase. Connors grossed over a million dollars from television rights for those four matches.

Beginning in 1974, Connors played in four successive Forest Hills finals, the first man to do that since Bill Tilden (1918–25), and his Flushing Meadow appearance in 1978 made it five straight U.S. finals for Connors. He was the first since Fred Perry (1933–34 and 1936) to win the U.S. title three years. Connors was beaten in the finals by Manolo Orantes in 1975 and by Guillermo Vilas in 1977.

Connors set a tournament prize-money record of $610,991 for the 1977 season, topped the following year by Vilas. Connors' winnings at the close of 1978 were $2,080,127, making him the first pro to exceed $2 million

in prize money, and he was edging toward the $3 million mark at the close of 1979.

MARGARET SMITH COURT
(1942–   )

For sheer strength of performance and accomplishment there has never been a tennis player to match Margaret Smith Court. As the most prolific winner of major championships, she rolled up 66 Big Four titles in singles, doubles, and mixed doubles between 1960 and 1975, and took the Australian, French, Wimbledon, and U.S. singles all within 1970 for the second female Grand Slam. She is the only player to achieve a Slam in doubles as well as in singles: Margaret and Ken Fletcher won the four titles in mixed in 1963.

Her closest rivals statistically are not close: Billie Jean King with 38 Big Four titles, and Roy Emerson leading the men with 28.

From the country town of Albury in New South Wales, where she was born July 16, 1942, Margaret was one of the first Australian notables to be developed outside of the principal cities. Tall and gangling, nearly six feet, she worked hard in the gym and on the road, as well as oncourt, to attain co-ordination and

Margaret Court: The Arm's incredible reach. *UPI*

to marshal her prodigious strength. She was self-made through determination and training. Her power and incredible reach ("I call her The Arm," said rival Billie Jean King) first paid off and called international attention to her when she won the Australian singles at 18 in 1960. It was the first of her record 11 conquests of her homeland, the first seven in a row.

In 1961 she traveled abroad for the first time and played in her first Wimbledon final, the doubles that she and countrywoman Jan Lehane lost to Karen Hantze and another historic figure, Mrs. King (then Billie Jean Moffitt), who was also in her first.

Margaret was to win three Wimbledon, five French, and seven U.S. singles championships, and the greatest of those victories was probably the 1970 Wimbledon final. In considerable pain with a sprained ankle, she held off Billie Jean, 14–12, 11–9, in possibly the finest of female finals there, and certainly the longest in point of games, 46 (two more than the Suzanne Lenglen-Dorothea Lambert Chambers record in 1919).

She retired momentarily upon marrying Barry Court in 1967, but was soon back on the trail of championships. Margaret was remarkable in that she continued to win major titles, such as the U.S. of 1973, after the birth of her first child and was still competing at 34 in 1977. She was shy, soft-spoken, and late in her career extremely religious.

Court was primarily an attacker, basing her game on a heavy serve and volley, and relying on athleticism and endurance. She could conquer with ground strokes, though, as she demonstrated in stopping clay court terror Chris Evert in the splendid French final of 1973. Sometimes Court fell prey to nerves, as in her 1971 Wimbledon final defeat by the crowd's favorite, Evonne Goolagong, or the bizarre televised challenge by 55-year-old Bobby Riggs in 1973, which she lost implausibly and badly. She couldn't reach the inspirational heights of her chief foe, King, but held a lifetime edge over Billie Jean, 22–10.

Representing Australia six times in the worldwide Federation Cup team competition, she played in the first in 1963 (a final-round defeat by the U.S.) and spearheaded Cup victories in 1964–65, 1968, and 1971. Her last extraordinary season was 1973, when she won 18 tournaments, among them the Australian, French, and U.S., and narrowly missed another singles Grand Slam by losing a Wimbledon semifinal to Evert in three sets.

MARGARET OSBORNE duPONT (1918–)

One of the most thoughtful players, Margaret Evelyn Osborne duPont was a collector of major championships second only to Margaret Court (66) and Billie Jean King (38). Although duPont's 37 Big Four victories in singles, doubles, and mixed doubles were well below Court's total, duPont accumulated hers in the U.S., Wimbledon, and French tournaments, never playing the Australian.

Peerless at doubles, she was the canny right-court player, superbly complementing Louise Brough in the most successful team of all time. Together they won a record 20 Big Four titles: 12 U.S., five Wimbledon, three French. She won the U.S. Doubles first with Sarah Palfrey Fabyan (later Mrs. Cooke) in 1941, and the next nine with Brough in a

Margaret Osborne duPont: Canny playmaker. *UPI*

208

record streak that ran from 1942 through 1950. Their record match win streak of 41 ended barely in the 1951 final, a 6–2, 7–9, 9–7 defeat by Shirley Fry and Doris Hart. As a team in the U.S. Championships, Brough and duPont won 12 of the 14 times they entered and 58 of 60 matches. DuPont was the playmaker, utilizing a devilish forehand chop, and a variety of other spins that kept the ball low. She lobbed and volleyed excellently, and set up her volley with an effective serve.

Although 31 of her Big Four titles were doubles and mixed doubles, she was just as tough in singles, reaching the U.S. final at Forest Hills five times and Wimbledon three times, the French twice. Her rivalry with Brough was as close as their friendship and partnership. They split two of the more spectacular finals at the two top championships. Brough won the 1949 Wimbledon final, 10–8, 1–6, 10–8, and duPont the 1948 Forest Hills, 4–6, 6–4, 15–13—48 games, the longest female final played there.

She won Forest Hills in 1948–50, Wimbledon in 1947, and the French singles in 1946 and 1949. In the U.S. Mixed Doubles Championship she set a record by winning nine times, 1943 through 1946 with Bill Talbert, 1950 with Ken McGregor, 1956 with Ken Rosewall, and 1958 through 1960 with Neale Fraser. In the 1948 semifinal she and Talbert won the longest mixed doubles ever played, 71 games, over Gussy Moran and Bob Falkenburg, 27–25, 5–7, 6–1.

Born March 4, 1918, at Joseph, Oregon, Margaret grew up in San Francisco. She made her initial appearance in the American Top Ten in 1938 at No. 7, and set a longevity record for U.S. females, ranking No. 5 two decades later at 40 in 1958. Over the 20 years she was ranked in the Top Ten 14 times, No. 1 in 1948–50. She married William duPont in 1947, and later interrupted her career to give birth to a son. She was one of the few women to win a major title after childbirth.

Hers was one of the finest Wightman Cup records. In nine years of the British-U.S. series, she was unbeaten in 10 singles and eight doubles, and did not play on a losing side between 1946 and 1962. She also captained the U.S. team nine times, presiding over eight victories.

In 1967 she was inducted into the International Tennis Hall of Fame.

ROY EMERSON (1936–   )

In the grand days for Australia of domination of the tennis world, nobody played as large a role as the country boy out of Black Butt in Queensland, Roy Stanley Emerson.

Emerson, a slim, quick, athletic farm kid who strengthened his wrists for tennis by milking innumerable cows on his father's property, played on eight winning Davis Cup teams between 1959 and 1967, a record. He won 28 of the Big Four singles and doubles championships—a record for men—including two Wimbledon singles in 1964–65 and two U.S. singles at Forest Hills in 1961 and 1964. His accomplishments as a right-court doubles player who could make anybody look good amounted to 16 Big Four titles with five different partners, the last in 1971 at Wimbledon with his old Queensland pal, Rod Laver. His best-known alliance was with Aussie left-

Roy Emerson: Fittest of the fit. *UPI*

hander Neale Fraser, with whom he won Wimbledon in 1959 and 1961, the U.S. title in 1959–60, and the doubles of the Davis Cup triumphs of 1959–61.

Known as "Emmo" to his wide circle of friends on the circuit, he was a rollicking, gregarious six-footer who could lead the partying and singing without jeopardizing his high standards of play. Fitness was his hall-mark. He trained hard and was always ready for strenuous matches and tournaments. Al-though primarily a serve-and-volley player, he could adapt to the rigors of slow courts, win-ning the French singles in 1963 and 1967, and leading the Davis Cup victory over the U.S. on clay in Cleveland in 1964. That year he was unbeaten in eight Davis Cup singles as the Aussies regained the Cup. Emmo had a singles winning streak of 55 matches during the summer and autumn while establishing himself as No. 1 in the amateur game by winning 17 tournaments and 109 of 115 matches. The only prize to elude him in that majestic 1964 was the French. Between 1961 and 1967, he won a record six Australian singles titles, the last five in a row.

An outstanding team player who could fire up his teammates, Emerson also took part in two Australian victories in the World Cup, the annual competition against the U.S.

He exemplified the Aussie code of sports-manship and competitiveness, stating it as, "You should never complain about an injury. We believe that if you play, then you aren't injured, and that's that."

Emerson was born November 3, 1936, at Black Butt, a crossroads, and his family moved to Brisbane, where he could get better competition and coaching when his tennis tal-ent became evident.

After resisting several professional offers, he turned pro in 1968 just before open tennis began, and was still competing in 1978 as player-coach of the Boston Lobsters in World Team Tennis, directing them to the semifinals of the league playoffs. Of all Australia's Davis Cup luminaries under Captain Harry Hopman, Emerson made the best record. While helping win the eight Cups, he won 22 of 24 singles and 13 of 15 doubles. When the Cup was on the line, the score tied 2–2 with one match to be played in 1964, he beat

American Chuck McKinley, 3–6, 6–2, 6–4, 6–4, to ice the 3–2 decision.

ALTHEA GIBSON (1927–)

No player overcame more obstacles to be-come a champion than Althea Gibson, the first black to win at Wimbledon and Forest Hills.

Her entry in the U.S. Championships of 1950 at Forest Hills was historic: the first appearance of an American black in that event. It took seven more years for Gibson to work her way to the championship there, in 1957.

Tennis was pretty much a segregated sport in the U.S. until the American Tennis Associ-ation, the governing body for black tourna-ments, prevailed on the U.S. Lawn Tennis Association to permit the ATA female cham-pion, Gibson, to enter Forest Hills. Two years earlier, in 1948, Dr. Reginald Weir, a New York physician, was the first black permitted in a USLTA championship, playing in the U.S. Indoor event.

Althea's first appearance at Forest Hills was

Althea Gibson: A big hitter. *UPI*

not only a notable occasion, it was nearly a moment of staggering triumph. In the second round she encountered third-seeded Louise Brough, the reigning Wimbledon champion, and came within one game of winning. Recovering from nerves, Althea led, 1–6, 6–3, 7–6, when providence intervened: A rainstorm struck Forest Hills, curtailing the match until the following day, when Brough reaffirmed her eminence by winning three straight games.

Born August 25, 1927, at Spring, South Carolina, Gibson grew up in the New York City ghetto of Harlem. Her family was poor, but she was fortunate in coming to the attention of Dr. Robert W. Johnson, a Lynchburg, Virginia, physician who was active in the black tennis community. He became her patron, as he would later be for Arthur Ashe, the black champion at Forest Hills (1968) and Wimbledon (1975). Through Dr. Johnson, Gibson received better instruction and competition, and contacts were set up with the USLTA to inject her into the recognized tennis scene.

Tall (5–11), strong, and extremely athletic, she would have come to prominence earlier but for segregation. She was 23 when she first played at Forest Hills, 30 when she won her first of two successive U.S. Championships, in 1957. During the two years she won Wimbledon, 1957 and 1958, she was ranked No. 1 in the U.S. and the world, but she was never completely at ease in amateur tennis for she realized that, despite her success, she was still unwelcome at some clubs where important tournaments were played. She was ranked ninth in 1952, her first inclusion in the U.S. Top Ten.

A mark of general acceptance, however, was her 1957 selection to represent the U.S. on the Wightman Cup team against Britain. She played two years, winning three of four singles, and two of two doubles.

Gibson was a big hitter with an awesome serve. She liked to attack, but developed consistency at the baseline eventually, and won the French and Italian Singles Championships on slow clay in 1956.

In all, Gibson won 11 major titles in singles and doubles. After six years of trying at Forest Hills she seemed ready to win in 1956, when she reached the final. But she appeared overanxious and lost to the steadier Shirley Fry. A year later Gibson was solidly in control, beating Darlene Hard, 6–3, 6–2, to take Wimbledon and following up with a 6–3, 6–2 triumph over Louise Brough in the Forest Hills final to at last rule her own country.

It was in doubles that Gibson accomplished the first major championship by a black, winning Wimbledon in 1956 alongside Englishwoman Angela Buxton.

After winning Forest Hills for a second time in 1958, Althea turned pro. She played a series of head-to-head matches in 1960 against Karol Fageros, who had been ranked eighth in the U.S. Their tour was played in conjunction with the Harlem Globetrotters, the matches staged on basketball courts prior to Trotter games. Gibson won almost every match. She said she earned over $100,000 in one year as her share of the gate, but there was no professional game in tennis for women then, and she turned to the pro golf tour for a few years. She showed an aptitude for that game, but was too late in starting.

Althea tried to play a few pro tennis events after open tennis began in 1968, but by then she was too old. She was married briefly to W. A. Darben, and worked as a tennis teaching pro after ceasing competition. She was inducted into the International Tennis Hall of Fame in 1971.

PANCHO GONZALES (1928–   )

Very much his own man, a loner, and an acerbic competitor, Ricardo Alonzo Gonzales was probably as good as anyone who ever played the game, if not better. Most of his great tennis was played beyond wide public attention, on the nearly secret pro tour amid a small band of gypsies of whom he was the ticket-selling mainstay.

His rages against opponents, officials, photographers, newsmen, and even spectators were frequently spectacular—but they only served to intensify his own play, and didn't disturb his concentration, as fits of temper do to most others. Pancho got mad and played better. "We hoped he wouldn't get upset; it

Pancho Gonzales: Thunderbolt service. *UPI*

just made him tougher," said Rod Laver. "Later when he got older, he would get into arguments to stall for time and rest, and we had to be careful that it didn't put us off our games."

Gonzales, born May 9, 1928, at Los Angeles, was always out of the tennis mainstream, a fact that seemed to goad him to play harder. Because he came from a Chicano family, he was never acceptable in the supposedly proper upper circles of his city's tennis establishment. And because he was a truant he wasn't permitted to play in Southern California junior tournaments. Once he got out of the Navy in 1946 there was no preventing him from mixing in the game, and beating everyone. He had a marvelously pure and effortless service action that delivered thunderbolts, and he grew up as an attacker on fast West Coast cement.

Although not regarded as anything more than promising on his second trip East in 1948, he was at age 20 ready to win the big one, the U.S. Championship at Forest Hills. Ranked 17th nationally at the time, he served and volleyed his way to the final, where he beat South African Eric Sturgess with ease.

The following year Gonzales met the favorite, a Southern California antagonist, Ted Schroeder. It was one of the gripping finals. Schroeder won the first two sets as expected, but they were demanding and exhausting, 18-16, 6-2, and after that Gonzales rolled up the next three, 6-1, 6-2, 6-4, for the title. In 1949 Pancho also helped the U.S. hold the Davis Cup against Australia, then went for the money, turning pro to tour against the monarch, Jack Kramer. Gonzales was too green for Kramer, losing, 96-27, and he faded from view for several agonizing years.

When Kramer retired, Gonzales won a tour over Don Budge, Pancho Segura, and Frank Sedgman in 1954 to determine Jack's successor, and stood himself as Emperor Pancho, proud and imperious, for a long while, through the challenges of Tony Trabert, Ken Rosewall, Lew Hoad, Ashley Cooper, Mal Anderson, Alex Olmedo, and Segura. For a decade Gonzales and pro tennis were synonymous. A promoter couldn't hope to rally crowds unless Pancho was on the bill. The other names meant little. During his reign Pancho won the U.S. Pro singles a record eight times.

By the time Rosewall and Laver were reaching their zeniths during the mid- and late 1960s, the aging Gonzales hung on as a dangerous foe, still capable of defeating all. In 1964, his last serious bid for his ninth U.S. Pro title, he lost the final to Laver in four hard sets. Yet there was still much more glory ahead. In 1969, at 41, he electrified Wimbledon by overcoming Charlie Pasarell in the tournament's longest match, 112 games, a first-rounder that consumed 5 hours, 12 minutes, beginning one afternoon and concluding on the next after darkness intervened. In winning, 22-24, 1-6, 16-14, 6-3, 11-9, Gonzales saved seven match points.

Later that year he beat John Newcombe, Rosewall, Stan Smith, and Arthur Ashe in succession to win a rich tournament at Las Vegas. Early in 1970, in the opener of a series of $10,000 winner-take-all challenge matches leading to a grand final, he toppled Laver. The Aussie, just off his Grand Slam year (and the eventual winner of this tournament), was clearly No. 1 in the world, but

Pancho warmed a crowd of 14,761 at New York's Madison Square Garden with a 7–5, 3–6, 2–6, 6–3, 6–2 victory. As late as 1972 he was ranked No. 9 in the U.S., tying Vic Seixas' American longevity record since he had first been a member of the Top Ten 24 years before.

In 1968 he was named to the International Tennis Hall of Fame and he was a consistent winner on the Grand Masters tour for the over-45 champs beginning in 1973. Although his high-speed serve, so effortlessly delivered, was a trademark, Gonzales, a 6-foot-2, 180-pounder, was a splendid athlete and tactician, who excelled at defense, too. "My legs, retrieving, lobs, and change-of-pace service returns meant as much or more to me than my power," he once said, "but people overlooked that because of the reputation of my serve." He won $911,078 between 1950 and 1972, and crossed the million mark as a Grand Master.

Doris Hart: The complete performer. *UPI*

DORIS HART (1925–   )

As a child Doris Jane Hart was certainly not a candidate for sports immortality. She was stricken by a serious knee infection later erroneously publicized as "polio," and faced the prospect of being crippled for life. She began to play tennis at six as therapy, and recovered so successfully that, despite bowed and uncertain-appearing legs, she became one of the all-time champions.

"One of the first newspaper stories on me described me as having recovered from polio," she once said. "It was a good story that just caught on. But it wasn't so."

Her total of 35 Big Four (Australian, French, Wimbledon, and U.S.) championships in singles, doubles, and mixed doubles ties her with Louise Brough, behind only Margaret Court (66), Billie Jean King (38), and Margaret duPont (37). Hart and Court are the only players in history, male or female, to win all 12 of the Big Four titles at least once, and she is one of nine to win all the Big Four singles within her career.

For 15 successive years between 1942 and 1955 she was ranked in the American Top Ten, standing at No. 1 in 1954–55.

Possibly her finest tournament was Wimble-don of 1951, when she scored a triple—championships in singles, doubles, and mixed—and lost only one set, that in the mixed. After handing her good friend and partner, Shirley Fry, one of the worst beatings in the tournament's history (6–1, 6–0), Doris united with Shirley for the doubles title, then annexed the mixed with Frank Sedgman. Doris won the mixed the following year with Sedgman, and the next three years with Vic Seixas, a Wimbledon record of five straight years.

After being a runner-up at Forest Hills for the U.S. Singles Championship four times, including 1952–53 to Maureen Connolly, Hart finally was rewarded on her 15th try at the title, beating Brough in a thriller, 6–8, 6–1, 8–6, in the 1954 title match. She retained that title, 6–4, 6–2, over Pat Ward, then retired to become a teaching pro.

Born June 20, 1925, in St. Louis, Hart grew up in Coral Gables, Florida. She was an intelligent and solid all-around player whose strokes were crisp and stylish. She moved very well, despite the early handicap of her legs, and had an excellent disposition. She was effective at the net, or in the backcourt, as attested by her championships in the

French singles of 1950 and 1952, and the U.S. Clay Court singles in 1950.

Hart and Fry were one of the outstanding doubles teams in history, winning the French a record five straight times beginning in 1950, Wimbledon three straight beginning in 1951. In the 1953 final they ended the record streak of Louise Brough and Margaret duPont at nine championships and 41 matches. In turn their own streak of four championships and 20 matches was stopped in the 1955 final by Brough and duPont.

During a decade of U.S. supremacy over Britain (1946–55) in the Wightman Cup, Hart won all 14 of her singles and eight of nine doubles. She captained the winning U.S. team in 1970.

Her U.S. championships on various surfaces amounted to 20 singles and doubles. In 1969 she was enshrined at the International Tennis Hall of Fame.

LEW HOAD (1934–   )

During his quarter-century career as a professional, Pancho Gonzales faced a vast array

Lew Hoad: His strength enabled him to lift many a cup. *UPI*

of first-rate players, and the one he considered the most devastating was Lewis Alan Hoad.

"When Lew's game was at its peak nobody could touch him," said Gonzales, who cited Hoad as his toughest foe during his years of head-to-head one-night-stand pro tours. Hoad, who turned pro in 1957, after winning his second successive Wimbledon singles, was one rookie who seemed able to dethrone Gonzales as the pro king. They were just about even when Hoad's troublesome back gave way during the winter of 1958. Gonzales won the tour, 51–36, but felt threatened all the way. It was Pancho's closest brush with defeat after taking over leadership in 1954.

Hoad, a strapping 175-pounder with a gorilla chest and iron wrists, may have been the strongest man to play tennis in the world class. He blistered the ball and became impatient with rallying, preferring to hit for winners. It was a flamboyant style, and made for some bad errors when he wasn't in tune. But when his power was focused along with his concentration, Hoad came on like a tidal wave. He was strong enough to use topspin as an offensive drive. He was assault-minded, but had enough control to win the French title on slow clay in 1956.

Born November 23, 1934, 21 days after Ken Rosewall in the same city, Sydney, Hoad was bracketed with Rosewall throughout his amateur days. Although entirely different in stature, style, and personality, the two were called Australia's tennis twins, the prodigies who drew attention as teen-agers and were rivals and teammates through 1956. Hoad was stronger, but less patient and consistent, more easygoing. His back problems cut his career short in the mid-1960s while Rosewall, whose style was less taxing, kept on going into the next decade.

His countrymen fondly remember Hoad's Davis Cup triumph of 1953 over Tony Trabert on a rainy Melbourne afternoon. At 19, he and Rosewall had been selected to defend the Cup. The U.S. led, 2–1, in the finale and seemed about to clinch the Cup when the more experienced Trabert, already the U.S. champion, caught up at two sets all. Hoad hung on to win, however, 13–11, 6–3, 3–6, 2–6, 7–5, and Rosewall beat Vic Seixas the following day to save the Cup, 3–2.

Although they lost it to the Americans the next year, Hoad and Rosewall were awesome in 1955, retaking the prize, 5–0, and defended the Davis Cup for the last time together in 1956.

Their first major titles came in 1953, when Lew and Ken were allied to win the Australian, French, and Wimbledon doubles. Lew won 13 major titles in singles and doubles, and in 1956 appeared on his way to win all of the Big Four (Australian, French, Wimbledon, and U.S.) singles within one year and thus achieve a rare Grand Slam. His Wimbledon final-round victory over the omni-present Rosewall meant he was three quarters of the way to a Slam. Yet it was Rosewall who stood as the immovable obstacle in the final at Forest Hills, spoiling a Slam with a four-set triumph. In his last significant tournament appearance in 1973, Lew reached the final of the South African doubles with Rob Maud, losing to Arthur Ashe and Tom Okker. He lost the final of the U.S. Pro singles to Gonzalez in 1958 and 1959.

Billie Jean King: A volleying trailblazer.
Russ Adams

BILLIE JEAN MOFFITT KING (1943–   )

The fireman's daughter, Billie Jean Moffitt King, began blazing through the tennis world in 1960 when she first appeared in the U.S. women's rankings at No. 4. She was 17. For almost two decades she continued as a glowing force in the game as the all-time Wimbledon champion, frequently the foremost player, a crusader in building the female professional game, and a million-dollar-plus winner on the tour.

Born November 22, 1943, at Long Beach, California, Billie Jean was named for her father, Bill Moffitt, a Long Beach fireman and an enthusiastic athlete, though not a tennis player. Her brother, Randy Moffitt, became a pitcher for the San Francisco Giants. She developed on the public courts of Long Beach, and first gained international recognition in 1961 by joining 18-year-year-old Karen Hantz for a surprising triumph in the Wimbledon women's doubles. They were the youngest team to win it. That was the first of 20 Wimbledon championships, making King the record winner of the most prestigious tourney.

Elizabeth Ryan's 19 titles (between 1914 and 1934) were all in doubles and mixed doubles. King won six singles, 10 doubles, and four mixed doubles between 1961 and 1979, and in 1979 lengthened another Wimbledon record by appearing in her 27th final, the doubles. Ryan was in 24 finals.

Billie Jean's has been a career of firsts. In 1968 she was the first woman of the open era to sign a pro contract to tour with a female tournament group, along with Rosie Casals, Franscoise Durr and Ann Haydon Jones as the women's auxiliary of National Tennis League, which also included six men (Rod Laver, Ken Rosewall, Pancho Gonzalez, Andres Gimeno, Fred Stolle, and Roy Emerson). A few women before King had turned pro to make head-to-head barnstorming tours, notably Suzanne Lenglen and Mary K. Browne, 1927; Alice Marble and Mary Hardwick, 1941; Pauline Betz and Sarah Palfrey Fabyan Cooke, 1947; Althea Gibson and Karol Fageros, 1960.

In 1971, King earned $117,000 in prize money, the first female athlete to win more than $100,000. In 1973 Billie Jean was the first woman to beat a man in a "Battle of the Sexes" challenge match, defeating 55-year-old ex-Wimbledon champ Bobby Riggs, 6–4, 6–3, 6–3, in a heavily publicized and nationally televised extravaganza that captured the nation's fancy and drew a record tennis crowd, 30,472, to Houston's Astrodome.

In 1974 she became the first woman to coach a professional team containing men when she served as player-coach of the Philadelphia Freedoms of World Team Tennis, a league she and her husband, Larry King, helped establish. Traded to the New York Apples, she led that team to WTT titles in 1976 and 1977 as a player.

An aggressive, emotional player who has often said, "You have to love to guts it out to win," Billie Jean specialized in serve-and-volley tactics, aided by quickness and a highly competitive nature. She overcame several knee operations to continue as a winner into her 37th year. As a big-match player she was unsurpassed, excelling in team situations when she represented the U.S. In nine years on the Federation Cup team in that worldwide team event, she helped the U.S. gain the final each time, and win seven times, by winning 51 of her 55 singles and doubles. In the Wightman Cup against Britain she played on only one losing side in 10 years, winning 21 of her 26 singles and doubles.

Outspoken on behalf of women's rights, in and out of sports—and the game of tennis in particular—she was possibly the most influential player in popularizing professional tennis in the United States. She worked tirelessly to promote the Virginia Slims tour during the early 1970s when the women realized they must separate from the men to achieve recognition and significant prize money on their own. With the financial backing of Virginia Slims, the organizational acumen of Gladys Heldman, and the salesmanship and winning verve of King, the women pros built an extremely profitable circuit.

Only one woman, Margaret Smith Court, has won more major championships than King. King's total is 38 Big Four (Australian, Wimbledon, U.S., French) titles in singles, doubles, and mixed. Court won 66. Margaret Osborne duPont also won 37. In regard to U.S. titles on all surfaces (grass, clay, hard court, indoor), King is second at 28 behind Hazel Hotchkiss Wightman's 34. King and Rosie Casals were the only doubles team to win U.S. titles on all four surfaces.

King's most important titles were the Wimbledon singles, 1966–68, 1972–73, and 1975, and the U.S. singles at Forest Hills, 1967, 1971–72, and 1974. She also won the French singles in 1972 and the Australian in 1968 and 1971, becoming the fifth woman to win all four Big Four singles titles. Ranked No. 1 in the U.S. seven times, she tied Molla Bjurstedt Mallory for most years at the top. Between 1960 and 1979 Billie Jean was ranked in the U.S. Top Ten 16 times, an accomplishment equalled only by Nancy Richey and Louise Brough. At the close of 1979 King's prize money amounted to more than $1.3 million.

JACK KRAMER (1921–   )

The impact of John Albert "Jake" Kramer on tennis has been fourfold: as great player, exceptional promoter, thoughtful innovator, and astute television commentator.

Kramer, born August 5, 1921, at Las Vegas, Nevada, grew up in the Los Angeles area. He achieved international notice as a teen-ager when he was selected to play doubles, alongside Joe Hunt, for the U.S. in the Davis Cup finale against Australia. At 18, Kramer was the youngest to play in the Cup title round, although John Alexander of Australia lowered the record to 17 by playing in 1968.

It was after World War II, however, that Kramer came to prominence as the dominant player in the game, so strong that he was voted fifth on a list of all-time greats selected by a panel of expert tennis journalists in 1969. He was the leading practitioner of the "big game," rushing to the net constantly behind his serve, and frequently attacking on return of serve. His serve put opponents off, setting them up for the volley, as did his forcing forehand.

A blistered racket hand probably prevented the Californian from winning Wimbledon in 1946, but he took the title the following year with an awesome performance, losing only 37 games in seven matches, the most lopsided

Jack Kramer: Power player and promoter. *UPI*

run to the championship. Kramer also won the U.S. singles title at Forest Hills in 1946 and 1947.

In December of 1946 he and Ted Schroeder journeyed to Melbourne to regain the Davis Cup in the first postwar showdown. Kramer was no longer the kid who had helped lose the Cup to the Aussies seven years before. Although the home side was favored, power players Kramer and Schroeder completely overwhelmed Adrian Quist and Dinny Pails in singles, and Quist and John Bromwich in doubles in a stunning 5–0 victory over Australia.

The following summer, Jake and Ted repelled the Australian challenge for the Cup at Forest Hills, and then Kramer closed out his amateur career memorably by overhauling Frankie Parker in the U.S. final. Kramer lost the first two sets, and was in danger of losing out on a lucrative professional contract as well as his championship. Counterpunching, Kramer won, 4–6, 2–6, 6–1, 6–0, 6–3, and set off in pursuit of Bobby Riggs, the reigning pro champ.

Kramer knocked Riggs off the summit by

winning their odyssey of one-nighters throughout the U.S., which was the test of professional supremacy of that day. Their opener was a phenomenon: New York was buried by a blizzard that brought the city to a stop, yet 15,114 customers made it on foot to the old Madison Square Garden on December 27, 1947, to watch Riggs win. Bobby couldn't keep it up. Kramer won the tour, 69–20, and stayed in action while Riggs took over as the promoter and signed Pancho Gonzales to challenge Kramer. Nobody was up to Kramer then. He bruised the rookie Gonzales, 96–27, on the longest of the tours. Kramer made $85,000 against Riggs as his percentage, and $72,000 against Gonzales.

In 1952 Kramer assumed the position of promoter himself, the boss of pro tennis, a role he would hold for over a decade, well past his playing days. Kramer's last tour as a principal was against the first man he recruited, Frank Sedgman, the Aussie who was tops among amateurs. Kramer won, 54–41. An arthritic back led to Kramer's retirement as a player, but he kept the tour going, resurrecting one of his victims, Gonzales, who became the strongman.

One of the shrewdest operators in tennis, Kramer was looked to for advice when the open era began in 1968. He devised the Grand Prix for the men's game, a series of tournaments leading to a Masters Championship for the top eight finishers, and a bonus pool to be shared by more than a score of the leading players. The Grand Prix, incorporating the most attractive tournaments around the world, has functioned since 1970. In 1972 he was instrumental in forming the Association of Tennis Pros, the male players' union, and was its first executive director. Later he served on the Men's International Professional Tennis Council, the world-wide governing board.

For more than 20 years Kramer has served as an analyst on tennis telecasts in many countries, notably for the British Broadcasting Corporation at Wimbledon and for all the American networks at Forest Hills and at other events.

Kramer, winner of 13 U.S. singles and doubles titles, was named to the International Tennis Hall of Fame in 1968.

ROD LAVER (1938–   )

Rod Laver was so scrawny and sickly as a child in the Australian bush that no one could guess he would become a left-handed whirlwind who would conquer the tennis world and be known as possibly the greatest player ever.

A little more than a month before Don Budge completed the first Grand Slam, Rodney George "Rocket" Laver was born, August 9, 1938, at Rockhampton, Queensland, Australia. Despite lack of size and early infirmities, Laver grew strong and tough on his father's cattle property and emulated Budge by making the second male Grand Slam in 1962 as an amateur—then became the only double Grand Slammer seven years later by taking the Big Four (Australian, French, Wimbledon, U.S. singles) as a pro.

Few champions have been as devastating and dominant as Laver was as amateur and pro during the 1960s. An incessant attacker, he was nevertheless a compleat player who glowed in backcourt and at the net. Laver's 145-pound body seemed to dangle from a massive left arm that belonged to a gorilla, an arm with which he bludgeoned the ball and was able to impart ferocious topspin. Although others had used topspin, Laver seemed to inspire a wave of heavy-hitting topspin practitioners of the 1970s such as Bjorn Borg and Guillermo Vilas. The stroke became basic after Laver.

Rod Laver: Ferocious attacker. *UPI*

As a teen-ager he was sarcastically nicknamed "Rocket" by Australian Davis Cup Captain Harry Hopman. "He was anything but a Rocket," Hopman recalled. "But Rod was willing to work harder than the rest, and it was soon apparent to me that he had more talent than any other of our fine Australian players."

His first international triumph came during his first trip abroad in 1956, when he won the U.S. Junior Championship at 17. Three years later he was ready to take his place among the world's best when he won the Australian singles and, with Bob Mark, the doubles, and was runner-up to Alex Olmedo for the Wimbledon championship. The Australian victories were the first of Laver's 20 titles in Big Four singles, doubles, and mixed that place him fourth among all-time winners, behind Roy Emerson (28), John Newcombe (25), and Frank Sedgman (22). Bill Tilden and Jean Borotra also won 20.

The losing Wimbledon final of 1959 was the beginning of an incredible run of success in that tournament. He was a finalist six straight times he entered: losing in 1960 to Neale Fraser, winning in 1961 and 1962, and—after a five-year absence because professionals were barred until 1968—winning again in 1968 and 1969. Only two others had played in six successive finals, back before the turn of the century: Willie Renshaw, 1881 through 1886; Wilfred Baddeley, 1891 through 1896. While winning Wimbledon four straight times (the only man since World War I to win four prior to Bjorn Borg), and proceeding to the fourth round in 1970, Laver set a tournament record of 31 consecutive match wins, ended by his loss to Roger Taylor.

The year 1969 was Laver's finest, one of the best experienced by any player, as he won 18 of 33 tournaments. Unlike his Grand Slam year of 1962 as an amateur, he was playing in tournaments that were open to all, amateur and pro, and this Slam was all the more impressive. It was endangered only a few times—Tony Roche forcing him to a fifth set in an exhausting 90-game semifinal in the Australian championships; Dick Crealy winning the first two sets of a second-rounder in the French; Premjit Lall winning the first two sets of a second-rounder at Wimbledon; Stan Smith threatening in the fifth set of a fourth-rounder at Wimbledon; Arthur Ashe and John Newcombe pushing him to four sets in the Wimbledon semifinal and final, respectively; Dennis Ralston leading 2 sets to 1 in the fourth round of the U.S.; Roche winning the opening set of the U.S. final.

But that year Laver could always accelerate to a much higher gear and bang his way out of trouble. The closest anyone came to puncturing either Slam was Marty Mulligan, who held a match point in the fourth set of their French quarterfinal in 1962.

After his second year running as the No. 1 amateur, 1962, and helping Australia win a fourth successive Davis Cup, Laver turned pro. It was a life of one-nighters, but Pancho Gonzales was no longer supreme. Kenny Rosewall was at the top and gave Laver numerous beatings as their long, illustrious rivalry began. Rosewall beat Laver to win the U.S. Pro singles in 1963, but the next year Laver defeated Rosewall and Gonzales to win the first of his five crowns, four of them in a row beginning in 1966. He had a record streak of 19 wins in the U.S. Pro until losing the 1970 final to Roche.

When open tennis dawned in 1968, Laver was ready to resume where he'd left off at the traditional tournaments, whipping Roche in less than an hour, 6–3, 6–4, 6–2, to take the first open Wimbledon.

In 1971 Laver won $292,717 in tournament prize money (a season record that stood until Arthur Ashe won $338,337 in 1975), the figure enabling him to become the first tennis player to make a million dollars on the court. Until the last days of 1978, when he was playing few tournaments, Laver was still the all-time leading money-winner with $1,564,-304. Jimmy Connors and Ilie Nastase then surpassed him.

In 1973 all professionals were permitted to play Davis Cup, and Laver honed himself for one last effort, after 11 years away. He was brilliant, teaming with John Newcombe to end a five-year U.S. reign, 5–0. Laver beat Tom Gorman in five sets on the first day, and paired with Newcombe for a crushing straight-set doubles victory over Stan Smith

and Erik van Dillen that clinched the Cup, Laver's fifth. Of all the marvelous Aussie Davis Cup performers he was the only one never to play in a losing match.

He was also a factor in winning three World Cups (1972, 1974–75) for Australia in the annual team competition against the U.S. In 1976, as his tournament career was winding down, Laver signed with San Diego in World Team Tennis and was named the league's Rookie of the Year at age 38!

CHRIS EVERT LLOYD (1954–   )

In 1970, at a small, insignificant tournament in North Carolina, 15-year-old Christine Marie Evert gave notice to the world that a dynamo was on the way up. Chrissie defeated Margaret Court, who had recently completed her singles Grand Slam and was the No. 1 player of the world.

A year later in the U.S. Open at Forest Hills, one of the two most significant tournaments, Evert reconfirmed by marching resolutely to the semifinals—at 16 years, 8 months, 20 days, the youngest at that time to reach that stage. Before losing to Billie Jean King,

Chris Evert: Her trademark a two-hand backhand. *Russ Adams*

the eventual champion, schoolgirl Evert bowled over a succession of seasoned pros— Edda Buding, Mary Ann Eisel, Francoise Durr, Lesley Hunt—captivating the American sporting public and filling the Forest Hills stadium day after day. Against Eisel, the No. 4 American player, Evert thrilled a national television audience by rescuing six match points with bold shotmaking while converting what seemed a certain defeat.

Although essentially a slow-court baseline specialist, raised on clay in Fort Lauderdale, Florida, where she was born December 20, 1954, Evert showed that booming ground-strokes could succeed on the fast Forest Hills grass. She was the Little Ice Maiden, a pony-tailed kid, deadpan, with metronomic strokes that seldom missed. Her two-handed back-hand, a powerful drive, stimulated a genera-tion of newcomers to copy her, even though her father, teaching pro Jimmy Evert, advised against it. "I didn't teach the two-hander to her," said her father, who had won the Cana-dian singles in 1947. "She started that way because she was too small and weak to swing the backhand with one hand. I hoped she'd change—but how can I argue with this suc-cess?"

It was such success that by the beginning of 1980 Evert had accumulated more than $2 million in prize money, an all-time female high, after seven professional seasons, becom-ing in 1976 the first woman to exceed a mil-lion dollars. She set a season tournament prize money record of $453,154 in 1977. Moreover, she had won 12 major titles in singles and doubles, including the Wimbledon singles in 1974–76, and the U.S. Open sin-gles at Forest Hills in 1975–77, and at Flush-ing Meadow in 1978, as well as the French singles in 1974–75 and 1979. By winning the U.S. title a fourth consecutive time, she was the first to do so since Helen Jacobs' run of 1932–35. Between 1973 and 1979 she won 125 consecutive matches on clay, including 24 tournaments. The streak came to an end in the semifinals of the Italian Open in Rome when she lost 6–4, 2–6, 7–6 to Tracy Austin. Evert's remarkable record in professional tour-naments for the nine seasons between 1970 and 1979 was 93 titles in 155 tournaments and

a singles won-lost record of 659–61. She was an amateur until 1973.

Her introduction to Goolagong was the 1972 Wimbledon semifinal, an exciting three-set struggle won by Goolagong, the defending champion. That was the start of the most compelling female rivalry of the 70s, one in which Evert had a 21–12 edge at the close of 1979. During the open era the Virginia Slims circuit and its championship became promi-nent in women's tennis. Evert won the first of her four Slims championships in 1972 at 17. In choosing to preserve her amateur status until her 18th birthday that year, she disdained more than $50,000 in prize money, including the $25,000 Slims award.

Once she entered tennis for a living, she was a thoroughgoing, exemplary professional in her relations with colleagues, press, and public, and perennially a hard but sporting competitor. Fairly soon she lost her status as the darling little girl, and became the heavy in almost every match she played, where the public's sympathy usually rested with her op-ponent. Her style is based on flawless bar-rages from the backcourt, and her constant winning seemed monotonous to many. Never-theless she is a smart player, able to maneu-ver a foe cleverly, scoring decisively with a well-disguised drop shot. She is also a better volleyer than given credit for, after overcom-ing an early distaste for the net. "I realize that a lot of fans think my game is boring, and they want to see me lose, or at least for somebody to give me a good fight all the time. But this is the game I play to win," she said. "Losing hurts me. I've always been de-termined to be No. 1 and I want to stay there as long as I play." She was No. 1 in the world 1975–78 and No. 1 in the U.S. rank-ings 1974–78, the first to stand at the top five straight times since Alice Marble (1936–40).

As one of five tennis-playing Evert chil-dren, she was clearly the star, but her sister, Jeanne, three years younger, was also a pro. In 1974 Jeanne ranked ninth in the U.S., and they were the first sisters to be ranked in the Top Ten since Florence (third) and Ethel Sut-ton (second) in 1913.

Chris and Jeanne were teammates on the victorious U.S. Wightman Cup team of 1973, the first sisters to play in the series against Britain. Chris also played on five other winning U.S. teams, winning all her 16 singles through 1979. In 1977–79 she helped the U.S. win the Federation Cup, the worldwide team competition, by taking all her 14 singles.

Her best remembered singles triumphs were the Forest Hills final of 1975 when she beat Goolagong, 5–7, 6–4, 6–2, and the Wimbledon final of 1976, a 6–3, 4–6, 8–6 decision over Goolagong. She played World Team Tennis for Phoenix in 1976–77, and for champion Los Angeles in 1978.

ILIE NASTASE (1946–   )

No player in history has been more gifted or mystifying than the Bucharest Buffoon, Ilie Nastase, noted both for his sorcery with the racket and his bizarre, even objectionable behavior. He was an entertainer second to none, amusing spectators with his antics and mimicry, also infuriating them with gaucheries and walkouts.

Despite a fragile nervous system and erratic temperament, Nastase—slender, quick, leggy and athletic—could do everything, and when

Ilie Nastase: The sorcerer's apprentice.
Jack Mecca

his concentration held together he was an artist creating with great originality and panache. His record in the Masters, the culmination of the annual Grand Prix circuit bringing together the top eight professionals, was spectacular. He won a record four times, 1971–73 and 1975, and was finalist to Guillermo Vilas in five sets in 1974.

Born July 19, 1946, at Bucharest, he was the first Romanian of international prominence, and largely through his play that small country rose to the Davis Cup final on three occasions, 1969, 1971, and 1972, losing each time to the U.S. At the end of 1977, after playing Davis Cup since 1966, Nastase ranked fourth among the most active players in Cup history, having won 90 of 115 singles and doubles engagements in 40 matches.

Romania was favored to lift the Cup from the U.S. in the 1972 finale on the friendly slow clay of Nastase's hometown. However, his nervousness combined with an inspirational performance by Stan Smith added up to an 11–9, 6–2, 6–3 victory for the American in the crucial opening singles, and the U.S. kept the Cup, 3–2. Nastase's foremost disappointment occurred three months prior, when Smith narrowly defeated him in the Wimbledon final, 4–6, 6–3, 6–3, 4–6, 7–5, one of the most exciting championship matches there. Nastase was in another Wimbledon singles final in 1976, but was beaten easily by Bjorn Borg.

Nastase first came to attention in 1966 when he and his first mentor, countryman Ion Tiriac, reached the final of the French doubles, losing to Clark Graebner and Dennis Ralston.

Nastase startled Wimbledon patrons in 1969 during Romania's Davis Cup semifinal against the favored British when he beat Mark Cox in the decisive singles, and co-operated with Tiriac in a doubles win, putting Romania in the final against the U.S., where they lost, 5–0. The next year Romania came closer against the U.S., 3–2, but it was Nastase's failure in the critical opener against Smith that was the difference, as it would be again in 1972.

By 1970 Nastase began to assert himself as a champion. He won the Italian singles and jolted Cliff Richey in the final of the U.S.

Indoors, 6–8, 3–6, 6–4, 9–7, 6–0, the only instance of a victor making up so big a deficit in the title match.

Despite his Davis Cup and Wimbledon heartaches of 1972, Nastase had the immeasurable consolation of winning the U.S. Open at Forest Hills from a seeming losing position (down 1–3 in the fourth set) against Arthur Ashe. The score: 3–6, 6–3, 6–7, 6–4, 6–3. It was his only major grass court singles prize.

His finest season was 1973, when he was regarded as No. 1 in the world after winning the Italian, French, and 13 other tournaments, and downing Tom Okker in the Masters final, 6–3, 7–5, 4–6, 6–3.

Though he provoked controversy, and his career was marred by fines, disqualifications, and suspensions, Nastase was good-natured and friendly offcourt. He had a sense of humor in his oncourt shenanigans, but frequently did not know when to stop and lost control of himself. "I am a little crazy," he said, "but I try to be a good boy."

He was expert at putting the ball just beyond an opponent's reach, and applying discomfiting spin. He lobbed and retrieved splendidly, in his prime possibly the fastest player of all, and he could play either baseline or serve-and-volley. In 1976 he was the first European to exceed $1 million in career prize money, and had made well over $2 million for 11 seasons as a pro at the end of 1979. Nastase played World Team Tennis for Hawaii in 1976 and Los Angeles in 1977–78, leading the Strings to the league title in 1978 as player-coach.

John Newcombe: The best server of his time. *Peter Mecca*

JOHN NEWCOMBE (1944–   )

When John Newcombe and Tony Roche, an Australian pair, won the Wimbledon doubles of 1965, it was the start not only of an extraordinary string of major titles for Newcombe but also for the two of them as a unit.

Two years earlier, though, Newcombe, at 19, attracted international attention as one of the youngest Aussies ever to play Davis Cup. He was selected for the finale to play singles against the U.S. Though he was beaten by both Dennis Ralston and Chuck McKinley during a 3–2 U.S. victory, Newcombe served notice that he was a player to reckon with when he pushed Wimbledon champion McKinley to four hard sets in the decisive fifth match.

Newcombe and the left-handed Roche, one of the great doubles teams in history, won five Wimbledons together, a modern record (topped only by the English Doherty brothers, who won eight between 1897 and 1905, and the English Renshaw brothers, who won seven between 1880 and 1889). Newcombe and Roche also won the U.S. in 1967, the French in 1967–69, and the Australian in 1965, 1967, 1971, and 1976, standing as one of only four teams to win all the Big Four titles during a career. Their three successive Wimbledons, 1968–70, enabled them to set a tourney record of 18 straight doubles match wins.

It was in singles, of course, that Newcombe made his name. He and Rod Laver are the only players to win the men's singles at

Wimbledon as amateurs and pros. Newcombe was the last amateur champion in 1967, and repeated in 1970 and 1971 during the open era. He, Bjorn Borg, and Laver were also the only three-time post-World War II champions by the close of 1978.

In all Newcombe won 25 major titles in singles, doubles, and mixed doubles to stand second behind Roy Emerson (28) in the list of all-time male championships.

John David Newcombe was born May 23, 1944, at Sydney, and was more interested in other sports as a youngster. Not until he was 17 did a career in tennis appeal to him. But he was powerful, athletic, and extremely competitive, and Australian Davis Cup Captain Harry Hopman was glad when Newcombe turned his full attention to tennis. Newcombe helped Hopman win four Cups, in 1964–67, and then returned to the Davis Cup in 1973, when all pros were reinstated, to be part of perhaps the strongest team ever, alongside Laver, Ken Rosewall, and Mal Anderson. In the finale that year Newcombe and Laver were overpowering. Both beat Stan Smith and Tom Gorman in singles, and teamed in crushing Smith and Erik van Dillen in the doubles during a 5–0 Australian victory that ended five-year possession of the Cup by the U.S.

Newcombe also played in the first World Cup in 1970, the inaugural of the annual team match between the Aussies and the U.S., and helped win five of those Cups for his country.

Newcombe's serve, forehand, and volleying were the backbone of his attacking game, which was at its best on grass. His heavy serve was possibly the best of his era. Grass was the setting for his foremost singles wins, the three Wimbledons plus two U.S. Championships at Forest Hills in 1967 and 1973. He and Laver are also the only men to win Forest Hills as amateurs and pros.

Newcombe regretted missing successive Wimbledons of 1972–73 when he felt he might have added to his string. In 1972 he was a member of the World Championship Tennis pro troupe that was banned because of the quarrels between its leader, Lamar Hunt, and the International Lawn Tennis Federation. In 1973 Newcombe was a member of the players union, Association of Tennis Pros,

which boycotted Wimbledon in another dispute with the ILTF. The following year he stretched his Wimbledon match win streak to 18 before losing to Rosewall in the quarterfinals. That year Newcombe won the World Championship Tennis singles over an adolescent named Bjorn Borg, 17.

Newcombe felt, "I'm at my best in a five-set match, especially if I get behind. My adrenalin starts pumping." This was evident in two of his outstanding triumphs, both over Stan Smith, a strong rival for world supremacy in the early 1970s. Newcombe beat Smith, 6–3, 5–7, 2–6, 6–4, 6–4, in the 1971 Wimbledon title match, and 6–1, 3–6, 6–3, 3–6, 6–4, during the 1973 Davis Cup finale, rating the latter as his finest performance.

In 1967 he was the No. 1 amateur in the world, and in 1970 and 1971 No. 1 of all. He was one of the first to sign a contract to play World Team Tennis (with Houston) in 1974, his presence helping give the new league credibility, although he played just that one season. Newcombe was still playing sporadically in 1978, and had $1,048,942 in prize money at the close of the year.

KEN ROSEWALL (1934–   )

As the Doomsday Stroking Machine, the remarkable Kenneth Robert "Muscles" Rosewall has been a factor in three decades of tennis, winning his first major titles, the Australian and French singles in 1953, and continuing as a tournament winner past his 43rd birthday and into 1978. At the close of the 1977 season he was still ranked as one of the top 15 players in the game on the Association of Tennis Pros' computer.

"It's something I enjoy and find I still do well," was his simple explanation of his prowess in 1977, "but I never imagined myself playing so long when I turned pro in 1957."

The son of a Sydney, New South Wales, Australia, grocer, Rosewall was born in that city on November 2, 1934, and grew up there. A natural left-hander, he was taught to play right-handed by his father, Robert Rosewall, and developed a peerless backhand. Some felt his lack of size (5-feet-7, 135

Ken Rosewall: The Iron Man and his backhand. *UPI*

pounds) would impede him, but it was never a problem. He moved quickly, with magnificent anticipation and perfect balance, and never suffered a serious injury. Though his serve wasn't formidable, he placed it well, and backed it up with superb volleying. Rosewall was at home on any surface, and at the baseline or the net. He had an even temperament, was shy and reticent, but good-natured.

Although Rosewall, the little guy, seemed always overshadowed by a rival, first Lew Hoad, then Pancho Gonzales and Rod Laver, he outlasted them all, and had the last competitive word. Even when Laver was acknowledged as the best in the world, Rosewall could bother him, and twice shocked Rod in the rich World Championship Tennis finals in Dallas in 1971 and 1972, snatching the $50,000 first prize from the favorite's grasp. The match, thought by many to be the greatest ever played—a 3½-hour struggle watched by millions on TV—went to Rosewall, 4–6, 6–0, 6–3, 6–7, 7–6, when he stroked two magnificent backhand returns to escape a seemingly untenable position in the decisive tie-breaker and win by two points (7 points to 5), the closest finish of an important championship.

Rosewall and Hoad, born only 21 days apart, Ken the elder, were linked as teammates and rivals almost from their first days on court. In 1952 as 17-year-olds they made an immediate impact on their first overseas tour, both reaching the quarterfinals of the U.S. championship at Forest Hills, Ken beating the No. 1 American, Vic Seixas. Late the following year (having won the Wimbledon doubles together), shortly after their 19th birthdays, they became the youngest Davis Cup defenders, joining for Australia to repel the U.S. challenge in the finale. Rosewall beat Seixas in the decisive last match to ensure a 3–2 victory.

Though Hoad was considerably stronger physically than Rosewall, who had been given the sardonic nickname "Muscles" by his countrymen, Ken always managed to keep up in the early days and often surpass. Hoad beat Rosewall in the 1956 Wimbledon final, but his bid for a Grand Slam was spoiled when Rosewall knocked him off in the U.S. final at Forest Hills.

After helping Australia win the Davis Cup over the U.S. in 1956, Rosewall turned pro to take on the professional king, Pancho Gonzales. Gonzales stayed on top, winning their head-to-head tour, 50–26, but it was apparent that Rosewall belonged at the uppermost level. Thus began one of the longest active professional careers, certainly the most distinguished in regard to significant victories over so long a span. Rosewall won the first of his three U.S. Pro singles titles over Laver in 1963, the second by beating Gonzales and Laver in succession in 1965 and the third over Cliff Drysdale in 1971.

He holds several longevity records. Fourteen years after his 1956 Forest Hills triumph over Hoad he beat the favored Tony Roche to win the U.S. Championship again. Eighteen years after, he was the finalist (having beaten favored John Newcombe) but lost in 1974 to Jimmy Connors. Twenty years after appearing in the first of four Wimbledon finals, he lost the 1974 final to Connors. The only big one Rosewall missed out on was Wimbledon singles, but he won the doubles twice. Nineteen years after his first major title, the Australian, he won it again, in 1972. Twenty years after his first Davis Cup appearance he returned to help Australia win once again in 1973. He played on four Australian Davis Cup winners and three World Cup winners in the annual team match against the U.S.

Altogether Rosewall won 18 Big Four titles (Australia, French, Wimbledon, U.S.) in singles, doubles, and mixed, the sixth highest total. In 1974 he tried World Team Tennis for a season, serving as player-coach of the Pittsburgh Triangles. He was the second tennis player to cross $1 million in prize money, following Laver, and had amassed $1,588,576 at the close of 1978.

MANUEL SANTANA (1938–   )

One of the masters of legerdemain, Manuel Martinez "Manolo" Santana was the first post-World War II European to gain universal respect because he not only won the most difficult clay court event, the French singles in 1961 and 1964, but also the grass court gems, Wimbledon of 1966 and the U.S. Championship of 1965 at Forest Hills. In doing so, the engaging Spaniard was the first European champ at Forest Hills since Frenchman Henri Cochet in 1928.

Manuel Santana: Magician on clay. *UPI*

"He was a magician on clay," said Rod Laver. "Manolo could hit the most incredible angles, drive you crazy with topspin lobs or drop shots. And he improved his volleying so that he was dangerous on grass, too."

In 1965 Santana became a national hero in Spain and was decorated by the country's leader, Francisco Franco, with the coveted Medal of Isabella, qualifying for the title Illustrissimo. That year Santa spearheaded the 4–1 upset of the U.S. at Barcelona during the Davis Cup campaign and led Spain all the way to the finale for the first time. Although the Spaniards were turned back, 4–1, Santana gave Roy Emerson his only defeat in 12 title-round singles. Two years later he drove Spain to the finale again, salvaging the only point in a 4–1 defeat by beating John Newcombe. Only Italian Nicola Pietrangeli (164 singles and doubles in 66 matches) played more Davis Cup than Santana, who won 92 of his 121 singles and doubles in 46 matches between 1958 and 1973. He set Cup records by winning 13 singles matches during the 1967 campaign, also by winning a total of 17 singles and doubles in 1965 and again in 1967, a mark topped in 1971 by Ilie Nastase's 18.

Born May 10, 1938, at Madrid, he worked as a ballboy at a local club where he picked up the game. He was a very appealing player who frequently smiled at play and was an admirable sportsman. His racket control was phenomenal, enabling him to hit with touch and power. He had great flair, the ability to improvise and to inspire himself and his partners and teammates. Never losing heart in the doubles of the 1965 Davis Cup aginast the U.S., he rallied partner Luis Arilla as they stormed back to beat Dennis Ralston and Clark Graebner, 4–6, 3–6, 6–3, 6–4, 11–9, in an emotional battle that clinched the decision. Cushions showered down on the two Spaniards as they were carried about the stadium court of the Real Club de Tenis in the manner of bullfighters. Santana and Arilla wept with joy at the most tremendous victory in Spanish tennis annals.

Less than a month later a similarly jubilant celebration was staged at Forest Hills after Santana jolted Cliff Drysdale in the U.S. final, 6–2, 7–9, 7–5, 6–1. A troupe of dancers from the World's Fair's Spanish Pavilion toted Santana from stadium to clubhouse, whereupon they serenaded him.

The following year was Santana's at Wimbledon, where he beat Ralston in the final, 6–4, 11–9, 6–4, and enthralled the gallery with his point and counterpoint thrusts.

His successes spurred the rapid development of tennis in Spain, where the sport was not much noticed prior to 1965. His protégé was Manuel Orantes, called Manolito (Little Manolo), who won the U.S. Championship at Forest Hills a decade after his own, though the surface had by then been transformed to clay.

Santana came out of retirement briefly in 1973 to play his last season of Davis Cup, and again in 1974 to act as player-coach for New York in the new World Team Tennis League.

FRANK SEDGMAN (1927–   )

The beginning of the most powerful dynasty in tennis history was in the strokes of Frank Allan Sedgman, the Australian savior of 1950.

Australia was sagging in the Davis Cup after World War II, losing four successive finales to the U.S. Then, in 1950, 22-year-old Sedgman—loser of both his singles the previous year—startled crowds at Forest Hills by spearheading a 4–1 victory for the Aussies. In the company of Ken McGregor that year, Mervyn Rose and McGregor the next, and McGregor again in 1952, Sedgman led the way to three straight Cups. In 1951 Sedgman became the first of numerous Aussies to win the U.S. Championship at Forest Hills and he repeated the following year.

Those Cup successes were the start of Captain Harry Hopman's stewardship under which Australia won the Davis trophy 15 times between 1950 and 1967. And also the start of Sedgman's nearly three years as the premier amateur.

Sedgman, tall, extremely athletic, was born at Mount Albert, Victoria, Australia, October 29, 1927, and was such a prolific winner of major titles during the late 1940s and early 1950s that he stands third among all-time male champions with 22 Big Four victories in

Frank Sedgman: The first $100,000-a-year man. *New York Herald Tribune*

singles, doubles, and mixed doubles, three behind John Newcombe and six behind Roy Emerson.

In 1951 Sedgman and McGregor scored the only Grand Slam in doubles by winning all the Big Four (Australian, Wimbledon, French, and U.S.) within a calender year. In 1952, his last season as an amateur, Sedgman was the last man to make a rare Wimbledon triple, adding the doubles (with McGregor) and mixed (with Doris Hart) to his singles conquest.

Speed, brilliant volleying, and a heavy forehand were his chief assets, plus a fighting—yet good-natured—spirit.

Jack Kramer, proprietor of the professional tour and its foremost player, enticed Sedgman to become his challenger in 1953, and they played the customary head-to-head tour between the amateur-king-turned-pro-rookie and the incumbent Kramer, who stayed on top, 54–41. However, Sedgman's share of the gate was $102,000, and he was the first tennis player to earn more than $100,000 in a season.

Sedgman continued to barnstorm with the pros into the 1960s. He was finalist to Pancho Gonzales for the U.S. Pro Singles championship in 1954 and won the U.S. Pro doubles with Andres Gimeno in 1961. Keeping himself unusually fit, he was able to launch a second professional career in 1974 when promoter Al Bunis formed the Grand Masters tour for ex-champs over 45. Sedgman won the Grand Masters championship in a season's-end play-off among the top eight players in 1975 and 1977–78, and in this second phase of professionalism won more than $250,000 over six seasons.

PANCHO SEGURA (1921–   )

A strange sight was Pancho Segura when he appeared on the American scene in 1942 and seized the No. 4 U.S. ranking. He had an unorthodox two-fisted forehand, and flimsy-looking bowed legs that seemed incapable of holding him up. Yet the little guy (5-6) was quick nimble, and extremely effective.

Francisco "Pancho" Segura was born June 20, 1921, at Guayaquil, Ecuador, and was raised there. A childhood attack of rickets deformed his legs but his will was strong, and he drove himself to play tennis well, even though he was so weak at first that he had to grip the racket with both hands. A right-hander, he was likely the first to utilize a two-fisted forehand.

Entering the University of Miami on a tennis scholarship, he won the U.S. Intercollegiate singles in 1943, 1944, and 1945, the only man in this century to take three straight. He won the U.S. Indoor title of 1946 and the U.S. Clay Court of 1944, but his best days were ahead of him, as a professional. After settling in the U.S., he left the amateurs in 1947, signing on to play mostly the secondary matches on the tour of one-nighters. Unfortunately for Segura, he was out of the limelight once he became a professional, but while he beat Dinny Pails, Frank Parker, and Ken McGregor in their series, sharpening his strokes and tactics and becoming one of the

Pancho Segura: First with the two-fisted fore-hand. *Russ Adams*

great players, he received little recognition. Jack Kramer and Pancho Gonzales were the stars, but Segura was making his mark in a small circle as a shrewd strategist, a cunning lobber, and a killer with a forehand.

He toured for nearly two decades and stands as one of the prominent figures in the history of the U.S. Pro Championships. Segura won the singles title three times in a row, first in 1950 over Frank Kovacs, then in 1951 and 1952 over Gonzales. Segura lost the title to Gonzales on three occasions, 1955, 1956, and 1957, and a fourth time, at age 41, to Butch Buchholz in 1962. Segura also won the doubles with Jack Kramer in 1948 and 1955, and with Gonzales in 1954 and 1958.

Hardy and good-natured, Segura was a favorite with crowds. He could always smile and crack a joke, yet was thoroughly professional and a constant competitor. He never made big money. Open tennis arrived too late for him, but he entered the doubles of the first open Wimbledon in 1968 with Alex Olmedo, and in the second round they won the longest doubles match of Wimbledon's open era, 94 games, over Abe Segal and Gordon Forbes,

32–30, 5–7, 6–4, 6–4. The 62-game set was the longest ever at Wimbledon.

Segura still makes appearances on the Grand Masters circuit for ex-champs over 45 but concentrates on teaching tennis and is regarded as one of the foremost instructors. One of his protégés was Jimmy Connors.

VIC SEIXAS (1923–   )

When Vic Seixas played—and won—the fifth longest singles match in tennis history, he was 42. That was in 1966, when he went 94 games to beat a 22-year-old Australian Davis Cup player, Bill Bowrey, 32–34, 6–4, 10–8, during the Pennsylvania Grass Championships at Philadelphia. It took nearly four hours.

Elias Victor Seixas, Jr., born August 30, 1923, at Philadelphia, was very hardy. He played the U.S. Championship at Forest Hills a record 28 times between 1939 and 1969, winning the singles in 1954, and played more Davis Cup matches than any other American,

winning 38 of 55 singles and doubles encounters during his seven years on the team between 1951 and 1957. Thirteen times he was ranked in the Top Ten in the U.S. between 1942 and 1966, setting an American longevity record of a 24-year span between his first and last entries (later equaled by Pancho Gonzales, 1948–72).

In 1954, when Seixas won the Wimbledon singles and led the U.S. to the Davis Cup, a brief cracking of the Australian monopoly of the time, he was considered No. 1 in the amateur world.

Although he helped the U.S. attain the finale every year he played Davis Cup, the team could win only once, the high spot of 1954 when he and Tony Trabert were victorious. After Trabert opened with a win over Lew Hoad, Seixas followed with a stunning 8–6, 6–8, 6–4, 6–3 triumph over his nemesis, Ken Rosewall. That put the U.S. ahead, 2–0, on the first day, and Seixas and Trabert clinched the Cup the following day with a doubles victory over Hoad and Rex Hartwig, 6–2, 4–6, 6–2, 10–8, before a record outdoor crowd of 25,578 at Sydney.

Seixas won 15 of the Big Four titles in singles and doubles, setting a Wimbledon record by winning the mixed doubles four successive years, 1953–55 with Doris Hart, and 1956 with Shirley Fry.

Among his 13 U.S. titles were the Clay Court singles in 1953 and 1957, the Hard Court doubles (with Ted Schroeder) in 1948, and the Indoor doubles (with Trabert) in 1955, making Seixas one of the few to win national titles on all four surfaces. In 1971 he was named to the International Tennis Hall of Fame.

Seixas was an attacker who won more on determination and conditioning than on outstanding form. His volleying was exceptional, and he had an excellent match temperament. His career was interrupted for three years by World War II, during which he served as a pilot in the U.S. Air Force. He graduated from the University of North Carolina. Seixas was one of the few extraordinary amateurs who did not join the pro tour. Eventually, though, after the age of 50, he did become a pro to compete on the Grand Masters circuit.

Vic Seixas: A longevity record to match. *UPI*

TONY TRABERT (1930–   )

One of the finest seasons ever achieved was the 1955 of Tony Trabert, who won three of the Big Four singles titles—Wimbledon, French, and U.S.—to earn acclaim as the No. 1 amateur of that year. Only two other men, Don Budge (1938) and Rod Laver (1962 and 1969), en route to their Grand Slams, have won those three uppermost championships within a calendar year.

Moreover, Trabert also won the U.S. Indoor and U.S. Clay Court titles, adding them to the pre-eminent American championship on grass at Forest Hills.

An exceptional athlete, Marion Anthony Trabert was born August 16, 1930, in Cincinnati, Ohio, where he grew up, and was a standout basketball player at the University of Cincinnati, where he won the National Intercollegiate singles title in 1951.

The French Championships has traditionally been the most difficult battleground for American men. Trabert won five titles in Paris, the singles in 1954 and 1955, and the doubles in 1950 (with Bill Talbert) and in 1954 and 1955 (with Vic Seixas). As of 1979, no American male since had won the French singles. Only a defeat by Ken Rosewall (the eventual champ) in the semifinals of the Australian Championships ruined Trabert's chance at a Grand Slam in 1955.

For five years Trabert was a mainstay of the U.S. Davis Cup team, along with Seixas. In each of those years the U.S. reached the Challenge Round finale, and Trabert's best-remembered match may have been a defeat, a tremendous struggle against Lew Hoad on a rainy afternoon in 1953 at Melbourne. Hoad won out, 7–5, in the fifth, and Australia kept the Cup. However, Trabert and Seixas returned to Australia a year later, where Trabert beat Hoad on the opening day in singles and he and Seixas won the doubles over Hoad and Rex Hartwig in a 3–2 triumph, the only U.S. seizure of the Cup from the Aussies during an eight-year stretch.

Tony Trabert: A champ for all surfaces. *UPI*

Trabert was an attacker with a powerful backhand and strong volley, exceptionally competitive. In winning the U.S. Singles at Forest Hills twice, 1953 and 1955, and Wimbledon, he did not lose a set, a rare feat.

Amassing 13 U.S. titles in singles and doubles he was one of two Americans (the other was Art Larsen) to win singles championships on all four surfaces: grass at Forest Hills, indoor, clay court, and hard court.

Following the custom of the time, Trabert, as the top amateur, signed on with the professionals to challenge the ruler, Pancho Gonzales, on a head-to-head tour in 1956. Gonzales won, 74–27. Trabert was runner-up to Alex Olmedo for the U.S. Pro singles title in 1960, having won the doubles with Hartwig in 1956.

When his playing career ended Trabert worked as a teaching pro and as a television commentator on tennis. In 1976 he returned to the Davis Cup scene as the U.S. captain, leading the Cup-winning teams of 1978–79.

7 } THE OFFICIALS

When tennis made its swift, tumultuous transition from a proper, country-club pastime to a billion-dollar, fiercely competitive business, it neglected to bring its officials along into the modern age.

Until the late 1960s tennis had remained, at least on the face of it, a purely amateur sport with only a handful of outcast professionals able to make a living at it.

Suddenly, with the speed of a booming service, tennis exploded into an extremely lucrative industry, reaching a point where single tournaments alone, such as the U.S. Open, offer prize money in excess of a half million dollars.

But even now, when thousands of dollars are riding on the outcome of a single call, the ladies and gentlemen charged with the awe-

This was the occasion of the annual meeting in the 1920s of the National Umpires' Association at Forest Hills. The man in the white suit is the association's first president, Edward C. Conlin. In the second row, second from the left, is F.P.A. (Franklin P. Adams), noted columnist ("The Conning Tower") and friend and admirer of Bill Tilden. F.P.A., according to notes in the photo album of the late William M. Fischer, was "a good umpire." *Fischer Collection*

some responsibility of making the snap decisions remain relics of the dark ages.

At the 1978 U.S. Open, for example, the army of officials was being paid approximately $300 each for two weeks of work. Since many of the officials came from outside New York, their recompense didn't even cover expenses.

Still, until the mid-1970s, officials didn't even receive this little consideration. In addition, they still lack sufficient disciplinary control proportionate to their reponsibility.

Adrian Clark, Jr., an outspoken and highly respected official since the 1950s, recognizes the incongruity of the situation.

"One time a few of us were gabbing in the Garden [Madison Square Garden]," he said, "and Rod Laver said to me, 'My God, I can make $10,000 in here tonight and you guys, who will determine whether or not I win it, are doing it for nothing. It's entirely wrong.'

"Unfortunately, it's an outgrowth of tennis antiquity, dating back to the polite social game it once was, and it places an unfair onus on the umpires trying to do a fair job. You have a situation where people aren't sufficiently trained and you have no way of controlling it. Fortunately, there are a lot of dedicated people in this business and a lot of us do a helluva good job."

There is general agreement among old-time officials that they never were taken seriously enough, and the situation hasn't improved commensurate with the other rapid developments of a high-pressure sport.

"Not even the officials took it very seriously," said Jack Stahr, considered one of the very best for some four decades. "It was more an honorific thing than a career, and we still have difficulty getting young ones to umpire because they'd rather be out playing instead. It wasn't until 1973 that the U.S. Open first made any money at all available to officials, and then it amounted to $5,000 to be distributed among 185 people. Before then all we received was perquisites, perhaps a dinner chit for a whole day's work.

"It is only recently that tournament organizers have begun to realize they should be more businesslike about where they get their officials and they have been engaging chair umpires, at least, at a fairly decent fee. It's been getting better, but there are only a few people who make their living out of tennis officiating."

For a major match, there will be as many as 13 officials working at courtside. Nevertheless, they aren't nearly as visible as a baseball umpire or basketball referee because they must remain seated, almost motionless, and except for the chair umpire they are virtually silent.

Still, there is an aspect of the spectacular surrounding special events, and certain individuals, such as Clark and Frank Hammond, transcend the soft surroundings and have become celebrities. Hammond, who has a booming voice and a commanding personality, has a reputation for controlling a match better than anyone.

"I think an umpire is very much like a conductor, without being hammy, and before you can concentrate on the players you'd better have great empathy with the people who are paying the money to come in," he said. "They're your reeds and your brass and your timpani, and the two players are your soloists.

"This business of talking down to the crowd, telling them to shut up and not to move, that's ridiculous. Instead, you should keep them informed and lead them. If they're yelling, 'Let's go, Jimmy,' or 'Let's go, Bjorn,' you can hush them by injecting a little humor and saying, 'The players thank you a lot but ssshhh, here we go.' Once you've got the crowd under control, you can concentrate on the players. I've umpired more than 5,000 matches and run 500 tournaments as a referee, and never have I had a major incident."

Hammond's comments were made before the 1979 U.S. Open in which he, indeed, would be involved in a major incident. It happened in a match between John McEnroe and Ilie Nastase, after Hammond had repeatedly called Nastase for stalling and had awarded first a point penalty, then a game, then the match to McEnroe.

The crowd became so unruly, booing and throwing refuse, that Mike Blanchard, the tourney referee, removed Hammond from the umpire's chair, reversed Hammond's decision, and directed that the match be resumed.

McEnroe still emerged the winner, and Hammond was an embarrassed loser. He later conceded that for the first time in more than three decades of officiating, he'd lost control of a match.

According to Blanchard, who has served as referee for many tournaments, including the U.S. Open, there are four prime qualifications for an official: He must know the rules, he must have good eyesight, he must be able to concentrate for long stretches of time, and he has to be in good enough health to sit for four hours under a broiling sun.

A full complement of officials includes 10 line umpires (three on each end and four for the service lines and baselines), a net-cord judge, a foot-fault judge, and the chair umpire.

The line umpires sit opposite the various lines on the court and call the balls that fall within their line. They call "out" if the ball is out, they say nothing if the ball is good.

The net-cord judge sits by the net post with his fingers on the net, at the same time looking along the length of the net. He listens, he feels, and he watches for serves that may clip the net as they cross into the other side of the court. Occasionally, a gust of wind may cause the net to tremble, sending a vibration to the fingers of the judge, but if he is also looking he can see that the ball didn't touch the net.

A foot-fault judge is employed only in the more important matches of major tournaments, and in such team competitions as the Davis Cup and the Wightman Cup. He sits on the baseline, shifting from one side of the court to the other, wherever the server might be.

The umpire sits in the high chair just beyond the net, and he has complete charge of the match. He calls the score, interprets rules, and now has the authority to overrule the call of an umpire or a judge. In addition, he can take the ultimate step of defaulting a player for bad conduct.

Not directly involved with the individual matches is the referee, but he is charged with control of all facets of play. Once the tournament director gets the site ready and does the other preliminary work, the referee takes charge. It is he who makes the draw and

assigns courts, it is he who sets a schedule and then makes whatever changes are required because of weather conditions, and it is he who must settle any appeals pertaining to law.

"Players are permitted to summon the referee for an interpretation of rules, a question of law," Blanchard said. "The umpire has charge of the court as to a question of fact—was the ball in? was the ball out? point penalties, and such things. The player may ask the referee to come to the court to interpret a rule."

If a fairly big tournament is held in a locality that doesn't have a strong umpire's association, the organizers may engage a name umpire to help out. In addition to being in the chair for some major matches, this chief umpire may give a clinic before the tournament starts so that local officials can brush up their technique and tactics.

A chief of umpires, such as Bob Bigelow, also is employed at the U.S. Open, but there his primary function is to manage the people working the assignments.

Many tournament matches are worked with as few as five officials, the minimum number permitted for Grand Prix competition. In such a case they are positioned with one on each of the two baselines, one on the far sideline, one on the center line, and one on the jump serve.

There is a code of dress for officials, although it isn't strictly enforced. Men should wear a blue shirt, blazer jacket, and gray pants, and women (they compose about 40 per cent of the USTA Umpires' Council) are requested to wear gray skirts with blue top jackets, or all navy blue suits.

Rules generally are consistent throughout the world, with some minor variations from sector to sector, such as a determination on which tie-breakers are to be used.

"There are subtle differences in the officiating," said Stahr, who worked at Wimbledon in 1973 and 1977. "Mainly, they stonewall things more in Britain than they do over here. A line umpire makes a call and no one thinks to question him, even if he's wrong.

"The players are disciplined by the aura of Wimbledon. The officiating at Wimbledon has a reputation for being superior, but I honestly think it has the reputation only because they stonewall it, and because it goes against tradition to even question a call."

In slow, painful degrees, tennis officials are being given the kind of power that allows them to exert full control over a match. Where not so long ago they had no disciplinary control over players, officials now can flex a soft muscle with a system of point penalties. First proposed in 1970 and then authorized in 1973, it wasn't until 1976 that the International Lawn Tennis Federation permitted their use on an experimental basis.

Under the point penalty provision, the umpire is empowered to assess penalties of one point or one game—depending on the frequency of violations—for such infractions as delay on changeover, delay of match, knocking the ball out of the enclosure, throwing a racket, profanity, obscenity, and verbal or physical abuse.

The umpire can even default a player for repeated offenses.

Curiously, there are no such point penalties in women's tennis.

Another critical change now allows an umpire to overrule a linesman's call if the umpire is certain it was wrong. Previously, an umpire could request a change if he felt one was warranted, but he couldn't force it.

This change, incidentally, probably was responsible for Jimmy Connors winning the U.S. Open in 1978. This is the way Adrian Clark, who was on the service line, recalls this important footnote to history:

"It was the fourth-round match against Adriano Panatta, and Connors was losing, 5–4 in the fifth set. In the 10th game, Panatta served to the deuce court and I called the ball good. But the umpire, sitting in front of me, never saw my hands go down, and he called a fault. In the meantime, Connors had returned the ball weakly and Panatta was in the process of putting it away, which would have given him advantage.

"Instead, he stopped his motion, went back, and served a second serve, which Connors put away, a beautiful cross-court winner. That made it advantage Connors. Panatta won the next point for deuce, but if my call had stood, that would have been Panatta's advantage and the next point he won would have been match point.

"Because of that one overrule, Connors won the match and didn't drop another set the rest of the way to win the championship."

Aside from having to make a snap judgment on a ball flying at speeds of up to 140 miles per hour, one of the more difficult facets of an official's life is dealing with the players, many of whom are cantankerous and love to showboat before a crowd.

"I try not to react physically, but a person never can be happy with players who are troublemakers," said Stahr, a low-key gentleman with an easy manner. "I keep thinking of the few players who are always protesting calls, that if I had the opportunity I'd like to sit down with them and say, 'Look, do you mean to say you're the only one who ever gets all these bad calls? These other players also get calls they doubt, but they don't make a big holler about it. Why don't you play the way the rest of them do? What gives you a special privilege to make trouble?'

"The only thing that bugs me is when you get a player who questions everything that possibly could be questioned."

Hammond, who is close to many of the players, contends that umpires must take responsibility for losing control.

"I insist that 80 per cent of the trouble with any player in the game is initiated from the chair," he said. "[Ilie] Nastase, 80 percent of the trouble he gets into is because of the incompetence of an umpire.

"If you could walk into a bank and legally take all the money you could carry in an hour, would you do it? I would. Now here's a guy in a chair. If a player can say, 'Fat Frank, I'm taking over your chair, I'm going to run your match for you, I'm going to tell you when the ball's in and out, when I want to play, when I don't want to play,' why shouldn't he do it?

"It's up to the chair umpire, without saying, 'I have a badge and I can rule the world,' to control the match. If a player knows that someone is controlling the match, he plays tennis and enjoys it."

Nastase stories are legendary among officials, and surprisingly they aren't all bad. The better officials seem to enjoy their association with him, and one top umpire said Nastase was the only player he would pay to see.

"There are ways of controlling players, and it's not done by embarrassing them over a microphone to get your point across," Hammond said. "I remember a match at Baltimore when I was the referee. A linesman called two foot faults on Nastase right away and he approached the chair. I was sitting by the court and Nastase said to me, 'Either he goes or I go.'

"There are two ways I could have handled this. I could have said something like 'either you play or you're out,' or I could have approached him the way I did. I said, 'Ilie, every person here has paid to see you play. If you don't play you'll destroy me, I've got to throw you out.' He went back and played like a pussycat."

Adrian Clark likes to talk about a match in 1973 between Nastase and Bob Carmichael, an Australian.

"Carmichael is such an intense person, and after he'd miss a shot he'd go through the motions of what he should've done," Clark related. "Nasty started imitating him behind his back, and the crowd loved it. Carmichael, sensing what was happening, turned around quickly, and there was Nasty looking around acting like he was watching for flies.

"It was a hot, sweltering day, and later in the match the guy calling center service called two foot faults on Nasty; so after one point Nasty drops his racket and says to the guy, 'My God, what eyes you got. You must be able to see Washington from here.' Later he goes back to the guy again and says, 'Why don't you go away 15 minutes? I have a good friend who'll buy you a cup of coffee.' At that point I couldn't resist and I said, 'Hey, Nasty, make it a cold pitcher of beer and I'll join him.'

"Another time in Madison Square Garden I called a foot fault on him at the baseline. He comes up to me, points his finger, then says, 'Don't move, they're taking our picture.' So you see how serious he is in most of these cases. It's only when the crowd gets nasty to

him that he loses his cool. He loves to clown, but he doesn't always know how to. That's his trouble."

In the revolution that shook tennis during the 1970s, one can't overlook World Team Tennis. And just as it introduced a new concept to the sport, WTT, for its relatively short life, also brought with it a more energized form of officiating.

The system, which utilized only six officials, was the innovation of Dick Roberson, supervisor of officials for WTT for two years before he moved on as Grand Prix tournament supervisor.

"To cut the number of men from 12, I figured out what lines needed to be covered," Roberson said. "Then I had to break the taboo barrier of having the line umpires move during a point. The players felt it couldn't be done, but I thought it could if the timing of the moves was right.

"Once the ball was on a player's racket, then the line umpires could move. The line umpire who called the service line had to move back to the baseline, and the other umpire moved from the center service line to the sideline. He moved again when the ball was being returned. The other two line umpires were stationary."

Along with the four line umpires, there were a referee and a scorekeeper. The referee stood on a box about 2½ feet high, from where he controlled the match and dealt with any disputes involving the rival coaches, and the scorekeeper called the nets as well as kept score.

"The big thing about the WTT system was that the referee was totally in charge of the match, and that's that main reason matches went so smoothly," Roberson said. "A player or coach could gripe, but the referee could order that play be continued. And he had the authority to assess point penalties or to default a player from a set."

There was a good deal of early skepticism about the effectiveness of "Roberson's Rovers" (Adrian Clark called them jumping jacks), but the system proved effective.

In such ways is progress made, but there still is a long road to travel to transport tennis officiating from the country-club era to the competitive industry it must govern.

Another important step was taken with the introduction of the super referee to the Grand Prix circuit. It is the function of the super referee to see that qualified officials are hired, that the rules are upheld, and that the code of conduct is followed.

"The change in tennis has been much too fast for everyone to keep up with," said Mike Blanchard, who started umpiring at the Longwood Cricket Club in Chestnut Hill, Massachusetts, in 1932. "About 20 years ago there might be six or seven of what you'd call really major tournaments in the U.S., known as the Eastern grass courts circuit, plus two in California that ended the season.

"The tournament season ran from about the latter part of June till the middle of October. Now you've got about three tournaments a week going on all over the country, and I'm talking about big tournaments. And there are thousands of smaller tourneys as tennis has grown to its present proportions.

To do justice to such growth, it is inherent on the wise men of tennis to stimulate a corresponding impetus in the depth and quality of officiating.

8 } EQUIPMENT

When you walk into any well-stocked tennis shop these days, you're likely to face decisions about equipment that a few years ago were relatively easy. More and more companies have begun to capitalize on the growth of the game in recent years, designing and producing a host of new products. Some of these new products represent true advances in design, durability, and playability—but there have also been a number of marginal items, and occasionally even some that were downright poor. The marketplace has especially seen a proliferation of new rackets and shoes, but even with balls and strings there have been dozens of new brands and specialized types.

Choosing equipment is a highly personal matter, but there are a number of useful criteria you need to consider when you start looking over today's array of equipment. The following guidelines are intended to help you to see what qualities you should look for to get the best value. The most fundamental point to observe, however, is a deceptively simple rule that many players seem to forget: Be comfortable with your choice, both physically and psychologically. A new racket should provide you with a comfortable feel and fit on the court, and so should a shoe: otherwise, it probably isn't the right choice for your game, no matter what anyone tells you. Further, you will generally find that equipment performs best—and feels best—when it's used for the proper playing conditions. Thus, you'll get a better game out of a regular ball (rather than a heavy-duty model) on a clay court, because that is where it was designed to be used. Equipment alone won't make anyone into a winning player, of course, but you will play better, and get more satisfaction out of the game, if you make enlightened choices.

RACKETS

Here are a few things to consider when you select a tennis racket:

Playing Style and Ability

One of the most important ways that tennis players differ is in their preference for a powerful serve-and-volley style of game as opposed to a slower, more controlled game. Generally, fast playing surfaces favor the power players, while slower surfaces like clay put a premium on control and the use of ground strokes. A player who wants more contol will usually find that a very flexible frame adds extra power to his shots, but diminishes control; while a stiffer frame increases a player's control but adds no power.

Men and women also tend to play different kinds of games; here the difference is chiefly one of physical strength. A few manufacturers have begun to market lightweight, highly mobile frames specially designed for women, but your choice of a racket should not necessarily be influenced by sex. Some women are better off with a frame that adds power; others play better with a stiff frame.

The same is true for beginners. It's often said that a beginner should start with a wood racket rather than a metal, Fiberglas, or composite model, because wood rackets offer better control. In reality, beginners are like every other player: They need both power and control. The only sensible argument for starting a player off with a wood racket is economics: A good wooden racket can be bought more cheaply that most metal or composite frames. The high-performance frames only really pay off for a player who has developed enough skill and interest in the game to justify investing in top equipment that will give years of service.

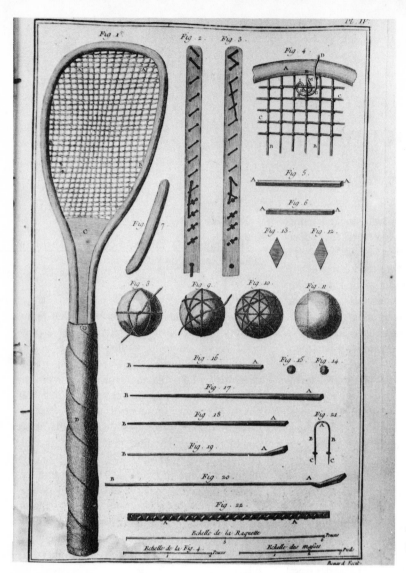

This is the way it was.
USLTA

Materials

Broadly speaking, there are five kinds of materials used to make tennis rackets—wood, steel, aluminum, Fiberglas, and various composites. Each of these has special playing characteristics, as well as strengths and weaknesses that should be considered when choosing a racket. Not all wood rackets play alike, nor do all Fiberglas rackets or aluminum rackets or steel rackets—but they have enough similarities that you can narrow your choice considerably by finding a material that seems to offer the qualities you want most.

Balance Point

Years ago, this characteristic wasn't as important as it is in today's game. But with a majority of world-class players using a lot of topspin on their ground strokes, head-light rackets have become more popular because it's easier to roll the racket over the ball and impart greater spin.

Basically, "balance point" refers to the point at which a racket will balance on a fulcrum. To find whether a racket is head-heavy, even-balanced, or head-light, measure the racket from the top of the head to the base of the grip, and divide this distance in half. If the racket balanced at exactly this midpoint, it is even-balanced; if it balances more toward the grip, it is head-light; and if it balances more toward the head, it is head-heavy. This test should be conducted with a strung racket, or with an equivalent weight attached to the racket head.

Before you decide automatically what kind of balance you want on your racket, it's essential to try a few demonstrator models first. You'll notice that if the frame is too light in the head for you, you won't feel much weight behind your shots—but if you have too much head weight it may make you a bit late on your shots, as well as tire your arm. A head-heavy racket can also contribute to arm problems if you aren't used to it.

Weight of Frame

There are no absolute standards in the tennis industry that determine a light, medium, or heavy racket frame, and in fact there are slight differences among different manufacturers. Thus, if you're changing brands, be sure to try different weights as well as different balance points to be sure you get exactly the right feel. Generally speaking, though, a light is about 12–12½ ounces unstrung; a medium is 12½–13¼ ounces; and a heavy is anything above that. (Add about ½ ounce to find the strung weight.)

The weight you pick is pretty much a matter of personal taste and individual strength. A physically strong player can generally use a heavy frame, but too heavy a frame will strain your arm muscles. Too light a frame, however, may cause you to use too much wrist action on your shots. If you decide to switch to a slightly heavier frame, be sure to do so gradually, because a sudden change may harm your arm.

Size of Grip

Grip sizes are determined by measuring the distance around the handle at midgrip, and one reason that grip sizes seem to vary from racket to racket is that some manufacturers use slightly different grip shapes that make the grip feel larger or smaller than it really is. The oval shape is used by Wilson, Spalding, ACRO, and others will make the grip seem larger, while a grip with an elongated top and bottom plane (for example, the Head Competition series) will seem smaller.

There are a number of ways to measure your hand to estimate the proper grip size, but don't feel obligated to accept the results of any measurement without question. One way to tell if you're using the wrong size grip is to hit with a racket for a while. Generally, if you are using a grip that is too large for you, your arm will tire faster because it must strain to control the racket. If the grip is too small, the racket will tend to twist in your hands on off-center hits. Either too large or too small a grip may contribute to arm problems after a while, though other factors are also involved.

Standard grip sizes today run from 4¼ inches to 4⅞ inches, with ⅛-inch intervals. Some junior rackets are sized as low as 4 inches, while an occasional frame may be sized as large as 5 inches. A few companies, including Davis, Dura-Fiber, and sometimes Adidas, use a European sizing system that substitutes whole numbers for the standard fractions. To translate, use the following chart:

AMERICAN	4 1/4	4 3/8	4 1/2	4 5/8	4 3/4	4 7/8
EUROPEAN	2	3	4	5	6	7

When you buy a racket, you should also check to see whether the grip is interchangeable with other sizes without adding tape or sanding down the grip base, and whether parts are easily available to do this. If not, a pro shop can change your grip size for you, but it's sometimes a complicated process.

Workmanship

It's also important to check for good workmanship when you buy a racket. The string holes on a wooden racket should be cleanly drilled, the finish should be smooth and clear and show no bubbling, the decal work should be clean, and the laminations should not be splitting. A metal racket should have adequate string protection, either a string strip or individual breakproof grommets (individual grommets do have a somewhat tarnished history). A composite frame should be checked carefully to see if it shows any sign of delaminating (that is, if the different layers are pulling apart), and a demonstrator should be inspected to see if the strings are pulling into the core material, which would eventually affect string tension.

Ease of Stringing

This is a factor that is important chiefly to the retailer or pro shop manager, rather than the consumer (though some players now string their own rackets). A number of rackets require unusual equipment or pose special difficulties in stringing, and if players are encouraged to buy them these rackets are likely to become a continuing source of annoyance for the shop and the owner.

Price

Like everything else, the cost of most tennis rackets has been rising streadily, under the combined impetus of inflation, labor costs, and higher materials costs. And there is a tremendous range in prices, anywhere from a few dollars for a prestrung wood import from Taiwan or Pakistan to upwards of $200 for a graphite composite, unstrung. Moreover, most prices are only suggested by the manufacturer.

As a rule of thumb, the least expensive frames are mostly wood; the highest priced are the composites. Typical price ranges for rackets are: wood, $25 to $60; steel, $30 to $50; aluminum, $35 to $50; Fiberglas, $65 to $90; composite, $55 and up; and graphite composites, $150 to $200. Naturally, there are many exceptions to these figures, but for the most part rackets are now carefully priced by their manufacturers to be competitive. If a racket costs substantially more than its competitors, chances are it has extra features that have pushed its price up. Too many companies have learned the hard way that it doesn't pay to overprice an inferior product.

SHOES

When you select tennis shoes, these are the points to consider:

Court Surface

If you're going to play on hard, abrasive court surfaces like asphalt or concrete, your choice of shoes starts with a trade-off between comfort and durability. Generally, sole materials that are best at absorbing shock also wear out fairly quickly on hard courts, but the soles (particularly the polyurethanes) that survive longest on these courts are also the most likely to transmit shock to your legs. If you don't play too often, the trade-off matters much less: Neither your shoes nor your legs will suffer from brief intervals of playing. But if you play heavily, something has to give.

Style of Play

As with rackets, there are some shoes that are better for power games, and others for the ground stroker. A player whose game is best suited to clay courts can count on a lot of running on a fairly slippery surface, and should therefore look for traction above all else. A serve-and-volley player, however, will probably play on hard courts, where traction is not usually as big a problem, but he will especially need good support and durability from his shoes,

Likewise, a social player can afford to wear shoes that provide a maximum of comfort; a tournament player will play harder and place more stress on his shoes, and therefore needs better support and a tighter fit.

Support

The amount of support you get from a shoe depends on several factors. One of these is the amount of cushioning and padding built into the shoe for extra comfort. A well-padded shoe usually will not offer a great deal of firm support for the foot under stress, since the padding tends to give rather than hold the foot firmly. The shape of the shoe itself also makes a difference, and this depends on the individual player's foot shape. Some shoes are narrow in the toe, others are wide; some are good for players with high arches, some for a variety of other conditions. It may take considerable trial and error to find a brand of shoe that is compatible with your foot shape, but the result should be worth the effort in improved support and comfort.

Materials

Pay most attention to the upper and the sole. Many brands of tennis shoe offer a choice between leather and canvas uppers; leather tends to provide better support, though it costs more than canvas. As for the soles, the choice is between various types of natural and synthetic rubbers, which absorb shock well but lack durability, and harder materials such as polyurethane, which resist abrasion but also transmit shock and can be slippery until broken in.

Weight

The tendency today is today is toward lighter-weight shoes, and this is easy to understand. A lightweight pair of shoes can save you from carrying around a good quarter pound of weight on your feet during a game. But, generally, there's a good trade-off between lighter weight and loss of support and durability, and this becomes especially important for anyone who plays heavily.

Price

Tennis shoes now cost anywhere from $12 to around $35 to $40. Some shoes can be resoled, and this can be a cost advantage.

BALLS

Balls are becoming increasingly specialized, so you should be sure that you get the right kind for your playing needs.

Court Surface

Because of variations in the nap of the ball, there are models that are adapted for clay courts ("championship"), hard courts ("heavy duty"), and grass. This should be indicated on the can.

Altitude

If a standard ball is used at high altitudes, the difference in air pressure will cause the ball to be too lively. Instead, there are special balls for high-altitude play with lower internal pressures.

Visibility

White used to be the standard color for all tennis balls, but white balls are easily stained and are less visible under most conditions than the yellow balls now in common use. For indoor play, studies have shown that the most visible color is yellow-orange or gold.

Price

Balls are often sold at discount prices of around $2.00 per can, and the more expensive brands can go as high as $4.00 for three balls. Cheaper balls can be obtained either by finding seconds of national brands, or by buying cheaper imports.

STRING

The major choice in string is between nylon and gut.

Durability vs. Playability

In general, the more durable a string is, the less sensitivity it has, and vice versa. Nylon strings tend to wear well, but gut has the edge on playability. Even among brands of nylon or gut, this trade-off seems to hold true; thus there are more durable nylons that do not play as well as other, less durable brands—and the same is true of gut.

Gauge

The thickness of a string is measured according to its gauge, which will range from a thick 15 gauge to an unusually thin 17 gauge. The thinner gauges are used mostly by tournament players, since they provide the best playability.

Price

Racket stringing prices include labor and string. A nylon stringing job can cost anywhere between $8.00 and $15; a gut stringing job will cost about $20 to $25.

Climate

Because gut is a natural material, it is easily affected by moisture and sudden rises or falls in temperature. Unless gut is protected from adverse climate, nylon is normally a better choice for most players.

9 } INTERNATIONAL TENNIS HALL OF FAME

It is fitting that the International Tennis Hall of Fame is housed in a casino in the town that once was the hub of high society, Newport, Rhode Island. Newport Casino was originally commissioned by James Gordon Bennett, Jr., publisher of the New York *Herald*, to be used as an exclusive men's club. It was designed by prestigious architect Stanford White, whose contributions to the American scene included Madison Square Garden when it was on Madison Square in New York.

The Casino became the cradle of U.S. tennis, hosting the men's National Singles Championships from their inception in 1881 until 1915, when they were shifted to the West Side Tennis Club's new facility in Forest Hills.

In 1952 James Van Alen, then president of the Casino, proposed formation of a National Tennis Hall of Fame to the U.S. Lawn Tennis Association, which sanctioned its establishment in 1954. The first induction ceremony was held in 1955, and to date more than 100 players or otherwise significant contributors to the game have been elected to membership in what is now called the International Tennis Hall of Fame.

The main building on Bellevue Avenue contains stores on the ground floor, with the rooms of the original club upstairs. To the rear are several acres of land on which the grass courts were laid out. White designed a ballroom-theater at the back of the property, linked by an ornate two-story porch with an enclosed tennis court. In spite of damage by fire and hurricane, these buildings are still in use, and the tennis courts are open to the public during the spring and summer.

The Hall of Fame, whose executive director is Colonel Robert S. Day, houses all sorts of memorabilia—rackets, cups, medals, scrapbooks, photographs, cartoons, paintings, books, and magazines. It all adds up to the largest tennis museum in the world.

The Casino hosted the Newport Invitational Tournament for many years, was a stop on the Virginia Slims circuit, and currently is the site of the Hall of Fame Classic, a Grand Prix event and the last significant grass court tournament in the U.S.

The members, with their year of induction:

1955

RICHARD DUDLEY SEARS
(1861–1943)

Richard Sears won the first seven U.S. singles titles, beginning at age 19 in 1881 and ending in 1887. He won the doubles title six straight years, with Dr. James Dwight, 1882–84, with Joseph Clark in 1885, and again with Dr. Dwight in 1886 and 1887. Sears later became president of the U.S.

Lawn Tennis Association. He was born October 26, 1861, lived in Boston and died April 8, 1943.

DR. JAMES DWIGHT
(1852–1917)

Hailed as the Father of American Lawn Tennis, Dr. James Dwight ranked second to Richard Sears, his frequent doubles partner, in 1885 and 1886. Dr. Dwight reached the

Newport, Rhode Island, 1891, site of the National Championship in which Oliver Campbell successfully defended hs title against Clarence Hobart in five sets. *Fischer Collection*

national singles final in 1883 and shared five U.S. Doubles titles with Sears. Dr. Dwight, credited by some historians for introducing the game to the U.S. in 1874, was president of the USLTA 1882–84 and 1894–1911, and refereed the U.S. Championships for more than 30 years. He supervised the first Davis Cup match in 1900. He was born July 14, 1852, in Boston and died July 13, 1917.

JOSEPH S. CLARK
(1861–1956)

Although he won the first Intercollegiate Singles Championship for Harvard in 1883, Joseph Clark achieved his greatest success in doubles, teaming with his brother Clarence to defeat Richard Sears and Dr. James Dwight in matches at Boston and New York and winning the National title with Sears in 1885. He served as president of the USLTA, 1889–91. Clark was born November 30, 1861, lived in Philadelphia, and died April 14, 1956.

HENRY W. SLOCUM, JR.
(1862–1948)

After losing to Richard Sears in the 1887 final, Henry Slocum became the second person to win the U.S. Singles Championship, reigning in 1888 and 1889. He also gained the final in 1890, losing to Oliver Campbell. Slocum and H. A. Taylor won the U.S. Doubles crown in 1889. He served as president of the USLTA, 1892–93. He was born May 28, 1862, lived in New York, and died January 22, 1948.

OLIVER S. CAMPBELL
(1871–1953)

The first American net rusher, Oliver Campbell wrested the U.S. Singles title from Henry Slocum in 1890, becoming the youngest male champion at 19, and withstood a five-set challenge by Clarence Hobart to retain it in 1891 and a four-set test by Fred Hovey in 1892. Campbell won three U.S. Doubles Championships, with Valentine Hall in 1888 and Robert Huntington in 1891 and 1892, and reached the finals in 1889 and 1893. He was born February 25, 1871, lived in New York, and died July 11, 1953.

ROBERT D. WRENN
(1873–1952)

The U.S. Singles champion in 1893, 1894, 1896, and 1897, Robert Wrenn also teamed with Malcolm Chace to win the U.S. Doubles title in 1895. Wrenn played on the 1903 U.S. Davis Cup team in singles and with his brother George in doubles. Robert Wrenn was president of the USLTA, 1912–15. He was born September 22, 1873, lived in New York, and died November 12, 1952.

MALCOLM D. WHITMAN
(1877–1932)

Malcolm Whitman was the U.S. Singles champion, 1898–1900, and played on the original Davis Cup team in 1900 and again in 1902 without losing a singles match. A dedicated student of the game's history, Whitman authored *Tennis Origins and Mysteries*, which was published in 1931. He was born March 15, 1877, lived in Boston and New York, and died December 28, 1932.

1956

MAY SUTTON BUNDY
(1887–1975)

The first American to win at Wimbledon, May Sutton reigned there, 1905 and 1907. She won the 1904 U.S. Singles title in Philadelphia and gained the final the following year. She won the U.S. Doubles crown with Miriam Hall in 1904. After a hiatus of several years from national competition, May Sutton still ranked fourth in the nation upon her return in 1921. She was born September 25, 1887, lived in California, and died October 4, 1975.

DWIGHT F. DAVIS
(1879–1945)

The donor of the Davis Cup, Dwight Davis was a superior player in his own right, winning the Intercollegiate singles for Harvard in 1899. He won the U.S. Doubles title with Holcombe Ward, 1899–1901. Davis played in the first two Davis Cup competitions, both won by the U.S. over the British Isles, in 1900 and 1902. He served as Secretary of War in the Coolidge Cabinet. He was born in St. Louis, July 5, 1879, and died November 28, 1945.

WILLIAM J. CLOTHIER
(1881–1962)

William Clothier was the U.S. Singles champion in 1906 and the All-Comers finalist at Wimbledon in 1909. He reached the U.S. finals in 1904 and 1909 and ranked in the Top Ten 11 times. He was a member of the Davis Cup team twice and played on the first squad to go abroad in 1905. Clothier was the first president of the Hall of Fame, serving from 1954 until his retirement in 1957. He was born September 27, 1881, in Philadelphia, and died September 4, 1962.

WILLIAM A. LARNED
(1872–1926)

The establisher of the first "dynasty" since Richard Sears, William Larned won the U.S. Singles title five times in a row and twice more between 1901 and 1911. During that decade he failed to reach the semifinals only once. When he won his first championship, at age 28, he had been finalist the previous year. When he defeated Maurice McLoughlin in the 1911 final Larned became, at age 38, the oldest player to have won the title. He played on the Davis Cup team in 1902, 1903, 1905, 1908, 1909, and 1911. He ranked first eight times and in the Top Ten a record 19 times between 1892 and 1911. He was born December 30, 1872, lived in Summit, New Jersey, and died December 16, 1926.

HOLCOMBE WARD
(1878–1967)

Holcombe Ward, a member of the original U.S. Davis Cup team in 1900, won the 1904 U.S. Singles title by defeating William Clothier, 10–8, 6–4, 9–7, but it was in doubles that he reached his greatest heights. He teamed with Dwight Davis to win the doubles title, 1899–1901, and with Beals Wright to win it, 1904–6. Ward was president of the USLTA, 1937–47. He was born in New York on November 23, 1878, and died January 23, 1967.

BEALS C. WRIGHT
(1879–1961)

In addition to the 1905 U.S. Singles title, which he won against his doubles partner, Holcombe Ward, Beals Wright reached the singles final three times. He and Ward won three U.S. Doubles titles. Wright played on four Davis Cup teams, registering key victories over Tony Wilding and Norman Brookes in the losing 1908 Challenge Round in Australia and beating those two in the 1905 victory over Australia that took the U.S. to the Challenge Round. He ranked in the Top Ten 11 times. Wright was born December 19, 1879, lived in Brookline, Massachusetts, and died August 19, 1961.

1957

MAURICE McLOUGHLIN
(1890–1957)

Although his tournament career was relatively short, ending with World War I, the California Comet, as Maurice McLoughlin was known, caused a sensation with his spectacular service. In a classic victory over Norman Brookes in the 1914 Davis Cup Challenge Round, McLoughlin won the first set, 17–15, without losing his service. He won the U.S. Singles title in 1912 and 1913 and reached the finals in 1911, 1914, and 1915. He won the U.S. Doubles Championship with T. C. Bundy, 1912–14, the same years he was ranked No. 1 in singles. McLoughlin was born January 7, 1890, lived in San Francisco, and died December 10, 1957.

HAZEL HOTCHKISS WIGHTMAN
(1886–1974)

The donor of the Wightman Cup, Hazel Hotchkiss was the first dominating force in women's tennis. She won the U.S. Singles title, 1909–11, and again in 1919, and was defeated in the 1915 final by Molla Bjurstedt. Mrs. Wightman won six National Doubles titles, 1909–11 and in 1915, 1924, and 1928, the last two with Helen Wills. Mrs. Wightman won five Mixed Doubles, two Indoor Singles, nine Indoor Doubles, and 11 Senior Doubles Championships, altogether 45 U.S. titles. After donating the Wightman Cup in 1923, she played on the U.S. team five times. She was born in December 20, 1886, in California, and lived in Boston until her death on December 5, 1974.

MARY K. BROWNE
(1897–1971)

One of the finest volleyers in the women's ranks, Mary Browne won the U.S. Singles Championship, 1912–14, and lost in the final to Molla Bjurstedt Mallory in 1921. Mary Browne won the U.S. Doubles in 1912, 1913, 1914, 1921, and 1925, and played on the Wightman Cup team in 1925 and 1926. She was born in 1897, lived in Los Angeles, and died in 1971.

RICHARD NORRIS WILLIAMS II
(1892–1968)

Richard Williams won the U.S. Singles title in 1914 and 1916 and reached the final in 1913. He and Vinnie Richards were the U.S. Doubles champions in 1925 and 1926, the same years they played doubles in the Davis Cup against France, and in the Top Ten 10 other years. He played on five winning U.S. Davis Cup teams, captaining four of them. Williams was ranked No. 1 nationally in 1916 and No. 2 to Maurice McLoughlin in 1914 despite a victory over him for the singles title, and in the Top Ten 10 other years. He played on five winning U. S. Davis Cup teams, captaining four of them. Williams was born in

Geneva, Switzerland, on January 29, 1892, was a survivor of the *Titanic*, and died in 1968.

1958

WILLIAM M. JOHNSTON
(1894–1946)

"Little Bill" Johnston won the U.S. singles title from Maurice McLoughlin in 1915 and from "Big Bill" Tilden in 1919. Five times in the next six years it was Tilden who defeated Johnston in the finals, although three times it took him five sets to do it. Johnston also reached the final in 1916 and was ranked in the Top Ten 12 times. He won Wimbledon in 1923 and teamed with Peck Griffin to win the U.S. Doubles title in 1915, 1916, and 1920. He was the U.S. Clay Court champion in 1919 and the U.S. Mixed Doubles winner with Mary Browne in 1921. His record in Davis Cup Challenge Round matches was 13–3, and he played on the team that brought the Cup back from Australia in 1920. He was born November 2, 1894, in San Francisco and died May 1, 1946.

MOLLA BJURSTEDT MALLORY
(1892–1959)

After coming to the U.S. from Norway in 1915, Molla Bjurstedt Mallory won seven U.S. Singles titles, eight if one includes the wartime Patriotic Tournament. After defeating Helen Wills in the 1922 final, Mallory lost to her in the following two finals. With Eleonora Sears, she won the U.S. Doubles title in 1916 and the Patriotic Championship in 1917. She won the mixed doubles title with Irving C. Wright in 1917 and with Bill Tilden in 1922 and 1923. She played on five Wightman Cup teams between 1923 and 1928 and ranked in the Top Ten 13 times, No. 1 a record seven times. She was born in 1892 and died November 22, 1959 as Mrs. Franklin Mallory.

R. LINDLEY MURRAY
(1893–1970)

The first time Bill Tilden reached the U.S.

Singles final, in 1918, he was turned back in three sets by Lindley Murray, who had won the Patriotic Tournament the year before. Murray also reached the semifinals in 1916, losing to Bill Johnston. A left-handed player with a strong serve, Murray was ranked No. 1 in the nation in 1918. He was born November 3, 1893, lived in Buffalo, and died in 1970.

MAUD BARGER-WALLACH
(1871–1954)

Maud Barger-Wallach won the U.S. Singles title from Evelyn Sears in 1908 at 38, the oldest winner, and reached the final two other times, losing to Helen Homans in 1906 and to Hazel Hotchkiss in 1909. A patron of the Newport Invitational Tournament much of her life, she was born in 1871 and died April 2, 1954.

1959

WILLIAM T. TILDEN II (1893–1953)

Considered by many the greatest player ever, Big Bill Tilden dominated tennis in the 1920s and was an important factor in the fledgling professional ranks until his death in 1953. He won his first U.S. title, mixed doubles, with Mary Browne in 1913. After losing the 1918 final to Lindley Murray and the 1919 final to Bill Johnston, Tilden reeled off six consecutive National Singles Championships and added a record seventh in 1929. He won Wimbledon in 1920 and 1921 and, at age 37 in 1930, defeated Wilmer Allison in straight sets for a third Wimbledon crown. He ranked No. 1 a record 10 times between 1920 and 1929. Tilden was the U.S. Doubles champion five times, three of them with Vinnie Richards, and won 13 straight singles matches in Davis Cup Challenge Round competition between 1920 and 1926. He turned professional in 1930 winning the U.S. Pro title in 1931 and 1935, and was still touring at the time of his death on June 5, 1953. He was born in Philadelphia on February 10, 1893.

HELEN WILLS MOODY (1905–   )

One of the legends of women's tennis, Helen Wills won eight Wimbledon and seven U.S. Singles titles, both records. She ruled Wimbledon, 1927–30, and won in 1932, 1933, 1935, and 1938 winding up with a record winning streak of 50 matches intact. Her U.S. reign was 1923–25, 1927–29, and was completed in 1931. Her record of 45 straight match wins ended in the 1933 final against Helen Jacobs. She won the French singles 1928–30 and in 1932. She won the Wimbledon Doubles with Hazel Wightman in 1924 and Elizabeth Ryan in 1927 and 1930. Helen's U.S. Doubles Championships were won with Wightman in 1924 and 1928, Mrs. J. B. Jessup in 1922, and Mary Browne in 1925. Helen won 18 of 20 singles matches in Wightman Cup competition and took gold medals in singles and doubles at the 1924 Paris Olympics. She ranked No. 1 in the U.S. a record seven times. Born October 6, 1905, she now lives in California as Mrs. Helen Moody.

1960 (No inductees)

1961

VINCENT RICHARDS (1903–59)

The only U.S. title to elude Vince Richards was in singles, which eluded a lot of quality players when Bill Tilden was at the height of his career. Richards became the youngest male player to win a national title when at age 15 he and Tilden took the U.S. Doubles crown in 1918. Richards went on to win four more U.S. Doubles Championships, in 1921 and 1922 with Tilden and in 1925 and 1926 with Richard Williams. Richards won the mixed doubles in 1919 with Marion Zinderstein and 1924 with Helen Wills, and captured gold medals in both singles and doubles at the 1924 Olympics. In 1926 Richards became the first "name" player to turn pro, and in a career that spanned two decades he won most of the world's professional titles, including the U.S. Pro Singles four times. His last, in 1945, was the U.S. Pro Doubles title with

Tilden. Richards was born March 20, 1903, in Yonkers, New York, and died September 28, 1959.

FRANCIS T. HUNTER (1894–   )

When Bill Tilden won his seventh U.S. Singles title in 1929, he needed five sets to defeat Frank Hunter, who had extended Henri Cochet to five sets in the final the year before. Hunter's greatest successes were indoors, where he was U.S. Singles champion in 1922 and U.S. Doubles champion with Vince Richards in 1922, 1924, and 1929. Hunter and Richards won the gold medal in doubles at the 1924 Olympics, and Hunter paired with Tilden to take the U.S. Doubles title in 1927. In the 1928 International championship in Holland, Hunter defeated Jean Borotra in the final. Hunter joined Tilden and Richards in the pro ranks in 1931. Hunter was born June 28, 1894, and lives in New York.

MALCOLM G. CHACE (1875–1955)

Although he gave up tournament tennis at the age of 21 upon his graduation from Yale, Malcolm Chace already had made his mark in the sport. He and Robert Wrenn won the U.S. Doubles title in 1895 and he had reached the U.S. Singles semifinals the year before. Chace won the U.S. interscholastic championship in 1892 and the Intercollegiate Singles and Doubles titles, 1893–95. He was a member of the U.S. team that played the English at Newport in 1900, before the donation of the Davis Cup. He was born in Rhode Island on March 12, 1875, and died July 16, 1955.

HAROLD H. HACKETT (1878–1937)

The captain of the 1913 Davis Cup team, Harold Hackett won the decisive doubles match with Maurice McLoughlin to defeat the British Isles, 3–2. Hackett and Fred Alexander reeled off four straight U.S. Doubles titles, 1907–10, and reached the finals in 1905 and 1906. He paired with Alexander to win three Indoor titles, 1906–8, and in 1912 Hackett won the U.S. Clay Court Doubles title with W. Merrill Hall. Hackett was a member of many committees of the USLTA and the West Side Tennis Club and served on the Davis Cup Committee in the 1920s. He was born July 17, 1878, lived in New York, and died November 20, 1937.

FRED ALEXANDER (1880–1969)

Known as part of the legendary doubles team of Hackett and Alexander, which won four consecutive U.S. titles, Fred Alexander also won the 1917 Patriotic Tournament Doubles title with Harold Throckmorton and four Indoor titles with Hackett. In 1914 he organized junior tournaments in New York, thus beginning the Junior Boy and Girl Development Program, and in 1917 he helped organize the Patriotic Tournaments, which benefited the Red Cross. Alexander won the Intercollegiate singles for Princeton in 1901 and played Davis Cup in 1908, the year he was the first foreigner to win the Australian title. He was born August 14, 1880, lived in New York, and died in 1969.

1962

JOHN HOPE DOEG (1908–   )

Best remembered for his powerful serve and topspin forehand, the left-handed John Doeg defeated Bill Tilden and Frank Shields en route to the 1930 U.S. Singles Championship and teamed with George Lott to win the U.S. Doubles title in 1929 and 1930. He was the country's junior champion in 1926 and a Wimbledon Doubles finalist in 1930. He was born December 7, 1908, in Mexico, and lives in California.

H. ELLSWORTH VINES, JR. (1911–   )

The pinnacle of Ellsworth Vines' career was 1932, when he won his second consecutive U.S. Singles title, teamed with Keith Gledhill to win the National Doubles crown, and also won the Wimbledon Singles. He and

Gledhill won the Junior Doubles Championship in 1929 and the Clay Court crown in 1931. In the 1932 Davis Cup Challenge Round against France, Vines beat Henri Cochet in five sets but lost to Jean Borotra in four. The following year Vines turned pro. He later embarked on a successful career as a professional golfer. He was born in Los Angeles on September 28, 1911.

HELEN HULL JACOBS (1908–   )

One of tennis' great rivalries existed between Helen Jacobs and Helen Wills, who both grew up in Berkeley, California, and it was usually the latter who won. Nevertheless, Helen Jacobs was the U.S. champion, 1932–35, beating Wills in the 1933 final, and finally won Wimbledon in 1936, on her fifth visit to the finals. She teamed with Sarah Palfrey to win the U.S. Doubles title in 1932, 1933, and 1935. In 1924 and 1925 Helen Jacobs was the U.S. girls' champion and in 1934 she teamed with George Lott to win the National Mixed Doubles crown. She played on the Wightman Cup team for 12 years. She was born in Globe, Arizona, on August 8, 1908, and lives on Long Island, New York.

1963

SARAH PALFREY FABYAN COOKE (1912–   )

While she won the U.S. Singles title in 1941 and 1945, and reached the final in 1934 and 1935, it is Sarah Palfrey's nine U.S. Doubles titles for which she is best known. After winning with Betty Nuthall in 1930, she won with Helen Jacobs in 1932, 1934, and 1935, with Alice Marble, 1937–40, and with Margaret Osborne in 1941. Sarah won the Wimbledon Doubles with Marble in 1938 and 1939, and won seven Wightman Cup matches, with Jacobs 1933–36 and with Marble 1937–39. She was born September 18, 1912, in Sharon, Massachusetts, and now lives in New York as Mrs. Sarah Palfrey Danzig.

WILMER ALLISON (1904–77)

Wilmer Allison won the U.S. Singles title in 1935 and teamed with John Van Ryn to win the National Doubles Championship in 1931 and 1935 and the Wimbledon title in 1929 and 1939; they won more Davis Cup matches (14) than any other American team. In 1930 he lost in the Wimbledon Singles final to Bill Tilden after defeating Henri Cochet in the semifinals, and he extended Fred Perry to five sets in the 1934 U.S. final. He was born in San Antonio, Texas, on December 8, 1904, and died on April 20, 1977.

JOHN VAN RYN (1906–   )

John Van Ryn teamed with Wilmer Allison in doubles to win the U.S. titles in 1931 and 1935 and reach the finals in 1930, 1932, 1934, and 1936. They also won Wimbledon in 1929 and 1930 and reached the final in 1935. They won more Davis Cup matches than any other U.S. pair, 14. In the 1929 Davis Cup Challenge Round they defeated Henri Cochet and Jean Borotra and in 1932 they beat Cochet and Jacques Brugnon. Van Ryn and George Lott won the Wimbledon and French Doubles titles in 1931. Van Ryn was born on June 30, 1906, in Newport News, Virginia.

JULIAN S. MYRICK (1880–1969)

A former president of the USLTA (1920–22), chairman of the Davis Cup and Wightman committees, Julian Myrick—the Elder Statesman of Tennis—was elected to the Hall of Fame for his distinguished service to the game. During his administration several programs for the development of junior tennis were begun, and he was largely responsible for the inauguration of the Wightman Cup competition and scheduling the first match in 1923 at the new Forest Hills Stadium. He was born March 1, 1880, lived in New York, and died January 4, 1969.

1964

J. DONALD BUDGE (1915–   )

After winning the U.S. and Wimbledon championships in 1937, Don Budge scored the first Grand Slam in 1938, sweeping Wimbledon, Forest Hills, and the French and Australian titles. With Gene Mako he won the Wimbledon Doubles in 1937 and 1938 and the U.S. Doubles in 1936 and 1938. He was a member of the team that won the Davis Cup in 1937 and defended it in 1938. In 1939 he began a distinguished professional career. He was born June 13, 1915, in California.

ALICE MARBLE (1913–   )

In addition to the U.S. Singles title in 1936 and 1938–40, Alice Marble won Wimbledon in 1939 and shared the U.S. Doubles title with Sarah Palfrey, 1937–40. Marble won the Wimbledon doubles title with Helen Jacobs in 1938 and was ranked No. 1 in the U.S., 1936–40. She won the Wimbledon Mixed Doubles Championship in 1937 and 1938 with Don Budge and in 1939 with Bobby Riggs. She also won four U.S. Mixed Doubles titles, in 1936 with George Mako, in 1938 with Budge, in 1939 with Harry Hopman, and in 1940 with Riggs. Marble ranked No. 1 in the U.S. a record five straight years, 1936–40. She was born September 28, 1913, in California.

GEORGE M. LOTT, JR. (1906–   )

George Lott won the U.S. Doubles title five times with three different partners. He reigned in 1928 with John Hennessey, in 1929 and 1930 with John Doeg, and in 1933 and 1934 with Lester Stoefen. Lott won the 1931 Wimbledon and French Doubles titles with John Van Ryn and the 1934 Wimbledon Championship with Stoefen. Lott reached the U.S. Singles final in 1931, bowing to Ellsworth Vines in four sets and was ranked in the Top Ten nine times. Lott won three U.S. Mixed Doubles titles and one at Wimbledon and competed for the Davis Cup team 1928–31 and 1933–34. He turned pro in 1934. Lott was born October 16, 1906, in Springfield, Illinois.

SIDNEY B. WOOD, JR. (1911–   )

At 19 Sidney Wood became the second youngest Wimbledon champion and the only one ever to receive a walk-over in the final when Frank Shields withdrew due to an injury in 1931. Wood reached the U.S. Singles final in 1935, when he was defeated by Wilmer Allison. Ranked 10 times in the Top Ten, Wood also reached the U.S. Singles semifinals in 1934 and 1938 and played on the Davis Cup team in 1931 and 1934. He was born November 1, 1911, in Black Rock, Connecticut, and lives in New York.

FRANCIS X. SHIELDS (1910–75)

Frank Shields reached the U.S. Singles final in 1930, bowing to John Doeg, 10–8, 1–6, 6–4, 16–14. Shields gained the Wimbledon final a year later but defaulted to Sidney Wood because of an injured knee. Shields reached the national semifinals in 1928 and 1933 and the Wimbledon semis in 1934 and teamed with Frank Parker to gain the 1933 U.S. Doubles final, which they lost to George Lott and Lester Stoefen. He was ranked in the Top Ten 10 times, No. 1 in 1933. Shields also played on the Davis Cup team in 1931–32 and 1934, and was captain in 1951. He was born November 18, 1910, in Oklahoma City, and died August 19, 1975.

GEORGE T. ADEE (1874–1948)

A Walter Camp All-America quarterback at Yale in 1894, George Adee was elected to the Hall of Fame because of his devoted service to tennis. He served as president of the USTA 1916–18, and the Davis Cup Committee and participated on the Amateur Rules Committee. He was born in 1874, lived in New York, and died in 1948.

1965

W. DONALD McNEILL (1918–   )

Although his career was interrupted by World War II, and the Davis Cup matches were suspended when he was in his prime,

Don McNeill still broke into the Top Ten six times and was ranked No. 1 in 1940. That year he defeated Jack Kramer in the U.S. semifinal and Bobby Riggs in the final at Forest Hills. In 1939 McNeill won the French Championships in singles, and in doubles with Charles Harris. In 1944 McNeill won the U.S. Doubles title with Robert Falkenburg and in 1946 reached the final with Frank Guernsey. McNeill was born April 30, 1918, in Chickasha, Oklahoma.

PAULINE BETZ (1919–   )

Pauline Betz won the U.S. Singles title in 1942, 1943, 1944, and 1946 and was runner-up in 1941 and 1945. Wimbledon was suspended during World War II, but when it resumed in 1946 she breezed to the Singles Championship without losing a set. In the French Championships that year she reached both the singles final and the doubles final, with Doris Hart. Betz also won her two singles matches and teamed with Hart to win at doubles in the 1946 Wightman Cup matches. She was born August 6, 1916, in Dayton, Ohio, and lives in Washington, D.C., married to sportswriter Bob Addie.

ELLEN FORDE HANSELL (1869–1937)

When the first U.S. Women's Championships were held at Philadelphia in 1887, Ellen Hansell emerged the winner. She was honored, along with Richard Sears, the first men's champion, at the Golden Jubilee celebration of the USLTA at Forest Hills in 1931. She was born on September 18, 1869, in Philadelphia and died in 1937 as Mrs. Ellen Allerdice.

JAMES H. VAN ALEN (1902–   )

Although he developed the Van Alen Streamlined Scoring System, which has helped to simplify tennis, James Van Alen, somewhat ironically, was a national champion in court tennis, the game's ancient forerunner. As president of the Newport Casino, he was responsible for the establishment of the Hall of Fame there, and he brought the first pro tournaments to the Casino in 1965. His tie-breakers, eliminating deuce sets, were adopted in the U.S. in 1970 and generally after that. He was born September 19, 1902, in Newport, Rhode Island.

WATSON WASHBURN (1894–1973)

With Richard Williams, Watson Washburn won the Davis Cup Challenge Round Doubles in 1921, reached the U.S. finals in 1921 and 1923, and was a Wimbledon finalist in 1924. He was a founder and long-time member of the board of directors of the Tennis Hall of Fame, and also served on many USLTA committees. He was born June 13, 1894, lived in New York, and died in 1973.

1966

JOSEPH R. HUNT (1919–44)

A lieutenant in the Navy, Joseph Hunt won the U.S. Singles Championship while on leave after serving in the Atlantic in 1943. He defeated Bill Talbert in the semifinals and Jack Kramer for the title. In 1939 and 1940 Hunt reached the semifinals, losing to Bobby Riggs both times. Hunt also played on the 1939 Davis Cup team. He was born February 17, 1919, in California and died in an accident while training to be a pilot on February 2, 1944.

FREDERICK R. SCHROEDER, JR. (1921–   )

In 1942 Ted Schroeder defeated Frank Parker for the U.S. Singles title. In 1949 Schroeder met Pancho Gonzales in the final winning the first two sets, 18–16 and 6–2, but losing the last three, 1–6, 2–6, 4–6. That same year he beat Jaroslav Drobny for the Wimbledon Championship. Schroeder teamed with Jack Kramer to win the U.S. Doubles title in 1940, 1941, and 1947, and was a finalist with Sidney Wood in 1942 and Frank Parker in 1948. Schroeder won the U.S. Mixed Doubles title with Louise Brough in 1942. He played on the teams that beat Australia for the

Davis Cup in 1946, 1947, 1948, and 1949 and lost to the Australians in 1950 and 1951. Schroeder was ranked in the Top Ten nine times, No. 1 in 1942. He was born in Newark, New Jersey.

FRANK A. PARKER (1916–   )

Frank Parker ranked in the Top Ten 17 consecutive years, 1933–49, No. 1 in 1944–45. While an Army sergeant, he won the U.S. Singles title in 1944 and 1945. In 1948 and 1949 he was the French Champion. He won the U.S. Doubles title with Jack Kramer in 1943 and the Wimbledon and French championships with Pancho Gonzales in 1949. Parker and Don Budge played singles on the 1937 team that brought the Davis Cup back to the U.S. after a 10-year hiatus. Parker also played on the 1937, 1939, 1946, and 1948 Davis Cup teams and won the U.S. Clay Court title five times. He later turned professional. He was born in Milwaukee on January 31, 1916.

THEODORE ROOSEVELT PELL (1879–1967)

Theodore Roosevelt Pell was inducted into the Hall of Fame not only for his playing ability but for the esteem in which he was held in the world of tennis. He was the U.S. Indoor champion in 1907, 1908, and 1911 in singles and 1905, 1909–11 in doubles, and was particularly admired for his backhand. He was born in 1879, lived in Sands Point, New York, and died in 1967.

1967

ROBERT L. RIGGS (1918–   )

Bobby Riggs was the U.S. Singles champion in 1939 and 1941 as well as a finalist in 1940, when he also won the U.S. Indoor title. He won the Wimbledon singles, doubles and mixed doubles titles in 1939, teaming with Elwood Cooke and Alice Marble and in 1940 he and Alice Marble were the U.S. Mixed Doubles champions. Riggs played on the Davis Cup team in 1938 and 1939. He was born in Los Angeles on February 25, 1918.

WILLIAM F. TALBERT (1918–)

One of tennis' premier doubles players, Bill Talbert won the U.S. title with Gardnar Mulloy in 1942, 1945, 1946, and 1948 and reached the finals in 1943 with Dave Freeman, 1944 with Pancho Segura, 1947 with Billy Sidwell, and 1950 and 1953 with Mulloy. Talbert and Tony Trabert won the French title in 1950. Talbert and Margaret Osborne won the U.S. Mixed Doubles, 1943–46. Talbert was the U.S. Clay Court Singles champion in 1945, the indoor champion in 1948 and 1951, and a national finalist in 1944 and 1945, losing to Frank Parker both years. Talbert played on the Davis Cup team in 1946 and 1948–53 and was its captain, 1953–57. He was born in Cincinnati on September 4, 1918, and lives in New York.

MARGARET OSBORNE duPONT (1918–)

After winning her first U.S. Doubles title with Sarah Palfrey in 1941, Margaret Osborne teamed with Louise Brough in the most successful tandem of all time, winning the next nine U.S. titles and three more, 1955–57. Osborne and Brough won Wimbledon in 1946, 1948–50, and in 1954, and the French Championship in 1946, 1947, and 1949. Brough and Osborne were fierce rivals in singles, however. Brough won the 1947 national title over Osborne, and Osborne defeated Brough, 4–6, 6–4, 15–13, the following year for the first of three successive U.S. Championships. Osborne was also a finalist in 1944. She won Wimbledon in 1947, lost to Brough in the finals in 1949 and 1950, and won the French Championship in 1946 and 1949. She played on the Wightman Cup team, 1946–50, 1954, 1955, and 1957, and won 10 singles and seven doubles matches without a loss. She was born March 4, 1918, in Joseph, Oregon, and lives in El Paso, Texas.

LOUISE BROUGH (1923–)

In addition to her legendary doubles accomplishments with Margaret Osborne, Louise Brough was the U.S. Singles champion in 1947 and reached the finals five other times. She won Wimbledon in 1948, 1949, 1950, and 1955, and was a finalist in 1946, 1952, and 1954. She won the U.S. Mixed Doubles in 1942, 1947, 1948, and 1949 with four different partners. She won the Wimbledon Mixed Doubles in 1946 and 1950, ranked in the Top Ten 16 times, and compiled a Wightman Cup record of 12 singles and 10 doubles victories without a defeat. She was born in Oklahoma City on March 11, 1923, lives in California, and married Dr. Edwin Clapp.

1968

ALLISON DANZIG (1898–)

The first journalist to be inducted into the Hall of Fame, Allison Danzig was the tennis writer for the New York *Times* for 45 years. In addition to newspaper articles, he wrote many magazine articles and books on tennis and other sports and covered several Olympic Games. He was born in Waco, Texas, on February 27, 1898, graduated from Cornell and lives in Roslyn, New York.

JOHN A. KRAMER (1921–)

The dominant player immediately after World War II, Jack Kramer won the 1946 and 1947 U.S. titles and the 1947 Wimbledon Championship. He won the 1947 Wimbledon Doubles with Robert Falkenburg and the U.S. title that year with Ted Schroeder as well as in 1940–41 and 1943. But it was as leader of the professional tour that Kramer gained his greatest fame, both as a player, promoter and innovator. In 1969 he conceived the present Grand Prix structure for the men's tournament game. He was born in Las Vegas on August 5, 1921.

RICHARD A. GONZALES (1928–)

After winning the National Singles title in 1948 and 1949, Pancho Gonzales turned professional at the age of 21. While a cannonball service highlighted his game, it was his stamina that provided some of tennis' classic matches. In the 1949 U.S. final he lost the first two sets to Ted Schroeder, 16–18 and 2–6, but won the next three. In the first round of Wimbledon in 1969, Gonzales and Charlie Pasarell played the longest singles match in the history of the Big Four tournaments, Gonzales again coming from two sets down, to win, 22–24, 1–6, 16–14, 6–3, 11–9. He was 41 at the time. His greatest success came prior to open tennis on pro tours, winning a record eight U.S. Pro singles and five doubles between 1953 and 1969. Gonzales was born in Los Angeles on May 9, 1928.

MAUREEN CONNOLLY (1934–69)

"Little Mo" Connolly became the youngest player to win the U. S. Singles when, at age 16, she conquered Forest Hills in 1951. It was her first of three successive National Championships. In 1953 she became the first woman to win the Grand Slam as she took the U.S., French, Australian, and the second of her three straight Wimbledon titles. She helped the U.S. win the Wightman Cup, 1951–54, winning all seven of her singles matches. A riding accident ended her tournament career prematurely. She was born in San Diego on September 17, 1934, and died June 21, 1969 as Mrs. Norman Brinker.

ELEONORA SEARS (1881–1967)

A trailblazer in women's sports, Eleonora Sears also was one of the game's top doubles players in the early part of this century. She won the U.S. title with Hazel Hotchkiss in 1911 and 1915 and with Molla Bjurstedt in 1916 and 1917. She won the U.S. Mixed Doubles in 1916 with Willis Davis. She reached the Singles Challenge Round in 1911, 1912, and 1916. She was born in 1881, lived in Boston, and died on March 26, 1967.

1969

DORIS HART (1925–   )

Doris Hart won the U.S. Singles title in 1954 and 1955 and reached the final in 1949,

1950, 1952, and 1953. She won Wimbledon in 1951 and reached the final in 1947, 1948, and 1953. She was the Australian champion in 1949, the French champion in 1950 and 1952, the Australian runner-up in 1950, and a French finalist in 1947, 1951, and 1953. She and Shirley Fry won the U.S. Doubles title, 1951–54, Wimbledon, 1951–53; and the French Championship, 1950–53. With Patricia Canning Todd, Hart won Wimbledon in 1947 and the French title in 1948. Hart won five consecutive U.S. Mixed Doubles titles, in 1951 and 1952 with Frank Sedgman and from 1953–55 with Vic Seixas. She was a member of the winning Wightman Cup teams, 1946–55, compiling records of 15–1 in singles and 7–1 in doubles. She was born in St. Louis on June 20, 1925.

ARTHUR LARSEN (1925–   )

Art Larsen, a left-hander, was the U.S. Singles champion in 1950. He reached the French final in 1954 and the U.S. and Australian semifinals in 1951. He was ranked in the Top Ten eight times, 1949–56, and in 1951 and 1952 he played on the Davis Cup team. By winning the Clay Court title in 1952, the Indoor in 1953, and the Hard Court in 1950 and 1952, he was one of two men to win all four national championships. His career ended prematurely when he received head injuries in a motorcycle accident. He was born in San Leandro, California on April 6, 1925.

CHARLES S. GARLAND (1898–1971)

A member of the 1920 U.S. team that reclaimed the Davis Cup from Australia, Chuck Garland was also the 1920 Wimbledon Doubles champion with Richard Williams. Garland was enshrined in the Hall of Fame because of his contributions as an officer and committeeman of the USLTA. He was born October 29, 1898, lived in Baltimore, and died January 28, 1971.

MARIE WAGNER (1883–1975)

Marie Wagner won the U.S. Indoor Championship six times, in 1908, 1909, 1911, 1913,

1914, and 1917, and lost in the U.S. Singles final to Mary Browne in 1914. She also won four Indoor doubles titles and served as a member of tournament and ranking committees. She organized the Junior Wightman Cup matches in New York in 1939. She was born February 3, 1883, and lived in Freeport, New York. She died April 1, 1975.

KARL H. BEHR (1885–1949)

Karl Behr ranked in the Top Ten seven times between 1906 and 1915, and was No. 3 in 1907, when he defeated William Larned in several matches. Against Australasia in the 1907 Davis Cup competition, Behr teamed with Beals Wright to defeat the legendary tandem of Norman Brookes and Tony Wilding. Behr was born May 30, 1885, and died October 15, 1949.

1970

TONY TRABERT (1930–   )

Tony Trabert won the 1953 and 1955 U.S. Singles titles and breezed through Wimbledon in 1955 without losing a set. He was the French champion in 1954 and 1955 and was the last American to win that title as 1980 began. In doubles he teamed with Vic Seixas to capture the 1954 U.S. title, the 1955 Australian crown, and the 1954 and 1955 French Championships. Trabert won the U.S. Hard Court title in 1953 and the Clay Court and Indoor titles in 1955. He played on the Davis Cup team, 1951–55, combining with Seixas to win in 1954, and turned pro in 1955, winning the U.S. Pro doubles in 1956. He became Davis Cup captain in 1976. He was born in Cincinnati on August 16, 1930.

SHIRLEY FRY (1927–   )

Shirley Fry and Doris Hart broke the spell of Louise Brough and Margaret Osborne in 1951 by ending their streak at eight U.S. Doubles titles and beginning a run of four of their own. They also won Wimbledon, 1951–53, and the French title, 1950–53. In singles Fry

won the U.S. and Wimbledon championships in 1956 and the French title in 1951, when she also reached the finals at Wimbledon and Forest Hills. She also won the Australian in 1957, becoming one of nine players to hold all the Big Four titles. She played on the Wightman Cup team in 1949 and 1950–56 and ranked in the Top Ten 13 times. She was born June 30, 1927, in Akron, Ohio, and became Mrs. Karl Irvin.

CLARENCE J. GRIFFIN (1888–1973)

"Peck" Griffin and Bill Johnston won the U.S. Doubles Championship in 1915, 1916, and 1920. With John Strachan, Griffin reached the U.S. Doubles final in 1913 and won the Clay Court Doubles title the following year. Griffin was also the 1914 Clay Court Singles champion. He was born September 4, 1888, in San Francisco and died in 1973.

PERRY JONES (1888–1970)

Known as "Mr. Tennis" on the West Coast, Perry Jones devoted much of his life to the game. As director of the Pacific Southwest Championships and president of the Southern California Tennis Association for more than 25 years, he helped raise funds and provide equipment and instruction for junior players. He was the nonplaying captain of the victorious 1958 U.S. Davis Cup team. He was born May 6, 1888, and died February 18, 1970.

1971

E. VICTOR SEIXAS (1923–   )

Between 1951 and 1957 Vic Seixas played in a U.S. record 55 matches in seven years of Davis Cup competition. He won the U.S. Singles title in 1954 and reached the finals in 1951 and 1953, the year he also won Wimbledon. He won the U.S. Doubles Championship with Mervyn Rose of Australia in 1952 and Tony Trabert in 1954. Seixas and Trabert won the Australian and French Doubles titles in

1953 and paired to seize the Davis Cup in 1954. Seixas and Doris Hart won every mixed doubles title at Wimbledon and Forest Hills, 1953–55, and he won the 1956 Wimbledon Mixed Doubles crown with Shirley Fry. Seixas was ranked No. 1 in 1951, 1954, and 1957 among his 13 times in the Top Ten between 1942 and 1966, a record for longevity. He was born in Philadelphia on August 30, 1923.

ALTHEA GIBSON (1927–   )

The first prominent black player, Althea Gibson won the singles championships at both Wimbledon and Forest Hills in 1957 and 1958 and reached the U.S. final in 1956, when she was beaten by Shirley Fry. She broke the color barrier at the U.S. Championships by first entering in 1950. Gibson won the U.S. Clay Court title in 1957 and played on the Wightman Cup team in 1957 and 1958. She won the Australian Doubles Championship in 1957 with Fry and reached the U.S. Doubles finals in 1957 with Darlene Hard and in 1958 with Maria Bueno. Gibson was the top-ranked player in 1957 and 1958. She later embarked on a career as a professional golfer. She was born in Silver, South Carolina, on August 25, 1927, and grew up in New York. She was married to William Darben.

ELIZABETH H. MOORE
(1877–1959)

One of the top players at the turn of the century, Elizabeth Moore won the U.S. Singles title in 1896, 1901, 1903, and 1905, and reached the finals in 1891, 1892, 1897, 1902, and 1904, thus standing as a finalist a record nine times. She won the Women's Doubles title in 1896 with Juliette P. Atkinson and in 1903 with Carrie B. Neely. Moore also won the Mixed Doubles Championship in 1902 and 1904 with Wylie C. Grant. She also won the Indoor title in 1907. Moore was born June 6, 1877, lived in Ridgewood, New Jersey, and died January 22, 1959.

ARTHUR C. NIELSEN (1894–   )

One of tennis' most generous patrons, A. C. Nielsen, chairman of the Nielsen market research company, which provides television ratings, has donated more than $3 million for the construction of tennis and squash facilities. He was captain of the University of Wisconsin tennis team, 1916–18 and won the U.S. Father and Son Doubles title in 1946 and 1948 with his son, Arthur, Jr. He was born on January 2, 1894.

1972

ELIZABETH RYAN
(1892–1979)

One of the top women's doubles players of all times, Elizabeth Ryan won 12 Wimbledon doubles titles, including six with Suzanne Lenglen and two with Helen Wills, and shared seven Wimbledon Mixed Doubles championships with five different partners to set a Wimbledon record for total championships that stood until Billie Jean King won a 20th in 1979. Ryan won the U.S. Doubles title in 1923 and the Mixed Doubles in 1926 and 1933. She won four French Doubles championships, in 1930, 1932, 1933, and 1934. In singles she reached the Wimbledon finals in 1921 and 1930. She also gained the U.S. final in 1926, losing to Molla Bjurstedt Mallory, 4–6, 6–4, 9–7. She has the distinction of being the last women's champion of Imperial Russia, a title she won in 1914. She was born on February 5, 1892, in Santa Monica, California, and died in London, July 6, 1979, ironically the day before King eclipsed her record.

BRYAN M. GRANT, JR.
(1910–   )

"Bitsy" Grant was the U.S. Clay Court champion in 1930, 1934, and 1935. He won the Southern Championship 11 times between

1927 and 1952 and was a U.S. Singles semifinalist in 1935 and 1936. He competed for the U.S. Davis Cup team, 1935–37, and was ranked in the Top Ten nine times, No. 3 twice. He was the U.S. Senior champion twice, the Senior 55 champion four times, and the Senior Clay Court champion six times. He ranked in the Top Ten 14 times, No. 1 in 1952, the year he reached the U.S. Singles final at 37. He was born in Atlanta December 25, 1910.

GARDNAR MULLOY (1914–   )

Gardnar Mulloy and Bill Talbert won the U.S. Doubles title in 1942, 1945, 1946, and 1948 and reached the finals in 1950 and 1953. In 1957, at age 44, Mulloy teamed with Budge Patty to win the Wimbledon doubles title and reach the U.S. final. Mulloy played on seven U.S. Davis Cup teams and was the playing captain twice. He ranked in the Top Ten 14 times, No. 1 in 1952, the year he reached the U.S. singles final at 37. He was born in Miami on November 22, 1914.

1973

DARLENE R. HARD (1936–   )

The U.S. Singles champion in 1960 and 1961 and a finalist in 1958 and 1962, Darlene Hard also won the French Championship in 1960 and reached the Wimbledon finals twice, in 1957, when she was beaten by Althea Gibson and in 1959, when she lost to Maria Bueno. Hard won four Wimbledon Doubles titles, including two with Bueno and one with Gibson, and three Wimbledon Mixed Doubles crowns, two of them with Rod Laver. She also won four U.S. and three French Women's Doubles championships and two French Mixed Doubles titles. She played on five Wightman Cup teams, one Federation Cup team and ranked No. 1 in the nation four times. She was born in Los Angeles on January 6, 1936, and won the Intercollegiate title for Pomona in 1958.

C. GENE MAKO (1916–   )

Gene Mako and Don Budge won the U.S. Doubles title in 1936 and 1938 and the Wimbledon crown in 1937 and 1938. In 1936 Mako won the U.S. Mixed Doubles title with Alice Marble. In the 1938 Singles final he lost to Budge in four sets as Budge went on to win the Grand Slam. Mako also played on the Davis Cup team in 1935–38. He was born January 24, 1916, in Hungary, grew up in California and won the Intercollegiate title for Southern California in 1934.

ALASTAIR B. MARTIN (1902–   )

Honored for his distinguished service to tennis, Alastair Martin served as president of the USLTA in 1969–70 and as vice president in 1967 and 1968, when he supported the British in their revolt that led to the sanctioning of open tournaments. In 1951 he founded the Eastern Tennis Patrons Association, and since retiring as head of the USLTA has served as president of the National Tennis Foundation, which recently merged with the Hall of Fame. In court tennis, Martin was one of the best players developed in this country. He was the amateur singles champion eight times and won the doubles title 10 times. He was born in 1902 and lives in Katonah, New York.

1974

BERTHA TOWNSEND
(1869–1909)

Bertha Townsend won the second and third U.S. Singles Championships, in 1888 and 1889, when they were held at the Philadelphia Cricket Club. She was the first left-handed champion. She was born in Philadelphia March 7, 1869, and died on May 12, 1909 as Mrs. Bertha Townsend Toumlin.

JULIETTE P. ATKINSON
(Dates unavailable)

One of the first outstanding women in tennis, Juliette Atkinson won the U.S. Singles title in 1895, 1897, and 1898 and was runner-up in 1896 and 1899. She won the U.S. Doubles Championship, 1894–98 and 1901–2 and the Mixed Doubles, 1894–96. She lived in Brooklyn.

FRED H. HOVEY *(1868–1945)*

Fred Hovey won the U.S. Singles title in 1895, defeating Robert Wrenn in the final. Hovey reached the final in 1892, 1893, and 1896, and the Challenge Round in 1891. Hovey and Clarence Hobart won the U.S. Doubles title in 1893 and 1894 as well as the championship at the 1893 World's Columbian Exposition at Chicago. In 1890–91 he won the Intercollegiate singles title for Harvard. Hovey was born on October 7, 1868, lived in Boston and died on October 18, 1945.

ROBERT FALKENBURG *(1926–   )*

Known for his powerful serve, Bob Falkenburg defeated John Bromwich, 7–5, 0–6, 6–2, 3–6, 7–5, to win the 1948 Wimbledon title, surviving three match points. Falkenburg won the U.S. Doubles Championship in 1944 with Don McNeill and reached the finals in 1945 with Jack Tuero. Falkenburg and Doris Hart reached the 1945 National Mixed Doubles final. He represented Brazil in the 1954 and 1955 Davis Cup competition. He was born January 29, 1926, in Los Angeles, and won the Intercollegiate title for Southern California.

1975

ELLEN C. ROOSEVELT
(1868–1954)

The U.S. Women's Singles champion in 1890, Ellen Roosevelt also won the National Doubles title that year with her sister, Grace Roosevelt, and the 1893 Mixed Doubles Championship with Clarence Hobart. She beat Grace for the 1890 title, the only U.S. final between sisters. She was born in 1868 in Hyde Park, New York, and died September 26, 1954.

LAWRENCE A. BAKER
(Dates unavailable)

A founder of the National Tennis Foundation, Lawrence Baker also is a former president of the USLTA 1948–50. He was a Davis Cup captain and later sponsored the Baker Cup, a tournament for seniors between the U.S. and Canada. He lives in East Hampton, New York.

FRED J. PERRY *(1909–   )*

One of the premier British players, Fred Perry won Wimbledon in 1934, 1935, and 1936, the U.S. Championship in 1933, 1934, and 1936, the French title in 1935 and 1936, and the Australian crown in 1934. He won the 1933 French and 1934 Australian Doubles titles with George Hughes, the U.S. Mixed Doubles with Sarah Palfrey in 1932, the Wimbledon Mixed Doubles with Dorothy Round in 1935 and 1936, and the French Mixed Doubles with Betty Nuthall in 1932. He was a member of the British Davis Cup team, 1931–36, helping his country win the Cup 1933–36. Then he turned pro. He was born May 18, 1909, in Stockport, Cheshire, England.

1976

JEAN-RENÉ LACOSTE
(1905–   )

The year 1976 was a very good one for the French, as the legendary Four Musketeers (Lacoste, Jean Borotra, Jacques Brugnon,

Henri Cochet) were enshrined in ceremonies held at Newport on Bastille Day. Known as the Crocodile, an insignia he has since made famous in the fashion world, René Lacoste became the first foreign player to win the U.S. title twice, with victories in 1926 and 1927. He won Wimbledon in 1925 and 1928 and the French Championship in 1925, 1927, and 1929. He and Borotra won the Wimbledon Doubles in 1925 and the French Doubles in 1924, 1925, and 1929. Lacoste, Borotra, Cochet, and Brugnon brought the Davis Cup to France for the first time in 1927. Although Lacoste had to retire in 1929 because of his health, the French defended the Cup every year until 1933, when they were defeated by the British. Lacoste was born in Paris on July 2, 1905.

JEAN BOROTRA (1898–   )

Jean Borotra won Wimbledon in 1924 and 1926, swept the Australian Singles, Doubles, and Mixed Doubles titles in 1928, and was the French Singles champion in 1931. He lost in the finals at Wimbledon to René Lacoste in 1925 and Henri Cochet in 1927 and 1929 and to Lacoste at Forest Hills in 1926. Borotra won the Wimbledon doubles in 1925 with Lacoste and in 1932 and 1933 with Jacques Brugnon. In addition to four French doubles titles, in 1925 and 1929 with Lacoste, 1934 with Brugnon, and 1936 with Marcel Bernard, Borotra won the French Mixed Doubles in 1927 and 1934, the U.S. Mixed Doubles in 1926 (with Elizabeth Ryan), and the Wimbledon mixed doubles in 1925 (with Suzanne Lenglen). Known as the Bounding Basque because of his acrobatic volleying ability, Borotra played on the French Davis Cup team in 1922, 1924–37, and 1947. He was born in Arbonne, France, on August 13, 1898.

JACQUES BRUGNON (1895–1978)

While he failed to achieve the success in singles of his Davis Cup teammates, Jacques Brugnon was perhaps the most adept doubles player of the Four Musketeers. He won four Wimbledon doubles titles, with Henri Cochet in 1926 and 1928 and with Jean Borotra in

1932 and 1933, and was runner-up with Cochet in 1927 and 1931 and Borotra in 1934. Brugnon won the French Doubles in 1922, 1927, 1928, 1930, 1932, and 1934, and the Australian Championship in 1928. He won the French Mixed Doubles five times, in 1921, 1922, 1923, 1925, and 1926. Brugnon played on the Davis Cup team, 1926–34. He was born in Paris on May 11, 1895, and died March 20, 1978.

HENRI COCHET (1901–   )

Although the Four Musketeers comprised a spectacular Davis Cup team, they were intense rivals in singles competition. After ending Bill Tilden's six-year reign as U.S. champion in the 1926 quarterfinals, Henri Cochet was defeated by René Lacoste in a five-set semifinal match. At Wimbledon Cochet defeated Jean Borotra in five sets to win the 1927 title and in three sets to win the 1929 championship. Cochet lost to Lacoste in the 1928 Wimbledon final. Cochet won the French Championship in 1922, 1926, 1928, 1930, and 1932 and finally won the U.S. title in 1928. He won the Wimbledon Doubles in 1926 and 1928, the French Doubles in 1927, 1930, and 1932, the U.S. Mixed Doubles in 1927, and the French Mixed Doubles in 1928 and 1929. He was born in Lyons, France, on December 14, 1901.

MABEL CAHILL
(Date unavailable)

A native of Ireland, Mabel Cahill won both the U.S. Singles and Doubles Championships in 1891 and 1892 as well as the Mixed Doubles in 1892. She was a member of the New York Tennis Club, but eventually returned to Ireland, where she died.

RICHARD SAVITT (1927–   )

At the zenith of his career in 1951, Dick Savitt won both the Wimbledon and Australian Singles Championships. He reached the semifinals at Forest Hills in 1950 and the Australian semifinals in 1952. He was the U.S. Indoor Singles champion in 1952, 1958, and 1961, and played on the Davis Cup team in 1951. He was born in Bayonne, New Jersey, on March 4, 1927.

1977

NORMAN EVERARD BROOKES
(1877–1968)

Sir Norman (he was knighted in 1939) was the first great Australian player and one of the best left-handers of all time. In 1907 he became the first male from overseas to win Wimbledon. He won Wimbledon again in 1914 and captured the Australian title in 1911. He won both the 1907 and 1914 Wimbledon Doubles titles with Tony Wilding, his partner in many Davis Cup matches. Brookes also won the 1919 U.S. and 1924 Australian Doubles Championships. He was a member of the Australasian Davis Cup team, 1905–20, and later served as president of the Lawn Tennis Association of Australia for 29 years. He was born in Melbourne, November 14, 1877, and died in 1968.

BARON GOTTFRIED von CRAMM
(1909–76)

The French Singles champion in 1934 and 1936, Baron von Cramm was the best player ever to come from Germany. He reached the Wimbledon finals in 1935, 1936, and 1937 and the U.S. final in 1937. He and Henner Henkel defeated Don Budge and Gene Mako for the 1937 U.S. Doubles title. Von Cramm was the German champion, 1932–35, as well as in 1948 and 1949, at the age of 40 and played more than 100 Davis Cup matches between 1923 and 1953. He was born July 7, 1909, in Germany and died November 8, 1976.

BETTY NUTHALL
(1911–   )

In 1927, at the age of 16, Betty Nuthall was runner-up to Helen Wills for the U.S. Championship. Three years later Nuthall became the first Briton to win the U.S. women's title. In 1931 she reached the finals of the French tournament. She won three U.S. Doubles Championships, in 1930 with Sarah Palfrey, in 1931 with Ellen Bennett Whittingstall, and in 1933 with Freda James. Nuthall played on the British Wightman Cup team in 1927, 1929, 1931–34, and in 1939. She was born in Surbiton, Surrey, on May 23, 1911, became Mrs. Betty Shomaker and lives in New York.

BUDGE PATTY *(1924–   )*

Although he won the Wimbledon and French Singles Championships in 1950, J. Edward "Budge" Patty is perhaps best known for a match he didn't win, in the third round at Wimbledon in 1953. He took Czechoslovakian exile Jaroslav Drobny to 93 games and held six match points before bowing, 8–6, 16–18, 3–6, 8–6, 12–10. Patty won the Wimbledon doubles with Gardnar Mulloy in 1957. Patty was born in Arkansas on February 11, 1924, grew up in California and has lived in Europe since World War II.

MANUEL ALONSO *(1896–   )*

The first world class player developed in Spain, Manuel Alonso came to the U.S. in 1923 to live for a few years. Although he never won the Wimbledon or U.S. title, he was a notable figure in some of the fiercest competition the game has ever known. He was ranked in the Top Ten three times and was a Forest Hills quarterfinalist three times. Bill Tilden called Alonso one of the world's great players. Alonso was born in San Sebastian, Spain, in 1896 and played Davis Cup seven years for his homeland.

1978

SUZANNE LENGLEN *(1899–1938)*

A legend in her time, Suzanne Lenglen, who was never beaten in a singles match at Wimbledon, won that tournament six times, 1919–23 and 1925. On her home soil she won the French title six times as well, 1920–23,

1925, and 1926. She won both the French Doubles and Mixed Doubles Championships in 1925 and 1926, the Wimbledon Doubles, 1919–23, and 1925 (the same years she won the singles title), and the Mixed Doubles in 1920, 1922, and 1925. She was the 1920 Olympic gold medalist in singles and doubles. After World War I she toured for promoter C.C. Pyle as the star of the first professional troupe. Lenglen was born May 24, 1899, and died May 27, 1938.

KATHLEEN McKANE GODFREE (1898–   )

The top British woman player in the early 1920s, Kitty McKane Godfree won the Wimbledon Singles Championship in 1924 and 1926. In 1924 she defeated Helen Wills, 4–6, 6–4, 6–4, for the title. In 1923 she reached the final but was beaten by Suzanne Lenglen. In 1925 at Forest Hills she lost to Wills in the final, 3–6, 6–0, 6–2. Kitty won the U.S. Doubles Championship in 1923 and 1927 and became the only player to win the Wimbledon Mixed Doubles with her husband when she and Leslie Godfree took the title in 1926. She was born in London in 1898.

HARRY C. HOPMAN (1906–   )

Best known as the captain of Australia's Davis Cup teams when they dominated the competition, winning in 1939, 1950–53, 1955–57, 1959–62, and 1964–67, Harry Hopman also was the Australian Mixed Doubles champion in 1930, 1936, 1937, and 1939 and won the U.S. Mixed Doubles title in 1939. He played Davis Cup five years. He was born in Sydney on December 8, 1906, and is currently a teaching pro in the U.S.

MARIA E. BUENO (1939–   )

The best woman tennis player to come out of South America, and a stylist of consummate grace, Brazilian Maria Bueno won the U.S. Singles title in 1959, 1963, 1964, and 1966, took the Wimbledon crown in 1959, 1960, and 1964, and won the Italian title in 1958, 1960, and 1961. She won the Wimble-

don Doubles in 1958, 1960, 1963, 1965, and 1966 and was the U.S. Doubles champion in 1960 and 1962 with Darlene Hard; in 1966 with Nancy Richey; and in 1968 with Margaret Court. She also won the French Doubles and Mixed Doubles titles in 1960. She was born in São Paolo, Brazil, on October 11, 1939.

PIERRE ETCHEBASTER (1893–   )

Pierre Etchebaster was the world champion in court tennis, retiring undefeated at the age of 61 in 1954. He had held the title for 26 years. He was born in St. Jean de Luiz, France, in 1893.

ANTHONY WILDING (1883–1915)

Tony Wilding was the Australian Singles champion in 1906 and 1909; the Doubles champion in 1906; and the German Doubles champion in 1905. A dashing figure, he charmed his British fans by winning the singles at Wimbledon four times, 1910–13, and the doubles in 1907, 1908, 1910, and 1914. He teamed with Norman Brookes to win four Davis Cups for Australasia. Wilding was born in Christchurch, New Zealand, on October 31, 1883, and was killed in action in France on May 9, 1915.

1979

JOHN H. CRAWFORD (1908–   )

Australia's Jack Crawford was 18 years old when he won his first tournament, the South Australian Junior Doubles. The year after winning the Singles in 1927, he visited Europe and America with the Australian Davis Cup team. He went on to win the Australian Singles in 1931, 1932, 1933, and 1935; the Doubles in 1929, 1930, and 1932; and the Mixed Doubles in 1931, 1932, 1933. At Wimbledon and the French Nationals he was Singles champ in 1933 and Doubles in 1935. In the U.S. Nationals he was runner-up to Fred Perry in the 1933 Singles. He was born on March 22, 1908, in Australia.

FRANK SEDGMAN (1927–   )

Born in Mont Albert, Victoria, Frank Sedgman developed into an outstanding forecourt player with a brilliant forehand. Noted equally for his singles and doubles play, he never lost a doubles match in Davis Cup competition, and was a triple winner in the 1952 Wimbledon championships. He was the U.S. Singles winner in 1951 and 1952, and Doubles champ in 1950 and 1951. In 1949 and 1950, he won the Australian Singles, and in 1951 and 1952 the Doubles, With his partner Doris Hart, he won numerous mixed doubles titles in Australia, France, and the U.S. He was born on October 29, 1927.

AL LANEY (1896–   )

Renowned sportswriter, editor, and author, Al Laney spans the continents and the ages from the Golden 20s to the early 70s. As a chronicler of the sporting scene for nearly six decades, his by-line appeared in the internationally known Paris *Herald*, the Dallas *Dispatch*, the Minneapolis *News,* and from 1935 to its demise, the New York *Herald Tribune.* Although his specialty was golf, Laney covered everything from tennis to big league baseball, and his articles, frequently award winners, have appeared in many anthologies. In 1914 he was present at the historic Maurice McLaughlin vs. Norman Brookes match at Forest Hills. He was born on January 11, 1896, in Pensacola, Florida, and lives in Spring Valley, New York.

MARGARET SMITH COURT (1942–   )

Australia's greatest woman tennis player, Margaret Court amassed a career-record 66 Big Four victories including a Grand Slam in 1970. She won the U.S. Singles in 1962, 1965, 1968, 1970, and 1973; the Doubles in 1963, 1968, 1969, 1970, 1973, and 1975; and Mixed Doubles in 1961–1965, 1969, 1970, and 1972. At Wimbledon she won the Singles in 1963, 1965 and 1970; the Doubles in 1964 and 1969; and Mixed Doubles in 1963, 1965, 1966, 1968, and 1975. In her native Australia, she took the Singles from 1960–66, and in 1969–71 and 1973; the Doubles from 1961–63, 1965, 1969–71, and 1973; the Mixed in 1963 and 1964. Margaret Court was born in Albury, New South Wales on July 16, 1942.

GLADYS HELDMAN (1922–   )

Gladys Heldman was the woman most responsible for the success of the women's professional tour which she guided via the Virginia Slims Circuit. She served as founding editor, owner and publisher of *World Tennis* magazine for over 20 years. Heldman, whose daughter Julie was a top-flight player, was born in New York on May 13, 1922, and lives in Houston, Texas.

RAFAEL OSUNA (1938–69)

The greatest Mexican player of all time, Osuna was noted for his volley and swiftness on court. He won the U.S. Singles in 1963 and the Doubles in 1962. At Wimbledon, he took the Doubles with Dennis Ralston in 1960 and again in 1963 with Antonio Palafox. Born in Mexico City on September 15, 1938, Osuna died in an air crash near Monterrey, Mexico in June 1969.

Jack Mecca

10 } TENNIS LINGO

Ace: An outright winning serve, either hit so hard or placed so accurately that the receiver has no chance of returning the ball, which sails past him untouched or barely touched.

Advantage: The point following deuce. The umpire generally calls the name of the player holding advantage (example, "Advantage Connors") whether he is server or receiver. Also called ad in informal play; ad-in is the score called when the server has the advantage; ad-out refers to the advantage being held by the receiver; ad-court refers to the left court, from which the advantage is always played.

Age-group tennis: Diaper-to-doomsday competition is available in the U.S., where sectional and national championships are determined for males and females of practically every age. It starts with the 12s (for those 12 years old and under) and continues through the 14s, 16s, 18s, and 21s. After that comes the usual adult tournaments. Then, for older adults, the 35s, 40s, 45s, 50s, 55s, 60s, 65s, 75s, and 80s. And on all four surfaces: grass, clay, indoor, and hard court.

All: The score is even. It can be 15-all, 30-all in a game; or 2-all, 3-all in a set score.

Alley: A 4½-foot-wide addition to the singles court on both sides in order to provide space for doubles play. This area, totaling nine feet, is in use during play following the serve.

Amateur: One who plays the game with no monetary reward involved, although some living expenses may be reimbursed. Prior to the advent of open tennis and the prize-money boom in 1968, the word was much abused. Amateurs at top tournaments were frequently referred to as "Shamateurs": players who accepted compensation under the well-known table and did not take checks or report their earnings as income. Alleged amateurs at the top sometimes earned more than the few outright touring professionals.

"Pro" was considered a dirty word in most tennis circles until open tennis and a flood of prize money made the profession respectable. There is still a semantic problem with "amateur" in the Communist countries, which continue to term their foremost players "amateurs," even though they are clearly professional and accept prize money. An absurdly titled event is the European Amateur championships, annually won by men and women from Communist countries whose annual incomes compare favorably to those of American professional basketball players.

American Formation: See I Formation.

American twist: A top-spinning serve that takes a high bounce and can present difficulties for the receiver, particularly on grass, where the bounce is tricky. It was originated by Holcombe Ward, a Harvard man, and developed by him with his college friend Dwight Davis around the turn of the century. Their use of the stroke during the first Davis Cup match in 1900 was a revelation to their English opponents, whom they baffled and beat. See also Kicker.

Approach shot: A drive followed to the net.

Around the post: A stroke hit by a player drawn so wide that it goes into the opposing court without clearing the net. In this rare case the shot is within the rules even if the flight of the ball is not higher than the net.

ATP: The Association of Tennis Pros, an

organization of male touring pros comparable to a union, embracing most of the leading pros. Founded in 1972, it has been influential in governing tournament conditions, conduct, prize-money amounts, and structure.

ATP computer rankings: A rating system including every male playing pro in the world, whether or not affiliated with ATP. The ratings are issued frequently, based on performance over the previous 12 months, and are used by most tournament committees to determine seedings and which players should be admitted to the draw should there be more entries than positions.

Australian Formation: See I Formation.

Avon Circuit: A series of women's prize money indoor tournaments in the U.S. during the first four months of the year. Total prize money was $2.2 million in 1979, the first year in operation as successor to the Virginia Slims circuit. The top eight finishers qualify for the Avon Championship, which, along with Wimbledon, the U.S. Open and the International Series Championship, is considered one of the four most important events for women. Feeding qualifiers into the circuit is the Avon Futures, tantamount to a minor league, where developing players compete for lower prize money and chances to advance to the major circuit.

Backhand: The stoke hit from the side of the body opposite the hand holding the racket—from the left for the right-hander and from the right for a left-hander.

Bagel job: A shutout set, 6–0. The loser's score looks like a bagel. A double bagel or triple bagel could be a shutout match. Also used as a verb: to bagel, or shut out. The term was coined by Eddie Dibbs, a leading American player, in 1973.

Ball: The bouncing object hit back and forth over the net by the players. It is two and a half inches in diameter and two ounces in weight. Balls are pressurized, with the pressure varying slightly according to national origin. The American ball is high pressure, thus livelier and more in use for the power game popular in the United States. The European ball is lower pressure, easier to control, yet harder to hit for an outright winning point. The nap of the ball also varies, depending on the surface on which it is played. It is thick for abrasive surfaces such as concrete and asphalt, medium for clay, and light for grass.

Ball boy, girl: Youngsters who retrieve balls during tournament matches. Must be as unobtrusive as possible in retrieving balls and throwing to server. For the U.S. Open there are tryouts (minimum age 14), with candidates tested for throwing arm, speed, agility, and knowledge of tennis. They are paid the prevailing minimum wage, receive free uniforms, and get a chance to see the matches free.

Baseline: The court's back line, joining the sidelines, from which the serve is delivered.

Baseliner: A player who hangs back at the rear of the court, generally quite steady, keeping the ball in play with ground strokes.

Bell Cup: A team competition between Australian and U.S. women, named for the donor, cosmetic manufacturer Jesse Bell, and held for three years, 1971–73. Australia won two of the matches. Subsequently it became a junior girls competition between the two nations.

Big Four: The championships of Australia, France, Britain (Wimbledon), and the U.S. These nations have been the leaders in tennis and were considered the Big Four because they were the only ones to win the Davis Cup until South Africa, Sweden, and Italy joined the club by winning in 1974, 1975, and 1976, respectively. Victory in all Big Four events in one year constitutes a Grand Slam.

Big W: Wimbledon, London, England; the site of the British National Championships. See also Wimbledon.

Break: A service break or loss of a service game. If the server loses the game, he or she is broken, sometimes in spirit as well as in fact.

Break point: Potentially the last point of a game being won by the receiver. If the receiver wins it, he breaks. If the server wins it, he prolongs the game and may eventually pull it out. Obviously a critical point. The following are break points (with the server's score first): 0–40, 15–40, 30–40, advantage out.

Cannonball: An extraordinarily swift serve. Maurice McLoughlin was the first of the big servers. At one time Pancho Gonzales' serve was said to be the fastest; his blasts were timed at 117 miles per hour. Later, Mike Sangster's serve was clocked in special tests at 154 miles per hour.

Carry: See Double Hit.

Centre Court: This is the cathedral of tennis, a covered stadium surrounding the principal court at Wimbledon, a structure much like an Elizabethan theater. On this grass court the championship finals are played along with the most important matches of the Wimbledon fortnight. It was built in 1922 to hold 14,000 spectators, 1,500 of them on each side in the open standing-room areas. That capacity was increased to about 15,000 in 1979. Also, center court can mean the main court in any arena.

Challenge Round: A type of final once common to tennis, particularly the Davis Cup, and now out of use, whereby the champion was privileged to stand aside the following year, waiting for a challenger to be determined by an elimination "all-comers" tournament. Then the challenger would face the reigning champion for the title. This format was discarded by the U.S. Championship in 1912, by Wimbledon in 1921, and by the Davis Cup in 1972. That year the Cup-holding U.S. played through the tournament along with the other nations entered, reached the final against Romania, and retained the title.

Change game: At the completion of each odd game of a match, beginning with the first game, the players change sides in order to equalize playing conditions—sun, wind, court surface, etc.

Chip: See Dink.

Choking: What a player is doing who can't perform to his normal ability when the going gets rough and the pressure is on. Most players recognize that it can happen to the best of them, and they are not ashamed to admit it.

Chop: A severe, slicing stroke that imparts underspin.

Court: The surface on which the game is played. A tennis court can be surfaced with anything from anthills (in Australia) to cow dung (in India) to wood, clay, grass, linoleum, canvas, concrete, asphalt or synthetic carpets. The dimensions are always the same: 78 feet long and 27 feet wide (36 feet wide for doubles). The game began on grass courts in England, but that is an uncommon surface now, although the biggest tournament of all, Wimbledon, is still a grass event.

Court speed: The "fastest" courts are those producing quick, low bounces such as grass and wood, and smooth, hard surfaces such as canvas stretched over wood or concrete, or concrete itself, or similar composition such as asphalt. The "slowest" courts are those producing high, lazy bounces and are usually clay or a similar soft surface, most often a gritty substance spread over earth. Power players favor fast surfaces where serve-and-volley tactics are rewarded, while retrievers and baseliners favor slow surfaces, which allow them more time to make a stroke. Indoor play, without wind resistance, is generally faster than outdoor, usually taking place on synthetic carpets. Outdoors, a damp court of clay or grass generally plays slower. Manufacturers of synthetic carpets can change the speed, as can manufacturers of outdoor hard courts by altering the texture, following the principle that the smoother a court the faster it plays. As of 1979 the Big Four were played on three different surfaces: Australia and Wimbledon on grass, French on clay, U.S. on a hard court at Flushing Meadow. All but the French, the premier clay court event in the world, favor power players. U.S. titles are determined on three surfaces: indoor, clay, and hard court (the U.S. Open), although a few grass court titles remain, such as the girls' 18 at Philadelphia.

Cross-court: A diagonal shot across the court from the left or the right.

Davis Cup: A competition (limited to males) open to teams representing nations throughout the world. It was originated at Boston's

Longwood Cricket Club in 1900 by Dwight Filley Davis, who was a student at Harvard and played on the first team, competing against the top players from Great Britain. The Americans won in the inaugural year, and have won a record 26 times through 1978.

Deuce: A game or set score meaning the opponents are even at a certain point. The deuce factor provides that games and sets can go on and on. In a game the score is deuce at 40-all or three points each. To win, a player must take two straight points from deuce. The first point after deuce is advantage, and the score keeps reverting to deuce unless one player wins the two straight points. A set becomes deuce when the score becomes five games apiece. To win the set, a player must be two games ahead, thus winning two straight games from 5-all, 6-all, 7-all, etc. The longest deuce set ever played was 49–47 during the longest match ever played: Dick Leach and Dick Dell beat Tom Mozur and Len Schloss, 3–6, 49–47, 22–20, in the 1967 Newport Invitation.

Dink: A softly sliced stroke intended to fall in the forecourt, between the net and service line at a net-rusher's feet. Also called a chip.

Donkeys: Consistent losers on the pro circuit.

Double fault: When the server misses with both serves, thus losing the point.

Double hit: Striking the ball twice during the same stroke, a misfortune that used to mean automatic loss of the point but now only if judged "intentional." Also called a carry.

Doubles: A team game with two players on each side of the net.

Down-the-line: A shot along either sideline.

Draw: The lineup for a customary elimination tournament. Names of the players are drawn blindly, usually from a cup, and placed in the order drawn on a bracketed draw sheet that indicates who opposes whom.

Drop Shot: A softly hit shot, intentionally aimed to barely clear the net in order to win a point outright, or to pull the opponent in close.

Elbow: Getting the elbow is choking or tightening up at a critical point, a bad reaction to pressure. However, tennis elbow is an actual physical affliction, a painful malfunctioning of the elbow that strikes not only tennis players. Physicians have not found a sure cure.

Error: A mistake that loses a point during a rally, such as hitting the ball out or into the net.

Fast court: See Court speed.

Fault: Failing to put the ball into play with the serve, either by serving into the net or beyond the confines of the service court. It is also a fault to step on the baseline while serving or to swing and miss the ball altogether. One fault isn't disastrous, but two lose the point.

Federation Cup: An annual worldwide women's team competition among nations comparable to the Davis Cup for men, which was begun in 1963. The format is best-of-three matches (two singles and a doubles) during the elimination tournament.

Fifteen: The first point either player or side wins.

First Ten or Top Ten: Two select groups set forth annually by the USTA, one of men and one of women who rank No. 1 through No. 10 in singles. The First Ten selections are based on tournament results of the previous season. This began in 1885 for men, when Dick Sears was No. 1, and in 1913 for women, when Mary K. Browne was No. 1. The most frequent selections have been Bill Larned, 19 years between 1892 and 1911 (he was No. 1 eight times); Louise Brough, 16 years between 1941 and 1957 (No. 1 once); Nancy Richey, 16 years between 1960 and 1976 (No. 1 four times); Billie Jean King, 16 years between 1960 and 1978 (No. 1 seven times). The rankings continue beyond the First Ten.

Flushing Meadow: A public park, site of the U.S. Open, held there for the first time in 1978. It is known as the USTA National Tennis Center, and is located in the borough of Queens in New York City. The principal court, Louis Armstrong Stadium, is the largest tennis arena in the world, seating 19,500. The courts are hard, an asphalt composition called DecoTurf. See also U.S. Open.

Foot fault: An infraction by the server when he steps on the baseline or serves from the wrong side of the center line. On a first serve it is not serious. On the second he loses the point, completing a double fault.

Forehand: The stroke hit from the same side of the body as the hand holding the racket—from the right for a right-hander, and the left for a left-hander.

Forest Hills: Scene of the U.S. National Championships (now the U.S. Open) for 60 years until the event moved to Flushing Meadow in 1978. Although the championships were played at the West Side Tennis Club, the tournament was generally referred to as Forest Hills, the section of the New York borough of Queens where the club is situated. The tournament moved from its original site, the Casino at Newport, Rhode Island, to Forest Hills in 1915 and was played there every year through 1977 with the exception of 1921–23, when it was shifted to Germantown Cricket Club at Philadelphia while the Forest Hills Stadium was constructed on the West Side grounds. This stadium was opened in 1923 by the inaugural Wightman Cup match between the U.S. and Great Britain, and became one of the world's great tennis arenas, whose record crowd was 16,253 for the 1976 finals. The tournament was played on grass at Forest Hills until 1975, when clay courts were installed for the Open. See also U.S. Open.

Foro Italico: Scene of the Italian Championships in Rome. A bastion of marble and pines alongside the Tiber, it is the world's most handsome setting for a major event and was built as Foro Mussolini during the dictator's reign.

Forty: The score for three points won by a side.

Game: The contest within a set and a match. One player serves throughout a game. To win a game, the player must win four points, unless the score is three points apiece, known as deuce. Then the player must get two straight points to win the game. The points in a game are called, 15, 30, 40, and game—in that order. To win a set, the player must win six games, unless the score is five games apiece. Then it is a deuce set, and the player must take two straight games from deuce to win. In some cases a tie-breaker game is played to determine winner of a set at six games apiece. See also Tie-breaker.

Grand Masters: A prize-money tournament circuit inaugurated in 1973 for the cream of the crocks—ex-champs over 45—by Cincinnati businessman Al Bunis. Dealing in nostalgia and featuring such yet imposing players as Pancho Gonzales, Frank Sedgman, and Torben Ulrich, it was a financial success. Sedgman won the championship tournament in 1975, 1977, and 1978, Ulrich in 1976, and Sven Davidson in 1979.

Grand Prix: A series of men's tournaments, including all the major championships across the world between January and December, in which bonus points are awarded for each victory. At the close of the year the leaders in points collect bonuses, and the top eight enter a playoff called the Masters.

Grand Slam: The rare feat of winning the four major championships (Australian, French, Wimbledon, U.S.) all in the same year. Don Budge did it in 1938, Maureen Connolly in 1953, Rod Laver in 1962 and 1969, and Margaret Court in 1970. Grand Slams have also been made in doubles (Frank Sedgman and Ken McGregor, 1951) and mixed doubles (Margaret Court and Ken Fletcher, 1963).

Grip: The method of holding the racket. Basic grips are the Eastern, Western, and Continental, but there are also numerous (but slight) variations adapted by individual players. Many players, notably Pancho Segura, Chris Evert, and Jimmy Connors, have done well with the unusual baseball grip—using both hands—but most common is the one-handed grip. Also, the leather wrapping around the handle of the racket, frequently changed by the top players to adjust to feel and wear. The diameter of the handle varies slightly and is a measurement that is marked for purposes of purchasing a racket. A player chooses one with a grip that is most comfortable for him or her.

Groundie: See Ground stroke.

Ground Stroke: A stroke hit from the backcourt area after the ball bounces. The return of serve is a ground stroke.

Gut: Animal intestines used to string rackets. The best gut comes from lambs.

Hacker: An ordinary player—a term applying to most of us; the tennis equivalent of the golfing duffer. Also used in good-natured ribbing by the pros. It came into vogue in 1966, when Aussie Fred Stolle, Wimbledon runner-up and German champion, came to Forest Hills to find himself surprisingly unseeded, "I guess they think I'm just an old hacker," He said. After he won the title, Fred said, "There's still some life in the old hacker." he was 27 and has been the Old Hacker since.

Half volley: The stroke by which the ball is blocked as soon as it hits the ground. Like trapping a baseball.

Hall of Fame: Located at the Newport Casino, Newport, Rhode Island, the cradle of American tennis, the International Tennis Hall of Fame was established as a valhalla for all-time greats of the game as well as a museum of tennis history and memorabilia. It was founded in 1954, the concept of tennis innovator Jimmy Van Alen, as the National Lawn Tennis Hall of Fame, and until 1975 enshrined only American players. That year the name and scope were changed to International with the induction of Englishman Fred Perry.

Hard court: This can be confusing because in the U.S. "hard court" means concrete, asphalt, or similar paving, such as U.S. Open courts at Flushing Meadow, while in Europe, Australia, and most other countries the term applies to clay courts. The U.S. annually held a National Hard Court championship on concrete until 1972. See also Court Speed.

I Formation: An unorthodox doubles alignment with the netman standing in the service court directly ahead of his partner, the server, instead of in the adjoining court. The purpose is to confuse the receiver. Also called the tandem formation, as well as the Australian formation (in the U.S.) and the American formation (in Australia).

International Series: A series of women's prize money tournaments throughout the year and the world, including the Big Four championships, in which bonus points are awarded for each victory, and bonuses are paid to the leading finishers. The top eight women qualify for the Series Championship playoff at the end of the season. Begun in 1977. Chris Evert won the championship in 1977–78.

In the zone: A state of great confidence when one is playing sensationally, even above expected ability. "I'm sure in the zone today." From "The Twilight Zone," a TV program about other-worldly behavior and situations.

IPA: Independent Players' Association, an organization founded in opposition to the ATP by Bill Riordan, tournament promoter, and then manager of Jimmy Connors. Connors appeared to be the only member of his private union, of which nothing has been heard since 1975.

ITF: The International Tennis Federation (originally the International Lawn Tennis Federation). Since 1913 it has been the world governing body of tennis, embracing the amateur bodies of nearly 100 countries. The ITF has little control over professional tennis other than the power to approve or disapprove open tournaments, but seats delegates on the Men's and Women's International Professional Tennis Councils.

Jag: A verb coined by Aussies meaning "to hit the ball unstylishly but somehow getting it over the net," as in Rod Laver remarking, "I just made up my mind to jag a few, keep it in play, until I found my timing."

Johnston Award: An award for outstanding sportsmanship presented annually to an American male by the U.S. Tennis Association. It was named for a tiny but indomitable competitor, the late Billy Johnston (1894–1946), who was national champion, 1915–19.

Kicker: An American Twist serve taking a high bounce to the right if served by a right-hander and to the left if served by a left-hander. See also American Twist.

Kill: To put a ball away, usually by hitting an overhead or smash that puts the ball past the opponent.

King's Cup: An indoor team competition for European nations, along the lines of the Davis Cup. It was named for the donor, King Gustav V of Sweden, the tennis fanatic who played into his nineties.

Kooyong: A stadium in Melbourne, Australia, where the third largest crowd in tennis history, 22,000, gathered for the Australian-U.S. Davis Cup finale in 1957. An aboriginal word, *kooyong* means "haunt of the wild fowl." Built in 1927, customary site of Australian Open, whose surface is grass.

Let: The signal for a replay. If a serve hits the top of the net and proceeds into the proper service court, the serve is replayed. If a point is interrupted or interfered with in any way (such as a ball from a nearby court rolling through), let is called, and the point is replayed.

Liner: A shot landing on or touching a line. It is a good shot.

Linesman/lineswoman: An official who judges whether a shot is out or good. A full squad of linesmen for a match is ten. Add the umpire, net judge, and foot-fault judge, and you have quite a crowd presiding over one match. The players feel outnumbered oncourt.

Lingering death: A tie-breaker based on Jimmy Van Alen's original theme, but adhering to the deuce principle of winning only if ahead by two or more points. The goal is to reach seven points, but the winner must be two points ahead; thus at 6–6 the tie-breaker could continue indefinitely. This form is usually called the 12-point tie-breaker, a misnomer since it may stretch well beyond 12. The record is 20–18, won by Bjorn Borg over Premjit Lall at Wimbledon in 1973. See also Tie-breaker.

Lob: A high, arching stroke meant either as a defensive shot (enabling the hitter to regain position) to to go over the head of an opponent at net. P. F. Hadow, the Wimbledon champion in 1878, is generally credited with originating this stroke.

Long: The term applied to a ball that lands behind the service line on a serve or behind the baseline to end a point.

Longwood: Longwood Cricket Club is the oldest significant tennis club in the U.S., dating from 1877 (although the New Orleans Lawn Tennis Club, 1876, is the oldest). Located in the Boston suburb of Chestnut Hill, Longwood has been the scene of top-flight tennis almost since its beginning. The first Davis Cup match was played there in 1900, the National Doubles Championships from 1917 through 1969, the U.S. Pro from 1964 to date. Among members were such tennis pioneers as Dwight Davis, donor of the Davis Cup; Hazel Wightman, donor of the Wightman Cup; Richard Sears, first U.S. champion; and Dr. James Dwight, who introduced tennis to the U.S. Courts are predominantly grass.

Love: A zero score. A love game is a blitz, with the winner taking four straight points. A love set is six games to nothing (see Bagel Job). Probably derived from the French word *l'oeuf,* meaning the egg—and implying the old goose egg.

Masters: The climax of the tennis year is the eight-man Masters playoff among the top eight finishers in the Grand Prix. Begun in 1970 at Tokyo, where Stan Smith won, the Masters has moved from city to city, settling in New York in 1977. Ilie Nastase won a record four times, 1971, 1972, 1973, and 1975.

Match: The overall contest. It may be a two-out-of-three-sets match or a three-out-of-five-sets match, meaning one player must win either two sets or three sets to win. The number of matches needed to win a tournament is determined by the size of the draw in a conventional elimination tournament, or by whatever rules prevail, as in a round-robin or medal-play event.

Match point: The point prior to completion of a match. The player in the lead needs only one more point to win. This can be a very dramatic spot, and sometimes the player behind in the score saves numerous match points and goes on to victory. Pancho Gonzales saved seven match points in a dramatic five-set victory over Charlie Pasarell during the 1969 Wimbledon, the longest match ever played there: 22–24, 1–6, 16–14, 6–3, 11–9—112 games.

MIPTC: Men's International Professional Tennis Council, a board of control for the male pro tournament game. Formed in

1974, it seeks to regulate schedules and conditions of play and conduct. It is made up of representatives from the ITF, ATP, and various tournaments.

Mixed doubles: Doubles with one male and one female on each side.

Moonball: A high, floating ground stroke used in base line rallying to slow down the pace. It's not as high as a lob and is usually hit with topspin. It is most associated with a leading American, Harold Solomon, who can hit them forever and who coined the term in 1972 when his moonballing epic, a marathon victory over Guillermo Vilas during the French Open, consumed more than five hours.

Net: The webbed barrier dividing the court at middle and over which the ball is to be hit. At the center point it is three feet high and at either end three and a half feet.

Net cord: A shot that hits the top of the net and drops into the opposite court. Also, the cord or wire cable that supports a net.

Net judge: An official seated at one end of the net below the umpire's chair to detect lets on serve. During the serve he rests his hand on top of the net to feel whether the ball hits the top of the net. If it does, he calls "Net!" and the serve is replayed as a let if the ball lands in the proper court.

Net rusher: An attacking player who follows his serve to the net and continually seeks the closeup position to make winning volleys.

Newport Casino: Cradle of American tennis, it is a private club designed by noted architect Stanford White and built in 1880 at Newport, Rhode Island, where the following year it was the scene of the first U.S. Championship, won by Richard Sears. The U.S. Men's Championships were played there each year through 1914, then moved to Forest Hills in New York. Prominent tournament tennis has continued on the grass courts to this date, including a men's amateur event from 1915 through 1967, and professional tournaments since 1965—Virginia Slims women's tourneys as well as a Grand Prix event in 1977–79, the last American pro courney on grass. The Casino is also the site of the International Tennis Hall of Fame.

No-ad: A form of scoring originated by Jimmy Van Alen that eliminates deuce and replaces love–15–30–40 with 0–1–2–3. The maximum points for a game are seven. At 3–3 (normally deuce) the next point is game point for both sides, with the receiver to elect choice of courts. No-ad has been adopted by World Team Tennis and the National Collegiate Athletic Association annual tournament. See also VASSS.

Not up: The call when a player hits the ball just as it has bounced the second time on a close play. Usually the net judge makes the ruling, but if there are no officials, it is up to the offending player to call it against himself and accept loss of the point.

NTL: The National Tennis League, an organization formed by George MacCall in 1967 to promote professional tournaments. Under contract were Rod Laver, Ken Rosewall, Pancho Gonzales, Andres Gimeno, Fred Stolle, Roy Emerson, Billie Jean King, Rosie Casals, Ann Jones, and Françoise Durr. By 1970 NTL had been put out of business and absorbed by rival WCT.

Open: A tournament that may be entered by both amateurs and professionals, generally offering prize money. Not until 1968 did the ILTF permit opens. The first, the British Hard Court Championship, was won by pro Ken Rosewall. Now all the leading national title events are open.

Overhead: A stroke, usually a smash, executed like a serve by raising the racket above the head and swinging down hard.

Passing shot: A ball hit past the opposing netman on either side beyond his reach.

Philadelphia Cricket Club: This private club in the Philadelphia suburb of Chestnut Hill was the site of the U.S. Women's Championships from inception in 1887 through 1920. In 1921 the tournament moved to Forest Hills, and in 1978 to Flushing Meadow.

Placement: A shot aimed at a particular sector and hit so well that the opponent can't touch it.

Poach: In doubles, when a player, hoping to make a winning volley, crosses in front of his partner.

Point: The smallest unit of scoring. A game is won by a player winning four points, except in the case of deuce. The first point of a game is called 15, the second 30, the third 40, and the fourth is game. At 40-all the score is deuce. Each point is begun with the serve, and one player serves an entire game. In keeping score, the server's score is called first—e.g., in 15–40, 15 is the server. and 40 is the receiver.

Professional: A player who plays prize-money events for money or a teacher who gives tennis lessons for money.

Pusher: A player who hopes to wear down the opponent by maddeningly returning everything with soft looping strokes. A pusher hangs back at the baseline, a good retriever, patiently waiting for a big hitter to blow his cool and the match. Also known as a pooper, puddler, or puffball artist.

Racket: The implement used in hitting the ball; an oval frame attached to a long, straight handle. The frame is crossed horizontally and vertically with strings. The best strings are made of lamb intestine, which is known as gut. Nylon is also widely used. A racket may be of any size or material. Although wood frames predominate, metal, namely steel and aluminum, has become extremely popular. Fiberglas and graphite rackets are also produced.

Rally: An exchange of shots during a point.

Ranking: A player's standing in regard to other players. National rankings lists are made up annually for tournament players by the governing associations in almost every country. Sectional rankings, too, are made within the U.S. Tennis Association. An annual world ranking is also selected by a group of sportwriters. In the U.S. the finest record was made by Bill Larned (1872–1926), who was placed in the Top Ten 19 times between 1892 and 1911 and was No. 1 eight times. Rankings are based on tournament performance. Computerized rankings, based on professional tournament performance, are issued at frequent intervals of the year by the ATP and the WTA.

Referee: The official in charge of tournament play and playing conditions.

Riordan circuit: The first viable indoor circuit for men in the U.S., organized by Bill Riordan, dynamic promoter from Salisbury, Maryland, and then manager of Jimmy Connors. He started in earnest in 1964 by transferring the nearly defunct U.S. Indoor Championship from New York to Salisbury, where it became a thriving event. He expanded to eight tournaments by 1975, its last year. A combative type, Riordan fought the growth of WCT and the ATP; founded his own players' organization, called the IPA (Independent Players' Association); and kept his series of winter tournaments going as a one-man operation under the aegis of the USLTA that he called the Independent circuit but that was generally known as the Riordan circuit. See also IPA.

Roland Garros: The 17,000 seat stadium and adjoining courts in Paris where the French Championship has been played yearly since 1928. Built primarily for the first French defense of the Davis Cup that year, it was named for a heroic French aviator of World War I. Surface is clay.

Rough: Trim cord is sometimes placed on the top and bottom of a string job. "Rough" refers to the rough side of this trimming; the side with the loops around the regular strings is the rough side. The other is referred to as smooth. These terms can be used after spinning the racket to determine who serves first and which side of the court opponents start on.

Rubber: An individual singles or doubles match in a team competition such as Davis Cup or Wightman Cup. The usage is British and European.

Scrambler: A player who hustles for every point and manages to get the ball back somehow, though probably not very stylishly. A dogged retriever, usually a pusher.

Seeding: The deliberate, instead of chance, placing of certain strong players so that they will not meet in the earlier rounds of an elimination tournament. It was introduced to major tennis at Wimbledon in 1924 and soon became standard procedure, adopted at Forest Hills in 1927. Seeded players (those judged by a tournament committee or according to computerized rankings to be the leaders on the basis of performance and ability) are listed in numbered order prior to the draw. Then the seeds are separated by being planted in positions specified by tournament regulations. Thus the top two players, Nos. 1 and 2, are located at opposite ends of the draw, and if the seeding runs true, they will meet in the final.

Service or serve: The act of putting the ball into play and beginning a point by hitting the ball from the baseline diagonally over the net and into opponent's service court. Any motion (underhand, sidearm, or whatever) is permissible. However, the overhead stroke is nearly universal.

Service Break: Winning the opponent's service.

Service court(s): There are two, since the server alternates from the right to the left side of the court with each point. The service courts are bounded by the sidelines, the net, and the service line, which is 21 feet from the net; they are divided from one another by the center line. Each court is 13½ feet wide by 21 feet deep.

Service winner: An unreturned serve, though not an ace.

Set: The second highest unit of scoring. The winner of six games takes the set, except when the score is 5-all in games. Then it is a deuce set, and the winner must win by two games, unless tie-breakers are used, usually at 6-all in games. In that case one tie-breaker game decides the outcome of the set, whose score would be 7–6.

Set Point: The point prior to the completion of a set. The player needs only one more point to win the set. But the player behind may still save the set point and go on to win the set himself, thanks to the deuce factor.

Sitter: An easy opportunity; a ball softly hit close to the net and well within reach, which can be smashed away for a point.

Slice: Hitting under the ball, which produces underspin and a low bounce.

Slims Circuit: The first notable attempt to bring women into the prize-money era of tennis was made successfully by Gladys Heldman, publisher of *World Tennis* magazine, who in 1970 began forming a circuit for the women separate from that of the men and sponsored by Virginia Slims cigarettes, lasting through 1978. With Ms. Heldman as the organizational wizard and Billie Jean King as spokeswoman and all-conquering champion, the women's game took off in 1971. By going it alone, the women no longer had to play second racket to the men in cash or publicity, and the women's prize money rose dramatically to $1.5 million in 1978 for 12 tournaments in the U.S. For women the Virginia Slims Championship—a play-off among the top eight women at the conclusion of the circuit in the spring—was, along with Wimbledon, the U.S. Open, and the International Series Championship, one of the four most important events. Chris Evert won the championship in 1972–73, 1975, and 1977; Goolagong in 1974 and 1976; and Martina Navratilova in 1978.

Slow court: See Court speed.

Smash: An overhead stroke brought down hard like a serve.

Spikes: Spiked shoes with ⅜-inch metal spikes that are sometimes worn on wet grass courts to help a player's footing.

Spin: Pronounced rotation of the ball according to how it is struck by the racket, and divided into three categories: topspin (overspin); slice (underspin); and sidespin. For topspin the racket brushes the ball from low to high producing a high bouncing ball, enabling one to hit the ball harder and still keep it deep but within the court. For slice the racket brushes from high to low, producing a low bounce. A serve slice is a chop, causing the ball to bound to the receiver's right if server is right-handed and to the left if server is left-handed. For sidespin the racket brushes across the ball on either side, producing a bounce to the left if ball struck on the right side, and vice versa.

Sudden death: A tie-breaker of definite length, either nine-point or 13-point, settled by a sudden-death point when the score is 4–4, or 6–6. It was conceived by Jimmy Van Alen, the Newport Bolshevik. See also Tie-breaker.

Supreme Court: The trade name for a synthetic carpet court favored for a majority of major professional indoor tournaments.

Tandem Formation: See I Formation.

Thirty: Two points.

Throat: The thin part of the racket between the handle and the head, sometimes open, particularly in metal rackets.

Tie: A team match between countries, such as Davis Cup or Federation Cup. It is an old expression, used mainly in Britain and Europe, seldom in the U.S. In the Davis Cup a tie is composed of five rubbers. See also Rubber.

Tie-breaker: A means of ending a tied set in one game, rather than continuing in a theoretically endless deuce set in which one side must be two games ahead to win after 5–5 in games. It's another scoring innovation from the fertile mind of Jimmy Van Alen. Usually the tie-breaker is invoked at 6–6 in games, although Wimbledon until 1979 preferred to wait until 8–8. Serve alternates during the tie-breaker, which is won by the first side to reach a specified number, depending on the form of tie-breaker. The most comprehensible is Van Alen's sudden-death nine-point maximum, won by the first to reach five points. There is also a sudden-death 13-point maximum, won by the first to reach seven, which is sometimes used by WCT. A variation on Van Alen's theme is the lingering death, won by the first to reach seven points, provided there is a two-point margin. Otherwise it continues until one side is ahead by two, and could theoretically last indefinitely. Tie-breakers came into noticeable use in 1970, when sudden death was adopted by the U.S. Pro Championships and the U.S. Open. The U.S. Open, and most other pro events, were using lingering death, recommended by the ITF, by 1975. See also Game.

Topspin: Spin produced by brushing the ball from low to high to create a high bounce. It also helps control a hard-hit ball, preventing it from traveling too far. See Spin.

Top Ten: See First Ten.

Tournament: The basic form of competition. The most common is a single-elimination tournament with a minimum of eight entries. Departure of losers cuts the field in half at each round as a tournament narrows

to two entries in the final. The world's three premier tournaments—Wimbledon, the U.S. Open, and the French Championships—normally have draws of 128 men and 96 women, with seven and six rounds of play.

Umpire: The official in charge of a match, keeping and calling score, usually from a high chair at one end of the net.

U.S. Open: See also Forest Hills and Flushing Meadow.

U.S. Pro Championship(s): The longest-running tournament for professionals is the U.S. Pro, won in 1927, its first year, by Vincent Richards at the long-since-vanished Notlek Tennis Club in Manhattan. Total prize money was $5,000. The largely unnoticed and unsuccessful event was played all over the country until moving to its present site, the Longwood Cricket Club in Boston, in 1964, where it prospered and was the fountainhead for the solid growth of the pro game, with prize money rising to $200,000 by 1978.

USTA: The United States Tennis Association (formerly U.S. Lawn Tennis Association), the governing organization of amateur tennis in the United States. It also operates the U.S. Open. Founded in 1881 as the U.S. National Lawn Tennis Association, it embraces seventeen sectional associations from New England to Southern California. In 1975 the "L" was dropped from the association abbreviation as dated, since so little tennis is now played on grass.

VASSS: The Van Alen Streamlined Scoring System. Devised by James Van Alen, who was anxious to make the game more readily understood by the general public and to eliminate long-drawn-out matches. VASSS replaced love–15–30–40 with 0–1–2–3 and eliminated deuce altogether. He devised the tie-breaker to avoid deuce sets. In VASSS no-ad the first player to win four points wins the game. In VASSS single point the scoring is changed altogether. The first player to reach 31 points wins the set, with the tie-breaker to be used if the score reaches 30–30. Few tournaments have adopted Van Alen's system, although World Team Tennis and the National Collegiate Athletic Association use no-ad.

Volley: To hit the ball during play before it touches the ground, usually at the net.

WCT: World Championship Tennis. This most ambitious and successful organization to promote professional tennis was formed in late 1967 by Dave Dixon of New Orleans in partnership with Dallas sportsman-oil millionaire Lamar Hunt. Dixon signed eight players, and the firm was in business, though shakily, and Hunt and his nephew, Al Hill, Jr., bought out Dixon after a few months' operation and huge losses. Gradually, under director Mike Davies, the concept of the World Championship of Tennis developed—a series of tournaments throughout the world involving most of the leading men and pointing to play-offs in May among the top eight finishers in singles and doubles. Ken Rosewall won first WCT play-off over Rod Laver in Dallas in 1971 and collected $50,000 first prize. WCT broadened its operations by constructing tennis resorts (Lakeway World of Tennis outside Austin, Texas, and Peachtree World of Tennis outside Atlanta), marketing tennis clothing, and opening tennis academies. Prize money for 30 WCT events in 1978 exceeded $2.4 million.

West Side: The West Side Tennis Club (see Forest Hills) had long been the scene of championship tennis, the site of the U.S. Championships for 60 years between 1915 and 1977 as well as 10 Davis Cup finales. This private club was founded in 1892 when situated in Manhattan on Central Park West between 88th Street and 89th Street, thus the name West Side. It occupied two other locations in Manhattan before moving to Forest Hills in 1913.

White City: A stadium in Sydney, Australia, where the second largest crowd in tennis history, 25,578, attended the Australia-U.S. Davis Cup finale in 1954. The tournament courts are grass.

Wide: To be out of the court on either side, thus a loss of point.

Wightman Cup: The annual women's team competition between Great Britain and the U.S., begun in 1923. The format is best-of-seven matches—five singles and two dou-

bles. The Cup was dominated by Mrs. Hazel Wightman of Boston (1886–1974), winner of a record 45 U.S. titles in singles and doubles. She played in the first Cup match, won by the United States, 7–0.

Wimbledon: The game's leading tournament, considered the world championship. Played on the grounds of the All England Lawn Tennis and Croquet Club in the London suburb of Wimbledon, the English title event is known formally as The Lawn Tennis Championships and called, universally, Wimbledon. Launched in 1877, it has always been played on grass and has been open to professionals as well as amateurs since 1968. Championships are decided in men's and women's singles and doubles, mixed doubles, junior boys' and girls' singles, and veterans' (over age 45) doubles. Always a sellout, the tourney draws over 250,000 spectators for 12 days. The record was 337,598 in 1975; the single-day record was 38,290 in 1978. See also Big W.

Winner: A shot hit for an outright point. Also called a placement.

WIPTC: Women's International Professional Tennis Council, a board of control for the female pro tournament game. Formed in 1975, it seeks to regulate schedules, conditions of play, and conduct. It is made up of representatives of the ITF, WTA, and various tournaments. See also MIPTC.

World Cup: An annual team competition between Australia and U.S. male pros, begun in 1970. The event has been played at Hartford, Connecticut, since 1972, and Australia led, 5–4, following a 6–1 victory in 1978.

WTA: The Women's Tennis Association, an organization of the leading female pros, similar to a union and comparable to the ATP. Billie Jean King was the guiding light in the 1974 founding, and she was the first president.

WTT: World Team Tennis. City franchises, the foundation of major pro sports in the U.S., came to tennis in 1974 with the establishment of World Team Tennis, a league with 16 teams from Boston to Honolulu. Founded by Dennis Murphy, Jordan Kaiser, and Larry King (husband of Billie

Jean), WTT was a radical undertaking, involving tennis players and equipment and some of the basics but actually creating a new game: team tennis. Women and men were on pro teams together for the first time, sharing the load; a match consisted of five sets (men's and women's singles, men's and women's doubles, and mixed doubles), with victory going to the team that scored more games cumulatively, using no-ad scoring. Large salaries for top players lured from the traditional tournament game during WTT's May–September season, and low attendance, resulted in huge financial losses, failure of several franchises, and realignment of WTT for 1975 with twelve teams. Losses remained heavy, but WTT operated through 1978, then folded.

Denver won the title in 1974 and promptly folded. Pittsburgh, led by Evonne Goolagong, won in 1975, New York in 1976–77, Los Angeles in 1978. The founding of WTT precipitated a war with the ILTF that was settled after numerous lawsuits. Most of the leading female players—including King, Virginia Wade, Goolagong, Rosie Casals, Françoise Durr, Betty Stove, Chris Evert, Kerry Melville Reid—signed on, as well as such men as John Newcombe, Tom Okker, Marty Riessen, Vijay Amritraj, and Fred Stolle. WTT encouraged a complete break with tennis customs, urging the customers to cheer and boo.

APPENDIX A: RULES

RULES OF TENNIS and CASES AND DECISIONS

EXPLANATORY NOTE

The appended Code of Rules and Cases and Decisions is the Official Code of the International Tennis Federation, of which the United States Tennis Association is a member.

Italicized EXPLANATIONS, EXAMPLES and COMMENTS have been prepared by the USTA Rules Interpretation Committee to amplify and facilitate interpretation of the formal code.

The Singles Game

Rule 1

Dimensions and Equipment

The course shall be a rectangle 78 feet (23.77m) long and 27 feet (8.23m) wide. It shall be divided across the middle by a net suspended from a cord or metal cable of a maximum diameter of one-third of an inch (0.8cm), the ends of which shall be attached to, or pass over, the tops of two posts, 3 feet 6 inches (1.07m) high, and not more than 6 inches (15cm) in diameter, the centers of which shall be 3 feet (0.91m) outside the court on each side. The net shall be extended fully so that it fills completely the space between the two posts and shall be of sufficiently small mesh to prevent the ball's passing through. Th height of the net shall be 3 feet (0.914m) at the center, where it shall be held down taut by a strap not more than 2 inches (5cm) wide and white in color. There shall be a band covering the cord or metal cable and the top of the net for not less than 2 inches (5cm) nor more than 2½ inches (6.3cm) in depth on each side and white in color. There shall be no advertisement on the net, strap, band or singles sticks. The lines bounding the ends and sides of the Court shall respectively be called the Baselines and the Sidelines. On each side of the net, at a distance of 21 feet (6.40m) from it and parallel with it, shall be drawn the Service lines. The space on each side of the net between the service line and the sidelines shall be divided into two equal parts, called the service courts, by the center service line, which must be 2 inches (5cm) in width, drawn half-way between, and parallel with, the sidelines. Each baseline shall be bisected by an imaginary continuation of the center service line to a line 4 inches (10cm) in length and 2 inches (5cm) in width called the center mark, drawn inside the Court at right angles to and in contact with such baselines. All other lines shall be not less than 1 inch (2.5cm) nor more than 2 inches (5cm) in width, except the baseline, which may be 4 inches (10cm) in width, and all measurements shall be made to the outside of the lines.

Note—In the case of the International Tennis Championship (Davis Cup) or other Official Championships of the International Federation, there shall be a space behind each baseline of not less than 21 feet (6.4m), and at the sides of not less than 12 feet (3.66m).

The center of the posts in doubles should be 3 feet outside the doubles court.

The net should be 33 feet in the clear for a singles court, and 42 feet wide for a doubles court. It should touch the ground along its entire length and come flush to the posts at all points.

It is important to have a stick 3 feet, 6 inches long, with a notch cut in at the 3-foot mark for the purpose of measuring the height of the net at the posts and in the center. These measurements, as well as the measurements of the court itself, always should be made before starting to play a match.

Rule 2

Permanent Fixtures

The permanent fixtures of the Court shall include not only the net, posts, cord or metal cable, strap and band, but also, where there are any such, the back and side stops, the stands, fixed or movable seats and chairs around the Court, and their occupants, all other fixtures around and above the Court, and the Chair Umpire, Net Umpire, Line Umpires and Ball Boys when in their respective places.

Rule 3

Ball—Size, Weight and Bound

The ball shall have a uniform outer surface and shall be white or yellow in color. If there are any seams they shall be stitchless. The ball shall be more than two and a half inches (6.35cm) and less than two and five-eighths inches (6.67cm) in diameter, and more than two ounces (56.7 grams) and less than two and one-sixteenth ounces (58.5 grams) in weight. The ball shall have a bound of more than 53 inches (135cm) and less than 58 inches (147cm) when dropped 100 inches (254cm) upon a concrete base. The ball shall have a forward deformation of more than .220 of an inch (.56cm) and less than .290 of an inch (.74cm) and a return deformation of more than .350 of an inch (.89cm) and less than .425 of an inch (1.08cm) at 18 lbs. (8.165kg) load. The two deformation figures shall be the averages of three individual readings along three axes of the ball and no two individual readings shall differ by more than .030 of an inch (.08cm) in each case. All tests for bound, size and deformation shall be made in accordance with the regulations in the Appendix hereto.

Note—At the Annual General Meeting of the I.T.F. held on 12th July, 1967, it was agreed that for the time being non-pressurized balls and low-pressure balls may not be used in the International Tennis Championship (Davis Cup), unless mutually agreed by the two nations taking part in any particular event.

Note—

"How often may the player have new balls?" The ball-change pattern is specified by the Referee before the match is started. According to Tournament Regulations the Chair Umpire may call for a ball change at other than the prescribed time when in his opinion abnormal conditions warrant so doing. In a non-officiated match the players should agree beforehand on this matter.

Rule 4

Server and Receiver

The Players shall stand on opposite sides of the net; the player who first delivers the ball shall be called the Server, and the other the Receiver.

Case 1. Does a player, attempting a stroke, lose the point if he crosses the imaginary line in the extension of the net, (a) before striking the ball (b) after striking the ball?

> Decision: He does not lose the point in either case by crossing the imaginary line provided he does not enter the lines bounding his opponent's court. (Rule 18 (e.) In regard to hindrance, his opponent may ask for the decision of the umpire under Rules 19 and 23.

Case 2. The Server claims that the Receiver must stand within the lines bounding his court. Is this necessary?

> Decision: No. the Receiver may stand wherever he pleases on his own side of the net.

Rule 5

Choice of Ends and Service

The choice of ends and the right to be Server or Receiver in the first game shall be decided by toss. The player winning the toss may choose, or require his opponent to choose:

(a) The right to be Server or Receiver, in which case the other player shall choose the end; or

(b) The end, in which case the other player shall choose the right to be Server or Receiver.

Note—These choices should be made promptly, and are irrevocable.

Rule 6

Delivery of Service

The service shall be delivered in the following manner. Immediately before commencing to serve, the Server shall stand with both feet at rest behind (i.e. farther from the net than) the base-line, and within the imaginary continuations of the center-mark and side-line. The Server shall then project the ball by hand into the air in any direction and before it hits the ground strike it with his racket, and the delivery shall be deemed to have been completed at the moment of the impact of the racket and the ball. A player with the use of only one arm may utilize his racket for the projection.

Case 1. May the Server in a singles game take his stand behind the portion of the base-line between the sidelines of the singles court and the doubles court?

> Decision. No.

Case 2. If a player, when serving, throws up two or more balls instead of one, does he lose that service?

> Decision. No. A let should be called, but if the umpire regards the action as deliberate he may take action under Rule 19.

Case 3. May a player serve underhand?

> Decision. Yes. There is no restriction regarding the kind of service which may be used; that is, the player may use an underhand or overhand service at his discretion.

Rule 7

Foot Fault

The Server shall throughout the delivery of the service:

(1) Not change his position by walking or running.

(b) Not touch, with either foot, any area other than that behind the base-line within the imaginary extension of the center-mark and side-line.

*Note—*The following interpretation of Rule 7 was approved by the International Federation on 9th July 1958:—

(a) The Server shall not, by slight movements of the feet which do not materially affect the location originally taken up by him, be deemed "to change his position by walking or running."

(b) The word "foot" means the extremity of the leg below the ankle.

COMMENT: This rule covers the most decisive stroke in the game, and there is no justification for its not being obeyed by players and enforced by officials. No tournament official has the right to request or attempt to instruct any umpires to disregard violations of it.

Rule 8

From Alternate Courts

(a) In delivering the service, the Server shall stand alternately behind the right and left Courts, beginning from the right in every game. If service from a wrong half of the Court occurs and is undetected, all play resulting from such wrong service or services shall stand, but the inaccuracy of the station shall be corrected immediately it is discovered.

(b) The ball served shall pass over the net and hit the ground within the Service Court which is diagonally opposite, or upon any line bounding such Court, before the Receiver returns it.

COMMENT: The Receiver is not allowed to volley a served ball, i.e., he must allow it to strike in his court first. (See Rule 16 (a).

Note: In matches played without umpires, it is customary for the Receiver to determine whether the service is good or fault; indeed each player makes the calls for all balls hit to his side of the net. (In doubles, the Receiver's partner makes the calls with respect to the service line. It is the prerogative of the Receiver, or his partner, to call a foot fault or faults, but only after all efforts (appeal to the server, requests for monitoring help, etc.) have failed, and the foot faulting is so flagrant as to be clearly perceptible from the Receiver's side.

Rule 9

Faults

The Service is a fault:

(a) If the Server commit any breach of Rules 6, 7, or 8;

(b) If he miss the ball in attempting to strike it;

(c) If the ball served touch a permanent fixture (other than the net, strap or band) before it hits the ground.

Case 1. After throwing a ball up preparatory to serving, the Server decides not to strike at it and catches it instead. Is it a fault?

Decision. No.

Case 2. In serving in a singles game played on a doubles court with doubles and singles net posts, the ball hits a singles post and then hits the ground within the lines of the correct service court. Is this a fault or a let?

Decision. In serving it is a fault, because the singles post, the doubles post, and that portion of the net, strap or band between them are permanent fixtures. (Rules 2 and 9, and note to Rule 22.)

EXPLANATION: The significant point governing Case 2 is that the part of the net and band "outside" the singles sticks is not part of the net over which this singles match is being played. Thus such a serve is a fault under the provisions of article (c) above . . . By the same token, this would be a fault also if it were a singles game played with permanent posts in the singles position. (See Case 1 under Rule 22 for difference between "service" and "good return" with respect to a ball's hitting a net post.)

COMMENT: In doubles, if the Server's delivery hits his partner, the serve is a fault (not necessarily loss of point). See Rule 37.

Rule 10

Service After a Fault

After a fault (if it be the first fault) the Server shall serve again from behind the same half of the Court from which he served that fault, unless the service was from the wrong half, when in accordance with Rule 8, the Server shall be entitled to one service only from behind the other half. A fault may not be claimed after the next service has been delivered.

Case 1. A player serves from a wrong court. He loses the point and then claims it was a fault because of his wrong station.

Decision. The points stands as played and the next service should be from the correct station according to the score.

Case 2. The point score being 15 all, the Server, by mistake, serves from the left-hand court. He wins the point. He then serves again from the right-hand court, delivering a fault. The mistake in station is then discovered. Is he entitled to the previous point? From which court should be next serve?

Decision. The previous point stands. The next service should be from the left-hand court, the score being 30/15, and the Server has served one fault.

Note: When a first service is belatedly determined by the officials to have been a fault–either during the ensuing rally or after the point has been played out the chair umpire is authorized to grant a full "let" (i.e., first service to come) on the ground of the nature and extent of the delay.

Rule 11

Receiver Must be Ready

The Server shall not serve until the Receiver is ready. If the latter attempts to return the service, he shall be deemed ready. If, however, the Receiver signifies that he is not ready, he may not claim a fault because the ball does not hit the ground within the limits fixed for the service.

Note: The Server must wait until the Receiver is ready for the second service as well as the first, and if the Receiver claims to be not ready and does not make any effort to return a service, the Server may not claim the point, even though the service was good.

Rule 12

A Let

Note: A service that touches the net in passing yet falls into the proper court, is a let. This word is used also when, because of an interruption while the ball is in play, or for any other reason, a point is to be replayed.

In all cases where a let has to be called under the rules, or to provide for an interruption to play, it shall have the following interpretations:

(a) When called solely in respect of a service, that one service only shall be replayed.

(b) When called under any other circumstance, the point shall be replayed.

Case 1. A service is interrupted by some cause outside those defined in Rule 13. Should the service only be re-played?

Decision. No, the whole point must be replayed.

EXPLANATION: The phrase "in respect of a service" in (a) means a let because a served ball has touched the net before landing in the proper court, OR because the Receiver was not ready . . . Case 1 refers to a second serve, and the decision means that if the interruption occurs during delivery of the second service, the Server gets two serves.

EXAMPLE: On a second service a Linesman calls "fault" and immediately corrects it (the Receiver meanwhile having let the ball go by). The Server is entitled to two serves, on this ground: The corrected call means that the Server had put the ball into play with a good service, and once the ball is in play and a let is called, the point must be replayed . . . Note, however, that if the serve were an unmistakable ace–that is, the Umpire was sure the erroneous call had no part in the Receiver's inability to play the ball–the point should be declared for the Server.
Case 2. If a ball in play becomes broken, should a let be called?
   Decision. Yes.

Note: A ball shall be regarded as having become "broken" if, in the opinion of the Chair Umpire, it is found to have lost compression to the point of being unfit for further play, or unfit for any reason, and it is clear the defective ball was the one in play.

Rule 13

The Service Is A Let

The service is a let:
 (a) If the ball served touches the net, strap or band, and is otherwise good, or, after touching the net, strap or band, touches the Receiver or anything which he wears or carries before hitting the ground.
 (b) If service or a fault be delivered when the Receiver is not ready (see Rule 11).

COMMENT: A "let" called for the reason the Receiver had indicated he is not ready, if called on second service, does not annul a fault on first serve.

Rule 14

When Receiver Becomes Server

At the end of the first game the Receiver shall become the Server, and the Server Receiver; and so on alternately in all the subsequent games of a match. If a player serves out of turn, the player who ought to have served shall serve as soon as the mistake is discovered, but all points scored before such discovery shall be reckoned. If a game shall have been completed before such discovery, the order of service remains as altered. A fault served before such discovery shall not be reckoned.

Note: If an error in serving sequence occurs and is discovered during a TIE-BREAKER game the serving sequence should be adjusted immediately so as to bring the number of points served by each player into the fairest possible balance. All completed points shall count.

Rule 15

Ball in Play Till Point Decided

A ball is in play from the moment at which it is delivered in service. Unless a fault or a let be called, it remains in play until the point is decided.

COMMENT: A point is not "decided" simply when, or because, a good shot has clearly passed a player, nor when an apparently bad shot passes over a baseline or sideline. An outgoing ball is still definitely "in play" until it actually strikes the ground, backstop or other fixture. The same applies to a good ball, bounding after it has landed in the proper court. A ball that becomes imbedded in the net is out of play.

Case 1. A ball is played into the net; the player on the other side, thinking that the ball is coming over, strikes at it and hits the net. Who loses the point?

Decision: If the player touches the net while the ball was still in play, he loses the point.

Rule 16

Server Wins Point

The Server wins the point:
- (a) If the ball served, not being a let under Rule 13, touch the Receiver or anything which he wears or carries, before it hits the ground;
- (b) If the Receiver otherwise loses the point as provided by Rule 18.

Rule 17

Receiver Wins Point

The Receiver wins the point:
- (a) If the Server serves two consecutive faults;
- (b) If the Server otherwise loses the point as provided by Rule 18.

Rule 18

Player Loses Point

A player loses the point if:
- (a) He fails, before the ball in play has hit the ground twice consecutively, to return it directly over the net (except as provided in Rule 22(a) or (c); or
- (b) He returns the ball in play so that it hits the ground, a permanent fixture, or other object, outside any of the lines which bound his opponent's Court (except as provided in Rule 22(a) and (c); or
- (c) He volleys the ball and fail to make a good return even when standing outside the Court; or
- (d) He touches or strikes the ball in play with his racket more than once in making a stroke; or

EXPLANATION: A player may be deemed to have touched the ball more than once if the ball takes an obvious second trajectory as it comes off the racket, or comes off the racket in such a way that the effect is that of a "sling" or "throw" rather than that of a "hit." Such strokes are informally referred to as "double hits" or "carries." Experienced umpires give the player the benefit of the doubt unless they see such a second trajectory or a definite "second push."

- (e) He or his racket (in his hand or otherwise) or anything which he wears or carries touches the net, post (singles stick, if they are in use), cord or metal cable, strap or band, or the ground within the opponent's Court at any time while the ball is in play; or
- (f) He volleys the ball before it has passed the net; or
- (g) The ball in play touches him or anything that he wears or carries, except his racket in his hand or hands; or

Note that this loss of point occurs regardless of whether the player is inside or outside the bounds of his court when the ball touches him. A player is considered to be "wearing or carrying" anything that he was wearing or carrying at the beginning of the point during which the touch occurred.

(h) He throws his racket at and hits the ball.

EXAMPLE: Player has let racket go out of his hand clearly before racket hits ball, but the ball rebounds from his racket into proper court. This is not a good return; player loses point.

Case 1. In delivering a first service which falls outside the proper court, the Server's racket slips out of his hand and flies into the net. Does he lose the point?

Decision. If his racket touches the net while the ball is in play, the Server loses the point (Rule 18 (e)).

Case 2. In serving, the racket flies from the Server's hand and touches the net before the ball has touched the ground. Is this a fault, or does the player lose the point?

Decision. The Server loses the point because his racket touched the net while the ball was in play. (Rule 18 (e)).

Case 3. A and B are playing against C and D. C touches the net before the ball touches the ground. A fault is then called because the service falls outside the service court. Do C and D lose the point?

Decision. The call "fault" is an erroneous one. C and D have already lost the point before "fault" could be called, because C touched the net while the ball was in play. (Rule 18 (e)).

Case 4. May a player jump over the net into the opponent's court· while the ball is in play and not suffer penalty?

Decision. No; he loses the point. (Rule 18 (e).)

Case 5. A cuts the ball just over the net, and it returns to A's side. B, unable to reach the ball, throws his racket and hits the ball. Both racket and ball fall over the net on A's court. A returns the ball outside of B's court. Does B win or lose the point?

Decision. B loses the point. (Rule 18 (e) and (h).)

Case 6. A player standing outside the service court is struck by the service ball before it has touched the ground. Does he win or lose the point?

Decision. The player struck loses the point (Rule 18 (g), except as provided under Rule 13 (a).)

EXPLANATION: The exception referred to is that of a served ball that has touched the net en route into the Receiver's court; in that circumstance it is a let service, not loss of point. Such a let does not annul a previous (first service) fault: therefore if it occurs on second service, the Server has one serve coming.

Case 7. A player standing outside the court volleys the ball or catches it in his hand and claims the point because the ball was certainly going out of court.

Decision. In no circumstance can he claim the point;

(1) If he catches the ball he loses the point under Rule 18 (g).

(2) If he volleys it and makes a bad return he loses the point under Rule 18 (c).

(3) If he volleys it and makes a good return, the rally continues.

Rule 19

Player Hinders Opponent

If a player commits any act either deliberate or involuntary which, in the opinion of the Umpire, hinders his opponent in making a stroke, the Umpire shall in the first case award the point to the opponent, and in the second case order the point to be replayed.

Case 1. Is a player liable to a penalty if in making a stroke he touches his opponent?

Decision. No. unless the Umpire deems it necessary to take action under Rule 19.

Case 2. When a ball bounds back over the net, the player concerned may reach over the net in order to play the ball. What is the ruling if the player is hindered from doing this by his opponent?

Decision. In accordance with Rule 19, the Umpire may either award the point to the player hindered, or order the point to be replayed. (See also Rule 23.)

USTA Interpretation: Upon appeal by a competitor that an opponent's action in discarding a "second ball" after a rally has started constitutes a distraction (hindrance), the Umpire, if he deems the claim valid, shall require the opponent to make some other, and satisfactory, disposition of the ball. Failure to comply with this instruction may result in loss of point(s) or disqualification.

Rule 20

Ball Falling on Line—Good

A ball falling on a line is regarded as falling in the Court bounded by that line.

COMMENT: In matches played without officials, it is customary for each player to make the calls on all balls hit to his side of the net, and if a player cannot call a ball out with surety he sould regard it as good.

Rule 21

Ball Touching Permanent Fixture

If the ball in play touches a permanent fixture (other than the net, posts, cord or metal cable, strap or band) after it has hit the ground, the player who struck it wins the point; if before it hits the ground his opponent wins the point.
Case 1. A return hits the Umpire or his chair or stand. The player claims that the ball was going into court.
　　　Decision. He loses the point.

Rule 22

Good Return

It is a good return:
　　(a) If the ball touch the net, post (singles stick, if they are in use), cord or metal cable, strap or band, provided that it passes over any of them and hits the ground within the Court; or
　　(b) If the ball, served or returned, hits the gound within the proper Court and rebound or be blown back over the net, and the player whose turn it is to strike reach over the net and play the ball, provided that neither he nor any part of his clothes or racket touch the net, post (singles stick), cord or metal cable, strap or band or the ground within his opponent's Court, and that the stroke be otherwise good; or
　　(c) If the ball be returned outside the post or singles stick, either above or below the level of the top of the net, even though it touch the (singles) post, provided that it hits the ground within the proper Court; or
　　(d) If a player's racket passes over the net after he has returned the ball, provided the ball pass the net before being played and be properly returned; or
　　(e) If a player succeeds in returning the ball, served or in play, which strikes a ball lying in the Court.

Note—If, for the sake of convenience, a doubles court be equipped with singles posts for the purpose of singles game, then the doubles post and those portions of the net, cord or metal cable and band outside such singles posts shall be regarded as "permanent fixtures *other than* net, post, strap or band," and therefore *not* posts or parts of the net of the singles game.

A return that passes under the net cord between the singles and adjacent doubles post without touching either net cord, net or doubles post and falls within the area of play, is a good return. (But in doubles this would be a "through"—loss of point.)

Case 1. A ball going out of court hits a net post and falls within the lines of the opponent's court. Is the stroke good?

>Decision. If a service; no, under Rule 9 (c). If other than a service; yes, under Rule 22 (a).

Case 2. Is it a good return if a player returns the ball holding his racket in both hands?

>Decision. Yes.

Case 3. The Service, or ball in play, strikes a ball lying in the court. Is the point won or lost thereby? (A ball that is touching a boundary line is considered to be "lying in the court".)

>Decision. No. Play must continue. If it is not clear to the Umpire that the right ball is returned a let should be called.

Case 4. May a player use more than one racket at any time during play?

>Decision. No. The whole implication of the rules is singular.

Case 5. Must a player's request for the removal of a ball or balls lying in the opponent's court be honored?

>Decision. Yes.

Rule 23

Interference

In case a player is hindered in making a stroke by anything not within his control except a permanent fixture of the Court, or except as provided for in Rule 19, the point shall be replayed.

Case 1. A spectator gets into the way of a player, who fails to return the ball. May the player then claim a let?

>Decision. Yes, If in the Umpire's opinion he was obstructed by circumstances beyond his control, but not if due to permanent fixtures of the Court or the arrangements of the ground.

Case 2. A player is interfered with as in Case 1, and the Umpire calls a let. The Server had previously served a fault. Has he the right to two services?

>Decision. Yes, as the ball was in play, the point, not merely the stroke, must be replayed as the rule provides.

Case 3. May a player claim a let under Rule 23 because he thought his opponent was being hindered, and consequently did not expect the ball to be returned?

>Decision: No.

Case 4. Is a stroke good when a ball in play hits another ball in the air?

>Decision. A let should be called unless the other ball is in the air by the act of one of the players, in which case the Umpire will decide under Rule 19.

Case 5. If an Umpire or other judge erroneously calls "fault" or "out" and then corrects himself, which of the calls shall prevail?

>Decision. A let must be called, unless, in the opinion of the Umpire, neither player is hindered in his game, in which case the corrected call shall prevail.

Case 6. If the first ball served—a fault—rebounds, interfering with the Receiver at the time of the second service, may the Receiver claim a let?

>Decision. Yes. But if he had an opportunity to remove the ball from the court and negligently failed to do so, he may not claim a let.

Case 7. Is it a good stroke if the ball touches a stationary or moving object on the court?

>Decision. It is a good stroke unless the stationary object came into court after the ball was put into play in which case a "let" must be called. If the ball in play strikes an object moving along or above the surface of the court a "let" must be called.

Case 8. What is the ruling if the first service is a fault, the second service correct, and it becomes necessary to call a let under the provisions of Rule 23 or if the Umpire is unable to decide the point?

>Decision. The fault shall be annulled and the whole point replayed.

COMMENT: See Rule 12 and Explanantion thereto.

Rule 24

The Game

If a player wins his first point, the score is called *15* for that player; on winning his second point, the score is called *30* for that player; on winning his third point, the score is called *40* for that player, and the fourth point won by a player is scored *game* for that player except as below:

If both players have won three points, the score is called *deuce*; and the next point won by a player is called *advantage for that player*. If the same player wins the next point, he wins the game; if the other player wins the next point the score is again called *deuce*; and so on until a player wins the two points immediately following the score at deuce, when the game is scored for that player.

COMMENT: In matches played without an umpire the Server should announce, in a voice audible to his opponent and spectators, the set score at the beginning of each game, and (audible at least to his opponent) point scores as the game goes on. Misunderstandings will be averted if this practice is followed.

Rule 25

The Set

A player (or players) who first wins six games wins a set; except that he must win by a margin of two games over his opponent and where necessary a set shall be extended until this margin be achieved. NOTE: See tiebreaker.

Rule 26

When Players Change Ends

The players shall change ends at the end of the first, third and every subsequent alternative game of each set, and at the end of each set unless the total number of games in such set be even, in which case the change is not made until the end of the first game of the next set.

Rule 27

Maximum Number of Sets

The maximum number of sets in a match shall be 5, or, where women take part, 3.

Rule 28

Rules Apply to Both Sexes

Except where otherwise stated, every reference in these Rules to the masculine includes the feminine gender.

Rule 29

Decisions of Umpire and Referee

In matches where a Chair Umpire is appointed his decision shall be final; but where a Referee is appointed an appeal shall lie to him from the decision of a Chair Umpire on a question of law, and in all such cases the decision of the Referee shall be final.

In matches where assistants to the Chair Umpire are appointed (Line Umpires, Net Umpires, Foot-fault Judge) their decisions shall be final on question of fact. When such an assistant is unable to give a decision he shall indicate this immediately to the Chair Umpire who shall give a decision. When the Chair is unable to give a decision on a question of fact he shall order a let to be called.

In Davis Cup and Wightman Cup and Bonne Bell Cup matches only, the decision of an assistant to the Chair Umpire, or of the Chair Umpire if the assistant is unable to make a decision, can be changed by the Referee, who may also authorize the Chair Umpire to change the decision of an assistant or order a let to be called.

The Referee, in his discretion, may at any time postpone a match on account of darkness or the condition of the ground or the weather. In any case of postponement the previous score and previous occupancy of courts shall hold good, unless the Referee and the players unanimously agree otherwise.

Rule 30

Play shall be continuous from the first service till the match be concluded; provided that after the third set, or, when women take part, the second set, either player is entitled to a rest, which shall not exceed 10 minutes, or in countries situated between Latitude 15 degrees North and Latitude 15 degrees South, 45 minutes, and provided further that when necessitated by circumstances not within the control of the players, the Umpire may suspend play for such a period as he may consider necessary. If play be suspended and be not resumed until a later day the rest may be taken only after the third set (or when women take part the second set) of play on such later day, completion of an unfinished set being counted as one set. These provisions shall be strictly construed, and play shall never be suspended, delayed or interfered with for the purpose of enabling a player to recover his strength or his wind, or to receive instruction or advice. The Chair Umpire shall be the sole judge of such suspension, delay or interference, and after giving due warning he may disqualify the offender.

(a) Any nation is at liberty to modify the first provision of Rule 30, or omit it from its regulations governing tournaments, matches, or competitions held in its own county, other than the International Lawn Tennis Championships (Davis Cup and Federation Cup).

(b) When chamging sides a maximum of one minute shall elapse from the cessation of the previous game to the time players are ready to begin the next game. (This provision became operative in 1968.)

Notes: Accepted practice in Grand Prix events (MIPTC-sanctioned) is that the changeover allowed time starts when the first player reaches the immediate vicinity of the umpire's chair.

Players and Chair Umpires should understand that the reminder: "15 seconds" by either the Chair or Net Umpire refers to the time play should actually resume. It does not mean there is 15 seconds more of sitting time.

Should a player, on account of physical unfitness or an unavoidable accident, not within his control, be unable to continue play, he must be defaulted.

If an Umpire decides that a player is deliberately stalling to gain time or unfairly disconcert his opponent he should warn the player once, and if the practice continues the Umpire should default him. (See Point Penalties System)

USTA Rules Regarding Rest Periods in Age-Limited Categories:

Regular MEN'S and WOMEN'S, and MEN'S 21 and WOMEN'S 21—The first paragraph of Rule 30 applies, except that a tournament using tie-breakers may eliminate rest periods provided advance notice is given.

BOYS' 18—All matches in this division shall be best of three sets with NO REST PERIOD, except that in interscholastic, state, sectional, and national championships the FINAL ROUND may be best-of-five. If such a final requires more than three sets to decide it, a rest of 10 minutes after the third set is mandatory. Special Note: In severe temperature-humidity conditions a Referee may rule that a 10-minute rest may be taken in a Boys' 18 best-of-three. However, to be valid this must be done before the match is started, and as a matter of the Referee's independent judgment.

BOYS' 16, 14 and 12. And GIRLS' 18, 16, 14 and 12—All matches in these categories shall be best of three sets. A 10-minute rest before the third set is MANDATORY in Girls' 12, 14, and 16, and in Boys' 12 and 14. The rest period is OPTIONAL in Girls' 18 and Boys' 16. (Optional means at the option of any competitor.)

All SENIOR divisions (35's, 40's, 45's, 50's and up), and Father-and-Son: Under conventional scoring, all matches best-of-three, with rest period optional.

WHEN 'NO-AD' SCORING IS USED IN A TOURNAMENT . . . A tournament committee may stipulate that there will be not rest periods, even in some age divisions where rest periods would be optional under conventional scoring. These divisions are: regular Men's (best-of-five) and Women's . . . Men's 21 . . . Men's 35 . . . Seniors (men 45 and over) . . . Father-and-Son.

N.B. Two conditions of this stipulation are: (1) Advance notice must be given on entry blanks for the event, and (2) The Referee is empowered to reinstate the normal rest periods for matches played under unusually severe temperature-humidity conditions; to be valid, such reinstatement must be announced before a given match or series of matches is started, and be a matter of the Referee's independent judgement.

COMMENT: *When a player competes in an event designed as for players of a bracket whose rules as to intermissions and length of match are geared to a different physical status, the player cannot ask for allowances based on his or her age, or her sex. For example, a female competing in an intercollegiate (men's) varsity team match would not be entitled to claim a rest period in a best-of-three-sets match unless that were the condition under which the team competition was normally held.*

Case 1. A player's clothing, footwear, or equipment becomes out of adjustment in such a way that it is impossible or undesirable for him to play on. May play be suspended while the maladjustment is rectified?

  Decision. If this occurs in circumstances not within the control of the player, of which circumstances the Umpire is the sole judge, a suspension may be allowed.

Case 2. If, owing to an accident, a player is unable to continue immediately, is there any limit to the time during which play may be suspended?

  Decision. No allowance may be made for natural loss of physical condition. Consideration may be given by the Umpire for accidental loss of physical ability or condition.

COMMENT: *Case 2 refers to an important distinction that should be made between a temporary disability caused by an accident during play, and disability caused by fatigue (cramps or muscle pull, for example). Not even momentary "rest" is allowed for recovery from "natural loss of physical condition." Even in case of accident, no more than three minutes should be spent in diagnosis/prognosis, and if bandaging or medication is going to require more than that, the decision as to whether any additional time is to be allowed should be reached by the Referee after considering the recommendation of the Chair Umpire; and, of course, taking into account the need for being fair to the non-injured player.*

Case 3. During a doubles game, may one of the partners leave the court while the remaining partner keeps the ball in play?

Decision. Yes, so long as the Umpire is satisfied that play is continuous within the meaning of the rules, and that there is no conflict with Rules 33 and 34. (See Case 1, of Rule 33)

Note: When a match is resumed following an interruption necessitated by weather conditions, it is allowable for the players to engage in a "re-warm-up" period. It may be of the same duration as the warm-up allowed at the start of the match: may be done using the balls that were in play at the time of the interruption, and the time for the next ball change shall not be affected by this.

The Doubles Game

Rule 31

The above Rules shall apply to the Doubles Game except as below.

Rule 32

Dimensions of Court

For the Doubles Game the Court shall be 36 feet (10.97m) in width, i.e., 4½ feet (1.37m) wider on each side than the Court for the Singles Game, and those portions of the singles sidelines which lie between the two service lines shall be called the service sidelines. In other respects, the Court shall be similar to that described in Rule 1, but the portions of the singles sidelines between the baseline and the service line on each side of the net may be omitted if desired.

Case 1. In doubles the Server claims the right to stand at the corner of the court as marked by the doubles side line. Is the foregoing correct or is it necessary that the Server stand within the limits of the center mark and the singles side line?

Decision. The Server has the right to stand anywhere between the center mark and the doubles sideline.

Rule 33

Order of Service

The order of serving shall be decided at the beginning of each set as follows:

The pair who have to serve in the first game of each set shall decide which partner shall do so and the opposing pair shall decide similarly for the second game. The partner of the player who served in the first game shall serve in the third; the partner of the player who served in the second game shall serve in the fourth, and so on in the same order in all the subsequent games of a set.

EXPLANATION: It is not required that the order of service, as between partners, carry over from one set to the next. Each team is allowed to decide which partner shall serve first for it, in each set. This same option applies with respect to the order of receiving service.

Case 1. In doubles, one player does not appear in time to play, and his partner claims to be allowed to play single-handed against the opposing players. May he do so?

Decision. No.

Rule 34

Order of Receiving

The order of Receiving the service shall be decided at the beginning of each set as follows:

The pair who have to receive the service in the first game shall decide which partner shall receive the first service, and that partner shall continue to receive the first service in every odd game throughout that set. The opposing pair shall likewise decide which partner shall receive the first service in the second game and that partner shall continue to receive the first service in every even game throughout that set. Partners shall receive the service alternately throughout each game.

EXPLANATION: The receiving formation of a doubles team may not be changed during a set; only at the start of a new set. Partners must receive throughout each set on the same sides of the court which they originally select when the set began. The first Server is not required to receive in the right court; he may select either side, but must hold this to the end of the set. Case 1. Is it allowable in doubles for the Server's partner to stand in a position that obstructs the view of the Receiver?

   Decision. Yes. The Server's partner may take any position on his side of the net in or out of the court that he wishes. (The same is true on the Receiver's partner).

Rule 35

Service Out of Turn

If a partner serves out of his turn, the partner who ought to have served shall serve as soon as the mistake is discovered, but all points scored, and any faults served before such discovery shall be reckoned. If a game shall have been completed before such discovery the order of service remains as altered.

Rule 36

Error in Order of Receiving

If during a game the order of receiving the service is changed by the receivers it shall remain as altered until the end of the game in which the mistake is discovered, but the partners shall resume their original order of receiving in the next game of that set in which they are receivers of the service.

Rule 37

Ball Touching Server's Partner Is Fault

The service is a fault as provided for by Rule 9, or if the ball served touches the Server's partner or anything he wears or carries; but if the ball served touches the partner of the Receiver or anything which he wears or carries, not being a let under Rule 13 (a), before it hits the ground, the Server wins the point.

Rule 38

Ball Struck Alternately

The ball shall be struck alternately by one or other player of the opposing pairs, and if a player touches the ball in play with his racket in contravention of this Rule, his opponents wins the point.

EXPLANATION: This means that, in the course of making one return, only one member of a doubles team may hit the ball. If both of them hit the ball, either simultaneously of consecutively, it is an illegal return. The partners themselves do not have to "alternate" in making returns. (Mere clashing of rackets does not make a return illegal, if it is clear that only one racket touched the ball.)

APPENDIX B: RECORDS

UNITED STATES CHAMPIONSHIPS

The United States Championships, now called the U.S. Open at the U.S. National Tennis Center, Flushing Meadow, New York, had separate beginnings for men and women. The first Championships, men only, was staged at the Newport Casino in 1881, and held there through 1914. The doubles championship was played along with the singles between 1881 and 1886. From 1887 through 1914, sectional doubles tournaments, East and West, sometimes North and South as well, were staged at various locations with the winners playing off for the title at Newport.

In 1915 the men's singles moved to the West Side Tennis Club, Forest Hills, New York, as did the doubles final for sectional winners. In 1917 the men's doubles championship, a complete tournament, was installed at the Longwood Cricket Club, Boston, and remained there through 1967, with two exceptions (1934 at Germantown Cricket Club, Philadelphia, and 1942 through 1945 at West Side, Forest Hills, during World War II).

The men's singles departed briefly from Forest Hills for a three-year stay at Germantown Cricket, Philadelphia, 1921 through 1923, and thereafter was staged at West Side where the newly constructed Stadium was ready in 1924.

The women's championships in singles and doubles began in 1887 at the Philadelphia Cricket Club, Philadelphia, and remained there through 1920, along with the mixed doubles, begun in 1892. In 1921 the women's singles and doubles moved to West Side, Forest Hills, but as an event prior to and separate from the men's championship, while the mixed doubles moved to Longwood, Boston, to be played concurrently with the men's doubles.

In 1935 the men's and women's singles championships were united at Forest Hills while the women's doubles moved to Longwood, Boston, as part of the National Doubles with men's and mixed events.

During World War II (1942–45) all five events—men's and women's singles and doubles and mixed—were played at Forest Hills. In 1946 the men's and women's doubles returned to Longwood but the mixed remained at West Side until 1967 when it was played again at Longwood.

In 1968, with the advent of open tennis, the Championships, an amateur event closed to professionals since inception, was moved to Longwood where men's and women's singles and doubles and mixed were played as amateur events in 1968–69. Forest Hills thus became the scene of the first U.S. Open in 1968, and remained so until the move to Flushing Meadow in 1978. Men's and women's singles and doubles and mixed were thereby open to professionals and amateurs alike, and prize money was offered from 1968 on. The original amateurs-only event was abandoned in Boston after 1969, eliminating the confusion of two U.S. championships on successive dates on the calendar.

The Championships began on grass courts and continued that way until 1975 when the Forest Hills surface was changed to clay. The present surface at Flushing Meadow is hard, an asphalt composition. Night play began with the installation of floodlights in 1975 at Forest Hills.

The following is a list of champions and finalists in men's and women's singles and doubles, and champions in mixed doubles. The challenge round system was in force from 1884 through

1911, meaning that the defending champion played only one match, waiting for a challenger to emerge from an all-comers tournament. Sometimes the champion did not defend, and the winner of the all-comers became champion. The system has not been used since 1911.

U.S. championships are also determined on clay courts and indoor courts at various locations for men and women. The indoor championships began in 1898 for men and 1907 for women; the clay court in 1910 for men, 1912 for women. A hard court championships for men and women, begun in 1948, was discontinued after 1971, and is obviously no longer called for since the U.S. Open is played on hard courts.

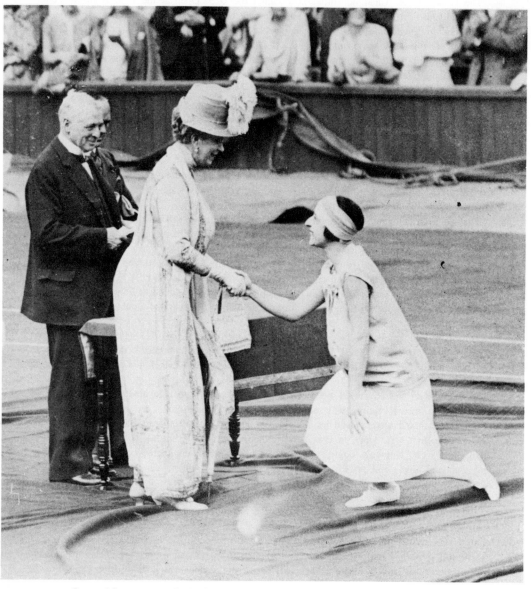

Queen Mary congratulates the queen of Wimbledon, Suzanne Lenglen. *UPI*

Men's Singles

Year

1881	Richard Sears d. W. Glyn 6–0, 6–3, 6–2
1882	Richard Sears d. Clarence Clark 6–1, 6–4, 6–0
1883	Richard Sears d. James Dwight 6–2, 6–0, 9–7
1884	Richard Sears d. Howard Taylor 6–0, 1–6, 6–0, 6–2
1885	Richard Sears d. G. Brinley 6–3, 4–6, 6–0, 6–3
1886	Richard Sears d. R. Beeckman 4–6, 6–1, 6–3, 6–4
1887	Richard Sears d. Henry Slocum 6–1, 6–3, 6–2
1888	Henry Slocum d. Howard Taylor 6–4, 6–1, 6–0
1889	Henry Slocum d. Q. Shaw 6–3, 6–1, 4–6, 6–2
1890	Oliver Campbell d. Henry Slocum 6–2, 4–6, 6–3, 6–1
1891	Oliver Campbell d. Clarence Hobart 2–6, 7–5, 7–9, 6–1, 6–2
1892	Oliver Campbell d. Fred Hovey 7–5, 3–6, 6–3, 7–5
1893	Robert Wrenn d. Fred Hovey 6–4, 3–6, 6–4, 6–4
1894	Robert Wrenn d. Manlove Goodbody 6–8, 6–1, 6–4, 6–4
1895	Fred Hovey d. Robert Wrenn 6–3, 6–2, 6–4
1896	Robert Wrenn d. Fred Hovey 7–5, 3–6, 6–0, 1–6, 6–1
1897	Robert Wrenn d. Wilberforce Eaves 4–6, 8–6, 6–3, 2–6, 6–2
1898	Malcolm Whitman d. Dwight Davis 2–6, 6–2, 6–2, 6–1
1899	Malcolm Whitman d. Parmely Paret 6–1, 6–2, 3–6, 7–5
1900	Malcolm Whitman d. Bill Larned 6–4, 1–6, 6–2, 6–2
1901	Bill Larned d. Beals Wright 6–2, 6–8, 6–4, 6–4
1902	Bill Larned d. Reggie Doherty 4–6, 6–2, 6–4, 8–6
1903	Laurie Doherty d. Bill Larned 6–0, 6–3, 10–8
1904	Holcolm Ward d. Bill Clothier 10–8, 6–4, 9–7
1905	Beals Wright d. Holcombe Ward 6–2, 6–1, 11–9
1906	Bill Clothier d. Beals Wright 6–3, 6–0, 6–4
1907	Bill Larned d. Bob LeRoy 6–2, 6–2, 6–4
1908	Bill Larned d. Beals Wright 6–1, 6–2, 8–6
1909	Bill Larned d. Bill Clothier 6–1, 6–2, 5–7, 1–6, 6–1
1910	Bill Larned d. Tom Bundy 6–1, 5–7, 6–0, 6–8, 6–1
1911	Bill Larned d. Maurice McLoughlin 6–4, 6–4, 6–2
1912	Maurice McLoughlin d. Wallace Johnson 3–6, 2–6, 6–2, 6–4, 6–2
1913	Maurice McLoughlin d. R. Norris Williams 6–4, 5–7, 6–3, 6–1
1914	R. Norris Williams d. Maurice McLougblin 6–3, 8–6, 10–8
1915	Bill Johnston d. Maurice McLoughlin 1–6, 6–0, 7–5, 10–8
1916	R. Norris Williams d. Bill Johnston 4–6, 6–4, 0–6, 6–2, 6–4
1917	R. Lindley Murray d. Nathaniel Niles 5–7, 8–6, 6–3, 6–3
1918	R. Lindley Murray d. Bill Tilden 6–3, 6–1, 7–5
1919	Bill Johnston d. Bill Tilden 6–4, 6–4, 6–3
1920	Bill Tilden d. Bill Johnston 6–1, 1–6, 7–5, 5–7, 6–3
1921	Bill Tilden d. Wallace Johnson 6–1, 6–3, 6–1
1922	Bill Tilden d. Bill Johnston 4–6, 3–6, 6–2, 6–3, 6–4
1923	Bill Tilden d. Bill Johnston 6–4, 6–1, 6–4
1924	Bill Tilden d. Bill Johnston 6–1, 9–7, 6–2
1925	Bill Tilden d. Bill Johnston 4–6, 11–9, 6–3, 4–6, 6–3
1926	René LaCoste d. Jean Borotra 6–4, 6–0, 6–4
1927	René LaCoste d. Bill Tilden 11–9, 6–3, 11–9
1928	Henri Cochet d. Francis Hunter 4–6, 6–4, 3–6, 7–5, 6–3
1929	Bill Tilden d. Francis Hunter 3–6, 6–3, 4–6, 6–2, 6–4
1930	John Doeg d. Frank Shields 10–8, 1–6, 6–4, 16–14
1931	Ellsworth Vines d. George Lott 7–9, 6–3, 9–7, 7–5
1932	Ellsworth Vines d. Henri Cochet 6–4, 6–4, 6–4
1933	Fred Perry d. Jack Crawford 6–3, 11–13, 4–6, 6–0, 6–1

1934	Fred Perry d. Wilmer Allison 6–4, 6–3, 1–6, 8–6	1962	Rod Laver d. Roy Emerson 6–2, 6–4, 5–7, 6–4
1935	Wilmer Allison d. Sidney Wood 6–2, 6–2, 6–3	1963	Rafael Osuna d. Frank Froehling 7–5, 6–4, 6–2
1936	Fred Perry d. Don Budge 2–6, 6–2, 8–6, 1–6, 10–8	1964	Roy Emerson d. Fred Stolle 6–4, 6–1, 6–4
1937	Don Budge d. Gottfried von Cramm 6–1, 7–9, 6–1, 3–6, 6–1	1965	Manuel Santana d. Cliff Drysdale 6–2, 7–9, 7–5, 6–1
1938	Don Budge d. Gene Mako 6–3, 6–8, 6–2, 6–1	1966	Fred Stolle d. John Newcombe 4–6, 12–10, 6–3, 6–4
1939	Bobby Riggs d. Welby Van Horn 6–4, 6–2, 6–4	1967	John Newcombe d. Clark Graebner 6–4, 6–4, 8–6
1940	Don McNeill d. Bobby Riggs 4–6, 6–8, 6–3, 6–3, 7–5	1968	Arthur Ashe d. Bob Lutz 4–6, 6–3, 8–10, 6–0, 6–4
1941	Bobby Riggs d. Frank Kovacs 5–7, 6–1, 6–3, 6–3	1968*	Arthur Ashe d. Tom Okker 14–12, 5–7, 6–3, 3–6, 6–3
1942	Ted Schroeder d. Frank Parker 8–6, 7–5, 3–6, 4–6, 6–2	1969	Stan Smith d. Bob Lutz 9–7, 6–3, 6–1
1943	Joe Hunt d. Jack Kramer 6–3, 6–8, 10–8, 6–0	1969*	Rod Laver d. Tony Roche 7–9, 6–1, 6–3, 6–2
1944	Frank Parker d. Bill Talbert 6–4, 3–6, 6–3, 6–3	1970	Ken Rosewall d. Tony Roche 2–6, 6–4, 7–6, 6–3
1945	Frank Parker d. Bill Talbert 14–12, 6–1, 6–2	1971	Stan Smith d. Jan Kodes 3–6, 6–3, 6–2, 7–6
1946	Jack Kramer d. Tom Brown 9–7, 6–3, 6–0	1972	Ilie Nastase d. Arthur Ashe 3–6, 6–3, 6–7, 6–4, 6–3
1947	Jack Kramer d. Frank Parker 4–6, 2–6, 6–1, 6–0, 6–3	1973	John Newcombe d. Jan Kodes 6–4, 1–6, 4–6, 6–2, 6–3
1948	Pancho Gonzales d. Eric Sturgess 6–2, 6–3, 14–12	1974	Jimmy Connors d. Ken Rosewall 6–1, 6–0, 6–1
1949	Pancho Gonzales d. Ted Schroeder 16–18, 2–6, 6–1, 6–2, 6–4	1975	Manuel Orantes d. Jimmy Connors 6–4, 6–3, 6–3
1950	Art Larsen d. Herbie Flam 6–3, 4–6, 5–7, 6–4, 6–3	1976	Jimmy Connors d. Bjorn Borg 6–4, 3–6, 7–6, 6–4
1951	Frank Sedgman d. Vic Seixas 6–4, 6–1, 6–1	1977	Guillermo Vilas d. Jimmy Connors 2–6, 6–3, 7–6, 6–0
1952	Frank Sedgman d. Gardnar Mulloy 6–1, 6–2, 6–3	1978	Jimmy Connors d. Bjorn Borg 6–4, 6–2, 6–2
1953	Tony Trabert d. Vic Seixas 6–3, 6–2, 6–3	1979	John McEnroe d. Vitas Gerulaitis 7–5, 6–3, 6–3
1954	Vic Seixas d. Rex Hartwig 3–6, 6–2, 6–4, 6–4		
1955	Tony Trabert d. Ken Rosewall 9–7, 6–3, 6–3		
1956	Ken Rosewall d. Lew Hoad 4–6, 6–2, 6–3, 6–3	*Men's Doubles*	
1957	Mal Anderson d. Ashley Cooper 10–8, 7–5, 6–4	*Year*	
1958	Ashley Cooper d. Mal Anderson 6–2, 3–6, 4–6, 10–8, 8–6	1881	Clarence Clark-Fred Taylor d. A. Van Rensselaer-A. Newbold
1959	Neale Fraser d. Alex Olmedo 6–3, 5–7, 6–2, 6–4	1882	Richard Sears-James Dwight d. W. Nightingale-G. Smith
1960	Neale Fraser d. Rod Laver 6–4, 6–4, 9–7	1883	Richard Sears-James Dwight d. A. Van Rensselaer-A. Newbold
1961	Roy Emerson d. Rod Laver 7–5, 6–3, 6–2		

*Open champions. In 1968 and 1969 there were both Amateur and Open Championships held. Thereafter there was only the Open.

1884	Richard Sears-James Dwight d. A. Van Rensselaer-W. Berry	1912	Maurice McLoughlin-Tom Bundy d. Ray Little-Gus Touchard
1885	Richard Sears-Joseph Clark d. Henry Slocum-W. Knapp	1913	Maurice McLoughlin-Tom Bundy d. John Strachan-Clarence Griffin
1886	Richard Sears-James Dwight d. Howard Taylor-G. Brinley	1914	Maurice McLoughlin-Tom Bundy d. George Church-Dean Mathey
1887	Richard Sears-James Dwight d. Howard Taylor-Henry Slocum	1915	Bill Johnston-Clarence Griffin d. Maurice McLoughlin-Tom Bundy
1888	Oliver Campbell-Valentine Hall d. Clarence Hobart-E. MacMullen	1916	Bill Johnston-Clarence Griffin d. Maurice McLoughlin-Ward Dawson
1889	Henry Slocum-Howard Taylor d. Valentine Hall-Oliver Campbell	1917	Fred Alexander-Harold Throckmorton d. Harry Johnson-Irving Wright
1890	Valentine Hall-Clarence Hobart d. J. Carver-J. Ryerson	1918	Bill Tilden-Vinnie Richards d. Fred Alexander-Beals Wright
1891	Oliver Campbell-Bob Huntington d. Valentine Hall-Clarence Hobart	1919	Norman Brookes-Gerald Patterson d. Bill Tilden-Vinnie Richards
1892	Oliver Campbell-Bob Huntington d. Valentine Hall-Edward Hall	1920	Bill Johnston-Clarence Griffin d. Willis Davis-Roland Roberts
1893	Clarence Hobart-Fred Hovey d. Oliver Campbell-Bob Huntington	1921	Bill Tilden-Vinnie Richards d. R. Norris Williams-Watson Washburn
1894	Clarence Hobart-Fred Hovey d. Carr Neel-Sam Neel	1922	Bill Tilden-Vinnie Richards d. Gerald Patterson-Pat Wood
1895	Malcolm Chace-Robert Wrenn d. J. Howland-Arthur Foote	1923	Bill Tilden-Brian Norton d. R. Norris Williams-Watson Washburn
1896	Carr Neel-Sam Neel d. Robert Wrenn-Malcolm Chace	1924	Howard Kinsey-Robert Kinsey d. Gerald Patterson-Pat Wood
1897	Leo Ware-George Sheldon d. Harold Mahony-H. Nisbet	1925	R. Norris Williams-Vinnie Richards d. Gerald Patterson-John Hawkes
1898	Leo Ware-George Sheldon d. Holcombe Ward-Dwight Davis	1926	R. Norris Williams-Vinnie Richards d. Bill Tilden-Al Chapin
1899	Holcombe Ward-Dwight Davis d. Leo Ware-George Sheldon	1927	Bill Tilden-Francis Hunter d. Bill Johnston-R. Norris Williams
1900	Holcombe Ward-Dwight Davis d. Fred Alexander-Ray Little	1928	George Lott-John Hennessey d. Gerald Patterson-John Hawkes
1901	Holcombe Ward-Dwight Davis d. Leo Ware-Beals Wright	1929	George Lott-John Doeg d. Berkeley Bell-Lewis White
1902	Reggie Doherty-Laurie Doherty d. Holcombe Ward-Dwight Davis	1930	George Lott-John Doeg d. John Van Ryn-Wilmer Allison
1903	Reggie Doherty-Laurie Doherty d. Kriegh Collins-Harry Waidner	1931	Wilmer Allison-John Van Ryn d. Greg Mangin-Berkeley Bell
1904	Holcombe Ward-Beals Wright d. Kriegh Collins-Ray Little	1932	Ellsworth Vines-Keith Gledhill d. Wilmer Allison-John Van Ryn
1905	Holcombe Ward-Beals Wright d. Fred Alexander-Harold Hackett	1933	George Lott-Lester Stoefen d. Frank Shields-Frank Parker
1906	Holcombe Ward-Beals Wright d. Fred Alexander-Harold Hackett	1934	George Lott-Lester Stoefen d. Wilmer Allison-John Van Ryn
1907	Fred Alexander-Harold Hackett d. Nat Thornton-B.M. Grant	1935	Wilmer Allison-John Van Ryn d. Don Budge-Gene Mako
1908	Fred Alexander-Harold Hackett d. Ray Little-Beals Wright	1936	Don Budge-Gene Mako d. Wilmer Allison-John Van Ryn
1909	Fred Alexander-Harold Hackett d. Maurice McLoughlin-George Janes	1937	Gottfried von Cramm-Henner Henkel d. Don Budge-Gene Mako
1910	Fred Alexander-Harold Hackett d. Tom Bundy-Trowbridge Hendrick	1938	Don Budge-Gene Mako d. Adrian Quist-John Bromwich
1911	Ray Little-Gus Touchard d. Fred Alexander-Harold Hackett	1939	Adrian Quist-John Bromwich d. Jack Crawford-Harry Hopman

Year		Year	
1940	Jack Kramer-Ted Schroeder d. Gardnar Mulloy-Henry Prussoff	1968	Bob Lutz-Stan Smith d. Bob Hewitt-Ray Moore
1941	Jack Kramer-Ted Schroeder d. Wayne Sabin-Gardnar Mulloy	1968*	Bob Lutz-Stan Smith d. Arthur Ashe-Andres Gimeno
1942	Gardnar Mulloy-Bill Talbert d. Ted Schroeder-Sidney Wood	1969	Dick Crealy-Allan Stone d. Bill Bowrey-Charlie Pasarell
1943	Jack Kramer-Frank Parker d. Bill Talbert-David Freeman	1969*	Ken Rosewall-Fred Stolle d. Charlie Pasarell-Dennis Ralston
1944	Don McNeill-Bob Falkenburg d. Bill Talbert-Pancho Segura	1970	Pierre Barthes-Nikki Pilic d. Roy Emerson-Rod Laver
1945	Gardnar Mulloy-Bill Talbert d. Bob Falkenburg-Jack Tuero	1971	John Newcombe-Roger Taylor d. Stan Smith-Erik van Dillen
1946	Gardnar Mulloy-Bill Talbert d. Don McNeill-Frank Guernsey	1972	Cliff Drysdale-Royer Taylor d. Owen Davidson-John Newcombe
1947	Jack Kramer-Ted Schroeder d. Bill Talbert-Bill Sidwell	1973	Owen Davidson-John Newcombe d. Rod Laver-Ken Rosewall
1948	Gardnar Mulloy-Bill Talbert d. Frank Parker-Ted Schroeder	1974	Bob Lutz-Stan Smith d. Pat Cornejo-Jaime Fillol
1949	John Bromwich-Bill Sidwell d. Frank Sedgman-George Worthington	1975	Jimmy Connors-Ilie Nastase d. Tom Okker-Marty Riessen
1950	John Bromwich-Frank Sedgman d. Bill Talbert-Gardnar Mulloy	1976	Tom Okker-Marty Riessen d. Paul Kronk-Cliff Letcher
1951	Ken McGregor-Frank Sedgman d. Don Candy-Mervyn Rose	1977	Bob Hewitt-Frew McMillan d. Brian Gottfried-Raul Ramirez
1952	Mervyn Rose-Vic Seixas d. Ken McGregor-Frank Sedgman	1978	Bob Lutz-Stan Smith d. Marty Riessen-Sherwood Stewart
1953	Rex Hartwig-Mervyn Rose d. Gardnar Mulloy-Bill Talbert	1979	John McEnroe-Peter Fleming d. Bob Lutz-Stan Smith
1954	Vic Seixas-Tony Trabert d. Lew Hoad-Ken Rosewall		
1955	Kosei Kamo-Atsushi Miyagi d. Gerald Moss-Bill Quillan		

Women's Singles

1956	Lew Hoad-Ken Rosewall d. Ham Richardson-Vic S
1957	Ashley Cooper-Neale Fraser d. Gardnar Mulloy-Budge Patty
1958	Alex Olmedo-Ham Richardson d. Sammy Giammalva-Barry MacKay
1959	Neale Fraser-Roy Emerson d. Alex Olmedo-Butch Buchholz
1960	Neale Fraser-Roy Emerson d. Rod Laver-Bob Mark
1961	Chuck McKinley-Dennis Ralston d. Rafael Osuna-Tony Palafox
1962	Rafael Osuna-Tony Palafox d. Chuck McKinley-Dennis Ralston
1963	Chuck McKinley-Dennis Ralston d. Rafael Osuna-Tony Palafox
1964	Chuck McKinley-Dennis Ralston d. Graham Stilwell-Mike Sangster
1965	Roy Emerson-Fred Stolle d. Frank Froehling-Charlie Pasarell
1966	Roy Emerson-Fred Stolle d. Clark Graebner-Dennis Ralston
1967	John Newcombe-Tony Roche d. Bill Bowrey-Owen Davidson

Women's Singles

Year

1887	Ellen Hansell d. Laura Knight 6–1, 6–0
1888	Bertha Townsend d. Marion Wright 6–2, 6–2
1889	Bertha Townsend d. Louise Voorhees 7–5, 6–2
1890	Ellen Roosevelt d. Grace Roosevelt 6–3, 6–1
1891	Mabel Cahill d. Elizabeth Moore 5–7, 6–3, 6–4, 4–6, 6–2
1892	Mabel Cahill d. Elizabeth Moore 5–7, 6–3, 6–4, 4–6, 6–2
1893	Aline Terry d. Mabel Cahill default
1894	Helen Helwig d. Aline Terry 7–5, 3–6, 6–0, 3–6, 6–3
1895	Juliette Atkinson d. Helen Helwig 6–4, 6–2, 6–1
1896	Elizabeth Moore d. Juliette Atkinson 6–4, 4–6, 6–2, 6–2
1897	Juliette Atkinson d. Elizabeth Moore 6–3, 6–3, 4–6, 3–6, 6–3

*Open champions. In 1968 and 1969 there were both Amateur and Open Championships held. Thereafter there was only the Open.

1898 Juliette Atkinson d. Marion Jones 6–3, 5–7, 6–4, 2–6, 7–5

1899 Marion Jones d. Juliette Atkinson default

1900 Myrtle McAteer d. Edith Parker 6–2, 6–2, 6–0

1901 Elizabeth Moore d. Myrtle McAteer 6–4, 3–6, 7–5, 2–6, 6–2

1902 Marion Jones d. Elizabeth Moore 6–1, 1–0 default

1903 Elizabeth Moore d. Marion Jones 7–5, 8–6

1904 May Sutton d. Elizabeth Moore 6–1, 6–2

1905 Elizabeth Moore d. Helen Homans 6–4, 5–7, 6–1

1906 Helen Homans d. Maud Barger-Wallach 6–4, 6–3

1907 Evelyn Sears d. Carrie Neely 6–3, 6–2

1908 Maud Barger-Wallach d. Evelyn Sears 6–2, 1–6, 6–3

1909 Hazel Hotchkiss d. Maud Barger-Wallach 6–0, 6–1

1910 Hazel Hotchkiss d. Louise Hammond 6–4, 6–2

1911 Hazel Hotchkiss d. Florence Sutton 8–10, 6–1, 9–7

1912 Mary Browne d. Eleonora Sears 6–4, 6–2

1913 Mary Browne d. Dorothy Green 6–2, 7–5

1914 Mary Browne d. Marie Wagner 6–2, 1–6, 6–1

1915 Molla Bjurstedt d. Hazel Hotchkiss Wightman 4–6, 6–2, 6–0

1916 Molla Bjurstedt d. Louise Hammond Raymond 4–6, 6–2, 6–0

1917 Molla Bjurstedt d. Marion Vanderhoef 4–6, 6–0, 6–2

1918 Molla Bjurstedt d. Eleanor Goss 6–4, 6–3

1919 Hazel Wightman d. Marion Zinderstein 6–1, 6–2

1920 Molla Bjurstedt Mallory d. Marion Zinderstein 6–3, 6–1

1921 Molla Mallory d. Mary Browne 4–6, 6–4, 6–2

1922 Molla Mallory d. Helen Wills 6–3, 6–1

1923 Helen Wills d. Molla Mallory 6–2, 6–1

1924 Helen Wills d. Molla Mallory 6–1, 6–3

1925 Helen Wills d. Kitty McKane 3–6, 6–0, 6–2

1926 Molla Mallory d. Elizabeth Ryan 4–6, 6–4, 9–7

1927 Helen Wills d. Betty Nuthall 6–1, 6–4

1928 Helen Wills d. Helen Jacobs 6–2, 6–1

1929 Helen Wills Moody d. Phoebe Watson 6–4, 6–2

1930 Betty Nuthall d. Anna Harper, 6–1, 6–4

1931 Helen Moody d. Eileen Whitingstall 6–4, 6–1

1932 Helen Jacobs d. Carolin Babcock 6–2, 6–2

1933 Helen Jacobs d. Helen Moody 8–6, 3–6, 3–0 default

1934 Helen Jacobs d. Sarah Palfrey Fabyan 6–1, 6–4

1935 Helen Jacobs d. Sarah Palfrey Fabyan 6–2, 6–4

1936 Alice Marble d. Helen Jacobs 4–6, 6–3, 6–2

1937 Anita Lizana d. Jadwiga Jedrzejowska 6–4, 6–2

1938 Alice Marble d. Nancye Wynne 6–0, 6–3

1939 Alice Marble d. Helen Jacobs 6–0, 8–10, 6–4

1940 Alice Marble d. Helen Jacobs 6–2, 6–3

1941 Sarah Palfrey Cooke d. Pauline Betz 7–5, 6–2

1942 Pauline Betz d. Louise Brough 4–6, 6–1, 6–4

1943 Pauline Betz d. Louise Brough 6–3, 5–7, 6–3

1944 Pauline Betz d. Margaret Osborne 6–3, 8–6

1945 Sarah Palfrey Cooke d. Pauline Betz 3–6, 8–6, 6–4

1946 Pauline Betz d. Pat Canning 11–9, 6–3

1947 Louise Brough d. Margaret Osborne duPont 8–6, 4–6, 6–1

1948 Margaret duPont d. Louise Brough 4–6, 6–4, 15–13

1949 Margaret duPont d. Doris Hart 6–4, 6–1

1950 Margaret duPont d. Doris Hart 6–3, 6–3

1951 Maureen Connolly d. Shirley Fry 6–3, 1–6, 6–4

1952 Maureen Connolly d. Doris Hart 6–3, 7–5

1953 Maureen Connolly d. Doris Hart 6–2, 6–4

1954 Doris Hart d. Louise Brough 6–8, 6–1, 8–6

1955	Doris Hart d. Pat Ward 6–4, 6–2
1956	Shirley Fry d. Althea Gibson 6–3, 6–4
1957	Althea Gibson d. Louise Brough 6–3, 6–2
1958	Althea Gibson d. Darlene Hard 3–6, 6–1, 6–2
1959	Maria Bueno d. Christine Truman 6–1, 6–4
1960	Darlene Hard d. Maria Bueno 6–4, 10–12, 6–4
1961	Darlene Hard d. Ann Haydon 6–3, 6–4
1962	Margaret Smith d. Darlene Hard 9–7, 6–4
1963	Maria Bueno d. Margaret Smith 7–5, 6–4
1964	Maria Bueno d. Carole Graebner 6–1, 6–0
1965	Margaret Smith d. Billie Jean Moffitt King 8–6, 7–5
1966	Maria Bueno d. Nancy Richey 6–3, 6–1
1967	Billie Jean King d. Ann Haydon Jones 11–9, 6–4
1968	Margaret Smith Court d. Maria Bueno 6–2, 6–2
1968*	Virginia Wade d. Billie Jean King 6–4, 6–4
1969	Margaret Court d. Virginia Wade 4–6, 6–3, 6–0
1969*	Margaret Court d. Nancy Richey 6–2, 6–2
1970	Margaret Court d. Rosie Casals 6–2, 2–6, 6–1
1971	Billie Jean King d. Rosie Casals 6–4, 7–6
1972	Billie Jean King d. Kerry Melville 6–3, 7–5
1973	Margaret Court d. Evonne Goolagong 7–6, 5–7, 6–2
1974	Billie Jean King d. Evonne Goolagong 3–6, 6–3, 7–5
1975	Chris Evert d. Evonne Goolagong 5–7, 6–4, 6–2
1976	Chris Evert d. Evonne Goolagong 6–3, 6–0
1977	Chris Evert d. Wendy Turnbull 7–6, 6–2
1978	Chris Evert d. Pam Shriver 7–5, 6–4
1979	Tracy Austin d. Chris Evert Lloyd 6–4, 6–3

*Open champions. In 1968 and 1969 there were both Amateur and Open Championships held. Thereafter there was only the Open.

Women's Doubles

Year

1890	Ellen Roosevelt-Grace Roosevelt
1891	Mabel Cahill-Mrs. W. F. Morgan
1892	Mabel Cahill-A. McKinley
1893	Aline Terry-Hattie Butler
1894	Helen Helwig-Juliette Atkinson d. Wistar-Louise Williams
1895	Helen Helwig-Juliette Atkinson d. Elizabeth Moore-Louise Williams
1896	Elizabeth Moore-Juliette Atkinson d. Wistar-Louise Williams
1897	Juliette Atkinson-Kathleen Atkinson d. Edwards-Elizabeth Rastall
1898	Juliette Atkinson-Kathleen Atkinson d. Carrie Neely-Marie Weimer
1899	Jane Craven-Myrtle McAteer d. Elizabeth Rastall-Banks
1900	Edith Parker-Hallie Champlin d. Myrtle McAteer-Marie Weimer
1901	Juliette Atkinson-Myrtle McAteer d. Elizabeth Moore-Marion Jones
1902	Juliette Atkinson-Marion Jones d. Maud Banks-Nona Closterman
1903	Elizabeth Moore-Carrie Neely d. Marion Jones-Miriam Hall
1904	May Sutton-Miriam Hall d. Elizabeth Moore-Carrie Neely
1905	Helen Homans-Carrie Neely d. Virginia Maule-Marjorie Oberteuffer
1906	Mrs. L. Coe-Mrs. D. Platt d. Helen Homans-Clover Boldt
1907	Marie Weimer-Carrie Neely d. Edna Wildey-Natalie Wildey
1908	Evelyn Sears-Margaret Curtis d. Carrie Neely-M. Steever
1909	Hazel Hotchkiss-Edith Rotch d. Dorothy Green-Lois Moyes
1910	Hazel Hotchkiss-Edith Rotch d. Browning-Edna Wildey
1911	Hazel Hotchkiss-Eleonora Sears d. Florence Sutton-Dorothy Green
1912	Dorothy Green-Mary Browne d. Maud Barger-Wallach-Mrs. F. Schmitz
1913	Mary Browne-Louise Williams d. Edna Wildey-Dorothy Green
1914	Mary Browne-Louise Williams d. Louise Raymond-Edna Wildey
1915	Hazel Hotchkiss Wightman-Eleonora Sears d. Helen McLean-Mrs. L. Chapman
1916	Molla Bjurstedt-Eleonora Sears d. Edna Wildey-Louise Raymond
1917	Molla Bjurstedt-Eleonora Sears d. Mrs. R. LeRoy-Phyllis Walsh

1918   Marion Zinderstein-Eleanor Goss d. Molla Bjurstedt-Mrs. J. Rogge

1919   Marion Zinderstein-Eleanor Goss d. Hazel Wightman-Eleonora Sears

1920   Marion Zinderstein-Eleanor Goss d. Eleanor Tennant-Helen Baker

1921   Mary Browne-Louise Williams d. Mrs. L. Morris-Helen Guilleaudeau

1922   Marion Zinderstein Jessup-Helen Wills d. Molla Bjurstedt Mallory-Edith Sigourney

1923   Kitty McKane-Phyllis Covell d. Hazel Wightman-Eleanor Goss

1924   Hazel Wightman-Helen Wills d. Eleanor Goss-Marion Jessup

1925   Mary Browne-Helen Wills d. May Bundy-Elizabeth Ryan

1926   Elizabeth Ryan-Eleanor Goss d. Mary Browne-Charlotte Chapin

1927   Kitty McKane Godfree-Ermyntrude Harvey d. Joan Fry-Betty Nuthall

1928   Hazel Wightman-Helen Wills d. Edith Cross-Anna Harper

1929   Phoebe Watson-Peggy Michell d. Phyllis Covell-Dorothy Barron

1930   Betty Nuthall-Sarah Palfrey d. Edith Cross-Anna Harper

1931   Betty Nuthall-Eileen Whittingstall d. Dorothy Round-Helen Jacobs

1932   Helen Jacobs-Sarah Palfrey d. Marjorie Painter-Alice Marble

1933   Betty Nuthall-Freda James d. Helen Wills Moody-Elizabeth Ryan

1934   Helen Jacobs-Sarah Palfrey d. Carolin Babcock-Dorothy Andrus

1935   Helen Jacobs-Sarah Palfrey Fabyan d. Carolin Babcock-Dorothy Andrus

1936   Marjorie Gladman Van Ryn-Carolin Babcock d. Helen Jacobs-Sarah Palfrey Fabyan

1937   Sarah Palfrey Fabyan-Alice Marble d. Carolin Babcock-Marjorie Van Ryn

1938   Sarah Palfrey Fabyan-Alice Marble d. Simone Mathieu-Jadwiga Jedrzejowska

1939   Sarah Palfrey Fabyan-Alice Marble d. Kay Stammers-Freda Hammersley

1940   Sara Palfrey Fabyan-Alice Marble d. Dorothy Bundy-Marjorie Van Ryn

1941   Sarah Palfrey Fabyan-Margaret Osborne d. Pauline Betz-Doris Hart

1942   Louise Brough-Margaret Osborne d. Pauline Betz-Doris Hart

1943   Louise Brough-Margaret Osborne d. Pauline Betz-Doris Hart

1944   Louise Brough-Margaret Osborne d. Pauline Betz-Doris Hart

1945   Louise Brough-Margaret Osborne d. Pauline Betz-Doris Hart

1946   Louise Brough-Margaret Osborne d. Mary Prentiss-Pat Todd

1947   Louise Brough-Margaret Osborne d. Doris Hart-Pat Todd

1948   Louise Brough-Margaret Osborne duPont d. Doris Hart-Pat Todd

1949   Louise Brough-Margaret duPont d. Doris Hart-Shirley Fry

1950   Louise Brough-Margaret duPont d. Doris Hart-Shirley Fry

1951   Shirley Fry-Doris Hart d. Pat Todd-Nancy Chaffee

1952   Shirley Fry-Doris Hart d. Louise Brough-Maureen Connolly

1953   Shirley Fry-Doris Hart d. Margaret duPont-Louise Brough

1954   Shirley Fry-Doris Hart d. Margaret duPont-Louise Brough

1955   Louise Brough-Margaret duPont d. Doris Hart-Shirley Fry

1956   Louise Brough-Margaret duPont d. Shirley Fry-Betty Pratt

1957   Louise Brough-Margaret duPont d. Althea Gibson-Darlene Hard

1958   Jeanne Arth-Darlene Hard d. Althea Gibson-Maria Bueno

1959   Jeanne Arth-Darlene Hard d. Maria Bueno-Sally Moore

1960   Maria Bueno-Darlene Hard d. Ann Haydon-Deidre Catt

1961   Darlene Hard-Lesley Turner d. Edda Buding-Yola Ramirez

1962   Darlene Hard-Maria Bueno d. Billie Jean Moffitt-Karen Susman

1963   Robyn Ebbern-Margaret Smith d. Darlene Hard-Maria Bueno

1964   Billie Jean Moffitt-Karen Susman d. Margaret Smith-Lesley Turner

1965   Carole Graebner-Nancy Richey d. Billie Jean Moffitt-Karen Susman

1966   Maria Bueno-Nancy Richey d. Billie Jean Moffitt King-Rosie Casals

1967   Billie Jean King-Rosie Casals d. Mary Ann Eisel-Donna Fales

1968   Maria Bueno-Margaret Smith Court d. Virginia Wade-Joyce Williams

1968* Maria Bueno-Margaret Court d. Rosie Casals-Billie Jean King

1969   Margaret Court-Virginia Wade d. Mary Ann Eisel Curtis-Val Ziegenfuss

1969* Françoise Durr-Darlene Hard d. Margaret Court-Virginia Wade

*Open champions. In 1968 and 1969 there were both Amateur and Open Championships held. Thereafter there was only the Open.

1970	Margaret Court-Judy Dalton d. Rosie Casals-Virginia Wade
1971	Rosie Casals-Judy Dalton d. Gail Chanfreau-Françoise Durr
1972	Françoise Durr-Betty Stove d. Margaret Court-Virginia Wade
1973	Margaret Court-Virginia Wade d. Billie Jean King-Rosie Casals
1974	Billie Jean King-Rosie Casals d. Françoise Durr-Betty Stove
1975	Margaret Court-Virginia Wade d. Billie Jean King-Rosie Casals
1976	Linky Boshoff-Ilana Kloss d. Virginia Wade-Olga Morozova
1977	Martina Navratilova-Betty Stove d. Renée Richards-Bettyann Stewart
1978	Martina Navratilova-Billie Jean King d. Kerry Reid-Wendy Turnbull
1979	Wendy Turnbull-Betty Stove d. Martina Navratilova-Billie Jean King

Mixed Doubles

Year

1892	Mabel Cahill-Clarence Hobart
1893	Ellen Roosevelt-Clarence Hobart
1894	Juliette Atkinson-Edwin Fischer
1895	Juliette Atkinson-Edwin Fischer
1896	Juliette Atkinson-Edwin Fischer
1897	Laura Hensen-D. Magruder
1898	Carrie Neely-Edwin Fischer
1899	Elizabeth Rastall-Al Hoskins
1900	Margaret Hunnewell-Al Codman
1901	Marion Jones-Ray Little
1902	Elizabeth Moore-Wylie Grant
1903	Helen Chapman-Harry Allen
1904	Elizabeth Moore-Wylie Grant
1905	Mr. and Mrs. Clarence Hobart
1906	Sarah Coffin-Ed Dewhurst
1907	May Sayres-Wallace Johnson
1908	Edith Rotch-Nathaniel Niles
1909	Hazel Hotchkiss-Wallace Johnson
1910	Hazel Hotchkiss-Joe Carpenter
1911	Hazel Hotchkiss-Wallace Johnson
1912	Mary Browne-R. Norris Williams
1913	Mary Browne-Bill Tilden
1914	Mary Browne-Bill Tilden
1915	Hazel Hotchkiss Wightman-Harry Johnson
1916	Eleonora Sears-Willis Davis
1917	Molla Bjurstedt-Irving Wright
1918	Hazel Wightman-Irving Wright
1919	Marion Zinderstein Jessup-Vinnie Richards

1920	Hazel Wightman-Wallace Johnson
1921	Mary Browne-Bill Johnston
1922	Molla Bjurstedt Mallory-Bill Tilden
1923	Molla Mallory-Bill Tilden
1924	Helen Wills-Vinnie Richards
1925	Kitty McKane-John Hawkes
1926	Elizabeth Ryan-Jean Borotra
1927	Eileen Bennett-Henri Cochet
1928	Helen Wills-John Hawkes
1929	Betty Nuthall-George Lott
1930	Edith Cross-Wilmer Allison
1931	Betty Nuthall-George Lott
1932	Sarah Palfrey-Fred Perry
1933	Elizabeth Ryan-Ellsworth Vines
1934	Helen Jacobs-George Lott
1935	Sarah Palfrey Fabyan-Enrique Maier
1936	Alice Marble-Gene Mako
1937	Sarah Palfrey Fabyan-Don Budge
1938	Alice Marble-Don Budge
1939	Alice Marble-Harry Hopman
1940	Alice Marble-Bobby Riggs
1941	Sarah Palfrey Cooke-Jack Kramer
1942	Louise Brough-Ted Schroeder
1943	Margaret Osborne-Bill Talbert
1944	Margaret Osborne-Bill Talbert
1945	Margaret Osborne-Bill Talbert
1946	Margaret Osborne-Bill Talbert
1947	Louise Brough-John Bromwich
1948	Louise Brough-Tom Brown
1949	Louise Brough-Eric Sturgess
1950	Margaret Osborne duPont-Ken McGregor
1951	Doris Hart-Frank Sedgman
1952	Doris Hart-Frank Sedgman
1953	Doris Hart-Vic Seixas
1954	Doris Hart-Vic Seixas
1955	Doris Hart-Vic Seixas
1956	Margaret duPont-Ken Rosewall
1957	Althea Gibson-Kurt Nielsen
1958	Margaret duPont-Neale Fraser
1959	Margaret duPont-Neale Fraser
1960	Margaret duPont-Neale Fraser
1961	Margaret Smith-Bob Mark
1962	Margaret Smith-Fred Stolle
1963	Margaret Smith-Ken Fletcher
1964	Margaret Smith-John Newcombe
1965	Margaret Smith-Fred Stolle
1966	Donna Floyd Fales-Owen Davidson
1967	Billie Jean King-Owen Davidson
1968	Mary Ann Eisel-Peter Curtis
1969	Patti Hogan-Paul Sullivan
1969*	Margaret Smith Court-Mary Riessen

*Open champions. In 1969 both Amateur and Open Championships were held. Thereafter there was only the Open.

1970	Margaret Court-Marty Riessen	
1971	Billie Jean King-Owen Davidson	
1972	Margaret Court-Marty Riessen	
1973	Billie Jean King-Owen Davidson	
1974	Pam Teeguarden-Geoff Masters	
1975	Rosie Casals-Dick Stockton	
1976	Billie Jean King-Phil Dent	
1977	Betty Stove-Frew McMillan	
1978	Betty Stove-Frew McMillan	
1979	Greer Stevens-Bob Hewitt	

All-time United States Championship Records

Most men's singles: 7—Dick Sears, 1881–87; Bill Larned, 1901–10; Bill Tilden, 1920–30

Most men's doubles: 6—Sears, 1882–87; Holcombe Ward, 1895–1905

Most men's mixed: 4—Edwin Fischer, 1894–98; Wallace Johnson, 1907–20; Tilden, 1913–23; Bill Talbert, 1943–46; Owen Davidson, 1966–73

Most men's altogether: 16—Tilden, 1913–30

Most women's singles: 8—Molla Bjurstedt Mallory, 1915–26

Most women's doubles: 13—Margaret Osborne du-Pont, 1941–57

Most women's mixed: 9—duPont, 1943–60

Most women's altogether: 25—duPont, 1941–60

Most men's doubles, team: 5—James Dwight and Sears, 1882–87

Most women's doubles, team: 12—Louise Brough and duPont, 1942–57

Most mixed doubles, team: 4—duPont and Talbert, 1943–46

U.S. NATIONAL MEN'S INTER-COLLEGIATE CHAMPIONS

Singles

Year		College
1883 (fall)	Howard Taylor	Harvard
1883 (spring)	Joseph Clark	Harvard
1884	W. Knapp	Yale
1885	W. Knapp	Yale
1886	G. Brinley	Trinity (Conn.)
1887	Philip Sears	Harvard
1888	Philip Sears	Harvard
1889	Bob Huntington	Yale
1890	Fred Hovey	Harvard
1891	Fred Hovey	Harvard
1892	Bill Larned	Cornell
1893	Malcolm Chace	Brown
1894	Malcolm Chace	Yale
1895	Malcolm Chace	Yale
1896	Malcolm Whitman	Harvard
1897	S. Thompson	Princeton
1898	Leo Ware	Harvard
1899	Dwight Davis	Harvard
1900	Ray Little	Princeton
1901	Fred Alexander	Princeton
1902	Bill Clothier	Harvard
1903	Ed Dewhurst	Pennsylvania
1904	Bob LeRoy	Columbia
1905	Ed Dewhurst	Pennsylvania
1906	Bob LeRoy	Columbia
1907	George Gardner	Harvard
1908	Nat Niles	Harvard
1909	Wallace Johnson	Pennsylvania
1910	R. Holden	Yale
1911	Edwin Whitney	Harvard
1912	George Church	Princeton
1913	R. Norris Williams	Harvard
1914	George Church	Princeton
1915	R. Norris Williams	Harvard
1916	Colket Caner	Harvard
1917–18	(not held)	
1919	Church Garland	Yale
1920	Maxwell Banks	Yale
1921	Phil Neer	Stanford
1922	Lucien Williams	Yale
1923	Carl Fischer	Philadelphia Osteo
1924	Wallace Scott	Washington
1925	Edward Chandler	California
1926	Edward Chandler	California
1927	Wilmer Allison	Texas
1928	Julius Seligson	Lehigh
1929	Berkeley Bell	Texas
1930	Cliff Sutter	Tulane
1931	Keith Gledhill	Stanford
1932	Cliff Sutter	Tulane
1933	Jack Tidball	UCLA
1934	Gene Mako	USC
1935	Wilbur Hess	Rice
1936	Ernie Sutter	Tulane
1937	Ernie Sutter	Tulane
1938	Frank Guernsey	Rice
1939	Frank Guernsey	Rice
1940	Don McNeill	Kenyon College
1941	Joe Hunt	US Naval Academy
1942	Ted Schroeder	Stanford
1943	Pancho Segura	Miami
1944	Pancho Segura	Miami

Year	Player	College	Year	Player	College
1945	Pancho Segura	Miami	1890	Quincey Shaw-Sam Chase	Harvard
1946	Bob Falkenburg	USC	1891	Fred Hovey-Robert Wrenn	Harvard
1947	Gardnar Larned	William & Mary	1892	Robert Wrenn-Fred Winslow	Harvard
1948	Harry Likas	San Francisco	1893	Malcolm Chace-C. Budlong	Brown
1949	Jack Tuero	Tulane	1894	Malcolm Chace-Arthur Foote	Yale
1950	Herbie Flam	UCLA	1895	Malcolm Chace-Arthur Foote	Yale
1951	Tony Trabert	Cincinnati	1896	Leo Ware-William Scudder	Harvard
1952	Hugh Stewart	USC	1897	Leo Ware-Malcolm Whitman	Harvard
1953	Ham Richardson	Tulane	1898	Leo Ware-Malcolm Whitman	Harvard
1954	Ham Richardson	Tulane	1899	Holcombe Ward-Dwight Davis	Harvard
1955	José Aguero	Tulane	1900	Fred Alexander-Ray Little	Princeton
1956	Alex Olmedo	USC	1901	H. Plummer-S. Russell	Yale
1957	Barry MacKay	Michigan	1902	Bill Clothier-Edgar Leonard	Harvard
1958	Alex Olmedo	USC	1903	B. Colston-E. Clapp	Yale
1959	Whitney Reed	San Jose State	1904	Karl Behr-George Bodman	Yale
1960	Larry Nagler	UCLA	1905	Ed Dewhurst-H. Register	Pennsylvania
1961	Allen Fox	UCLA	1906	E. Wells-Alfred Spaulding	Yale
1962	Rafael Osuna	USC	1907	Nathaniel Niles-A. Dabney	Harvard
1963	Dennis Ralston	USC	1908	Herbert Tilden-A. Thayer	Pennsylvania
1964	Dennis Ralston	USC	1909	Wallace Johnson-A. Thayer	Pennsylvania
1965	Arthur Ashe	UCLA	1910	Dean Mathey-Burnham Dell	Princeton
1966	Charlie Pasarell	UCLA	1911	Dean Mathey-C. Butler	Princeton
1967	Bob Lutz	USC	1912	George Church-W. Mace	Princeton
1968	Stan Smith	USC	1913	Watson Washburn-Joseph Armstrong	Harvard
1969	Joaquin Loyo-Mayo	USC	1914	Norris Williams-Richard Harte	Harvard
1970	Jeff Borowiak	UCLA	1915	Norris Williams-Richard Harte	Harvard
1971	Jimmy Connors	UCLA	1916	Colket Caner-Richard Harte	Harvard
1972	Dick Stockton	Trinity	1917–18	(not held)	
1973	Sandy Mayer	Stanford	1919	Chuck Garland-K. Hawkes	Yale
1974	John Whitlinger	Stanford			
1975	Billy Martin	UCLA			
1976	Bill Scanlon	Trinity			
1977	Matt Mitchell	Stanford			
1978	John McEnroe	Stanford			
1979	Kevin Curran	Texas			

Doubles

Year		College
1883 (spring)	Joseph Clark-Howard Taylor	Harvard
1883 (fall)	Howard Taylor-Palmer Presbrey	Harvard
1884	W. Knapp-W. Thorne	Yale
1885	W. Knapp-A. Shipman	Yale
1886	W. Knapp-W. Thacher	Yale
1887	Philip Sears-Quincy Shaw	Harvard
1888	Valentine Hall-Oliver Campbell	Columbia
1889	Oliver Campbell-A. Wright	Columbia

1920	A. Wilder-L. Wiley	Yale
1921	J. Brooks Fenno-Bill Fiebleman	Harvard
1922	Jim Davies-Phil Neer	Stanford
1923	L. White-Louis Thalheimer	Texas
1924	L. White-Louis Thalheimer	Texas
1925	Gervais Hills-Gerald Stratford	California
1926	Edward Chandler-Tom Stowe	California
1927	John Van Ryn-Ken Appel	Princeton
1928	Ralph McElevenny-Alan Herrington	Stanford
1929	Benjamin Gorchakoff-Arthur Kussman	Occidental
1930	Dolf Muehleisen-Bob Muench	California
1931	Bruce Barnes-Karl Kamrath	Texas
1932	Keith Gledhill-Joe Coughlin	Stanford
1933	Joe Coughlin-Sam Lee	Stanford
1934	Gene Mako-Phil Castlen	USC
1935	Paul Newton-Richard Bennett	California
1936	Bennett Dey-Bill Seward	Stanford
1937	Richard Bennett-Paul Newton	California
1938	Joe Hunt-Lewis Wetherell	USC
1939	Doug Imhoff-Bob Peacock	California
1940	Larry Dee-Jim Wade	Stanford
1941	Charles Olewine-Charles Mattman	USC
1942	Ted Schroeder-Larry Dee	Stanford
1943	John Hickman-Walt Driver	Texas
1944	John Hickman-Felix Kelley	Texas
1945	Pancho Segura-Tom Burke	Miami
1946	Bob Falkenburg-Tom Falkenburg	USC
1947	Sam Match-Bobby Curtis	Rice
1948	Fred Kovaleski-Tut Bartzen	William & Mary
1949	Jim Brink-Fred Fisher	Washington
1950	Herbie Flam-Gene Garrett	UCLA
1951	Earl Cochell-Hugh Stewart	USC
1952	Hugh Ditzler-Cliff Mayne	California
1953	Larry Huebner-Bob Perry	UCLA
1954	Ron Livingston-Bob Perry	UCLA
1955	Pancho Contreras-Joaquin Reyes	USC
1956	Pancho Contreras-Alex Olmedo	USC
1957	Crawford Henry-Ron Holmberg	Tulane
1958	Ed Atkinson-Alex Olmedo	USC
1959	Crawford Henry-Ron Holmberg	Tulane
1960	Larry Nagler-Allen Fox	UCLA
1961	Rafael Osuna-Ramsey Earnhart	USC
1962	Rafael Osuna-Ramsey Earnhart	USC
1963	Rafael Osuna-Dennis Ralston	USC
1964	Bill Bond-Dennis Ralston	USC
1965	Arthur Ashe-Ian Crookenden	UCLA
1966	Ian Crookenden-Charlie Pasarell	UCLA
1967	Bob Lutz-Stan Smith	USC
1968	Bob Lutz-Stan Smith	USC
1969	Joaquin Loyo-Mayo-Marcelo Lara	USC
1970	Pat Cramer-Luis Garcia	Miami
1971	Jeff Borowiak-Haroon Rahim	UCLA
1972	Sandy Mayer-Roscoe Tanner	Stanford
1973	Sandy Mayer-Jim Delaney	Stanford
1974	Jim Delaney-John Whitlinger	Stanford

1975	Bruce Manson- Butch Walts	USC
1976	Peter Fleming-Ferdi Taygan	UCLA
1977	Bruce Manson-Chris Lewis	USC
1978	John Austin-Bruce Nichols	UCLA
1979	Erick Iskersky-Ben McKowen	Trinity

U.S. NATIONAL WOMEN'S INTER-COLLEGIATE CHAMPIONS

Singles

Year		College
1958	Darlene Hard	Pomona
1959	Donna Floyd	William & Mary
1960	Linda Vail	Oakland City College
1961	Tory Fretz	Occidental
1962	Roberta Allison	Alabama
1963	Roberta Allison	Alabama
1964	Jane Albert	Stanford
1965	Mimi Henreid	UCLA
1966	Ceci Martinez	San Francisco State
1967	Patsy Rippy	Odessa Junior College
1968	Emilie Burrer	Trinity
1969	Emilie Burrer	Trinity
1970	Laura DuPont	North Carolina
1971	Pam Richmond	Arizona State
1972	Janice Metcalf	Redlands
1973	Janice Metcalf	Redlands
1974	Carrie Meyer	Marymount College
1975	Stephanie Tolleson	Trinity
1976	Barbara Hallquist	USC
1977	Barbara Hallquist	USC
1978	Stacy Margolin	USC
1979	Kathy Jordan	Stanford

Doubles

Year	
1958	Sue Metzger (St. Mary's Notre Dame)- Erika Puetz (Webster)
1959	Joyce Pniewski (Mich. St.)-Phyllis Saganski (Mich. St.)

1960	Susan Butt (U. of British Columbia)- Linda Vail (Oakland City)
1961	Tory Fretz (Occidental)-Mary Sherar (Yakima Valley Jr. College)
1962	Linda Yeomans (Stanford)-Carol Hanks (Stanford)
1963	Roberta Alison (U. of Alabama)-Justina Bricka (Washington U., Mo.)
1964	Connie Jaster (Cal. State at LA)-Carol Loop (Cal. State at LA)
1965	Nancy Falkenberg (Mary Baldwin)- Cynthia Goeltz (Mary Baldwin)
1966	Yale Stockwell (USC)-Libby Weiss (USC)
1967	Jane Albert (Stanford)-Julie Anthony (Stanford)
1968	Emilie Burrer (Trinity)-Becky Vest (Trinity)
1969	Emilie Burrer (Trinity)-Becky Vest (Trinity)
1970	Pam Farmer (Odessa Jr. College)-Con- nie Capozzi (Odessa Jr. College)
1972	Peggy Michel (Ariz. St.)-Pam Rich- mond (Ariz. St.)
1973	Cathy Beene (Lamar)-Linda Rupert (Lamar)
1974	Ann Lebedeff (San Diego St.)-Karen Reinke (San Diego St.)
1975	JoAnne Russell (Trinity)-Donna Stock- ton (Trinity)
1976	Susie Hagey (Stanford)-Diane Morrison (Stanford)
1977	Jodi Applebaum (Miami)-Terry Saiganik (Miami)
1978	Sherry Acker (Florida State)-Judy Acker (Florida State)
1979	Kathy Jordan (Stanford)-Alycia Moulton (Stanford)

U.S. INTERSCHOLASTIC CHAMPIONS

Boys

Year		School
1891	Robert Wrenn	Cambridge Latin (MA)
1892	Malcolm Chace	Univ. Grammar (RI)
1893	Clarence Budlong	Providence High (RI)
1894	W. Parker	Tutor (NY)
1895	Leo Ware	Roxbury Latin (MA)

1896	Rex Fincke	Hotchkiss (CT)
1897	Rex Fincke	Hotchkiss (CT)
1898	Beals Wright	Hopkinson (MA)
1899	Beals Wright	Hopkinson (MA)
1900	Irving Wright	Hopkinson (MA)
1901	Edward Larned	Lawrenceville (NJ)
1902	Hendricks Whitman	Noble's School (MA)
1903	Karl Behr	Lawrenceville (NJ)
1904	Nathaniel Niles	Boston Latin (MA)
1905	Nathaniel Niles	Volkmann (MA)
1906	J. Allen Ross	Hyde Park High, (IL)
1907	Wallace Johnson	Haverford (PA)
1908	Dean Mathey	Pingry (PA
1909	Maurice McLoughlin	San Francisco High (CA)
1910	Edwin Whitney	Stone's (MA)
1911	George Church	Irving (MA
1912	Clifton Herd	Exeter Academy (NH)
1913	Colket Caner	St. Mark's (MA)
1914	Leonard Beekman	Pawling (NY)
1915	Harold Throckmorton	Woodridge High (NY)
1916–22	Not Held	
1923	John Whitbeck	Loomis (CT)
1924	Horace Orser	Stuyvesant (NY)
1936	Robert Lowe	Choate (CT)
1937	William Gillespie	Scarborough (RI)
1938	Jack Kramer	Montebello High (CA)
1939	Chuck Olewine	Santa Monica High (CA)
1940	Bob Carothers	Coronado High (CA)
1941	Vic Seixas	Penn Charter (PA)
1942	Bob Falkenburg	Fairfax High (CA)
1943	Chuck Oliver	Perth Amboy High (NJ)
1944	Tut Bartzen	San Angelo High (TX)

1945	Herbie Flam	Beverly Hills High (CA)
1946	Hugh Stewart	So. Pasadena High (CA)
1947	Herb Behrens	Fort Lauderdale High (Fl)
1948	Gil Bogley	Landon (MD)
1949	Keston Deimling	Oak Park High (IL)
1950	Ham Richardson	Univ. High (LA)
1951	Herb Browne	Dreher High (SC)
1952	Ed Rubinoff	Miami Beach High (FL)
1953	Mike Green	Miami Beach High (FL)
1954	Greg Grant	South Pasadena High (CA)
1955	Crawford Henry	Grady High (GA)
1956	Clarence Sledge	Highland Park High (TX)
1957	Butch Buchholz	John Burroughs High (MO)
1958	Ray Senkowski	Hamtramck High (MI)
1959	Bill Lenoir	Tucson High (AR)
1960	Bill Lenoir	Tucson High (AR)
1961	Arthur Ashe	Sumner High (MO)
1962	Jackie Cooper	St. Xavier High (KY)
1963	Mike Belkin	Miami Beach High (FL)
1964	Bob Goeltz	Landon (MD)
1965	Bob Goeltz	Landon (MD)
1966	Bob Goeltz	Landon (MD)
1967	Zan Guerry	Baylor (TN)
1968	Charlie Owens	Tuscaloosa High (AL)
1969	Fred McNair	Landon (MD)
1970	Harold Solomon	Springbrook (CT)
1971	John Whitlinger	Shattuck High (WI)
1972	Bill Matyastik	Univ. High (LA)
1973	Dave Parker	Galesburg High (IL)
1974	Chris Delaney	Georgetown (MD)
1975	Pem Guerry	Baylor (TN)
1976	Jim Hodges	Landon (MD)

1977	Jay Lapidus	Lawrenceville (NJ)
1978	Jeff Turpin	St. Mark's (MA)
1979	Mike DePalmer	Bradenton High (FL)

Girls

Year		School
1978	Mary Lou Piatek	Whiting High (IN)
1979	Connie Yowell	Marlboro (MA)

WIMBLEDON

Men's Singles

Year

1877 Spencer Gore d. William Marshall 6–1, 6–2, 6–4

1878 Frank Hadow d. Spencer Gore 7–5, 6–1, 9–7

1879 John Hartley d. V. St. Leger Gould 6–2, 6–4, 6–2

1880 John Hartley d. Herbert Lawford 6–3, 6–2, 2–6, 6–3

1881 Willie Renshaw d. John Hartley 6–0, 6–2, 6–1

1882 Willie Renshaw d. Ernest Renshaw 6–1, 2–6, 4–6, 6–2, 6–2

1883 Willie Renshaw d. Ernest Renshaw 2–6, 6–3, 6–3, 4–6, 6–3

1884 Willie Rensaw d. Herbert Lawford 6–0, 6–4, 9–7

1885 Willie Renshaw d. Herbert Lawford 7–5, 6–2, 4–6, 7–5

1886 Willie Renshaw d. Herbert Lawford 6–0, 5–7, 6–3, 6–4

1887 Herbert Lawford d. Ernest Renshaw 1–6, 6–3, 3–6, 6–4, 6–4

1888 Ernest Renshaw d. Herbert Lawford 6–3, 7–5, 6–0

1889 Willie Renshaw d. Ernest Renshaw 6–4, 6–1, 3–6, 6–0

1890 W. Hamilton d. Willie Renshaw 6–8, 6–2, 3–6, 6–1, 6–1

1891 Wilfred Baddeley d. Joshua Pim 6–4, 1–6, 7–5, 6–0

1892 Wilfred Baddeley d. Joshua Pim 4–6, 6–3, 6–3, 6–2

1893 Joshua Pim d. Wilfred Baddeley 3–6, 6–1, 6–3, 6–2

1894 Joshua Pim d. Wilfred Baddeley 10–8, 6–2, 8–6

1895 Wilfred Baddeley d. Wilberforce Eaves 4–6, 2–6, 8–6, 6–2, 6–3

1896 Harold Mahony d. Wilfred Baddeley 6–2, 6–8, 5–7, 8–6, 6–3

1897 Reggie Doherty d. Harold Mahony 6–4, 6–4, 6–3

1898 Reggie Doherty d. Laurie Doherty 6–3, 6–3, 2–6, 5–7, 6–1

1899 Reggie Doherty d. Arthur Gore 1–6, 4–6, 6–2, 6–3, 6–3

1900 Reggie Doherty d. Sidney Smith 6–8, 6–3, 6–1, 6–2

1901 Arthur Gore d. Reggie Doherty 4–6, 7–5, 6–4, 6–4

1902 Laurie Doherty d. Arthur Gore 6–4, 6–3, 3–6, 6–0

1903 Laurie Doherty d. Frank Riseley 7–5, 6–3, 6–0

1904 Laurie Doherty d. Frank Riseley 6–1, 7–5, 8–6

1905 Laurie Doherty d. Norman Brookes 8–6, 6–2, 6–4

1906 Laurie Doherty d. Frank Riseley 6–4, 4–6, 6–2, 6–3

1907 Norman Brookes d. Arthur Gore 6–4, 6–2, 6–2

1908 Arthur Gore d. Roper Barrett 6–3, 6–2, 4–6, 3–6, 6–4

1909 Arthur Gore d. J. Ritchie 6–8, 1–6, 6–2, 6–2, 6–2

1910 Tony Wilding d. Arthur Gore 6–4, 7–5, 4–6, 6–2

1911 Tony Wilding d. Roper Barrett 6–4, 4–6, 2–6, 6–3 retired

1912 Tony Wilding d. Arthur Gore 6–4, 6–4, 4–6, 6–4

1913 Tony Wilding d. Maurice McLoughlin 8–6, 6–3, 10–8

1914 Norman Brookes d. Tony Wilding 6–4, 6–4, 7–5

1915–18 Not held

1919 Gerald Patterson d. Norman Brookes 6–3, 7–5, 6–2

1920 Bill Tilden d. Gerald Patterson 2–6, 6–3, 6–2, 6–4

1921 Bill Tilden d. Brian Norton 4–6, 2–6, 6–1, 6–0, 7–5

1922 Gerald Patterson d. Randolf Lycett 6–3, 6–4, 6–2

1923 Bill Johnston d. Francis Hunter 6–0, 6–3, 6–1

1924 Jean Borotra d. René Lacoste 6–1, 3–6, 6–1, 3–6, 6–4

1925	René Lacoste d. Jean Borotra 6–3, 6–3, 4–6, 8–6
1926	Jean Borotra d. Howard Kinsey 8–6, 6–1, 6–3
1927	Henri Cochet d. Jean Borotra 4–6, 4–6, 6–3, 6–4, 7–5
1928	René Lacoste d. Henri Cochet 6–1, 4–6, 6–4, 6–2
1929	Henri Cochet d. Jean Borotra 6–4, 6–3, 6–4
1930	Bill Tilden d. Wilmer Allison 6–3, 9–7, 6–4
1931	Sidney Wood d. Frank Shields default
1932	Ellsworth Vines d. Bunny Austin 6–4, 6–2, 6–0
1933	Jack Crawford d. Ellsworth Vines 4–6, 11–9, 6–2, 2–6, 6–4
1934	Fred Perry d. Jack Crawford 6–3, 6–0, 7–5
1935	Fred Perry d. Gottfried von Cramm 6–2, 6–4, 6–4
1936	Fred Perry d. Gottfried von Cramm 6–1, 6–1, 6–0
1937	Don Budge d. Gottfried von Cramm 6–3, 6–4, 6–2
1938	Don Budge d. Bunny Austin 6–1, 6–0, 6–3
1939	Bobby Riggs d. Elwood Cooke 2–6, 8–6, 3–6, 6–3, 6–2
1940–45	Not held
1946	Yvon Petra d. Geoff Brown 6–2, 6–4, 7–9, 5–7, 6–4
1947	Jack Kramer d. Tom Brown 6–1, 6–3, 6–2
1948	Bob Falkenburg d. John Bromwich 7–5, 0–6, 6–2, 3–6, 7–5
1949	Ted Schroeder d. Jaroslav Drobny 3–6, 6–0, 6–3, 4–6, 6–4
1950	Budge Patty d. Frank Sedgman 6–1, 8–10, 6–2, 6–3
1951	Dick Savitt d. Ken McGregor 6–4, 6–4, 6–4
1952	Frank Sedgman d. Jaroslav Drobny 4–6, 6–2, 6–3, 6–2
1953	Vic Seixas d. Kurt Nielsen 9–7, 6–3, 6–4
1954	Jaroslav Drobny d. Ken Rosewall 13–11, 4–6, 6–2, 9–7
1955	Tony Trabert d. Kurt Nielsen 6–3, 7–5, 6–1
1956	Lew Hoad d. Ken Rosewall 6–2, 4–6, 7–5, 6–4
1957	Lew Hoad d. Ashley Cooper 6–2, 6–1, 6–2
1958	Ashley Cooper d. Neale Fraser 3–6, 6–3, 6–4, 13–11

1959	Alex Olmedo d. Rod Laver 6–4, 6–3, 6–4
1960	Neale Fraser d. Rod Laver 6–4, 3–6, 9–7, 7–5
1961	Rod Laver d. Chuck McKinley 6–3, 6–1, 6–4
1962	Rod Laver d. Marty Mulligan 6–2, 6–2, 6–1
1963	Chuck McKinley d. Fred Stolle 9–7, 6–1, 6–4
1964	Roy Emerson d. Fred Stolle 6–4, 12–10, 4–6, 6–3
1965	Roy Emerson d. Fred Stolle 6–2, 6–4, 6–4
1966	Manuel Santana d. Dennis Ralston 6–4, 11–9, 6–4
1967	John Newcombe d. Willie Bungert 6–3, 6–1, 6–1
1968	Rod Laver d. Tony Roche 6–3, 6–4, 6–2
1969	Rod Laver d. John Newcombe 6–4, 5–7, 6–4, 6–4
1970	John Newcombe d. Ken Rosewall 5–7, 6–3, 6–2, 3–6, 6–1
1971	John Newcombe d. Stan Smith 6–3, 5–7, 2–6, 6–4, 6–4
1972	Stan Smith d. Ilie Nastase 4–6, 6–3, 6–3, 4–6, 7–5
1973	Jan Kodes d. Alex Metreveli 6–1, 9–8, 6–3
1974	Jimmy Connors d. Ken Rosewall 6–1, 6–1, 6–4
1975	Arthur Ashe d. Jimmy Connors 6–1, 6–1, 5–7, 6–4
1976	Bjorn Borg d. Ilie Nastase 6–4, 6–2, 9–7
1977	Bjorn Borg d. Jimmy Connors 3–6, 6–2, 6–1, 5–7, 6–4
1978	Bjorn Borg d. Jimmy Connors 6–2, 6–2, 6–3
1979	Bjorn Borg d. Roscoe Tanner 6–7, 6–1, 3–6, 6–3, 6–4

Men's Doubles

Year	
1879	R. Erskine-Herbert Lawford d. F. Durant-G. Tabor
1880	Willie Renshaw-Ernest Renshaw d. O. Woodhouse-C. Cole
1881	Willie Renshaw-Ernest Renshaw d. W. Down-H. Vaughan
1882	John Hartley-R. Richardson d. J. Horn-C. Russell

1883   C. Grinstead-C. Welldon d. C. Russell-R. Milford

1884   Willie Renshaw-Ernest Renshaw d. E. Lewis-E. Williams

1885   Willie Renshaw-Ernest Renshaw d. C. Farrar-A. Stanley

1886   Willie Renshaw-Ernest Renshaw d. C. Farrar-A. Stanley

1887   Herb Wiberforce-P. Lyon d. J. Crips-Barratt Smith

1888   Willie Renshaw-Ernest Renshaw d. P. Wiberforce-P. Lyon

1889   Willie Renshaw-Ernest Renshaw d. E. Lewis-George Hillyard

1890   Joshua Pim-F. Stoker d. E. Lewis-G. Hillyard

1891   Wilfred Baddeley-Herbert Baddeley d. Joshua Pim-F. Stoker

1892   E. Lewis-H. Barlow d. Wilfred Baddeley-Herbert Baddeley

1893   Joshua Pim-F. Stoker d. E. Lewis-H. Barlow

1894   Wilfred Baddeley-Herbert Baddeley d. H. Barlow-C. Martin

1895   Wilfred Baddeley-Herbert Baddeley d. E. Lewis-Wilberforce Eaves

1896   Wilfred Baddeley-Herbert Baddeley d. Reggie Doherty-H. Nisbet

1897   Reggie Doherty-Laurie Doherty d. Wilfred Baddeley-Herbert Baddeley

1898   Reggie Doherty-Laurie Doherty d. H. Nisbet-Clarence Hobart

1899   Reggie Doherty-Laurie Doherty d. H. Nisbet-Clarence Hobart

1900   Reggie Doherty-Laurie Doherty d. Roper Barrett-H. Nisbet

1901   Reggie Doherty-Laurie Doherty d. Dwight Davis-Holcombe Ward

1902   Sidney Smith-Frank Riseley d. Reggie Doherty-Laurie Doherty

1903   Reggie Doherty-Laurie Doherty d. Sidney Smith-Frank Risely

1904   Reggie Doherty-Laurie Doherty d. Sidney Smith-Frank Riseley

1905   Reggie Doherty-Laurie Doherty d. Sidney Smith-Frank Riseley

1906   Sidney Smith-Frank Riseley d. Reggie Doherty-Laurie Doherty

1907   Norman Brookes-Tony Wilding d. Beals Wright-Karl Behr

1908   Tony Wilding-M. Ritchie d. Arthur Gore-Roper Barrett

1909   Arthur Gore-Roper Barrett d. Stanley Doust-H. Parker

1910   Tony Wilding-M. Ritchie d. Arthur Gore-Roper Barrett

1911   Andre Gobert-Max Decugis d. Tony Wilding-J. Ritchie

1912   Roper Barrett-Charles Dixon d. Andre Gobert-Max Decugis

1913   Roper Barrett-Charles Dixon d. Frederick Rahe-Hans Kleinschroth

1914   Norman Brookes-Tony Wilding d. Roper Barrett-Charles Dixon

1915-18   Not held

1919   R. Thomas-Pat Wood d. Randolph Lycett-Rodney Heath

1920   R. Norris Williams-Charles Garland d. Algernon Kingscote-James Parke

1921   Randolph Lycett-Max Woosnam d. Arthur Lowe-Frank Lowe

1922   James Anderson-Randolph Lycett d. Gerald Patterson-Pat Wood

1923   Leslie Godfree-Randolf Lycett d. Count de Gomar-E. Flaquer

1924   Frank Hunter-Vinnie Richards d. Norris Williams-W. Washburn

1925   Jean Borotra-Rene Lacoste d. J. Hennessey-R. Casey

1926   Jacques Brugnon-Henri Cochet d. H. Kinsey-Vinnie Richards

1927   Frank Hunter-Bill Tilden d. Jacques Brugnon-Henri Cochet

1928   Jacques Brugnon-Henri Cochet d. Gerald Patterson-John Hawkes

1929   Wilmer Allison-John Van Ryn d. J. Colin Gregory-Ian Collins

1930   Wilmer Allison-John Van Ryn d. George Lott-John Doeg

1931   George Lott-John Van Ryn d. Jacques Brugnon-Henri Cochet

1932   Jean Borotra-Jacques Brugnon d. Fred Perry-Pat Hughes

1933   Jean Borotra-Jacques Brugnon d. R. Nunoi-J. Sato

1934   George Lott-Lester Stoefen d. Jean Borotra-Jacques Brugnon

1935   Jack Crawford-Adrian Quist d. Wilmer Allison-John Van Ryn

1936   Pat Hughes-Ray Tuckey d. Charlie Hare-Frank Wilde

1937   Don Budge-Gene Mako d. Pat Hughes-Ray Tuckey

1938   Don Budge-Gene Mako d. Henner Henkel-G. von Metaxa

1939   Ellwood Cooke-Bobby Riggs d. Charlie Hare-Frank Wilde

1940-45   Not held

1946   Tom Brown-Jack Kramer d. Geoff Brown-Dinny Pails

1947   Bob Falkenburg-Jack Kramer d. Tony Mottram-Billy Sidwell

1948	John Bromwich-Frank Sedgman d. Tom Brown-Gardnar Mulloy
1949	Pancho Gonzales-Frank Parker d. Gardnar Mulloy-Ted Schroeder
1950	John Bromwich-Adrian Quist d. Geoff Brown-Billy Sidwell
1951	Ken McGregor-Frank Sedgman d. Jaroslav Drobny-Eric Sturgess
1952	Ken McGregor-Frank Sedgman d. Vic Seixas-Eric Sturgess
1953	Lew Hoad-Ken Rosewall d. Rex Hartwig-Mervyn Rose
1954	Rex Hartwig-Mervyn Rose d. Vic Seixas-Tony Trabert
1955	Rex Hartwig-Lew Hoad d. Neale Fraser-Ken Rosewall
1956	Lew Hoad-Ken Rosewall d. Nicola Pietrangeli-Orlando Sirola
1957	Budge Patty-Gardnar Mulloy d. Neale Fraser-Lew Hoad
1958	Sven Davidson-Ulf Schmidt d. Ashley Cooper-Neale Fraser
1959	Roy Emerson-Neale Fraser d. Rod Laver-Bob Mark
1960	Rafael Osuna-Dennis Ralston d. Mike Davies-Bobby Wilson
1961	Roy Emerson-Neal Fraser d. Bob Hewitt-Fred Stolle
1962	Bob Hewitt-Fred Stolle d. Boro Jovanovic-Nikki Pilic
1963	Rafael Osuna-Tony Palafox d. Jean Claude Barclay-Pierre Darmon
1964	Bob Hewitt-Fred Stolle d. Roy Emerson-Ken Fletcher
1965	John Newcombe-Tony Roche d. Ken Fletcher-Bob Hewitt
1966	Ken Fletcher-John Newcombe d. Bill Bowrey-Owen Davidson
1967	Bob Hewitt-Frew McMillan d. Roy Emerson-Ken Fletcher
1968	John Newcombe-Tony Roche d. Ken Rosewall-Fred Stolle
1969	John Newcombe-Tony Roche d. Tom Okker-Marty Riessen
1970	John Newcombe-Tony Roche d. Ken Rosewall-Fred Stolle
1971	Roy Emerson-Rod Laver d. Arthur Ashe-Dennis Ralston
1972	Bob Hewitt-Frew McMillan d. Stan Smith-Erik Van Dillen
1973	Jimmy Connors-Ilie Nastase d. John Cooper-Neale Fraser
1974	John Newcombe-Tony Roche d. Stan Smith-Bob Lutz
1975	Vitas Gerulaitis-Sandy Mayer d. Colin Dowdeswell-Allan Stone
1976	Brian Gottfried-Raul Ramirez d. Ross Case-Geoff Masters
1977	Ross Case-Geoff Masters d. John Alexander-Phil Dent
1978	Bob Hewitt-Frew McMillan d. John McEnroe-Peter Fleming
1979	John McEnroe-Peter Fleming d. Brian Gottfried-Raul Ramirez

Women's Singles

Year

1884	Maud Watson d. Lillian Watson 6-8, 6-3, 6-3
1885	Maud Watson d. Blanche Bingley 6-1, 7-5
1886	Blanche Bingley d. Maud Watson 6-3, 6-3
1887	Lottie Dod d. Blanche Bingley Hillyard 6-2, 6-0
1888	Lottie Dod d. Blanche Hillyard 6-3, 6-3
1889	Blanche Hillyard d. L. Rice 4-6, 8-6, 6-4
1890	L. Rice d. M. Jacks 6-4, 6-1
1891	Lottie Dod d. Blanche Hillyard 6-2, 6-1
1892	Lottie Dod d. Blanche Hillyard 6-1, 6-1
1893	Lottie Dod d. Blanche Hillyard 6-8, 6-1, 6-4
1894	Blanche Hillyard d. L. Austin 6-1, 6-1
1895	Charlotte Cooper d. H. Jackson 7-5, 8-6
1896	Charlotte Cooper d. Mrs. W. Pickering 6-2, 6-3
1897	Blanche Hillyard d. Charlotte Cooper 5-7, 7-5, 6-2
1898	Charlotte Cooper d. L. Martin 6-4, 6-4
1899	Blanche Hillyard d. Charlotte Cooper 6-2, 6-3
1900	Blanche Hillyard d. Charlotte Cooper 4-6, 6-4, 6-4
1901	Charlotte Cooper Sterry d. Blanche Hillyard 6-2, 6-2
1902	Muriel Robb d. Charlotte Sterry 7-5, 6-1
1903	Dorothea Douglass d. Ethel Thomson 4-6, 6-4, 6-2
1904	Dorothea Douglass d. Charlotte Sterry 6-0, 6-3
1905	May Sutton d. Dorothea Douglass 6-3, 6-4

1906	Dorothea Douglass d. May Sutton 6–3, 9–7
1907	May Sutton d. Dorothea Douglass Lambert Chambers 6–1, 6–4
1908	Charlotte Sterry d. A. Morton 6–4, 6–4
1909	Dora Boothby d. A. Morton 6–4, 4–6, 8–6
1910	Dorothea Lambert Chambers d. Dora Boothby 6–2, 6–2
1911	Dorothea Lambert Chambers d. Dora Boothby 6–0, 6–0
1912	Ethel Thomson Larcombe d. Charlotte Sterry 6–3, 6–1
1913	Dorothera Lambert Chambers d. Mrs. R. McNair 6–0, 6–4
1914	Dorothea Lambert Chambers d. Ethel Larcombe 7–5, 6–4
1915–18	Not held
1919	Suzanne Lenglen d. Dorothea Lambert Chambers 10–8, 4–6, 9–7
1920	Suzanne Lenglen d. Dorothea Lambert Chambers 6–3, 6–0
1921	Suzanne Lenglen d. Elizabeth Ryan 6–2, 6–0
1922	Suzanne Lenglen d. Molla Mallory 6–2, 6–0
1923	Suzanne Lenglen d. Kitty McKane 6–2, 6–2
1924	Kitty McKane d. Helen Wills 4–6, 6–4, 6–4
1925	Suzanne Lenglen d. Joan Fry 6–2, 6–0
1926	Kitty McKane Godfree d. Lili d' Alvarez 6–2, 4–6, 6–3
1927	Helen Wills d. Lili d' Alvarez 6–2, 6–4
1928	Helen Wills d. Lili d' Alvarez 6–2, 6–3
1929	Helen Wills d. Helen Jacobs 6–1, 6–2
1930	Helen Wills Moody d. Elizabeth Ryan 6–2, 6–2
1931	Cilly Aussem d. Hilda Krahwinkel 6–2, 7–5
1932	Helen Moody d. Helen Jacobs 6–3, 6–1
1933	Helen Moody d. Dorothy Round 6–4, 6–8, 6–3
1934	Dorothy Round d. Helen Jacobs 6–2, 5–7, 6–3
1935	Helen Moody d. Helen Jacobs 6–3, 3–6, 7–5
1936	Helen Jacobs d. Hilda Krahwinkel-Sperling 6–2, 4–6, 7–5
1937	Dorothy Round d. Jadwiga Jedrzejowska 6–2, 2–6, 7–5
1938	Helen Moody d. Helen Jacobs 6–4, 6–0
1939	Alice Marble d. Kay Stammers 6–2, 6–0
1940–45	Not held
1946	Pauline Betz d. Louise Brough 6–2, 6–4
1947	Margaret Osborne d. Doris Hart 6–2, 6–4
1948	Louise Brough d. Doris Hart 6–3, 8–6
1949	Louise Brough d. Margaret Osborne duPont 10–8, 1–6, 10–8
1950	Louise Brough d. Margaret duPont 6–1, 3–6, 6–1
1951	Doris Hart d. Shirley Fry 6–1, 6–0
1952	Maureen Connolly d. Louise Brough 7–5, 6–3
1953	Maureen Connolly d. Doris Hart 8–6, 7–5
1954	Maureen Connolly d. Louise Brough 6–2, 7–5
1955	Louise Brough d. Beverly Baker Fleitz 7–5, 8–6
1956	Shirley Fry d. Angela Buxton 6–3, 6–1
1957	Althea Gibson d. Darlene Hard 6–3, 6–2
1958	Althea Gibson d. Angela Mortimer 8–6, 6–2
1959	Maria Bueno d. Darlene Hard 6–4, 6–3
1960	Maria Bueno d. Sandra Reynolds 8–6, 6–0
1961	Angela Mortimer d. Christine Truman 4–6, 6–4, 7–5
1962	Karen Hantze Susman d. Vera Sukova 6–4, 6–4
1963	Margaret Smith d. Billie Jean Moffitt 6–3, 6–4
1964	Maria Bueno d. Margaret Smith 6–4, 7–9, 6–3
1965	Margaret Smith d. Maria Bueno 6–4, 7–5
1966	Billie Jean Moffitt King d. Maria Bueno 6–3, 3–6, 6–1
1967	Billie Jean King d. Ann Jones 6–3, 6–4
1968	Billie Jean King d. Judy Tegart 9–7, 7–5
1969	Ann Jones d. Billie Jean King 3–6, 6–3, 6–2
1970	Margaret Smith Court d. Billie Jean King 14–12, 11–9
1971	Evonne Goolagong d. Margaret Court 6–4, 6–1
1972	Billie Jean King d. Evonne Goolagong 6–3, 6–3

1973 Billie Jean King d. Chris Evert 6–0, 7–5

1974 Chris Evert d. Olga Morozova 6–0, 6–4

1975 Billie Jean King d. Evonne Goolagong 6–0, 6–1

1976 Chris Evert d. Evonne Goolagong 6–3, 4–6, 8–6

1977 Virginia Wade d. Betty Stove 4–6, 6–3, 6–1

1978 Martina Navratilova d. Chris Evert 2–6, 6–4, 7–5

1979 Martina Navratilova d. Chris Evert Lloyd 6–4, 6–4

Women's Doubles

Year

1913 Mrs. R. McNair-Dora Boothby d. Charlotte Cooper Sterry-Dorothy Lambert Chambers

1914 Elizabeth Ryan-A. Morton d. Edith Larcombe-Mrs. F. Hannam

1915–18 Not held

1919 Suzanne Lenglen-Elizabeth Ryan d. Edith Larcombe-Dorothea Lambert Chambers

1920 Suzanne Lenglen-Elizabeth Ryan d. Edith Larcombe-Dorothea Lambert Chambers

1921 Suzanne Lenglen-Elizabeth Ryan d. Geraldine Beamish-Mrs. G. Peacock

1922 Suzanne Lenglen-Elizabeth Ryan d. Kitty McKane-Mrs. A. Stocks

1923 Suzanne Lenglen-Elizabeth Ryan d. Joan Austin-Edith Colyer

1924 Hazel Hotchkiss Wightman-Helen Wills d. Phyllis Covel-Kitty McKane

1925 Suzanne Lenglen-Elizabeth Ryan d. Mrs. A. Bridge-Mrs. C. McIlquham

1926 Mary Browne-Elizabeth Ryan d. Kitty McKane Godfree-Edith Colyer

1927 Helen Wills-Elizabeth Ryan d. G. Peacock-Bobbie Heine

1928 Peggy Saunders-Phoebe Watson d. Ermytrude Harvey-Eileen Bennett

1929 Peggy Michell-Phoebe Watson d. Phyllis Covel-Dorothy Barron

1930 Helen Wills Moody-Elizabeth Ryan d. Sarah Palfrey-Eleanor Cross

1931 Phyllis Mudford-Dorothy Barron d. Doris Metaxa-Josane Sigart

1932 Doris Metaxa-Josane Sigart d. Helen Jacobs-Elizabeth Ryan

1933 Elizabeth Ryan-Simone Mathieu d. Freda James-Billie Yorke

1934 Elizabeth Ryan-Simone Mathieu d. Dorothy Andrus-Sylvia Henrotin

1935 Freda James-Kay Stammers d. Simone Mathieu-Hilda Krahwinkel Sperling

1936 Freda James-Kay Stammers d. Helen Jacobs-Sarah Palfrey Fabyan

1937 Simone Mathieu-Billie Yorke d. Phyllis Mudford King-Elsie Pittman

1938 Sarah Palfrey Fabyan-Alice Marble d. Simone Mathieu-Billie Yorke

1939 Sarah Palfrey Fabyan-Alice Marble d. Helen Jacobs-Billie Yorke

1940–45 Not held

1946 Louise Brough-Margaret Osborne d. Pauline Betz-Doris Hart

1947 Pat Todd-Doris Hart d. Louise Brough-Margaret Osborne duPont

1948 Louise Brough-Margaret duPont d. Pat Todd-Doris Hart

1949 Louise Brough-Margaret duPont d. Pat Todd-Gussy Moran

1950 Louise Brough-Margaret duPont d. Doris Hart-Shirley Fry

1951 Doris Hart-Shirley Fry d. Louise Brough-Margaret duPont

1952 Doris Hart-Shirley Fry d. Louise Brough-Maureen Connolly

1953 Doris Hart-Shirley Fry d. Julie Sampson-Maureen Connolly

1954 Louise Brough-Margaret duPont d. Doris Hart-Shirley Fry

1955 Angela Mortimer-Anne Shilcock d. Shirley Bloomer-Pat Ward

1956 Angela Buxton-Althea Gibson d. Daphne Seeney-Fay Muller

1957 Althea Gibson-Darlene Hard d. Thelma Long-Mary Hawton

1958 Maria Bueno-Althea Gibson d. Margaret duPont-Margaret Varner

1959 Jeanne Arth-Darlene Hard d. Beverly Fleitz-Christine Truman

1960 Maria Bueno-Darlene Hard d. Sandra Reynolds-Renée Schuurman

1961 Karen Hantze-Billie Jean Moffitt d. Jan Lehane-Margaret Smith

1962 Billie Jean Moffitt-Karen Hantze Susman d. Sandra Reynolds-Renée Schuurman

1963 Maria Bueno-Darlene Hard d. Robyn Ebbern-Margaret Smith

1964 Margaret Smith-Lesley Turner d. Billie Jean Moffitt-Karen Susman

1965 Maria Bueno-Billie Jean Moffitt d. Françoise Durr-Jan Lieffrig

1966 Maria Bueno-Nancy Richey d. Margaret Smith-Judy Tegart

1967	Rosie Casals-Billie Jean Moffitt King d. Maria Bueno-Nancy Richey
1968	Rosie Casals-Billie Jean King d. Fran-coise Durr-Ann Jones
1969	Margaret Court-Judy Tegart d. Patti Hogan-Peggy Michel
1970	Rosie Casals-Billie Jean King d. Fran-coise Durr-Virginia Wade
1971	Rosie Casals-Billie Jean King d. Margaret Court-Evonne Goolagong
1972	Billie Jean King-Betty Stove d. Judy Tegart Dalton-Françoise Durr
1973	Rosie Casals-Billie Jean King d. Fran-coise Durr-Betty Stove
1974	Evonne Goolagong-Peggy Michel d. Helen Gourlay-Karen Krantzcke
1975	Ann Kiyomura-Kazuko Sawamatsu d. Françoise Durr-Betty Stove
1976	Chris Evert-Martina Navratilova d. Billie Jean King-Betty Stove
1977	Helen Gourlay-JoAnne Russell d. Martina Navratilova-Betty Stove
1978	Kerry Reid-Wendy Turnbull d. Virginia Ruzici-Mima Jausovec
1979	Billie Jean King-Martina Navratilova d. Betty Stove-Wendy Turnbull

Mixed Doubles

Year

1913	Mrs. C. Tuckey-Hope Crisp d. Edith Larcombe-James Parke
1914	Edith Larcombe-James Parke d. Marquerite Broquedis-Tony Wilding
1915–18	Not held
1919	Elizabeth Ryan-Randolph Lycett d. Dorothea Lambert Chambers-Albert Prebble
1920	Suzanne Lenglen-Gerald Patterson d. Elizabeth Ryan-Randolph Lycett
1921	Elizabeth Ryan-Randolph Lycett d. P. Howkins-Max Woosnam
1922	Suzanne Lenglen-Pat Wood d. Elizabeth Ryan-Randolph Lycett
1923	Elizabeth Ryan-Randolph Lycett d. Dorothy Barron-L. Deane
1924	Kitty McKane-Brian Gilbert d. Dorothy Barron-Leslie Godfree
1925	Suzanne Lenglen-Jean Borotra d. Elizabeth Ryan-H. de Morpurgo
1926	Kitty McKane Godfree-Leslie Godfree d. Mary Browne-Harry Kinsey
1927	Elizabeth Ryan-Frank Hunter d. Kitty McKane Godfree-Leslie Godfree

1928	Elizabeth Ryan-Pat Spence d. Daphne Akhurst-Jack Crawford
1929	Helen Wills-Frank Hunter d. Joan Fry-Ian Collins
1930	Elizabeth Ryan-Jack Crawford d. Hilda Krahwinkel-Daniel Prenn
1931	Louise Harper-George Lott d. Joan Ridley-Ian Collins
1932	Elizabeth Ryan-Enrique Maier d. Josane Sigart-Harry Hopman
1933	Hilda Krahwinkel-Gottfried von Cramm d. Mary Heeley-Norman Farquharson
1934	Dorothy Round-Ryuki Miki d. Dorothy Barron-Bunny Austin
1935	Dorothy Round-Fred Perry d. Nell Hopman-Harry Hopman
1936	Dorothy Round-Fred Perry d. Sarah Palfrey Fabyan-Don Budge
1937	Alice Marble-Don Budge d. Simone Mathieu-Yvon Petra
1938	Alice Marble-Don Budge d. Sarah Palfrey Fabyan-Henner Henkel
1939	Alice Marble-Bobby Riggs d. Nina Brown-Frank Wilde
1940–45	Not held
1946	Louise Brough-Tom Brown d. Dorothy Bundy-Geoff Brown
1947	Louise Brough-John Bromwich d. Nancye Bolton-Colin Long
1948	Louise Brough-John Bromwich d. Doris Hart-Frank Sedgman
1949	Sheila Summers-Eric Sturgess d. Louise Brough-John Bromwich
1950	Louise Brough-Eric Sturgess d. Pat Todd-Geoff Brown
1951	Doris Hart-Frank Sedgman d. Nancye Bolton-Mervyn Rose
1952	Doris Hart-Frank Sedgman d. Thelma Long-Enrique Morea
1953	Doris Hart-Vic Seixas d. Shirley Fry-Enrique Morea
1954	Doris Hart-Vic Seixas d. Margaret Osborne duPont-Ken Rosewall
1955	Doris Hart-Vic Seixas d. Louise Brough-Enrique Morea
1956	Shirley Fry-Vic Seixas d. Althea Gibson-Gardnar Mulloy
1957	Darlene Hard-Mervyn Rose d. Althea Gibson-Neale Fraser
1958	Loraine Coghlan-Bob Howe d. Althea Gibson-Kurt Nielsen
1959	Darlene Hard-Rod Laver d. Maria Bueno-Neale Fraser
1960	Darlene Hard-Rod Laver d. Maria Bueno-Bob Howe

1961	Lesley Turner-Fred Stolle d. Edda Buding-Bob Howe
1962	Margaret duPont-Neale Fraser d. Ann Haydon-Dennis Ralston
1963	Margaret Smith-Ken Fletcher d. Darlene Hard-Bob Hewitt
1964	Lesley Turner-Fred Stolle d. Margaret Smith-Ken Fletcher
1965	Margaret Smith-Ken Fletcher d. Judy Tegart-Tony Roche
1966	Margaret Smith-Ken Fletcher d. Billie Jean King-Dennis Ralston
1967	Billie Jean King-Owen Davidson d. Maria Bueno-Ken Fletcher
1968	Margaret Smith Court-Ken Fletcher d. Olga Morozova-Alex Mètreveli
1969	Ann Haydon Jones-Fred Stolle d. Judy Tegart-Tony Roche
1970	Rosie Casals-Ilie Nastase d. Olga Morozova-Alex Metreveli
1971	Billie Jean King-Owen Davidson d. Margaret Court-Marty Riessen
1972	Rosie Casals-Ilie Nastase d. Evonne Goolagong-Kim Warwick
1973	Billie Jean King-Owen Davidson d. Janet Newberry-Raul Ramirez
1974	Billie Jean King-Owen Davidson d. Lesley Charles-Mark Farrell
1975	Margaret Court-Marty Riessen d. Betty Stove-Allan Stone
1976	Françoise Durr-Tony Roche d. Rosie Casals-Dick Stockton
1977	Greer Stevens-Bob Hewitt d. Betty Stove-Frew McMillan
1978	Betty Stove-Frew McMillan d. Billie Jean King-Ray Ruffels
1979	Greer Stevens-Bob Hewitt d. Betty Stove-Frew McMillan

All-time Wimbledon Championship Records

Most men's singles: 7—Willie Renshaw, 1881–89

Most men's doubles: 8—Reggie Doherty, 1897–1905; Laurie Doherty, 1897–1905

Most men's, mixed: 4—Ken Fletcher, 1963–68; Owen Davidson, 1967–74

Most men's altogether: 13—Laurie Doherty, 1897–1905

Most women's singles: 8—Helen Wills Moody, 1927–38

Most women's doubles: 12—Elizabeth Ryan, 1914–34

Most women's, mixed: 7—Ryan, 1919–32

Most women's altogether: 20—Billie Jean King, 1961–79

Most men's doubles, team: 8—Reggie and Laurie Doherty (brothers), 1897–1905

Most women's doubles, team: 6—Suzanne Lenglen and Ryan, 1919–25

Most mixed doubles, team: 4—Court and Fletcher, 1963–68; King and Davidson, 1967–74

AUSTRALIAN CHAMPIONSHIPS

Men's Singles

Year	
1905	Rodney Heath
1906	Tony Wilding
1907	Horace Rice
1908	Fred Alexander
1909	Tony Wilding
1910	Rodney Heath
1911	Norman Brookes
1912	James Parke
1913	E. Parker
1914	Arthur O'Hara Wood
1915	Francis Lowe
1916–18	Not held
1919	Algernon Kingscote
1920	Pat O'Hara Wood
1921	Rice Gemmell
1922	Jim Anderson
1923	Pat O'Hara Wood
1924	Jim Anderson
1925	Jim Anderson
1926	John Hawkes
1927	Gerald Patterson
1928	Jean Borotra
1929	John Gregory
1930	Gar Moon
1931	Jack Crawford
1932	Jack Crawford
1933	Jack Crawford
1934	Fred Perry
1935	Jack Crawford
1936	Adrian Quist
1937	Viv McGrath
1938	Don Budge
1939	John Bromwich
1940	Adrian Quist
1941–45	Not held
1946	John Bromwich
1947	Dinny Pails
1948	Adrian Quist
1949	Frank Sedgman
1950	Frank Sedgman
1951	Dick Savitt
1952	Ken McGregor

1953	Ken Rosewall	1925	Gerald Patterson-Pat Wood
1954	Mervyn Rose	1926	Gerald Patterson-John Hawkes
1955	Ken Rosewall	1927	Gerald Patterson-John Hawkes
1956	Lew Hoad	1928	Jean Borotra-Jacques Brugnon
1957	Ashley Cooper	1929	Jack Crawford-Harry Hopman
1958	Ashley Cooper	1930	Jack Crawford-Harry Hopman
1959	Alex Olmedo	1931	Charlie Donohoe-Ray Dunlop
1960	Rod Laver	1932	Jack Crawford-E. Moon
1961	Roy Emerson	1933	Ellsworth Vines-Keith Gledhill
1962	Rod Laver	1934	Fred Perry-George Hughes
1963	Roy Emerson	1935	Jack Crawford-Viv McGrath
1964	Roy Emerson	1936	Adrian Quist-Don Turnbull
1965	Roy Emerson	1937	Adrian Quist-Don Turnbull
1966	Roy Emerson	1938	Adrian Quist-John Bromwich
1967	Roy Emerson	1939	Adrian Quist-John Bromwich
1968	Bill Bowrey	1940	Adrian Quist-John Bromwich
1969	Rod Laver	1941–45	Not held
1970	Arthur Ashe	1946	Adrian Quist-John Bromwich
1971	Ken Rosewall	1947	Adrian Quist-John Bromwich
1972	Ken Rosewall	1948	Adrian Quist-John Bromwich
1973	John Newcombe	1949	Adrian Quist-John Bromwich
1974	Jimmy Connors	1950	Adrian Quist-John Bromwich
1975	John Newcombe	1951	Frank Sedgman-Ken McGregor-
1976	Mark Edmondson	1952	Frank Sedgman-Ken McGregor
1977*	Roscoe Tanner	1953	Lew Hoad-Ken Rosewall
1977*	Vitas Gerulaitis	1954	Red Hartwig-Mervyn Rose
1978	Guillermo Vilas	1955	Vic Seixas-Tony Trabert
		1956	Lew Hoad-Ken Rosewall
		1957	Lew Hoad-Neale Fraser
		1958	Ashley Cooper-Neale Fraser

Men's Doubles

Year

		1959	Rod Laver-Bob Mark
		1960	Rod Laver-Bob Mark
		1961	Rod Laver-Bob Mark
1905	Tom Tachell-Randolph Lycett	1962	Roy Emerson-Neale Fraser
1906	Tony Wilding-Rodney Heath	1963	Bob Hewitt-Fred Stolle
1907	Harry Parker-W. Gregg	1964	Bob Hewitt-Fred Stolle
1908	Fred Alexander-Alfred Dunlop	1965	John Newcombe-Tony Roche
1909	E. Parker-J. Keane	1966	Roy Emerson-Fred Stolle
1910	Horace Rice-Ashley Campbell	1967	John Newcombe-Tony Roche
1911	Rodney Heath-Randolph Lycett	1968	Dick Crealy-Allan Stone
1912	James Parke-Charles Dixon	1969	Roy Emerson-Rod Laver
1913	E. Parker-A. Hedemann	1970	Bob Lutz-Stan Smith
1914	Ashley Campbell-Gerald Patterson	1971	John Newcombe-Tony Roche
1915	Horace Rice-Clarence Todd	1972	Owen Davidson-Ken Rosewall
1916–18	Not held	1973	Mal Anderson-John Newcombe
1919	Pat O'Hara Wood-Ronald Thomas	1974	Ross Case-Geoff Masters
1920	Pat O'Hara Wood-Ronald Thomas	1975	John Alexander-Phil Dent
1921	Rice Gemmell-S. Eaton	1976	John Newcombe-Tony Roche
1922	Gerald Patterson-John Hawkes	1977*	Arthur Ashe-Tony Roche
1923	Pat O'Hara Wood-C. St. John	1977*	Allan Stone-Ray Ruffels
1924	Norman Brookes-Jim Anderson	1978	Wojtek Fibak-Kim Warwick

*There were two championships held in 1977 when the tournament was switched from January to December, Tanner winning in January.

*There were two championships held in 1977 when the tournament was switched from January to December.

Women's Singles

Year

1922	Mal Molesworth
1923	Mal Molesworth
1924	Sylvia Lance
1925	Daphne Akhurst
1926	Daphne Akhurst
1927	Esna Boyd
1928	Daphne Akhurst
1929	Daphne Akhurst
1930	Daphne Akhurst
1931	Coral Buttsworth
1932	Coral Buttsworth
1933	Joan Hartigan
1934	Joan Hartigan
1935	Dorothy Round
1936	Joan Hartigan
1937	Nancye Wynne
1938	Dorothy Bundy
1939	Emily Westacott
1940	Nancye Wynne
1941–45	Not held
1946	Nancye Wynne Bolton
1947	Nancye Bolton
1948	Nancye Bolton
1949	Doris Hart
1950	Louise Brough
1951	Nancye Bolton
1952	Thelma Long
1953	Maureen Connolly
1954	Thelma Long
1955	Beryl Penrose
1956	Mary Carter
1957	Shirley Fry
1958	Angela Mortimer
1959	Mary Carter Reitano
1960	Margaret Smith
1961	Margaret Smith
1962	Margaret Smith
1963	Margaret Smith
1964	Margaret Smith
1965	Margaret Smith
1966	Margaret Smith
1967	Nancy Richey
1968	Billie Jean King
1969	Margaret Smith Court
1970	Margaret Court
1971	Margaret Court
1972	Virginia Wade
1973	Margaret Court
1974	Evonne Goolagong
1975	Evonne Goolagong
1976	Evonne Goolagong
1977*	Kerry Reid
1977*	Evonne Goolagong
1978	Chris O'Neil

Women's Doubles

Year

1922	Esna Boyd-M. Mountain
1923	Esna Boyd-Sylvia Lance
1924	Daphne Akhurst-Sylvia Lance
1925	Daphne Akhurst-Sylvia Lance Harper
1926	Mrs. Pat Wood-Esna Boyd
1927	Mrs. Pat Wood-Louie Bickerton
1928	Daphne Akhurst-Esna Boyd
1929	Daphne Akhurst-Louie Bickerton
1930	Mal Molesworth-Emily Hood
1931	Daphne Akhurst Cozens-Louie Bickerton
1932	Coral Buttsworth-Marjorie Crawford
1933	Mal Molesworth-Emily Westacott
1934	Mal Molesworth-Emily Westacott
1935	Evelyn Dearman-Nancye Lyle
1936	Thelma Coyne-Nancye Wynne
1937	Thelma Coyne-Nancye Wynne
1938	Thelma Coyne-Nancye Wynne
1939	Thelma Coyne-Nancye Wynne
1940	Thelma Coyne-Nancye Wynne
1941–45	Not held
1946	Joyce Fitch-Mary Bevis
1947	Thelma Coyne Long-Nancye Wynne Bolton
1948	Thelma Long-Nancye Bolton
1949	Thelma Long-Nancye Bolton
1950	Louise Brough-Doris Hart
1951	Thelma Long-Nancye Bolton
1952	Thelma Long-Nancye Bolton
1953	Maureen Connolly-Julie Sampson
1954	Mary Bevis Hawton-Beryl Penrose
1955	Mary Hawton-Beryl Penrose
1956	Mary Hawton-Thelma Long
1957	Althea Gibson-Shirley Fry
1958	Mary Hawton-Thelma Long
1959	Renée Schuurman-Sandra Reynolds
1960	Maria Bueno-Christine Truman
1961	Mary Reitano-Margaret Smith
1962	Margaret Smith-Robyn Ebbern
1963	Margaret Smith-Robyn Ebbern
1964	Judy Tegart-Lesley Turner
1965	Margaret Smith-Lesley Turner
1966	Carole Graebner-Nancy Richey
1967	Lesley Turner-Judy Tegart
1968	Karen Krantzcke-Kerry Melville
1969	Margaret Smith Court-Judy Tegart
1970	Margaret Court-Judy Tegart Dalton
1971	Margaret Court-Evonne Goolagong

*There were two championships held in 1977 when the tournament was switched from January to December.

1972	Kerry Harris-Helen Gourlay
1973	Margaret Court-Virginia Wade
1974	Evonne Goolagong-Peggy Michel
1975	Evonne Goolagong-Peggy Michel
1976	Evonne Goolagong-Helen Gourlay
1977*	Dianne Fromholtz-Helen Gourlay
1977**	Evonne Goolagong-Helen Gourlay Cawley
	Chris Matison-Pam Whytcross
1978	Renata Tomanova-Betsy Nagelsen

Mixed Doubles
Year

1922	Esna Boyd-John Hawkes
1923	Sylvia Lance-Horace Rice
1924	Daphne Akhurst-John Willard
1925	Daphne Akhurst-John Willard
1926	Esna Boyd-John Hawkes
1927	Esna Boyd-John Hawkes
1928	Daphne Akhurst-Jean Borotra
1929	Daphne Akhurst-Gar Moon
1930	Nell Hall-Harry Hopman
1931	Marjorie Crawford-Jack Crawford
1932	Marjorie Crawford-Jack Crawford
1933	Marjorie Crawford-Jack Crawford
1934	Joan Hartigan-Gar Moon
1935	Louie Bickerton-Christian Boussus
1936	Nell Hall Hopman-Harry Hopman
1937	Nell Hopman-Harry Hopman
1938	M. Wilson-John Bromwich
1939	Nell Hopman-Harry Hopman
1940	Nancye Wynne-Colin Long
1941–45	Not held
1946	Nancye Wynne Bolton-Colin Long
1947	Nancye Bolton-Colin Long
1948	Nancye Bolton-Colin Long
1949	Doris Hart-Frank Sedgman
1950	Doris Hart-Frank Sedgman
1951	Thelma Long-George Worthington
1952	Thelma Long-George Worthington
1953	Julie Sampson-Rex Hartwig
1954	Thelma Long-Rex Hartwig
1955	Thelma Long-George Worthington
1956	Beryl Penrose-Neale Fraser
1957	Fay Muller-Mal Anderson
1958	Mary Hawton-Bob Howe
1959	Sandra Reynolds-Bob Mark
1960	Jan Lehane-Trevor Fancutt
1961	Jan Lehane-Bob Hewitt
1962	Lesley Turner-Fred Stolle
1963	Margaret Smith-Ken Fletcher
1964	Margaret Smith-Ken Fletcher
1965	event unfinished

*There were two 1977 championships as the tournament switched dates from January back to December.
**Shared because finals rained out.

1966	Judy Tegart-Tony Roche
1967	Lesley Turner-Owen Davidson
1968	Billie Jean King-Dick Crealy
1969	event unfinished
1970–79	Not held

All-time Australian Championship Records

Most men's singles: 6—Roy Emerson, 1961–67
Most men's doubles: 10—Adrian Quist, 1936–50
Most men's, mixed: 4—Colin Long, 1940–48; Harry Hopman, 1930–39
Most men's altogether: 13—Quist, 1936–50
Most women's singles: 11—Margaret Court, 1960–73
Most women's doubles: 12—Thelma Long, 1936–58
Most women's, mixed: 4—Nell Hopman, 1930–39; Long, 1951–55; Nancy Bolton, 1940–48
Most women's altogether: 21—Court, 1960–75
Most men's doubles, team: 8—Quist and Jack Bromwich, 1938–50
Most women's doubles, team: 10—Long and Bolton, 1936–52
Most mixed doubles, team: 4—Nell and Harry Hopman (husband-wife), 1930–39; Bolton and Colin Long, 1940–48

FRENCH CHAMPIONSHIPS

Men's Singles
Year

1891	J. Briggs
1892	J. Schopfer
1893	L. Riboulet
1894	Andre Vacherot
1895	Andre Vacherot
1896	Andre Vacherot
1897	P. Ayme
1898	P. Ayme
1899	P. Ayme
1900	P. Ayme
1901	Andre Vacherot
1902	M. Vacherot
1903	Max Decugis
1904	Max Decugis
1905	Maurice Germot
1906	Maurice Germot
1907	Max Decugis
1908	Max Decugis
1909	Max Decugis
1910	Maurice Germot

1911	André Gobert
1912	Max Decugis
1913	Max Decugis
1914	Max Decugis
1915–19	Not held
1920	André Gobert
1921	Jean Samazeuilh
1922	Henri Cochet
1923	Pierre Blanchy
1924	Jean Borotra
1925*	René Lacoste
1926	Henri Cochet
1927	René Lacoste
1928	Henri Cochet
1929	René Lacoste
1930	Henri Cochet
1931	Jean Borotra
1932	Henri Cochet
1933	Jack Crawford
1934	Gottfried von Cramm
1935	Fred Perry
1936	Gottfried von Cramm
1937	Henner Henkel
1938	Don Budge
1939	Don McNeill
1940–45	Not held
1946	Marcel Bernard
1947	Joseph Asboth
1948	Frank Parker
1949	Frank Parker
1950	Budge Patty
1951	Jaroslav Drobny
1952	Jaroslav Drobny
1953	Ken Rosewall
1954	Tony Trabert
1955	Tony Trabert
1956	Lew Hoad
1957	Sven Davidson
1958	Mervyn Rose
1959	Nicola Pietrangeli
1960	Nicola Pietrangeli
1961	Manuel Santana
1962	Rod Laver
1963	Roy Emerson
1964	Manuel Santana
1965	Fred Stolle
1966	Tony Roche
1967	Roy Emerson
1968	Ken Rosewall
1969	Rod Laver
1970	Jan Kodes
1971	Jan Kodes
1972	Andres Gimeno
1973	Ilie Nastase

*Tournament henceforth open to non-French citizens.

1975	Bjorn Borg
1976	Adriano Panatta
1977	Guillermo Vilas
1978	Bjorn Borg
1979	Bjorn Borg

Men's Doubles

Year

1891	B. Desjoyau-Legrand
1892	Diaz Albertini-Havet
1893	Schopfer-Goldsmith
1894	Brosselin-Lesage
1895	André Vacherot-Winzer
1896	Warden-Wynn
1897	P. Ayme-Lebreton
1898	André Vacherot-Casdagli
1899	P. Ayme-Lebreton
1900	P. Ayme-Lebreton
1901	André Vacherot-M. Vacherot
1902	Max Decugis-J. Worth
1903	Max Decugis-J. Worth
1904	Max Decugis-Maurice Germot
1905	Max Decugis-J. Worth
1906	Max Decugis-Maurice Germot
1907	Max Decugis-Maurice Germot
1908	Max Decugis-Maurice Germot
1909	Max Decugis-Maurice Germot
1910	Max Decugis-Marcel Dupont
1911	Max Decugis-Maurice Germot
1912	Max Decugis-Maurice Germot
1913	Max Decugis-Maurice Germot
1914	Max Decugis-Maurice Germot
1915–19	Not held
1920	Max Decugis-Maurice Germot
1921	André Gobert-William Laurentz
1922	Jacques Brugnon-Marcel Dupont
1923	Pierre Blanchy-Jean Samazeuilh
1924	Jean Borotra-René Lacoste
1925*	Jean Borotra-René Lacoste
1926	Vinnie Richards-Howard Kinsey
1927	Henri Cochet-Jacques Brugnon
1928	Jean Borotra-Jacques Brugnon
1929	Jean Borotra-René Lacoste
1930	Henri Cochet-Jacques Brugnon
1931	George Lott-John Van Ryn
1932	Henri Cochet-Jacques Brugnon
1933	George Hughes-Fred Perry
1934	Jean Borotra-Jacques Brugnon
1935	Jack Crawford-Adrian Quist
1936	Jean Borotra-Marcel Bernard
1937	Gottfried von Cramm-Henner Henkel
1938	Bernard Destremau-Yvon Petra

*Tournament henceforth open to non-French citizens.

1939	Don McNeill-Charles Harris
1940–45	Not held
1946	Marcel Bernard-Yvon Petra
1947	Eustace Fannin-Eric Sturgess
1948	Lennart Bergelin-Jaroslav Drobny
1949	Frank Parker-Pancho Gonzales
1950	Bill Talbert-Tony Trabert
1951	Ken McGregor-Frank Sedgman
1952	Ken McGregor-Frank Sedgman
1953	Lew Hoad-Ken Rosewall
1954	Vic Seixas-Tony Trabert
1955	Vic Seixas-Tony Trabert
1956	Don Candy-Robert Perry
1957	Mal Anderson-Ashley Cooper
1958	Ashley Cooper-Neale Fraser
1959	Nicola Pietrangeli-Orlando Sirola
1960	Roy Emerson-Neale Fraser
1961	Roy Emerson-Rod Laver
1962	Roy Emerson-Neale Fraser
1963	Roy Emerson-Manuel Santana
1964	Roy Emerson-Ken Fletcher
1965	Roy Emerson-Fred Stolle
1966	Clark Graebner-Dennis Ralston
1967	John Newcombe-Tony Roche
1968	Ken Rosewall-Fred Stolle
1969	John Newcombe-Tony Roche
1970	Ilie Nastase-Ion Tiriac
1971	Arthur Ashe-Marty Riessen
1972	Bob Hewitt-Frew McMillan
1973	John Newcombe-Tom Okker
1974	Dick Crealy-Onny Parun
1975	Brian Gottfried-Raul Ramirez
1976	Fred McNair-Sherwood Stewart
1977	Brian Gottfried-Raul Ramirez
1978	Hank Pfister-Gene Mayer
1979	Sandy Mayer-Gene Mayer

Women's Singles

Year

1897	Cecilia Masson
1898	Cecilia Masson
1899	Cecilia Masson
1900	Cecilia Prevost
1901	P. Girod
1902	Cecilia Masson
1903	Cecilia Masson
1904	Katie Gillou
1905	Katie Gillou
1906	Katie Fenwick
1907	M. deKermel
1908	Katie Fenwick
1909	Jeanne Mattey
1910	Jeanne Mattey
1911	Jeanne Mattey

1912	Jeanne Mattey
1913	Marguerite Broquedis
1914	Marguerite Broquedis
1915–19	Not held
1920	Suzanne Lenglen
1921	Suzanne Lenglen
1922	Suzanne Lenglen
1923	Suzanne Lenglen
1924	Suzanne Lenglen
1925*	Suzanne Lenglen
1926	Suzanne Lenglen
1927	Kea Bouman
1928	Helen Wills
1929	Helen Wills
1930	Helen Wills Moody
1931	Cilly Aussem
1932	Helen Wills Moody
1933	Margaret Scriven
1934	Margaret Scriven
1935	Hilda Sperling
1936	Hilda Sperling
1937	Hilda Sperling
1938	Simone Mathieu
1939	Simone Mathieu
1940–45	Not held
1946	Margaret Osborne
1957	Pat Todd
1948	Nelly Landry
1949	Margaret Osborne duPont
1950	Doris Hart
1951	Shirley Fry
1952	Doris Hart
1953	Maureen Connolly
1954	Maureen Connolly
1955	Angela Mortimer
1956	Althea Gibson
1957	Shirley Bloomer
1958	Suzie Kormoczi
1959	Christine Truman
1960	Darlene Hard
1961	Ann Haydon
1962	Margaret Smith
1963	Lesley Turner
1964	Margaret Smith
1965	Lesley Turner
1966	Ann Haydon Jones
1967	Françoise Durr
1968	Nancy Richey
1969	Margaret Smith Court
1970	Margaret Court
1971	Evonne Goolagong
1972	Billie Jean King
1973	Margaret Court
1974	Chris Evert

*Tournament henceforth open to non-French citizens.

1975	Chris Evert
1976	Sue Barker
1977	Mima Jausovec
1978	Virginia Ruzici
1979	Chris Evert Lloyd

1973	Margaret Smith Court-Virginia Wade
1974	Chris Evert-Olga Morozova
1975	Chris Evert-Martina Navratilova
1976	Fiorella Bonicelli-Gail Chanfreau Lovera
1977	Regina Marsikova-Pam Teeguarden
1978	Mima Jausovec-Virginia Ruzici
1979	Betty Stove-Wendy Turnbull

Women's Doubles

Year

1925*	Suzanne Lenglen-Diddi Vlasto
1926	Suzanne Lenglen-Diddi Vlasto
1927	Irene Peacock-Esther Heine
1928	Phoebe Watson-Eileen Bennett
1929	Lili d'Alvarez-Kea Bouman
1930	Helen Wills Moody-Elizabeth Ryan
1931	Eileen Bennett Whittingstall-Betty Nuthall
1932	Helen Wills Moody-Elizabeth Ryan
1933	Simone Mathieu-Elizabeth Ryan
1934	Simone Mathieu-Elizabeth Ryan
1935	Margaret Scriven-Kay Stammers
1936	Simone Mathieu-Adeline Yorke
1937	Simone Mathieu-Adeline Yorke
1938	Simone Mathieu-Adeline Yorke
1939	Simone Mathieu-Jadwiga Jedrezejowska
1940–45	Not held
1946	Louise Brough-Margaret Osborne
1947	Louise Brough-Margaret Osborne
1948	Doris Hart-Pat Todd
1949	Louise Brough-Margaret Osborne duPont
1950	Doris Hart-Shirley Fry
1951	Doris Hart-Shirley Fry
1952	Doris Hart-Shirley Fry
1953	Doris Hart-Shirley Fry
1954	Maureen Connolly-Nell Hopman
1955	Beverly Fleitz-Darlene Hard
1956	Angela Buxton-Althea Gibson
1957	Shirley Bloomer-Darlene Hard
1958	Rosie Reyes-Yola Ramirez
1959	Sandra Reynolds-Renée Schuurman
1960	Maria Bueno-Darlene Hard
1961	Sandra Reynolds-Renée Schuurman
1962	Sandra Reynolds-Renée Schuurman
1963	Ann Jones-Renée Schuurman
1964	Margaret Smith-Lesley Turner
1965	Margaret Smith-Lesley Turner
1966	Margaret Smith-Judy Tegart
1967	Françoise Durr-Gail Sheriff
1968	Françoise Durr-Ann Jones
1969	Françoise Durr-Ann Jones
1970	Françoise Durr-Gail Chanfreau
1971	Françoise Durr-Gail Chanfreau
1972	Billie Jean King-Betty Stove

Mixed Doubles

Year

1925*	Suzanne Lenglen-Jacques Brugnon
1926	Suzanne Lenglen-Jacques Brugnon
1927	M. Bordes-Jean Borotra
1928	Eileen Bennett-Henri Cochet
1929	Eileen Bennett-Henri Cochet
1930	Cilly Aussem-Bill Tilden
1931	Betty Nuthall-Patrick Spence
1932	Betty Nuthall-Fred Perry
1933	Margaret Scriven-Jack Crawford
1934	Colette Rosanbert-Jean Borotra
1935	Lolette Payot-Marcel Bernard
1936	Adeline Yorke-Marcel Bernard
1937	Simone Mathieu-Yvon Petra
1938	Simone Mathieu-Dragutin Mitic
1939	Sarah Palfrey Fabyan-Elwood Cooke
1940–45	Not held
1946	Pauline Betz-Budge Patty
1947	Sheila Summers-Eric Sturgess
1948	Pat Todd-Jaroslav Drobny
1949	Sheila Summers-Eric Sturgess
1950	Barbara Scofield-Enrique Morea
1951	Doris Hart-Frank Sedgman
1952	Doris Hart-Frank Sedgman
1953	Doris Hart-Vic Seixas
1954	Maureen Connolly-Lew Hoad
1955	Darlene Hard-Gordon Forbes
1956	Thelma Long-Luis Ayala
1957	Vera Puzejova-Jiri Javorsky
1958	Shirley Bloomer-Nicola Pietrangeli
1959	Yola Ramirez-Billy Knight
1960	Maria Bueno-Bob Howe
1961	Darlene Hard-Rod Laver
1962	Renée Schuurman-Bob Howe
1963	Margaret Smith-Ken Fletcher
1964	Margaret Smith-Ken Fletcher
1965	Margaret Smith-Ken Fletcher
1966	Annette Van Zyl-Frew McMillan
1967	Billie Jean King-Owen Davidson
1968	Françoise Durr-Jean Claude Barclay
1969	Margaret Smith Court-Marty Riessen
1970	Billie Jean King-Bob Hewitt
1971	Françoise Durr-Jean Claude Barclay
1972	Evonne Goolagong-Kim Warwick

*Tournament henceforth open to non-French citizens.

*Tournament henceforth open to non-French citizens.

1973	Françoise Durr-Jean Claude Barclay
1974	Martina Navratilova-Ivan Molina
1975	Fiorella Bonicelli-Tom Koch
1976	Not held
1977	Mary Carillo-John McEnroe
1978	Renata Tomanova-Pavel Slozil
1979	Wendy Turnbull-Bob Hewitt

All-time French Championship Records

(Only since 1925 when championships were opened to non-French)

Most men's singles: 4—Henri Cochet, 1926–32; Bjorn Borg, 1974–79

Most men's doubles: 6—Roy Emerson, 1960–65

Most men's, mixed: 3—Ken Fletcher, 1963–65

Most men's altogether: 9—Cochet, 1926–32

Most women's singles: 5—Margaret Court, 1962–73

Most women's doubles: 6—Simone Mathieu, 1933–39

Most women's, mixed: 4—Court, 1963–69

Most women's altogether: 13—Court, 1960–75

Most men's doubles, team: 4—Cochet and Jacques Brugnon, 1927–32

Most women's doubles, team: 4—Doris Hart and Shirley Fry, 1950–53

Most mixed doubles, team: 3—Françoise Durr and Jean Claude Barclay, 1968–73; Court and Ken Fletcher, 1963–65

ITALIAN CHAMPIONSHIPS

Men's Singles

Year

1930	Bill Tilden
1931	Pat Hughes
1932	Andre Merlin
1933	Emanuele Sertorio
1934	Giovanni Palmieri
1935	Wilmer Hines
1936–49	Not held
1950	Jaroslav Drobny
1951	Jaroslav Drobny
1952	Frank Sedgman
1953	Jaroslav Drobny
1954	Budge Patty
1955	Fausto Gardini
1956	Lew Hoad
1957	Nicola Pietrangeli
1958	Mervyn Rose
1959	Luis Ayala
1960	Barry MacKay
1961	Nicola Pietrangeli
1962	Rod Laver
1963	Marty Mulligan
1964	Jan Erik Lundquist
1965	Marty Mulligan
1966	Tony Roche
1967	Marty Mulligan
1968	Tom Okker
1969	John Newcombe
1970	Ilie Nastase
1971	Rod Laver
1972	Manuel Orantes
1973	Ilie Nastase
1974	Bjorn Borg
1975	Raul Ramirez
1976	Adriano Panatta
1977	Vitas Gerulaitis
1978	Bjorn Borg
1979	Vitas Gerulaitis

Men's Doubles

Year

1930	Bill Tilden-Wilbur Coen
1931	Alberto DelBono-Pat Hughes
1932	Giorgio DeStefani-Pat Hughes
1933	Gene Lesuer-Marty Legeay
1934	Giovanni Palmieri-George Rogers
1935	Jack Crawford-Viv McGrath
1936–49	Not held
1950	Bill Talbert-Tony Trabert
1951	Jaroslav Drobny-Dick Savitt
1952	Jaroslav Drobny-Frank Sedgman
1953	Lew Hoad-Ken Rosewall
1954	Jaroslov Drobny-Enrique Morea
1955	Art Larsen-Enrique Morea
1956	Jaroslav Drobny-Lew Hoad
1957	Lew Hoad-Neale Fraser
1958	Kurt Nielsen-Anton Jansco
1959	Neale Fraser-Roy Emerson
1960	Not completed
1961	Neale Fraser-Roy Emerson
1962	Rod Laver-John Fraser
1963	Bob Hewitt-Fred Stolle
1964	Bob Hewitt-Fred Stolle
1965	John Newcombe-Tony Roche
1966	Roy Emerson-Fred Stolle
1967	Bob Hewitt-Frew McMillan
1968	Tom Okker-Marty Riessen
1969	Not completed
1970	Ilie Nastase-Ion Tiriac
1971	John Newcombe-Tony Roche
1972	Ilie Nastase-Ion Tiriac

1973	John Newcombe-Tom Okker
1974	Brian Gottfried-Raul Ramirez
1975	Brian Gottfried-Raul Ramirez
1976	Brian Gottfried-Raul Ramirez
1977	Brian Gottfried-Raul Ramirez
1978	Victor Pecci-Belus Prajoux
1979	Peter Fleming-Tomaz Smid

Women's Singles

Year

1930	Lili d'Alvarez
1931	Lucia Valerio
1932	Ida Adamoff
1933	Elizabeth Ryan
1934	Helen Jacobs
1935	Hilda Sperling
1936–49	Not held
1950	Annalios Bossi
1951	Doris Hart
1952	Susan Partridge
1953	Doris Hart
1954	Maureen Connolly
1955	Pat Ward
1956	Althea Gibson
1957	Shirley Bloomer
1958	Maria Bueno
1959	Christine Truman
1960	Suzie Kormoczi
1961	Maria Bueno
1962	Margaret Smith
1963	Margaret Smith
1964	Margaret Smith
1965	Maria Bueno
1966	Ann Jones
1967	Lesley Turner
1968	Lesley Turner Bowrey
1969	Julie Heldman
1970	Billie Jean King
1971	Virginia Wade
1972	Linda Tuero
1973	Evonne Goolagong
1974	Chris Evert
1975	Chris Evert
1976	Mima Jausovec
1977	Janet Newberry
1978	Regina Marsikova
1979	Tracy Austin

Women's Doubles

Year

| 1930 | Lucia Valerio-Lili d'Alvarez |
| 1931 | Anna Luzzatti-Rosetta Gagliardi |

1932	Colette Rosambert-Lolette Payot
1933	Dorothy Burke-Ida Adamoff
1934	Helen Jacobs-Elizabeth Ryan
1935	Evelyn Dearman-Nancy Lyle
1936–49	Not held
1950	Jean Quertier-Jean Smith
1951	Doris Hart-Shirley Fry
1952	Thelma Long-Nell Hopman
1953	Maureen Connolly-Julie Sampson
1954	Pat Ward-Elaine Watson
1955	Pat Ward-Christiane Mercelis
1956	Thelma Long-Mary Hawton
1957	Thelma Long-Mary Hawton
1958	Shirley Bloomer-Christine Truman
1959	Yola Ramirez-Rosie Reyes
1960	Yola Ramirez-Rosie Reyes
1961	Lesley Turner-Jan Lehane
1962	Maria Bueno-Darlene Hard
1963	Margaret Smith-Robyn Ebbern
1964	Margaret Smith-Lesley Turner
1965	Madonna Schacht-Annette Van Zyl
1966	Norma Baylon-Annette Van Zyl
1967	Rosie Casals-Lesley Turner
1968	Margaret Smith Court-Virginia Wade
1969	Françoise Durr-Ann Jones
1970	Rosie Casals-Billie Jean King
1971	Helga Masthoff-Virginia Wade
1972	Lesley Hunt-Olga Morozova
1973	Virginia Wade-Olga Morozova
1974	Chris Evert-Olga Morozova
1975	Chris Evert-Martina Navratilova
1976	Delina Boshoff-Ilana Kloss
1977	Brigitte Cuypers-Marise Kruger
1978	Mima Jausovec-Virgina Ruzici
1979	Betty Stove-Wendy Turnbull

Mixed Doubles

Year

1930	Lili d'Alvarez-Umberto de Morpurgo
1931	Lucia Valerio-Pat Hughes
1932	Lolette Payot-J. Bonte
1933	Dorothy Burke-Marty Legeay
1934	Elizabeth Ryan-Henry Culley
1935	Jadwiga Jedrzejowska-Harry Hopman
1936–49	Not held
1950	Not completed
1951	Shirley Fry-Felicissimo Ampon
1952	Arvilla McGuire-Kurt Nielsen
1953	Doris Hart-Vic Seixas
1954	Divided
1955	Divided
1956	Thelma Long-Luis Ayala
1957	Thelma Long-Luis Ayala
1958	Shirley Bloomer-Giorgio Fachini

1959	Rosie Reyes-Francisco Contreras
1960	Not played
1961	Margaret Smith-Roy Emerson
1962	Lesley Turner-Fred Stolle
1963	Canceled
1964	Margaret Smith-John Newcombe
1965	Carmen Coronado-Edison Mandarino
1966	Not played
1967	Lesley Turner-Bill Bowrey
1968	Margaret Smith Court-Marty Riessen
1969–79	Not played

DAVIS CUP

A 21-year-old Harvard graduate, Dwight Filley Davis (1879–1945), launched the international team competition for men that eventually bore his name: the Davis Cup. Davis was just out of Harvard in 1900 when he commissioned a sterling bowl for $750 from a Boston jeweler and offered it for competition among nations. That year only Great Britain, whose team was called British Isles, showed interest, and sent a team to Boston to challenge the United States on the grass of Longwood Cricket Club.

Davis himself, along with schoolmates Holcombe Ward and Malcolm Whitman, formed the U.S. team that defeated the Britons, 3–0. In the first three years of the competition (1900, 1902–3), only Britain and the U.S. entered, and their match determined who would hold the Cup. In 1904 other nations showed interest, and Belgium and France entered (the U.S. did not). It was then that the Challenge Round format was put into use. Belgium defeated France for the right to challenge the defender, Britain, for the Cup. Gradually more nations entered and the prize, entitled the International Lawn Tennis Challenge Trophy, became known as the Davis Cup.

It became necessary to divide the world into zones for preliminary tournaments to determine one challenger for the championship nation. The champion was required to play only the title match—the Challenge Round—the following year against the winner of the preliminary tournament. That system was changed in 1972, when all nations were required to play in the eliminations in their respective zones: American (North and South sections), European (A and B sections) and Eastern. That year the Cup-defending U.S. reached the final against Romania in Bucharest and won, 3–2.

A total of 63 nations have appeared in the competition, with a record number of 59 playing in 1977. But only seven have won the Cup: the U.S. (26 times), Australia (24), Britain (9), France (6),

South Africa (1), Sweden (1), and Italy (1). Nine nations besides the seven winners have qualified for the Challenge Round and/or final: Romania (3 times), India (2), Spain (2), Belgium (1), Japan (1), Mexico (1), West Germany (1), Czechoslovakia (1), and Chile (1).

The competition was confined to amateurs until 1969, when certain professionals, those with ties to their national federations, became eligible. In 1973 it became a truly open event, with all players welcome, and Australia won with possibly the strongest team ever, a group of pros who had been away from Davis Cup for years: Rod Laver, Ken Rosewall, John Newcombe, Mal Anderson.

The format for a match (or tie) is four singles and one doubles, a best-of-five meeting over three days. A team may be composed of no more than four players. Two players are nominated for singles and each faces the two men from the opposing team. A draw determines who plays whom. Opponents on the first day are reversed on the third. The doubles is played on the second day.

Nations visit one another for matches, a scheduling formula determining which of two opponents has choice of ground.

By 1923, when 17 nations entered, it was necessary to divide the world into two zones, American and European. In 1955 an Eastern Zone was added, and in 1966 the European Zone was split into sections A and B. In 1967 the American Zone was split into North and South sections.

Early Australian success was achieved under the banner of Australasia, a joint effort by Australia and New Zealand. This ended in 1924, when each county began to enter separate teams.

Through 1979 the competition had been held 68 times, the annual flow interrupted only by two world wars and hiatuses of 1901 and 1910.

Title-round Standings

	Challenge Rounds		Final Rounds (since 1972)		Total	
	W	L	W	L	W	L
United States	23	24	3	1	26	25
Australia	22	15	2	0	24	15
Britain	9	7	0	1	9	8
France	6	3	0	0	6	3
Italy	0	2	1	2	1	4
Sweden	0	0	1	0	1	0
South Africa	0	0	1	0	1	0
Romania	0	2	0	1	0	3
Spain	0	2	0	0	0	2
India	0	1	0	1	0	2
Belgium	0	1	0	0	0	1

	Challenge Rounds		Final Rounds (since 1972)		Total	
	W	L	W	L	W	L
Japan	0	1	0	0	0	1
Mexico	0	1	0	0	0	1
West Germany	0	1	0	0	0	1
Czechoslovakia	0	0	0	1	0	1
Chile	0	0	0	1	0	1

Davis Cup Final Round Results

1900 United States d. British Isles 3–0 (Boston, Mass.)
Malcolm Whitman d. Arthur Gore 6–1, 6–3, 6–2
Dwight Davis d. E. Black 4–6, 6–2, 6–4, 6–4
Holcombe Ward-Dwight Davis d. E. Black-Roper Barrett 6–4, 6–4, 6–4
Malcolm Whitman vs. E. Black not played
Dwight Davis vs. Arthur Gore 9–7, 9–9 abandoned

1901 No competition

1902 United States d. British Isles 3–2 (Brooklyn, N.Y.)
Reggie Doherty (B) d. Bill Larned 2–6, 3–6, 6–3, 6–4, 6–4
Malcolm Whitman d. Joshua Pim 6–1, 6–1, 1–6, 6–0
Reggie Doherty-Laurie Doherty (B) d. Holcombe Ward-Dwight Davis 3–6, 10–8, 6–3, 6–4
Bill Larned d. Joshua Pim 6–3, 6–2, 6–3
Malcolm Whitman d. Reggie Doherty 6–1, 7–5, 6–4

1903 British Isles d. United States 4–1 (Boston, Mass.)
Laurie Doherty d. Robert Wrenn 6–0, 6–3, 6–4
Bill Larned (US) d. Reggie Doherty default
Reggie Doherty-Laurie Doherty d. Robert Wrenn-George Wrenn 7–5, 9–7, 2–6, 6–3
Laurie Doherty d. Bill Larned 6–3, 6–8, 6–0, 2–6, 7–5
Reggie Doherty d. Robert Wrenn 6–4, 3–6, 6–3, 6–8, 6–4

1904 British Isles d. Belgium 5–0 (Wimbledon)
Laurie Doherty d. Paul de Borman 6–4, 6–1, 6–1
Frank Riseley d. Willie Lemaire 6–1, 6–4, 6–2
Reggie Doherty-Laurie Doherty d. Paul de Borman-Willie Lemaire 6–0, 6–1, 6–3

Laurie Doherty d. Willie Lemaire default
Frank Riseley d. Paul de Borman 4–6, 6–2, 8–6, 7–5

1905 British Isles d. United States 5–0 (Wimbledon)
Laurie Doherty d. Holcombe Ward 7–9, 4–6, 6–1, 6–2, 6–0
Sidney Smith d. Bill Larned 6–4, 6–4, 5–7, 6–4
Reggie Doherty-Laurie Doherty d. Holcombe Ward-Beals Wright 8–10, 6–2, 6–2, 4–6, 8–6
Sidney Smith d. Bill Clothier 4–6, 6–1, 6–4, 6–3
Laurie Doherty d. Bill Larned 6–4, 2–6, 6–8, 6–4, 6–2

1906 British Isles d. United States 5–0 (Wimbledon)
Sidney Smith d. Ray Little 6–4, 6–4, 6–1
Laurie Doherty d. Holcombe Ward 6–2, 8–6, 6–3
Reggie Doherty-Laurie Doherty d. Holcombe Ward-Ray Little 3–6, 11–9, 9–7, 6–1
Sidney Smith d. Holcombe Ward 6–1, 6–0, 6–4
Laurie Doherty d. Ray Little 3–6, 6–3, 6–8, 6–1, 6–3

1907 Australasia d. British Isles 3–2 (Wimbledon)
Norman Brookes d. Arthur Gore 7–5, 6–1, 7–5
Tony Wilding d. Roper Barrett 1–6, 6–4, 6–3, 7–5
Arthur Gore-Roper Barrett (B) d. Norman Brookes-Tony Wilding 3–6, 4–6, 7–5, 6–2, 13–11
Norman Brookes d. Roper Barrett 6–2, 6–0, 6–3
Arthur Gore (B) d. Tony Wilding 3–6, 6–3, 7–5, 6–2

1908 Australasia d. United States 3–2 (Melbourne, Australia)
Norman Brookes d. Fred Alexander 5–7, 9–7, 6–2, 4–6, 6–3
Beals Wright (US) d. Tony Wilding 3–6, 7–5, 6–3, 6–1
Norman Brookes-Tony Wilding (A) d. Beals Wright-Fred Alexander 6–4, 6–2, 5–7, 1–6, 6–4
Tony Wilding d. Fred Alexander 6–3, 6–4, 6–1
Beals Wright d. Norman Brookes 0–6, 3–6, 7–5, 6–2, 12–10

1909   Australasia d. United States 5–0 (Sydney, Australia)

Norman Brookes d. Maurice McLoughlin 6–2, 6–2, 6–4

Tony Wilding d. Melville Long 6–2, 7–5, 6–1

Norman Brookes-Tony Wilding d. Maurice McLoughlin-Melville Long 12–10, 9–7, 6–3

Norman Brookes d. Melville Long 6–4, 7–5, 8–6

Tony Wilding d. Maurice McLoughlin 3–6, 8–6, 6–2, 6–3

1910   No competition

1911   Australasia d. United States 5–0 (Christchurch, New Zealand)

Norman Brookes d. Beals Wright 6–4, 2–6, 6–3, 6–3

Rod Heath d. Bill Larned 2–6, 6–1, 7–5, 6–2

Norman Brookes-Alfred Dunlop d. Beals Wright-Maurice McLoughlin 6–4, 5–7, 7–5, 6–4

Norman Brookes d. Maurice McLoughlin 6–4, 3–6, 4–6, 6–3, 6–4

Rod Heath d. Beals Wright default

1912   British Isles d. Australasia 3–2 (Melbourne, Australia)

Cecil Parke d. Norman Brookes 8–6, 6–3, 5–7, 6–2

Charles Dixon d. Rod Heath 5–7, 6–4, 6–4

Norman Brookes-Alfred Dunlop (A) d. Cecil Parke-Alfred Beamish 6–4, 6–1, 7–5

Cecil Parke d. Rod Heath 6–2, 6–4, 6–4

Norman Brookes (A) d. Charles Dixon 6–2, 6–4, 6–4

1913   United States d. British Isles 3–2 (Wimbledon)

Cecil Parke (B) d. Maurice McLoughlin 8–10, 7–5, 6–4, 1–6, 7–5

Norris Williams d. Charles Dixon 8–6, 3–6, 6–2, 1–6, 7–5

Harold Hackett-Maurice McLoughlin d. Roper Barrett-Charles Dixon 5–7, 6–1, 2–6, 7–5, 6–4

Maurice McLoughlin d. Charles Dixon 8–6, 6–3, 6–2

Cecil Parker (B) d. Norris Williams 6–2, 5–7, 5–7, 6–4, 6–2

1914   Australasia d. United States 3–2 (Forest Hills, N.Y.)

Tony Wilding d. Norris Williams 7–5, 6–2, 6–3

Maurice McLoughlin (US) d. Norman Brookes 17–15, 6–3, 6–3

Norman Brookes d. Norris Williams 6–1, 6–2, 8–10, 6–3

Maurice McLoughlin (US) d. Tony Wilding 6–2, 6–3, 2–6, 6–2

Norman Brookes-Tony Wilding d. Maurice McLoughlin-Tom Bundy 6–3, 8–6, 9–7

1915–18   No competition

1919   Australasia d. British Isles 4–1 (Sydney, Australia)

Gerald Patterson d. Arthur Lowe 6–4, 6–3, 2–6, 6–3

Algernon Kingscote (B) d. Jim Anderson 7–5, 6–2, 6–4

Norman Brookes-Gerald Patterson d. Algernon Kingscote-Alfred Beamish 6–0, 6–0, 6–2

Gerald Patterson d. Algernon Kingscote 6–4, 6–4, 8–6

Jim Anderson d. Arthur Lowe 6–4, 5–7, 6–3, 4–6, 12–10

1920   United States d. Australasia 5–0 (Auckland, New Zealand)

Bill Tilden d. Norman Brookes 10–8, 6–4, 1–6, 6–4

Bill Johnston d. Gerald Patterson 6–3, 6–1, 6–1

Bill Tilden-Bill Johnston d. Norman Brookes-Gerald Patterson 4–6, 6–4, 6–0, 6–4

Bill Tilden d. Gerald Patterson 5–7, 6–2, 6–3, 6–3

Bill Johnston d. Norman Brookes 5–7, 7–5, 6–3. 6–3

1921   United States d. Japan 5–0 (Forest Hills, N.Y.)

Bill Tilden d. Zenzo Shimizu 5–7, 4–6, 7–5, 6–2, 6–1

Bill Johnston d. Ichiya Kumagae 6–2, 6–4, 6–2

Norris Williams-Watson Washburn d. Zenzo Shimizu-Ichiya Kumagae 6–2, 7–5, 4–6, 7–5

Bill Tilden d. Ichiya Kumagae 9–7, 6–4, 6–1

Bill Johnston d. Zenzo Shimizu 6–3, 5–7, 6–2, 6–4

1922   United States d. Australasia 4–1 (Forest Hills, N.Y.)

Bill Tilden d. Gerald Patterson 7–5, 10–8, 6–0

Bill Johnston d. Jim Anderson 6–1, 6–2, 6–3

Gerald Patterson-Pat O'Hara Wood (A) d. Bill Tilden-Vinnie Richards 6–3, 6–0, 6–4

Bill Johnston d. Gerald Patterson 6–2, 6–2, 6–1

Bill Tilden d. Jim Anderson 6–4, 5–7, 3–6, 6–4, 6–2

1923 United States d. Australasia 4–1 (Forest Hills, N.Y.)

Jim Anderson (A) d. Bill Johnston 4–6, 6–2, 2–6, 7–5, 6–2

Bill Tilden d. John Hawkes 6–4, 6–2, 6–1

Bill Tilden-Norris Williams d. Jim Anderson-John Hawkes 17–15, 11–13, 2–6, 6–3, 6–2

Bill Johnston d. John Hawkes 6–0, 6–2, 6–1

Bill Tilden d. Jim Anderson 6–2, 6–3, 1–6, 7–5

1924 United States d. Australasia 5–0 (Philadelphia, Pa.)

Bill Tilden d. Gerald Patterson 6–4, 6–2, 6–2

Vincent Richards d. Pat O'Hara Wood 6–3, 6–2, 6–4

Bill Tilden-Bill Johnston d. Gerald Patterson-Pat O'Hara Wood 5–7, 6–3, 6–4, 6–1

Bill Tilden d. Pat O'Hara Wood 6–2, 6–1, 6–1

Vincent Richards d. Gerald Patterson 6–3, 7–5, 6–4

1925 United States d. France 5–0 (Philadelphia, Pa.)

Bill Tilden d. Jean Borotra 4–6, 6–0, 2–6, 9–7, 6–4

Bill Johnston d. René Lacoste 6–1, 6–1, 6–8, 6–3

Vincent Richards-Norris Williams d. René Lacoste-Jean Borotra 6–4, 6–4, 6–3

Bill Tilden d. René Lacoste 3–6, 10–12, 8–6, 7–5, 6–2

Bill Johnston d. Jean Borotra 6–1, 6–4, 6–0

1926 United States d. France 4–1 (Philadelphia, Pa.)

Bill Johnston d. René Lacoste 6–0, 6–4, 0–6, 6–0

Bill Tilden d. Jean Borotra 6–2, 6–3, 6–3

Norris Williams-Vincent Richards d. Henri Cochet-Jacques Brugnon 6–4, 6–4, 6–2

Bill Johnston d. Jean Borotra 8–6, 6–4, 9–7

René Lacoste (F) d. Bill Tilden 4–6, 6–4, 8–6, 8–6

1927 France d. United States 3–2 (Philadelphia, Pa.)

René Lacoste d. Bill Johnston 6–3, 6–2, 6–2

Bill Tilden (US) d. Henri Cochet 6–4, 2–6, 6–2, 8–6

Bill Tilden-Frank Hunter (US) d. Jean Bor-

otra-Jacques Brugnon 3–6, 6–3, 6–3, 4–6, 6–0

René Lacoste d. Bill Tilden 6–3, 4–6, 6–3, 6–2

Henri Cochet d. Bill Johnston 6–4, 4–6, 6–2, 6–4

1928 France d. United States 4–1 (Paris, France)

Bill Tilden (US) d. René Lacoste 1–6, 6–4, 6–4, 2–6, 6–3

Henri Cochet d. John Hennessey 5–7, 9–7, 6–3, 6–0

Henri Cochet-Jean Borotra d. Bill Tilden-Frank Hunter 6–4, 6–8, 7–5, 4–6, 6–2

Henri Cochet d. Bill Tilden 9–7, 8–6, 6–4

René Lacoste d. John Hennessey 4–6, 6–1, 7–5, 6–3

1929 France d. United States 3–2 (Paris, France)

Henri Cochet d. Bill Tilden 6–3, 6–1, 6–2

Jean Borotra d. George Lott 6–1, 3–6, 6–4, 7–5

John Van Ryn-Wilmer Allison (US) d. Henri Cochet-Jean Borotra 6–1, 8–6, 6–4

Bill Tilden (US) d. Jean Borotra 4–6, 6–1, 6–4, 7–5

Henri Cochet d. George Lott 6–1, 3–6, 6–0, 6–3

1930 France d. United States 4–1 (Paris, France)

Bill Tilden (US) d. Jean Borotra 2–6, 7–5, 6–4, 7–5

Henri Cochet d. George Lott 6–4, 6–2, 6–2

Henri Cochet-Jacques Brugnon d. Wilmer Allison-John Van Ryn 6–3, 7–5, 1–6, 6–2

Jean Borotra d. George Lott 5–7, 6–3, 2–6, 6–2, 8–6

Henri Cochet d. Bill Tilden 4–6, 6–3, 6–1, 7–5

1931 France d. Great Britain 3–2 (Paris, France)

Henri Cochet d. Bunny Austin 3–6, 11–9, 6–2, 6–4

Fred Perry (B) d. Jean Borotra 4–6, 10–8, 6–0, 4–6, 6–4

Henri Cochet-Jacques Brugnon d. George Hughes-Charles Kingsley 6–1, 5–7, 6–3, 8–6

Bunny Austin (B) d. Jean Borotra 7–5, 6–3, 3–6, 7–5

Henri Cochet d. Fred Perry 6–4, 1–6, 9–7, 6–3

1932 France d. United States 3–2 (Paris, France)

Jean Borotra d. Ellsworth Vines 6–4, 6–2, 3–6, 6–4

Henri Cochet d. Wilmer Allison 5–7, 7–5, 7–5, 6–2

Wilmer Allison-John Van Ryn (US) d. Henri Cochet-Jacques Brugnon 6–3, 11–13, 7–5, 4–6, 6–4

Jean Borotra d. Wilmer Allison 1–6, 3–6, 6–4, 6–2, 7–5

Ellsworth Vines (U.S.) d. Henri Cochet 4–6, 0–6, 7–5, 8–6, 6–2

1933   Great Britain d. France 3–2 (Paris, France)

Bunny Austin d. André Merlin 6–3, 6–4, 6–0

Fred Perry d. Henri Cochet 8–10, 6–4, 8–6, 3–6, 6–1

Jean Borotra-Jacques Brugnon (F) d. George Hughes-Harold Lee 6–3, 8–6, 6–2

Henri Cochet (F) d. Bunny Austin 5–7, 6–4, 4–6, 6–4, 6–4

Fred Perry d. André Merlin 4–6, 8–6, 6–2, 7–5

1934   Great Britain d. United States 4–1 (Wimbledon)

Bunny Austin d. Frank Shields 6–4, 6–4, 6–1

Fred Perry d. Sidney Wood 6–1, 4–6, 5–7, 6–0, 6–3

George Lott-Lester Stoefen (US) d. George Hughes-Harold Lee 7–5, 6–0, 4–6, 9–7

Fred Perry d. Frank Shields 6–4, 4–6, 6–2, 15–13

Bunny Austin d. Sydney Wood 6–4, 6–0, 6–8, 6–3

1935   Great Britain d. United States 5–0 (Wimbledon)

Bunny Austin d. Wilmer Allison 6–2, 2–6, 4–6, 6–3, 7–5

Fred Perry d. Don Budge 6–0, 6–8, 6–3, 6–4

George Hughes-Charles Tuckey d. Wilmer Allison-John Van Ryn 6–2, 1–6, 6–8, 6–3, 6–3

Bunny Austin d. Don Budge 6–2, 6–4, 6–8, 7–5

Fred Perry d. Wilmer Allison 4–6, 6–4, 7–5, 6–3

1936   Great Britain d. Australia 3–2 (Wimbledon)

Bunny Austin d. Jack Crawford 4–6, 6–3, 6–3, 6–1

Fred Perry d. Adrian Quist 6–3, 4–6, 7–5, 6–2

Jack Crawford-Adrian Quist (A) d. George Hughes-Charles Tuckey 6–4, 2–6, 7–5, 10–8

Adrian Quist (A) d. Bunny Austin 6–4, 3–6, 7–5, 6–3

Fred Perry d. Jack Crawford 6–2, 6–2, 6–3

1937   United States d. Great Britain 4–1 (Wimbledon)

Bunny Austin (B) d. Frank Parker 6–3, 6–2, 7–5

Don Budge d. Charlie Hare 15–13, 6–1, 6–2

Don Budge-Gene Mako d. Charles Tuckey-Frank Wilde 6–3, 7–5, 7–9, 12–10

Frank Parker d. Charlie Hare 6–2, 6–4, 6–2

Don Budge d. Bunny Austin 8–6, 3–6, 6–4, 6–3

1938   United States d. Australia 3–2 (Philadelphia, Pa.)

Bobby Riggs d. Adrian Quist 4–6, 6–0, 8–6, 6–1

Don Budge d. John Bromwich 6–2, 6–3, 4–6, 7–5

Adrian Quist-John Bromwich A. d. Don Budge-Gene Mako 0–6, 6–3, 6–4, 6–2

Don Budge d. Adrian Quist 8–6, 6–1, 6–2

John Bromwich (A) d. Bobby Riggs 6–4, 4–6, 6–0, 6–2

1939   Australia d. United States 3–2 (Haverford, Pa.)

Bobby Riggs (US) d. John Bromwich 6–4, 6–0, 7–5

Frank Parker (US) d. Adrian Quist 6–3, 6–4, 1–6, 7–5

Adrian Quist-John Bromwich d. Jack Kramer-Joe Hunt 5–7, 6–2, 7–5, 6–2

Adrian Quist d. Bobby Riggs 6–1, 6–4, 3–6, 3–6, 6–4

John Bromwich d. Frank Parker 6–0, 6–3, 6–1

1940–45 No competition

1946   United States d. Australia 5–0 (Melbourne, Australia)

Ted Schroeder d. John Bromwich 3–6, 6–1, 6–2, 0–6, 6–3

Jack Kramer d. Dinny Pails 8–6, 6–2, 9–7

Jack Kramer-Ted Schroeder d. John Bromwich-Adrian Quist 6–2, 7–5, 6–4

Jack Kramer d. John Bromwich 8–6, 6–4, 6–4

Gardnar Mulloy d. Dinny Pails 6–3, 6–3, 6–4

1947   United States d. Australia 4–1 (Forest Hills, N.Y.)

Jack Kramer d. Dinny Pails 6–2, 6–1, 6–2

Ted Schroeder d. John Bromwich 6–4, 5–7, 6–3, 6–4

John Bromwich-Colin Long (A) d. Jack Kramer-Ted Schroeder 6–4, 2–6, 6–2, 6–4

Ted Schroeder d. Dinny Pails 6–3, 8–6, 4–6, 9–11, 10–8

Jack Kramer d. John Bromwich 6–3, 6–2, 6–2

1948 United States d. Australia 5–0 (Forest Hills, N.Y.)

Frank Parker d. Bill Sidwell 6–4, 6–4, 6–4

Ted Schroeder d. Adrian Quist 6–3, 4–6, 6–0, 6–0

Bill Talbert-Gardnar Mulloy d. Bill Sidwell-Colin Long 8–6, 9–7, 2–6, 7–5

Ted Schroeder d. Bill Sidwell 6–2, 6–1, 6–1

Frank Parker d. Adrian Quist 6–2, 6–2, 6–3

1949 United States d. Australia 4–1 (Forest Hills, N.Y.)

Ted Schroeder d. Bill Sidwell 6–1, 5–7, 4–6, 6–2, 6–3

Pancho Gonzalez d. Frank Sedgman 8–6, 6–4, 9–7

Bill Sidwell-John Bromwich (A) d. Bill Talbert-Gardnar Mulloy 3–6, 4–6, 10–8, 9–7, 9–7

Ted Schroeder d. Frank Sedgman 6–4, 6–3, 6–3

Pancho Gonzalez d. Bill Sidwell 6–1, 6–3, 6–3

1950 Australia d. United States 4–1 (Forest Hills, N.Y.)

Frank Sedgman d. Tom Brown 6–0, 8–6, 9–7

Ken McGregor d. Ted Schroeder 13–11, 6–3, 6–4

Frank Sedgman-John Bromwich d. Ted Schroeder-Gardnar Mulloy 4–6, 6–4, 6–2, 4–6, 6–4)

Frank Sedgman d. Ted Schroeder 6–2, 6–2, 6–2

Tom Brown (US) d. Ken McGregor 9–11, 8–10, 11–9, 6–1, 6–4

1951 Australia d. United States 3–2 (Sydney, Australia)

Vic Seixas (US) d. Mervyn Rose 6–3, 6–4, 9–7

Frank Sedgman d. Ted Schroeder 6–4, 6–3, 4–6, 6–4

Ken McGregor-Frank Sedgman d. Ted Schroeder-Tony Trabert 6–2, 9–7, 6–3

Ted Schroeder (US) d. Mervyn Rose 6–4, 13–11, 7–5

Frank Sedgman d. Vic Seixas 6–4, 6–2, 6–2

1952 Australia d. United States 4–1 (Adelaide, Australia)

Frank Sedgman d. Vic Seixas 6–3, 6–4, 6–2

Ken McGregor d. Tony Trabert 11–9, 6–4, 6–1

Ken McGregor-Frank Sedgman d. Vic Seixas-Tony Trabert 6–3, 6–4, 1–6, 6–2

Frank Sedgman d. Tony Trabert 7–5, 6–4, 10–8

Vic Seixas (US) d. Ken McGregor 6–3, 8–6, 6–3

1953 Australia d. United States 3–2 (Melbourne, Australia)

Lew Hoad d. Vic Seixas 6–4, 6–2, 6–3

Tony Trabert (US) d. Ken Rosewall 6–3, 6–4, 6–4

Vic Seixas-Tony Trabert (US) d. Rex Hartwig-Lew Hoad 6–2, 6–4, 6–4

Lew Hoad d. Tony Trabert 13–11, 6–3, 2–6, 3–6, 7–5

Ken Rosewall d. Vic Seixas 6–2, 2–6, 6–3, 6–4

1954 United States d. Australia 3–2 (Syndey, Australia)

Tony Trabert d. Lew Hoad 6–4, 2–6, 12–10, 6–3

Vic Seixas d. Ken Rosewall 8–6, 6–8, 6–4, 6–3

Vic Seixas-Tony Trabert d. Lew Hoad-Ken Rosewall 6–2, 4–6, 6–2, 10–8

Ken Rosewall (A) d. Tony Trabert 9–7, 7–5, 6–3

Rex Hartwig (A) d. Vic Seixas 4–6, 6–3, 6–2, 6–3

1955 Australia d. United States 5–0 (Forest Hills, N.Y.)

Ken Rosewall d. Vic Seixas 6–3, 10–8, 4–6, 6–2

Lew Hoad d. Tony Trabert 4–6, 6–3, 6–3, 8–6

Lew Hoad-Rex Hartwig d. Tony Trabert-Vic Seixas 12–14, 6–4, 6–3, 3–6, 7–5

Lew Hoad d. Vic Seixas 7–9, 6–1, 6–4, 6–4

Ken Rosewall d. Ham Richardson 6–4, 3–6, 6–1, 6–4

1956 Australia d. United States 5–0 (Adelaide, Australia)

Lew Hoad d. Herbie Flam 6–2, 6–3, 6–3

Ken Rosewall d. Vic Seixas 6–1, 6–4, 4–6, 6–1

Lew Hoad-Ken Rosewall d. Sammy Giammalva-Vic Seixas 1–6, 6–1, 7–5, 6–4

Ken Rosewall d. Sammy Giammalva 4–6, 6–1, 8–6, 7–5

Lew Hoad d. Vic Seixas 6–2, 7–5, 6–3

1957   Australia d. United States 3–2 (Melbourne, Australia)

Mal Anderson d. Barry MacKay 6–3, 7–5, 3–6, 7–9, 6–3

Ashley Cooper d. Vic Seixas 3–6, 7–5, 6–1, 1–6, 6–3

Mal Anderson-Mervyn Rose d. Barry MacKay-Vic Seixas 6–4, 6–4, 8–6

Vic Seixas (US) d. Mal Anderson 6–3, 4–6, 6–3, 0–6, 13–11

Barry MacKay (US) d. Ashley Cooper 6–4, 1–6, 4–6, 6–4, 6–3

1958   United States d. Australia 3–2 (Brisbane, Australia)

Alex Olmedo d. Mal Anderson 8–6, 2–6, 9–7, 8–6

Ashley Cooper (A) d. Barry MacKay 4–6, 6–3, 6–2, 6–4

Alex Olmedo-Ham Richardson (A) d. Mal Anderson-Neale Fraser 10–12, 3–6, 16–14, 6–3, 7–5

Alex Olmedo d. Ashley Cooper 6–3, 4–6, 6–4, 8–6

Mal Anderson d. Barry MacKay 7–5, 13–11, 11–9

1959   Australia d. United States 3–2 (Forest Hills, N.Y.)

Neale Fraser d. Alex Olmedo 8–6, 6–8, 6–4, 8–6

Barry MacKay (US) d. Rod Laver 7–5, 6–4, 6–1

Neale Fraser-Roy Emerson d. Alex Olmedo-Butch Buchholz 7–5, 7–5, 6–4

Alex Olmedo (US) d. Rod Laver 9–7, 4–6, 10–8, 12–10

Neale Fraser d. Barry MacKay 8–6, 3–6, 6–2, 6–4

1960   Australia d. Italy 4–1 (Sydney, Australia)

Neale Fraser d. Orlando Sirola 4–6, 6–3, 6–3, 6–3

Rod Laver d. Nicola Pietrangeli 8–6, 6–4, 6–3

Neale Fraser-Roy Emerson d. Nicola Pietrangeli-Orlando Sirola 10–8, 5–7, 6–2, 6–4

Rod Laver d. Orlando Sirola 9–7, 6–2, 6–3

Nicola Pietrangeli (I) d. Neale Fraser 11–9, 6–3, 1–6, 6–2

1961   Australia d. Italy 5–0 (Melbourne, Australia)

Roy Emerson d. Nicola Pietrangeli 8–6, 6–4, 6–0

Rod Laver d. Orlando Sirola 6–1, 6–4, 6–3

Neale Fraser-Roy Emerson d. Nicola Pietrangeli-Orlando Sirola 6–2, 6–3, 6–4

Rod Laver d. Nicola Pietrangeli 6–3, 3–6, 4–6, 6–3, 8–6

Roy Emerson d. Orlando Sirola 6–3, 6–3, 4–6, 6–2

1962   Australia d. Mexico 5–0 (Brisbane, Australia)

Rod Laver d. Rafael Osuna 6–2, 6–1, 7–5

Neale Fraser d. Tony Palafox 7–9, 6–3, 6–4, 11–9

Roy Emerson-Rod Laver d. Rafael Osuna-Tony Palafox 7–5, 6–2, 6–4

Neale Fraser d. Rafael Osuna 3–6, 11–9, 6–1, 3–6, 6–4

Rod Laver d. Tony Palafox 6–1, 4–6, 6–4, 8–6

1963   United States d. Australia 3–2 (Adelaide, Australia)

Dennis Ralston d. John Newcombe 6–4, 6–1, 3–6, 4–6, 7–5

Roy Emerson (A) d. Chuck McKinley 6–3, 3–6, 7–5, 7–5

Chuck McKinley-Dennis Ralston d. Roy Emerson-Neale Fraser 6–3, 4–6, 11–9, 11–9

Roy Emerson (A) d. Dennis Ralston 6–2, 6–3, 3–6, 6–2

Chuck McKinley d. John Newcombe 10–12, 6–2, 9–7, 6–2

1964   Australia d. United States 3–2 (Cleveland, O.)

Chuck McKinley (US) d. Fred Stolle 6–1, 9–7, 4–6, 6–2

Roy Emerson d. Dennis Ralston 6–3, 6–4, 6–2

Chuck McKinley-Dennis Ralston (US) d. Roy Emerson-Fred Stolle 6–4, 4–6, 4–6, 6–3, 6–4

Fred Stolle d. Dennis Ralston 7–5, 6–3, 3–6, 9–11, 6–4

Roy Emerson d. Chuck McKinley 3–6, 6–2, 6–4, 6–4

1965   Australia d. Spain 4–1 (Sydney, Australia)

Fred Stolle d. Manuel Santana 10–12, 3–6, 6–1, 6–4, 7–5

Roy Emerson d. Juan Gisbert 6–3, 6–2, 6–2

John Newcombe-Tony Roche d. Luis Arilla-Manuel Santana 6–3, 4–6, 7–5, 6–2

Manuel Santana (S) d. Roy Emerson 2–6, 6–3, 6–4, 15–13

Fred Stolle d. Juan Gisbert 6–2, 6–4, 8–6

1966   Australia d. India 4–1 (Melbourne, Australia)

Fred Stolle d. Ramanathan Krishnan 6–3, 6–2, 6–4

Roy Emerson d. Jai Mukerjea 7–5, 6–4, 6–2

Ramanathan Krishnan-Jai Mukerjea (I) d. John Newcombe-Tony Roche 4–6, 7–5, ·6–4, 6–4

Roy Emerson d. Ramanathan Krishnan 6–0, 6–2, 10–8

Fred Stolle d. Jai Mukerjea 7–5, 6–8, 6–3, 5–7, 6–3

1967 Australia d. Spain 4–1 (Brisbane, Australia)
Roy Emerson d. Manuel Santana 6–4, 6–1, 6–1

John Newcombe d. Manuel Orantes 6–3, 6–3, 6–2

John Newcombe-Tony Roche d. Manuel Santana-Manuel Orantes 6–4, 6–4, 6–4

Manuel Santana (S) d. John Newcombe 7–5, 6–4, 6–2

Roy Emerson d. Manuel Orantes 6–1, 6–1, 2–6, 6–4

1968 United States d. Australia 4–1 (Adelaide, Australia)
Clark Graebner d. Bill Bowrey 8–10, 6–4, 8–6, 3–6, 6–1

Arthur Ashe d. Ray Ruffels 6–8, 7–5, 6–3, 6–3

Bob Lutz-Stan Smith d. John Alexander-Ray Ruffels 6–4, 6–4, 6–2

Clark Graebner d. Ray Ruffels 3–6, 8–6, 2–6, 6–3, 6–1

Bill Bowrey (A) d. Arthur Ashe 2–6, 6–3, 11–9, 8–6

1969 United States d. Romania 5–0 (Cleveland, O.)
Arthur Ashe d. Ilie Nastase 6–2, 15–13, 7–5

Stan Smith d. Ion Tiriac 6–8, 6–3, 5–7, 6–4, 6–4

Bob Lutz-Stan Smith d. Ilie Nastase-Ion Tiriac 8–6, 6–1, 11–9

Stan Smith d. Ilie Nastase 4–6, 4–6, 6–4, 6–1, 11–9

Arthur Ashe d. Ion Tiriac 6–3, 8–6, 3–6, 4–0 default

1970 United States d. Germany 5–0 (Cleveland, O.)
Arthur Ashe d. Willie Bungert 6–2, 10–8, 6–2

Cliff Richey d. Christian Kuhnke 6–3, 6–4, 6–2

Bob Lutz-Stan Smith d. Christian Kuhnke-Willie Bungert 6–3, 7–5, 6–4

Cliff Richey d. Willie Bungert 6–4, 6–4, 7–5

Arthur Ashe d. Christian Kuhnke 6–8, 10–12, 9–7, 13–11, 6–4

1971 United States d. Romania 3–2 (Charlotte, N.C.)
Stan Smith d. Ilie Nastase 7–5, 6–3, 6–1

Frank Froehling d. Ion Tiriac 3–6, 1–6, 6–3, 6–1, 8–6

Ilie Nastase-Ion Tiriac (R) d. Stan Smith-Erik van Dillen 7–5, 6–4, 8–6

Stan Smith d. Ion Tiriac 8–6, 6–3, 6–0

Ilie Nastase (R) d. Frank Froehling 6–3, 6–1, 4–6, 6–4

1972 United States d. Romania 3–2 (Bucharest, Romania)
Stan Smith d. Ilie Nastase 11–9, 6–2, 6–3

Ion Tiriac (R) d. Tom Gorman 4–6, 2–6, 6–4, 6–3, 6–2

Stan Smith-Erik van Dillen d. Ilie Nastase-Ion Tiriac 6–2, 6–0, 6–3

Stan Smith d. Ion Tiriac 4–6, 6–2, 6–4, 2–6, 6–0

Ilie Nastase (R) d. Tom Gorman 6–1, 6–2, 5–7, 10–8

1973 Australia d. United States 5–0 (Cleveland, O.)
John Newcombe d. Stan Smith 6–1, 3–6, 6–3, 3–6, 6–4

Rod Laver d. Tom Gorman 8–10, 8–6, 6–8, 6–3, 6–1

John Newcombe-Rod Laver d. Erik van Dillen-Stan Smith 6–1, 6–2, 6–4

John Newcombe d. Tom Gorman 6–2, 6–1, 6–3

Rod Laver d. Stan Smith 6–3, 6–4, 3–6, 6–2

1974 South Africa d. India (default—India refused to play, a protest against the South African government's policy of apartheid. The South African team was: Bob Hewitt, Fred McMillan, Ray Moore, and Rob Maud. The Indian team was: Vijay Amritraj, Anand Amritraj, Jas Singh, and Sashi Menon.)

1975 Sweden d. Czechoslovakia 3–2 (Stockholm, Sweden)
Bjorn Borg d. Jiri Hrebec 6–1, 6–3, 6–0

Jan Kodes (C) d. Ove Bengtson 4–6, 6–2, 7–5, 6–4

Bjorn Borg-Ove Bengtson d. Jan Kodes-Vladimir Zednik 6–4, 6–4, 6–4

Bjorn Borg d. Jan Kodes 6–4, 6–2, 6–2

Jiri Hrebec (C) d. Ove Bengtson 1–6, 6–3, 6–1, 6–4

1976 Italy d. Chile 4–1 (Santiago, Chile)
Corrado Barazzutti d. Jaime Fillol 7–5, 4–6, 7–5, 6–1

Adriano Panatta d. Pat Cornejo 6–3, 6–1, 6–3

Adriano Panatta-Paolo Bertolucci d. Pat
Cornejo-Jaime Fillol 3–6, 6–2, 9–7, 6–3
Adriano Panatta d. Jamie Fillol 8–6, 6–4,
3–6, 10–8
Belus Prajoux (C) d. Antonio Zugarelli
6–4, 6–4, 6–2
1977   Australia d. Italy 3–1 (Sydney, Australia)
Tony Roche d. Adriano Panatta 6–3, 6–4,
6–4
John Alexander d. Corrado Barazzutti 6–4,
8–6, 4–6, 6–2
Adriano Panatta–Paolo Bertolucci (I) d.
John Alexander-Phil Dent 6–4, 6–4, 7–5
John Alexander d. Adriano Panatta 6–4,
4–6, 2–6, 8–6, 11–9
Tony Roche vs. Corrado Barazzutti 12–12
abandoned
1978   United States d. Great Britain 4–1 (Rancho
Mirage, Calif.)
John McEnroe d. John Lloyd 6–1, 6–2,
6–2
Buster Mottram (B) d. Brian Gottfried 4–6,
2–6, 10–8, 6–4, 6–3
Stan Smith-Bob Lutz d. David Lloyd-Mark
Cox 6–2, 6–2, 6–3
John McEnroe d. Buster Mottram 6–2,
6–2, 6–1
Brian Gottfried d. John Lloyd 6–1, 6–2,
6–4
1979   United States d. Italy 5–0 (San Francisco,
Calif.)
Vitas Gerulaitis d. Corrado Barazzutti 6–2
default
John McEnroe d. Adriano Panatta 6–2,
6–3, 6–4
Stan Smith-Bob Lutz d. Paolo Bertolucci-
Adriano Panatta 6–4, 12–10, 6–2
John McEnroe d. Antonio Zugarelli 6–4,
6–3, 6–1
Vitas Gerulaitis d. Adriano Panatta 6–1,
6–3, 6–3

All-time Davis Cup Records

Individual

Most Cup-winning years: 8—Roy Emerson, Aus-
tralia, 1959–67
Most years in Challenge Round and/or final: 11—
Bill Tilden, U.S., 1920–30
Most years played: 21—Torben Ulrich, Denmark,
1948–68
Most team matches played: 66—Nicola Pietrangeli,
Italy, 1954–72
Most singles played: 110—Pietrangeli
Most singles won: 78—Pietrangeli

Most doubles played: 54—Pietrangeli
Most doubles won: 42—Pietrangeli
Most singles and doubles altogether: 164—
Pietrangeli
Most singles and doubles won altogether: 120—
Pietrangeli
Most consecutive singles wins: 31—Bjorn Borg,
Sweden, 1973–79
Longest singles: 86 games—Arthur Ashe, U.S., d.
Christian Kuhnke, West Germany, 6–8, 10–12,
9–7, 13–11, 6–4; Challenge Round, Cleveland,
1970
Longest doubles: 122 games—Stan Smith and Erik
van Dillen, U.S., d. Jaime Fillol and Pat Cor-
nejo, Chile, 7–9, 37–39, 8–6, 6–1, 6–3; zone
match, Little Rock, Ark., 1973
Best record in Challenge Rounds and/or finals: 7–0
in singles, 5–0 in doubles—Laurie Doherty,
Britain, 1902–6
Most Cups won as captain:16—Harry Hopman,
Australia, 1939–67

Team

Most Cups won: 26—United States
Most matches won: 145—U.S.
Most consecutive Cups won: 7—U.S., 1920–26
Most consecutive matches won: 17—U.S.,
1968–73

U.S. Davis Cup Records

Individual

Most Cup-winning years: 7—Bill Tilden, 1920–26;
Stan Smith, 1968–79
Most years played: 11—Tilden, 1920–30
Most team matches played: 24—John Van Ryn,
1929–36; Wilmer Allison, 1928–36
Most singles played: 36—Vic Seixas, 1951–57
Most singles won: 27—Arthur Ashe, 1963–78
Most doubles played: 23—Van Ryn
Most doubles won: 21—Van Ryn
Most singles and doubles altogether: 55—Seixas
Most singles and doubles won altogether: 38—
Seixas
Most consecutive singles won: 16—Tilden,
1920–27
Best winning percentage, 25 or more wins, singles
and doubles altogether: .903—Van Ryn, 28
wins, 3 losses
Best doubles team record (12–1) Stan Smith and
Bob Lutz, 1968–79
Best winning percentage singles, 15 or more wins:
1.000—Tut Bartzen, 1952–61, 15 wins
Best winning percentage doubles, 10 or more wins:
.923—Bob Lutz, 1968–78, 12 wins, 1 loss

Most Cups won as captain: 6—R. Norris Williams, 1921–26

Most matches won as captain: 13—Tony Trabert, 1976–79

FEDERATION CUP

In response to a growing interest in a worldwide women's team competition similar to the men's Davis Cup, the International Tennis Federation put the Federation Cup into play in 1963, marking the ITF's 50th birthday. Sixteen countries entered the competition that year in London at Queen's Club, and the United States edged Australia for the Cup, 2–1, as Billie Jean King and Darlene Hard beat Margaret Court and Lesley Turner in the decisive doubles, 3–6, 13–11, 6–3

The format differs from the Davis Cup in that all teams gather at one location each year for an elimination tournament to be played within one week. Each one-day engagement is best-of-three matches, two singles and a doubles. A team consists of a minimum of two players and a maximum of four, with players nominated for Nos. 1 and 2 singles facing respective opponents. The competition has grown to a 32 draw annually, with a qualifying tournament if more than that number enter. It was confined to amateurs until 1969, when it became an open event. Prize money has been offered since 1976. Only four countries have won the Cup: U.S. (8 times), Australia (7), South Africa (1), Czechoslovakia (1).

Title-round Standings

	W	L
United States	8	3
Australia	7	6
South Africa	1	1
Czechoslovakia	1	0
West Germany	0	2
Great Britain	0	3

Federation Cup Final Round Results

1963 United States d. Australia 2–1 (London, England)
Margaret Smith (A) d. Darlene Hard 6–3, 6–0
Billie Jean Moffitt d. Lesley Turner 5–7, 6–0, 6–3
Darlene Hard-Billie Jean Moffitt d. Margaret Smith-Lesley Turner 3–6, 13–11, 6–3

1964 Australia d. United States 2–1 (Philadelphia, Pa.)
Margaret Smith d. Billie Jean Moffitt 6–2, 6–3
Lesley Turner d. Nancy Richey 7–5, 6–1
Billie Jean Moffitt-Karen Susman (US) d. Margaret Smith-Lesley Turner 4–6, 7–5, 6–1

1965 Australia d. United States 2–1 (Melbourne, Australia)
Lesley Turner d. Carole Graebner 6–3, 2–6, 6–3
Margaret Smith d. Billie Jean Moffitt 6–4, 8–6
Billie Jean Moffitt-Carole Graebner (US) d. Margaret Smith-Judy Tegart 7–5, 4–6, 6–4

1966 United States d. Germany 3–0 (Turin, Italy)
Julie Heldman d. Helga Niessen 4–6, 7–5, 6–1
Billie Jean Moffitt King d. Edda Buding 6–3, 3–6, 6–1
Carole Graebner-Billie Jean King d. Helga Schultze-Edda Buding 6–4, 6–2

1967 United States d. Great Britain 2–0 (Berlin, West Germany)
Rosie Casals d. Virginia Wade 9–7, 8–6
Billie Jean King d. Ann Jones 6–3, 6–4
Doubles match called at set-all

1968 Australia d. Netherlands 3–0 (Paris, France)
Kerry Melville d. Marijke Jansen 4–6, 7–5, 6–3
Margaret Court d. Astrid Suurbeek 6–1, 6–3
Margaret Court-Kerry Melville d. Astrid Suurbeek-Lidy Venneboer 6–3, 6–8, 7–5

1969 United States d. Australia 2–1 (Athens, Greece)
Nancy Richey d. Kerry Melville 6–4, 6–3
Margaret Court (A) d. Julie Heldman 6–1, 8–6
Peaches Bartkowicz-Nancy Richey d. Margaret Court-Judy Tegart 6–4, 6–4

1970 Australia d. Germany 3–0 (Freiburg, West Germany)
Karen Krantzcke d. Helga Hoesl 6–2, 6–3
Judy Tegart Dalton d. Helga Niessen 4–6, 6–3, 6–3
Karen Krantzcke-Judy Dalton d. Helga Hoesl-Helga Niessen 6–2, 7–5

1971 Australia d. Great Britain 3–0 (Perth, Australia)
Margaret Court d. Ann Jones 6–3, 6–8, 6–2
Evonne Goolagong d. Virginia Wade 6–4, 6–1
Margaret Court-Lesley Hunt d. Virginia Wade-Winnie Shaw 6–4, 6–4

1972   South Africa d. Great Britain 2–1 (Johannesburg, South Africa)

Virginia Wade (GB) d. Pat Pretorious 6–3, 6–2

Brenda Kirk d. Winnie Shaw 4–6, 7–5, 6–0

Brenda Kirk-Pat Pretorious d. Winnie Shaw-Virginia Wade 6–1, 7–5

1973   Australia d. South Africa 3–0 (Bad Homburg, West Germany)

Evonne Goolagong d. Pat Pretorious 6–0, 6–2

Patti Coleman d. Brenda Kirk 10–8, 6–0

Evonne Goolagong-Janet Young d. Brenda Kirk-Pat Pretorious 6–1, 6–2

1974   Australia d. United States 2–1 (Naples, Italy)

Evonne Goolagong d. Julie Heldman 6–1, 7–5

Jeanne Evert (US) d. Dianne Fromholtz 2–6, 7–5, 6–4

Evonne Goolagong-Janet Young d. Julie Heldman-Sharon Walsh 7–5, 8–6

1975   Czechoslovakia d. Australia 3–0 (Aix-En-Provence, France)

Martina Navratilova d. Evonne Goolagong 6–3, 6–4

Renata Tomanova d. Helen Gourlay 6–4, 6–2

Martina Navratilova-Renata Tomanova d. Dianne Fromholtz-Helen Gourlay 6–3, 6–1

1976   United States d. Australia 2–1 (Philadelphia, Pa.)

Kerry Reid (A) d. Rosie Casals 1–6, 6–3, 7–5

Billie Jean King d. Evonne Goolagong 7–6, 6–4

Billie Jean King-Rosie Casals d. Evonne Goolagong-Kerry Reid 7–5, 6–3

1977   United States d. Australia 2–1 (Eastbourne, England)

Billie Jean King d. Dianne Fromholtz 6–1, 2–6, 6–2

Chris Evert d. Kerry Reid 7–5, 6–3

Kerry Reid-Wendy Turnbull (A) d. Chris Evert-Rosie Casals 6–3, 6–3

1978   United States d. Australia 2–1 (Melbourne, Australia)

Kerry Reid (A) d. Tracy Austin 6–3, 6–3

Chris Evert d. Wendy Turnbull 3–6, 6–1, 6–1

Chris Evert-Billie Jean King d. Wendy Turnbull-Kerry Reid 4–6, 6–1, 6–4

1979   United States d. Australia 3–0 (Madrid, Spain)

Tracy Austin d. Kerry Reid 6–3, 6–0

Chris Evert Lloyd d. Dianne Fromholtz 2–6, 6–3, 8–6

Billie Jean King-Rosie Casals d. Wendy Turnbull-Kerry Reid 3–6, 6–3, 8–6

All-time Federation Cup Records

Individual

Most Cup-winning years: 7—Billie Jean Moffitt King, U.S., 1963–79

Most years played: 13—Virginia Wade, Britain, 1967–79

Most team matches played: 41—Wade

Most singles played: 41—Wade

Most singles won: 29—Wade

Most doubles played: 29—Wade

Most doubles won: 27—King

Most singles and doubles played altogether: 70—Wade

Most singles and doubles won altogether: 50—Wade

Most consecutive singles won: 22—Margaret Smith Court, Australia, 1963–71

Best winning percentage singles, 20 or more wins: 1.000—Court, 22 wins, 0 losses

Best winning percentage doubles, 20 or more matches: 1.000—King, 27 wins, 0 losses

Best doubles team record: 10–0—Rosie Casals and King, 1967–79

Longest singles: 44 games—Leena Mutanen, Finland, d. Beatriz Araujo, Argentina, 9–7, 8–10, 6–4, 1972

Longest doubles: 46 games—Betty Stove and Trudy Walhof, Netherlands, d. Marilyn Pryde and Robyn Hunt, New Zealand, 15–13, 10–8, 1972

WIGHTMAN CUP

Hoping to stimulate international interest in women's tennis as the Davis Cup did in men's, Hazel Hotchkiss Wightman, an all-time champion from Boston, donated a sterling vase to the U.S. Tennis Association as a prize for such a team competition. It was decided to invite Great Britain to challenge for the prize in 1923 to open the new Forest Hills Stadium at the West Side Tennis Club in New York. With Mrs. Wightman as player-captain, the U.S. won the inaugural, 7–0. The rivalry was rewarding to both countries and soon developed into a close competition, an annual match between the two with the prize soon known as the Wightman Cup. The matches are played in even years in Britain and in odd years in the U.S.

Interrupted only by World War II, the series has been dominated by the U.S., which held a 39–9 edge after 1978.

The format is five singles and two doubles, a best-of-seven match engagement. Each team contains a maximum of six players and a minimum of four. Three singles players are nominated as Nos. 1, 2, and 3. Nos. 1 and 2 of each team play against each other in reverse singles. Nos. 3 play against each other once. Two doubles complete the program.

Wightman Cup Results

1923   United States d. Great Britain 7–0 (Forest Hills, New York)
Helen Wills d. Kitty McKane 6–2, 7–5
Molla Mallory d. M. Clayton 6–1, 8–6
Eleanor Goss d. Geraldine Beamish 6–2, 7–5
Helen Wills d. M. Clayton 6–2, 6–3
Molla Mallory d. Kitty McKane 6–2, 6–3
Hazel Wightman-Eleanor Goss d. Kitty McKane-Phyllis Covell 10–8, 5–7, 6–4
Molla Mallory-Helen Wills Moody d. Geraldine Beamish-M. Clayton 6–3, 6–2

1924   Great Britain d. United States 6–1 (Wimbledon)
Phyllis Covell d. Helen Wills 6–2, 6–4
Kitty McKane d. Molla Mallory 6–3, 6–3
Kitty McKane d. Helen Wills 6–2, 6–2
Phyllis Covell d. Molla Mallory 6–2, 5–7, 6–3
Geraldine Beamish d. Eleanor Goss 6–1, 8–10, 6–3
Phyllis Covell-Dorothy Shepherd-Barron d. Marion Jessup-Eleanor Goss 6–2, 6–2
Hazel Wightman-Helen Wills (US) d. Kitty McKane-Evelyn Colyer 2–6, 6–2, 6–4

1925   Great Britain d. United States 4–3 (Forest Hills, N.Y.)
Kitty McKane d. Molla Mallory 6–4, 5–7, 6–0
Helen Wills (US) d. Joan Fry 6–0, 7–5
Dorothea Lambert Chambers d. Eleanor Goss 7–5, 3–6, 6–1
Helen Wills (US) d. Kitty McKane 6–1, 1–6, 9–7
Molla Mallory (US) d. Joan Fry 6–3, 6–0
Dorothea Lambert Chambers-Ermyntrude Harvey (GB) d. Molla Mallory-May Sutton Bundy 10–8, 6–1
Kitty McKane-Evelyn Colyer (GB) d. Helen Wills-Mary Browne 6–0, 6–3

1926   United States d. Great Britain 4–3 (Wimbledon)
Elizabeth Ryan d. Joan Fry 6–1, 6–3
Kitty McKane Godfree (GB) d. Mary Browne 6–1, 7–5
Joan Fry (GB) d. Mary Browne 3–6, 6–0, 6–4
Kitty Godfree (GB) d. Elizabeth Ryan 6–1, 5–7, 6–4
Marion Jessup d. Dorothy Shepherd Barron 6–1, 5–7, 6–4
Marion Jessup-Eleanor Goss d. Dorothea Lambert Chambers-Dorothy Shepherd Barron 6–4, 6–2
Mary Browne-Elizabeth Ryan d. Kitty Godfree-Evelyn Colyer 3–6, 6–2, 6–4

1927   United States d. Great Britain 5–2 (Forest Hills, N.Y.)
Helen Wills d. Joan Fry 6–2, 6–0
Molla Mallory d. Kitty Godfree 6–4, 6–2
Betty Nuthall (GB) d. Helen Jacobs 6–3, 2–6, 6–1
Helen Wills d. Kitty Godfree 6–1, 6–1
Molla Mallory d. Joan Fry 6–2, 11–9
Gwendolyn Sterry-Betty Hill (GB) d. Eleanor Goss-Charlotte Chapin 5–7, 7–5, 7–5
Helen Wills-Hazel Wightman d. Kitty Godfree-Ermyntrude Harvey 6–4, 4–6, 6–3

1928   Great Britain d. United States 4–3 (Wimbledon)
Helen Wills (US) d. Phoebe Watson 6–1, 6–2
Eileen Bennett d. Molla Mallory 6–1, 6–3
Helen Wills (US) d. Eileen Bennett 6–3, 6–2
Phoebe Watson d. Molla Mallory 2–6, 6–1, 6–2
Helen Jacobs (US) d. Betty Nuthall 6–3, 6–1
Ermyntrude Harvey-Peggy Saunders d. Eleanor Goss-Helen Jacobs 6–4, 6–1
Eileen Bennett-Phoebe Watson d. Helen Wills-Penelope Anderson 6–2, 6–1

1929   United States d. Great Britain 4–3 (Forest Hills, N.Y.)
Helen Wills d. Phoebe Watson 6–1, 6–4
Helen Jacobs d. Betty Nuthall 7–5, 8–6
Phoebe Watson (GB) d. Helen Jacobs 6–3, 6–2
Edith Cross d. Peggy Michell 6–3, 3–6, 6–3
Helen Wills d. Betty Nuthall 8–6, 8–6
Phoebe Watson-Peggy Michell (GB) d. Helen Wills-Edith Cross 6–4, 6–1
Phyllis Covell-Dorothy Shepherd Barron

(GB) d. Hazel Wightman-Helen Jacobs 6–2, 6–1

1930   Great Britain d. United States 4–3 (Wimbledon)

Helen Wills Moody (US) d. Joan Fry 6–1, 6–1

Phoebe Watson d. Helen Jacobs 2–6, 6–2, 6–4

Helen Moody (US) d. Phoebe Watson 7–5, 6–1

Helen Jacobs (US) d. Joan Fry 6–0, 6–3

Phyllis Mudford d. Sarah Palfrey 6–0, 6–2

Joan Fry-Ermyntrude Harvey d. Sarah Palfrey-Edith Cross 2–6, 6–2, 6–4

Phoebe Watson-Kitty Godfree d. Helen Moody-Helen Jacobs 7–5, 1–6, 6–4

1931   United States d. Great Britain 5–2 (Forest Hills, N.Y.)

Helen Moody d. Betty Nuthall 6–4, 6–2

Anna Harper d. Dorothy Round 6–3, 4–6, 9–7

Helen Jacobs d. Phyllis Mudford 6–4, 6–2

Helen Moody d. Phyllis Mudford 6–1, 6–4

Helen Jacobs d. Betty Nuthall 8–6, 6–4

Phyllis Mudford-Dorothy Shepherd Barron (GB) d. Sarah Palfrey-Hazel Wightman 6–4, 10–8

Betty Nuthall-Eileen Whittingstall (GB) d. Helen Moody-Ann Harper 8–6, 5–7, 6–3

1932   United States d. Great Britain 4–3 (Wimbledon)

Helen Jacobs d. Dorothy Round 6–4, 6–3

Helen Moody d. Eileen Whittingstall 6–4, 6–2

Helen Moody d. Dorothy Round 6–2, 6–3

Eileen Whittingstall (GB) d. Helen Jacobs 6–4, 2–6, 6–1

Phyllis Mudford King (GB) d. Anna Harper 3–6, 6–3, 6–1

Anna Harper-Helen Jacobs d. Peggy Saunders Michell-Dorothy Round 6–4, 6–1

Eileen Whittingstall-Betty Nuthall (GB) d. Helen Moody-Sarah Palfrey 6–3, 1–6, 10–8

1933   United States d. Great Britain 4–3 (Forest Hills, N.Y.)

Helen Jacobs d. Dorothy Round 6–4, 6–2

Sarah Palfrey d. Margaret Scriven 6–3, 6–1

Betty Nuthall (GB) d. Carolin Babcock 1–6, 6–1, 6–3

Dorothy Round (GB) d. Sarah Palfrey 6–4, 10–8

Helen Jacobs d. Margaret Scriven 5–7, 6–2, 7–5

Helen Jacobs-Sarah Palfrey d. Dorothy Round-Mary Heeley 6–4, 6–2

Betty Nuthall-Freda James (GB) d. Alice Marble-Marjorie Van Ryn 7–5, 6–2

1934   United States d. Great Britain 5–2 (Wimbledon)

Sarah Palfrey d. Dorothy Round 6–3, 3–6, 8–6

Helen Jacobs d. Margaret Scriven 6–1, 6–1

Helen Jacobs d. Dorothy Round 6–4, 6–4

Sarah Palfrey d. Margaret Scriven 4–6, 6–2, 8–6

Betty Nuthall (GB) d. Carolin Babcock 5–7, 6–3, 6–4

Nancy Lyle-Evelyn Dearman (GB) d. Carolin Babcock-Josephine Cruickshank 7–5, 7–5

Helen Jacobs-Sarah Palfrey d. Kitty Godfree-Betty Nuthall 5–7, 6–3, 6–2

1935   United States d. Great Britain 4–3 (Forest Hills, N.Y.)

Kay Stammers (GB) d. Helen Jacobs 5–7, 6–1, 9–7

Dorothy Round (GB) d. Ethel Arnold 6–0, 6–3

Sarah Palfrey Fabyan d. Phyllis King 6–0, 6–3

Helen Jacobs d. Dorothy Round 6–3, 6–2

Ethel Arnold d. Kay Stammers 6–2, 1–6, 6–3

Helen Jacobs-Sarah Palfrey Fabyan d. Kay Stammers-Freda James 6–3, 6–2

Nancy Lyle-Evelyn Dearman (GB) d. Dorothy Andrus-Carolin Babcock 3–6, 6–4, 6–1

1936   United States d. Great Britain 4–3 (Wimbledon)

Kay Stammers (GB) d. Helen Jacobs 12–10, 6–1

Dorothy Round (GB) d. Sarah Palfrey Fabyan 6–3, 6–4

Sarah Palfrey Fabyan d. Kay Stammers 6–3, 6–4

Dorothy Round (GB) d. Helen Jacobs 6–3, 6–3

Carolin Babcock d. Mary Hardwick 6–4, 4–6, 6–2

Carolin Babcock-Marjorie Van Ryn d. Evelyn Dearman-Nancy Lyle 6–2, 1–6, 6–3

Helen Jacobs-Sarah Palfrey Fabyan d. Kay Stammers-Freda James 1–6, 6–3, 7–5

1937   United States d. Great Britain 6–1 (Forest Hills, N.Y.)

Alice Marble d. Mary Hardwick 4–6, 6–2, 6–4

Helen Jacobs d. Kay Stammers 6–1, 4–6, 6–4

Helen Jacobs d. Mary Hardwick 2–6, 6–4, 6–2

Alice Marble d. Kay Stammers 6–3, 6–1

Sarah Palfrey Fabyan d. Margot Lumb 6–3, 6–1

Alice Marble-Sarah Palfrey Fabyan d. Evelyn Dearman-Joan Ingram 6–3, 6–2

Kay Stammers-Freda James (GB) d. Marjorie Van Ryn-Dorothy Bundy 6–3, 10–8

1938 United States d. Great Britain 5–2 (Wimbledon)

Kay Stammers (GB) d. Alice Marble 3–6, 7–5, 6–3

Helen Moody d. Margaret Scriven 6–0, 7–5

Sarah Palfrey Fabyan d. Margot Lumb 5–7, 6–2, 6–3

Alice Marble d. Margaret Scriven 6–3, 3–6, 6–0

Helen Moody d. Kay Stammers 6–2, 3–6, 6–3

Alice Marble-Sarah Palfrey Fabyan d. Margot Lumb-Freda James 6–4, 6–2

Evelyn Dearman-Joan Ingram (GB) d. Helen Moody-Dorothy Bundy 6–2, 7–5

1939 United States d. Great Britain 5–2 (Forest Hills, N.Y.)

Alice Marble d. Mary Hardwick 6–3, 6–4

Kay Stammers (GB) d. Helen Jacobs 6–2, 1–6, 6–3

Valerie Scott (GB) d. Sarah Palfrey Fabyan 6–3, 6–4

Alice Marble d. Kay Stammers 3–6, 6–3, 6–4

Helen Jacobs d. Mary Hardwick 6–2, 6–2

Dorothy Bundy-Mary Arnold d. Betty Nuthall-Nina Brown 6–3, 6–1

Alice Marble-Sarah Palfrey Fabyan d. Kay Stammers-Freda James Hammersley 7–5, 6–2

1940–45 Not held

1946 United States d. Great Britain 7–0 (Wimbledon)

Pauline Betz d. Jean Bostock 6–2, 6–4

Margaret Osborne d. Jean Bostock 6–1, 6–4

Margaret Osborne d. Kay Stammers Menzies 6–3, 6–2

Louise Brough d. Joan Curry 8–6, 6–3

Pauline Betz d. Kay Menzies 6–4, 6–4

Margaret Osborne-Louise Brough d. Jean Bostock-Mary Halford 6–2, 6–1

Pauline Betz-Doris Hart d. Betty Passingham-Molly Lincoln 6–1, 6–3

1947 United States d. Great Britain 7–0 (Forest Hills)

Margaret Osborne d. Jean Bostock 6–4, 2–6, 6–2

Louise Brough d. Kay Menzies 6–4, 6–2

Doris Hart d. Betty Hilton 4–6, 6–3, 7–5

Louise Brough d. Jean Bostock 6–4, 6–4

Margaret Osborne d. Kay Menzies 7–5, 6–2

Doris Hart-Pat Todd d. Joy Gannon-Jean Quertier 6–1, 6–2

Margaret Osborne-Louise Brough d. Jean Bostock-Betty Hilton 6–1, 6–4

1948 United States d. Great Britain 6–1 (Wimbledon)

Margaret Osborne duPont d. Jean Bostock 6–4, 8–6

Louise Brough d. Betty Hilton 6–1, 6–1

Margaret duPont d. Betty Hilton 6–3, 6–4

Louise Brough d. Jean Bostock 6–2, 4–6, 7–5

Doris Hart d. Joy Gannon 6–1, 6–4

Louise Brough-Margaret duPont d. Kay Menzies-Betty Hilton 6–2, 6–2

Jean Bostock-Molly Lincoln Blair (GB) d. Doris Hart-Pat Todd 6–3, 6–4

1949 United States d. Great Britain 7–0 (Haverford, Pa.)

Doris Hart d. Jean Smith 6–3, 6–1

Margaret duPont d. Betty Hilton 6–1, 6–3

Doris Hart d. Betty Hilton 6–1, 6–3

Margaret duPont d. Jean Smith 6–4, 6–2

Beverly Baker d. Jean Quertier 6–4, 7–5

Doris Hart-Shirley Fry d. Jean Quertier-Molly Lincoln Blair 6–1, 6–2

Gussy Moran-Pat Todd d. Betty Hilton-Kay Tuckey 6–4, 8–6

1950 United States d. Great Britain 7–0 (Wimbledon)

Margaret duPont d. Betty Hilton 6–3, 6–4

Doris Hart d. Joan Curry 6–2, 6–4

Louise Brough d. Betty Hilton 2–6, 6–2, 7–5

Margaret duPont d. Jean Smith 6–3, 6–2

Louise Brough d. Jean Smith 6–0, 6–0

Pat Todd-Doris Hart d. Jean Smith-Jean Quertier 6–2, 6–3

Louise Brough-Margaret duPont d. Betty Hilton-Kay Tuckey 6–2, 6–0

1951 United States d. Great Britain 6–1 (Chestnut Hill, Mass.)

Doris Hart d. Jean Quertier 6–4, 6–4

Shirley Fry d. Jean Walker Smith 6–1, 6–4

Maureen Connolly d. Kay Tuckey 6–1, 6–3

Doris Hart d. Jean Smith 6–4, 2–6, 7–5

Jean Quertier (GB) d. Shirley Fry 6–3, 8–6

Pat Todd-Nancy Chaffee d. Pat Ward-Joy Mottram 7–5, 6–3

Shirley Fry-Doris Hart d. Jean Quertier-Kay Tuckey 6–3, 6–3

1952 United States d. Great Britain 7–0 (Wimbledon)

Doris Hart d. Jean Quertier-Rinkel 6–3, 6–3

Maureen Connolly d. Jean Smith 3–6, 6–1, 7–5

Doris Hart d. Jean Smith 7–5, 6–2

Maureen Connolly d. Jean Rinkel 9–7, 6–2

Shirley Fry d. Susan Partridge 6–0, 8–6

Shirley Fry-Doris Hart d. Helen Fletcher-Jean Rinkel 8–6, 6–4

Louise Brough-Maureen Connolly d. Joy Mottram-Pat Ward 6–0, 6–3

1953 United States d. Great Britain 7–0 (Rye, N.Y.)

Maureen Connolly d. Angela Mortimer 6–1, 6–1

Doris Hart d. Helen Fletcher 6–4, 7–5

Shirley Fry d. Jean Rinkel 6–2, 6–4

Maureen Connolly d. Helen Fletcher 6–1, 6–1

Doris Hart d. Angela Mortimer 6–1, 6–1

Maureen Connolly-Louise Brough d. Angela Mortimer-Ann Shilcock 6–2, 6–3

Doris Hart-Shirley Fry d. Jean Rinkel-Helen Fletcher 6–2, 6–1

1954 United States d. Great Britain 7–0 (Wimbledon)

Maureen Connolly d. Helen Fletcher 6–1, 6–3

Doris Hart d. Ann Shilcock 6–4, 6–1

Doris Hart d. Helen Fletcher 6–1, 6–8, 6–2

Louise Brough d. Angela Buxton 8–6, 6–2

Maureen Connolly d. Ann Shilcock 6–2, 6–2

Louise Brough-Margaret duPont d. Angela Buxton-Pat Hird 2–6, 6–4, 7–5

Helen Fletcher-Ann Shilcock vs Shirley Fry-Doris Hart not played

1955 United States d. Great Britain 6–1 (Rye, N.Y.)

Angela Mortimer (GB) d. Doris Hart 6–4, 1–6, 7–5

Louise Brough d. Shirley Bloomer 6–2, 6–4

Louise Brough d. Angela Mortimer 6–0, 6–2

Dorothy Knode d. Angela Buxton 6–3, 6–3

Doris Hart d. Shirley Bloomer 7–5, 6–3

Louise Brough-Margaret duPont d. Shirley Bloomer-Pat Ward 6–3, 6–3

Doris Hart-Shirley Bloomer d. Angela Mortimer-Angela Buxton 3–6, 6–2, 7–5

1956 United States d. Great Britain 5–2 (Wimbledon)

Louise Brough d. Angela Mortimer 3–6, 6–4, 7–5

Shirley Fry d. Angela Buxton 6–2, 6–8, 7–5

Louise Brough d. Angela Buxton 3–6, 6–3, 6–4

Shirley Bloomer (GB) d. Dorothy Knode 6–4, 6–4

Angela Mortimer (GB) d. Shirley Fry 6–4, 6–3

Dorothy Knode-Beverly Fleitz d. Shirley Bloomer-Pat Ward 6–1, 6–4

Louise Brough-Shirley Fry d. Angela Buxton-Angela Mortimer 6–2, 6–2

1957 United States d. Great Britain 6–1 (Sewickley, Pa.)

Althea Gibson d. Shirley Bloomer 6–4, 4–6, 6–2

Dorothy Head Knode d. Christine Truman 6–2, 11–9

Ann Haydon (GB) d. Darlene Hard 6–3, 3–6, 6–4

Dorothy Knode d. Shirley Bloomer 5–7, 6–1, 6–2

Althea Gibson d. Christine Truman 6–4, 6–2

Althea Gibson-Darlene Hard d. Shirley Bloomer-Sheila Armstrong 6–3, 6–4

Louise Brough-Margaret duPont d. Ann Shilcock-Ann Haydon 6–4, 6–1

1958 Great Britain d. United States 4–3 (Wimbledon)

Althea Gibson (US) d. Shirley Bloomer 6–3, 6–4

Christine Truman d. Dorothy Knode 6–4, 6–4

Dorothy Knode (US) d. Shirley Bloomer 6–4, 6–2

Christine Truman d. Althea Gibson 2–6, 6–3, 6–4

Ann Haydon d. Mimi Arnold 6–3, 5–7, 6–3

Christine Truman-Shirley Bloomer d. Karol Fageros-Dorothy Knode 6–2, 6–3

Althea Gibson-Janet Hopps (US) d. Anne Shilcock-Pat Ward 6–4, 3–6, 6–3

1959 United States d. Great Britain 4–3 (Sewickley, Pa.)

Beverly Fleitz d. Angela Mortimer 6–2, 6–1

Christine Truman (GB) d. Darlene Hard 6–4, 2–6, 6–3

Darlene Hard d. Angela Mortimer 6–3, 6–8, 6–4

Beverly Fleitz d. Christine Truman 6–4, 6–4

Ann Haydon (GB) d. Sally Moore 6–1, 6–1

Darlene Hard-Jeanne Arth d. Shirley Bloomer Brasher-Christine Truman 9–7, 9–7

Ann Haydon-Angela Mortimer (GB) d. Janet Hopps-Sally Moore 6–2, 6–4

1960 Great Britain d. United States 4–3 (Wimbledon)

Ann Haydon d. Karen Hantze 2–6, 11–9, 6–1

Darlene Hard (US) d. Christine Truman 4–6, 6–3, 6–4

Darlene Hard (US) d. Ann Haydon 5–7, 6–2, 6–1

Christine Truman d. Karen Hantze 7–5, 6–3

Angela Mortimer d. Janet Hopps 6–8, 6–4, 6–1

Karen Hantze-Darlene Hard (US) d. Ann Haydon-Angela Mortimer 6–0, 6–0

Christine Truman-Shirley Brasher d. Janet Hopps-Dorothy Knode 6–4, 9–7

1961 United States d. Great Britain 6–1 (Chicago, Ill.)

Karen Hantze d. Christine Truman 7–9, 6–1, 6–1

Billie Jean Moffitt d. Ann Haydon 6–4, 6–4

Karen Hantze d. Ann Haydon 6–1, 6–4

Christine Truman (GB) d. Billie Jean Moffitt 6–3, 6–2

Justina Bricka d. Angela Mortimer 10–8, 4–6, 6–3

Karen Hantze-Billie Jean Moffitt d. Christine Truman-Deidre Catt 7–5, 6–2

Margaret duPont-Margaret Varner d. Angela Mortimer-Ann Haydon default

1962 United States d. Great Britain 4–3 (Wimbledon)

Darlene Hard d. Christine Truman 6–2, 6–2

Ann Haydon (GB) d. Karen Hantze Susman 10–8, 7–5

Deidre Catt (GB) d. Nancy Richey 6–1, 7–5

Darlene Hard d. Ann Haydon 6–3, 6–8, 6–4

Karen Susman d. Christine Truman 6–4, 7–5

Margaret duPont-Margaret Varner d. Deidre Catt-Elizabeth Starkie 6–2, 3–6, 6–2

Christine Truman-Ann Haydon (GB) d.

Darlene Hard-Billie Jean Moffitt 6–4, 6–3

1963 United States d. Great Britain 6–1 (Cleveland, O.)

Ann Haydon Jones (GB) d. Darlene Hard 6–1, 0–6, 8–6

Billie Jean Moffitt d. Christine Truman 6–4, 19–17

Nancy Richey d. Deidre Catt 14–12, 6–3

Darlene Hard d. Christine Truman 6–3, 6–0

Billie Jean Moffitt d. Ann Jones 6–4, 4–6, 6–3

Darlene Hard-Billie Jean Moffitt d. Christine Truman-Ann Jones 4–6, 7–5, 6–2

Nancy Richey-Donna Fales d. Deidre Catt-Elizabeth Starkie 6–4, 6–8, 6–2

1964 United States d. Great Britain 5–2 (Wimbledon)

Nancy Richey d. Deidre Catt 4–6, 6–4, 7–5

Billie Jean Moffitt d. Ann Jones 4–6, 6–2, 6–3

Carole Caldwell d. Elizabeth Starkie 6–4, 1–6, 6–3

Nancy Richey d. Ann Jones 7–5, 11–9

Billie Jean Moffitt d. Deidre Catt 6–3, 4–6, 6–3

Deidre Catt-Ann Jones (GB) d. Carole Caldwell-Billie Jean Moffitt 6–2, 4–6, 6–0

Angela Mortimer-Elizabeth Starkie (GB) d. Nancy Richey-Donna Fales 2–6, 6–3, 6–4

1965 United States d. Great Britain 5–2 (Cleveland, O.)

Ann Jones (GB) d. Billie Jean Moffitt 6–2, 6–4

Nancy Richey d. Elizabeth Starkie 6–1, 6–0

Carole Caldwell Graebner d. Virginia Wade 3–6, 10–8, 6–4

Billie Jean Moffitt d. Elizabeth Starkie 6–3, 6–2

Ann Jones (GB) d. Nancy Richey 6–4, 8–6

Carole Graebner-Nancy Richey d. Nell Truman-Elizabeth Starkie 6–1, 6–0

Billie Jean Moffitt-Karen Susman d. Ann Jones-Virginia Wade 6–3, 8–6

1966 United States d. Great Britain 4–3 (Wimbledon)

Ann Jones (GB) d. Nancy Richey 2–6, 6–4, 6–3

Billie Jean Moffitt King d. Virginia Wade 6–2, 6–3

Winnie Shaw (GB) d. Mary Ann Eisel 6–3, 6–3

Nancy Richey d. Virginia Wade 2–6, 6–2, 7–5

Billie Jean King d. Ann Jones 5–7, 6–2, 6–3

Ann Jones-Virginia Wade (GB) d. Billie Jean King-Jane Albert 7–5, 6–2

Nancy Richey-Mary Ann Eisel d. Rita Bentley-Elizabeth Starkie 6–1, 6–2

1967   United States d. Great Britain 6–1 (Cleveland, O.)

Billie Jean King d. Virginia Wade 6–3, 6–2

Nancy Richey d. Ann Jones 6–2, 6–2

Christine Truman (GB) d. Rosie Casals 3–6, 7–5, 6–1

Nancy Richey d. Virginia Wade 3–6, 8–6, 6–2

Billie Jean King d. Ann Jones 6–1, 6–2

Rosie Casals-Billie Jean King d. Ann Jones-Virginia Wade 10–8, 6–4

Mary Ann Eisel-Carole Graebner d. Winnie Shaw-Joyce Williams 8–6, 12–10

1968   Great Britain d. United States 4–3 (Wimbledon)

Nancy Richey (US) D. Christine Truman Janes 6–1, 8–6

Virginia Wade d. Mary Ann Eisel 6–0, 6–1

Peaches Bartkowicz (US) d. Winnie Shaw 7–5, 3–6, 6–4

Mary Ann Eisel (US) d. Christine Janes 6–4, 6–3

Virginia Wade d. Nancy Richey 6–4, 2–6, 6–3

Virginia Wade-Winnie Shaw d. Nancy Richey-Mary Ann Eisel 5–7, 6–4, 6–3

Nell Truman-Christine Janes d. Stephanie DeFina-Kathy Harter 6–3, 2–6, 6–3

1969   United States d. Great Britain 5–2 (Cleveland, O.)

Julie Heldman d. Virginia Wade 3–6, 6–1, 8–6

Nancy Richey d. Winnie Shaw 8–6, 6–2

Peaches Bartkowicz d. Christine Janes 8–6, 6–0

Christine Janes-Nell Truman (GB) d. Mary Ann Eisel-Val Ziegenfuss 6–1, 3–6, 6–4

Virginia Wade (GB) d. Nancy Richey 6–3, 2–6, 6–3

Julie Heldman d. Winnie Shaw 6–3, 6–4

Julie Heldman-Peaches Bartkowicz d. Winnie Shaw-Virginia Wade 6–4, 6–2

1970   United States d. Great Britain 4–3 (Wimbledon)

Billie Jean King d. Virginia Wade 8–6, 6–4

Ann Jones (GB) d. Nancy Richey 6–3, 6–3

Julie Heldman d. Joyce Williams 6–3, 6–2

Virginia Wade (GB) d. Nancy Richey 6–3, 6–2

Billie Jean King d. Ann Jones 6–4, 6–2

Ann Jones-Joyce Williams (GB) d. Mary Ann Eisel-Julie Heldman 6–3, 6–2

Billie Jean King-Peaches Bartkowicz d. Virginia Wade-Winnie Shaw 7–5, 6–8, 6–2

1971   United States d. Great Britain 4–3 (Cleveland, O.)

Chris Evert d. Winnie Shaw 6–0, 6–4

Virginia Wade (GB) d. Julie Heldman 7–5, 7–5

Joyce Williams (GB) d. Kristy Pigeon 7–5, 3–6, 6–4

Mary Ann Eisel-Val Ziegenfuss d. Christine Janes-Nell Truman 6–1, 6–4

Val Ziegenfuss d. Winnie Shaw 6–4, 4–6, 6–3

Chris Evert d. Virginia Wade 6–1, 6–1

Virginia Wade-Joyce Williams (GB) d. Carole Graebner-Chris Evert 10–8, 4–6, 6–1

1972   United States d. Great Britain 5–2 (Wimbledon)

Joyce Williams (GB) d. Wendy Overton 6–3, 3–6, 6–3

Chris Evert d. Virginia Wade 6–4, 6–4

Chris Evert-Patti Hogan d. Winnie Shaw-Nell Truman 7–5, 6–4

Patti Hogan d. Corinne Molesworth 6–8, 6–4, 6–2

Chris Evert d. Joyce Williams 6–2, 6–3

Virginia Wade (GB) d. Wendy Overton 8–6, 7–5

Val Ziegenfuss-Wendy Overton d. Virginia Wade-Joyce Williams 6–3, 6–3

1973   United States d. Great Britain 5–2 (Brookline, Mass.)

Chris Evert d. Virginia Wade 6–4, 6–2

Patti Hogan d. Veronica Burton 6–4, 6–3

Linda Tuero d. Glynis Coles 7–5, 6–2

Virginia Wade-Glynis Coles (GB) d. Chris Evert-Marita Redondo 6–3, 6–4

Chris Evert d. Veronica Burton 6–3, 6–0

Virginia Wade (GB) d. Patti Hogan 6–2, 6–2

Patti Hogan-Jeanne Evert d. Lindsey Beaven-Lesley Charles 6–3, 4–6, 8–6

1974   Great Britain d. United States 6–1 (Queensferry, North Wales)

Virginia Wade d. Julie Heldman 5–7, 9–7, 6–4

Glynis Coles d. Janet Newberry 4–6, 6–1, 6–3

Sue Barker d. Jeanne Evert 4–6, 6–4, 6–1

Lesley Charles-Sue Barker d. Janet Newberry-Betsy Nagelsen 4–6, 6–2, 6–1

Glynis Coles d. Julie Heldman 6–0, 6–4

Virginia Wade d. Janet Newberry 6–1, 6–3

Julie Heldman-Mona Schallau (US) d. Virginia Wade-Glynis Coles 7–5, 6–4

1975 Great Britain d. United States 5–2 (Cleveland, O.)

Virginia Wade d. Mona Schallau 6–2, 6–2

Chris Evert (US) d. Glynis Coles 6–4, 6–1

Sue Barker d. Janet Newberry 6–4, 7–5

Virginia Wade-Ann Jones d. Janet Newberry-Julie Anthony 6–2, 6–3

Chris Evert (US) d. Virginia Wade 6–3, 7–6

Glynis Coles d. Mona Schallau 6–3, 7–6

Glynis Coles-Sue Barker d. Chris Evert-Mona Schallau 7–5, 6–4

1976 United States d. Great Britain 5–2 (Wimbledon)

Chris Evert d. Virginia Wade 6–2, 3–6, 6–3

Sue Barker (GB) d. Rosie Casals 1–6, 6–3, 6–2

Terry Holladay d. Glynis Coles 3–6, 6–1, 6–4

Chris Evert-Rosie Casals d. Virginia Wade-Sue Barker 6–0, 5–7, 6–1

Virginia Wade (GB) d. Rosie Casals 3–6, 9–7 ret.

Chris Evert d. Sue Barker 2–6, 6–2, 6–2

Ann Kiyomura-Mona Schallau Guerrant d. Sue Mappin-Lesley Charles 6–2, 6–2

1977 United States d. Great Britain 7–0 (Oakland, Calif.)

Chris Evert d. Virginia Wade 7–5, 7–6

Billie Jean King d. Sue Barker 6–1, 6–4

Rosie Casals d. Michele Tyler 6–2, 3–6, 6–4

Billie Jean King-JoAnne Russell d. Sue Mappin-Lesley Charles 6–0, 6–1

Billie Jean King d. Virginia Wade 6–4, 3–6, 8–6

Chris Evert d. Sue Barker 6–1, 6–2

Chris Evert-Rosie Casals d. Virginia Wade-Sue Barker 6–2, 6–4

1978 Great Britain d. United States 4–3 (London)

Chris Evert (US) d. Sue Barker 6–2, 6–1

Michele Tyler d. Pam Shriver 5–7, 6–3, 6–3

Virginia Wade d. Tracy Austin 3–6, 7–5, 6–3

Billie Jean King-Tracy Austin (US) d. Sue Mappin-Ann Hobbs 6–2, 4–6, 6–2

Chris Evert (US) d. Virginia Wade 6–0, 6–1

Sue Barker d. Tracy Austin 6–3, 3–6, 6–0

Virginia Wade-Sue Barker d. Chris Evert-Pam Shriver 6–0, 5–7, 6–4

1979 United States d. Great Britain 7–0 (Palm Beach, Fla.)

Chris Evert Lloyd d. Sue Barker 7–5, 6–2

Kathy Jordan d. Ann Hobbs 6–4, 6–7, 6–2

Tracy Austin d. Virginia Wade 6–1, 6–4

Tracy Austin-Ann Kiyomura d. Joanne Durie-Debbie Jevans 6–3, 6–1

Tracy Austin d. Sue Barker 6–4, 6–2

Chris Evert Lloyd d. Virginia Wade 6–1, 6–1

Chris Evert Lloyd-Rosie Casals d. Virginia Wade-Sue Barker 6–0, 6–1

All-time Wightman Cup Records

Individual

Most Cup-winning years: 11—Helen Jacobs, U.S., 1927–39

Most years played:14—Virginia Wade, Britain, 1965–79

Most singles played: 29—Wade

Most singles won: 18—Helen Wills Moody, U.S., 1923–38

Most doubles played: 15—Wade

Most doubles won: 10—Louise Brough, U.S., 1946–57

Most singles and doubles altogether: 38—Wade

Most singles and doubles won altogether: 22—Brough

Most consecutive singles won: 16—Chris Evert, U.S., 1971–79

Best winning percentage, 15 or more wins, singles and doubles altogether: 1.000—Brough, 22 wins, 0 losses

Best winning percentage singles, 10 or more wins: 1.000—Evert, 16–0

Best winning percentage doubles, 5 or more wins: 1.000—Brough, 10 wins, 0 losses

Best doubles team record: 7–0—Margaret Osborne duPont and Brough, 1946–57

Longest singles: 46 games—Billie Jean Moffitt King, U.S., d. Christine Truman, 19–17, 6–4, 1963

Longest doubles: 40 games—Hazel Hotchkiss Wightman and Eleanor Goss, U.S., d. Kathleen McKane and Phyllis Covel, 10–8, 5–7, 6–4, 1923

Most Cups won by captain: 12—Wightman, 1923–48

GRAND PRIX MASTERS

The Grand Prix Masters is a playoff for the top eight players at the end of a year-long series of Grand Prix tournaments. The players earn the right to play the Masters by accumulating points in tournaments throughout the year. It became a prestigious event from the time the first Masters was played under the sponsorship of Pepsi in 1970. Commercial Union sponsored the Grand Prix and the Masters from 1972 through 1976, and then Colgate 1977–79.

Meanwhile, Colgate established the Colgate International Series for women in 1976. This meant that the women had their own Grand Prix, and when the top eight women assembled in Palm Springs for the Colgate Series Championship, the tournament was a female version of the Masters.

Grand Prix Masters Champions (Men)

1970	(Tokyo) Stan Smith
1971	(Paris) Ilie Nastase
1972	(Barcelona) Ilie Nastase d. Stan Smith 6–3, 6–2, 3–6, 2–6, 6–3
1973	(Boston) Ilie Nastase d. Tom Okker 6–3, 7–5, 4–6, 6–3
1944	(Melbourne) Guillermo Vilas d. Ilie Nastase 7–6, 6–2, 3–6, 3–6, 6–4
1975	(Stockholm) Ilie Nastase d. Bjorn Borg 6–2, 6–2, 6–1
1976	(Houston) Manuel Orantes d. Wojtek Fibak 5–7, 6–2, 0–6, 7–6, 6–1
1977	(New York) Jimmy Connors d. Bjorn Borg 6–4, 1–6, 6–4
1978	(New York) John McEnroe d. Arthur Ashe 6–7, 6–3, 7–5

Colgate Series Champions (Women)

1976	(Palm Springs, Calif.) Chris Evert d. Françoise Durr 6–1, 6–2
1977	(Palm Springs, Calif.) Chris Evert d. Billie Jean King 6–2, 6–2
1978	(Palm Springs, Calif.) Chris Evert d. Martina Navratilova 6–3, 6–3

VIRGINIA SLIMS/AVON

In the fall of 1970, eight leading women (including Billie Jean King) signed pro contracts with Gladys Heldman, founder of *World Tennis* maga-

zine. They played a few small events that fall but by 1971 the Virginia Slims circuit had quickly expanded and the women competed for almost $200,-000 in prize money. With interest growing faster than the players could ever have imagined, the first Virginia Slims Championship was played in Boca Raton, Florida, in October of 1972. The top 32 players played the initial event. Eventually the Slims became a winter indoor circuit.

The field was reduced to sixteen players in 1974, when the tournament was moved to Los Angeles, and the format was changed to a round robin with two groups of four players in 1976. The format remained the same through 1978, but a political struggle between the Women's Tennis Association and Virginia Slims resulted in the women electing to establish a new circuit with a new sponsor.

Avon, which had begun a Futures circuit designed to help young players get the opportunity to move up to the big tour, signed an agreement with the WTA to take over the Virginia Slims, and the sponsor continued the tradition of a circuit championship for the top eight players when it launched the first Avon Championship at Madison Square Garden in New York in March 1979.

Virginia Slims Champions

1972	(Boca Raton, Fla.) Chris Evert d. Kerry Reid 7–5, 6–4
1973	(Boca Raton, Fla.) Chris Evert d. Nancy Richey 6–3, 6–3
1974	(Los Angeles) Evonne Goolagong d. Chris Evert 6–3, 6–4
1975	(Los Angeles) Chris Evert d. Martina Navratilova 6–4, 6–2
1976	(Los Angeles) Evonne Goolagong d. Chris Evert 6–3, 5–7, 6–3
1977	(New York) Chris Evert d. Sue Barker 2–6, 6–1, 6–1
1978	(Oakland) Martina Navratilova d. Evonne Goolagong 7–6, 6–4

Avon Champions

1979	(New York) Martina Navratilova d. Tracy Austin 6–3, 3–6, 6–2

WORLD CHAMPIONSHIP TENNIS

World Championship Tennis (WCT) is a Dallas-based professional tennis organization headed by Lamar Hunt. WCT became involved in tennis in

1967, the year before Open Tennis, when it signed up eight leading players to pro contracts and called them "The Handsome Eight." What began as a small pro circuit with these eight players (Dennis Ralston, Butch Buchholz, John Newcombe, Tony Roche, Nikki Pilic, Cliff Drysdale, Pierre Barthes, and Roger Taylor) grew into an important part of the international game.

WCT established a circuit of its own, and starting in 1971 the top eight players on the basis of points earned throughout the circuit came to Dallas for the WCT finals, the circuit championship. The first WCT finals was played in November 1971, but thereafter WCT established a May date for the annual event in Dallas. The WCT tournaments were eventually incorporated into the Grand Prix.

WCT Finals

1971   Ken Rosewall d. Rod Laver 6–4, 1–6, 7–6, 7–6

1972   Ken Rosewall d. Rod Laver 4–6, 6–0, 6–3, 6–7, 7–6

1973   Stan Smith d. Arthur Ashe 6–3, 6–3, 4–6, 6–4

1974   John Newcombe d. Bjorn Borg 4–6, 6–3, 6–2, 6–3

1975   Arthur Ashe d. Bjorn Borg 3–6, 6–4, 6–4, 6–0

1976   Bjorn Borg d. Guillermo Vilas 1–6, 6–1, 7–5, 6–1

1977   Jimmy Connors d. Dick Stockton 6–7, 6–1, 6–4, 6–3

1978   Vitas Gerulaitis d. Eddie Dibbs 6–3, 6–2, 6–1

1979   John McEnroe d. Bjorn Borg 7–5, 4–6, 6–2, 7–6

UNITED STATES TENNIS ASSOCIATION RANKINGS

(Editor's Note: Every year the United States Tennis Association, formerly the U.S. Lawn Tennis Association, releases annual rankings for the leading male and female players in the country. Until 1972, these rankings included only amateur players, but when Open Tennis arrived in 1968, bringing the pros and amateurs together under the same roof, it was inevitable that the American rankings would soon include all players.)

USTA Men's Rankings

1885

1. Richard Sears
2. James Dwight
3. W. Berry
4. G. Brinley
5. Joseph Clark
6. A. Moffat
7. Livingstone Beeckman
8. Howard Taylor
9. Fred Mansfield
10. W. Knapp

1886

1. Richard Sears
2. James Dwight
3. Livingstone Beeckman
4. Howard Taylor
5. Joseph Clark
6. Henry Slocum
7. G. Brinley
8. Fred Mansfield
9. A. Moffat
10. J. Conover

1887

1. Richard Sears
2. Henry Slocum
3. Livingstone Beeckman
4. Howard Taylor
5. Joseph Clark
6. Fred Mansfield
7. Philip Sears
8. G. Brinley
9. E. MacMullen
10. Quincy Shaw

1888

1. Henry Slocum
2. Howard Taylor
3. James Dwight
4. Joseph Clark
5. C. Chase
6. Philip Sears
7. E. MacMullen
8. Oliver Campbell
9. Livingstone Beeckman
10. Fred Mansfield

1889

1. Henry Slocum
2. Quincy Shaw
3. Oliver Campbell
4. Howard Taylor
5. C. Chase
6. Joseph Clark
7. W. Knapp
8. Bob Huntington
9. Philip Sears
10. Fred Mansfield

1890

1. Oliver Campbell
2. Bob Huntington
3. W. Knapp
4. Henry Slocum
5. Fred Hovey
6. Clarence Hobart
7. Philip Sears
8. Howard Taylor
9. C. Chase
10. Valentine Hall

1891

1. Oliver Campbell
2. Clarence Hobart
3. Bob Huntington
4. Fred Hovey
5. Edward Hall
6. Valentine Hall
7. Philip Sears
8. S. Chase
9. C. Lee
10. M. Smith

1892

1. Oliver Campbell
2. Edward Hall
3. W. Knapp
4. Clarence Hobart
5. Fred Hovey
6. Bill Larned
7. Malcolm Chace
8. Robert Wrenn
9. Richard Stevens
10. Charles Hubbard

1893

1. Robert Wrenn
2. Clarence Hobart
3. Fred Hovey
4. Malcolm Chace
5. Bill Larned
6. Edward Hall
7. Richard Stevens
8. Arthur Foote
9. John Howland
10. Clarence Budlong

1894

1. Robert Wrenn
2. Bill Larned
3. Manlove Goodbody
4. Fred Hovey
5. Malcolm Chace
6. Clarence Hobart
7. Richard Stevens
8. Clarence Budlong
9. Arthur Foote
10. W. Parker

1895

1. Fred Hovey
2. Bill Larned
3. Malcolm Chace
4. John Howland
5. Robert Wrenn
6. Carr Neel
7. Clarence Hobart
8. Richard Stevens
9. Arthur Foote
10. Clarence Budlong

1896

1. Robert Wrenn
2. Bill Larned
3. Carr Neel
4. Fred Hovey
5. Edwin Fischer
6. George Wrenn
7. Richard Stevens
8. Malcolm Whitman
9. Leo Ware
10. George Sheldon

1897

1. Robert Wrenn
2. Bill Larned
3. Wilberforce Eaves
4. H. Nisbet
5. Harold Mahony
6. George Wrenn
7. Malcolm Whitman
8. Kreigh Collins
9. Edwin Fischer
10. W. Bond

1898

1. Malcolm Whitman
2. Leo Ware
3. W. Bond
4. Dwight Davis
5. Clarence Budlong
6. Edwin Fischer
7. George Wrenn
8. Richard Stevens
9. Stephen Millett
10. G. Bieden

1899

1. Malcolm Whitman
2. Dwight Davis
3. Bill Larned
4. Parmely Paret
5. Kriegh Collins
6. George Wrenn
7. Leo Ware
8. Beals Wright
9. Holcombe Ward
10. Bob Huntington

1900

1. Malcolm Whitman
2. Dwight Davis
3. Bill Larned
4. Beals Wright
5. Kriegh Collins
6. George Wrenn
7. Holcombe Ward
8. Leo Ware
9. John Allen
10. Ray Little

1901

1. Bill Larned
2. Beals Wright
3. Dwight Davis
4. Leo Ware
5. Clarence Hobart
6. Ray Little
7. Holcombe Ward
8. Kriegh Collins
9. Edwin Fischer
10. Bill Clothier

1902

1. Bill Larned
2. Malcolm Whitman
3. Beals Wright
4. Holcombe Ward
5. Bill Clothier
6. Leo Ware
7. Ray Little
8. Kriegh Collins
9. Harold Hackett
10. Clarence Hobart

1903

1. Bill Larned
2. Holcombe Ward
3. Bill Clothier
4. Beals Wright
5. Kriegh Collins
6. Edwin Larned
7. Harry Allen
8. Edgar Leonard
9. R. Carleton
10. Ken Horton

1904

1. Holcombe Ward
2. Bill Clothier
3. Bill Larned
4. Beals Wright
5. Kriegh Collins
6. Ray Little
7. Fred Alexander
8. Richard Stevens
9. A. Bell
10. Edgar Leonard

1905

1. Beals Wright
2. Holcombe Ward
3. Bill Larned
4. Bill Clothier
5. Fred Alexander
6. Clarence Hobart
7. Richard Stevens
8. Kriegh Collins
9. Ray Little
10. Fred Anderson

1906

1. Bill Clothier
2. Bill Larned
3. Beals Wright
4. Fred Alexander
5. Karl Behr
6. Ray Little
7. Harold Hackett
8. Fred Anderson
9. Ed Dewhurst
10. Irving Wright

1907

1. Bill Larned
2. Beals Wright
3. Karl Behr
4. Ray Little
5. Bob LeRoy
6. Clarence Hobart
7. Edwin Larned
8. R. Seaver
9. Irving Wright
10. Fred Colston

1908

1. Bill Larned
2. Beals Wright
3. Fred Alexander
4. Bill Clothier
5. Ray Little
6. Bob LeRoy
7. Nat Emerson
8. Nathaniel Niles
9. Wallace Johnson
10. Presbrey Palmer

1909

1. Bill Larned
2. Bill Clothier
3. Wallace Johnson
4. Nathaniel Niles
5. Ray Little
6. Maurice McLoughlin
7. Melville Long
8. Karl Behr
9. Edwin Larned
10. Bob LeRoy

1910

1. Bill Larned
2. Tom Bundy
3. Beals Wright
4. Maurice McLoughlin
5. Melville Long
6. Nathaniel Niles
7. Gustave Touchard
8. Theodore Pell
9. Fred Colston
10. C. Gardner

1911

1. Bill Larned
2. Maurice McLoughlin
3. Tom Bundy
4. Gustave Touchard
5. Melville Long
6. Nathaniel Niles
7. Theodore Pell
8. Ray Little
9. Karl Behr
10. Walter Hall

1912

1. Maurice McLoughlin
2. R. Norris Williams
3. Wallace Johnson
4. Bill Clothier
5. Nathaniel Niles
6. Tom Bundy
7. Karl Behr
8. Ray Little
9. George Gardner
10. Gustave Touchard

1913

1. Maurice McLoughlin
2. R. Norris Williams
3. Bill Clothier
4. Bill Johnston
5. Theodore Pell
6. Nathaniel Niles
7. Wallace Johnson
8. Gustave Touchard
9. George Gardner
10. John Strachan

1914

1. Maurice McLoughlin
2. R. Norris Williams
3. Karl Behr
4. R. Lindley Murray
5. Bill Clothier
6. Bill Johnston
7. George Church
8. Fred Alexander
9. Watson Washburn
10. Elia Fottrell

1915

1. Bill Johnston
2. R. Norris Williams
3. Maurice McLoughlin
4. Karl Behr
5. Theodore Pell
6. Nathaniel Niles
7. Clarence Griffin
8. Watson Washburn
9. George Church
10. Walter Hall

1916

1. R. Norris Williams
2. Bill Johnston
3. George Church
4. R. Lindley Murray
5. Ichiya Kumagae
6. Clarence Griffin
7. Watson Washburn
8. Wallace Davis
9. Joseph Armstrong
10. Dean Mathey

1917 No rankings

1918

1. R. Lindley Murray
2. Bill Tilden
3. Fred Alexander
4. Walter Hall
5. Walter Hayes
6. Nathanial Niles
7. Ichiya Kumagae
8. Chuck Garland
9. Howard Voshell
10. Theodore Pell

1919

1. Bill Johnston
2. Bill Tilden
3. Ichiya Kumagae
4. R. Lindley Murray
5. Wallace Johnson
6. R. Norris Williams
7. Roland Roberts
8. Chuck Garland
9. Walter Hayes
10. Watson Washburn

1920

1. Bill Tilden
2. Bill Johnston
3. R. Norris Willams
4. Ichiya Kumagae
5. Willis Davis
6. Clarence Griffin
7. Watson Washburn
8. Chuck Garland
9. Nathaniel Niles
10. Wallace Johnson

1921

1. Bill Tilden
2. Bill Johnston
3. Vinnie Richards
4. Wallace Johnson
5. Watson Washburn
6. R. Norris Williams
7. Ichiya Kumagae
8. Howard Voshell
9. Larry Rice
10. Nathaniel Niles

1922

1. Bill Tilden
2. Bill Johnston
3. Vinnie Richards
4. R. Norris Williams
5. Wallace Johnson
6. Bob Kinsey
7. Zenzo Shimizu
8. Howard Kinsey
9. Francis Hunter
10. Watson Washburn

1923

1. Bill Tilden
2. Bill Johnston
3. R. Norris Williams
4. Vinnie Richards
5. Francis Hunter
6. Howard Kinsey
7. Carl Fischer
8. Brian Norton
9. Harvey Snodgrass
10. Bob Kinsey

1924

1. Bill Tilden
2. Vinnie Richards
3. Bill Johnston
4. Howard Kinsey
5. Wallace Johnson
6. Harvey Snodgrass
7. John Hennessey
8. Brian Norton
9. George Lott
10. Clarence Griffin

1925

1. Bill Tilden
2. Bill Johnston
3. Vinnie Richards
4. R. Norris Williams
5. Manuel Alonso
6. Howard Kinsey
7. Takeichi Harada
8. Cranston Holman
9. Brian Norton
10. Wray Brown

1926

1. Bill Tilden
2. Manuel Alonso
3. Takeichi Harada
4. Bill Johnston
5. Ed Chandler
6. Lewis White
7. Al Chapin
8. Brian Norton
9. George Lott
10. George King

1927

1. Bill Tilden
2. Francis Hunter
3. George Lott
4. Manuel Alonso
5. John Hennessey
6. John Van Ryn
7. Arnold Jones
8. John Doeg
9. Lewis White
10. Cranston Holman

1928

1. Bill Tilden
2. Francis Hunter
3. George Lott
4. John Hennessey
5. Wilmer Allison
6. John Van Ryn
7. Fred Mercur
8. John Doeg
9. Julius Seligson
10. Frank Shields

1929

1. Bill Tilden
2. Francis Hunter
3. John Doeg
4. George Lott
5. John Van Ryn
6. Fred Mercur
7. Wilmer Allison
8. Wilbur Coen
9. Berkeley Bell
10. Greg Mangin

1930

1. John Doeg
2. Frank Shields
3. Wilmer Allison
4. Sidney Wood
5. Cliff Sutter
6. Greg Mangin
7. George Lott
8. Ellsworth Vines
9. John Van Ryn
10. Bitsy Grant

1931

1. Ellsworth Vines
2. George Lott
3. Frank Shields
4. John Van Ryn
5. John Doeg
6. Cliff Sutter
7. Sidney Wood
8. Keith Gledhill
9. Wilmer Allison
10. Berkeley Bell

1932

1. Ellsworth Vines
2. Wilmer Allison
3. Cliff Sutter
4. Sidney Wood
5. Frank Shields
6. Lester Stoefen
7. Greg Mangin
8. Keith Gledhill
9. John Van Ryn
10. David Jones

1933

1. Frank Shields
2. Wilmer Allison
3. Lester Stoefen
4. Cliff Sutter
5. Greg Mangin
6. Sidney Wood
7. Bitsy Grant
8. Frank Parker
9. Keith Gledhill
10. George Lott

1934

1. Wilmer Allison
2. Sidney Wood
3. Frank Shields
4. Frank Parker
5. Lester Stoefen
6. George Lott
7. Berkeley Bell
8. Cliff Sutter
9. Don Budge
10. Bitsy Grant

1935

1. Wilmer Allison
2. Don Budge
3. Bitsy Grant
4. Frank Shields
5. Sidney Wood
6. Greg Mangin
7. Frank Parker
8. Gilbert Hall
9. Wilmer Hines
10. Berkeley Bell

1936

1. Don Budge
2. Frank Parker
3. Bitsy Grant
4. Bobby Riggs
5. George Mangin
6. John Van Ryn
7. John McDiarmid
8. Chuck Harris
9. Joe Hunt
10. Arthur Hendrix

1937

1. Don Budge
2. Bobby Riggs
3. Frank Parker
4. Bitsy Grant
5. Joe Hunt
6. Wayne Sabin
7. Harold Surface
8. Gene Mako
9. Don McNeill
10. John Van Ryn

1938

1. Don Budge
2. Bobby Riggs
3. Gene Mako
4. Sidney Wood
5. Joe Hunt
6. Bitsy Grant
7. Elwood Cooke
8. Frank Parker
9. Gilbert Hunt
10. Frank Kovacs

1939

1. Bobby Riggs
2. Frank Parker
3. Don NcNeill
4. Welby Van Horn
5. Wayne Sabin
6. Elwood Cooke
7. Bitsy Grant
8. Gardnar Mulloy
9. Gilbert Hunt
10. Henry Prusoff

1940

1. Don McNeill
2. Bobby Riggs
3. Frank Kovacs
4. Joe Hunt
5. Frank Parker
6. Jack Kramer
7. Gardnar Mulloy
8. Henry Prusoff
9. Elwood Cooke
10. Ted Schroeder

1941

1. Bobby Riggs
2. Frank Kovacs
3. Frank Parker
4. Don McNeill
5. Ted Schroeder
6. Wayne Sabin
7. Gardnar Mulloy
8. Bitsy Grant
9. Jack Kramer
10. Bill Talbert

1942

1. Ted Schroeder
2. Frank Parker
3. Gardnar Mulloy
4. Pancho Segura
5. Bill Talbert
6. Sidney Wood
7. Seymour Greenberg
8. George Richards
9. Vic Seixas
10. Ladislav Hecht

1943

1. Joe Hunt
2. Jack Kramer
3. Pancho Segura
4. Bill Talbert
5. Seymour Greenberg
6. Sidney Wood
7. Bob Falkenburg
8. Frank Parker
9. Jim Brink
10. Jack Tuero

1944

1. Frank Parker
2. Bill Talbert
3. Pancho Segura
4. Don McNeill
5. Seymour Greenberg
6. Bob Falkenburg
7. Jack Jossi
8. Charles Oliver
9. Jack McManis
10. Gilbert Hall

1945

1. Frank Parker
2. Bill Talbert
3. Pancho Segura
4. Elwood Cooke
5. Sidney Wood
6. Gardnar Mulloy
7. Frank Shields
8. Hal Surface
9. Seymour Greenberg
10. Jack McManis

1946

1. Jack Kramer
2. Ted Schroeder
3. Frank Parker
4. Tom Brown
5. Gardnar Mulloy
6. Bill Talbert
7. Don McNeill
8. Bob Falkenburg
9. Eddie Moylan
10. Pancho Segura

1947

1. Jack Kramer
2. Frank Parker
3. Ted Schroeder
4. Gardnar Mulloy
5. Bill Talbert
6. Pancho Segura
7. Bob Falkenburg
8. Eddie Moylan
9. Earl Cochell
10. Seymour Greenberg

1948

1. Pancho Gonzales
2. Ted Schroeder
3. Frank Parker
4. Bill Talbert
5. Bob Falkenburg
6. Earl Cochell
7. Vic Seixas
8. Gardnar Mulloy
9. Herbie Flam
10. Harry Likas

1949

1. Pancho Gonzales
2. Ted Schroeder
3. Bill Talbert
4. Frank Parker
5. Gardnar Mulloy
6. Art Larsen
7. Earl Cochell
8. Sammy Match
9. Eddie Moylan
10. Herbie Flam

1950

1. Art Larsen
2. Herbie Flam
3. Ted Schroeder
4. Gardnar Mulloy
5. Bill Talbert
6. Dick Savitt
7. Earl Cochell
8. Vic Seixas
9. Tom Brown
10. Sammy Match

1951

1. Vic Seixas
2. Dick Savitt
3. Tony Trabert
4. Herbie Flam
5. Bill Talbert
6. Art Larsen
7. Ted Schroeder
8. Gardnar Mulloy
9. Ham Richardson
10. Budge Patty

1952

1. Gardnar Mulloy
2. Vic Seixas
3. Art Larsen
4. Dick Savitt
5. Herbie Flam
6. Bill Talbert
7. Ham Richardson
8. Tom Brown
9. Noel Brown
10. Harry Likas

1953

1. Tony Trabert
2. Vic Seixas
3. Art Larsen
4. Gardnar Mulloy
5. Straight Clark
6. Ham Richardson
7. Tut Bartzen
8. Tom Brown
9. Noel Brown
10. Grant Golden

1954

1. Vic Seixas
2. Tony Trabert
3. Ham Richardson
4. Art Larsen
5. Gardnar Mulloy
6. Tom Brown
7. Eddie Moylan
8. Tut Bartzen
9. Bill Talbert
10. Gilbert Shea

1955

1. Tony Trabert
2. Vic Seixas
3. Art Larsen
4. Tut Bartzen
5. Eddie Moylan
6. Gilbert Shea
7. Ham Richardson
8. Herbie Flam
9. Sammy Giammalva
10. Tom Brown

1956

1. Ham Richardson
2. Herbie Flam
3. Vic Seixas
4. Eddie Moylan
5. Tut Bartzen
6. Bob Perry
7. Sammy Giammalva
8. Art Larsen
9. Gilbert Shea
10. Grant Golden

1957

1. Vic Seixas
2. Herbie Flam
3. Dick Savitt
4. Gilbert Shea
5. Barry MacKay
6. Ron Holmberg
7. Tom Brown
8. Whitney Reed
9. Tut Bartzen
10. William Quillian

1958

1. Ham Richardson
2. Alex Olmedo
3. Barry MacKay
4. Tut Bartzen
5. Herbie Flam
6. Dick Savitt
7. Sammy Giammalva
8. Vic Seixas
9. Butch Buchholz
10. Tom Brown

1959

1. Alex Olmedo
2. Tut Bartzen
3. Barry MacKay
4. Ron Holmberg
5. Dick Savitt
6. Butch Buchholz
7. Mike Franks
8. Noel Brown
9. Whitney Reed
10. Vic Seixas

1960

1. Barry MacKay
2. Tut Bartzen
3. Butch Buchholz
4. Chuck McKinley
5. Dennis Ralston
6. Jon Douglas
7. Ron Holmberg
8. Whitney Reed
9. Donald Dell
10. Chris Crawford

1961

1. Whitney Reed
2. Chuck McKinley
3. Tut Bartzen
4. Jon Douglas
5. Donald Dell
6. Frank Froehling
7. Ron Holmberg
8. Allen Fox
9. Jack Frost
10. Bill Bond

1962

1. Chuck McKinley
2. Frank Froehling
3. Ham Richardson
4. Allen Fox
5. Jon Douglas
6. Whitney Reed
7. Donald Dell
8. Gene Scott
9. Marty Riessen
10. Charlie Pasarell

1963

1. Chuck McKinley
2. Dennis Ralston
3. Frank Froehling
4. Gene Scott
5. Marty Riessen
6. Arthur Ashe
7. Ham Richardson
8. Allen Fox
9. Tom Edlefsen
10. Charlie Pasarell

1964

1. Dennis Ralston
2. Chuck McKinley
3. Arthur Ashe
4. Frank Froehling
5. Gene Scott
6. Ron Holmberg
7. Ham Richardson
8. Allen Fox
9. Clark Graebner
10. Marty Riessen

1965

1. Dennis Ralston
2. Arthur Ashe
3. Cliff Richey
4. Chuck McKinley
5. Charlie Pasarell
6. Ham Richardson
7. Mike Belkin
8. Marty Riessen
9. Ron Holmberg
10. Tom Edlefsen

1966

1. Dennis Ralston
2. Arthur Ashe
3. Clark Graebner
4. Charlie Pasarell
5. Cliff Richey
6. Ron Holmberg
7. Marty Riessen
8. Frank Froehling
9. Vic Seixas
10. Chuck McKinley

1967

1. Charlie Pasarell
2. Arthur Ashe
3. Cliff Richey
4. Clark Graebner
5. Marty Riessen
6. Ron Holmberg
7. Stan Smith
8. Allen Fox
9. Gene Scott
10. Bob Lutz

1968

1. Arthur Ashe
2. Clark Graebner
3. Stan Smith
4. Cliff Richey
5. Bob Lutz
6. Ron Holmberg
7. Charlie Pasarell
8. Jim Osborne
9. Jim McManus
10. Gene Scott

1969

1. Stan Smith
2. Arthur Ashe
3. Cliff Richey
4. Clark Graebner
5. Charlie Pasarell
6. Bob Lutz
7. Tom Edlefsen
8. Roy Barth
9. Jim Osborne
10. Jim McManus

1970

1. Cliff Richey
2. Stan Smith
3. Arthur Ashe
4. Clark Graebner
5. Bob Lutz
6. Tom Gorman
7. Jim Osborne
8. Jim McManus
9. Barry MacKay
10. Charlie Pasarell

1971

1. Stan Smith
2. Cliff Richey
3. Clark Graebner
4. Tom Gorman
5. Jimmy Connors
6. Erik van Dillen
7. Frank Froehling
8. Roscoe Tanner
9. Alex Olmedo
10. Harold Solomon

1972

1. Stan Smith
2. Tom Gorman
3. Jimmy Connors
4. Dick Stockton
5. Roscoe Tanner
6. Harold Solomon
7. Erik van Dillen
8. Clark Graebner
9. Pancho Gonzalez
10. Brian Gottfried

1973

1. Jimmy Connors and Stan Smith
3. Arthur Ashe
4. Tom Gorman
5. Cliff Richey
6. Charlie Pasarell
7. Marty Riessen
8. Erik Van Dillen
9. Brian Gottfried
10. Bob Lutz

1974

1. Jimmy Connors
2. Stan Smith
3. Marty Riessen
4. Roscoe Tanner
5. Arthur Ashe
6. Tom Gorman
7. Dick Stockton
8. Harold Solomon
9. Charlie Pasarell
10. Jeff Borowiak

1975

1. Arthur Ashe
2. Jimmy Connors
3. Roscoe Tanner
4. Vitas Gerulaitis
5. Eddie Dibbs
6. Brian Gottfried
7. Harold Solomon
8. Bob Lutz
9. Cliff Richey
10. Dick Stockton

1976

1. Jimmy Connors
2. Eddie Dibbs
3. Arthur Ashe
4. Harold Solomon
5. Brian Gottfried
6. Roscoe Tanner
7. Dick Stockton
8. Stan Smith
9. Vitas Gerulaitis
10. Bob Lutz

1977

1. Jimmy Connors
2. Brian Gottfried
3. Vitas Gerulaitis
4. Eddie Dibbs
5. Dick Stockton
6. Harold Solomon
7. Stan Smith
8. Roscoe Tanner
9. Bob Lutz
10. John McEnroe

1978

1. Jimmy Connors
2. Vitas Gerulaitis
3. Brain Gottfried
4. Eddie Dibbs
5. John McEnroe
6. Sandy Mayer
7. Harold Solomon
8. Roscoe Tanner
9. Arthur Ashe
10. Dick Stockton

1979

1. John McEnroe
2. Jimmy Connors
3. Roscoe Tanner
4. Vitas Gerulaitis
5. Arthur Ashe
6. Eddie Dibbs
7. Harold Solomon
8. Peter Fleming
9. Gene Mayer
10. Brian Gottfried

USTA Women's Rankings

1913

1. Mary Browne
2. Ethel Bruce
3. Florence Sutton
4. Helen McLean
5. Louise Williams
6. Marie Wagner
7. Dorothy Briggs
8. Edith Rotch
9. Anita Myers
10. Gwendolyn Rees

1914

1. Mary Browne
2. Florence Sutton
3. Marie Wagner
4. Louise Raymond
5. Edith Rotch
6. Eleonora Sears
7. Louise Williams
8. Sarita Wood
9. Mrs. H. Niemeyer
10. Sara Livingstone

1915

1. Molla Bjurstedt
2. Hazel Wightman
3. Helen McLean
4. Florence Sutton
5. Maud Barger-Wallach
6. Marie Wagner
7. Anita Myers
8. Sara Livingstone
9. Clare Cassel
10. Eleonora Sears

1916

1. Molla Bjurstedt
2. Louise Raymond
3. Evelyn Sears
4. Anita Myers
5. Sara Livingstone
6. Marie Wagner
7. Adelaide Green
8. Martha Guthrie
9. Eleonora Sears
10. Maud Barger-Wallach

1917 No rankings

1918

1. Molla Bjurstedt
2. Hazel Wightman
3. Adelaide Green
4. Eleanor Goss
5. Marie Wagner
6. Carrie Neely
7. Corinne Gould
8. Helene Pollak
9. Edith Handy
10. Clare Cassel

1919

1. Hazel Wightman
2. Eleanor Goss
3. Molla Bjurstedt Mallory
4. Marion Zinderstein
5. Helen Baker
6. Louise Raymond
7. Helen Gilleaudeau
8. Marie Wagner
9. Corinne Gould
10. Helene Pollak

1920

1. Molla Mallory
2. Marion Zinderstein
3. Eleanor Tennant
4. Helen Baker
5. Eleanor Goss
6. Louise Raymond
7. Marie Wagner
8. Helene Pollak Falk
9. Edith Sigourney
10. Margaret Grove

1921

1. Molla Mallory
2. Mary Browne
3. Marion Zinderstein Jessup
4. May Sutton Bundy
5. Eleanor Goss
6. Helen Gilleaudeau
7. Nancy Cole
8. Leslie Bancroft
9. Louise Raymond
10. Margaret Grove

1922

1. Molla Mallory
2. Leslie Bancroft
3. Helen Wills
4. Marion Jessup
5. May Bundy
6. Martha Bayard
7. Helen Gilleaudeau
8. Mollie Thayer
9. Marie Wagner
10. Florence Ballin

1923

1. Helen Wills
2. Molla Mallory
3. Eleanor Goss
4. Lillian Scharman
5. Helen Lockhorn
6. Mayme MacDonald
7. Edith Sigourney
8. Leslie Bancroft
9. Martha Bayard
10. Helen Hooker

1924

1. Helen Wills
2. Mary Browne
3. Molla Mallory
4. Eleanor Goss
5. Marion Jessup
6. Martha Bayard
7. Mayme MacDonald
8. Nancy Cole
9. Mollie Thayer
10. Leslie Bancroft

1925

1. Helen Wills
2. Elizabeth Ryan
3. Molla Mallory
4. Marion Jessup
5. Eleanor Goss
6. Mary Browne
7. Martha Bayard
8. May Bundy
9. Charlotte Hosmer
10. Edith Sigourney

1926

1. Molla Mallory
2. Elizabeth Ryan
3. Eleanor Goss
4. Martha Bayard
5. Charlotte Chapin
6. Betty Corbiere
7. Margaret Blake
8. Penelope Anderson
9. Edna Roeser
10. Mrs. Ellis Endicott

1927

1. Helen Wills
2. Molla Mallory
3. Charlotte Chapin
4. Helen Jacobs
5. Eleanor Goss
6. Betty Corbiere
7. Penelope Anderson
8. Margaret Blake
9. Edna Roeser
10. Alice Francis

1928

1. Helen Wills
2. Helen Jacobs
3. Edith Cross
4. Molla Mallory
5. May Bundy
6. Marjorie Morrill
7. Marjorie Gladman
8. Anna Harper
9. Charlotte Chapin
10. Betty Corbiere

1929

1. Helen Wills Moody
2. Helen Jacobs
3. Edith Cross
4. Sarah Palfrey
5. Anna Harper
6. Mary Greef
7. Eleanor Goss
8. Ethel Burkhardt
9. Marjorie Gladman
10. Josephine Cruickshank

1930

1. Anna Harper
2. Marjorie Morrill
3. Dorothy Weisel
4. Virginia Hilleary
5. Josephine Cruickshank
6. Ethel Burkhardt
7. Marjorie Van Ryn
8. Sarah Palfrey
9. Mary Greef
10. Edith Cross

1931

1. Helen Moody
2. Helen Jacobs
3. Anna Harper
4. Marion Jessup
5. Mary Greef
6. Marjorie Morrill
7. Sarah Palfrey
8. Marjorie Van Ryn
9. Virginia Hilleary
10. Dorothy Burke

1932

1. Helen Jacobs
2. Anna Harper
3. Carolin Babcock
4. Marjorie Painter
5. Josephine Cruickshank
6. Virginia Hilleary
7. Alice Marble
8. Marjorie Van Ryn
9. Virginia Rice
10. Marjorie Sachs

1933

1. Helen Jacobs
2. Helen Moody
3. Alice Marble
4. Sarah Palfrey
5. Carolin Babcock
6. Josephine Cruickshank
7. Maud Levi
8. Marjorie Van Ryn
9. Virginia Rice
10. Agnes Lamme

1934

1. Helen Jacobs
2. Sarah Palfrey Fabyan
3. Carolin Babcock
4. Dorothy Andrus
5. Maude Levi
6. Jane Sharp
7. Marjorie Painter
8. Mary Greef Harris
9. Marjorie Sachs
10. Catherine Wolf

1935

1. Helen Jacobs
2. Ethel Burkhardt Arnold
3. Sarah Palfrey Fabyan
4. Carolin Babcock
5. Marjorie Van Ryn
6. Gracyn Wheeler
7. Mary Harris
8. Agnes Lamme
9. Dorothy Andrus
10. Catherine Wolf

1936

1. Alice Marble
2. Helen Jacobs
3. Sarah Palfrey Fabyan
4. Gracyn Wheeler
5. Carolin Babcock
6. Helen Pedersen
7. Marjorie Van Ryn
8. Dorothy Bundy
9. Katharine Winthrop
10. Mary Harris

1937

1. Alice Marble
2. Helen Jacobs
3. Dorothy Bundy
4. Marjorie Van Ryn
5. Gracyn Wheeler
6. Sarah Palfrey Fabyan
7. Dorothy Andrus
8. Helen Pedersen
9. Carolin Babcock Stark
10. Katharine Winthrop

1938

1. Alice Marble
2. Sarah Palfrey Fabyan
3. Dorothy Bundy
4. Barbara Winslow
5. Gracyn Wheeler
6. Dorothy Workman
7. Margaret Osborne
8. Helen Pedersen
9. Virginia Wolfenden
10. Katharine Winthrop

1939

1. Alice Marble
2. Helen Jacobs
3. Sarah Palfrey Fabyan
4. Helen Bernhard
5. Virginia Wolfenden
6. Dorothy Bundy
7. Dorothy Workman
8. Pauline Betz
9. Katharine Winthrop
10. Mary Arnold

1940

1. Alice Marble
2. Helen Jacobs
3. Pauline Betz
4. Dorothy Bundy
5. Gracyn Wheeler Kelleher
6. Sarah Palfrey Cooke
7. Virginia Wolfenden
8. Helen Bernhard
9. Mary Arnold
10. Hope Knowles

1941

1. Sarah Palfrey Cooke
2. Pauline Betz
3. Dorothy Bundy
4. Margaret Osborne
5. Helen Jacobs
6. Helen Bernhard
7. Hope Knowles
8. Mary Arnold
9. Virginia Wolfenden Kovacs
10. Louise Brough

1942

1. Pauline Betz
2. Louise Brough
3. Margaret Osborne
4. Helen Bernhard
5. Mary Arnold
6. Doris Hart
7. Pat Todd
8. Helen Pedersen Rihbany
9. Madge Vosters
10. Katharyn Winthrop

1943

1. Pauline Betz
2. Louise Brough
3. Doris Hart
4. Margaret Osborne
5. Dorothy Bundy
6. Mary Arnold
7. Dorothy Head
8. Helen Bernhard
9. Helen Rihbany
10. Katharine Winthrop

1944

1. Pauline Betz
2. Margaret Osborne
3. Louise Brough
4. Dorothy Bundy
5. Mary Arnold
6. Doris Hart
7. Virginia Kovacs
8. Shirley Fry
9. Pat Todd
10. Dorothy Head

1945

1. Sarah Palfrey Cooke
2. Pauline Betz
3. Margaret Osborne
4. Louise Brough
5. Pat Todd
6. Doris Hart
7. Shirley Fry
8. Mary Arnold Prentiss
9. Dorothy Bundy
10. Helen Rihbany

1946

1. Pauline Betz
2. Margaret Osborne
3. Louise Brough
4. Doris Hart
5. Pat Todd
6. Dorothy Bundy Cheney
7. Shirley Fry
8. Mary Prentiss
9. Virginia Kovacs
10. Dorothy Head

1947

1. Louise Brough
2. Margaret Osborne duPont
3. Doris Hart
4. Pat Todd
5. Shirley Fry
6. Barbara Krase
7. Dorothy Head
8. Mary Prentiss
9. Gussy Moran
10. Helen Rihbany

1948

1. Margaret duPont
2. Louise Brough
3. Doris Hart
4. Gussy Moran
5. Beverly Baker
6. Pat Todd
7. Shirley Fry
8. Helen Perez
9. Virginia Kovacs
10. Helen Rihbany

1949

1. Margaret duPont
2. Louise Brough
3. Doris Hart
4. Pat Todd
5. Helen Perez
6. Shirley Fry
7. Gussy Moran
8. Beverly Baker Beckett
9. Dorothy Head
10. Barbara Scofield

1950

1. Margaret duPont
2. Doris Hart
3. Louise Brough
4. Beverly Baker
5. Pat Todd
6. Nancy Chaffee
7. Barbara Scofield
8. Shirley Fry
9. Helen Perez
10. Maureen Connolly

1951

1. Maureen Connolly
2. Doris Hart
3. Shirley Fry
4. Nancy Chaffee Kiner
5. Pat Todd
6. Beverly Baker Fleitz
7. Dorothy Head
8. Betty Pratt
9. Magda Rurac
10. Baba Lewis

1952

1. Maureen Connolly
2. Doris Hart
3. Shirley Fry
4. Louise Brough
5. Nancy Kiner
6. Anita Kanter
7. Pat Todd
8. Baba Lewis
9. Althea Gibson
10. Julie Sampson

1953

1. Maureen Connolly
2. Doris Hart
3. Shirley Fry
4. Louise Brough
5. Margaret duPont
6. Helen Perez
7. Althea Gibson
8. Baba Lewis
9. Anita Kanter
10. Julie Sampson

1954

1. Doris Hart
2. Louise Brough
3. Beverly Fleitz
4. Shirley Fry
5. Betty Pratt
6. Barbara Breit
7. Darlene Hard
8. Lois Felix
9. Helen Perez
10. Barbara Davidson

1955

1. Doris Hart
2. Shirley Fry
3. Louise Brough
4. Dorothy Head Knode
5. Beverly Fleitz
6. Barbara Davidson
7. Barbara Breit
8. Althea Gibson
9. Darlene Hard
10. Dorothy Cheney

1956

1. Shirley Fry
2. Althea Gibson
3. Louise Brough
4. Margaret duPont
5. Betty Pratt
6. Dorothy Knode
7. Darlene Hard
8. Karol Fageros
9. Janet Hopps
10. Miriam Arnold

1957

1. Althea Gibson
2. Louise Brough
3. Dorothy Knode
4. Darlene Hard
5. Karol Fageros
6. Miriam Arnold
7. Jeanne Arth
8. Sally Moore
9. Janet Hopps
10. Mary Ann Mitchell

1958

1. Althea Gibson
2. Beverly Fleitz
3. Darlene Hard
4. Dorothy Knode
5. Margaret duPont
6. Jeanne Arth
7. Janet Hopps
8. Sally Moore
9. Gwyneth Thomas
10. Mary Ann Mitchell

1959

1. Beverly Fleitz
2. Darlene Hard
3. Dorothy Knode
4. Sally Moore
5. Janet Hopps
6. Karen Hantze
7. Barbara Weigandt
8. Karol Fageros
9. Miriam Arnold
10. Lois Felix

1960

1. Darlene Hard
2. Karen Hantze
3. Nancy Richey
4. Billie Jean Moffitt
5. Donna Floyd
6. Janet Hopps
7. Gwyneth Thomas
8. Vicki Palmer
9. Kathy Chabot
10. Carol Hanks

1961

1. Darlene Hard
2. Karen Hantze
3. Billie Jean Moffitt
4. Kathy Chavot
5. Justina Bricka
6. Gwyneth Thomas
7. Marilyn Montgomery
8. Judy Alvarez
9. Carole Caldwell
10. Donna Floyd

1962

1. Darlene Hard
2. Karen Hantze Susman
3. Billie Jean Moffitt
4. Carole Caldwell
5. Donna Floyd
6. Nancy Richey
7. Vicki Palmer
8. Gwyneth Thomas
9. Justina Bricka
10. Judy Alvarez

1963

1. Darlene Hard
2. Billie Jean Moffitt
3. Nancy Richey
4. Carole Caldwell
5. Gwyneth Thomas
6. Judy Alvarez
7. Carol Hanks
8. Tory Fretz
9. Donna Floyd Fales
10. Julie Heldman

1964

1. Nancy Richey
2. Billie Jean Moffitt
3. Carole Caldwell Graebner
4. Karen Susman
5. Carol Hanks Aucamp
6. Jane Albert
7. Julie Heldman
8. Justina Bricka
9. Tory Fretz
10. Mary Ann Eisel

1965

1. Nancy Richey and Billie Jean Moffitt King
3. Carole Graebner
4. Jane Albert
5. Mary Ann Eisel
6. Carol Aucamp
7. Kathy Harter
8. Julie Heldman
9. Tory Fretz
10. Donna Fales

1966

1. Billie Jean King
2. Nancy Richey
3. Rosie Casals
4. Tory Fretz
5. Peaches Bartkowicz
6. Mary Ann Eisel
7. Donna Fales
8. Carol Aucamp
9. Stephanie DeFina
10. Fern Kellmeyer

1967

1. Billie Jean King
2. Nancy Richey
3. Mary Ann Eisel
4. Peaches Bartkowicz
5. Rosie Casals
6. Carole Graebner
7. Stephanie DeFina
8. Kathy Harter
9. Lynne Abbes
10. Vicky Rogers

1968

1. Nancy Richey
2. Julie Heldman
3. Vicky Rogers
4. Mary Ann Eisel
5. Kathy Harter
6. Kristy Pigeon
7. Peaches Bartkowicz
8. Linda Tuero
9. Stephanie DeFina
10. Patti Hogan

1969

1. Nancy Richey
2. Julie Heldman
3. Mary Ann Eisel Curtis
4. Peaches Bartkowicz
5. Patti Hogan
6. Kristy Pigeon
7. Betty Ann Grubb
8. Denise Carter
9. Val Ziegenfuss
10. Linda Tuero

1970

1. Billie Jean King
2. Rosie Casals
3. Nancy Richey Gunter
4. Mary Ann Curtis
5. Patti Hogan
6. Peaches Bartkowicz
7. Val Ziegenfuss
8. Kristy Pigeon
9. Stephanie DeFina Johnson
10. Denise Carter Triolo

1971

1. Billie Jean King
2. Rosie Casals
3. Chris Evert
4. Nancy Gunter
5. Mary Ann Eisel
6. Julie Heldman
7. Peaches Bartkowicz
8. Linda Tuero
9. Patti Hogan
10. Denise Triolo

1972

1. Billie Jean King
2. Nancy Gunter
3. Chris Evert
4. Rosie Casals
5. Wendy Overton
6. Patti Hogan
7. Linda Tuero
8. Julie Heldman
9. Pam Teeguarden
10. Janet Newberry

1973

1. Billie Jean King
2. Chris Evert
3. Rosie Casals
4. Nancy Gunter
5. Julie Heldman
6. Pam Teeguarden
7. Kristien Kemmer
8. Janet Newberry
9. Val Ziegenfuss
10. Wendy Overton

1974

1. Chris Evert
2. Billie Jean King
3. Rosie Casals
4. Nancy Gunter
5. Julie Heldman
6. Kathy Kuykendall
7. Pam Teeguarden
8. Val Ziegenfuss
9. Jeanne Evert
10. Marcie Louie

1975

1. Chris Evert
2. Nancy Gunter
3. Julie Heldman
4. Wendy Overton
5. Marcie Louie
6. Mona Schallau
7. Kathy Kuykendall
8. Janet Newberry
9. Terry Holladay
10. Rosie Casals

1976

1. Chris Evert
2. Rosie Casals
3. Nancy Richey
4. Terry Holladay
5. Marita Redondo
6. Mona Schallau Guerrant
7. Kathy May
8. JoAnne Russell
9. Janet Newberry
10. Kathy Kuykendall

1977

1. Chris Evert
2. Billie Jean King
3. Rosie Casals
4. Tracy Austin
5. JoAnne Russell
6. Kathy May
7. Terry Holladay
8. Kristien Kemmer Shaw
9. Janet Newberry
10. Laura DuPont

1978

1. Chris Evert
2. Billie Jean King
3. Tracy Austin
4. Rosie Casals
5. Pam Shriver
6. Marita Redondo
7. Kathy May Teacher
8. Anne Smith
9. JoAnne Russell
10. Jeanne DuVall

1979

1. Martina Navratilova
2. Chris Evert Lloyd
3. Tracy Austin
4. Billie Jean King
5. Kathy Jordan
6. Ann Kiyomura
7. Caroline Stoll
8. Kathy May Teacher
9. Kate Latham
10. Terry Holladay

WORLD RANKINGS

World rankings always provide good controversy in tennis, all the more because there is no official ranking of the tennis players in the world. The national associations of each of the countries customarily issue rankings that include only their own players. There are a number of unofficial world ranking lists produced by magazines and newspaper people, and in recent years the Association of Tennis Professionals (ATP) and Women's Tennis Association (WTA) have each issued computer ranking lists, which add to the debate.

What is fact is that since 1914 there have been men's ratings and since 1925 there have been women's ratings, all unofficial but rendered by respected tennis journalists. From 1914 through 1938, with time off for World War I, A. Wallis Myers of the London *Daily Telegraph* was the ratings master. In the years since, through 1951, except for World War II (1940–45), F. Gordon Lowe, Pierre Gillow, and John Olliff were the sources for the world rankings. Starting in 1952, Lance Tingay of the London *Daily Telegraph* has made the rankings, and these are included here through 1967. The rankings for the open era, from 1968 on, are those of Bud Collins.

World Rankings

Men

1914

1. Maurice McLoughlin, U.S.
2. Norman Brookes, Australia
3. Tony Wilding, New Zealand
4. Otto Froitzheim, Germany
5. R. Norris Williams, U.S.
6. J. Cecil Parke, Ireland
7. Arthur Lowe, England
8. Frank Lowe, England
9. Heinrich Kleinschroth, Germany
10. Max Decugis, France

1919

1. Gerald Patterson, Australia
2. Bill Johnston, U.S.
3. André Gobert, France
4. Bill Tilden, U.S.
5. Norman Brookes, Australia
6. Algernon Kingscote, England
7. R. Norris Williams, U.S.
8. Percival Davson, England
9. Willis Davis, U.S.
10. William Laurentz, France

1920

1. Bill Tilden, U.S.
2. Bill Johnston, U.S.
3. Algernon Kingscote, England
4. J. Cecil Parke, England
5. André Gobert, France
6. Norman Brookes, Australia
7. R. Norris Williams, U.S.
8. William Laurentz, France
9. Zenzo Shimizu, Japan
10. Gerald Patterson, Australia

1921

1. Bill Tilden, U.S.
2. Bill Johnston, U.S.
3. Vincent Richards, U.S.
4. Zenzo Shimizu, Japan
5. Gerald Patterson, Australia
6. Jim Anderson, Australia
7. Brian Norton, S. Africa
8. Manuel Alonso, Spain
9. R. Norris Williams, U.S.
10. André Gobert, France

1922

1. Bill Tilden, U.S.
2. Bill Johnston, U.S.
3. Gerald Patterson, Australia
4. Vincent Richards, U.S.
5. Jim Anderson, Australia
6. Henri Cochet, France
7. Pat O'Hara Wood, Australia
8. R. Norris Williams, U.S.
9. Algernon Kingscote, England
10. Andres Gobert, France

1923

1. Bill Tilden, U.S.
2. Bill Johnston, U.S.
3. Jim Anderson, Australia
4. R. Norris Williams, U.S.
5. Francis Hunter, U.S.
6. Vincent Richards, U.S.
7. Brian Norton, S. Africa
8. Manuel Alonso, Spain
9. Philippe Washer, Belgium
10. Henri Cochet, France

1924

1. Bill Tilden, U.S.
2. Vincent Richards, U.S.
3. Jim Anderson, Australia
4. Bill Johnston, U.S.
5. René Lacoste, France
6. Jean Borotra, France,
7. Howard Kinsey, U.S.
8. Gerald Patterson, Australia
9. Henri Cochet, France
10. Manuel Alonso, Spain

Men   Women

1925

1. Bill Tilden, U.S.
2. Bill Johnston, U.S.
3. Vincent Richards, U.S.
4. René Lacoste, France
5. R. Norris Williams, U.S.
6. Jean Borotra, France
7. Gerald Patterson, Australia
8. Manuel Alonso, Spain
9. Brian Norton, S. Africa
10. Takeichi Harada, Japan

1925

1. Suzanne Lenglen, France
2. Helen Wills, U.S.
3. Kitty McKane, England
4. Elizabeth Ryan, U.S.
5. Molla Mallory, U.S.
6. Eleanor Goss, U.S.
7. Dorothea Chambers, England
8. Joan Fry, England
9. Mrs. B. Billout, France
10. Marion Jessup, U.S.

1926

1. René Lacoste, France
2. Jean Borotra, France
3. Henri Cochet, France
4. Bill Johnston, U.S.
5. Bill Tilden, U.S.
6. Vincent Richards, U.S.
7. Takeichi Harada, Japan
8. Manuel Alonso, Spain
9. Howard Kinsey, U.S.
10. Jacques Brugnon, France

1926

1. Suzanne Lenglen, France
2. Kitty McKane Godfree, England
3. Lili d'Alvarez, Spain
4. Molla Mallory, U.S.
5. Elizabeth Ryan, U.S.
6. Mary Browne, U.S.
7. Joan Fry, England
8. Phoebe Watson, England
9. Marion Jessup, U.S.
10. Diddi Vlasto, France

1927

1. René Lacoste, France
2. Bill Tilden, U.S.
3. Henri Cochet, France
4. Jean Borotra, France
5. Manuel Alonso, Spain
6. Francis Hunter, U.S.
7. George Lott, U.S.
8. John Hennessey, U.S.
9. Jacques Brugnon, France
10. Karel Kozeluh, Czechoslovakia

1927

1. Helen Wills, U.S.
2. Lili d'Alvarez, Spain
3. Elizabeth Ryan, U.S.
4. Molla Mallory, U.S.
5. Kitty Godfree, England
6. Betty Nuthall, England
7. Easther Heine, S. Africa
8. Joan Fry, England
9. Kea Bouman, Holland
10. Charlotte Chapin, U.S.

1928

1. Henri Cochet, France
2. René Lacoste, France
3. Bill Tilden, U.S.
4. Francis Hunter, U.S.
5. Jean Borotra, France
6. George Lott, U.S.
7. Bunny Austin, England
8. John Hennessey, U.S.
9. Umberto de Morpurgo, Italy
10. John Hawkes, Australia

1928

1. Helen Wills, U.S.
2. Lili d'Alvarez, Spain
3. Daphne Akhurst, Australia
4. Eileen Bennett, England
5. Phoebe Watson, England
6. Elizabeth Ryan, U.S.
7. Cilly Aussem, Germany
8. Kea Bouman, Holland
9. Helen Jacobs, U.S.
10. Esna Boyd, Australia

Men   **Women**

1929

1. Henri Cochet, France
2. René Lacoste, France
3. Jean Borotra, France
4. Bill Tilden, U.S.
5. Francis Hunter, U.S.
6. George Lott, U.S.
7. John Doeg, U.S.
8. John Van Ryn, U.S.
9. Bunny Austin, England
10. Umberto de Morpurgo, Italy

1930

1. Henri Cochet, France
2. Bill Tilden, U.S.
3. Jean Borotra, France
4. John Doeg, U.S.
5. Francis Shields, U.S.
6. Wilmer Allison, U.S.
7. George Lott, U.S.
8. Umberto de Morpurgo, Italy
9. Christian Boussus, France
10. Bunny Austin, England

1931

1. Henri Cochet, France
2. Bunny Austin, England
3. Ellsworth Vines, U.S.
4. Fred Perry, England
5. Francis Shields, U.S.
6. Sidney Wood, U.S.
7. Jean Borotra, France
8. George Lott, U.S.
9. Jiro Satoh, Japan
10. John Van Ryn, U.S.

1932

1. Ellsworth Vines, U.S.
2. Henri Cochet, France
3. Jean Borotra, France
4. Wilmer Allison, U.S.
5. Cliff Sutter, U.S.
6. Daniel Prenn, Germany
7. Fred Perry, England
8. Gottfried von Cramm, Germany
9. Bunny Austin, England
10. Jack Crawford, Australia

1929

1. Helen Wills, U.S.
2. Phoebe Watson, England
3. Helen Jacobs, U.S.
4. Betty Nuthall, England
5. Esther Heine, S. Africa
6. Simone Mathieu, France
7. Eileen Bennett, England
8. Paula von Reznicek, Germany
9. Peggy Michell, England
10. E. A. Goldsack, England

1930

1. Helen Wills, U.S.
2. Cilly Aussem, Germany
3. Phoebe Watson, England
4. Elizabeth Ryan, U.S.
5. Simone Mathieu, France
6. Helen Jacobs, U.S.
7. Phyllis Mudford, England
8. Lili d'Alvarez, Spain
9. Betty Nuthall, England
10. Hilda Krahwinkel, Germany

1931

1. Helen Moody, U.S.
2. Cilly Aussem, Germany
3. Eileen Whittingstall, England
4. Helen Jacobs, U.S.
5. Betty Nuthall, England
6. Hilda Krahwinkel, Germany
7. Simone Mathieu, France
8. Lili d'Alvarez, Spain
9. Phyllis Mudford, England
10. Elsie Pittman, England

1932

1. Helen Moody, U.S.
2. Helen Jacobs, U.S.
3. Simone Mathieu, France
4. Lolette Payot, Switzerland
5. Hilda Krahwinkel, Germany
6. Mary Heeley, England
7. Eileen Whittingstall, England
8. Marie-Louise Horn, Germany
9. Kay Stammers, England
10. Josane Sigart, Belgium

Men	Women

1933

Men:
1. Jack Crawford, Australia
2. Fred Perry, England
3. Jiro Satoh, Japan
4. Bunny Austin, England
5. Ellsworth Vines, U.S.
6. Henri Cochet, France
7. Francis Shields, U.S.
8. Sidney Wood, U.S.
9. Gottfried von Cramm, Germany
10. Lester Stoefen, U.S.

Women (**1933**):
1. Helen Moody, U.S.
2. Helen Jacobs, U.S.
3. Dorothy Round, England
4. Hilda Krahwinkel, Germany
5. Margaret Scriven, England
6. Simone Mathieu, France
7. Sarah Palfrey, U.S.
8. Betty Nuthall, England
9. Lolette Payot, Switzerland
10. Alice Marble, U.S.

1934

Men:
1. Fred Perry, England
2. Jack Crawford, Australia
3. Gottfried von Cramm, Germany
4. Bunny Austin, England
5. Wilmer Allison, U.S.
6. Sidney Wood, U.S.
7. Roderick Menzel, Czechoslovakia
8. Francis Shields, U.S.
9. Giorgio de Stefani, Italy
10. Christian Boussus, France

Women (**1934**):
1. Dorothy Round, England
2. Helen Jacobs, U.S.
3. Hilda Krahwinkel Sperling, Denmark
4. Sarah Palfrey, U.S.
5. Margaret Scriven, England
6. Simone Mathieu, France
7. Lolette Payot, Switzerland
8. Joan Hartigan, Australia
9. Cilly Aussem, Germany
10. Carolin Babcock, U.S.

1935

Men:
1. Fred Perry, England
2. Jack Crawford, Australia
3. Gottfried von Cramm, Germany
4. Wilmer Allison, U.S.
5. Bunny Austin, England
6. Don Budge, U.S.
7. Francis Shields, U.S.
8. Vivian McGrath, Australia
9. Christian Boussus, France
10. Sidney Wood, U.S.

Women (**1935**):
1. Helen Moody, U.S.
2. Helen Jacobs, U.S.
3. Kay Stammers, England
4. Hilda Sperling, Denmark
5. Sarah Palfrey Fabyan, U.S.
6. Dorothy Round, England
7. Mary Arnold, U.S.
8. Simone Mathieu, France
9. Joan Hartigan, Australia
10. Margaret Scriven, England

1936

Men:
1. Fred Perry, England
2. Gottfried von Cramm, Germany
3. Don Budge, U.S.
4. Adrian Quist, Australia
5. Bunny Austin, England
6. Jack Crawford, Australia
7. Wilmer Allison, U.S.
8. Bitsy Grant, U.S.
9. Henner Henkel, Germany
10. Vivian McGrath, Australia

Women (**1936**):
1. Helen Jacobs, U.S.
2. Hilda Sperling, Denmark
3. Dorothy Round, England
4. Alice Marble, U.S.
5. Simone Mathieu, France
6. Jadwiga Jedrzejowska, Poland
7. Kay Stammers, England
8. Anita Lizana, Chile
9. Sarah Fabyan, U.S.
10. Carolin Babcock, U.S.

Men	Women

1937

1. Don Budge, U.S.
2. Gottfried von Cramm, Germany
3. Henner Henkel, Germany
4. Bunny Austin, England
5. Bobby Riggs, U.S.
6. Bitsy Grant, U.S.
7. Jack Crawford, Australia
8. Roderic Menzel, Czechoslovakia
9. Frank Parker, U.S.
10. Charlie Hare, England

1937

1. Anita Lizana, Chile
2. Dorothy Round Little, England
3. Jadwiga Jedrzejowska, Poland
4. Hilda Sperling, Denmark
5. Simone Mathieu, France
6. Helen Jacobs, U.S.
7. Alice Marble, U.S.
8. Mary-Louise Horn, Germany
9. Mary Hardwick, England
10. Dorothy Bundy, U.S.

1938

1. Don Budge, U.S.
2. Bunny Austin, U.S.
3. John Bromwich, Australia
4. Bobby Riggs, U.S.
5. Sidney Wood, U.S.
6. Adrian Quist, Australia
7. Roderic Menzel, Czechoslovakia
8. Jiro Yamagishi, Japan
9. Gene Mako, U.S.
10. Franjo Puncec, Yugoslavia

1938

1. Helen Moody, U.S.
2. Helen Jacobs, U.S.
3. Alice Marble, U.S.
4. Hilda Sperling, Denmark
5. Simone Mathieu, France
6. Jadwiga Jedrzejowska, Poland
7. Sarah Fabyan, U.S.
8. Esther Miller, S. Africa
9. Kay Stammers, England
10. Nancye Wynne, Australia

1939

1. Bobby Riggs, U.S.
2. John Bromwich, Australia
3. Adrian Quist, Australia
4. Franjo Puncec, Yugoslavia
5. Frank Parker, U.S.
6. Henner Henkel, Germany
7. Don McNeill, U.S.
8. Elwood Cooke, U.S.
9. Welby Van Horn, U.S.
10. Joseph Hunt, U.S.

1939

1. Alice Marble, U.S.
2. Kay Stammers, England
3. Helen Jacobs, U.S.
4. Hilda Sperling, Denmark
5. Simone Mathieu, France
6. Sarah Fabyan, U.S.
7. Jadwiga Jerzejowska, Poland
8. Mary Hardwick, England
9. Virginia Wolfenden, U.S.
10. Valery Scott, England

1946

1. Jack Kramer, U.S.
2. Ted Schroeder, U.S.
3. Jaroslav Drobny, Czechoslovakia
4. Yvon Petra, France
5. Marcel Bernard, France
6. John Bromwich, Australia
7. Tom Brown, U.S.
8. Gardnar Mulloy, U.S.
9. Frank Parker, U.S.
10. Geoffrey Brown, Australia

1946

1. Pauline Betz, U.S.
2. Margaret Osborne, U.S.
3. Louise Brough, U.S.
4. Doris Hart, U.S.
5. Pat Todd, U.S.
6. Dorothy Bundy, U.S.
7. Nelly Landry, France
8. Kay Stammers Menzies, England
9. Shirley Fry, U.S.
10. Virginia Wolfenden Kovacs, U.S.

Men	Women

1947

Men	Women
1. Jack Kramer, U.S.	1. Margaret Osborne, U.S.
2. Ted Schroeder, U.S.	2. Louise Brough, U.S.
3. Frank Parker, U.S.	3. Doris Hart, U.S.
4. John Bromwich, Australia	4. Nancye Wynne Bolton, Australia
5. Jaroslav Drobny, Czechoslovakia	5. Pat Todd, U.S.
6. Dinny Pails, Australia	6. Sheila Summers, S. Africa
7. Tom Brown, U.S.	7. Jean Bostock, England
8. Budge Patty, U.S.	8. Barbara Krase, U.S.
9. Jozsef Asboth, Hungary	9. Betty Hilton, England
10. Gardnar Mulloy, U.S.	10. Magda Rurac, Romania

1948

Men	Women
1. Frank Parker, U.S.	1. Margaret Osborne duPont, U.S.
2. Ted Schroeder, U.S.	2. Louise Brough, U.S.
3. Pancho Gonzales, U.S.	3. Doris Hart, U.S.
4. John Bromwich, Australia	4. Nancye Bolton, Australia
5. Jaroslav Drobny, Czechoslovakia	5. Pat Todd, U.S.
6. Eric Sturgess, S. Africa	6. Jean Bostock, England
7. Bob Falkenburg, U.S.	7. Sheila Summers, S. Africa
8. Jozsef Asboth, Hungary	8. Shirley Fry, U.S.
9. Lennart Bergelin, Sweden	9. Magda Rurac, Romania
10. Adrian Quist, Australia	10. Nelly Landry, France

1949

Men	Women
1. Pancho Gonzales, U.S.	1. Margaret duPont, U.S.
2. Ted Schroeder, U.S.	2. Louise Brough, U.S.
3. Bill Talbert, U.S.	3. Doris Hart, U.S.
4. Frank Sedgman, Australia	4. Nancye Bolton, Australia
5. Frank Parker, U.S.	5. Pat Todd, U.S.
6. Eric Sturgess, S. Africa	6. Betty Hilton, England
7. Jaroslav Drobny, Czechoslovakia	7. Sheila Summers, S. Africa
8. Budge Patty, U.S.	8. Anna Bossi, Italy
9. Gardnar Mulloy, U.S.	9. Joan Curry, England
10. Billy Sidwell, Australia	10. Jean Walker-Smith, England

1950

Men	Women
1. Budge Patty, U.S.	1. Margaret duPont, U.S.
2. Frank Sedgman, Australia	2. Louise Brough, U.S.
3. Art Larsen, U.S.	3. Doris Hart, U.S.
4. Jaroslav Drobny, Czechoslovakia	4. Pat Todd, U.S.
5. Herbie Flam, U.S.	5. Barbara Scofield, U.S.
6. Ted Schroeder, U.S.	6. Nancy Chaffee, U.S.
7. Vic Seixas, U.S.	7. Beverly Baker, U.S.
8. Ken McGregor, Australia	8. Shirley Fry, U.S.
9. Bill Talbert, U.S.	9. Anna Bossi, Italy
10. Eric Sturgess, S. Africa	10. Maria Weiss, Argentina

Men   **Women**

1951   **1951**

1. Frank Sedgman, Australia   1. Doris Hart, U.S.
2. Dick Savitt, U.S.   2. Maureen Connolly, U.S.
3. Jaroslav Drobny, Czechoslovakia   3. Shirley Fry, U.S.
4. Vic Seixas, U.S.   4. Nancy Chaffee Kiner, U.S.
5. Tony Trabert, U.S.   5. Jean Walker Smith, England
6. Ted Schroeder, U.S.   6. Jean Quertier, England
7. Ken McGregor, Australia   7. Louise Brough, U.S.
8. Herbie Flam, U.S.   8. Beverly Baker Fleitz, U.S.
9. Art Larsen, U.S.   9. Pat Todd, U.S.
10. Mervyn Rose, Australia   10. Mrs. J. Maule, England

1952   **1952**

1. Frank Sedgman, Australia   1. Maureen Connolly, U.S.
2. Jaroslav Drobny, Czechoslovakia   2. Doris Hart, U.S.
3. Ken McGregor, Australia   3. Louise Brough, U.S.
4. Mervyn Rose, Australia   4. Shirley Fry, U.S.
5. Vic Seixas, U.S.   5. Pat Todd, U.S.
6. Herbie Flam, U.S.   6. Nancy Kiner, U.S.
7. Gardnar Mulloy, U.S.   7. Thelma Long, Australia
8. Eric Sturgess, S. Africa   8. Jean Walker Smith, England
9. Dick Savitt, U.S.   9. Jean Quertier Rinkel, England
10. Ken Rosewall, Australia, and Lew Hoad,   10. Dorothy Head Knode, U.S.
    Australia

1953   **1953**

1. Tony Trabert, U.S.   1. Maureen Connolly, U.S.
2. Ken Rosewall, Australia   2. Doris Hart, U.S.
3. Vic Seixas, U.S.   3. Louise Brough, U.S.
4. Jaroslav Drobny, Czechoslovakia   4. Shirley Fry, U.S.
5. Lew Hoad, Australia   5. Margaret duPont, U.S.
6. Mervyn Rose, Australia   6. Dorothy Knode, U.S.
7. Kurt Nielsen, Denmark   7. Suzie Kormoczi, Hungary
8. Budge Patty, U.S.   8. Angela Mortimer, England
9. Sven Davidson, Sweden   9. Helen Fletcher, England
10. Enrique Morea, Argentina   10. Jean Quertier-Rinkel, England

1954   **1954**

1. Jaroslav Drobny, Czechoslovakia   2. Maureen Connolly, U.S.
2. Tony Trabert, U.S.   2. Doris Hart, U.S.
3. Ken Rosewall, Australia   3. Beverly Fleitz, U.S.
4. Vic Seixas, U.S.   4. Louise Brough, U.S.
5. Rex Hartwig, Australia   5. Margaret duPont, U.S.
6. Mervyn Rose, Australia   6. Shirley Fry, U.S.
7. Lew Hoad, Australia   7. Betty Pratt, Jamaica
8. Budge Patty, U.S.   8. Helen Fletcher, England
9. Art Larsen, U.S.   9. Angela Mortimer, England
10. Enrique Morea, Argentina; Ham Richardson,   10. Ginette Bucaille, France, and
    U.S.; Sven Davidson, Sweden   Thelma Long, Australia

Men

Women

1955

1. Tony Trabert, U.S.
2. Ken Rosewall, Australia
3. Lew Hoad, Australia
4. Vic Seixas, U.S.
5. Rex Hartwig, Australia
6. Budge Patty, U.S.
7. Ham Richardson, U.S.
8. Kurt Nielson, Denmark
9. Jaroslav Drobny, Czechoslovakia
10. Sven Davidson, Sweden, and Mervyn Rose, Australia

1955

1. Louise Brough, U.S.
2. Doris Hart, U.S.
3. Beverly Fleitz, U.S.
4. Angela Mortimer, England
5. Dorothy Knode, U.S.
6. Barbara Breit, U.S.
7. Darlene Hard, U.S.
8. Beryl Penrose, Australia
9. Pat Ward, England
10. Suzie Kormoczi, Hungary, and Shirley Fry, U.S.

1956

1. Lew Hoad, Australia
2. Ken Rosewall, Australia
3. Ham Richardson, U.S.
4. Vic Seixas, U.S.
5. Sven Davidson, Sweden
6. Neale Fraser, Australia
7. Ashley Cooper, Australia
8. Dick Savitt, U.S.
9. Herbie Flam, U.S.
10. Budge Patty, U.S. and Nicola Pietrangeli, Italy

1956

1. Shirley Fry, U.S.
2. Althea Gibson, U.S.
3. Louise Brough, U.S.
4. Angela Mortimer, England
5. Suzie Kormoczi, Hungary
6. Angela Buxton, England
7. Shirley Bloomer, England
8. Pat Ward, England
9. Betty Pratt, Jamaica
10. Margaret duPont. U.S., and Darlene Hard, U.S.

1957

1. Ashley Cooper, Australia
2. Mal Anderson, Australia
3. Sven Davidson, Sweden
4. Herbie Flam, U.S.
5. Neale Fraser, Australia
6. Mervyn Rose, Australia
7. Vic Seixas, U.S.
8. Budge Patty, U.S.
9. Nicola Pietrangeli, Italy
10. Dick Savitt, U.S.

1957

1. Althea Gibson, U.S.
2. Darlene Hard, U.S.
3. Shirley Bloomer, England
4. Louise Brough, U.S.
5. Dorothy Knode, U.S.
6. Vera Puzejova, Czechoslovakia
7. Ann Haydon, England
8. Yola Ramirez, Mexico
9. Christine Truman, England
10. Margaret duPont, U.S.

1958

1. Ashley Cooper, Australia
2. Mal Anderson, Australia
3. Mervyn Rose, Australia
4. Neale Fraser, Australia
5. Luis Ayala, Chile
6. Ham Richardson, U.S.
7. Ulf Schmidt, Sweden
9. Barry MacKay, U.S.
10. Sven Davidson, Sweden

1958

1. Althea Gibson, U.S.
2. Suzie Kormoczi, Hungary
3. Beverly Fleitz, U.S.
4. Darlene Hard, U.S.
5. Shirley Bloomer, England
6. Christine Truman, England
8. Ann Haydon, England
9. Maria Bueno, Brazil
10. Dorothy Knode, U.S.

Men

1959

1. Neale Fraser, Australia
2. Alex Olmedo, U.S.
3. Nicola Pietrangeli, Italy
4. Barry MacKay, U.S.
5. Rod Laver, Australia
6. Luis Ayala, Chile
7. Roy Emerson, Australia
8. Tut Bartzen, U.S.
9. Ramanathan Krishnan, India
10. Ian Vermaak, S. Africa

1960

1. Neale Fraser, Australia
2. Rod Laver, Australia
3. Nicola Pietrangeli, Italy
4. Barry MacKay, U.S.
5. Butch Buchholz, U.S.
6. Roy Emerson, Australia
7. Luis Ayala, Chile
8. Ramanathan Krishnan, India
9. Jan Erik Lundquist, Sweden
10. Dennis Ralston, U.S.

1961

1. Rod Laver, Australia
2. Roy Emerson, Australia
3. Manuel Santana, Spain
4. Nicola Pietrangeli, Italy
5. Chuck McKinley, U.S.
6. Ramanathan Krishnan, India
7. Luis Ayala, Chile
8. Neale Fraser, Australia
9. Jan Erik Lundquist, Sweden
10. Ulf Schmidt, Sweden

1962

1. Rod Laver, Australia
2. Roy Emerson, Australia
3. Manuel Santana, Spain
4. Neale Fraser, Australia
5. Chuck McKinley, U.S.
6. Rafael Osuna, Mexico
7. Marty Mulligan, Australia
8. Bob Hewitt, Australia
9. Ramanathan Krishnan, India
10. Willie Bungert, Germany

Women

1959

1. Maria Bueno, Brazil
2. Christine Truman, England
3. Darlene Hard, U.S.
4. Beverly Fleitz, U.S.
5. Sandra Reynolds, S. Africa
6. Angela Mortimer, England
7. Ann Haydon, England
8. Suzie Kormoczi, Hungary
9. Sally Moore, U.S.
10. Yola Ramirez, Mexico

1960

1. Maria Bueno, Brazil
2. Darlene Hard, U.S.
3. Sandra Reynolds, S. Africa
4. Christine Truman, England
5. Suzie Kormoczi, Hungary
6. Ann Haydon, England
7. Angela Mortimer, England
8. Jan Lehane, Australia
9. Yola Ramirez, Mexico
10. Renée Schuurman, S. Africa

1961

1. Angela Mortimer, England
2. Darlene Hard, U.S.
3. Ann Haydon, England
4. Margaret Smith, Australia
5. Sandra Reynolds, S. Africa
6. Yola Ramirez, Mexico
7. Christine Truman, England
8. Suzie Kormoczi, Hungary
9. Renée Schuurman, S. Africa
10. Karen Hantze, U.S.

1962

1. Margaret Smith, Australia
2. Maria Bueno, Brazil
3. Darlene Hard, U.S.
4. Karen Hantze Susman, U.S.
5. Vera Sukova, Czechoslovakia
6. Sandra Reynolds Price, S. Africa
7. Lesley Turner, S. Africa
8. Ann Haydon, England
9. Renée Schuurman, S. Africa
10. Angela Mortimer, England

Men

Women

1963

1. Rafael Osuna, Mexico
2. Chuck McKinley, U.S.
3. Roy Emerson, Australia
4. Manuel Santana, Spain
5. Fred Stolle, Australia
6. Frank Froehling, U.S.
7. Dennis Ralston, U.S.
8. Boro Jovanovic, Yugoslavia
9. Mike Sangster, England
10. Marty Mulligan, Australia

1963

1. Margaret Smith, Australia
2. Lesley Turner, Australia
3. Maria Bueno, Brazil
4. Billie Jean Moffitt, U.S.
5. Ann Haydon Jones, England
6. Darlene Hard, U.S.
7. Jan Lehane, Australia
8. Renée Schuurman, S. Africa
9. Nancy Richey, U.S.
10. Vera Sukova, Czechoslovakia

1964

1. Roy Emerson, Australia
2. Fred Stolle, Australia
3. Jan Erik Lundquist, Sweden
4. Willie Bungert, Germany
5. Chuck McKinley, U.S.
6. Manuel Santana, Spain
7. Nicola Pietrangeli, Italy
8. Christian Kuhnke, Germany
9. Dennis Ralston, U.S.
10. Rafael Osuna, Mexico

1964

1. Margaret Smith, Australia
2. Maria Bueno, Brazil
3. Lesley Turner, Australia
4. Carole Caldwell Graebner, U.S.
5. Helga Schultze, Germany
6. Nancy Richey, U.S.
7. Billie Jean Moffitt, U.S.
8. Karen Susman, U.S.
9. Robyn Ebbern, Australia
10. Jan Lehane, Australia

1965

1. Roy Emerson, Australia
2. Manuel Santana, Spain
3. Fred Stolle, Australia
4. Cliff Drysdale, S. Africa
5. Marty Mulligan, Australia
6. Jan Erik Lundquist, Sweden
7. Tony Roche, Australia
8. John Newcombe, Australia
9. Dennis Ralston, U.S.
10. Arthur Ashe, U.S.

1965

1. Margaret Smith, Australia
2. Maria Bueno, Brazil
3. Lesley Turner, Australia
4. Billie Jean Moffitt King, U.S.
5. Ann Jones, England
6. Annette Van Zyl, S. Africa
7. Christine Truman, England
8. Nancy Richey, U.S.
9. Carole Graebner, U.S.
10. Françoise Durr, France

1966

1. Manuel Santana, Spain
2. Fred Stolle, Australia
3. Roy Emerson, Australia
4. Tony Roche, Australia
5. Dennis Ralston, U.S.
6. John Newcombe, Australia
7. Arthur Ashe, U.S.
8. Istvan Gulyas, Hungary
9. Cliff Drysdale, S. Africa
10. Ken Fletcher, Australia

1966

1. Billie Jean King, U.S.
2. Margaret Smith, Australia
3. Maria Bueno, Brazil
4. Ann Jones, England
5. Nancy Richey, U.S.
6. Annette Van Zyl, S. Africa
7. Norma Baylon, Argentina
8. Françoise Durr, France
9. Rosie Casals, U.S.
10. Kerry Melville, Australia

Men   **Women**

1967

1. John Newcombe, Australia
2. Roy Emerson, Australia
3. Manuel Santana, Spain
4. Marty Mulligan, Australia
5. Tony Roche, Australia
6. Bob Hewitt, S. Africa
7. Nikki Pilic, Yugoslavia
8. Clark Graebner, U.S.
9. Arthur Ashe, U.S.
10. Jan Leschley, Denmark; Willie Bungert, Germany; Cliff Drysdale, S. Africa

1967

1. Billie Jean King, U.S.
2. Ann Jones, England
3. Françoise Durr, France
4. Nancy Richey, U.S.
5. Lesley Turner, Australia
6. Rosie Casals, U.S.
7. Maria Bueno, Brazil
8. Virginia Wade, England
9. Kerry Melville, Australia
10. Judy Tegart, Australia

1968

1. Rod Laver, Australia
2. Arthur Ashe, U.S.
3. Ken Rosewall, Australia
4. Tony Roche, Australia
5. Tom Okker, Netherlands
6. John Newcombe, Australia
7. Clark Graebner, U.S.
8. Dennis Ralston, U.S.
9. Cliff Drysdale, S. Africa
10. Pancho Gonzales, U.S.

1968

1. Billie Jean King, U.S.
2. Virginia Wade, England
3. Nancy Richey, U.S.
4. Margaret Smith Court, Australia
5. Maria Bueno, Brazil
6. Ann Jones, England
7. Judy Tegart, Australia
8. Lesley Turner Bowrey, Australia
9. Annette Van Zyl duPlooy, S. Africa
10. Rosie Casals, U.S.

1969

1. Rod Laver, Australia
2. Tony Roche, Australia
3. John Newcombe, Australia
4. Ken Rosewall, Australia
5. Tom Okker, Netherlands
6. Pancho Gonzales, U.S.
7. Stan Smith, U.S.
8. Arthur Ashe, U.S.
9. Cliff Drysdale, S. Africa
10. Andres Gimeno, Spain

1969

1. Margaret Court, Australia
2. Ann Jones, England
3. Billie Jean King, U.S.
4. Nancy Richey, U.S.
5. Julie Heldman, U.S.
6. Rosie Casals, U.S.
7. Kerry Melville, Australia
8. Mary Ann Eisel, U.S.
9. Virginia Wade, England
10. Lesley Bowrey, Australia

1970

1. John Newcombe, Australia
2. Ken Rosewall, Australia
3. Tony Roche, Australia
4. Rod Laver, Australia
5. Ilie Nastase, Romania
6. Tom Okker, Netherlands
7. Cliff Richey, U.S.
8. Stan Smith, U.S.
9. Arthur Ashe, U.S.
10. Andres Gimeno, Spain

1970

1. Margaret Court, Australia
2. Billie Jean King, U.S.
3. Rosie Casals, U.S.
4. Nancy Richey, U.S.
5. Virginia Wade, England
6. Helga Niessen Masthoff, Germany
7. Ann Jones, England
8. Kerry Melville, Australia
9. Karen Krantzcke, Australia
10. Françoise, Durr, France

Men

Women

1971

1. John Newcombe, Australia
2. Stan Smith, U.S.
3. Ken Rosewall, Australia
4. Rod Laver, Australia
5. Jan Kodes, Czechoslovakia
6. Arthur Ashe, U.S.
7. Ilie Nastase, Romania
8. Tom Okker, Netherlands
9. Cliff Drysdale, S. Africa
10. Marty Riessen, U.S.

1971

1. Billie Jean King, U.S.
2. Evonne Goolagong, Australia
3. Margaret Court, Australia
4. Rosie Casals, U.S.
5. Kerry Melville, Australia
6. Françoise Durr, France
7. Virginia Wade, England
8. Helga Masthoff, Germany
9. Judy Tegart, Australia
10. Chris Evert, U.S.

1972

1. Stan Smith, U.S
2. Ken Rosewall, Australia
3. Ilie Nastase, Romania
4. Rod Laver, Australia
5. Arthur Ashe, U.S.
6. John Newcombe, Australia
7. Bob Lutz, U.S.
8. Tom Okker, Netherlands
9. Marty Riessen, U.S.
10. Andres Gimeno, Spain

1972

1. Billie Jean King, U.S.
2. Margaret Court, Australia
3. Nancy Richey Gunter, U.S.
4. Chris Evert, U.S.
5. Virginia Wade, England
6. Evonne Goolagong, Australia
7. Rosie Casals, U.S.
8. Kerry Melville, Australia
9. Françoise Durr, France
10. Olga Morozova, U.S.S.R.

1973

1. Ilie Nastase, Romania
2. John Newcombe, Australia
3. Stan Smith, U.S.
4. Rod Laver, Australia
5. Ken Rosewall, Australia
6. Jimmy Connors, U.S.
7. Tom Okker, Netherlands
8. Jan Kodes, Czechoslovakia
9. Arthur Ashe, U.S.
10. Manolo Orantes, Spain

1973

1. Margaret Court, Australia
2. Billie Jean King, U.S.
3. Evonne Goolagong, Australia
4. Chris Evert, U.S.
5. Rosie Casals, U.S.
6. Virginia Wade, England
7. Kerry Melville, Australia
8. Nancy Richey Gunter, U.S.
9. Julie Heldman, U.S.
10. Helga Masthoff, Germany

1974

1. Jimmy Connors, U.S.
2. Guillermo Vilas, Argentina
3. John Newcombe, Australia
4. Bjorn Borg, Sweden
5. Rod Laver, Australia
6. Ilie Nastase, Romania
7. Ken Rosewall, Australia
8. Stan Smith, U.S.
9. Manolo Orantes, Spain
10. Arthur Ashe, U.S.

1974

1. Billie Jean King, U.S.
2. Evonne Goolagong, Australia
3. Chris Evert, U.S.
4. Virginia Wade, England
5. Julie Heldman, U.S.
6. Rosie Casals, U.S.
7. Kerry Melville, Australia
8. Olga Morozova, U.S.S.R.
9. Lesley Hunt, Australia
10. Françoise Durr, France

Men

Women

1975

1. Arthur Ashe, U.S.
2. Bjorn Borg, Sweden
3. Manolo Orantes, Spain
4. Jimmy Connors, U.S.
5. Ilie Nastase, Romania
6. Guillermo Vilas, Argentina
7. Rod Laver, Australia
8. Raul Ramirez, Mexico
9. John Alexander, Australia
10. Ken Rosewall, Australia

1975

1. Chris Evert, U.S.
2. Billie Jean King, U.S.
3. Evonne Goolagong, Australia
4. Martina Navratilova, Czechoslovakia
5. Virginia Wade, England
6. Margaret Court, Australia
7. Olga Morozova, U.S.S.R.
8. Nancy Richey Gunter, U.S.
9. Françoise Durr, France
10. Rosie Casals, U.S.

1976

1. Jimmy Connors, U.S.
2. Bjorn Borg, Sweden
3. Ilie Nastase, Romania
4. Manolo Orantes, Spain
5. Adriano Panatta, Italy
6. Harold Solomon, U.S.
7. Raul Ramirez, Mexico
8. Roscoe Tanner, U.S.
9. Eddie Dibbs, U.S.
10. Wojtek Fibak, Poland

1. Chris Evert, U.S.
2. Evonne Goolagong, Australia
3. Virginia Wade, England
4. Martina Navratilova, Czechoslovakia
5. Sue Barker, England
6. Betty Stove, Netherlands
7. Dianne Fromholtz, Australia
8. Mima Jausovec, Yugoslavia
9. Rosie Casals, U.S.
10. Françoise Durr, France

1977

1. Bjorn Borg, Sweden
2. Guillermo Vilas, Argentina
3. Jimmy Connors, U.S.
4. Vitas Gerulaitis, U.S.
5. Brian Gottfried, U.S.
6. Manolo Orantes, Spain
7. Dick Stockton, U.S.
8. Eddie Dibbs, U.S.
9. Ilie Nastase, Romania
10. Raul Ramirez, Mexico

1977

1. Chris Evert, U.S.
2. Billie Jean King, U.S.
3. Virginia Wade, England
4. Martina Navratilova, Czechoslovakia
5. Sue Barker, England
6. Wendy Turnbull, Australia
7. Betty Stove, Netherlands
8. Rosie Casals, U.S.
9. Dianne Fromholtz, Australia
10. Kerry Melville Reid, U.S.

1978

1. Bjorn Borg, Sweden
2. Jimmy Connors, U.S.
3. John McEnroe, U.S.
4. Vitas Gerulaitis, U.S.
5. Eddie Dibbs, U.S.
6. Guillermo Vilas, Argentina
7. Brian Gottfried, U.S.
8. Raul Ramirez, Mexico
9. Harold Solomon, U.S.
10. Arthur Ashe, U.S.

1978

1. Martina Navratilova, Czechoslovakia
2. Chris Evert, U.S.
3. Evonne Goolagong, Australia
4. Virginia Wade, England
5. Billie Jean King, U.S.
6. Tracy Austin, U.S.
7. Pam Shriver, U.S.
8. Virginia Ruzici, Romania
9. Wendy Turnbull, Australia
10. Kerry Reid, U.S

Men

1979

1. Bjorn Borg, Sweden
2. John McEnroe, U.S.
3. Jimmy Connors, U.S.
4. Vitas Gerulaitis, U.S.
5. Roscoe Tanner, U.S.
6. Guillermo Vilas, Argentina
7. Harold Solomon, U.S.
8. Jose Higueras, Spain
9. Victor Pecci, Paraguay
10. Wojtek Fibak, Poland

MISCELLANEOUS ALL-TIME RECORDS

Longest Matches

Men's singles: 126 games—Roger Taylor, Britain, d. Wieslaw Gasiorek, Poland, 27–29, 31–29, 6–4. King's Cup match, Warsaw, 1966.

Men's doubles: 147 games—Dick Leach, Arcadia, Calif., and Dick Dell, Bethesda, Md., d. Len Schloss, Baltimore, and Tom Mozur, Sweetwater, Tenn., 3–6, 49–47, 22–20. Second round, Newport (R.I.) Casino Invitation, 1967.

Women's singles: 62 games—Kathy Blake, Pacific Palisades, Calif., d. Elena Subirats, Mexico, 12–10, 6–8, 14–12. First round, Piping Rock Invitation, Locust Valley, N.Y., 1966.

Women's doubles: 81 games—Nancy Richey, San Angelo, Tex., and Carole Graebner, New York, d. Carol Hanks and Justina Bricka, both St. Louis, 31–33, 6–1, 6–4. Semifinal, Eastern Grass Championship, South Orange, N.J., 1964.

Mixed doubles: 71 games—Margaret duPont, Wilmington, Dela., and Bill Talbert, New York, d. Gussy Moran, Santa Monica, Calif., and Bob Falkenburg, Los Angeles, 27–25, 5–7, 6–1. Semifinal, U.S. Championships, Forest Hills, 1948.

Longest Sets

Men's singles: 70 games—John Brown, Australia, d. Bill Brown, Omaha, Neb., *36–34*, 6–1. Third Round, Heart of America tourney, Kansas City, Mo., 1968.

Men's doubles: 96 games—Dell and Leach d. Schloss and Mozur, 3–6, *49–47*, 22–20 (see above).

Women

1979

1. Martina Navratilova, U.S.
2. Tracy Austin, U.S.
3. Chris Evert Lloyd, U.S.
4. Evonne Goolagong, Australia
5. Billie Jean King, U.S.
6. Wendy Turnbull, Australia
7. Dianne Fromholtz, Australia
8. Kerry Melville Reid, Australia
9. Virginia Wade, England
10. Regina Marsikova, Czechoslovakia

Women's singles: 36 games—Billie Jean King, U.S., d. Christine Truman, Britain, 6–4, *19–17*.Wightman Cup, Cleveland, 1963.

Women's doubles: 64 games—Richey and Graebner d. Hanks and Bricka, *31–33*, 6–1, 6–4 (see above).

Mixed doubles: 52 games—duPont and Talbert d. Moran and Falkenburg, *27–25*, 5–7, 6–1 (see above).

Longest Tie-breakers

Men's singles: 20–18—Third set, Bjorn Borg, Sweden, d. Premjit Lall, India, 6–3, 6–4, *9–8*.First round, Wimbledon, London, 1973. Tie-breaker played at 8 games-all.

Women's singles: 14–12—Second set, Martina Navratilova, Czechoslovakia, d. Helga Masthoff, West Germany, 4–6, *7–6*, 7–6. Quarterfinal, Italian Open, Rome, 1974. Second set, Margaret Court, Australia, d. Billie Jean King, Long Beach, Calif., 6–3, *7–6*; final, Philadelphia Indoor, 1970.

Mixed doubles: 18–16—Third set, Mareen Louie, San Francisco, and Andy Lucchesi d. Diane Desfor, Long Beach, Calif., and Horace Reid, New York, 6–2, 6–7, *7–6*. Second round, U.S. Open, Flushing Meadow, N.Y., 1978.

Championships

(This pertains to the major titles, the Big Four championships of Australia, France, Britain/

Wimbledon, and the United States, with years between first and last championship indicated.)

Most men's singles: 12—Roy Emerson, 1961–67 (6 Aus, 2 Fr, 2 Wim., 2 U.S.)

Most men's doubles: 17—John Newcombe, 1965–76 (5 Aus., 3 Fr., 6 Wim., 3 U.S.)

Most men's mixed: 8—Vic Seixas, 1953–56 (1 Fr., 4 Wim., 3 U.S.); Frank Sedgman, 1949–52 (2 Aus., 2 Fr., 2 Wim., 2 U.S.)

Most men's altogether: 28—Emerson, 1959–71.

Most women's singles: 26—Margaret Smith Court, 1960–73 (11 Aus., 5 Fr., 3 Wim., 7 U.S.)

Most women's doubles: 21—Court, 1960–75 (8 Aus., 4 Fr., 2 Wim., 7 U.S.); Margaret Osborne duPont, 1941–60 (3 Fr., 5 Wim., 13 U.S.)

Most women's mixed: 19—Court, 1961–75 (2 Aus., 4 Fr., 5 Wim., 8 U.S.)

Most women's altogether: 66—Court, 1960–75

Most men's doubles, team: 12—Newcombe and Tony Roche, 1965–75 (4 Aus., 2 Fr., 5 Wim., 1 U.S.)

Most women's doubles, team: 19—duPont and Louise Brough, 1942–57 (3 Fr., 4 Wim., 12 U.S.)

Most mixed doubles, team: 10—Court and Ken Fletcher, 1963–68 (2 Aus., 3 Fr., 4 Wim., 1 U.S.)

Prize Money

(Figures, as of close of 1978 season, are based on recognized tournament prize money and circuit bonuses, and do not include exhibitions, endorsements, or World Team Tennis salaries.)

Men's season high: $800,642—Guillermo Vilas, 1977

Women's season high: $453,154—Chris Evert, 1977

Men's career high: $2,080,127—Jimmy Connors, 1972–78.

Women's career high: $1,834,224—Evert, 1973–78.

Men's tournament high: $100,000—Connors, winner of 1977 Masters, New York; John McEnroe,

winner of 1978 Masters, New York. (A few other tournaments also offered $100,000 first prize but the Masters was the most significant.)

Women's tournament high: $75,000—Evert, winner of International Series Championship, 1977 and 1978, Rancho Mirage, Calif.

Tournament total high: $552,480—U.S. Open, Flushing Meadow, 1978.

The Millionaires in Career Prize Money

Men

1.	Jimmy Connors, 1972–78	$2,080,127
2.	Ilie Nastase, 1969–78	$1,976,799
3.	Guillermo Vilas, 1972–78	$1,784,529
4.	Raul Ramirez, 1973–78	$1,679,340
5.	Ken Rosewall, 1957–78	$1,588,576
6.	Arthur Ashe, 1969–78	$1,582,362
7.	Rod Laver, 1963–78	$1,564,304
8.	Bjorn Borg, 1973–78	$1,517,726
9.	Brian Gottfried, 1972–78	$1,404,864
10.	Eddie Dibbs, 1972–78	$1,315,991
11.	Stan Smith, 1969–78	$1,314,088
12.	Manolo Orantes, 1968–77	$1,273,447
13.	Tom Okker, 1968–78	$1,119,714
14.	Harold Solomon, 1972–78	$1,086,035
15.	John Newcombe, 1968–78	$1,055,240

Women

1.	Chris Evert, 1973–78	$1,834,224
2.	Billie Jean King, 1968–78	$1,183,840
3.	Martina Navratilova, 1973–78	$1,044,019

Attendance

Indoor high: 30,472—Astrodome, Houston, Tex., Sept. 20, 1973. Billie Jean King d. Bobby Riggs, 6–4, 6–3, 6–3, mixed singles challenge.

Outdoor high: 25,578—White City Stadium, Sydney, Australia, Dec. 27–29, 1954. Australia d. U.S., 3–2, Davis Cup Challenge Round.

Tournament high: 337,598—Wimbledon, 1975 (12 sessions). One session high, 38,290, June 28, 1978.

INDEX

cil, 231; as U.S. Lawn Tennis Association (USLTA), formerly U.S. National Lawn Tennis Association (USNLTA), 6–8, 9, 31–32, 137, 148, 151, 155, 160, 172

U.S. Women's Championships, West Side Tennis Club as home of (1920), 13

Van Alen, James H. (Jimmy), xxii, 126, 240, 248–49; in Hall of Fame, 248–49; and VASSS tie-breaker, 126, 131, 267, 268, 270, 271–72

Van Alen Streamlined Scoring System (VASSS), 126, 131, 267, 268, 270, 271–72

Van Dillen, Erik, 149, 155, 160

Van Horn, Welby, 50, 51–52, 88

Van Ryn, John, 34, 35, 36, 38, 44, 56; in Hall of Fame, 247

Van Ryn, Marjorie, 46

Varner, Margaret, 119

Vasselin, Christopher Roger, 184

VASSS. See Van Alen Streamlined Scoring System

Vermaak, Ian, 112

Vessies-Appel, Elli, 179

Victorian Championship meeting (1879), 8

Vilas, Guillermo, xix, 164, 168, 169, 170, 174, 178, 180–81, 182, 184, 187, 189, 190, 195, 197; biography, described, championships, 180–81, 190; ill., 181; and prize money, 164, 181, 182, 374

Vines, H. Ellsworth, Jr., 35, 36, 37–38, 43, 44, 46, 50–51, 57, 62, 69, 77–78, 85, 87, 246; biography, described, championships, 36, 37–38, 77–78; and Budge, 52, 59; and Crawford, 40; in Hall of Fame, 246; ill., 37, 78; and Kramer, 85, 87; and Perry, 48–49, 50–51, 52, 74, 78; and Tilden, 78

Virginia Slims Circuit, xx, xxi, 145, 150–51, 152, 156, 160, 161, 193, 215, 219, 220, 270; championship records (1972–79), 338

Volley, defined, 272

Von Cramm, Baron Gottfried, 36, 42, 44, 45–46, 74, 78–79, 93, 257; biography, described, championships, 78–79, 257; and Budge, 47–48, 49, 59, 76; in Hall of Fame, 257; ill., 79

Voshell, S. Howard, 49

Wade, Virginia, xix, 42, 131, 138, 139, 140, 141, 143, 147, 151, 152, 156, 160, 161, 165, 166, 171, 172, 177, 178, 179–80, 183, 184, 192, 196, 199

Wagner, Marie, 251–52; in Hall of Fame, 251–52

Walkden, Pat, 141

Wallach, Maud Berger, 13. See also Barger-Wallach, Maud

Walsh, Sharon, 151

Walters, O. S., ill., 16

Ward, Holcombe, 9, 10, 51, 59, 243, 261; in Hall of Fame, 243; ill., 9, 51

Ward, Patricia (Pat), 105, 212

Warwick, Kim, 174

Washburn, Watson, 16, 21, 81, 249; in Hall of Fame, 249; ill., 16

Washington Star International, 139–40

Watson, Lilian, 7

Watson, Maud, 7

Watson, Phoebe, 34, 35–36

WCT. See World Championship Tennis (WCT)

Weigandt, Barbara Green, 202

Weir, Reginald, 209

Wembly, England, 106

West Side Tennis Club, N.Y.C., 22, 26, 84, 91, 182, 272 (see also Forest Hills, N.Y.); start of, 13

White, Stanford, 240

White City (stadium) (Sydney, Australia), 272

Whitman, Malcolm D., 9, 10; in Hall of Fame, 242

Whittingstall, Eileen, 37

Wide, defined, 272

Wightman, Mrs. George W. (Hazel Hotchkiss), xiv, 13, 18, 22, 26, 31, 53, 56, 61, 68, 90, 161, 166, 243, 272, 330; in Hall of Fame, 243; ill., 24; and Wightman Cup (see Wightman Cup)

Wightman Cup, 13, 22, 24, 26, 56, 82, 272, 330–37; all-time championship records, 337; championships (1923–79), 330–37

Wilding, Anthony (Tony), 11, 12, 13, 58, 70, 79–80, 196, 258; biography, described, championships, 79–80, 258; in Hall of Fame, 258; ill., 12, 80

Williams, Joyce, 156

Williams, Louise, 14; ill., 14

Williams, Owen, 140

Williams, Richard Norris, II (Dick), 13, 15, 16, 21, 22, 27, 30, 71, 80–81, 245; biography, described, championships, 80–81, 243–44; in Hall of Fame, 243–44; ill., 15, 16, 80

Wills (Wills Moody), Helen. See Moody, Helen Wills

Wilson, Bobby, 110, 114, 117, 135, 139

Wimbledon (Wimbledon Lawn Tennis Championship), xi, xv, xix, 56, 82, 83–84, 85, 114, 120, 129, 130, 272; all-time championship records, 311, 373–74; as "Big W," 262; boycott of (1973), 159; Centennial (Centennial Medal winners); 63, 70, 178–80; Centre Court, xv, 263; championship records (1877–1979), 304–11; early matches and championships, 5–6, 7, 8, 9, 11, 12–13, 14–15, 17–18, 24–25, 26; first open tournament, 136–37; and officials (officiating), 231; Wightman Cup play and (see Wightman Cup); World War II bombings of, 52

Wingfield, Walter, C., xii, xiii, 1–3, 4, 156; ill., 1

Winner, defined, 272

Winship, Tom, xxii

WIPTC (Women's International Professional Tennis Council), xxi, 126, 272

Women (see also specific championships, development, individuals by name, organizations,